WORDSWORTH CLASSICS
OF WORLD LITERATURE

General Editor: Tom Griffith

SCOTT'S LAST
EXPEDITION

D1494679

Scott's
Last Expedition

Volume One being the Journals of
Captain R. F. Scott, R. N., C. V. O.

Volume Two being the reports of the
journeys and the scientific work undertaken
by Dr E. A. Wilson and the surviving
members of the expedition

Arranged by Leonard Huxley

with an introduction by Beau Riffenburgh

**WORDSWORTH CLASSICS
OF WORLD LITERATURE**

For my husband
Anthony John Ranson

with love from your wife, the publisher
Eternally grateful for your unconditional
love, not just for me but for our children
Simon, Andrew and Nichola Trayler

I

Customers interested in other titles from
Wordsworth Editions are invited to visit our
website at www.wordsworth-editions.com

For our latest list and a full mail order service contact
Bibliophile Books, Unit 5 Datapoint,
South Crescent, London E16 4TL
Tel: +44 020 74 74 24 74
Fax: +44 020 74 74 85 89
orders@bibliophilebooks.com

This edition published 2011 by Wordsworth Editions Limited
8B East Street, Ware, Hertfordshire SG12 9HJ

ISBN 978 1 84022 669 0

Typeset in Great Britain by Roperford Editorial
Printed and bound by Clays Ltd, St Ives plc

CONTENTS

ILLUSTRATIONS

DIAGRAMS

MAPS

INTRODUCTION

The concluding diary entries and last letters of Robert Falcon Scott are unquestionably among the most eloquent pieces of prose produced in the history of exploration, some would say of any writing in the English language. The conditions in which they were composed – facing death as a fierce blizzard raged unceasingly outside his lonely tent far out on the desolate Great Ice Barrier at the conclusion of his party's courageous but ill-fated return from the South Pole – add a poignancy to these documents that has perhaps never been surpassed in the literature of travel and exploration. Moreover, in a time of national doubt about the greatness of the British Empire and her sons, Scott's tale of strength, courage, and fortitude served as an inspiration of the highest order to the British public. It helped immortalise not only him and his four companions, but also the book subsequently published – and reprinted here – as *Scott's Last Expedition*.

Today, Scott is still remembered as one of the greatest heroes of both Antarctic exploration and the pre-Great War British Empire. The many exhibitions, books, and other centenary celebrations of his *Terra Nova* Expedition show that his actions, achievements, and personal dignity continue to have an impact on the consciousness and pride of people from virtually all ages and walks of life. Concurrently, the oft-quoted passages from his diaries and letters show that his words still touch the human spirit in a remarkable way.

Although Scott's final writings are his most memorable, they were by no means the first time that he made an impression on the wide readership then fascinated with tales from exploring expeditions throughout the world. His initial expedition account, *The Voyage of the Discovery*, had been extolled as a masterpiece when it appeared in two volumes in October 1905. One critic from *The Nation*, for example, stated that 'The narrative of Capt. Scott easily takes rank among the foremost books of travel and discovery which a half-century has brought out.'[1] That book told the story of Scott's initial effort as leader of an exploring endeavour – the British National Antarctic Expedition (B.N.A.E.) – which was one of the first major attempts to penetrate into the mysteries of the Antarctic continent, and which introduced Scott to the arena in which he would gain immortality.

The B.N.A.E. had been the brainchild of Sir Clements Markham, the president of the Royal Geographical Society (RGS). Scott had initially come to Markham's attention, legend has it, in 1887, when, as a midshipman, he won a sailing race that Markham was watching. In the summer of 1899, Scott, then a 31-year-old torpedo lieutenant serving in HMS *Majestic*, happened to see Markham across a road in London and engaged the older man in a conversation that led to a discussion about Markham's proposed Antarctic expedition. Although Scott acknowledged later that he had had no previous interest in polar exploration, within days he had applied to command the expedition. Markham was convinced that Scott was the right man for the job, and, as was his wont, he battled and intrigued tenaciously for what he wanted – in this case Scott's appointment. With Markham ultimately overriding all opposition, Scott was placed in charge of the expedition and promoted from lieutenant to commander.

Departing Britain in 1901 in the purpose-built expedition ship *Discovery*, Scott and the members of his expedition eventually reached the Ross Sea, far south of New Zealand, where they established a base at Hut Point on Ross Island, at the southern end of McMurdo Sound. Here, adjacent to the Great Ice Barrier (now known as the Ross Ice Shelf) – a massive sheet of floating ice that averages some 1200 feet thick and covers 209,000 square miles, an area larger than Spain – *Discovery* was frozen into the ice. Throughout and beyond the winter, Scott's party made pioneering scientific studies and compiled meteorological, biological, geological, and other data.

In November 1902, Scott and two companions – junior surgeon Dr Edward Wilson and third officer Ernest Shackleton – began what would be the expedition's most publicised effort, an attempt to cross the Barrier and reach the South Pole. Before long, the journey became a misery, as the three men, not truly understanding the dynamics of driving the dogs that initially pulled their sledges – and therefore unable to prod the creatures into hauling properly – had to go into harness themselves and begin man-hauling, a terrible task once described as the hardest work ever done by free men. On 30 December, they reached 82°17'S, a point farther south than had ever previously been attained. But with supplies dwindling, they were forced to turn for home, and, physically weakened and plagued by scurvy, the return became a dreadful struggle. Despite terrible adversity, they somehow managed to reach Hut Point on 3 February 1903. Shortly thereafter, while most of the members of the expedition remained in the Antarctic for another winter, Scott sent Shackleton back to Britain on a relief ship, ostensibly for medical reasons.

A year later, the rest of the expedition returned to Britain, where Scott became a national hero and was promoted to captain. Subsequently, the success both critically and in sales of *The Voyage of the Discovery* helped establish him as one of Britain's foremost polar figures. However, his homecoming also meant an eventual return to the day-to-day life of an officer in the Royal Navy. With such duties, Scott found he could only dream of a return to the far south and of eventually becoming the first man to attain the South Pole.

In 1907, Shackleton, who felt he had been unjustly 'invalided' home and wanted to prove he possessed the fortitude and abilities to be a successful Antarctic explorer, launched his own expedition to reach the Pole. Scott had nascent plans in that direction, too, so Shackleton's sudden appearance as a competitor led to a bitter rivalry between the two men. This was heightened by Scott extricating a promise from Shackleton not to use the McMurdo Sound region as his base, and the younger man eventually being forced to break the promise due to his inability to make what he considered a safe landing farther east on the Barrier.

Meanwhile, the realities of his commitments to the Royal Navy and his relationship with the sculptress Kathleen Bruce – whom he married in September 1908 – meant that when Shackleton sailed south, Scott could only wait helplessly and hope that the Pole would remain unattained when his former subordinate reappeared. That *is*, in fact, what occurred in 1909. To Scott's relief, although Shackleton and three companions had made one of the most amazing journeys in Antarctic history – one that took them across the Barrier, up the previously unknown Beardmore Glacier, and across the central Polar Plateau to 88°23'S, only 97 geographical miles from the Pole – the southernmost place on Earth remained virgin territory.

Scott wasted little time in staking his claim to be the person to complete those remaining 97 miles. On 19 June 1909, in an after-dinner speech at an event honouring Shackleton at London's famed Savage Club, Scott urged that every effort be made to assure that an Englishman was the first to the Pole, adding that he was willing 'to go forth in search of that object' himself, and that 'All I have to do now is to thank Mr Shackleton for so nobly showing the way.'[2]

Three months later, on 13 September 1909, the day before his son Peter was born, Scott formally announced his second Antarctic venture. 'The main object of this Expedition is to reach the South Pole,' he wrote both for the press and in a fund-raising document, 'and to secure for the British Empire the honour of that achievement.'[3] At the same time, Scott had a true interest in scientific research, and he planned to establish a scientific programme that would exceed even the lauded results from his first expedition. In charge of that component of the expedition was his close friend and old sledging-mate Edward Wilson.

Scott's first major challenge was raising the funds required for such a large venture, and it proved a difficult challenge, even after E. R. G. R. 'Teddy' Evans, a naval officer who had been organising his own expedition, joined Scott's as second-in-command, bring-ing with him the donations he had already received. Finally, a grant of £20,000 was made by Prime Minister Herbert Asquith's Liberal government, allowing Scott to purchase the former whal-ing ship *Terra Nova*. Finding men to accompany the expedition was not, on the surface, such a difficult challenge, as more than 8000 applied for positions. Two of those ultimately selected were able to purchase their positions on the shore party by contributing £1000 each – Captain L. E. G. Oates of the Inniskilling Dragoons, who was placed in charge of the expedition's ponies, and Apsley Cherry-Garrard, the assistant biologist.

Terra Nova sailed from Cardiff on 15 June 1910, and Scott, who remained behind to continue fund-raising efforts, joined her at

Cape Town. On 12 October, the ship arrived at Melbourne, where Scott received a mysterious telegram: 'Beg leave to inform you, *Fram* proceeding Antarctic. Amundsen.' It was clearly from the famed Norwegian explorer Roald Amundsen, who several years earlier had become the first man to navigate the entire Northwest Passage. But Amundsen had been planning a drift through the Arctic basin, so the meaning of the message remained, for the time being, unclear.

Shortly thereafter, *Terra Nova* proceeded to New Zealand, and it is there that Scott began recording his account of the expedition in the journals that would be used as the basis for *Scott's Last Expedition*. On 29 November, the ship sailed for the Ross Sea from Port Chalmers. The journey south was plagued by a violent gale and, as *Terra Nova* tried to enter the Ross Sea, by unremitting ice. Therefore, it was not until 4 January 1911 that, with the way to Hut Point blocked by miles of ice, Scott decided to establish his new base at a small promontory a dozen miles north of his original station, at a place he named Cape Evans in honour of his second-in-command.

Immediately after establishing his winter quarters, Scott led a party south to lay supply depots for the journey toward the Pole, which would leave the next spring. At the same time, the Australian geologist Griffith Taylor led a small party across McMurdo Sound to investigate the geology and physiography of the western mountains. And *Terra Nova* sailed east to drop a party under the command of Victor Campbell at King Edward VII Land on the far side of the Great Ice Barrier. Unable to reach its destination, that party sought a place to land on the Barrier itself, and at a location Shackleton had named the Bay of Whales, the men unexpectedly came across *Fram* moored against the ice edge. Amundsen had arrived three weeks earlier and, they discovered, had set up a base with the goal of becoming the first to reach the Pole. After cordial interactions with the Norwegians, Campbell hurried back to Cape Evans to report the discovery of Amundsen. *Terra Nova* then headed north, dropping off Campbell and five others at Cape Adare, where they were left to winter, before proceeding back to New Zealand.

Meanwhile, Scott established his southernmost supply station, One Ton Depot, at 79°29'S, some 30 geographical miles short of his original goal. Six ponies were lost on the return journey, which would help lead Scott to postpone his spring departure until the temperatures seemed more conducive for the ponies. On his return from the depot trip, he received a message from Campbell letting him know beyond doubt that he was now in a race with Amundsen for priority at the Pole.

Throughout the long, dark winter that followed, the members of Scott's party conducted scientific studies and prepared for the upcoming sledging. But the most famous occurrence of the period was a brutal journey made by Wilson, Cherry-Garrard, and Lieutenant Henry 'Birdie' Bowers to the emperor penguin colony at Cape Crozier on the far side of Ross Island. Wilson had long been keen to study emperor penguins, which he considered the most 'primitive' of birds, and to collect their eggs in order to test theories about the origin of birds and the relation of reptilian scales to feathers. The journey needed to be made in the dead of winter, when the emperors incubated, and the glaciers, ice falls, and dangerous rises of Mount Erebus, the active volcano on Ross Island, meant they could not travel over land. So the three men headed south from Cape Evans at the end of June and slowly hauled their two heavy sledges across the rough surfaces near the edge of the Barrier in the continual dark with temperatures plummeting to a low of −61°C. At Cape Crozier, they built a small igloo near the colony and gathered eggs. Then, after facing a devastating gale, they slogged back the 57 miles (105 km) to base. The effort had taken them more than a month, and their tortuous effort was later immortalised in Cherry-Garrard's book *The Worst Journey in the World*.

On 1 November 1911, Scott finally set out for the Pole, with his transport comprising 10 ponies and their handlers, a team of dogs in the charge of Cecil Meares, and two motor sledges under the command of 'Teddy' Evans. Frustratingly, the expensive motorised equipment soon broke down, and Evans's party was forced to begin man-hauling. In the following weeks a number of the ponies wore out due to the hard work and being in an environment for which they were not well-adapted; each had to be shot. Slowly Scott sent back a trickle of support personnel, and at the base of the Beardmore Glacier, the remaining ponies were put down and the dogs sent back to base. Scott and his men would now man-haul the rest of the way, following the route pioneered three years before by Shackleton – ascending the Beardmore Glacier to the Polar Plateau. Once on the Plateau, Scott eventually sent Evans and the last support party back to base and led a final party of five on toward the Pole.

On 17 January 1912, Scott, Wilson, Bowers, Oates, and Petty Officer Edgar Evans reached what had been their cherished goal. But their excitement had already been tempered the day before when they had discovered a black flag and then the remains of a camp. It was immediately apparent that the Norwegians had arrived before them. In fact, Amundsen had beaten them by more than a month, his five-man party and their dog teams having reached the Pole on 14 December. The disheartened British explorers – already dangerously exhausted from the incredible exertions of man-hauling – could do little more than take pictures of themselves and dejectedly head north. 'Now for the run home and a desperate struggle,' wrote Scott. 'I wonder if we can do it.'[4]

Sadly, they could not. On the return journey of some 800 miles, dejected emotionally and struggling against both inadequate supplies of food and fuel and worsening weather conditions, they simply wore out. First, Evans died near the base of the Beardmore Glacier. Then, having sledged most of the way across the Barrier, Oates, whose feet were so badly damaged by frostbite and gangrene that he felt he could not travel at the rate necessary to safely reach the next depot, walked out of the tent to his death so as not to hinder his companions' progress. But only days later, Scott, Wilson, and Bowers were halted by a fierce storm, and the three eventually weakened and died in their tent, only 11 geographical miles (20 km) short of One Ton Depôt, which, had it been placed where Scott originally intended, would have supplied them with the food and fuel that would have saved them.

The expedition members back at Cape Evans had made various efforts to assist the return of the Polar Party, but had been hampered not only by poor weather, but by a lack of clear directions as to what Scott wanted them to do. When *Terra Nova*, which had returned to Cape Evans with the hope of picking up the entire party, was forced to head back north to

New Zealand to avoid wintering in the Antarctic, a number of the expedition members sailed on her. Others remained to wait for the Polar Party and to continue the scientific work, but, as winter approached, they realised that Scott and his men would not be coming back, and there was no longer anything they could do to save them. Therefore, the next spring, when conditions allowed, they went in search of their lost comrades. On 12 November 1912, a party under surgeon Edward Atkinson found the bodies of Scott, Wilson, and Bowers, and were able to retrieve their journals, correspondence, and photographs. Thus, the entire, tragic fate of the Polar Party became known.

The loss of Scott and his four companions – initially told in news releases carefully constructed by a committee of expedition members on the voyage from Antarctica to New Zealand – caused a sensation in Britain. Amundsen had already received acclaim, praise, and occasional disapproval for his journey to the Pole, but much of the British geographical and scientific hierarchy, as well as the public, had anxiously awaited the reports of the achievements of Scott and his expedition. When their fate was finally revealed, the members of the Polar Party quickly became heroes, and were viewed by many as martyrs to science. Perhaps most importantly, they served as proof that British manhood was still ascendant in a period in which many had feared its decline.

Scott's powerful 'Message to the Public' – written at the back of his last notebook as, clearly, one of his last acts – had a particularly profound effect after it was released in the press. His plea 'to our countrymen to see that those who depend on us are properly provided for'[5] helped lead to the establishment of several funds that, when combined, raised more than £75,000 (the equivalent of more than £4.5 million today), which was earmarked to provide for the families of the lost men, publish the expedition's scientific results, and erect memorials in honour of the expedition's members and its achievements. Part of that funding was eventually used to help found the Scott Polar Research Institute in Cambridge.

The first significant use of Scott's journals for publication was for a four-part serialisation in the *Strand Magazine*, which appeared between June and September 1913. Thus, the public was already familiar with the tragic details of the expedition when Reginald Smith, a dear friend of both Scott and Wilson and the head of the publishing house of Smith, Elder – which had earlier brought out *The Voyage of the Discovery* – published *Scott's Last Expedition* in two volumes on 6 November 1913.

The final form of the book was the handiwork of Leonard Huxley, the chief editor at Smith, Elder, who arranged and edited Scott's dozen Antarctic journals in consultation with Smith and Kathleen Scott. It was Huxley who made the first volume of the book a continuous narrative from Scott's original writings, no easy task, since the expedition leader's different notebooks at times included multiple versions of some incidents. Huxley also integrated Scott's letters to Kathleen into the text and broke the book up into chapters that would conform to the style and format of the standard expedition account. And he altered or omitted numerous comments that presented a less-than-favourable image of Scott because they were so caustically or pettily critical of Shackleton, Amundsen, or members of his expedition, such as Charles Wright, Griffith Taylor, or Tryggve Gran.

With all these revisions, it is doubtful that one would agree with Huxley's assessment that 'the revising hand has managed to remain unobtrusive.' However, there could be no doubt that he was honest in writing that 'the labour has been seasoned with love, & at the end whatever one has managed to do, one longs to have devised some way of doing it better.'[6]

Certainly, Huxley retained Scott's eloquent prose, and, as has been pointed out many times, the explorer's literary gifts helped make the work a classic of exploration literature, one that immediately was translated into numerous different languages.[7] And nowhere was Scott's writing more powerful, more articulate, and more moving than in his final journal entries, his last letters, and his 'Message to the Public'. The letters and 'Message' were placed near the end of the first volume, which immediately preceding them had already reached an emotional high point, as Scott's last entry – 'For God's sake look after our people' – had been withheld from the serialisation in *Strand Magazine* and therefore was breathtakingly new to the public. Following the final journal entry were eight pages of Scott's last letters and then his 'Message to the

Public', which was also made more immediate and powerful by a facsimile of the original.

The second volume told the stories of those parts of the expedition in which Scott did not actively participate. Thus, the tale of the mid-winter journey to Cape Crozier, the two years spent by the members of the Northern Party, including their horrific second winter, the investigations by the two Western Parties, the final year at Cape Evans, an ascent of Mount Erebus, and the voyages of *Terra Nova* were detailed. In addition, summaries or brief reports of a variety of the scientific findings were included.

The praise lavished on *Scott's Last Expedition* was all that Huxley, Smith, or Kathleen Scott could have wanted. 'It is a great book,' bubbled the *Daily Graphic*, 'perhaps the greatest ever written, because of the grandeur of its tragedy.'[8] And no less an authority on literature than Winston Churchill, then the First Lord of the Admiralty, wrote to Kathleen Scott that the book was 'a worthy memorial of one of the great achievements of our time'.[9]

The book itself was an extravagant production, with expensive, vertically straight-grained blue cloth and the covers, spine, and borders lettered and ruled in gilt. The two volumes had 204 plates, which included 237 photographs in black and white or sepia (most by the famed 'camera artist' Herbert Ponting), 18 coloured plates (17 from paintings by Wilson) with tissue paper guards, two folding plates with photographic panoramas, three double-page plates, and eight folding maps. Its extremely high quality was reflected in its cost of 42 shillings (approximately £125 today), but it had nevertheless sold out in a matter of weeks. A second and third printing, with minor additions or changes, were published before the end of the year, and two more came out in January 1914.

The fourth edition, from which this reprint is taken, has long been considered the best, as the typographical errors and mistakes of the earlier editions had been corrected. A new map and new authorship attributions (which caused an extension of the preliminaries) were also added in the second volume.

The sales of *Scott's Last Expedition* – particularly considering the price – were nothing short of amazing. By the end of 1913, 9663 sets of the Smith, Elder edition were recorded as having been sold, and some 3400 more sets were printed by February of 1914.[10] The book also sold well in the United States, where Dodd, Mead printed three editions by the end of 1913. MacMillan's 'Empire Library' edition, which was in a smaller format 'intended for circulation only in India and the British Dominions over the Seas'[11] sold more than 10,000 copies.

In fact, so keen was the public that in 1914 Smith, Elder produced a one-volume condensation with extracts from Scott's journals from both his Antarctic expeditions. Titled *The Voyages of Captain Scott*, this included a now well-known 'Biographical Intro- duction' by J.M. Barrie, the author of *Peter Pan* and one of Scott's close friends.

Due in part to the cost difficulties imposed by the First World War, in part to the death of Reginald Smith in 1916, and perhaps in part to the success of *The Voyages of Captain Scott* (which sold out its 10,000-copy print run), it was a decade before the common practice of the time of abridging a two-volume first edition into a one-volume 'Popular' or 'Cheap' edition was followed. In 1923, the publishing house of John Murray – which had purchased Smith, Elder's backlist – produced such a volume, which omitted virtually all of the second volume of the original. It did, however, include Barrie's 'Biographical Introduction'; a new essay on the finding of the bodies of Scott's party, written by Surgeon Atkinson; and a much-reduced set of 16 photographs. Within 18 months, the new edition had sold 10,000 copies at a published price of 7s 6d.

In the years since, a number of editions of *Scott's Last Expedition*, both one-volume and two-, have been released, demonstrating the continued fascination with the story of Scott and his final journey. Despite such a variety of editions, copies of the full, two-volume work can now demand a very high price. There- fore, it should be much appreciated that this current edition – containing two volumes in one – allows the reader to become familiar both with what was a hugely significant expedition, and with a classic account by a man who was not simply a remark- able explorer, but one of the most talented, commanding, and articulate writers ever in the field of polar exploration.

Indeed, it is appropriate that the original copy of Scott's last journal – which has been regularly on display since first being loaned to the nation and exhibited in the British Museum in 1914 – now rests opposite the first folio of William Shakespeare's plays in the British Library. For as a literary effort, Scott's journals – represented here in *Scott's Last Expedition* – remain to the literature of travel and exploration much the same as do the works of Shakespeare in the realm of theatre: classics of the English language unlikely ever to be surpassed in their genres.

BEAU RIFFENBURGH
Scott Polar Research Institute
Cambridge

References

1 *The Nation*, 82 (2114), pages 13–14.
2 *The Observer*, 20 June 1909.
3 Scott, R. F. 1909. The South Pole. *The Times* 13 September 1909. Scott, R.F. 1909. *Antarctic Expedition for 1910*. London: Spottiswoode and Co.
4 Scott, R. F. 1913. *Scott's Last Expedition*. (page 380 in this edition)
5 Scott, R. F. 1913. *Scott's Last Expedition*. (page 426 in this edition)
6 Huxley, L. 1913. Letter to R. Smith, 5 November 1913.
7 For example, Scott, R. F. 1913. *Kapitan Scott: Letzte Fahrt*. Leipzig: F. A. Brockhaus. Scott, R. F. 1913. *Scott's Sidste Rejse*. København: Steen Hasselbalogs. Scott, R. F. 1914. *Le Pole Meurtrier: Journal du Capitaine Scott*. Paris: Hachette.
8 *Daily Graphic*, 6 November 1913.
9 Churchill, W. 1913. Letter to Kathleen Scott, 12 November 1913.
10 Jones, M. 2005. Composition and Publication History. In: *Robert Falcon Scott Journals*. Oxford: Oxford University Press, page xlv.
11 Scott, R. F. 1913. *Scott's Last Expedition*. London: Macmillan.

FURTHER READING

Baughman, T. H. 1999. *Pilgrims on the Ice: Robert Falcon Scott's First Antarctic Expedition*. Lincoln: University of Nebraska Press.

Cherry-Garrard, Apsley. 1922. *The Worst Journey in the World*. 2 vols. London: Constable.

Crane, David. 2005. *Scott of the Antarctic*. London: Harper Collins.

Evans, E. R. G. R. 1921. *South With Scott*. London: Collins.

Fiennes, Ranulph. 2003. *Captain Scott*. London: Hodder & Stoughton.

Holland, Clive (editor). 1986. *Antarctic Obsession: A Personal Narrative of the British National Antarctic Expedition 1901–1904 by Sir Clements Markham*. Alburgh: Bluntisham Books and Erskine Press.

Howgego, Raymond John. 2006. *Encyclopedia of Exploration 1850 to 1940: The Oceans, Islands and Polar Regions*. Potts Point, New South Wales: Hordern House.

Huntford, Roland. 1979. *Scott and Amundsen*. London: Hodder & Stoughton.

Huxley, Elspeth. 1977. *Scott of the Antarctic*. London: Weidenfeld and Nicolson.

Johnson, Anthony. 1995. *Scott of the Antarctic and Cardiff*. Cardiff: Captain Scott Society.

Jones, Max. 2003. *The Last Great Quest: Captain Scott's Antarctic Sacrifice*. Oxford: Oxford University Press.

Ponting, Herbert. 1921. *The Great White South*. London: Duckworth.

Pound, Reginald. 1966. *Scott of the Antarctic*. London: Cassell.

Priestley, Raymond. 1914. *Antarctic Adventure: Scott's Northern Party*. London: T. Fisher Unwin.

Riffenburgh, Beau. 2004. *Nimrod: Ernest Shackleton and the Extra-ordinary Story of the 1907–09 British Antarctic Expedition*. London: Bloomsbury.

Solomon, Susan. 2001. *The Coldest March: Scott's Fatal Antarctic Expedition*. New Haven, CT: Yale University Press.

Spufford, Francis. 1996. *I May Be Some Time: Ice and the English Imagination*. London: Faber & Faber.

Taylor, T. Griffith. 1916. *With Scott: the Silver Lining*. London: Smith, Elder.

Wheeler, Sara. 1996. *Terra Incognita: Travels in Antarctica*. London: Cape.

Wilson, Edward. 1972. *Diary of the 'Terra Nova' Expedition to the Antarctic 1910–1912*. London: Blandford Press.

Yelverton, David. 2000. *Antarctica Unveiled: Scott's First Expedition and the Quest for the Unknown Continent*. Boulder, CO: University Press of Colorado.

VOLUME ONE

PREFACE

Fourteen years ago Robert Falcon Scott was a rising naval officer, able, accomplished, popular, highly thought of by his superiors, and devoted to his noble profession. It was a serious responsibility to induce him to take up the work of an explorer; yet no man living could be found who was so well fitted to command a great Antarctic Expedition. The undertaking was new and unprecedented. The object was to explore the unknown Antarctic Continent by land. Captain Scott entered upon the enterprise with enthusiasm tempered by prudence and sound sense. All had to be learnt by a thorough study of the history of Arctic travelling, combined with experience of different conditions in the Antarctic Regions. Scott was the initiator and founder of Antarctic sledge-travelling.

His discoveries were of great importance. The survey and soundings along the Barrier cliffs, the discovery of King Edward Land, the discovery of Ross Island and the other volcanic islets, the examination of the Barrier surface, the discovery of the Victoria Mountains – a range of great height and many hundreds of miles in length, which had only before been seen from a distance out at sea – and above all the discovery of the great ice cap on which the South Pole is situated, by one of the most remarkable Polar journeys on record. His small but excellent scientific staff worked hard and with trained intelligence, their results being recorded in twelve large quarto volumes.

The great discoverer had no intention of losing touch with his beloved profession – though resolved to complete his Antarctic work. The exigencies of the naval service called him to the command of battleships and to confidential work of the Admiralty; so that five years elapsed before he could resume his Antarctic labours.

The object of Captain Scott's second expedition was mainly scientific, to complete and extend his former work in all branches of science. It was his ambition that in his ship there should be the most completely equipped expedition for scientific purposes connected with the Polar regions, both as regards men and material, that ever left these shores. In this he succeeded. He had on board a fuller complement of geologists, one of them especially trained for the study of physiography, biologists, physicists, and surveyors than ever before composed the staff of a Polar expedition. Thus Captain Scott's objects were strictly scientific, including the completion and extension of his former discoveries. The results will be explained in the second volume of this work. They will be found to be extensive and important. Never before, in the Polar regions, have meteorological, magnetic and tidal observations been taken, in one locality, during five years. It was also part of Captain Scott's plan to reach the South Pole by a long and most arduous journey, but here again his intention was, if possible, to achieve scientific results on the way, especially hoping to discover fossils which would throw light on the former history of the great range of mountains which he had made known to science.

The principal aim of this great man – for he rightly has his niche among the Polar *Di Majores* – was the advancement of knowledge. From all aspects Scott was among the most remarkable men of our time, and the vast number of readers of his journal will be deeply impressed with the beauty of his character. The chief traits which shone forth through his life were conspicuous in the hour of death. There are few events in history to be compared, for grandeur and pathos, with the last closing scene in that silent wilderness of snow. The great leader, with the bodies of his dearest friends beside him, wrote and wrote until the pencil dropped from his dying grasp. There was no thought of himself, only the earnest desire to give comfort and consolation to others in their sorrow. His very last lines were written lest he who induced him to enter upon Antarctic work should now feel regret for what he had done.

'If I cannot write to Sir Clements, tell him I thought much of him, and never regretted his putting me in command of the *Discovery*.'

CLEMENTS R. MARKHAM
September 1913

BRITISH ANTARCTIC EXPEDITION 1910

SHORE PARTIES

Officers

Name	Rank, &c
Robert Falcon Scott	Captain, C.F.O., R.N.
Edward R. G. R. Evans	Lieutenant, R.N.
Victor L. A. Campbell	Lieutenant, R.N. (Emergency List)
Henry R. Bowers	Lieutenant, R.I.M.
Lawrence E. G. Oates	Captain, 6th Inniskilling Dragoons
G. Murray Levick	Surgeon, R.N.
Edward L. Atkinson	Surgeon, R.N., Parasitologist

Scientific Staff

Name	Rank, &c
Edward Adrian Wilson	B.A., M.S. (Cantab), Chief of the Scientific Staff, and Zoologist
George C. Simpson	D.Sc., Meteorologist
T. Griffith Taylor	B.A., B.Sc., B.E., Geologist
Edward W. Nelson	Biologist
Frank Debenham	B.A., B.Sc., Geologist
Charles S. Wright	B.A., Physicist
Raymond E. Priestley	Geologist
Herbert G. Ponting	F.R.G.S., Camera Artist
Cecil H. Meares	In Charge of Dogs
Bernard C. Day	Motor Engineer
Apsley Cherry-Garrard	B.A., Asst. Zoologist
Tryggve Gran	Sub-Lieutenant, Norwegian N.R., B.A., Ski Expert.

SHORE PARTIES (continued)

Men

Name	Rank, &c
W. Lashly	Chief Stoker, R.N.
W. W. Archer	Chief Steward, late R.N.
Thomas Clissold	Cook, late R.N.
Edgar Evans	Petty Officer, R.N.
Robert Forde	Petty Officer, R.N.
Thomas Crean	Petty Officer, R.N.
Thomas S. Williamson	Petty Officer, R.N.
Patrick Keohane	Petty Officer, R.N.
George P. Abbott	Petty Officer, R.N.
Frank V. Browning	Petty Officer, 2nd Class, R.N.
Harry Dickason	Able Seaman, R.N.
F. J. Hooper	Steward, late R.N.
Anton Omelchenko	Groom
Demetri Gerof	Dog Driver

SHIP'S PARTY

Officers, &c

Name	Rank, &c
Harry L. L. Pennell	Lieutenant, R.N.
Henry E. de P. Rennick	Lieutenant, R.N.
Wilfred M. Bruce	Lieutenant, R.N.R.
Francis R. H. Drake	Asst. Paymaster, R.N. (Retired), Secretary & Meteorologist in Ship
Denis G. Lillie	M.A., Biologist in Ship
James R. Dennistoun	In Charge of Mules in Ship
Alfred B. Cheetham	R.N.R. , Boatswain
William Williams	Chief Engine-room Artificer, R.N., Engineer
William A. Horton	Eng. Rm. Art., 3rd Cl, R.N., 2nd Engineer
Francis E. C. Davies	Leading Shipwright, R.N.
Frederick Parsons	Petty Officer, R.N.
William L. Heald	Late P.O., R.N.
Arthur S. Bailey	Petty Officer, 2nd Class, R.N.
Albert Balson	Leading Seaman, R.N.

SHIP'S PARTY (continued)

Name	*Rank, &c*
Joseph Leese	Able Seaman, R.N.
John Hugh Mather	Petty Officer, R.N.F.R.
Robert Oliphant	Able Seaman
Thomas F. McLeod	Able Seaman
Mortimer McCarthy	Able Seaman
William Knowles	Able Seaman
Charles Williams	Able Seaman
James Skelton	Able Seaman
William McDonald	Able Seaman
James Paton	Able Seaman
Robert Brissenden	Leading Stoker, R.N.
Edward A. McKenzie	Leading Stoker, R.N.
William Burton	Leading Stoker, R.N.
Bernard J. Stone	Leading Stoker, R.N.
Angus McDonald	Fireman
Thomas McGillon	Fireman
Charles Lammas	Fireman
W. H. Neale	Steward

GLOSSARY

Barrier, the immense sheet of ice, over 400 miles wide and of still greater length, which lies south of Ross Island to the west of Victoria Land.

Brash, small ice fragments from a floe that is breaking up.

Drift, snow swept from the ground like dust and driven before the wind.

Finnesko, fur boots.

Flense, flence, to cut the blubber from a skin or carcase.

Frost smoke, a mist of water vapour above the open leads, condensed by the severe cold.

Hoosh, a thick camp-soup with a basis of pemmican.

Ice-foot, properly the low fringe of ice formed about Polar lands by the sea spray. More widely, the banks of ice of varying height which skirt many parts of the Antarctic shores.

Nunatak, a 'lonely peak' of rock in the midst of the ice; when rounded by glacial action, a *Nunakol*.

Piedmont, coastwise stretches of the ancient ice-sheet which once covered the Antarctic Continent, remaining either on the land, or wholly or partially afloat.

Pram, a Norwegian skiff, with a spoon bow.

Primus, a portable stove for cooking.

Ramp, a great embankment of morainic material with ice beneath, once part of the glacier, on the lowest slopes of Erebus at the landward end of C. Evans.

Saennegras, a kind of fine Norwegian hay, used as packing in the finnesko to keep the feet warm and to make the fur boot fit firmly.

Sastrugus, an irregularity formed by the wind on a snow-plain. 'Snow wave' is not completely descriptive, as the sastrugus has often a fantastic shape unlike the ordinary conception of a wave.

Skua, a large gull.

Tank, a large canvas 'holdall' for sledge use.

Working Crack, an open crack which leaves the ice free to move with the movement of the water beneath.

NOTES

Passages enclosed in inverted commas are taken from home letters of Captain Scott.

A number following a word in the text refers to a corresponding note at the end of this volume.

To prevent confusion between the officer and the seaman on the Expedition who both bore the name of Evans, it should be noted that the former is referred to as Lieutenant E. or E. R. Evans, and 'Teddie' Evans: the latter as Seaman, Petty Officer (P.O.), or Edgar Evans.

CHAPTER ONE

Through stormy seas
The final preparations in New Zealand

The first three weeks of November have gone with such a rush that I have neglected my diary and can only patch it up from memory.

The dates seem unimportant, but throughout the period the officers and men of the ship have been unremittingly busy.

On arrival the ship was cleared of all the shore party stores, including huts, sledges, &c. Within five days she was in dock. Bowers attacked the ship's stores, surveyed, relisted, and restowed them, saving very much space by unstowing numerous cases and stowing the contents in the lazarette. Meanwhile our good friend Miller attacked the leak and traced it to the stern. We found the false stem split, and in one case a hole bored for a long-stem through-bolt which was much too large for the bolt. Miller made the excellent job in overcoming this difficulty which I expected, and since the ship has been afloat and loaded the leak is found to be enormously reduced. The ship still leaks, but the amount of water entering is little more than one would expect in an old wooden vessel.

The stream which was visible and audible inside the stern has been entirely stopped. Without steam the leak can now be kept under with the hand pump by two daily efforts of a quarter of an hour to twenty minutes. As the ship was, and in her present heavily laden condition, it would certainly have taken three to four hours each day.

Before the ship left dock, Bowers and Wyatt were at work again in the shed with a party of stevedores, sorting and relisting the shore party stores. Everything seems to have gone without a hitch. The various gifts and purchases made in New Zealand were collected – butter, cheese, bacon, hams, some preserved meats, tongues.

Meanwhile the huts were erected on the waste ground beyond the harbour works. Everything was overhauled, sorted, and marked afresh to prevent difficulty in the South. Davies, our excellent carpenter, Forde, Abbott, and Keohane were employed in this work. The large green tent was put up and proper supports made for it.

When the ship came out of dock she presented a scene of great industry. Officers and men of the ship, with a party of stevedores, were busy storing the holds. Miller's men were building horse stalls, caulking the decks, resecuring the deck-houses, putting in bolts and various small fittings. The engine-room staff and Anderson's people on the engines; scientists were stowing their laboratories; the cook refitting his galley, and so forth – not a single spot but had its band of workers.

We prepared to start our stowage much as follows: the main hold contains all the shore party provisions and part of the huts; above this on the main deck is packed in wonderfully close fashion the remainder of the wood of the huts, the sledges, and travelling equipment, and the larger instruments and machines to be employed by the scientific people; this encroaches far on the men's space, but the extent has been determined by their own wish; they have requested, through Evans, that they should not be considered: they were prepared to pig it anyhow, and a few cubic feet of space didn't matter – such is their spirit.

The men's space, such as it is, therefore, extends from the fore hatch to the stem on the main deck.

Under the forecastle are stalls for fifteen ponies, the maximum the space would hold; the narrow irregular space in front is packed tight with fodder.

Immediately behind the forecastle bulkhead is the small booby hatch, the only entrance to the men's mess deck in bad weather. Next comes the foremast, and between that and the fore hatch the galley and winch; on the port side of the fore hatch are stalls for four ponies – a very stout wooden structure.

Abaft the fore hatch is the ice-house. We managed to get 3 tons of ice, 162 carcases of mutton, and three carcases of beef, besides some boxes of sweetbreads and kidneys, into this space. The carcases are stowed in tiers with wooden battens between the tiers – it looks a triumph of orderly stowage, and I have great hope that it will ensure fresh mutton throughout our winter.

On either side of the main hatch and close up to the ice-house are two out of our three motor sledges; the third rests across the break of the poop in a space formerly occupied by a winch.

In front of the break of the poop is a stack of petrol cases; a further stack surmounted with bales of fodder stands between the main hatch and the mainmast, and cases of petrol, paraffin, and alcohol, arranged along either gangway.

We have managed to get 405 tons of coal in bunkers and main hold, 25 tons in a space left in the fore hold, and a little over 30 tons on the upper deck.

The sacks containing this last, added to the goods already mentioned, make a really heavy deck cargo, and one is naturally anxious concerning it; but everything that can be done by lashing and securing has been done.

The appearance of confusion on deck is completed by our thirty-three dogs[1] chained to stanchions and bolts on the ice-house and on the main hatch between the motor sledges.

With all these stores on board the ship still stood two inches above her load mark. The tanks are filled with compressed forage, except one, which contains 12 tons of fresh water – enough, we hope, to take us to the ice.

Forage. I originally ordered 30 tons of compressed oaten hay from Melbourne. Oates has gradually persuaded us that this is insufficient, and our pony food weight has gone up to 45 tons, besides 3 or 4 tons for immediate use. The extra consists of 5 tons of hay, 5 or 6 tons of oil-cake, 4 or 5 tons of bran, and some crushed oats. We are not taking any corn.

We have managed to wedge in all the dog biscuits, the total weight being about 5 tons; Meares is reluctant to feed the dogs on seal, but I think we ought to do so during the winter.

We stayed with the Kinseys at their house 'Te Han' at Clifton. The house stands at the edge of the cliff, 400 feet above the sea, and looks far over the Christchurch plain and the long northern beach which limits it; close beneath one is the harbour bar and winding estuary of the two small rivers, the Avon and Waimakariri. Far away beyond the plains are the mountains, ever changing their aspect, and yet farther in over this northern sweep of sea can be seen in clear weather the beautiful snow-capped peaks of the Kaikouras. The scene is wholly enchanting, and such a view from some sheltered sunny corner in a garden which blazes with masses of red and golden flowers tends to feelings of inexpressible satisfaction with all things. At night we slept in this garden under peaceful clear skies; by day I was off to my office in Christchurch, then perhaps to the ship or the Island, and so home by the mountain road over the Port Hills. It is a pleasant time to remember in spite of interruptions and it gave time for many necessary consultations with Kinsey. His interest in the expedition is wonderful, and such interest on the part of a thoroughly shrewd business man is an asset of which I have taken full advantage. Kinsey will act as my agent in Christchurch during my absence; I have given him an ordinary power of attorney, and I think have left him in possession of all facts. His kindness to us was beyond words.

The voyage out

Saturday, November 26. – We advertised our start at 3 p.m., and at three minutes to that hour the *Terra Nova* pushed off from the jetty. A great mass of people assembled. K. and I lunched with a party in the New Zealand Company's ship *Ruapehu*. Mr Kinsey. Ainsley, the Arthur and George Rhodes, Sir George Clifford, &c.[2] K. and I went out in the ship, but left her inside the heads after passing the *Cambrian*, the only Naval ship present. We came home in the Harbour Tug; two other tugs followed the ship out and innumerable small boats. Ponting busy with cinematograph. We walked over the hills to Sumner. Saw the *Terra Nova*, a little dot to the S.E.

Monday, November 28. – Caught 8 o'clock express to Port Chalmers, Kinsey saw us off. Wilson joined train. Rhodes met us Timaru. Telegram to say *Terra Nova* had arrived Sunday night. Arrived Port Chalmers at 4.30. Found all well.

Tuesday, November 29. – Saw Fenwick *re* Central News agreement – to town. Thanked Glendenning for handsome gift, 130 grey jerseys. To Town Hall to see Mayor. Found all well on board.

We left the wharf at 2.30 – bright sunshine – very gay scene. If anything more craft following us than at Lyttelton – Mrs Wilson, Mrs Evans, and K. left at Heads and back in Harbour Tug. Other tugs followed farther with Volunteer Reserve Gunboat – all left about 4.30. Pennell 'swung' the ship for compass adjustment, then 'away'.

Evening. – Loom of land and Cape Saunders Light blinking.

Wednesday, November 30. – Noon 110 miles. Light breeze from northward all day, freshening towards nightfall and turning to N.W. Bright sunshine. Ship pitching with south-westerly swell. All in good spirits except one or two sick.

We are away, sliding easily and smoothly through the water, but burning coal – 8 tons in 24 hours reported 8 p.m.

Thursday, December 1. – The month opens well on the whole. During the night the wind increased; we worked up to 8, to 9, and to 9.5 knots. Stiff wind from N.W. and confused sea. Awoke to much motion.

The ship a queer and not altogether cheerful sight under the circumstances.

Below one knows all space is packed as tight as human skill can devise – and on deck! Under the forecastle fifteen ponies close side by side, seven one side, eight the other, heads together and groom between – swaying, swaying continually to the plunging, irregular motion.

One takes a look through a hole in the bulkhead and sees a row of heads with sad, patient eyes come swinging up together from the starboard side, whilst those on the port swing back; then up come the port heads, whilst the starboard recede. It seems a terrible ordeal for these poor beasts to stand this day after day for weeks together, and indeed though they continue to feed well the strain quickly drags down their weight and condition; but nevertheless the trial cannot be gauged from human standards. There are horses which never lie down, and all horses can sleep standing; anatomically they possess a ligament in each leg which takes their weight without strain. Even our poor animals will get rest and sleep in spite of the violent motion. Some 4 or 5 tons of fodder and the ever watchful Anton take up the remainder of the forecastle space. Anton is suffering badly from sea-sickness, but last night he smoked a cigar. He smoked a little, then had an interval of evacuation, and back to his cigar whilst he rubbed his stomach and remarked to Oates 'No good' – gallant little Anton!

There are four ponies outside the forecastle and to leeward of the fore hatch, and on the whole, perhaps, with shielding tarpaulins, they have a rather better time than their comrades. Just behind the ice-house and on either side of the main hatch are two enormous packing-cases containing motor sledges, each 16 x 5 x 4; mounted as they are several inches above the deck they take a formidable amount of space. A third sledge stands across the break of the poop in the space hitherto occupied by the after winch. All these cases are covered with stout tarpaulin and lashed with heavy chain and rope lashings, so that they may be absolutely secure.

The petrol for these sledges is contained in tins and drums protected in stout wooden packing-cases which are ranged across the deck immediately in front of the poop and abreast the motor sledges. The quantity is 2½ tons and the space occupied considerable.

Round and about these packing-cases, stretching from the galley forward to the wheel aft, the deck is stacked with coal bags forming our deck cargo of coal, now rapidly diminishing.

We left Port Chalmers with 462 tons of coal on board, rather a greater quantity than I had hoped for, and yet the load mark was 3 inches above the water. The ship was over 2 feet by the stern, but this will soon be remedied.

Upon the coal sacks, upon and between the motor sledges and upon the ice-house are grouped the dogs, thirty-three in all. They must perforce be chained up and they are given what shelter is afforded on deck, but their position is not enviable. The seas continually break on the weather bulwarks and scatter clouds of heavy spray over the backs of all who must venture into the waist of the ship. The dogs sit with their tails to this invading water, their coats wet and dripping. It is a pathetic attitude, deeply significant of cold and misery; occasionally some poor beast emits a long pathetic whine. The group forms a picture of wretched dejection; such a life is truly hard for these poor creatures.

We manage somehow to find a seat for everyone at our cabin table, although the wardroom contains twenty-four officers. There are generally one or two on watch, which eases matters, but it is a squash. Our meals are simple enough, but it is really remarkable to see the manner in which our two stewards, Hooper and Neald, provide for all requirements – washing up, tidying cabin, and making themselves generally useful in the cheerfullest manner.

With such a large number of hands on board, allowing nine seamen in each watch, the ship is easily worked, and Meares and Oates have their appointed assistants to help them in custody of dogs and ponies, but on such a night as the last with the prospect of dirty weather, the 'after guard' of volunteers is awake and exhibiting its delightful enthusiasm in the cause of safety and comfort – some are ready to lend a hand if there is difficulty with ponies and dogs, others in shortening or trimming sails, and others again in keeping the bunkers filled with the deck coal.

I think Priestley is the most seriously incapacitated by sea-sickness – others who might be as bad have had some experience of the ship and her movement. Ponting cannot face meals but sticks to his work; on the way to Port Chalmers I am told that he posed several groups before the cinematograph, though obliged repeatedly to retire to the ship's side. Yesterday he was developing plates with the developing dish in one hand and an ordinary basin in the other!

We have run 190 miles today: a good start, but inconvenient in one respect – we have been making for Campbell Island, but early this morning it became evident that our rapid progress would bring us to the Island in the middle of the night, instead of tomorrow, as I had anticipated. The delay of waiting for daylight would not be advisable under the circumstances, so we gave up this item of our programme.

Later in the day the wind has veered to the westward, heading us slightly. I trust it will not go further round; we are now more than a point to eastward of our course to the ice, and three points to leeward of that to Campbell Island, so that we should not have fetched the Island anyhow.

Friday, December 2. – A day of great disaster. From 4 o'clock last night the wind freshened with great rapidity, and very shortly we were under topsails, jib, and staysail only. It blew very hard and the sea got up at once. Soon we were plunging heavily and taking much water over the lee rail. Oates and Atkinson with intermittent assistance from others were busy keeping the ponies on their legs. Cases of petrol, forage, &c., began to break loose on the upper deck; the principal trouble was caused by the loose coal-bags, which were bodily lifted by the seas and swung against the lashed cases. 'You know how carefully everything had been lashed, but no lashings could have withstood the onslaught of these coal sacks for long;' they acted like battering rams. 'There was nothing for it but to grapple with the evil, and nearly all hands were labouring for hours in the waist of the ship, heaving coal sacks overboard and re-lashing the petrol cases, &c., in the best manner possible under such difficult and dangerous circumstances. The seas were continually breaking over these people and now and again they would be completely submerged. At such times they had to cling for dear life to some fixture to prevent themselves being washed overboard, and with coal bags and loose cases washing about, there was every risk of such hold being torn away.

'No sooner was some semblance of order restored than some exceptionally heavy wave would tear away the lashing and the work had to be done all over again.'

The night wore on, the sea and wind ever rising, and the ship ever plunging more distractedly; we shortened sail to main topsail and staysail, stopped engines and hove to, but to little purpose. Tales of ponies down came frequently from forward, where Oates and Atkinson laboured through the entire night. Worse was to follow, much worse – a report from the engine-room that the pumps had choked and the water risen over the gratings.

From this moment, about 4 a.m., the engine-room became the centre of interest. The water gained in spite of every effort. Lashly, to his neck in rushing water, stuck gamely to the work of clearing suctions. For a time, with donkey engine and bilge pump sucking, it looked as though the water would be got under; but the hope was short-lived: five minutes of pumping invariably led to the same result – a general choking of the pumps.

The outlook appeared grim. The amount of water which was being made, with the ship so roughly handled, was most uncertain. 'We knew that normally the ship was not making much water, but we also knew that a considerable part of the water washing over the upper deck must be finding its way below; the decks were leaking in streams. The ship was very deeply laden; it did not need the addition of much water to get her waterlogged, in which condition anything might have happened.' The hand pump pro-duced only a dribble, and its suction could not be got at; as the water crept higher it got in contact with the boiler and grew warmer – so hot at last that no one could work at the suctions.

Williams had to confess he was beaten and must draw fires. What was to be done? Things for the moment appeared very black. The sea seemed higher than ever; it came over lee rail and poop, a rush of green water; the ship wallowed in it; a great piece of the bulwark carried clean away. The bilge pump is dependent on the main engine. To use the pump it was necessary to go ahead. It was at such times that the heaviest seas swept in over the lee rail; over and over [again] the rail, from the forerigging to the main, was covered by a solid sheet of curling water which swept aft and high on the poop. On one occasion I was waist deep when standing on the rail of the poop.

The scene on deck was devastating, and in the engine-room the water, though really not great in quantity, rushed over the floor plates and frames in a fashion that gave it a fearful significance.

The afterguard were organised in two parties by Evans to work buckets; the men were kept steadily going on the choked hand-pumps – this seemed all that could be done for the moment, and what a measure to count as the sole safeguard of the ship from sinking, practically an attempt to bale her out! Yet strange as it may seem the effort has not been wholly fruitless – the string of buckets which has now been kept going for four hours,* together with the dribble from the pump, has kept the water under – if anything there is a small decrease.

Meanwhile we have been thinking of a way to get at the suction of the pump: a hole is being made in the engine-room bulkhead, the coal between this and the pump shaft will be removed, and a hole made in the shaft. With so much water coming on board, it is impossible to open the hatch over the shaft. We are not out of the wood, but hope dawns, as indeed it should for me, when I find myself so wonderfully served. Officers and men are singing chanties over their arduous work. Williams is working in sweltering heat behind the boiler to get the door made in the bulkhead. Not a single one has lost his good spirits. A dog was drowned last night, one pony is dead and two others in a bad condition – probably they too will go. Occasionally a heavy sea would bear one of them away, and he was only saved by his chain. Meares with some helpers had constantly to be rescuing these wretched creatures from hanging, and trying to find them

* It was continued a night and a day.

better shelter, an almost hopeless task. One poor beast was found hanging when dead; one was washed away with such force that his chain broke and he disappeared overboard; the next wave miraculously washed him onboard again and he is now fit and well.' The gale has exacted heavy toll, but I feel all will be well if we can only cope with the water. Another dog has just been washed overboard – alas! Thank God, the gale is abating. The sea is still mountainously high, but the ship is not labouring so heavily as she was. I pray we may be under sail again before morning.

Saturday, December 3. – Yesterday the wind slowly fell towards evening; less water was taken on board, therefore less found its way below, and it soon became evident that our baling was gaining on the engine-room. The work was steadily kept going in two-hour shifts. By 10 p.m. the hole in the engine-room bulk-head was completed, and (Lieut.) Evans, wriggling over the coal, found his way to the pump shaft and down it. He soon cleared the suction 'of the coal balls (a mixture of coal and oil) which choked it', and to the joy of all a good stream of water came from the pump for the first time. From this moment it was evident we should get over the difficulty, and though the pump choked again on several occasions the water in the engine-room steadily decreased. It was good to visit that spot this morning and to find that the water no longer swished from side to side. In the forenoon fires were laid and lighted – the hand pump was got into complete order and sucked the bilges almost dry, so that great quantities of coal and ashes could be taken out.

Now all is well again, and we are steaming and sailing steadily south within two points of our course. Campbell and Bowers have been busy relisting everything on the upper deck. This afternoon we got out the two dead ponies through the forecastle skylight. It was a curious proceeding, as the space looked quite inadequate for their passage. We looked into the ice-house and found it in the best order.

Though we are not yet safe, as another gale might have disastrous results, it is wonderful to realise the change which has been wrought in our outlook in twenty-four hours. The others have confessed the gravely serious view of our position which they shared with me yesterday, and now we are all hopeful again.

As far as one can gather, besides the damage to the bulwarks of the ship, we have lost two ponies, one dog, '10 tons of coal', 65 gallons of petrol, and a case of the biologists' spirit – a serious loss enough, but much less than I expected. 'All things considered we have come off lightly, but it was bad luck to strike a gale at such a time.' The third pony which was down in a sling for some time in the gale is again on his feet. He looks a little groggy, but may pull through if we don't have another gale. Osman, our best sledge dog, was very bad this morning, but has been lying warmly in hay all day, and is now much better. 'Several more were in a very bad way and needed nursing back to life.' The sea and wind seem to be increasing again, and there is a heavy southerly swell, but the glass is high; we ought not to have another gale till it falls.[3]

Monday, December 5. – Lat. 56° 40'. – The barometer has been almost steady since Saturday, the wind rising and falling slightly, but steady in direction from the west. From a point off course we have crept up to the course itself. Everything looks prosperous except the ponies. Up to this morning, in spite of favourable wind and sea, the ship has been pitching heavily to a south-westerly swell. This has tried the animals badly, especially those under the forecastle. We had thought the ponies on the port side to be pretty safe, but two of them seem to me to be groggy, and I doubt if they could stand more heavy weather without a spell of rest. I pray there may be no more gales. We should be nearing the limits of the westerlies, but one cannot be sure for at least two days. There is still a swell from the S.W., though it is not nearly so heavy as yesterday, but I devoutly wish it would vanish altogether. So much depends on fine weather. December ought to be a fine month in the Ross Sea; it always has been, and just now conditions point to fine weather. Well, we must be prepared for anything, but I'm anxious, anxious about these animals of ours.

The dogs have quite recovered since the fine weather – they are quite in good form again.

Our deck cargo is getting reduced; all the coal is off the upper deck and the petrol is re-stored in better fashion; as far as that is concerned we should not mind another blow. Campbell and Bowers have been untiring in getting things straight on deck.

The idea of making our station Cape Crozier has again come on the tapis. There would be many advantages: the ease of getting there at an early date, the fact that none of the autumn or summer parties could be cut off, the fact that the main Barrier could be reached without crossing crevasses and that the track to the Pole would be due south from the first: the mild condition and absence of blizzards at the penguin rookery, the opportunity of studying the Emperor penguin incubation, and the new interest of the geology of Terror, besides minor facilities, such as the getting of ice, stones for shelters, &c. The disadvantages mainly consist in the possible difficulty of landing stores – a swell would make things very unpleasant, and might possibly prevent the landing of the horses and motors. Then again it would be certain that some distance of bare rock would have to be traversed before a good snow surface was reached from the hut, and possibly a climb of 300 or 400 feet would intervene. Again, it might be difficult to handle the ship whilst stores were being landed, owing to current, bergs, and floe ice. It remains to be seen, but the prospect is certainly alluring. At a pinch we could land the ponies in McMurdo Sound and let them walk round.

The sun is shining brightly this afternoon, everything is drying, and I think the swell continues to subside.

Tuesday, December 6. – Lat. 59° 7'. Long. 177° 51' E. Made good S. 17 E. 153; 457' to Circle. The promise of yesterday has been fulfilled, the swell has continued to subside, and this afternoon we go so steadily that we have much comfort. I am truly thankful – mainly for the sake of the ponies; poor things, they look thin and scraggy enough, but generally brighter and fitter. There is no doubt the forecastle is a bad place for them, but in any case some must have gone there. The four midship ponies, which were expected to be subject to the worst conditions, have had a much better time than their fellows. A few ponies have swollen legs, but all are feeding well. The wind failed in the morning watch and later a faint breeze came from the eastward; the barometer has been falling, but not on a steep gradient; it is still above normal. This afternoon it is overcast with a Scotch mist. Another day ought to put us beyond the reach of westerly gales.

We still continue to discuss the project of landing at Cape Crozier, and the prospect grows more fascinating as we realise it. For instance, we ought from such a base to get an excellent idea of the Barrier movement, and of the relative movement amongst the pressure ridges. There is no doubt it would be a tremendous stroke of luck to get safely landed there with all our paraphernalia.

Everyone is very cheerful – one hears laughter and song all day – it's delightful to be with such a merry crew. A week from New Zealand today.

Wednesday, December 7. – Lat. 61° 22'. Long. 179° 56' W. Made good S. 25 E. 150; Ant. Circle 313'. The barometer descended on a steep regular gradient all night, turning suddenly to an equally steep up grade this morning. With the turn a smart breeze sprang up from the S.W. and forced us three points off our course. The sea has remained calm, seeming to show that the ice is not far off; this afternoon temperature of air and water both 34°, supporting the assumption. The wind has come fair and we are on our course again, going between 7 and 8 knots.

Quantities of whale birds about the ship, the first fulmars and the first McCormick* skua seen. Last night saw 'hour glass' dolphins about. Sooty and black-browed albatrosses continue, with Cape chickens. The cold makes people hungry and one gets just a tremor on seeing the marvellous disappearance of consumables when our twenty-four young appetites have to be appeased.

Last night I discussed the Western Geological Party, and explained to Ponting the desirability of his going with it. I had thought he ought to be in charge, as the oldest and most experienced traveller, and mentioned it to him – then to Griffith Taylor. The latter was evidently deeply disappointed. So we three talked the matter out between us, and Ponting at once disclaimed any right, and announced cheerful agreement with Taylor's leadership; it was a satisfactory arrangement, and shows Ponting in a very pleasant light. I'm sure he's a very nice fellow.

I would record here a symptom of the spirit which actuates the men. After the gale the main deck under the forecastle space in which the ponies are stabled leaked badly, and the dirt of the stable leaked through on hammocks and bedding. Not a word has been said; the men living in that part have done their best to fend off the nuisance with oilskins and canvas, but without sign of complaint. Indeed the discomfort throughout the mess deck

* McCormick, after whom the bird was named, was doctor-naturalist on the *Erebus* with Ross in 1839–43.

has been extreme. Everything has been thrown about, water has found its way down in a dozen places. There is no daylight, and air can come only through the small forehatch; the artificial lamplight has given much trouble. The men have been wetted to the skin repeatedly on deck, and have no chance of drying their clothing. Ail things considered, their cheerful fortitude is little short of wonderful.

First Ice. – There was a report of ice at dinner tonight. Evans corroborated Cheetham's statement that there was a berg far away to the west, showing now and again as the sun burst through the clouds.

Thursday, December 8. – 63° 20'. 177° 22'. S. 31 E. 138': to Circle 191'. The wind increased in the first watch last night to a moderate gale. The ship close hauled held within two points of her course. Topgallant sails and mainsail were furled, and later in the night the wind gradually crept ahead. At 6 a.m. we were obliged to furl everything, and throughout the day we have been plunging against a stiff breeze and moderate sea. This afternoon by keeping a little to eastward of the course, we have managed to get fore and aft sail filled. The barometer has continued its steady upward path for twenty-four hours; it shows signs of turning, having reached within 1/10th of 30 inches. It was light throughout last night (always a cheerful condition), but this head wind is trying to the patience, more especially as our coal expenditure is more than I estimated. We manage 62 or 63 revolutions on about 9 tons, but have to distil every three days at expense of half a ton, and then there is a weekly half-ton for the cook. It is certainly a case of fighting one's way South.

I was much disturbed last night by the motion; the ship was pitching and twisting with short sharp movements on a confused sea, and with every plunge my thoughts flew to our poor ponies. This afternoon they are fairly well, but one knows that they must be getting weaker as time goes on, and one longs to give them a good sound rest with the ship on an even keel. Poor patient beasts! One wonders how far the memory of such fearful discomfort will remain with them – animals so often remember places and conditions where they have encountered difficulties or hurt. Do they only recollect circumstances which are deeply impressed by some shock of fear or sudden pain, and does the remembrance of prolonged strain pass away? Who can tell? But it would seem strangely merciful if nature should blot out these weeks of slow but inevitable torture.

The dogs are in great form again; for them the greatest circumstance of discomfort is to be constantly wet. It was this circumstance prolonged throughout the gale which nearly lost us our splendid leader 'Osman'. In the morning he was discovered utterly exhausted and only feebly trembling; life was very nearly out of him. He was buried in hay, and lay so for twenty-four hours, refusing food – the wonderful hardihood of his species was again shown by the fact that within another twenty-four hours he was to all appearance as fit as ever.

Antarctic petrels have come about us. This afternoon one was caught.

Later, about 7 p.m. Evans saw two icebergs far on the port beam; they could only be seen from the masthead. Whales have been frequently seen – *Balaenoptera Sibbaldi* – supposed to be the biggest mammal that has ever existed.[4]

Friday, December 9. – 65° 8'. 177° 41'. Made good S.4 W. 109'; Scott Island S. 22 W. 147'. At six this morning bergs and pack were reported ahead; at first we thought the pack might consist only of fragments of the bergs, but on entering a stream we found small worn floes – the ice not more than two or three feet in thickness. 'I had hoped that we should not meet it till we reached latitude 66½ or at least 66.' We decided to work to the south and west as far as the open water would allow, and have met with some success. At 4 p.m., as I write, we are still in open water, having kept a fairly straight course and come through five or six light streams of ice, none more than 300 yards across.

We have passed some very beautiful bergs, mostly tabular. The heights have varied from 60 to 80 feet, and I am getting to think that this part of the Antarctic yields few bergs of greater altitude.

Two bergs deserve some description. One, passed very close on port hand in order that it might be cinematographed, was about 80 feet in height, and tabular. It seemed to have been calved at a comparatively recent date.

The above picture* shows its peculiarities, and points to the desirability of close examination of other berg faces. There seemed

* Not reproduced in this edition.

to be a distinct difference of origin between the upper and lower portions of the berg, as though a land glacier had been covered by layer after layer of seasonal snow. Then again, what I have described as 'intrusive layers of blue ice' was a remarkable feature; one could imagine that these layers represent surfaces which have been transformed by regelation under hot sun and wind.

This point required investigation.

The second berg was distinguished by innumerable vertical cracks. These seemed to run criss-cross and to weaken the structure, so that the various seracs formed by them had bent to different angles and shapes, giving a very irregular surface to the berg, and a face scarred with immense vertical fissures.

One imagines that such a berg has come from a region of ice disturbance such as King Edward's Land.

We have seen a good many whales today, rorquals with high black spouts – *Balaenoptera Sibbaldi*.

The birds with us: Antarctic and snow petrel – a fulmar – and this morning Cape pigeon.

We have pack ice farther north than expected, and it's impossible to interpret the fact. One hopes that we shall not have anything heavy, but I'm afraid there's not much to build upon.

10 p.m. – We have made good progress throughout the day, but the ice streams thicken as we advance, and on either side of us the pack now appears in considerable fields. We still pass quantities of bergs, perhaps nearly one-half the number tabular, but the rest worn and fantastic.

The sky has been wonderful, with every form of cloud in every condition of light and shade; the sun has continually appeared through breaks in the cloudy heavens from time to time, brilliantly illuminating some field of pack, some steep-walled berg, or some patch of bluest sea. So sunlight and shadow have chased each other across our scene. Tonight there is little or no swell – the ship is on an even keel, steady, save for the occasional shocks on striking ice.

It is difficult to express the sense of relief this steadiness gives after our storm-tossed passage. One can only imagine the relief and comfort afforded to the ponies, but the dogs are visibly cheered and the human element is full of gaiety. The voyage seems full of promise in spite of the imminence of delay.

If the pack becomes thick I shall certainly put the fires out and wait for it to open. I do not think it ought to remain close for long in this meridian. Tonight we must be beyond the 66th parallel.

Saturday, December 10. – Dead Reckoning 66° 38'. Long. 178° 47'. Made good S. 17 W. 94. C. Crozier 688'. Stayed on deck till midnight. The sun just dipped below the southern horizon. The scene was incomparable. The northern sky was gloriously rosy and reflected in the calm sea between the ice, which varied from burnished copper to salmon pink; bergs and pack to the north had a pale greenish hue with deep purple shadows, the sky shaded to saffron and pale green. We gazed long at these beautiful effects. The ship made through leads during the night; morning found us pretty well at the end of the open water. We stopped to water ship from a nice hummocky floe. We made about 8 tons of water. Rennick took a sounding, 1960 fathoms; the tube brought up two small lumps of volcanic lava with the usual globigerina ooze.

Wilson shot a number of Antarctic petrel and snowy petrel. Nelson got some crustaceans and other beasts with a vertical tow net, and got a water sample and temperatures at 400 metres. The water was warmer at that depth. About 1.30 we proceeded at first through fairly easy pack, then in amongst very heavy old floes grouped about a big berg; we shot out of this and made a detour, getting easier going; but though the floes were less formidable as we proceeded south, the pack grew thicker. I noticed large floes of comparatively thin ice – very sodden and easily split; these are similar to some we went through in the *Discovery*, but tougher by a month.

At three we stopped and shot four crab-eater seals; tonight we had the livers for dinner – they were excellent.

Tonight we are in very close pack – it is doubtful if it is worth pushing on, but an arch of clear sky which has shown to the southward all day makes me think that there must be clearer water in that direction; perhaps only some 20 miles away – but 20 miles is much under present conditions. As I came below to bed at 11 p.m. Bruce was slogging away, making fair progress, but now and again brought up altogether. I noticed the ice was becoming much smoother and thinner, with occasional signs of pressure, between which the ice was very thin.

'We had been very carefully into all the evidence of former
voyages to pick the best meridian to go south on, and I thought
and still think that the evidence points to the 178° W. as the best.
We entered the pack more or less on this meridian, and have
been rewarded by encountering worse conditions than any ship
has had before – worse, in fact, than I imagined would have been
possible on any other meridian of those from which we could
have chosen.

'To understand the difficulty of the position you must appreciate
what the pack is and how little is known of its movements.

'The pack in this part of the world consists (1) of the ice which has
formed over the sea on the fringe of the Antarctic continent during
the last winter; (2) of very heavy old ice floes which have broken
out of bays and inlets during the previous summer, but have not had
time to get north before the winter set in; (3) of comparatively
heavy ice formed over the Ross Sea early in the last winter; and (4)
of comparatively thin ice which has formed over parts of the Ross
Sea in middle or towards the end of the last winter.

'Undoubtedly throughout the winter all ice-sheets move and
twist, tear apart and press up into ridges, and thousands of bergs
charge through these sheets, raising hummocks and lines of
pressure and mixing things up; then of course where such rents
are made in the winter the sea freezes again, forming a newer and
thinner sheet.

'With the coming of summer the northern edge of the sheet
decays and the heavy ocean swell penetrates it, gradually breaking
it into smaller and smaller fragments. Then the whole body moves
to the north and the swell of the Ross Sea attacks the southern edge
of the pack.

'This makes it clear why at the northern and southern limits
the pieces or ice-floes are comparatively small, whilst in the
middle the floes may be two or three miles across; and why the
pack may and does consist of various natures of ice-floes in
extraordinary confusion.

'Further it will be understood why the belt grows narrower and
the floes thinner and smaller as the summer advances.

'We know that where thick pack may be found early in January,
open water and a clear sea may be found in February, and broadly
that the later the date the easier the chance of getting through.

'A ship going through the pack must either break through the floes, push them aside, or go round them, observing that she cannot push floes which are more than 200 or 300 yards across.

'Whether a ship can get through or not depends on the thickness and nature of the ice, the size of the floes and the closeness with which they are packed together, as well as on her own power.

'The situation of the main bodies of pack and the closeness with which the floes are packed depend almost entirely on the prevailing winds. One cannot tell what winds have prevailed before one's arrival; therefore one cannot know much about the situation or density.

'Within limits the density is changing from day to day and even from hour to hour; such changes depend on the wind, but it may not ncessarily be a local wind, so that at times they seem almost mysterious. One sees the floes pressing closely against one another at a given time, and an hour or two afterwards a gap of a foot or more may be seen between each.

'When the floes are pressed together it is difficult and sometimes impossible to force a way through, but when there is release of pressure the sum of many little gaps allows one to take a zigzag path.'

CHAPTER TWO

In the pack

Sunday, December 11. – The ice grew closer during the night, and at 6 it seemed hopeless to try and get ahead. The pack here is very regular; the floes about 2½ feet thick and very solid. They are pressed closely together, but being irregular in shape, open spaces frequently occur, generally triangular in shape.

It might be noted that such ice as this occupies much greater space than it originally did when it formed a complete sheet – hence if the Ross Sea were wholly frozen over in the spring, the total quantity of pack to the north of it when it breaks out must be immense.

This ice looks as though it must have come from the Ross Sea, and yet one is puzzled to account for the absence of pressure.

We have lain tight in the pack all day; the wind from 6 a.m. strong from W. and N.W., with snow; the wind has eased tonight, and for some hours the glass, which fell rapidly last night, has been stationary. I expect the wind will shift soon; pressure on the pack has eased, but so far it has not opened.

This morning Rennick got a sounding at 2015 fathoms from bottom similar to yesterday, with small pieces of basic lava; these two soundings appear to show a great distribution of this volcanic rock by ice. The line was weighed by hand after the soundings. I read Service in the wardroom.

This afternoon all hands have been away on ski over the floes. It is delightful to get the exercise. I'm much pleased with the ski and ski boots – both are very well adapted to our purposes.

This waiting requires patience, though I suppose it was to be expected at such an early season. It is difficult to know when to try and push on again.

Monday, December 12. – The pack was a little looser this morning; there was a distinct long swell apparently from N.W. The floes were not apart but barely touching the edges, which were hard pressed yesterday; the wind still holds from N.W., but lighter. Gran, Oates, and Bowers went on ski towards a reported island about which there had been some difference of opinion. I felt certain it was a berg, and it proved to be so; only of a very curious dome shape with very low cliffs all about.

Fires were ordered for 12, and at 11.30 we started steaming with plain sail set. We made, and are making fair progress on the whole, but it is very uneven. We escaped from the heavy floes about us into much thinner pack, then through two water holes, then back to the thinner pack consisting of thin floes of large area fairly easily broken. All went well till we struck heavy floes again, then for half an hour we stopped dead. Then on again, and since alternately bad and good – that is, thin young floes and hoary older ones, occasionally a pressed-up berg, very heavy.

The best news of yesterday was that we drifted 15 miles to the S.E., so that we have not really stopped our progress at all, though it has, of course, been pretty slow.

I really don't know what to think of the pack, or when to hope for open water.

We tried Atkinson's blubber stove this afternoon with great success. The interior of the stove holds a pipe in a single coil pierced with holes on the under side. These holes drip oil on to an asbestos burner. The blubber is placed in a tank suitably built around the chimney; the overflow of oil from this tank leads to the feed pipe in the stove, with a cock to regulate the flow. A very simple device, but as has been shown a very effective one; the stove gives great heat, but, of course, some blubber smell. However, with such stoves in the South one would never lack cooked food or warm hut.

Discussed with Wright the fact that the hummocks on sea ice always yield fresh water. We agreed that the brine must simply run down out of the ice. It will be interesting to bring up a piece of sea ice and watch this process. But the fact itself is interesting as showing that the process producing the hummock is really producing fresh water. It may also be noted as a phenomenon which makes all the difference to the ice navigator.[5]

Truly the getting to our winter quarters is no light task; at first the gales and heavy seas, and now this continuous fight with the pack ice.

8 p.m. – We are getting on with much bumping and occasional 'hold ups'.

Tuesday, December 13. – I was up most of the night. Never have I experienced such rapid and complete changes of prospect. Cheetham in the last dog-watch was running the ship through sludgy new ice, making with all sail set four or five knots. Bruce, in the first, took over as we got into heavy ice again; but after a severe tussle got through into better conditions. The ice of yesterday loose with sludgy thin floes between. The middle watch found us making for an open lead, the ice around hard and heavy. We got through, and by sticking to the open water and then to some recently frozen pools made good progress. At the end of the middle watch trouble began again, and during this and the first part of the morning we were wrestling with the worst conditions we have met. Heavy hummocked bay ice, the floes standing 7 or 8 feet out of water, and very deep below. It was just such ice as we encountered at King Edward's Land in the *Discovery*. I have never seen anything more formidable. The last part of the morning watch was spent in a long recently-frozen lead or pool, and the ship went well ahead again.

These changes sound tame enough, but they are a great strain on one's nerves – one is for ever wondering whether one has done right in trying to come down so far east, and having regard to coal, what ought to be done under the circumstances.

In the first watch came many alterations of opinion; time and again it looks as though we ought to stop when it seemed futile to be pushing and pushing without result; then would come a stretch of easy going and the impression that all was going very well with us. The fact of the matter is, it is difficult not to imagine the conditions in which one finds oneself to be more extensive than they are. It is wearing to have to face new conditions every hour. This morning we met at breakfast in great spirits; the ship has been boring along well for two hours; then Cheetham suddenly ran her into a belt of the worst and we were held up immediately. We can push back again, I think, but meanwhile we have taken advantage of the conditions to water ship. These big floes are very handy for that purpose at any rate. Rennick got a sounding – 2124 fathoms, similar bottom including volcanic lava.

Terra Nova in the pack

December 13 (cont.). – 67° 30' S. 177 °58' W. Made good S. 20 E. 27'. C. Crozier S. 21 W. 644'. We got in several tons of ice, then pushed off and slowly and laboriously worked our way to one of the recently frozen pools. It was not easily crossed, but when we came to its junction with the next part to the S.W. (in which direction I proposed to go) we were quite hung up. A little inspection showed that the big floes were tending to close. It seems as though the tenacity of the 6 or 7 inches of recent ice over the pools is enormously increased by lateral pressure. But whatever the cause, we could not budge.

We have decided to put fires out and remain here till the conditions change altogether for the better. It is sheer waste of coal to make further attempts to break through as things are at present.

We have been set to the east during the past days; is it the normal set in the region, or due to the prevalence of westerly winds? Possibly much depends on this as concerns our date of release. It is annoying, but one must contain one's soul in patience and hope for a brighter outlook in a day or two. Meanwhile we shall sound, and do as much biological work as is possible.

The pack is a sunless place as a rule; this morning we had bright sunshine for a few hours, but later the sky clouded over from the north again, and now it is snowing dismally. It is calm.

Wednesday, December 14. – Position, N. 2', W. ½'. The pack still close around. From the masthead one can see a few patches of open water in different directions, but the main outlook is the same scene of desolate hummocky pack. The wind has come from the S.W., force 2; we have bright sunshine and good sights. The ship has swung to the wind and the floes around are continually moving. They change their relative positions in a slow, furtive, creeping fashion. The temperature is 35°, the water 29.2° to 29.5°. Under such conditions the thin sludgy ice ought to be weakening all the time; a few inches of such stuff should allow us to push through anywhere.

One realises the awful monotony of a long stay in the pack, such as Nansen and others experienced. One can imagine such days as these lengthening into interminable months and years.

For us there is novelty, and everyone has work to do or makes work, so that there is no keen sense of impatience.

Nelson and Lillie were up all night with the current meter; it is not quite satisfactory, but some result has been obtained. They will also get a series of temperatures and samples and use the vertical tow net.

The current is satisfactory. Both days the fixes have been good – it is best that we should go north and west. I had a great fear that we should be drifted east and so away to regions of permanent pack. If we go on in this direction it can only be a question of time before we are freed.

We have all been away on ski on the large floe to which we anchored this morning. Gran is wonderfully good and gives instruction well. It was hot, and garments came off one by one – the Soldier* and Atkinson were stripped to the waist eventually, and have been sliding round the floe for some time in that condition. Nearly everyone has been wearing goggles; the glare is very bad. Ponting tried to get a colour picture, but unfortunately the ice colours are too delicate for this.

Tonight Campbell, E. Evans, and I went out over the floe, and each in turn towed the other two; it was fairly easy work – that is, to pull 310 to 320 lb. One could pull it perhaps more easily on foot, yet it would be impossible to pull such a load on a sledge. What a puzzle this pulling of loads is! If one could think that this captivity was soon to end there would be little reason to regret it; it is giving practice with our deep-sea gear, and has made everyone keen to learn the proper use of ski.

The swell has increased considerably, but it is impossible to tell from what direction it comes; one can simply note that the ship and brash ice swing to and fro, bumping into the floe.

We opened the ice-house today, and found the meat in excellent condition – most of it still frozen.

Thursday, December 15. – 66° 23' S. 177° 59' W. Sit. N. 2', E. 5½'. In the morning the conditions were unaltered. Went for a ski run before breakfast. It makes a wonderful difference to get the blood circulating by a little exercise.

After breakfast we served out ski to the men of the landing party. They are all very keen to learn, and Gran has been out morning and afternoon giving instruction.

Meares got some of his dogs out and a sledge – two lots of seven;

* Captain Oates's nickname.

those that looked in worst condition (and several are getting very fat) were tried. They were very short of wind; it is difficult to understand how they can get so fat, as they only get two and a half biscuits a day at the most. The ponies are looking very well on the whole, especially those in the outside stalls.

Rennick got a sounding today – 1,844 fathoms; reversible thermometers were placed close to bottom and 500 fathoms up. We shall get a very good series of temperatures from the bottom up during the wait. Nelson will try to get some more current observations tonight or tomorrow.

It is very trying to find oneself continually drifting north, but one is thankful not to be going east.

Tonight it has fallen calm and the floes have decidedly opened; there is a lot of water about the ship, but it does not look to extend far. Meanwhile the brash and thinner floes are melting; everything of that sort must help – but it's trying to the patience to be delayed like this.

We have seen enough to know that with a north-westerly or westerly wind the floes tend to pack and that they open when it is calm. The question is, will they open more with an easterly or south-easterly wind – that is the hope.

Signs of open water round and about are certainly increasing rather than diminishing.

Friday, December 16. – The wind sprang up from the N.E. this morning, bringing snow, thin light hail, and finally rain; it grew very thick and has remained so all day.

Early the floe on which we had done so much ski-ing broke up, and we gathered in our ice anchors, then put on head sail, to which she gradually paid off. With a fair wind we set sail on the foremast, and slowly but surely she pushed the heavy floes aside. At lunch time we entered a long lead of open water, and for nearly half an hour we sailed along comfortably in it. Entering the pack again, we found the floes much lighter and again pushed on slowly. In all we may have made as much as three miles.

I have observed for some time some floes of immense area forming a chain of lakes in this pack, and have been most anxious to discover their thickness. They are most certainly the result of the freezing of comparatively recent pools in the winter pack, and it follows that they must be getting weaker day by day. If one could be certain, first, that these big areas extend to the south, and, secondly, that the ship could go through them, it would be worth getting up steam. We have arrived at the edge of one of these floes, and the ship will not go through under sail, but I'm sure she would do so under steam. Is this a typical floe? And are there more ahead?

One of the ponies got down this afternoon – Oates thinks it was probably asleep and fell, but the incident is alarming; the animals are not too strong. On this account this delay is harassing – otherwise we should not have much to regret.

Saturday, December 17. – 67° 24'. 177° 34'. Drift for 48 hours S. 82 E. 9.7'. It rained hard and the glass fell rapidly last night with every sign of a coming gale. This morning the wind increased to force 6 from the west with snow. At noon the barograph curve turned up and the wind moderated, the sky gradually clearing.

Tonight it is fairly bright and clear; there is a light south-westerly wind. It seems rather as though the great gales of the Westerlies must begin in these latitudes with such mild disturbances as we have just experienced. I think it is the first time I have known rain beyond the Antarctic circle – it is interesting to speculate on its effect in melting the floes.

We have scarcely moved all day, but bergs which have become quite old friends through the week are on the move, and one has approached and almost circled us. Evidently these bergs are moving about in an irregular fashion, only they must have all travelled a little east in the forty-eight hours as we have done. Another interesting observation tonight is that of the slow passage of a stream of old heavy floes past the ship and the lighter ice in which she is held.

There are signs of water sky to the south, and I'm impatient to be off, but still one feels that waiting may be good policy, and I should certainly contemplate waiting some time longer if it weren't for the ponies.

Everyone is wonderfully cheerful; there is laughter all day long. Nelson finished his series of temperatures and samples today with an observation at 1800 metres.

Series of sea temperatures

	Depth in metres	Temp. (uncorrected)
Dec. 14	0	−1.67
	10	−1.84
	20	−1.86
	30	−1.89
	50	−1.92
	75	−1.93
	100	−1.80
	125	−1.11
	150	−0.63
	200	+0.24
	500	+1.18
	1500	+0.935
Dec. 17	1800	+0.61
	2300	+0.48
Dec. 15	2800	+0.28
	3220	+0.11
	3650	−0.13 no sample
	3891	bottom
Dec. 20	2300 (1260 fms.)	+0.48° C.
	3220 (1760 fms.)	+0.11° C.
	3300	bottom

A curious point is that the bottom layer is 2 tenths higher on the 20th, remaining in accord with the same depth on the 15th.

Sunday, December 18. – In the night it fell calm and the floes opened out. There is more open water between the floes around us, yet not a great deal more.

In general what we have observed on the opening of the pack means a very small increase in the open water spaces, but enough to convey the impression that the floes, instead of wishing to rub shoulders and grind against one another, desire to be apart. They touch lightly where they touch at all – such a condition makes much difference to the ship in attempts to force her through, as each floe is freer to move on being struck.

If a pack be taken as an area bounded by open water it is evident that a small increase of the periphery or a small outward movement of the floes will add much to the open water spaces and create a general freedom.

The opening of this pack was reported at 3 a.m., and orders were given to raise steam. The die is cast, and we must now make a determined push for the open southern sea.

There is a considerable swell from the N.W.; it should help us to get along.

Evening. – Again extraordinary differences of fortune. At first things looked very bad – it took nearly half an hour to get started, much more than an hour to work away to one of the large area floes to which I have referred; then to my horror the ship refused to look at it. Again by hard fighting we worked away to a crack running across this sheet, and to get through this crack required many stoppages and engine reversals.

Then we had to shoot away south to avoid another unbroken floe of large area, but after we had rounded this things became easier; from 6 o'clock we were almost able to keep a steady course, only occasionally hung up by some thicker floe. The rest of the ice was fairly recent and easily broken. At 7 the leads of recent ice became easier still, and at 8 we entered a long lane of open water. For a time we almost thought we had come to the end of our troubles, and there was much jubilation. But, alas! at the end of the lead we have come again to heavy bay ice. It is undoubtedly this mixture of bay ice which causes the open leads, and I cannot but think that this is the King Edward's Land pack. We are making S.W. as best we can.

What an exasperating game this is! one cannot tell what is going to happen in the next half or even quarter of an hour. At one moment everything looks flourishing, the next one begins to doubt if it is possible to get through.

New fish. – Just at the end of the open lead tonight we capsized a small floe and thereby jerked a fish out on top of another one. We stopped and picked it up, finding it a beautiful silver-grey, genus *Notothenia* – I think a new species.

Snow squalls have been passing at intervals the wind continues in the N.W. It is comparatively warm.

We saw the first full-grown Emperor penguin tonight.

Monday, December 19. – On the whole, in spite of many bumps, we made good progress during the night, but the morning (present) outlook is the worst we've had. We seem to be in the midst of a terribly heavy screwed pack; it stretches in all directions as far as the eye can see, and the prospects are alarming from all points of view. I have decided to push west – anything to get out of these terribly heavy floes. Great patience is the only panacea for our ill case. It is bad luck.

We first got amongst the very thick floes at 1 a.m., and jammed through some of the most monstrous I have ever seen. The pressure ridges rose 24 feet above the surface – the ice must have extended at least 30 feet below. The blows given us gave the impression of irresistible solidity. Later in the night we passed out of this into long lanes of water and some of thin brash ice, hence the progress made. I'm afraid we have strained our rudder; it is stiff in one direction. We are in difficult circumstances altogether. This morning we have brilliant sunshine and no wind.

Noon 67° 54.5' S., 178° 28' W. Made good S. 34 W. 37'; C. Crozier 606'. Fog has spread up from the south with a very light southerly breeze.

There has been another change of conditions, but I scarcely know whether to call it for the better or the worse. There are fewer heavy old floes; on the other hand, the one-year floes, tremendously screwed and doubtless including old floes in their mass, have now enormously increased in area.

A floe which we have just passed must have been a mile across; this argues lack of swell and from that one might judge the open water to be very far. We made progress in a fairly good direction this morning, but the outlook is bad again – the ice seems to be closing. Again patience, we must go on steadily working through.

5.30. – We passed two immense bergs in the afternoon watch, the first of an irregular tabular form. The stratified surface had clearly faulted. I suggest that an uneven bottom to such a berg giving unequal buoyancy to parts causes this faulting. The second berg was domed, having a twin peak. These bergs are still a puzzle. I rather cling to my original idea that they become domed when stranded and isolated.

These two bergs had left long tracks of open water in the pack. We came through these making nearly 3 knots, but, alas! only in a direction which carried us a little east of south. It was difficult to get from one tract to another, but the tracts themselves were quite clear of ice. I noticed with rather a sinking that the floes on either side of us were assuming gigantic areas; one or two could not have been less than 2 or 3 miles across. It seemed to point to very distant open water.

But an observation which gave greater satisfaction was a steady reduction in the thickness of the floes. At first they were still much pressed up and screwed. One saw lines and heaps of pressure dotted over the surface of the larger floes, but it was evident from the upturned slopes that the floes had been thin when these disturbances took place.

At about 4.30 we came to a group of six or seven low tabular bergs some 15 or 20 feet in height. It was such as these that we saw in King Edward's Land, and they might very well come from that region. Three of these were beautifully uniform, with flat tops and straight perpendicular sides, and others had overhanging cornices, and some sloped towards the edges.

No more open water was reported on the other side of the bergs, and one wondered what would come next. The conditions have proved a pleasing surprise. There are still large floes on either side of us, but they are not much hummocked; there are pools of water on their surface, and the lanes between are filled with light brash and only an occasional heavy floe. The difference is wonderful. The heavy floes and gigantic pressure ice struck one most alarmingly – it seemed impossible that the ship could win her way through them, and led one to imagine all sorts of possibilities, such as remaining to be drifted north and freed later in the season, and the contrast now that the ice all around is little more than 2 or 3 feet thick is an immense relief. It seems like release from a horrid captivity. Evans has twice suggested stopping and waiting today, and on three occasions I have felt my own decision trembling in the balance. If this condition holds I need not say how glad we shall be that we doggedly pushed on in spite of the apparently hopeless outlook.

In any case, if it holds or not, it will be a great relief to feel that there is this plain of negotiable ice behind one.

Saw two sea leopards this evening, one in the water making short, lazy dives under the floes. It had a beautiful sinuous movement.

I have asked Pennell to prepare a map of the pack; it ought to give some idea of the origin of the various forms of floes, and their general drift. I am much inclined to think that most of the pressure ridges are formed by the passage of bergs through the comparatively young ice. I imagine that when the sea freezes very solid it carries bergs with it, but obviously the enormous mass of a berg would need a great deal of stopping. In support of this view I notice that most of the pressure ridges are formed by pieces of a sheet which did not exceed one or two feet in thickness – also it seems that the screwed ice which we have passed has occurred mostly in the regions of bergs. On one side of the tabular berg passed yesterday pressure was heaped to a height of 15 feet – it was like a ship's bow wave on a large scale. Yesterday there were many bergs and much pressure; last night no bergs and practically no pressure; this morning few bergs and comparatively little pressure. It goes to show that the unconfined pack of these seas would not be likely to give a ship a severe squeeze.

Saw a young Emperor this morning, and whilst trying to capture it one of Wilson's new whales with the sabre dorsal fin rose close to the ship. I estimated this fin to be 4 feet high.

It is pretty to see the snow petrel and Antarctic petrel diving on to the upturned and flooded floes. The wash of water sweeps the Euphausia* across such submerged ice. The Antarctic petrel has a pretty crouching attitude.

Notes on nicknames

Evans	Teddy
Wilson	Bill, Uncle Bill, Uncle
Simpson	Sunny Jim
Ponting	Ponco
Meares	
Day	
Campbell	The Mate, Mr Mate
Pennell	Penelope
Rennick	Parnie
Bowers	Birdie
Taylor	Griff and Keir Hardy
Nelson	Marie and Bronte
Gran	
Cherry-Garrard	Cherry

* A species of shrimp on which the seabirds feed.

Wright	Silas, Toronto
Priestley	Raymond
Debenham	Deb
Bruce	
Drake	Francis
Atkinson	Jane, Helmin, Atchison
Oates	Titus, Soldier, 'Farmer Hayseed' (by Bowers)
Levick	Toffarino, the Old Sport
Lillie	Lithley, Hercules, Lithi[6]

Tuesday, December 20. – Noon 68° 41' S., 179° 28' W. Made good S. 36 W. 58; C. Crozier S. 20 W. 563'. The good conditions held up to midnight last night; we went from lead to lead with only occasional small difficulties. At 9 o'clock we passed along the western edge of a big stream of very heavy bay ice – such ice as would come out late in the season from the inner reaches and bays of Victoria Sound, where the snows drift deeply. For a moment one imagined a return to our bad conditions, but we passed this heavy stuff in an hour and came again to the former condition, making our way in leads between floes of great area.

Bowers reported a floe of 12 square miles in the middle watch. We made very fair progress during the night, and an excellent run in the morning watch. Before eight a moderate breeze sprang up from the west and the ice began to close. We have worked our way a mile or two on since, but with much difficulty, so that we have now decided to bank fires and wait for the ice to open again; meanwhile we shall sound and get a haul with tow nets. I'm afraid we are still a long way from the open water; the floes are large, and where we have stopped they seem to be such as must have been formed early last winter. The signs of pressure have increased again. Bergs were very scarce last night, but there are several around us today. One has a number of big humps on top. It is curious to think how these big blocks became perched so high. I imagine the berg must have been calved from a region of hard-pressure ridges. [*Later*] This is a mistake – on closer inspection it is quite clear that the berg has tilted and that a great part of the upper strata, probably 20 feet deep, has slipped off, leaving the humps as islands on top.

It looks as though we must exercise patience again; progress is more difficult than in the worst of our experiences yesterday, but the outlook is very much brighter. This morning there were many dark shades of open water sky to the south; the westerly wind ruffling the water makes these cloud shadows very dark.

The barometer has been very steady for several days and we ought to have fine weather: this morning a lot of low cloud came from the S.W., at one time low enough to become fog – the clouds are rising and dissipating, and we have almost a clear blue sky with sunshine.

Evening. – The wind has gone from west to W.S.W. and still blows nearly force 6. We are lying very comfortably alongside a floe with open water to windward for 200 or 300 yards. The sky has been clear most of the day, fragments of low stratus occasionally hurry across the sky and a light cirrus is moving with some speed. Evidently it is blowing hard in the upper current. The ice has closed – I trust it will open well when the wind lets up. There is a lot of open water behind us. The berg described this morning has been circling round us, passing within 800 yards; the bearing and distance have altered so un-uniformly that it is evident that the differential movement between the surface water and the berg-driving layers (from 100 to 200 metres down) is very irregular. We had several hours on the floe practising ski running, and thus got some welcome exercise. Coal is now the great anxiety – we are making terrible inroads on our supply – we have come 240 miles since we first entered the pack streams.

The sounding today gave 1804 fathoms – the water bottle didn't work, but temperatures were got at 1300 and bottom.

The temperature was down to 20° last night and kept 2 or 3 degrees below freezing all day.

The surface for ski-ing today was very good.

Wednesday, December 21. – The wind was still strong this morning, but had shifted to the south-west. With an overcast sky it was very cold and raw. The sun is now peeping through, the wind lessening and the weather conditions generally improving. During the night we had been drifting towards two large bergs, and about breakfast time we were becoming uncomfortably close to one of them – the big floes were binding down on one another, but there seemed to be open water to the S.E., if we could work out in that direction.

(*Note.* All directions of wind are given 'true' in this book.)

Noon position. – 68° 25' S., 179° 11' W. Made good S. 26 E. 2.5'. Set of current N., 32 E. 9.4'. Made good 24 hours – N. 40 E. 8'. We got the steam up and about 9 a.m. commenced to push through. Once or twice we have spent nearly twenty minutes pushing through bad places, but it looks as though we are getting to easier water. It's distressing to have the pack so tight, and the bergs make it impossible to lie comfortably still for any length of time. Ponting has made some beautiful photographs and Wilson some charming pictures of the pack and bergs; certainly our voyage will be well illustrated. We find quite a lot of sketching talent. Day, Taylor, Debenham, and Wright all contribute to the elaborate record of the bergs and ice features met with.

5 p.m. – The wind has settled to a moderate gale from S.W. We went 2½ miles this morning, then became jammed again. The effort has taken us well clear of the threatening bergs. Some others to leeward now are a long way off, but they are there and to leeward, robbing our position of its full measure of security. Oh! but it's mighty trying to be delayed and delayed like this, and coal going all the time – also we are drifting N. and E. – the pack has carried us 9' N. and 6' E. It really is very distressing. I don't like letting fires go out with these bergs about.

Wilson went over the floe to capture some penguins and lay flat on the surface. We saw the birds run up to him, then turn within a few feet and rush away again. He says that they came towards him when he was singing, and ran away again when he stopped. They were all one-year birds, and seemed exceptionally shy; they appear to be attracted to the ship by a fearful curiosity.[7]

A chain of bergs must form a great obstruction to a field of pack ice, largely preventing its drift and forming lanes of open water. Taken in conjunction with the effect of bergs in forming pressure ridges, it follows that bergs have a great influence on the movement as well as the nature of pack.

Thursday, December 22. – Noon 68° 26' 2" S., 197° 8' 5" W. Sit. N. 5 E. 8.5'. – No change. The wind still steady from the S.W., with a clear sky and even barometer. It looks as though it might last any time. This is sheer bad luck. We have let the fires die out;

there are bergs to leeward and we must take our chance of clearing them – we cannot go on wasting coal.

There is not a vestige of swell, and with the wind in this direction there certainly ought to be if the open water was reasonably close. No, it looks as though we'd struck a streak of real bad luck; that fortune has determined to put every difficulty in our path. We have less than 300 tons of coal left in a ship that simply eats coal. It's alarming – and then there are the ponies going steadily down-hill in condition. The only encouragement is the persistence of open water to the east and south-east to south; big lanes of open water can be seen in that position, but we cannot get to them in this pressed-up pack.

Atkinson has discovered a new tapeworm in the intestines of the Adélie penguin – a very tiny worm one-eighth of an inch in length with a propeller-shaped head.

A crumb of comfort comes on finding that we have not drifted to the eastward appreciably.

Friday, December 23. – The wind fell light at about ten last night and the ship swung round. Sail was set on the fore, and she pushed a few hundred yards to the north, but soon became jammed again. This brought us dead to windward of and close to a large berg with the wind steadily increasing. Not a very pleasant position, but also not one that caused much alarm. We set all sail, and with this help the ship slowly carried the pack round, pivoting on the berg until, as the pressure relieved, she slid out into the open water close to the berg. Here it was possible to 'wear ship', and we saw a fair prospect of getting away to the east and afterwards south. Following the leads up we made excellent progress during the morning watch, and early in the forenoon turned south, and then south-west.

We had made 8½' S. 22 E. and about 5' S.S.W. by 1 p.m., and could see a long lead of water to the south, cut off only by a broad strip of floe with many water holes in it: a composite floe. There was just a chance of getting through, but we have stuck half-way, advance and retreat equally impossible under sail alone. Steam has been ordered but will not be ready till near midnight. Shall we be out of the pack by Christmas Eve?

The floes today have been larger but thin and very sodden. There are extensive water pools showing in patches on the surface, and one notes some that run in line as though extending from cracks; also here and there close water-free cracks can be seen. Such floes might well be termed '*composite*' floes, since they evidently consist of old floes which have been frozen together – the junction being concealed by more recent snowfalls.

A month ago it would probably have been difficult to detect inequalities or differences in the nature of the parts of the floes, but now the younger ice has become waterlogged and is melting rapidly, hence the pools.

I am inclined to think that nearly all the large floes as well as many of the smaller ones are 'composite' and this would seem to show that the cementing of two floes does not necessarily mean a line of weakness, provided the difference in the thickness of the cemented floes is not too great; of course, young ice or even a single season's sea ice cannot become firmly attached to the thick old bay floes, and hence one finds these isolated even at this season of the year.

Very little can happen in the personal affairs of our company in this comparatively dull time, but it is good to see the steady progress that proceeds unconsciously in cementing the happy relationship that exists between the members of the party. Never could there have been a greater freedom from quarrels and trouble of all sorts. I have not heard a harsh word or seen a black look. A spirit of tolerance and good humour pervades the whole community, and it is glorious to realise that men can live under conditions of hardship, monotony, and danger in such bountiful good comradeship.

Preparations are now being made for Christmas festivities. It is curious to think that we have already passed the longest day in the southern year.

Saw a whale this morning – estimated 25 to 30 feet. Wilson thinks a new species. Find Adélie penguins in batches of twenty or so. Do not remember having seen so many together in the pack.

After midnight, December 23. – Steam was reported ready at 11 p.m. After some pushing to and fro we wriggled out of our ice prison and followed a lead to opener waters.

We have come into a region where the open water exceeds the ice; the former lies in great irregular pools 3 or 4 miles or more across and connecting with many leads. The latter – and the fact is puzzling – still contain floes of enormous dimensions; we have just passed one which is at least 2 miles in diameter. In such a scattered sea we cannot go direct, but often have to make longish detours; but on the whole in calm water and with a favouring wind we make good progress. With the sea even as open as we find it here it is astonishing to find the floes so large, and clearly there cannot be a southerly swell. The floes have water pools as described this afternoon, and none average more than 2 feet in thickness. We have two or three bergs in sight.

Saturday, December 24, Christmas Eve. – 69° 1' S., 178° 29' W. S. 22 E. 29'; C. Crozier 551'. Alas! alas! at 7 a.m. this morning we were brought up with a solid sheet of pack extending in all directions, save that from which we had come. I must honestly own that I turned in at three thinking we had come to the end of our troubles; I had a suspicion of anxiety when I thought of the size of the floes, but I didn't for a moment suspect we should get into thick pack again behind those great sheets of open water.

All went well till four, when the white wall again appeared ahead – at five all leads ended and we entered the pack; at seven we were close up to an immense composite floe, about as big as any we've seen. She wouldn't skirt the edge of this and she wouldn't go through it. There was nothing to do but to stop and bank fires. How do we stand? – Any day or hour the floes may open up, leaving a road to further open water to the south, but there is no guarantee that one would not be hung up again and again in this manner as long as these great floes exist. In a fortnight's time the floes will have crumbled somewhat, and in many places the ship will be able to penetrate them.

What to do under these circumstances calls for the most difficult decision.

If one lets fires out it means a dead loss of over 2 tons, when the boiler has to be heated again. But this 2 tons would only cover a day under banked fires, so that for anything longer than twenty-four hours it is economy to put the fires out. At each stoppage one is called upon to decide whether it is to be for more or less than twenty-four hours.

Last night we got some five or six hours of good going ahead – but it has to be remembered that this costs 2 tons of coal in addition to that expended in doing the distance.

If one waits one probably drifts north – in all other respects conditions ought to be improving, except that the southern edge of the pack will be steadily augmenting.

Rough summary of current in pack

Dec.	Current	Wind
11–12	S. 48 E. 12' ?	N. by W. 3–5
13–14	N. 20 W. 2'	N.W. by W. 0–2
14–15	N. 2 E. 5.2'	S.W. 1–2
15–17	apparently little current	variable light
20–21	N. 32 E. 9.4	N.W. to W.S.W. 4–6
21–22	N. 5 E. 8.5	West 4–5

The above seems to show that the drift is generally with the wind. We have had a predominance of westerly winds in a region where a predominance of easterly might be expected.

Now that we have an easterly, what will be the result?

Sunday, December 25, Christmas Day. – Dead reckoning 69° 5' S., 178° 30' E. The night before last I had bright hopes that this Christmas Day would see us in open water. The scene is altogether too Christmassy. Ice surrounds us, low nimbus clouds intermittently discharging light snow flakes obscure the sky, here and there small pools of open water throw shafts of black shadow on to the cloud – this black predominates in the direction from whence we have come, elsewhere the white haze of ice blink is pervading.

We are captured. We do practically nothing under sail to push through, and could do little under steam, and at each step forward the possibility of advance seems to lessen.

The wind which has persisted from the west for so long fell light last night, and today comes from the N.E. by N., a steady breeze from 2 to 3 in force. Since one must have hope, ours is pinned to the possible effect of a continuance of easterly wind. Again the call is for patience and again patience. Here at least we seem to enjoy full security. The ice is so thin that it could not hurt by pressure – there are no bergs within reasonable distance – indeed the thinness of the ice is one of the most tantalising conditions. In spite of the unpropitious prospect everyone on board is cheerful and one foresees a merry dinner tonight.

The mess is gaily decorated with our various banners. There was full attendance at the Service this morning and a lusty singing of hymns.

Should we now try to go east or west?

I have been trying to go west because the majority of tracks lie that side and no one has encountered such hard conditions as ours – otherwise there is nothing to point to this direction, and all through the last week the prospect to the west has seemed less promising than in other directions; in spite of orders to steer to the S.W. when possible it has been impossible to push in that direction.

An event of Christmas was the production of a family by Crean's rabbit. She gave birth to 17, it is said, and Crean has given away 22!

I don't know what will become of the parent or family; at present they are warm and snug enough, tucked away in the fodder under the forecastle.

Midnight. – Tonight the air is thick with falling snow; the temperature 28°. It is cold and slushy without.

A merry evening has just concluded. We had an excellent dinner: tomato soup, penguin breast stewed as an entrée, roast beef, plum pudding, and mince pies, asparagus, champagne, port and liqueurs – a festive menu. Dinner began at 6 and ended at 7. For five hours the company has been sitting round the table singing lustily; we haven't much talent, but everyone has contributed more or less, 'and the choruses are deafening. It is rather a surprising circumstance that such an unmusical party should be so keen on singing. On Xmas night it was kept up till 1 a.m., and no work is done without a chanty. I don't know if you have ever heard sea chanties being sung. The merchant sailors have quite a repertoire, and invariably call on it when getting up anchor or hoisting sails. Often as not they are sung in a flat and throaty style, but the effect when a number of men break into the chorus is generally inspiriting.'

The men had dinner at midday – much the same fare, but with beer and some whisky to drink. They seem to have enjoyed themselves much. Evidently the men's deck contains a very merry band.

There are three groups of penguins roosting on the floes quite close to the ship. I made the total number of birds 39. We could easily capture these birds, and so it is evident that food can always be obtained in the pack.

Tonight I noticed a skua gull settle on an upturned block of ice at the edge of a floe on which several penguins were preparing for rest. It is a fact that the latter held a noisy confabulation with the skua as subject – then they advanced as a body towards it; within a few paces the foremost penguin halted and turned, and then the others pushed him on towards the skua. One after another they jibbed at being first to approach their enemy, and it was only with much chattering and mutual support that they gradually edged towards him.

They couldn't reach him as he was perched on a block, but when they got quite close the skua, who up to that time had appeared quite unconcerned, flapped away a few yards and settled close on the other side of the group of penguins. The latter turned and repeated their former tactics until the skua finally flapped away altogether. It really was extraordinarily interesting to watch the timorous protesting movements of the penguins. The frame of mind producing every action could be so easily imagined and put into human sentiments.

On the other side of the ship part of another group of penguins were quarrelling for the possession of a small pressure block which offered only the most insecure foothold. The scrambling antics to secure the point of vantage, the ousting of the bird in possession, and the incontinent loss of balance and position as each bird reached the summit of his ambition was almost as entertaining as the episode of the skua. Truly these little creatures afford much amusement.

Monday, December 26. – Obs. 69° 9' S., 178° 13' W. Made good 48 hours, S. 35 E. 10'. The position tonight is very cheerless. All hope that this easterly wind will open the pack seems to have vanished. We are surrounded with compacted floes of immense area. Openings appear between these floes and we slide crab-like from one to another with long delays between. It is difficult to keep hope alive. There are streaks of water sky over open leads to the north, but everywhere to the south we have the uniform white sky. The day has been overcast and the wind force 3 to 5 from the E.N.E. – snow has fallen from time to time. There could scarcely be a more dreary prospect for the eye to rest upon.

As I lay in my bunk last night I seemed to note a measured crush on the brash ice, and today first it was reported that the floes had become smaller, and then we seemed to note a sort of measured send alongside the ship. There may be a long low swell, but it is not helping us apparently; tonight the floes around are indisputably as large as ever and I see little sign of their breaking or becoming less tightly locked.

It is a very, very trying time.

We have managed to make 2 or 3 miles in a S.W. (?) direction under sail by alternately throwing her aback, then filling sail and pressing through the narrow leads; probably this will scarcely make up for our drift. It's all very disheartening. The bright side is that everyone is prepared to exert himself to the utmost – however poor the result of our labours may show.

Rennick got a sounding again today, 1843 fathoms.

One is much struck by our inability to find a cause for the periodic opening and closing of the floes. One wonders whether there is a reason to be found in tidal movement. In general, however, it seems to show that our conditions are governed by remote causes. Somewhere well north or south of us the wind may be blowing in some other direction, tending to press up or release pressure; then again such sheets of open water as those through which we passed to the north afford space into which bodies of pack can be pushed. The exasperating uncertainty of one's mind in such captivity is due to ignorance of its cause and inability to predict the effect of changes of wind. One can only vaguely comprehend that things are happening far beyond our horizon which directly affect our situation.

Tuesday, December 27. – Dead reckoning 69° 12' S., 178° 18' W. We made nearly 2 miles in the first watch – half push, half drift. Then the ship was again held up. In the middle the ice was close around, even pressing on us, and we didn't move a yard. The wind steadily increased and has been blowing a moderate gale, shifting in direction to E.S.E. We are reduced to lower topsails.

In the morning watch we began to move again, the ice opening out with the usual astonishing absence of reason. We have made a mile or two in a westerly direction in the same manner as yesterday. The floes seem a little smaller, but our outlook is very limited; there is a thick haze, and the only fact that can be known is that there are pools of water at intervals for a mile or two in the direction in which we go.

We commence to move between two floes, make 200 or 300 yards, and are then brought up bows on to a large lump. This may mean a wait of anything from ten minutes to half an hour, whilst the ship swings round, falls away, and drifts to leeward. When clear she forges ahead again and the operation is repeated. Occasionally when she can get a little way on she cracks the obstacle and slowly passes through it. There is a distinct swell – very long, very low. I counted the period as about nine seconds. Everyone says the ice is breaking up. I have not seen any distinct evidence myself, but Wilson saw a large floe which had recently cracked into four pieces in such a position that the ship could not have caused it. The breaking up of the big floes is certainly a hopeful sign.

'I have written quite a lot about the pack ice when under ordinary conditions I should have passed it with few words. But you will scarcely be surprised when I tell you what an obstacle we have found it on this occasion.'

I was thinking during the gale last night that our position might be a great deal worse than it is. We were lying amongst the floes perfectly peacefully whilst the wind howled through the rigging. One felt quite free from anxiety as to the ship, the sails, the bergs or ice pressures. One calmly went below and slept in the greatest comfort. One thought of the ponies, but after all, horses have been carried for all time in small ships, and often enough for very long voyages. The Eastern Party* will certainly benefit by any delay we may make; for them the later they get to King Edward's Land the better. The depôt journey of the Western Party will be curtailed, but even so if we can get landed in January there should be time for a good deal of work. One must confess that things might be a great deal worse and there would be little to disturb one if one's release was certain, say in a week's time.

I'm afraid the ice-house is not going on so well as it might. There is some mould on the mutton and the beef is tainted. There

* The party headed by Lieutenant Campbell, which, being unable to disembark on King Edward's Land, was ultimately taken by the *Terra Nova* to the north part of Victoria Land, and so came to be known as the Northern Party. The Western Party here mentioned includes all who had their base at Cape Evans: the depôts to be laid were for the subsequent expedition to the Pole.

is a distinct smell. The house has been opened by order when the temperature has fallen below 28°. I thought the effect would be to 'harden up' the meat, but apparently we need air circulation. When the temperature goes down tonight we shall probably take the beef out of the house and put a wind-sail in to clear the atmosphere. If this does not improve matters we must hang more carcases in the rigging.

Later, 6 p.m. – The wind has backed from S.E. to E.S.E. and the swell is going down – this seems to argue open water in the first but not in the second direction and that the course we pursue is a good one on the whole.

The sky is clearing but the wind still gusty, force 4 to 7; the ice has frozen a little and we've made no progress since noon.

9 p.m. – One of the ponies went down tonight. He has been down before. It may mean nothing; on the other hand it is not a circumstance of good omen.

Otherwise there is nothing further to record, and I close this volume of my Journal under circumstances which cannot be considered cheerful.

A FRESH MS. BOOK. 1910–11

[*on the flyleaf*]   And in regions far
                      Such heroes bring ye forth
                         As those from whom we came
                         And plant our name
                         Under that star
                      Not known unto our North.
                         'To the Virginian Voyage' – DRAYTON

But be the workemen what they may be, let us speake of the
worke; that is, the true greatnesse of Kingdom and estates; and
the meanes thereof. –   BACON

Still in the ice

Wednesday, December 28, 1910. – Obs. Noon, 69° 17' S., 179° 42' W. Made good since 26th S. 74 W. 31'; C. Crozier S. 22 W. 530'. The gale has abated. The sky began to clear in the middle watch; now we have bright, cheerful, warm sunshine (temp. 28°). The wind lulled in the middle watch and has fallen to force 2 to 3. We made 1½ miles in the middle and have added nearly a mile since. This movement has brought us amongst floes of decidedly smaller area and the pack has loosened considerably. A visit to the crow's nest shows great improvement in the conditions. There is ice on all sides, but a large percentage of the floes is quite thin and even the heavier ice appears breakable. It is only possible to be certain of conditions for three miles or so – the limit of observation from the crow's nest; but as far as this limit there is no doubt the ship could work through with ease. Beyond there are vague signs of open water in the southern sky. We have pushed and drifted south and west during the gale and are now near the 180th meridian again. It seems impossible that we can be far from the southern limit of the pack.

On strength of these observations we have decided to raise steam. I trust this effort will carry us through.

The pony which fell last night has now been brought out into the open. The poor beast is in a miserable condition, very thin, very weak on the hind legs, and suffering from a most irritating skin affection which is causing its hair to fall out in great quantities. I think a day or so in the open will help matters; one or two of the other ponies under the forecastle are also in poor condition, but none so bad as this one. Oates is unremitting in his attention and care of the animals, but I don't think he quite realises that whilst in the pack the ship must remain steady and that, therefore, a certain limited scope for movement and exercise is afforded by the open deck on which the sick animal now stands.

If we can get through the ice in the coming effort we may get all the ponies through safely, but there would be no great cause for surprise if we lost two or three more.

These animals are now the great consideration, balanced as they are against the coal expenditure.

This morning a number of penguins were diving for food around and under the ship. It is the first time they have come so close to the ship in the pack, and there can be little doubt that the absence of motion of the propeller has made them bold.

The Adélie penguin on land or ice is almost wholly ludicrous. Whether sleeping, quarrelling, or playing, whether curious, fright-ened, or angry, its interest is continuously humorous; but the Adélie penguin in the water is another thing: as it darts to and fro a fathom or two below the surface, as it leaps porpoise-like into the air or swims skimmingly over the rippling surface of a pool, it excites nothing but admiration. Its speed probably appears greater than it is, but the ability to twist and turn and the general control of movement is both beautiful and wonderful.

As one looks across the barren stretches of the pack, it is sometimes difficult to realise what teeming life exists immediately beneath its surface.

A tow-net is filled with diatoms in a very short space of time, showing that the floating plant life is many times richer than that of temperate or tropic seas. These diatoms mostly consist of three or four well-known species. Feeding on these diatoms are countless thousands of small shrimps (*Euphausia*); they can be seen swimming at the edge of every floe and washing about on the overturned pieces. In turn they afford food for creatures great and small: the crab-eater or white seal, the penguins, the Antarctic and snowy petrel, and an unknown number of fish.

These fish must be plentiful, as shown by our capture of one on an overturned floe and the report of several seen two days ago by some men leaning over the counter of the ship. These all exclaimed together, and on inquiry all agreed that they had seen half a dozen or more a foot or so in length swimming away under a floe. Seals and penguins capture these fish, as also, doubtless, the skuas and the petrels.

Coming to the larger mammals, one occasionally sees the long lithe sea-leopard, formidably armed with ferocious teeth and doubtless containing a penguin or two and perhaps a young crab-eating seal. The killer whale (*Orca gladiator*), unappeasably voracious, devouring or attempting to devour every smaller animal, is less common in the pack but numerous on the coasts. Finally, we have the great browsing whales of various species, from the vast blue whale (*Balaenoptera Sibbaldi*), the largest mammal of all time, to the smaller and less common bottle-nose and such species as have not yet been named. Great numbers of these huge animals are seen, and one realises what a demand they must make on their food supply and therefore how immense a supply of small sea beasts these seas must contain. Beneath the placid ice floes and under the calm water pools the old universal warfare is raging incessantly in the struggle for existence.

Both morning and afternoon we have had brilliant sunshine, and this afternoon all the after-guard lay about on the deck sunning themselves. A happy, care-free group.

10 p.m. – We made our start at eight, and so far things look well. We have found the ice comparatively thin, the floes 2 to 3 feet in thickness except where hummocked; amongst them are large sheets from 6 inches to 1 foot in thickness as well as fairly numerous water pools. The ship has pushed on well, covering at least 3 miles an hour, though occasionally almost stopped by a group of hummocked floes. The sky is overcast: stratus clouds come over from the N.N.E. with wind in the same direction soon after we started. This may be an advantage, as the sails give great assistance and the officer of the watch has an easier time when the sun is not shining directly in his eyes. As I write the pack looks a little closer; I hope to heavens it is not generally closing up again – no sign of open water to the south. Alas!

12 p.m. – saw two sea-leopards playing in the wake.

Thursday, December 29. – No sights. At last the change for which I have been so eagerly looking has arrived and we are steaming amongst floes of small area evidently broken by swell, and with edges abraded by contact. The transition was almost sudden. We made very good progress during the night with one or two checks and one or two slices of luck in the way of open water. In one pool we ran clear for an hour, capturing 6 good miles.

This morning we were running through large continuous sheets of ice from 6 inches to 1 foot in thickness, with occasional water holes and groups of heavier floes. This forenoon it is the same tale, *except* that the sheets of thin ice are broken into comparatively regular figures, none more than 30 yards across. It is the hopefullest sign of the approach to the open sea that I have seen.

The wind remains in the north helping us, the sky is overcast and slight sleety drizzle is falling; the sun has made one or two attempts to break through but without success.

Last night we had a good example of the phenomenon called 'Glazed Frost'. The ship everywhere, on every fibre of rope as well as on her more solid parts, was covered with a thin sheet of ice caused by a fall of light super-cooled rain. The effect was pretty and interesting.

Our passage through the pack has been comparatively uninteresting from the zoologist's point of view, as we have seen so little of the rarer species of animals or of birds in exceptional plumage. We passed dozens of crab-eaters, but have seen no Ross seals nor have we been able to kill a sea leopard. Today we see very few penguins. I'm afraid there can be no observations to give us our position.

Release after twenty days in the pack

Friday, December 30. – Obs. 72° 17' S. 177° 9' E. Made good in 48 hours, S. 19 W. 190'; C. Crozier S. 21 W. 334'. We are out of the pack at length and at last; one breathes again and hopes that it will be possible to carry out the main part of our programme, but the coal will need tender nursing.

Yesterday afternoon it became darkly overcast with falling snow. The barometer fell on a very steep gradient and the wind increased to force 6 from the E.N.E. In the evening the snow fell heavily and the glass still galloped down. In any other part of the world one would have felt certain of a coming gale. But here by experience we know that the barometer gives little indication of wind.

Throughout the afternoon and evening the water holes became more frequent and we came along at a fine speed. At the end of the first watch we were passing through occasional streams of ice; the wind had shifted to north and the barometer had ceased to fall. In the middle watch the snow held up, and soon after – 1 a.m. – Bowers steered through the last ice stream.

At six this morning we were well in the open sea, the sky thick and overcast with occasional patches of fog. We passed one small berg on the starboard hand with a group of Antarctic petrels on one side and a group of snow petrels on the other. It is evident that these birds rely on sea and swell to cast their food up on ice ledges – only a few find sustenance in the pack where, though food is plentiful, it is not so easily come by. A flight of Antarctic petrel accompanied the ship for some distance, wheeling to and fro about her rather than following in the wake as do the more northerly sea birds.

It is [good] to escape from the captivity of the pack and to feel that a few days will see us at Cape Crozier, but it is sad to remember the terrible inroad which the fight of the last fortnight has made on our coal supply.

2 p.m. – The wind failed in the forenoon. Sails were clewed up, and at eleven we stopped to sound. The sounding showed 1111 fathoms – we appear to be on the edge of the continental shelf. Nelson got some samples and temperatures.

The sun is bursting through the misty sky and warming the air. The snowstorm had covered the ropes with an icy sheet – this is now peeling off and falling with a clatter to the deck, from which the moist slush is rapidly evaporating. In a few hours the ship will be dry – much to our satisfaction; it is very wretched when, as last night, there is slippery wet snow underfoot and on every object one touches.

Our run has exceeded our reckoning by much. I feel confident that our speed during the last two days had been greatly under-estimated, and so it has proved. We ought to be off C. Crozier on New Year's Day.

8 p.m. – Our calm soon came to an end, the breeze at 3 p.m. coming strong from the S.S.W., dead in our teeth – a regular southern blizzard. We are creeping along a bare 2 knots. I begin to wonder if fortune will ever turn her wheel. On every possible occasion she seems to have decided against us. Of course, the ponies are feeling the motion as we pitch in a short, sharp sea – it's damnable for them and disgusting for us.

Summary of the pack

We may be said to have entered the pack at 4 p.m. on the 9th in latitude 65½ S. We left it at 1 a.m. on 30th in latitude 71½ S. We have taken twenty days and some odd hours to get through, and covered in a direct line over 370 miles, an average of 18 miles a day. We entered the pack with 342 tons of coal and left with 281 tons; we have, therefore, expended 61 tons in forcing our way through – an average of 6 miles to the ton.

These are not pleasant figures to contemplate, but considering the exceptional conditions experienced I suppose one must conclude that things might have been worse.

9th. Loose streams, steaming	19th. Noon, heavy pack and leads, steaming.
10th. Close pack	20th. Forenoon, banked fires.
11th. 6 a.m. close pack, stopped	21st. 9 a.m. started. 11 a.m. banked.
12th. 11.30 a.m. started	22nd. 11 a.m. banked.

13th. 8 a.m. heavy pack, stopped 8 p.m, out fires	23rd. Midnight, started.
14th. Fires out.	24th. 7 a.m. stopped.
15th. Fires out.	25th. Fires out.
16th. Fires out.	26th. Fires out.
17th. Fires out.	27th. Fires out.
18th. Noon, heavy pack and leads, steaming.	28th. 7.30 p.m. steaming.
	29th. Steaming.
	30th. Steaming.

These columns show that we were steaming for nine out of twenty days. We had two long stops, one of *five* days and one of *four and a half* days. On three other occasions we stopped for short intervals without drawing fires.

I have asked Wright to plot the pack with certain symbols on the chart made by Pennell. It promises to give a very graphic representation of our experiences.

'We hold the record for reaching the northern edge of the pack, whereas three or four times the open Ross Sea has been gained at an earlier date.

'I can imagine few things more trying to the patience than the long wasted days of waiting. Exasperating as it is to see the tons of coal melting away with the smallest mileage to our credit, one has at least the satisfaction of active fighting and the hope of better fortune. To wait idly is the worst of conditions. You can imagine how often and how restlessly we climbed to the crow's nest and studied the outlook. And strangely enough there was generally some change to note. A water lead would mysteriously open up a few miles away or the place where it had been would as mysteriously close. Huge icebergs crept silently towards or past us, and continually we were observing these formidable objects with range finder and compass to determine the relative movement, sometimes with misgiving as to our ability to clear them. Under steam the change of conditions was even more marked. Sometimes we would enter a lead of open water and proceed for a mile or two without hindrance; sometimes we would come to big sheets of thin ice which broke easily as our iron-shod prow struck them, and sometimes even a thin sheet would resist all our attempts to break it; sometimes we would push big floes with comparative ease and sometimes a small floe would bar our passage with such obstinacy that one would almost believe it possessed of an evil spirit; sometimes we passed through acres of sludgy sodden ice which hissed as it swept along the side, and sometimes the hissing ceased seemingly without rhyme or reason, and we found our screw churning the sea without any effect.

'Thus the steaming days passed away in an ever-changing environment and are remembered as an unceasing struggle.

The ship behaved splendidly – no other ship, not even the *Discovery*, would have come through so well. Certainly the *Nimrod* would never have reached the south water had she been caught in such pack. As a result I have grown strangely attached to the *Terra Nova*. As she bumped the floes with mighty shocks, crushing and grinding a way through some, twisting and turning to avoid others, she seemed like a living thing fighting a great fight. If only she had more economical engines she would be suitable in all respects.

'Once or twice we got among floes which stood 7 or 8 feet above water, with hummocks and pinnacles as high as 25 feet. The ship could have stood no chance had such floes pressed against her, and at first we were a little alarmed in such situations. But familiarity breeds contempt; there never was any pressure in the heavy ice, and I'm inclined to think there never would be.

'The weather changed frequently during our journey through the pack. The wind blew strong from the west and from the east; the sky was often darkly overcast; we had snowstorms, flaky snow, and even light rain. In all such circumstances we were better placed in the pack than outside of it. The foulest weather could do us little harm. During quite a large percentage of days, however, we had bright sunshine, which, even with the temperature well below freezing, made everything look bright and cheerful. The sun also brought us wonderful cloud effects, marvellously delicate tints of sky, cloud, and ice, such effects as one might travel far to see. In spite of our impatience we would not willingly have missed many of the beautiful scenes which our sojourn in the pack afforded us. Ponting and Wilson have been busy catching these effects, but no art can reproduce such colours as the deep blue of the icebergs.

'Scientifically we have been able to do something. We have managed to get a line of soundings on our route showing the raising of the bottom from the ocean depths to the shallow water on the continental shelf, and the nature of the bottom. With these soundings we have obtained many interesting observations of the temperature of different layers of water in the sea.

'Then we have added a great deal to the knowledge of life in the pack from observation of the whales, seals, penguins, birds, and fishes as well as of the pelagic beasts which are caught in tow-nets. Life in one form or another is very plentiful in the pack, and the struggle for existence here as elsewhere is a fascinating subject for study.

'We have made a systematic study of the ice also, both the bergs and sea ice, and have got a good deal of useful information concerning it. Also Pennell has done a little magnetic work.

'But of course this slight list of activity in the cause of science is a very poor showing for the time of our numerous experts; many have had to be idle in regard to their own specialities, though none are idle otherwise.

'All the scientific people keep night watch when they have no special work to do, and I have never seen a party of men so anxious to be doing work or so cheerful in doing it. When there is anything to be done, such as making or shortening sail, digging ice from floes for the water supply, or heaving up the sounding line, it goes without saying that all the afterguard turn out to do it. There is no hesitation and no distinction. It will be the same when it comes to landing stores or doing any other hard manual labour.

'The spirit of the enterprise is as bright as ever. Everyone strives to help everyone else, and not a word of complaint or anger has been heard on board. The inner life of our small community is very pleasant to think upon and very wonderful considering the extremely small space in which we are confined.

'The attitude of the men is equally worthy of admiration. In the forecastle as in the wardroom there is a rush to be first when work is to be done, and the same desire to sacrifice selfish consideration to the success of the expedition. It is very good to be able to write in such high praise of one's companions, and I feel that the possession of such support ought to ensure success. Fortune would be in a hard mood indeed if it allowed such a combination of knowledge, experience, ability, and enthusiasm to achieve nothing.'

CHAPTER THREE

Land

Saturday, December 31. *New Year's Eve.* – Obs. 72° 54' S., 174° 55' E. Made good S. 45 W. 55'; C. Crozier S. 17 W. 286'. – 'The New Year's Eve found us in the Ross Sea, but not at the end of our misfortunes.' We had a horrible night. In the first watch we kept away 2 points and set fore and aft sail. It did not increase our comfort but gave us greater speed. The night dragged slowly through. I could not sleep thinking of the sore strait for our wretched ponies. In the morning watch the wind and sea increased and the outlook was very distressing, but at six ice was sighted ahead. Under ordinary conditions the safe course would have been to go about and stand to the east. But in our case we must risk trouble to get smoother water for the ponies. We passed a stream of ice over which the sea was breaking heavily, and one realised the danger of being amongst loose floes in such a sea. But soon we came to a compacter body of floes, and running behind this we were agreeably surprised to find comparatively smooth water. We ran on for a bit, then stopped and lay to. Now we are lying in a sort of ice bay – there is a mile or so of pack to windward, and two horns which form the bay embracing us. The sea is damped down to a gentle swell, although the wind is as strong as ever. As a result we are lying very comfortably. The ice is drifting a little faster than the ship so that we have occasionally to steam slowly to leeward.

So far so good. From a dangerous position we have achieved one which only directly involved a waste of coal. The question is, which will last longest, the gale or our temporary shelter?

Rennick has just obtained a sounding of 187 fathoms; taken in conjunction with yesterday's 1111 fathoms and Ross's sounding of 180, this is interesting, showing the rapid gradient of the continental shelf. Nelson is going to put over the 8 feet Agassiz trawl.

Unfortunately we could not clear the line for the trawl – it is stowed under the fodder. A light dredge was tried on a small manilla line – very little result. First the weights were insufficient to carry it to the bottom; a second time, with more weight and line, it seems to have touched for a very short time only; there was little of value in the catch, but the biologists are learning the difficulties of the situation.

Evening. – Our protection grew less as the day advanced but saved us much from the heavy swell. At 8 p.m. we started to steam west to gain fresh protection, there being signs of pack to south and west; the swell is again diminishing. The wind which started south yesterday has gone to S.S.W. (true), the main swell in from S.E. by S. or S.S.E. There seems to be another from south but none from the direction from which the wind is now blowing. The wind has been getting squally: now the squalls are lessening in force, the sky is clearing and we seem to be approaching the end of the blow. I trust it may be so and that the New Year will bring us better fortune than the Old.

If so, it will be some pleasure to write 1910 for the last time. – Land oh!

At 10 p.m. tonight as the clouds lifted to the west a distant but splendid view of the great mountains was obtained. All were in sunshine; Sabine and Whewell were most conspicuous – the latter from this view is a beautiful sharp peak, as remarkable a landmark as Sabine itself. Mount Sabine was 110 miles away when we saw it. I believe we could have seen it at a distance of 30 or 40 miles farther – such is the wonderful clearness of the atmosphere.

FINIS 1910

1911

Sunday, January 1. – Obs. 73° 5′ S. 174° 11′ E. Made good S. 48 W. 13.4; C. Crozier S. 15 W. 277′. – At 4 a.m. we proceeded, steaming slowly to the S.E. The wind having gone to the S.W. and fallen to force 3 as we cleared the ice, we headed into a short steep swell, and for some hours the ship pitched most uncomfortably.

At 8 a.m. the ship was clear of the ice and headed south with fore and aft sail set. She is lying easier on this course, but there is still a good deal of motion, and would be more if we attempted to increase speed.

Oates reports that the ponies are taking it pretty well.

Soon after 8 a.m. the sky cleared, and we have had brilliant sunshine throughout the day; the wind came from the N.W. this forenoon, but has dropped during the afternoon. We increased to 55 revolutions at 10 a.m. The swell is subsiding but not so quickly as I had expected.

Tonight it is absolutely calm, with glorious bright sunshine. Several people were sunning themselves at 11 o'clock! sitting on deck and reading.

The land is clear tonight. Coulman Island 75 miles west.

> Sounding at 7 p.m.   187 fathoms.
> Sounding at 4 a.m.   310

Monday, January 2. – Obs. 75° 3', 173° 41'. Made good S. 3 W. 119'; C. Crozier S. 22 W. 159'. It has been a glorious night followed by a glorious forenoon; the sun has been shining almost continuously. Several of us drew a bucket of sea water and had a bath with saltwater soap on the deck. The water was cold, of course, but it was quite pleasant to dry oneself in the sun. The deck bathing habit has fallen off since we crossed the Antarctic circle, but Bowers has kept going in all weathers.

There is still a good deal of swell – difficult to understand after a day's calm – and less than 200 miles of water to windward.

Wilson saw and sketched the new white-stomached whale seen by us in the pack.

At 8.30 we sighted Mount Erebus, distant about 115 miles; the sky is covered with light cumulus and an easterly wind has sprung up, force 2 to 3. With all sail set we are making very good progress.

Tuesday, January 3, 10 a.m. – The conditions are very much the same as last night. We are only 24 miles from C. Crozier and the land is showing up well, though Erebus is veiled in stratus cloud.

It looks finer to the south and we may run into sunshine soon, but the wind is alarming and there is a slight swell which has little effect on the ship, but makes all the difference to our landing.

For the moment it doesn't look hopeful. We have been continuing our line of soundings. From the bank we crossed in latitude 71° the water has gradually got deeper, and we are now getting 310 to 350 fathoms against 180 on the bank.

The *Discovery* soundings give depths up to 450 fathoms east of Ross Island.

6 p.m. – No good!! Alas! Cape Crozier with all its attractions is denied us.

We came up to the Barrier five miles east of the Cape soon after 1 p.m. The swell from the E.N.E. continued to the end. The Barrier was not more than 60 feet in height. From the crow's nest one could see well over it, and noted that there was a gentle slope for at least a mile towards the edge. The land of Black (or White?) Island could be seen distinctly behind, topping the huge lines of pressure ridges. We plotted the Barrier edge from the point at which we met it to the Crozier cliffs; to the eye it seems scarcely to have changed since *Discovery* days, and Wilson thinks it meets the cliff in the same place.

The Barrier takes a sharp turn back at 2 or 3 miles from the cliffs, runs back for half a mile, then west again with a fairly regular surface until within a few hundred yards of the cliffs; the interval is occupied with a single high-pressure ridge – the evidences of pressure at the edge being less marked than I had expected.

Ponting was very busy with cinematograph and camera. In the angle at the corner near the cliffs Rennick got a sounding of 140 fathoms and Nelson some temperatures and samples. When lowering the water bottle on one occasion the line suddenly became slack at 100 metres, then after a moment's pause began to run out again. We are curious to know the cause, and imagine the bottle struck a seal or whale.

Meanwhile, one of the whale boats was lowered and Wilson, Griffith Taylor, Priestley, Evans, and I were pulled towards the shore. The after-guard are so keen that the proper boat's crew was displaced and the oars manned by Oates, Atkinson, and Cherry-Garrard, the latter catching several crabs.

The swell made it impossible for us to land. I had hoped to see whether there was room to pass between the pressure ridge and the cliff, a route by which Royds once descended to the Emperor rookery; as we approached the corner we saw that a large piece of sea floe ice had been jammed between the Barrier and the cliff and had buckled up till its under surface stood 3 or 4 ft. above the water. On top of this old floe we saw an old Emperor moulting and a young one shedding its down. (The down had come off the head and flippers and commenced to come off the breast in a vertical line similar to the ordinary moult.) This is an age and stage of development of the Emperor chick of which we have no knowledge, and it would have been a triumph to have secured the chick, but, alas! there was no way to get at it. Another most curious sight was the feet and tails of two chicks and the flipper of an adult bird projecting from the ice on the under side of the jammed floe; they had evidently been frozen in above and were being washed out under the floe.

Finding it impossible to land owing to the swell, we pulled along the cliffs for a short way. These Crozier cliffs are remarkably interesting. The rock, mainly volcanic tuff, includes thick strata of columnar basalt, and one could see beautiful designs of jammed and twisted columns as well as caves with whole and half pillars very much like a miniature Giant's Causeway. Bands of bright yellow occurred in the rich brown of the cliffs, caused, the geologists think, by the action of salts on the brown rock. In places the cliffs overhung. In places, the sea had eaten long low caves deep under them, and continued to break into them over a shelving beach. Icicles hung pendent everywhere, and from one fringe a continuous trickle of thaw water had swollen to a miniature water-fall. It was like a big hose playing over the cliff edge. We noticed a very clear echo as we passed close to a perpendicular rock face. Later we returned to the ship, which had been trying to turn in the bay – she is not very satisfactory in this respect owing to the difficulty of starting the engines either ahead or astern – several minutes often elapse after the telegraph has been put over before there is any movement of the engines.

It makes the position rather alarming when one is feeling one's way into some doubtful corner. When the whaler was hoisted we proceeded round to the penguin rookery; hopes of finding a quiet landing had now almost disappeared.[8]

There were several small grounded bergs close to the rookery; going close to these we got repeated soundings varying from 34 down to 12 fathoms. There is evidently a fairly extensive bank at the foot of the rookery. There is probably good anchorage behind some of the bergs, but none of these afford shelter for landing on the beach, on which the sea is now breaking incess-antly; it would have taken weeks to land the ordinary stores, and heaven only knows how we could have got the ponies and motor sledges ashore. Reluctantly and sadly we have had to abandon our cherished plan – it is a thousand pities. Every detail of the shore promised well for a wintering party. Comfortable quarters for the hut, ice for water, snow for the animals, good slopes for ski-ing, vast tracks of rock for walks. Proximity to the Barrier and to the rookeries of two types of penguins – easy ascent of Mount Terror – good ground for biological work – good peaks for observation of all sorts – fairly easy approach to the Southern Road, with no chance of being cut off – and so forth. It is a thousand pities to have to abandon such a spot.

On passing the rookery it seemed to me we had been wrong in assuming that all the guano is blown away. I think there must be a pretty good deposit in places. The penguins could be seen very clearly from the ship. On the large rookery they occupy an immense acreage, and one imagines have extended as far as shelter can be found. But on the small rookery they are patchy and there seems ample room for the further extension of the colonies. Such unused spaces would have been ideal for a wintering station if only some easy way could have been found to land stores.

I noted many groups of penguins on the snow slopes over-looking the sea far from the rookeries, and one finds it difficult to understand why they meander away to such places.

A number of killer whales rose close to the ship when we were opposite the rookery. What an excellent time these animals must have with thousands of penguins passing to and fro!

We saw our old *Discovery* post-office pole sticking up as erect as when planted, and we have been comparing all we have seen with old photographs. No change at all seems to have taken place anywhere, and this is very surprising in the case of the Barrier edge.

From the penguin rookeries to the west it is a relentless coast with high ice cliffs and occasional bare patches of rock showing through. Even if landing were possible, the grimmest crevassed snow slopes lie behind to cut one off from the Barrier surface; there is no hope of shelter till we reach Cape Royds.

Meanwhile all hands are employed making a running survey. I give an idea of the programme below. Terror cleared itself of cloud some hours ago, and we have had some change in views of it. It is quite certain that the ascent would be easy. The Bay on the north side of Erebus is much deeper than shown on the chart.

The sun has been obstinate all day, peeping out occasionally and then shyly retiring; it makes a great difference to comfort.

Programme

Bruce continually checking speed with hand log.

{ Bowers taking altitudes of objects as they come abeam.
{ Nelson noting results.

{ Pennell taking verge plate bearings on bow and quarter.
{ Cherry-Garrard noting results.

{ Evans taking verge plate bearings abeam.
{ Atkinson noting results.

{ Campbell taking distances abeam with range finder.
{ Wright noting results.

{ Rennick sounding with Thomson machine.
{ Drake noting results.

Beaufort Island looks very black from the south.

10.30. – We find pack off Cape Bird; we have passed through some streams and there is some open water ahead, but I'm afraid we may find the ice pretty thick in the Strait at this date.

Wednesday, January 4, 1 a.m. – We are around Cape Bird and in sight of our destination, but it is doubtful if the open water extends so far.

We have advanced by following an open water lead close along the land. Cape Bird is a very rounded promontory with many headlands; it is not easy to say which of these is the Cape.

The same grim unattainable ice-clad coast line extends continuously from the Cape Crozier Rookery to Cape Bird. West of C. Bird there is a very extensive expanse of land, and on it one larger and several small penguin rookeries.

On the uniform dark reddish brown of the land can be seen numerous grey spots; these are erratic boulders of granite. Through glasses one could be seen perched on a peak at least 1,300 feet above the sea.

Another group of killer whales were idly diving off the penguin rookery; an old one with a very high straight dorsal fin and several youngsters. We watched a small party of penguins leaping through the water towards their enemies. It seemed impossible that they should have failed to see the sinister fins during their frequent jumps into the air, yet they seemed to take no notice whatever – stranger still, the penguins must have actually crossed the whales, yet there was no commotion whatever, and presently the small birds could be seen leaping away on the other side. One can only suppose the whales are satiated.

As we rounded Cape Bird we came in sight of the old well-remembered landmarks – Mount Discovery and the Western Mountains – seen dimly through a hazy atmosphere. It was good to see them again, and perhaps after all we are better this side of the Island. It gives one a homely feeling to see such a familiar scene.

4 a.m. – The steep exposed hillsides on the west side of Cape Bird look like high cliffs as one gets south of them and form a most conspicuous landmark. We pushed past these cliffs into streams of heavy bay ice, making fair progress; as we proceeded the lanes became scarcer, the floes heavier, but the latter remain loose. 'Many of us spent the night on deck as we pushed through the pack.' We have passed some very large floes evidently frozen in the strait. This is curious, as all previous evidence has pointed to the clearance of ice sheets north of Cape Royds early in the spring.

I have observed several floes with an entirely new type of surface. They are covered with scales, each scale consisting of a number of little flaky ice sheets superimposed, and all 'dipping' at the same angle. It suggests to me a surface with sastrugi and layers of fine dust on which the snow has taken hold.

We are within 5 miles of Cape Royds and ought to get there.

Wednesday, January 4, p.m. – This work is full of surprises.

At 6 a.m. we came through the last of the Strait pack some three miles north of Cape Royds. We steered for the Cape, fully expecting to find the edge of the pack ice ranging westward from it. To our astonishment we ran on past the Cape with clear water or thin sludge ice on all sides of us. Past Cape Royds, past Cape Barne, past the glacier on its south side, and finally round and past Inaccessible Island, a good 2 miles south of Cape Royds. 'The Cape itself was cut off from the south.' We could have gone farther, but the last sludge ice seemed to be increasing in thickness, and there was no wintering spot to aim for but Cape Armitage.* 'I have never seen

---

* The extreme S. point of the Island, a dozen miles farther, on one of whose minor headlands, Hut Point, stood the *Discovery* hut.

the ice of the Sound in such a condition or the land so free from snow. Taking these facts in conjunction with the exceptional warmth of the air, I came to the conclusion that it had been an exceptionally warm summer. At this point it was evident that we had a considerable choice of wintering spots. We could have gone to either of the small islands, to the mainland, the Glacier Tongue, or pretty well anywhere except Hut Point. My main wish was to choose a place that would not be easily cut off from the Barrier, and my eye fell on a cape which we used to call the Skuary a little behind us. It was separated from old *Discovery* quarters by two deep bays on either side of the Glacier Tongue, and I thought that these bays would remain frozen until late in the season, and that when they froze over again the ice would soon become firm.' I called a council and put these propositions: to push on to the Glacier Tongue and winter there; to push west to the 'tombstone' ice and to make our way to an inviting spot to the northward of the cape we used to call 'the Skuary'. I favoured the latter course, and on discussion we found it obviously the best, so we turned back close around Inaccessible Island and steered for the fast ice off the Cape at full speed. After piercing a small fringe of thin ice at the edge of the fast floe the ship's stem struck heavily on hard bay ice about a mile and a half from the shore. Here was a road to the Cape and a solid wharf on which to land our stores. We made fast with ice anchors. Wilson, Evans, and I went to the Cape, which I had now rechristened Cape Evans in honour of our excellent second in command. A glance at the land showed, as we expected, ideal spots for our wintering station. The rock of the Cape consists mainly of volcanic agglomerate with olivine kenyte; it is much weathered and the destruction had formed quantities of coarse sand. We chose a spot for the hut on a beach facing N.W. and well protected by numerous small hills behind. This spot seems to have all the local advantages (which I must detail later) for a winter station, and we realised that at length our luck had turned. The most favourable circumstance of all is the strong chance of communication with Cape Armitage being established at an early date.

It was in connection with this fact that I had had such a strong desire to go to Mount Terror, and such misgivings if we had been forced to go to Cape Royds. It is quite evident that the ice south of Cape Royds does not become secure till late in the season, probably in May. Before that, all evidence seems to show that the part between Cape Royds and Cape Barne is continually going out. How, I ask myself, was our depôt party to get back to home quarters? I feel confident we can get to the new spot we have chosen at a comparatively early date; it will probably only be necessary to cross the sea ice in the deep bays north and south of the Glacier Tongue, and the ice rarely goes out of there after it has first formed. Even if it should, both stages can be seen before the party ventures upon them.

After many frowns fortune has treated us to the kindest smile – for twenty-four hours we have had a calm with brilliant sunshine. Such weather in such a place comes nearer to satisfying my ideal of perfection than any condition that I have ever experienced. The warm glow of the sun with the keen invigorating cold of the air forms a combination which is inexpressibly health-giving and satisfying to me, whilst the golden light on this wonderful scene of mountain and ice satisfies every claim of scenic magnificence. No words of mine can convey the impressiveness of the wonderful panorama displayed to our eyes. Ponting is enraptured and uses expressions which in anyone else and alluding to any other subject might be deemed extravagant.

The landing: a week's work

Whilst we were on shore Campbell was taking the first steps towards landing our stores. Two of the motor sledges were soon hoisted out, and Day with others was quickly unpacking them. Our luck stood again. In spite of all the bad weather and the tons of sea water which had washed over them the sledges and all the accessories appeared as fresh and clean as if they had been packed on the previous day – much credit is due to the officers who protected them with tarpaulins and lashings. After the sledges came the turn of the ponies – there was a good deal of difficulty in getting some of them into the horse box, but Oates rose to the occasion and got most in by persuasion, whilst others were simply lifted in by the sailors. Though all are thin and some few looked pulled down I was agreeably surprised at the evident vitality which they still possessed – some were even skittish. I cannot express the relief when the whole seventeen were safely picketed on the floe. From the moment of getting on the snow they seemed to take a new lease of life, and I haven't a doubt they will pick up very rapidly. It really is a triumph to have got them through safely and as well as they are. Poor brutes, how they must have enjoyed their first roll, and how glad they must be to have freedom to scratch themselves! It is evident all have suffered from skin irritation – one can imagine the horror of suffering from such an ill for weeks without being able to get at the part that itched. I note that now they are picketed together they administer kindly offices to each other; one sees them gnawing away at each other's flanks in most amicable and obliging manner.

Meares and the dogs were out early, and have been running to and fro most of the day with light loads. The great trouble with them has been due to the fatuous conduct of the penguins. Groups of these have been constantly leaping on to our floe. From the moment of landing on their feet their whole attitude expressed devouring curiosity and a pig-headed disregard for their own safety. They waddle forward, poking their heads to and fro in their usually absurd way, in spite of a string of howling dogs straining to get at them. 'Hulloa!' they seem to say, 'here's a game – what do all you ridiculous things want?' And they come a few steps nearer. The dogs make a rush as far as their leashes or harness allow. The penguins are not daunted in the least, but their ruffs go up and they squawk with semblance of anger, for all the world as though they were rebuking a rude stranger – their attitude might be imagined to convey 'Oh, that's the sort of animal you are; well, you've come to the wrong place – we aren't going to be bluffed and bounced by you,' and then the final fatal steps forward are taken and they come within reach. There is a spring, a squawk, a horrid red patch on the snow, and the incident is closed. Nothing can stop these silly birds. Members of our party rush to head them off, only to be met with evasions – the penguins squawk and duck as much as to say, 'What's it got to do with you, you silly ass? Let us alone.'

With the first spilling of blood the skua gulls assemble, and soon, for them at least, there is a gruesome satisfaction to be reaped. Oddly enough, they don't seem to excite the dogs; they simply alight within a few feet and wait for their turn in the drama, clamouring and quarrelling amongst themselves when the spoils accrue. Such incidents were happening constantly today, and seriously demoralising the dog teams. Meares was exasperated again and again.

The motor sledges were running by the afternoon, Day managing one and Nelson the other. In spite of a few minor breakdowns they hauled good loads to the shore. It is early to call them a success, but they are certainly extremely promising.

The next thing to be got out of the ship was the hut, and the large quantity of timber comprising it was got out this afternoon.

And so tonight, with the sun still shining, we look on a very different prospect from that of 48 or even 24 hours ago.

I have just come back from the shore.

The site for the hut is levelled and the erecting party is living on shore in our large green tent with a supply of food for eight days. Nearly all the timber, &c., of the hut is on shore, the remainder half-way there. The ponies are picketed in a line on a convenient snow slope so that they cannot eat sand. Oates and Anton are sleeping ashore to watch over them. The dogs are tied to a long length of chain stretched on the sand; they are coiled up after a long day, looking fitter already. Meares and Demetri are sleeping in the green tent to look after them. A supply of food for ponies and dogs as well as for the men has been landed. Two motor sledges in good working order are safely on the beach.

A fine record for our first day's work. All hands start again at 6 a.m. tomorrow.

It's splendid to see at last the effect of all the months of preparation and organisation. There is much snoring about me as I write (2 a.m.) from men tired after a hard day's work and preparing for such another tomorrow. I also must sleep, for I have had none for 48 hours – but it should be to dream happily.

Thursday, January 5. – All hands were up at 5 this morning and at work at 6. Words cannot express the splendid way in which everyone works and gradually the work gets organised. I was a little late on the scene this morning, and thereby witnessed a most extraordinary scene. Some 6 or 7 killer whales, old and young, were skirting the fast floe edge ahead of the ship; they seemed excited and dived rapidly, almost touching the floe. As we watched, they suddenly appeared astern, raising their snouts out of water. I had heard weird stories of these beasts, but had never associated serious danger with them. Close to the water's edge lay the wire stern rope of the ship, and our two Esquimaux dogs were tethered to this. I did not think of connecting the movements of the whales with this fact, and seeing them so close I shouted to Ponting, who was standing abreast of the ship. He seized his camera and ran towards the floe edge to get a close picture of the beasts, which had momentarily disappeared. The next moment the whole floe under him and the dogs heaved up and split into fragments. One could hear the 'booming' noise as the whales rose under the ice and struck it with their backs. Whale after whale rose under the ice, setting it rocking fiercely; luckily Ponting kept his feet and was able to fly to security. By an extraordinary chance also, the splits had been made around and between the dogs, so that neither of them fell into the water. Then it was clear that the whales shared our astonishment, for one after another their huge hideous heads shot vertically into the air through the cracks which they had made. As they reared them to a height of 6 or 8 feet it was possible to see their tawny head markings, their small glistening eyes, and their terrible array of teeth – by far the largest and most terrifying in the world. There cannot be a doubt that they looked up to see what had happened to Ponting and the dogs.

The latter were horribly frightened and strained to their chains, whining; the head of one killer must certainly have been within 5 feet of one of the dogs.

After this, whether they thought the game insignificant, or whether they missed Ponting is uncertain, but the terrifying creatures passed on to other hunting grounds, and we were able to rescue the dogs, and what was even more important, our petrol – 5 or 6 tons of which was waiting on a piece of ice which was not split away from the main mass.

Of course, we have known well that killer whales continually skirt the edge of the floes and that they would undoubtedly snap up anyone who was unfortunate enough to fall into the water; but the facts that they could display such deliberate cunning, that they were able to break ice of such thickness (at least 2½ feet), and that they could act in unison, were a revelation to us. It is clear that they are endowed with singular intelligence, and in future we shall treat that intelligence with every respect.

Notes on the Killer or Grampus [Orca gladiator]

One killed at Greenwich, 31 feet.

Teeth about 2½ inches above jaw; about 3½ inches total length.

British Quadrupeds, Bell: 'The fierceness and voracity of the killer, in which it surpasses all other known cetaceans.'

In stomach of a 21 ft. specimen were found remains of 13 porpoises and 14 seals.

A herd of white whales has been seen driven into a bay and literally torn to pieces.

Teeth large, conical, and slightly recurved, 11 or 12 on each side of either jaw.

Mammals, Flower and Lydekker: 'Distinguished from all their allies by great strength and ferocity.'

'Combine in packs to hunt down and destroy . . . full-sized whales.'

Marine Mammalia, Scammon: adult males average 20 feet; females 15 feet.

Strong sharp conical teeth which interlock. Combines great strength with agility.

Spout 'low and bushy'.

Habits exhibit a boldness and cunning peculiar to their carnivorous propensities.

Three or four do not hesitate to grapple the largest baleen whales, who become paralysed with terror – frequently evince no efforts to escape.

Instances have occurred where a band of orcas laid siege to whales in tow, and although frequently lanced and cut with boat spades, made away with their prey.

Inclined to believe it rarely attacks larger cetaceans.

Possessed of great swiftness.

Sometimes seen peering above the surface with a seal in their bristling jaws, shaking and crushing their victims and swallowing them apparently with gusto.

Tear white whales into pieces.

Ponting has been ravished yesterday by a view of the ship seen from a big cave in an iceberg, and wished to get pictures of it. He succeeded in getting some splendid plates. This forenoon I went to the iceberg with him and agreed that I had rarely seen anything more beautiful than this cave. It was really a sort of crevasse in a tilted berg parallel to the original surface; the strata on either side had bent outwards; through the back the sky could be seen through a screen of beautiful icicles – it looked a royal purple, whether by contrast with the blue of the cavern or whether from optical illusion I do not know. Through the larger entrance could be seen, also partly through icicles, the ship, the Western Mountains, and a lilac sky; a wonderfully beautiful picture.

Ponting is simply entranced with this view of Mt Erebus, and with the two bergs in the foreground and some volunteers he works up foregrounds to complete his picture of it.

I go to bed very satisfied with the day's work, but hoping for better results with the improved organisation and familiarity with the work.

Today we landed the remainder of the woodwork of the hut, all the petrol, paraffin and oil of all descriptions, and a quantity of oats for the ponies besides odds and ends. The ponies are to begin work tomorrow; they did nothing today, but the motor sledges did well – they are steadying down to their work and made nothing but non-stop runs today. One begins to believe they will be reliable, but I am still fearing that they will not take such heavy loads as we hoped.

Day is very pleased and thinks he's going to do wonders, and Nelson shares his optimism. The dogs find the day work terribly heavy and Meares is going to put them on to night work.

The framework of the hut is nearly up; the hands worked till 1 a.m. this morning and were at it again at 7 a.m. – an instance of the spirit which actuates everyone. The men teams formed of the after-guard brought in good loads, but they are not yet in condition. The hut is about 11 or 12 feet above the water as far as I can judge. I don't think spray can get so high in such a sheltered spot even if we get a northerly gale when the sea is open.

In all other respects the situation is admirable. This work makes one very tired for Diary-writing.

Friday, *January 6*. – We got to work at 6 again this morning. Wilson, Atkinson, Cherry-Garrard, and I took each a pony, returned to the ship, and brought a load ashore; we then changed ponies and repeated the process. We each took three ponies in the morning, and I took one in the afternoon.

Bruce, after relief by Rennick, took one in the morning and one in the afternoon – of the remaining five Oates deemed two unfit for work and three requiring some breaking in before getting to serious business.

I was astonished at the strength of the beasts I handled; three out of the four pulled hard the whole time and gave me much exercise. I brought back loads of 700 lbs. and on one occasion over 1000 lbs.

With ponies, motor sledges, dogs, and men parties we have done an excellent day of transporting – another such day should practically finish all the stores and leave only fuel and fodder (60 tons) to complete our landing. So far it has been remarkably expeditious.

The motor sledges are working well, but not very well; the small difficulties will be got over, but I rather fear they will never draw the loads we expect of them. Still they promise to be a help, and they are lively and attractive features of our present scene as they drone along over the floe. At a little distance, without silencers, they sound exactly like threshing machines.

The dogs are getting better, but they only take very light loads still and get back from each journey pretty dead beat. In their present state they don't inspire confidence, but the hot weather is much against them.

The men parties have done splendidly. Campbell and his Eastern Party made eight journeys in the day, a distance over 24 miles. Everyone declares that the ski sticks greatly help pulling; it is surprising that we never thought of using them before.

Atkinson is very bad with snow blindness tonight; also Bruce. Others have a touch of the same disease. It's well for people to get experience of the necessity of safeguarding their eyes.

The only thing which troubles me at present is the wear on our sledges owing to the hard ice. No great harm has been done so far, thanks to the excellent wood of which the runners are made, but we can't afford to have them worn. Wilson carried out a suggestion of his own tonight by covering the runners of a 9-ft. sledge with strips from the skin of a seal which he killed and flensed for the purpose. I shouldn't wonder if this acted well, and if it does we will cover more sledges in a similar manner. We shall also try Day's new under-runners tomorrow. After 48 hours of brilliant sunshine we have a haze over the sky.

List of sledges:

12 ft.	{	11 in use
	{	14 spare
10 ft.		10 not now used
9 ft.		10 in use

Today I walked over our peninsula to see what the southern side was like. Hundreds of skuas were nesting and attacked in the usual manner as I passed. They fly round shrieking wildly until they have gained some altitude. They then swoop down with great impetus directly at one's head, lifting again when within a foot of it. The bolder ones actually beat on one's head with their wings as they pass. At first it is alarming, but experience shows that they never strike except with their wings. A skua is nesting on a rock between the ponies and the dogs. People pass every few minutes within a pace or two, yet the old bird has not deserted its chick. In fact, it seems gradually to be getting confidence, for it no longer attempts to swoop at the intruder. Today Ponting went within a few feet, and by dint of patience managed to get some wonderful cinematograph pictures of its movements in feeding and tending its chick, as well as some photographs of these events at critical times.

The main channel for thaw water at Cape Evans is now quite a rushing stream.

Evans, Pennell, and Rennick have got sight for meridian distance; we ought to get a good longitude fix.

Saturday, January 7. – The sun has returned. Today it seemed better than ever and the glare was blinding. There are quite a number of cases of snow blindness.

We have done splendidly. Tonight all the provisions except some in bottles are ashore and nearly all the working paraphernalia of the scientific people – no light item. There remains some hut furniture, 2½ tons of carbide, some bottled stuff, and some odds and ends which should occupy only part of tomorrow; then we come to the two last and heaviest items – coal and horse fodder.

If we are not through in the week we shall be very near it. Meanwhile the ship is able to lay at the ice edge without steam; a splendid saving.

There has been a steady stream of cases passing along the shore route all day and transport arrangements are hourly improving.

Two parties of four and three officers made ten journeys each, covering over 25 miles and dragging loads one way which averaged 250 to 300 lbs. per man.

The ponies are working well now, but beginning to give some excitement. On the whole they are fairly quiet beasts, but they get restive with their loads, mainly but indirectly owing to the smoothness of the ice. They know perfectly well that the swingle trees and traces are hanging about their hocks and hate it. (I imagine it gives them the nervous feeling that they are going to be carried off their feet.) This makes it hard to start them, and when going they seem to appreciate the fact that the sledges will overrun them should they hesitate or stop. The result is that they are constantly fretful and the more nervous ones tend to become refractory and unmanageable.

Oates is splendid with them – I do not know what we should do without him.

I did seven journeys with ponies and got off with a bump on the head and some scratches.

One pony got away from Debenham close to the ship, and galloped the whole way in with its load behind; the load capsized just off the shore and the animal and sledge dashed into the station. Oates very wisely took this pony straight back for another load.

Two or three ponies got away as they were being harnessed, and careered up the hill again. In fact there were quite a lot of minor incidents which seemed to endanger life and limb to the animals if not the men, but which all ended safely.

One of Meares's dog teams ran away – one poor dog got turned over at the start and couldn't get up again (Mukaka). He was dragged at a gallop for nearly half a mile; I gave him up as dead, but apparently he was very little hurt.

The ponies are certainly going to keep things lively as time goes on and they get fresher. Even as it is, their condition can't be half as bad as we imagined; the runaway pony wasn't much done even after the extra trip.

The station is beginning to assume the appearance of an orderly camp. We continue to find advantages in the situation; the long level beach has enabled Bowers to arrange his stores in the most systematic manner. Everything will be handy and there will never be a doubt as to the position of a case when it is wanted. The hut is advancing apace – already the matchboarding is being put on. The framework is being clothed. It should be extraordinarily warm and comfortable, for in addition to this double coating of insulation, dry seaweed in quilted sacking, I propose to stack the pony fodder all around it.

I am wondering how we shall stable the ponies in the winter.

The only drawback to the present position is that the ice is getting thin and sludgy in the cracks and on some of the floes. The ponies drop their feet through, but most of them have evidently been accustomed to something of the sort; they make no fuss about it. Everything points to the desirability of the haste which we are making – so we go on tomorrow, Sunday.

A whole host of minor ills besides snow blindness have come upon us. Sore faces and lips, blistered feet, cuts and abrasions; there are few without some troublesome ailment, but, of course, such things are 'part of the business'. The soles of my feet are infernally sore.

'Of course the elements are going to be troublesome, but it is good to know them as the only adversary and to feel there is so small a chance of internal friction.'

Ponting had an alarming adventure about this time. Bent on getting artistic photographs with striking objects, such as hummocked floes or reflecting water, in the foreground, he used to depart with his own small sledge laden with cameras and cinematograph to journey alone to the grounded icebergs. One morning as he tramped along harnessed to his sledge, his snow glasses clouded with the mist of perspiration, he suddenly felt the ice giving under his feet. He describes the sensation as the worst he ever experienced, and one can well believe it; there was no one near to have lent assistance had he gone through. Instinctively he plunged forward, the ice giving at every step and the sledge dragging through water. Providentially the weak area he had struck was very limited, and in a minute or two he pulled out on a firm surface. He remarked that he was perspiring very freely!

Looking back it is easy to see that we were terribly incautious in our treatment of this decaying ice.

CHAPTER FOUR

Settling in

Sunday, January 8. – A day of *disaster*. I stupidly gave permission for the third motor to be got out this morning. This was done first thing and the motor placed on firm ice. Later Campbell told me one of the men had dropped a leg through crossing a sludgy patch some 200 yards from the ship. I didn't consider it very serious, as I imagined the man had only gone through the surface crust. About 7 a.m. I started for the shore with a single man load, leaving Campbell looking about for the best crossing for the motor. I sent Meares and the dogs over with a can of petrol on arrival. After some twenty minutes he returned to tell me the motor had gone through. Soon after Campbell and Day arrived to confirm the dismal tidings. It appears that getting frightened of the state of affairs Campbell got out a line and attached it to the motor – then manning the line well he attempted to rush the machine across the weak place. A man on the rope, Williamson, suddenly went through to the shoulders, but was immediately hauled out. During the operation the ice under the motor was seen to give, and suddenly it and the motor disappeared. The men kept hold of the rope, but it cut through the ice towards them with an ever increasing strain, obliging one after another to let go. Half a minute later nothing remained but a big hole. Perhaps it was lucky there was no accident to the men, but it's a sad incident for us in any case. It's a big blow to know that one of the two best motors, on which so much time and trouble have been spent, now lies at the bottom of the sea. The actual spot where the motor disappeared was crossed by its fellow motor with a very heavy load as well as by myself with heavy ponies only yesterday.

Meares took Campbell back and returned with the report that the ice in the vicinity of the accident was hourly getting more dangerous.

It was clear that we were practically cut off, certainly as regards heavy transport. Bowers went back again with Meares and managed to ferry over some wind clothes and odds and ends. Since that no communication has been held; the shore party have been working, but the people on board have had a half-holiday.

At 6 I went to the ice edge farther to the north. I found a place where the ship could come and be near the heavy ice over which sledging is still possible. I went near the ship and semaphored directions for her to get to this place as soon as she could, using steam if necessary. She is at present wedged in with the pack, and I think Pennell hopes to warp her along when the pack loosens.

Meares and I marked the new trail with kerosene tins before returning. So here we are waiting again till fortune is kinder. Meanwhile the hut proceeds; altogether there are four layers of boarding to go on, two of which are nearing completion; it will be some time before the rest and the insulation is on.

It's a big job getting settled in like this and a tantalising one when one is hoping to do some depôt work before the season closes.

We had a keen north wind tonight and a haze, but wind is dropping and sun shining brightly again. Today seemed to be the hottest we have yet had; after walking across I was perspiring freely, and later as I sat in the sun after lunch one could almost imagine a warm summer day in England.

This is my first night ashore. I'm writing in one of my new domed tents, which makes a very comfortable apartment.

Monday, January 9. – I didn't poke my nose out of my tent till 6.45, and the first object I saw was the ship, which had not previously been in sight from our camp. She was now working her way along the ice edge with some difficulty. I heard afterwards that she had started at 6.15 and she reached the point I marked yesterday at 8.15. After breakfast I went on board and was delighted to find a good solid road right up to the ship. A flag was hoisted immediately for the ponies to come out, and we commenced a good day's work. All day the sledges have been coming to and fro, but most of the pulling work has been done by the ponies: the track is so good that these little animals haul anything from 12 to 18 cwt. Both dogs and men parties have been a useful addition to the haulage – no party or no single man comes over without a load averaging 300 lbs. per man. The dogs, working five to a team, haul 5 to 6 cwt. and of course they travel much faster than either ponies or men.

In this way we transported a large quantity of miscellaneous stores; first about 3 tons of coal for present use, then 2½ tons of carbide, all the many stores, chimney and ventilators for the hut, all the biologists' gear – a big pile, the remainder of the physicists' gear and medical stores, and many old cases; in fact a general clear up of everything except the two heavy items of forage and fuel. Later in the day we made a start on the first of these, and got 7 tons ashore before ceasing work. We close with a good day to our credit, marred by an unfortunate incident – one of the dogs, a good puller, was seen to cough after a journey; he was evidently trying to bring something up – two minutes later he was dead. Nobody seems to know the reason, but a post-mortem is being held by Atkinson and I suppose the cause of death will be found. We can't afford to lose animals of any sort.

All the ponies except three have now brought loads from the ship. Oates thinks these three are too nervous to work over this slippery surface. However, he tried one of the hardest cases tonight, a very fine pony, and got him in successfully with a big load.

Tomorrow we ought to be running some twelve or thirteen of these animals.

Griffith Taylor's bolted on three occasions, the first two times more or less due to his own fault, but the third owing to the stupidity of one of the sailors. Nevertheless a third occasion couldn't be overlooked by his messmates, who made much merriment of the event. It was still funnier when he brought his final load (an exceptionally heavy one) with a set face and ardent pace, vouchsafing not a word to anyone he passed.

We have achieved fair organisation today. Evans is in charge of the road and periodically goes along searching for bad places and bridging cracks with boards and snow.

Bowers checks every case as it comes on shore and dashes off to the ship to arrange the precedence of different classes of goods. He proves a perfect treasure; there is not a single case he does not know or a single article of any sort which he cannot put his hand on at once.

Rennick and Bruce are working gallantly at the discharge of stores on board.

Williamson and Leese load the sledges and are getting very clever and expeditious. Evans (seaman) is generally superintending the sledging and camp outfit. Forde, Keohane, and Abbott are regularly assisting the carpenter, whilst Day, Lashly, Lillie, and others give intermittent help.

Wilson, Cherry-Garrard, Wright, Griffith Taylor, Debenham, Crean, and Browning have been driving ponies, a task at which I have assisted myself once or twice. There was a report that the ice was getting rotten, but I went over it myself and found it sound throughout. The accident with the motor sledge has made people nervous.

The weather has been very warm and fine on the whole, with occasional gleams of sunshine, but tonight there is a rather chill wind from the south. The hut is progressing famously. In two more working days we ought to have everything necessary on shore.

Tuesday, January 10. – We have been six days in McMurdo Sound and tonight I can say we are landed. Were it impossible to land another pound we could go on without hitch. Nothing like it has been done before; nothing so expeditious and complete. This morning the main loads were fodder. Sledge after sledge brought the bales, and early in the afternoon the last (except for about a ton stowed with Eastern Party stores) was brought on shore. Some addition to our patent fuel was made in the morning, and later in the afternoon it came in a steady stream. We have more than 12 tons and could make this do if necessity arose.

In addition to this oddments have been arriving all day – instruments, clothing, and personal effects. Our camp is becoming so perfect in its appointments that I am almost suspicious of some drawback hidden by the summer weather.

The hut is progressing apace, and all agree that it should be the most perfectly comfortable habitation. 'It amply repays the time and attention given to the planning.' The sides have double boarding inside and outside the frames, with a layer of our excellent quilted seaweed insulation between each pair of boardings. The roof has a single matchboarding inside, but on the outside is a matchboarding, then a layer of 2-ply 'ruberoid', then a layer of quilted seaweed, then a second matchboarding, and finally a cover of 3-ply 'ruberoid'. The first floor is laid, but over this there will be a quilting, a felt layer, a second boarding, and finally linoleum; as the plenteous volcanic sand can be piled well up on every side it is impossible to imagine that draughts can penetrate into the hut from beneath, and it is equally impossible to imagine great loss of heat by contact or radiation in that direction. To add to the wall insulation the south and east sides of the hut are piled high with compressed-forage bales, whilst the north side is being prepared as a winter stable for the ponies. The stable will stand between the wall of the hut and a wall built of forage bales, six bales high and two bales thick. This will be roofed with rafters and tarpaulin, as we cannot find enough boarding. We shall have to take care that too much snow does not collect on the roof, otherwise the place should do excellently well.

Some of the ponies are very troublesome, but all except two have been running today, and until this evening there were no excitements. After tea Oates suggested leading out the two intract-able animals behind other sledges; at the same time he brought out the strong, nervous grey pony. I led one of the supposedly safe ponies, and all went well whilst we made our journey; three loads were safely brought in. But whilst one of the sledges was being unpacked the pony tied to it suddenly got scared. Away he dashed with sledge attached; he made straight for the other ponies, but finding the incubus still fast to him he went in wider circles, galloped over hills and boulders, narrowly missing Ponting and his camera, and finally dashed down hill to camp again pretty exhausted – oddly enough, neither sledge nor pony was much damaged. Then we departed again in the same order. Half-way over the floe my rear pony got his foreleg foul of his halter, then got frightened, tugged at his halter, and lifted the unladen sledge to which he was tied – then the halter broke and away he went. But by this time the damage was done. My pony snorted wildly and sprang forward as the sledge banged to the ground. I just managed to hold him till Oates came up, then we started again; but he was thoroughly frightened – all my blandishments failed when he reared and plunged a second time, and I was obliged to let go. He galloped back and the party dejectedly returned. At the camp P. O. Evans got hold of the pony, but in a moment it was off again, knocking Evans off his legs. Finally he was captured and led forth once more between Oates and Anton. He remained fairly well on the outward journey, but on the homeward grew restive again; Evans, who was now leading him, called for Anton, and both tried to hold him, but to no purpose – he dashed off, upset his load, and came back to camp with the sledge. All these troubles arose after he had made three journeys without a hitch and we had come to regard him as a nice, placid, gritty pony. Now I'm afraid it will take a deal of trouble to get him safe again, and we have three very troublesome beasts instead of two. I have written this in some detail to show the unexpected difficulties that arise with these animals, and the impossibility of knowing exactly where one stands. The majority of our animals seem pretty quiet now, but any one of them may break out in this way if things go awry. There is no doubt that the bumping of the sledges close at the heels of the animals is the root of the evil.

The weather has the appearance of breaking. We had a strongish northerly breeze at midday with snow and hail storms, and now the wind has turned to the south and the sky is overcast with threatenings of a blizzard. The floe is cracking and pieces may go out – if so the ship will have to get up steam again. The hail at noon made the surface very bad for some hours; the men and dogs felt it most.

The dogs are going well, but Meares says he thinks that several are suffering from snow blindness. I never knew a dog get it before, but Day says that Shackleton's dogs suffered from it. The post-mortem on last night's death revealed nothing to account for it. Atkinson didn't examine the brain, and wonders if the cause lay there. There is a certain satisfaction in believing that there is nothing infectious.

Wednesday, January 11. – A week here today – it seems quite a month, so much has been crammed into a short space of time.

The threatened blizzard materialised at about four o'clock this morning. The wind increased to force six or seven at the ship, and continued to blow, with drift, throughout the forenoon.

Campbell and his sledging party arrived at the Camp at 8.0 a.m. bringing a small load: there seemed little object, but I suppose they like the experience of a march in the blizzard. They started to go back, but the ship being blotted out, turned and gave us their company at breakfast. The day was altogether too bad for outside work, so we turned our attention to the hut interior, with the result that tonight all the match-boarding is completed. The floor linoleum is the only thing that remains to be put down; outside, the roof and ends have to be finished. Then there are several days of odd jobs for the carpenter, and all will be finished. It is a first-rate building in an extraordinarily sheltered spot; whilst the wind was raging at the ship this morning we enjoyed comparative peace. Campbell says there was an extraordinary change as he approached the beach.

I sent two or three people to dig into the hard snow drift behind the camp; they got into solid ice immediately, became interested in the job, and have begun the making of a cave which is to be our larder. Already they have tunnelled 6 or 8 feet in and have begun side channels. In a few days they will have made quite a spacious apartment – an ideal place to keep our meat store. We had been speculating as to the origin of this solid drift and attached great antiquity to it, but the diggers came to a patch of earth with skua feathers, which rather knocks our theories on the head.

The wind began to drop at midday, and after lunch I went to the ship. I was very glad to learn that she can hold steam at two hours' notice on an expenditure of 13 cwt. The ice anchors had held well during the blow.

As far as I can see the open water extends to an east and west line which is a little short of the Glacier Tongue.

Tonight the wind has dropped altogether and we return to the glorious conditions of a week ago. I trust they may last for a few days at least.

Thursday, January 12. – Bright sun again all day, but in the afternoon a chill wind from the S.S.W. Again we are reminded of the shelter afforded by our position; tonight the anemometers on Observation Hill show a 20-mile wind – down in our valley we only have mild puffs.

Sledging began as usual this morning; seven ponies and the dog teams were hard at it all the forenoon. I ran six journeys with five dogs, driving them in the Siberian fashion for the first time. It was not difficult, but I kept forgetting the Russian words at critical moments: 'Ki' – 'right'; 'Tchui' – 'left'; 'Itah' – 'right ahead'; [here is a blank in memory and in Diary] – 'get along'; 'Paw' – 'stop'. Even my short experience makes me think that we may have

to reorganise this driving to suit our particular requirements. I
am inclined for smaller teams and the driver behind the sledge.
However, it's early days to decide such matters, and we shall learn
much on the depôt journey.

Early in the afternoon a message came from the ship to say
that all stores had been landed. Nothing remains to be brought
but mutton, books and pictures, and the pianola. So at last we
really are a self-contained party ready for all emergencies. We are
LANDED eight days after our arrival – a very good record.

The hut could be inhabited at this moment, but probably we
shall not begin to live in it for a week. Meanwhile the carpenter
will go on steadily fitting up the dark room and various other
compartments as well as Simpson's Corner.[*]

The grotto party are making headway into the ice for our larder,
but it is slow and very arduous work. However, once made it will
be admirable in every way.

Tomorrow we begin sending ballast off to the ship; some 30 tons
will be sledged off by the ponies. The hut and grotto parties will
continue, and the arrangements for the depôt journey will be
commenced. I discussed these with Bowers this afternoon – he is
a perfect treasure, enters into one's ideas at once, and evidently
thoroughly understands the principles of the game.

I have arranged to go to Hut Point with Meares and some dogs
tomorrow to test the ice and see how the land lies. As things are at
present we ought to have little difficulty in getting the depôt party
away any time before the end of the month, but the ponies will
have to cross the Cape[†] without loads. There is a way down on the
south side straight across, and another way round, keeping the land
on the north side and getting on ice at the Cape itself. Probably the
ship will take the greater part of the loads.

Saturday, January 14. – The completion of our station is approaching with steady progress. The wind was strong from the S.S.E.
yesterday morning, sweeping over the camp; the temperature fell
to 15°, the sky became overcast. To the south the land outlines
were hazy with drift, so my dog tour was abandoned. In the
afternoon, with some moderation of conditions, the ballast party
went to work, and wrought so well that more than 10 tons were

[*] Here were the meteorological instruments.
[†] Cape Evans, which lay on the S. side of the new hut.

got off before night. The organisation of this work is extremely good. The loose rocks are pulled up, some 30 or 40 feet up the hillside, placed on our heavy rough sledges and rushed down to the floe on a snow track; here they are laden on pony sledges and transported to the ship. I slept on board the ship and found it colder than the camp – the cabins were below freezing all night and the only warmth existed in the cheery spirit of the company. The cold snap froze the water in the boiler and Williams had to light one of the fires this morning. I shaved and bathed last night (the first time for 10 days) and wrote letters from breakfast till tea time today. Meanwhile the ballast team has been going on merrily, and tonight Pennell must have some 26 tons on board.

It was good to return to the camp and see the progress which had been made even during such a short absence. The grotto has been much enlarged and is, in fact, now big enough to hold all our mutton and a considerable quantity of seal and penguin.

Close by Simpson and Wright have made surprising progress in excavating for the differential magnetic hut. They have already gone in 7 feet and, turning a corner, commenced the chamber, which is to be 13 feet x 5 feet. The hard ice of this slope is a godsend and both grottoes will be ideal for their purposes.

The cooking range and stove have been placed in the hut and now chimneys are being constructed; the porch is almost finished as well as the interior; the various carpenters are busy with odd jobs and it will take them some time to fix up the many small fittings that different people require.

I have been making arrangements for the depôt journey, telling off people for ponies and dogs, &c.[9]

Tomorrow is to be our first rest day, but next week everything will be tending towards sledging preparations. I have also been discussing and writing about the provisions of animals to be brought down in the *Terra Nova* next year.

The wind is very persistent from the S.S.E., rising and falling; tonight it has sprung up again, and is rattling the canvas of the tent.

Some of the ponies are not turning out so well as I expected; they are slow walkers and must inevitably impede the faster ones. Two of the best had been told off for Campbell by Oates, but I must alter the arrangement. Then I am not quite *sure* they are going to stand the cold well, and on this first journey they may have to face pretty severe conditions. Then, of course, there is the danger of losing them on thin ice or by injury sustained in rough places. Although we have fifteen now (two having gone for the Eastern Party) it is not at all certain that we shall have such a number when the main journey is undertaken next season. One can only be careful and hope for the best.

Sunday, January 15. – We had decided to observe this day as a 'day of rest', and so it has been.

At one time or another the majority have employed their spare hours in writing letters.

We rose late, having breakfast at nine. The morning promised well and the day fulfilled the promise: we had bright sunshine and practically no wind.

At 10 a.m. the men and officers streamed over from the ship, and we all assembled on the beach and I read Divine Service, our first Service at the camp and impressive in the open air. After Service I told Campbell that I should have to cancel his two ponies and give him two others. He took it like the gentleman he is, thoroughly appreciating the reason.

He had asked me previously to be allowed to go to Cape Royds over the glacier and I had given permission. After our talk we went together to explore the route, which we expected to find much crevassed. I only intended to go a short way, but on reaching the snow above the uncovered hills of our Cape I found the surface so promising and so free from cracks that I went quite a long way. Eventually I turned, leaving Campbell, Gran, and Nelson roped together and on ski to make their way onward, but not before I felt certain that the route to Cape Royds would be quite easy. As we topped the last rise we saw Taylor and Wright some way ahead on the slope; they had come up by a different route. Evidently they are bound for the same goal.

I returned to camp, and after lunch Meares and I took a sledge and nine dogs over the Cape to the sea ice on the south side and started for Hut Point, We took a little provision and a cooker and our sleeping-bags. Meares had found a way over the Cape which was on snow all the way except about 100 yards. The dogs pulled well, and we went towards the Glacier Tongue at a brisk pace; found much of the ice uncovered. Towards the Glacier Tongue there were some heaps of snow much wind-blown. As we rose the glacier we saw the *Nimrod* depôt some way to the right and made for it. We found a good deal of compressed fodder and boxes of maize, but no grain crusher as expected. The open water was practically up to the Glacier Tongue.

We descended by an easy slope ¼ mile from the end of the Glacier Tongue, but found ourselves cut off by an open crack some 15 feet across and had to get on the glacier again and go some ½ mile farther in. We came to a second crack, but avoided it by skirting to the west. From this point we had an easy run without difficulty to Hut Point. There was a small pool of open water and a longish crack off Hut Point. I got my feet very wet crossing the latter. We passed hundreds of seals at the various cracks.

On the arrival at the hut to my chagrin we found it filled with snow. Shackleton reported* that the door had been forced by the wind, but that he had made an entrance by the window and found shelter inside – other members of his party used it for shelter. But they actually went away and left the window (which they had forced) open; as a result, nearly the whole of the interior of the hut is filled with hard icy snow, and it is now impossible to find shelter inside.

Meares and I were able to clamber over the snow to some extent and to examine the neat pile of cases in the middle, but they will take much digging out. We got some asbestos sheeting from the magnetic hut and made the best shelter we could to boil our cocoa.

There was something too depressing in finding the old hut in such a desolate condition. I had had so much interest in seeing all the old landmarks and the huts apparently intact. To camp outside and feel that all the old comfort and cheer had departed, was dreadfully heartrending. I went to bed thoroughly depressed. It seems a fundamental expression of civilised human sentiment that men who come to such places as this should leave what comfort they can to welcome those who follow, and finding that such a simple duty had been neglected by our immediate predecessors oppressed me horribly.

Monday, January 16. – We slept badly till the morning and, therefore, late. After breakfast we went up the hills; there was a keen S.E. breeze, but the sun shone and my spirits revived. There

* On the *Nimrod* expedition, 1907–9

was very much less snow everywhere than I had ever seen. The ski run was completely cut through in two places, the Gap and Observation Hill almost bare, a great bare slope on the side of Arrival Heights, and on top of Crater Heights an immense bare table-land. How delighted we should have been to see it like this in the old days! The pond was thawed and the confervae green in fresh water. The hole which we had dug in the mound in the pond was still there, as Meares discovered by falling into it up to his waist and getting very wet.

On the south side we could see the Pressure Ridges beyond Pram Point as of old – Horseshoe Bay calm and unpressed – the sea ice pressed on Pram Point and along the Gap ice foot, and a new ridge running around C. Armitage about 2 miles off. We saw Ferrar's old thermometer tubes standing out of the snow slope as though they'd been placed yesterday. Vince's cross might have been placed yesterday – the paint was so fresh and the inscription so legible.

The flagstaff was down, the stays having carried away, but in five minutes it could be put up again. We loaded some asbestos sheeting from the old magnetic hut on our sledges for Simpson, and by standing ¼ mile off Hut Point got a clear run to Glacier Tongue. I had hoped to get across the wide crack by going west, but found that it ran for a great distance and had to get on the glacier at the place at which we had left it. We got to camp about teatime. I found our larder in the grotto completed and stored with mutton and penguins – the temperature inside has never been above 27°, so that it ought to be a fine place for our winter store. Simpson has almost completed the differential magnetic cave next door. The hut stove was burning well and the interior of the building already warm and homelike – a day or two and we shall be occupying it.

I took Ponting out to see some interesting thaw effects on the ice cliffs east of the Camp. I noted that the ice layers were pressing out over thin dirt bands as though the latter made the cleavage lines over which the strata slid.

It has occurred to me that although the sea ice may freeze in our bays early in March it will be a difficult thing to get ponies across it owing to the cliff edges at the side. We must therefore be prepared to be cut off for a longer time than I anticipated. I heard that all the people who journeyed towards C. Royds yesterday reached their destination in safety. Campbell, Levick, and Priestley had just departed when I returned.[10]

Tuesday, January 17. – We took up our abode in the hut today and are simply overwhelmed with its comfort. After breakfast this morning I found Bowers making cubicles as I had arranged, but I soon saw these would not fit in, so instructed him to build a bulkhead of cases which shuts off the officers' space from the men's, I am quite sure to the satisfaction of both. The space between my bulkhead and the men's I allotted to five: Bowers, Oates, Atkinson, Meares, and Cherry-Garrard. These five are all special friends and have already made their dormitory very habitable. Simpson and Wright are near the instruments in their corner. Next come Day and Nelson in a space which includes the latter's 'Lab' near the big window; next to this is a space for three – Debenham, Taylor, and Gran; they also have already made their space part dormitory and part workshop.

It is fine to see the way everyone sets to work to put things straight; in a day or two the hut will become the most comfortable of houses, and in a week or so the whole station, instruments, routine, men and animals, &c., will be in working order.

It is really wonderful to realise the amount of work which has been got through of late.

It will be *a fortnight tomorrow* since we arrived in McMurdo Sound, and here we are absolutely settled down and ready to start on our depôt journey directly the ponies have had a proper chance to recover from the effects of the voyage. I had no idea we should be so expeditious.

It snowed hard all last night; there were about three or four inches of soft snow over the camp this morning and Simpson tells me some six inches out by the ship. The camp looks very white. During the day it has been blowing very hard from the south, with a great deal of drift. Here in this camp as usual we do not feel it much, but we see the anemometer racing on the hill and the snow clouds sweeping past the ship. The floe is breaking between the point and the ship, though curiously it remains fast on a direct route to the ship. Now the open water runs parallel to our ship road and only a few hundred yards south of it. Yesterday the whaler was rowed in close to the camp, and if the ship had steam

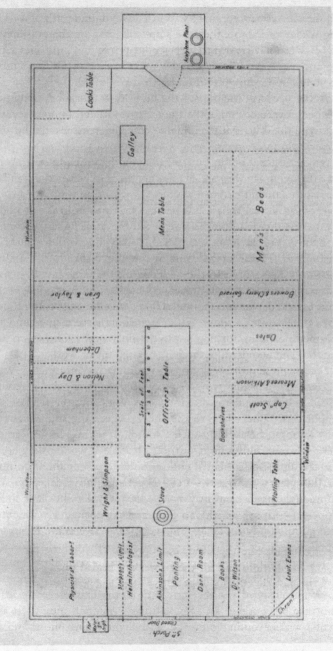

Plan of hut

up she could steam round to within a few hundred yards of us. The big wedge of ice to which the ship is holding on the outskirts of the Bay can have very little grip to keep it in and must inevitably go out very soon. I hope this may result in the ship finding a more sheltered and secure position close to us.

A big iceberg sailed past the ship this afternoon. Atkinson declares it was the end of the Cape Barne Glacier. I hope they will know in the ship, as it would be interesting to witness the birth of a glacier in this region.

It is clearing tonight, but still blowing hard. The ponies don't like the wind, but they are all standing the cold wonderfully and all their sores are healed up.

Wednesday, January 18. – The ship had a poor time last night; steam was ordered, but the floe began breaking up fast at 1 a.m., and the rest of the night was passed in struggling with ice anchors; steam was reported ready just as the ship broke adrift. In the morning she secured to the ice edge on the same line as before but a few hundred yards nearer. After getting things going at the hut, I walked over and suggested that Pennell should come round the corner close in shore. The ice anchors were tripped and we steamed slowly in, making fast to the floe within 200 yards of the ice foot and 400 yards of the hut.

For the present the position is extraordinarily comfortable. With a southerly blow she would simply bind on to the ice, receiving great shelter from the end of the Cape. With a northerly blow she might turn rather close to the shore, where the soundings run to 3 fathoms, but behind such a stretch of ice she could scarcely get a sea or swell without warning. It looks a wonderfully comfortable little nook, but, of course, one can be certain of nothing in this place; one knows from experience how deceptive the appearance of security may be. Pennell is truly excellent in his present position – he's invariably cheerful, unceasingly watchful, and continuously ready for emergencies. I have come to possess implicit confidence in him.

The temperature fell to 4° last night, with a keen S.S.E. breeze; it was very unpleasant outside after breakfast. Later in the forenoon the wind dropped and the sun shone forth. This afternoon it fell almost calm, but the sky clouded over again and now there is a gentle warm southerly breeze with light falling snow and an overcast sky. Rather significant of a blizzard if we had not had such a lot of wind lately. The position of the ship makes the casual transport that still proceeds very easy, but the ice is rather thin at the edge. In the hut all is marching towards the utmost comfort.

Bowers has completed a store-room on the south side, an excellent place to keep our travelling provisions. Every day he conceives or carries out some plan to benefit the camp. Simpson and Wright are worthy of all admiration: they have been unceasingly active in getting things to the fore and I think will be ready for routine work much earlier than was anticipated. But, indeed, it is hard to specialise praise where everyone is working so indefatigably for the cause.

Each man in his way is a treasure.

Clissold the cook has started splendidly, has served seal, penguin, and skua now, and I can honestly say that I have never met these articles of food in such a pleasing guise; 'this point is of the greatest practical importance, as it means the certainty of good health for any number of years.' Hooper was landed today, much to his joy. He got to work at once, and will be a splendid help, freeing the scientific people of all dirty work. Anton and Demetri are both most anxious to help on all occasions; they are excellent boys.

Thursday, January 19. – The hut is becoming the most comfortable dwelling-place imaginable. We have made unto ourselves a truly seductive home, within the walls of which peace, quiet, and comfort reign supreme.

Such a noble dwelling transcends the word 'hut', and we pause to give it a more fitting title only from lack of the appropriate suggestion. What shall we call it?

'The word "hut" is misleading. Our residence is really a house of considerable size, in every respect the finest that has ever been erected in the Polar regions; 50 ft. long by 25 wide and 9 ft. to the eaves.

'If you can picture our house nestling below this small hill on a long stretch of black sand, with many tons of provision cases ranged in neat blocks in front of it and the sea lapping the ice-foot below, you will have some idea of our immediate vicinity. As for our wider surroundings, it would be difficult to describe their beauty in sufficiently glowing terms. Cape Evans is one of the many spurs of Erebus and the one that stands closest under the mountain, so that always towering above us we have the grand snowy peak with its smoking summit. North and south of us are deep bays, beyond which great glaciers come rippling over the lower slopes to thrust high blue-walled snouts into the sea. The sea is blue before us, dotted with shining bergs or ice floes, whilst far over the Sound, yet so bold and magnificent as to appear near, stand the beautiful Western Mountains with their numerous lofty peaks, their deep glacial valley and clear cut scarps, a vision of mountain scenery that can have few rivals.

'Ponting is the most delighted of men; he declares this is the most beautiful spot he has ever seen and spends all day and most of the night in what he calls "gathering it in" with camera and cinematograph.'

The wind has been boisterous all day, to advantage after the last snow fall, as it has been drifting the loose snow along and hardening the surfaces. The horses don't like it, naturally, but it wouldn't do to pamper them so soon before our journey. I think the hardening process must be good for animals though not for men; nature replies to it in the former by growing a thick coat with wonderful promptitude. It seems to me that the shaggy coats of our ponies are already improving. The dogs seem to feel the cold little so far, but they are not so exposed.

A milder situation might be found for the ponies if only we could picket them off the snow.

Bowers has completed his southern store-room and brought the wing across the porch on the windward side, connecting the roofing with that of the porch. The improvement is enormous and will make the greatest difference to those who dwell near the door.

The carpenter has been setting up standards and roof beams for the stables, which will be completed in a few days. Internal affairs have been straightening out as rapidly as before, and every hour seems to add some new touch for the better.

This morning I overhauled all the fur sleeping-bags and found them in splendid order – on the whole the skins are excellent. Since that I have been trying to work out sledge details, but my head doesn't seem half as clear on the subject as it ought to be.

I have fixed the 25th as the date for our departure. P.O. Evans is to get all the sledges and gear ready whilst Bowers superintends the filling of provision bags.

Griffith Taylor and his companions have been seeking advice as to their Western trip. Wilson, dear chap, has been doing his best to coach them.

Ponting has fitted up his own dark room – doing the carpentering work with extraordinary speed and to everyone's admiration. To-night he made a window in the dark room in an hour or so.

Meares has become enamoured of the gramophone. We find we have a splendid selection of records. The pianola is being brought in sections, but I'm not at all sure it will be worth the trouble. Oates goes steadily on with the ponies – he is perfectly excellent and untiring in his devotion to the animals.

Day and Nelson, having given much thought to the proper fitting up of their corner, have now begun work. There seems to be little doubt that these ingenious people will make the most of their allotted space.

I have done quite a lot of thinking over the autumn journeys and a lot remains to be done, mainly on account of the prospect of being cut off from our winter quarters; for this reason we must have a great deal of food for animals and men.

Friday, January 20. – Our house has assumed great proportions. Bowers's annexe is finished, roof and all thoroughly snow-tight; an excellent place for spare clothing, furs, and ready use stores, and its extension affording complete protection to the entrance porch of the hut. The stables are nearly finished – a thoroughly stout well-roofed lean-to on the north side. Nelson has a small extension on the east side and Simpson a pre-arranged projection on the S.E. corner, so that on all sides the main building has thrown out limbs. Simpson has almost completed his ice cavern, light-tight lining, niches, floor and all. Wright and Forde have almost completed the absolute hut, a patchwork building for which the framework only was brought – but it will be very well adapted for our needs.

Gran has been putting 'record' on the ski runners. Record is a mixture of vegetable tar, paraffin, soft soap, and linseed oil, with some patent addition which prevents freezing – this according to Gran.

P.O. Evans and Crean have been preparing sledges; Evans shows himself wonderfully capable, and I haven't a doubt as to the working of the sledges he has fitted up.

We have been serving out some sledging gear and wintering boots. We are delighted with everything. First the felt boots and felt slippers made by Jaeger and then summer wind clothes and fur mits – nothing could be better than these articles. Finally tonight we have overhauled and served out two pairs of finnesko (fur boots) to each traveller. They are excellent in quality. At first I thought they seemed small, but a stiffness due to cold and dryness misled me – a little stretching and all was well. They are very good indeed. I have an idea to use putties to secure our wind trousers to the finnesko. But indeed the whole time we are thinking of devices to make our travelling work easier.

'We have now tried most of our stores, and so far we have not found a single article that is not perfectly excellent in quality and preservation. We are well repaid for all the trouble which was taken in selecting the food list and the firms from which the various articles could best be obtained, and we are showering blessings on Mr Wyatt's head for so strictly safeguarding our interests in these particulars.

'Our clothing is as good as good. In fact first and last, running through the whole extent of our outfit, I can say with some pride that there is not a single arrangement which I would have had altered.'

An Emperor penguin was found on the Cape well advanced in moult, a good specimen skin. Atkinson found cysts formed by a tapeworm in the intestines. It seems clear that this parasite is not transferred from another host, and that its history is unlike that of any other known tapeworm – in fact, Atkinson scores a discovery in parasitology of no little importance.

The wind has turned to the north tonight and is blowing quite fresh. I don't much like the position of the ship as the ice is breaking away all the time. The sky is quite clear and I don't think the wind often lasts long under such conditions.

The pianola has been erected by Rennick. He is a good fellow and one feels for him much at such a time – it must be rather dreadful for him to be returning when he remembers that he was once practically one of the shore party.[11] The pianola has been his special care, and it shows well that he should give so much pains in putting it right for us.

Day has been explaining the manner in which he hopes to be able to cope with the motor sledge difficulty. He is hopeful of getting things right, but I fear it won't do to place more reliance on the machines.

Everything looks hopeful for the depôt journey if only we can get our stores and ponies past the Glacier Tongue.

We had some seal rissoles today so extraordinarily well cooked that it was impossible to distinguish them from the best beef rissoles. I told two of the party they were beef, and they made no comment till I enlightened them after they had eaten two each. It is the first time I have tasted seal without being aware of its particular flavour. But even its own flavour is acceptable in our cook's hands – he really is excellent.

Saturday, January 21. – My anxiety for the ship was not unfounded. Fearing a little trouble I went out of the hut in the middle of the night and saw at once that she was having a bad time – the ice was breaking with a northerly swell and the wind increasing, with the ship on dead lee shore; luckily the ice anchors had been put well in on the floe and some still held. Pennell was getting up steam and his men struggling to replace the anchors.

We got out the men and gave some help. At 6 steam was up, and I was right glad to see the ship back out to windward, leaving us to recover anchors and hawsers.

She stood away to the west, and almost immediately after a large berg drove in and grounded in the place she had occupied.

We spent the day measuring our provisions and fixing up clothing arrangements for our journey; a good deal of progress has been made.

In the afternoon the ship returned to the northern ice edge; the wind was still strong (about N. 30 W.) and loose ice all along the edge – our people went out with the ice anchors and I saw the ship pass west again. Then as I went out on the floe came the report that she was ashore. I ran out to the Cape with E. Evans and saw that the report was only too true. She looked to be firmly fixed and in a very uncomfortable position. It looked as though she had been trying to get round the Cape, and therefore I argued she must have been going a good pace as the drift was making rapidly to the south. Later Pennell told me he had been trying to look behind the berg and had been going astern some time before he struck.

My heart sank when I looked at her and I sent Evans off in the whaler to sound, recovered the ice anchors again, set the people to work, and walked disconsolately back to the Cape to watch.

Visions of the ship failing to return to New Zealand and of sixty people waiting here arose in my mind with sickening pertinacity, and the only consolation I could draw from such imaginations was the determination that the southern work should go on as before – meanwhile the least ill possible seemed to be an extensive lightening of the ship with boats as the tide was evidently high when she struck – a terribly depressing prospect.

Some three or four of us watched it gloomily from the shore whilst all was bustle on board, the men shifting cargo aft. Pennell tells me they shifted 10 tons in a very short time.

The first ray of hope came when by careful watching one could see that the ship was turning very slowly, then one saw the men running from side to side and knew that an attempt was being made to roll her off. The rolling produced a more rapid turning movement at first and then she seemed to hang again. But only for a short time; the engines had been going astern all the time and presently a slight movement became apparent. But we only knew she was getting clear when we heard cheers on board and more cheers from the whaler.

Then she gathered stern way and was clear. The relief was enormous.

The wind dropped as she came off, and she is now securely moored off the northern ice edge, where I hope the greater number of her people are finding rest. For here and now I must record the splendid manner in which these men are working. I find it difficult to express my admiration for the manner in which the ship is handled and worked under these very trying circumstances.

From Pennell down there is not an officer or man who has not done his job nobly during the past weeks, and it will be a glorious thing to remember the unselfish loyal help they are giving us.

Pennell has been over to tell me all about it tonight; I think I like him more every day.

Campbell and his party returned late this afternoon – I have not heard details.

Meares and Oates went to the Glacier Tongue and satisfied themselves that the ice is good. It only has to remain another three days, and it would be poor luck if it failed in that time.

Sunday, January 22. – A quiet day with little to record.

The ship lies peacefully in the bay; a brisk northerly breeze in the forenoon died to light airs in the evening – it is warm enough, the temperature in the hut was 63° this evening. We have had a long busy day at clothing – everyone sewing away diligently. The Eastern Party ponies were put on board the ship this morning.

Monday, January 23. – Placid conditions last for a very short time in these regions. I got up at 5 this morning to find the weather calm and beautiful, but to my astonishment an opening lane of water between the land and the ice in the bay. The latter was going out in a solid mass.

The ship discovered it easily, got up her ice anchors, sent a boat ashore, and put out to sea to dredge. We went on with our preparations, but soon Meares brought word that the ice in the south bay was going in an equally rapid fashion. This proved an exaggeration, but an immense piece of floe had separated from the land. Meares and I walked till we came to the first ice. Luckily we found that it extends for some 2 miles along the rock of our Cape, and we discovered a possible way to lead ponies down to it. It was plain that only the ponies could go by it – no loads.

Since that everything has been rushed – and a wonderful day's work has resulted; we have got all the forage and food sledges and equipment off to the ship – the dogs will follow in an hour, I hope, with pony harness, &c., that is everything to do with our depôt party, except the ponies.

As at present arranged they are to cross the Cape and try to get over the Southern Road* tomorrow morning. One breathes a

---

* The Southern Road was the one feasible line of communication between the new station at C. Evans and the *Discovery* hut at Hut Point, for the rugged mountains and crevassed ice slopes of Ross Island forbade a passage by land. The Road afforded level going below the cliffs of the ice-foot, except where disturbed by the descending glacier, and there it was necessary to cross the body of the glacier itself. It consisted of the more enduring ice in the bays and the sea-ice along the coast, which only stayed fast for the season.

Thus it was of the utmost importance to get safely over the precarious part of the Road before the seasonal going-out of the sea-ice. To wait until all the ice should go out and enable the ship to sail to Hut Point would have meant long uncertainty and delay. As it happened, the Road broke up the day after the party had gone by.

prayer that the Road holds for the few remaining hours. It goes in one place between a berg in open water and a large pool of the glacier face – it may be weak in that part, and at any moment the narrow isthmus may break away. We are doing it on a very narrow margin.

If all is well I go to the ship tomorrow morning after the ponies have started, and then to Glacier Tongue.

CHAPTER FIVE

Depôt laying to One Ton Camp

Tuesday, January 24. – People were busy in the hut all last night – we got away at 9 a.m. A boat from the *Terra Nova* fetched the Western Party and myself as the ponies were led out of the camp. Meares and Wilson went ahead of the ponies to test the track. On board the ship I was taken in to see Lillie's catch of sea animals. It was wonderful, quantities of sponges, isopods, pentapods, large shrimps, corals, &c., &c.; but the *pièce de résistance* was the capture of several bucketsfull of cephalodiscus of which only seven pieces had been previously caught. Lillie is immensely pleased, feeling that it alone repays the whole enterprise.

In the forenoon we skirted the Island, getting 30 and 40 fathoms of water north and west of Inaccessible Island. With a telescope we could see the string of ponies steadily progressing over the sea ice past the Razorback Islands. As soon as we saw them well advanced we steamed on to the Glacier Tongue. The open water extended just round the corner and the ship made fast in the narrow angle made by the sea ice with the glacier, her port side flush with the surface of the latter. I walked over to meet the ponies whilst Campbell went to investigate a broad crack in the sea ice on the Southern Road. The ponies were got on to the Tongue without much difficulty, then across the glacier, and picketed on the sea ice close to the ship. Meanwhile Campbell informed me that the big crack was 30 feet across: it was evident we must get past it on the glacier, and I asked Campbell to peg out a road clear of cracks. Oates reported the ponies ready to start again after tea, and they were led along Campbell's road, their loads having already been taken on the floe – all went well until the animals got down on the floe level and Oates led across an old snowed-up crack. His and the next pony got across, but the third made a jump at the edge and sank to its stomach in the middle. It couldn't move, and with such struggles as it made it sank deeper till only its head and forelegs showed above the slush. With some trouble we got ropes on these, and hauling together pulled the poor creature out looking very weak and miserable and trembling much.

We led the other ponies round farther to the west and eventually got all out on the floe, gave them a small feed, and started them off with their loads. The dogs meanwhile gave some excitement. Starting on hard ice with a light load nothing could hold them, and they dashed off over everything – it seemed wonderful that we all reached the floe in safety. Wilson and I drive one team, whilst E. Evans and Meares drive the other. I withhold my opinion of the dogs, in much doubt as to whether they are going to be a real success – but the ponies are going to be real good. They work with such extraordinary steadiness, stepping out briskly and cheerfully, following in each other's tracks. The great drawback is the ease with which they sink in soft snow: they go through in lots of places where the men scarcely make an impression – they struggle pluckily when they sink, but it is trying to watch them. We came with the loads noted below and one bale of fodder (105 lbs.) added to each sledge. We are camped 6 miles from the glacier and 2 from Hut Point – a cold east wind; tonight the temperature 19°.

Autumn Party to start January 25, 1911

12 men,* 8 ponies, 26 dogs.

First load estimated 5,385 lbs., including 14 weeks' food and fuel for men – taken to Cache No. 1.

Ship transports following to Glacier Tongue:

	lbs.
130 bales compressed fodder	13,650
24 cases dog biscuit	1400
10 sacks of oats	1,600 ?
	16,650

Teams return to ship to transport this load to Cache No. 1. Dog teams also take on 500 lbs. of biscuit from Hut Point.

---

* viz. Atkinson and Crean, who were left at Safety Camp; E. Evans, Forde and Keohane, who returned with the weaker ponies on Feb. 13; Meares and Wilson with the dog teams; and Scott, Bowers, Oates, Cherry-Garrard, and Gran.

Pony sledges

		lbs.
On all sledges	Sledge with straps and tank	52
	Pony furniture	25
	Driver's ski and sleeping-bag, &c.	40
Nos. 1 & 5	Cooker and primus instruments	40
	Tank containing biscuit	172
	Sack of oats	160
	Tent and poles	28
	Alpine rope	5
	1 oil can and spirit can	15
		530
Nos. 2 & 6	Oil	100
	Tank contents: food bags	285
	Ready provision bag	63
	2 picks	20
		576
Nos. 3 & 7	Oil	100
	Tank contents: biscuit	196
	Sack of oats	160
	2 shovels	9
		570
Nos. 4 & 8	Box with tools, &c.	35
	Cookers, &c	105
	Tank contents food bags	252
	Sack of oats	160
	3 long bamboos and spare gear	15
		567

Spare gear per man

2 pairs under socks
2 pairs outer socks
1 pair hair socks
1 pair night socks
1 pyjama jacket
1 pyjama trousers
1 woollen mits

2 finnesko
Skein   = 10 lbs.
Books, diaries, tobacco, &c,   2 lbs.
                                            12 lbs.

Dress

Vest and drawers	Wind suit
Woollen shirt	Two pairs socks
Jersey	Ski boots
Balaclava	

Dogs

No. 1	lbs.	No 2	lbs.
Sledge straps and tank	54	Sledge straps and tank	54
Drivers' bags and ski	80	Drivers' bags and ski	80
Cooker primus and		Tank contents: food bags	324
instruments	50	Tent and poles	33
Tank contents: biscuit	221		
Alpine rope	5		
Lamps and candles	4		
2 shovels	9		
Ready provision bag	63		
Sledge-meter			
	486		491

10-ft. sledge: men's harness, extra tent.

Thursday, January 26. – Yesterday I went to the ship with a dog team. All went well till the dogs caught sight of a whale breeching in the 30 ft. lead and promptly made for it! It was all we could do to stop them before we reached the water.

Spent the day writing letters and completing arrangements for the ship – a brisk northerly breeze sprang up in the night and the ship bumped against the glacier until the pack came in as protection from the swell. Ponies and dogs arrived about 1 p.m., and at 5 we all went out for the final start.

A little earlier Pennell had the men aft and I thanked them for their splendid work. They have behaved like bricks and a finer lot of fellows never sailed in a ship. It was good to get their hearty send-off. Before we could get away Ponting had his half-hour photographing us, the ponies and the dog teams – I hope he will have made a good thing of it. It was a little sad to say farewell to all these good fellows and Campbell and his men. I do most heartily trust that all will be successful in their ventures, for indeed their unselfishness and their generous high spirit deserves reward. God bless them.

So here we are with all our loads. One wonders what the upshot will be. It will take three days to transport the loads to complete safety; the break-up of the sea ice ought not to catch us before that. The wind is from the S.E. again tonight.

Friday, January 27. Camp 2. – Started at 9.30 and moved a load of fodder 3¾ miles south – returned to camp to lunch – then shifted camp and provisions. Our weights are now divided into three loads: two of food for ponies, one of men's provisions with some ponies' food. It is slow work, but we retreat slowly but surely from the chance of going out on the sea ice.

We are camped about a mile south of C. Armitage. After camping I went to the east till abreast of Pram Point, finding the ice dangerously thin off C. Armitage. It is evident we must make a considerable detour to avoid danger. The rest of the party went to the *Discovery* hut to see what could be done towards digging it out. The report is unfavourable, as I expected. The drift inside has become very solid – it would take weeks of work to clear it. A great deal of biscuit and some butter, cocoa, &c., were seen, so that we need not have any anxiety about provisions if delayed in returning to Cape Evans.

The dogs are very tired tonight. I have definitely handed the control of the second team to Wilson. He was very eager to have it and will do well I'm sure – but certainly also the dogs will not pull heavy loads – 500 pounds proved a back-breaking load for 11 dogs today – they brought it at a snail's pace. Meares has estimated to give them two-thirds of a pound of biscuit a day. I have felt sure he will find this too little.

The ponies are doing excellently. Their loads run up to 800 and 900 lbs. and they make very light of them. Oates said he could have gone on for some time tonight.

Saturday, January 28. Camp 2. – The ponies went back for the last load at Camp 1, and I walked south to find a way round the great pressure ridge. The sea ice south is covered with confused irregular

sastrugi well remembered from *Discovery* days. The pressure ridge
is new. The broken ice of the ridge ended east of the spot I
approached and the pressure was seen only in a huge domed wave,
the hollow of which on my left was surrounded with a countless
number of seals – these lay about sleeping or apparently gambolling in the shallow water. I imagine the old ice in this hollow has
gone well under and that the seals have a pool above it which may
be warmer on such a bright day.

It was evident that the ponies could be brought round by this
route, and I returned to camp to hear that one of the ponies
(Keohane's) had gone lame. The Soldier took a gloomy view of
the situation, but he is not an optimist. It looks as though a tendon
had been strained, but it is not at all certain. Bowers's pony is also
weak in the forelegs, but we knew this before: it is only a question
of how long he will last. The pity is that he is an excellently strong
pony otherwise. Atkinson has a bad heel and laid up all day –
his pony was tied behind another sledge, and went well, a very
hopeful sign.

In the afternoon I led the ponies out 2¾ miles south to the
crossing of the pressure ridge, then east 1¼ till we struck the
barrier edge and ascended it. Going about ½ mile in we dumped
the loads – the ponies sank deep just before the loads were
dropped, but it looked as though the softness was due to some rise
in the surface.

We saw a dark object a quarter of a mile north as we reached the
Barrier. I walked over and found it to be the tops of two tents
more than half buried – Shackleton's tents we suppose. A moulting Emperor penguin was sleeping between them. The canvas on
one tent seemed intact, but half stripped from the other.

The ponies pulled splendidly today, as also the dogs, but we have
decided to load both lightly from now on, to march them easily,
and to keep as much life as possible in them. There is much to be
learnt as to their powers of performance.

Keohane says, 'Come on, lad; you'll be getting to the Pole' by
way of cheering his animal – all the party are cheerful, there never
were a better set of people.

Sunday, January 29. – Camp 2. This morning after breakfast I
read prayers. Excellent day. The seven good ponies have made
two journeys to the Barrier, covering 18 geographical miles,

half with good loads – none of them were at all done. Oates's pony, a spirited, nervous creature, got away at start when his head was left for a moment and charged through the camp at a gallop; finally his sledge cannoned into another, the swingle tree broke, and he galloped away, kicking furiously at the dangling trace. Oates fetched him when he had quieted down, and we found that nothing had been hurt or broken but the swingle tree.

Gran tried going on ski with his pony. All went well while he was alongside, but when he came up from the back the swish of the ski frightened the beast, who fled faster than his pursuer – that is, the pony and load were going better than the Norwegian on ski.

Gran is doing very well. He has a lazy pony and a good deal of work to get him along, and does it very cheerfully.

The dogs are doing excellently – getting into better condition every day.

They ran the first load 1 mile 1200 yards past the stores on the Barrier, to the spot chosen for 'Safety Camp', the big home depôt.

I don't think that any part of the Barrier is likely to go, but it's just as well to be prepared for everything, and our camp must deserve its distinctive title of 'Safety'.

In the afternoon the dogs ran a second load to the same place – covering over 24 geographical miles in the day – an excellent day's work.[12]

Evans and I took a load out on foot over the pressure ridge. The camp load alone remains to be taken to the Barrier. Once we get to Safety Camp we can stay as long as we like before starting our journey. It is only when we start that we must travel fast.

Most of the day it has been overcast, but tonight it has cleared again. There is very little wind. The temperatures of late have been ranging from 9° at night to 24° in the day. Very easy circumstances for sledging.

Monday, January 30. – Camp 3. Safety Camp. Bearings: Lat. 77.55; Cape Armitage N. 64 W.; Camel's Hump of Blue Glacier left, extreme; Castle Rock N. 40 W. Called the camp at 7.30. Finally left with ponies at 11.30. There was a good deal to do, which partly accounts for delays, but we shall have to 'buck up' with our camp arrangement. Atkinson had his foot lanced and should be well in a couple of days.

I led the lame pony; his leg is not swelled, but I fear he's developed a permanent defect – there are signs of ringbone and the hoof is split.

A great shock came when we passed the depôted fodder and made for this camp. The ponies sank very deep and only brought on their loads with difficulty, getting pretty hot. The distance was but 1½ miles, but it took more out of them than the rest of the march. We camped and held a council of war after lunch. I unfolded my plan, which is to go forward with five weeks' food for men and animals: to depôt a fortnight's supply after twelve or thirteen days and return here. The loads for ponies thus arranged work out a little over 600 lbs., for the dog teams 700 lbs., both apart from sledges. The ponies ought to do it easily if the surface is good enough for them to walk, which is doubtful – the dogs may have to be lightened; such as it is, it is the best we can do under the circumstances!

This afternoon I went forward on ski to see if the conditions changed. In 2 or 3 miles I could see no improvement.

Bowers, Garrard, and the three men went and dug out the *Nimrod* tent. They found a cooker and provisions and remains of a hastily abandoned meal. One tent was half full of hard ice, the result of thaw. The Willesden canvas was rotten except some material used for the doors. The floor cloth could not be freed.

The Soldier doesn't like the idea of fetching up the remainder of the loads to this camp with the ponies. I think we will bring on all we can with the dogs and take the risk of leaving the rest.

The *Nimrod* camp was evidently made by some relief or ship party, and if that has stood fast for so long there should be little fear for our stuff in a single season. Tomorrow we muster stores, build the depôt, and pack our sledges.

Tuesday, January 31. – Camp 3. We have everything ready to start – but this afternoon we tried our one pair of snow-shoes on 'Weary Willy'. The effect was magical. He strolled around as though walking on hard ground in places where he floundered woefully without them. Oates hasn't had any faith in these shoes at all, and I thought that even the quietest pony would need to be practised in their use.

Immediately after our experiment I decided that an effort must be made to get more, and within half an hour Meares and Wilson were on their way to the station more than 20 miles away. There is just the chance that the ice may not have gone out, but it is a very poor one I fear. At present it looks as though we might double our distance with the snow-shoes.

Atkinson is better today, but not by any means well, so that the delay is in his favour. We cannot start on till the dogs return with or without the shoes. The only other hope for this journey is that the Barrier gets harder farther out, but I feel that the prospect of this is not very bright. In any case it is something to have discovered the possibilities of these shoes.

Low temperature at night for first time. Min. 2.4°. Quite warm in tent.

Wednesday, February 1. – Camp 3. A day of comparative inactivity and some disappointment. Meares and Wilson returned at noon, reporting the ice out beyond the Razorback Island – no return to Cape Evans – no pony snow-shoes – alas! I have decided to make a start tomorrow without them. Late tonight Atkinson's foot was examined: it is bad and there's no possibility of its getting right for some days. He must be left behind – I've decided to leave Crean with him. Most luckily we now have an extra tent and cooker. How the ponies are to be led is very doubtful. Well, we must do the best that circumstances permit. Poor Atkinson is in very low spirits.

I sent Gran to the *Discovery* hut with our last mail. He went on ski and was nearly 4 hours away, making me rather anxious, as the wind had sprung up and there was a strong surface-drift; he narrowly missed the camp on returning and I am glad to get him back.

Our food allowance seems to be very ample, and if we go on as at present we shall thrive amazingly.

Thursday, February 2. – Camp 4. Made a start at last. Roused out at 7, left camp about 10.30. Atkinson and Crean remained behind – very hard on the latter. Atkinson suffering much pain and mental distress at his condition – for the latter I fear I cannot have much sympathy, as he ought to have reported his trouble long before. Crean will manage to rescue some more of the forage from the Barrier edge – I am very sorry for him.

On starting with all the ponies (I leading Atkinson's) I saw with some astonishment that the animals were not sinking deeply, and to my pleased surprise we made good progress at once. This lasted for more than an hour, then the surface got comparatively bad again – but still most of the ponies did well with it, making 5 miles. Birdie's * animal, however, is very heavy and flounders where the others walk fairly easily. He is eager and tries to go faster as he flounders. As a result he was brought in, in a lather. I inquired for our one set of snow-shoes and found they had been left behind. The difference in surface from what was expected makes one wonder whether better conditions may not be expected during the night and in the morning, when the temperatures are low. My suggestion that we should take to night marching has met with general approval. Even if there is no improvement in the surface the ponies will rest better during the warmer hours and march better in the night.

So we are resting in our tents, waiting to start tonight. Gran has gone back for the snow-shoes – he volunteered good-naturedly – certainly his expertness on ski is useful.

Last night the temperature fell to −6° after the wind dropped – today it is warm and calm.

Impressions

The seductive folds of the sleeping-bag.

The hiss of the primus and the fragrant steam of the cooker issuing from the tent ventilator.

The small green tent and the great white road.

The whine of a dog and the neigh of our steeds.

The driving cloud of powdered snow.

The crunch of footsteps which break the surface crust.

The wind-blown furrows.

The blue arch beneath the smoky cloud.

The crisp ring of the ponies' hoofs and the swish of the following sledge.

The droning conversation of the march as driver encourages or chides his horse.

The patter of dog pads.

The gentle flutter of our canvas shelter.

* The favourite nickname for Bowers.

Its deep booming sound under the full force of a blizzard.

The drift snow like finest flour penetrating every hole and corner –
  flickering up beneath one's head covering, pricking sharply as a
  sand blast.

The sun with blurred image peeping shyly through the wreathing
  drift giving pale shadowless light.

The eternal silence of the great white desert. Cloudy columns
  of snow drift advancing from the south, pale yellow wraiths,
  heralding the coming storm, blotting out one by one the sharp-
  cut lines of the land.

The blizzard, Nature's protest – the crevasse, Nature's pitfall –
  that grim trap for the unwary – no hunter could conceal his
  snare so perfectly – the light rippled snow bridge gives no hint
  or sign of the hidden danger, its position unguessable till man
  or beast is floundering, clawing and struggling for foothold on
  the brink.

The vast silence broken only by the mellow sounds of the marching column.

Friday, February 3, 8 a.m. – Camp 5. Roused the camp at 10
p.m. and we started marching at 12.30. At first surface bad, but
gradually improving. We had two short spells and set up temporary camp to feed ourselves and ponies at 3.20. Started again at
5 and marched till 7. In all covered 9 miles. Surface seemed to
have improved during the last part of the march till just before
camping time, when Bowers, who was leading, plunged into soft
snow. Several of the others following close on his heels shared his
fate, and soon three ponies were plunging and struggling in a
drift. Garrard's pony, which has very broad feet, found hard stuff
beyond and then my pony got round. Forde and Keohane led
round on comparatively hard ground well to the right, and the
entangled ponies were unharnessed and led round from patch
to patch till firmer ground was reached. Then we camped and
the remaining loads were brought in. Then came the *triumph of
the snow-shoe again*. We put a set on Bowers's big pony – at first
he walked awkwardly (for a few minutes only) then he settled
down, was harnessed to his load, brought that in and another
also – all over places into which he had been plunging. If
we had more of these shoes we could certainly put them on

seven out of eight of our ponies – and after a little I think on the eighth, Oates's pony, as certainly the ponies so shod would draw their loads over the soft snow patches without any difficulty. It is trying to feel that so great a help to our work has been left behind at the station.

Impressions

It is pathetic to see the ponies floundering in the soft patches. The first sink is a shock to them and seems to brace them to action. Thus they generally try to rush through when they feel themselves sticking. If the patch is small they land snorting and agitated on the harder surface with much effort. And if the patch is extensive they plunge on gamely until exhausted. Most of them after a bit plunge forward with both forefeet together, making a series of jumps and bringing the sledge behind them with jerks. This is, of course, terribly tiring for them. Now and again they have to stop, and it is horrid to see them half engulfed in the snow, panting and heaving from the strain. Now and again one falls and lies trembling and temporarily exhausted. It must be terribly trying for them, but it is wonderful to see how soon they recover their strength. The quiet, lazy ponies have a much better time than the eager ones when such troubles arise.

The soft snow which gave the trouble is evidently in the hollow of one of the big waves that continue through the pressure ridges at Cape Crozier towards the Bluff. There are probably more of these waves, though we crossed several during the last part of the march – so far it seems that the soft parts are in patches only and do not extend the whole length of the hollow. Our course is to pick a way with the sure-footed beasts and keep the others back till the road has been tested.

What extraordinary uncertainties this work exhibits! Every day some new fact comes to light – some new obstacle which threatens the gravest obstruction. I suppose this is the reason which makes the game so well worth playing.

Impressions

The more I think of our sledging outfit the more certain I am that we have arrived at something near a perfect equipment for civilised man under such conditions.

The borderline between necessity and luxury is vague enough.

We might save weight at the expense of comfort, but all possible saving would amount to but a mere fraction of one's loads. Supposing it were a grim struggle for existence and we were forced to drop everything but the barest necessities, the total saving on this three weeks' journey would be:

	lbs.
Fuel for cooking	100
Cooking apparatus	45
Personal clothing, &c., say	100
Tent, say	30
Instruments, &c	100
	375

This is half of one of ten sledge-loads, or about one-twentieth of the total weight carried. If this is the only part of our weights which under any conceivable circumstances could be included in the category of luxuries, it follows the sacrifice to comfort is negligible. Certainly we could not have increased our mileage by making such a sacrifice.

But beyond this it may be argued that we have an unnecessary amount of food: 32 oz. per day per man is our allowance. I well remember the great strait of hunger to which we were reduced in 1903 after four or five weeks on 26 oz., and am perfectly confident that we were steadily losing stamina at that time. Let it be supposed that 4 oz. per day per man might conceivably be saved. We have then 3 lbs. a day saved in the camp, or 63 lbs. in the three weeks, or 1/100th part of our present loads.

The smallness of the fractions on which the comfort and physical well-being of the men depend is due to the fact of travelling with animals whose needs are proportionately so much greater than those of the men. It follows that it must be sound policy to keep the men of a sledge party keyed up to a high pitch of well-fed physical condition as long as they have animals to drag their loads. The time for short rations, long marches and carefullest scrutiny of detail comes when the men are dependent on their own traction efforts.

6 p.m. – It has been blowing from the S.W., but the wind is dying away – the sky is overcast – I write after 9 hours' sleep, the others still peacefully slumbering. Work with animals means long

intervals of rest which are not altogether easily occupied. With our present routine the dogs remain behind for an hour or more, trying to hit off their arrival in the new camp soon after the ponies have been picketed. The teams are pulling very well, Meares's especially. The animals are getting a little fierce. Two white dogs in Meares's team have been trained to attack strangers – they were quiet enough on board ship, but now bark fiercely if anyone but their driver approaches the team. They suddenly barked at me as I was pointing out the stopping place to Meares, and Osman, my erstwhile friend, swept round and nipped my leg lightly. I had no stick, and there is no doubt that if Meares had not been on the sledge the whole team, following the lead of the white dogs, would have been at me in a moment.

Hunger and fear are the only realities in dog life: an empty stomach makes a fierce dog. There is something almost alarming in the sudden fierce display of natural instinct in a tame creature. Instinct becomes a blind, unreasoning, relentless passion. For instance, the dogs are as a rule all very good friends in harness: they pull side by side rubbing shoulders, they walk over each other as they settle to rest, relations seem quite peaceful and quiet. But the moment food is in their thoughts, however, their passions awaken; each dog is suspicious of his neighbour, and the smallest circumstance produces a fight. With like suddenness their rage flares out instantaneously if they get mixed up on the march – a quiet, peaceable team which has been lazily stretching itself with wagging tails one moment will become a set of raging, tearing, fighting devils the next. It is such stern facts that resign one to the sacrifice of animal life in the effort to advance such human projects as this.

The Corner Camp. [Bearings: Obs. Hill < Bluff 86°; Obs. Hill < Knoll 80½°; Mt. Terror N. 4 W.; Obs. Hill N. 69 W.]

Saturday, February 4, 8 a.m., 1911. – Camp 6. A satisfactory night march, covering 10 miles and some hundreds of yards.

Roused party at 10, when it was blowing quite hard from the S.E., with temperature below zero. It looked as though we should have a pretty cold start, but by the end of breakfast the wind had dropped and the sun shone forth.

Started on a bad surface – ponies plunging a good deal for 2 miles or so, Bowers's 'Uncle Bill' walking steadily on his snow-shoes. After this the surface improved and the marching became steadier.

We camped for lunch after 5 miles. Going still better in the afternoon, except that we crossed several crevasses. Oates's pony dropped his legs into two of these and sank into one – oddly the other ponies escaped and we were the last. Some 2 miles from our present position the cracks appeared to cease, and in the last march we have got on to quite a hard surface on which the ponies drag their loads with great ease. This part seems to be swept by the winds which so continually sweep round Cape Crozier, and therefore it is doubtful if it extends far to the south, but for the present the going should be good. Had bright moonshine for the march, but now the sky has clouded and it looks threatening to the south. I think we may have a blizzard, though the wind is northerly at present.

The ponies are in very good form; 'James Pigg' remarkably recovered from his lameness.

8 p.m. – It is blowing a blizzard – wind moderate – temperature mild.

Impressions

The deep, dreamless sleep that follows the long march and the satisfying supper.

The surface crust which breaks with a snap and sinks with a snap, startling men and animals.

Custom robs it of dread but not of interest to the dogs, who come to imagine such sounds as the result of some strange freak of hidden creatures. They become all alert and spring from side to side, hoping to catch the creature. The hope clings in spite of continual disappointment.[13]

A dog must be either eating, asleep, or *interested*. His eagerness to snatch at interest, to chain his attention to something, is almost pathetic. The monotony of marching kills him.

This is the fearfullest difficulty for the dog driver on a snow plain without leading marks or objects in sight. The dog is almost human in its demand for living interest, yet fatally less than human in its inability to foresee.

The dog lives for the day, the hour, even the moment. The human being can live and support discomfort for a future.

Sunday, *February* 5. – Corner Camp, No. 6. The blizzard descended on us at about 4 p.m. yesterday; for twenty-four hours it continued with moderate wind, then the wind shifting slightly to the west came with much greater violence. Now it is blowing very hard and our small frail tent is being well tested. One imagines it cannot continue long as at present, but remembers our proximity to Cape Crozier and the length of the blizzards recorded in that region. As usual we sleep and eat, conversing as cheerfully as may be in the intervals. There is scant news of our small outside world – only a report of comfort and a rumour that Bowers's pony has eaten one of its putties!!

11 p.m. – Still blowing hard – a real blizzard now with dusty, floury drift – two minutes in the open makes a white figure. What a wonderful shelter our little tent affords! We have just had an excellent meal, a quiet pipe, and fireside conversation within, almost forgetful for the time of the howling tempest without – now, as we lie in our bags warm and comfortable, one can scarcely realise that 'hell' is on the other side of the thin sheet of canvas that protects us.

Monday, February 6. – Corner Camp, No. 6. 6 p.m. The wind increased in the night. It has been blowing very hard all day. No fun to be out of the tent but there are no shirkers with us. Oates has been out regularly to feed the ponies; Meares and Wilson to attend to the dogs; the rest of us as occasion required. The ponies are fairly comfortable, though one sees now what great improvements could be made to the horse clothes. The dogs ought to be quite happy. They are curled snugly under the snow and at meal times issue from steaming warm holes. The temperature is high, luckily. We are comfortable enough in the tent, but it is terribly trying to the patience – over fifty hours already and no sign of the end. The drifts about the camp are very deep – some of the sledges almost covered. It is the old story – eat and sleep, sleep and eat – and it's surprising how much sleep can be put in.

Tuesday, February 7, 5 p.m. – Corner Camp, No. 6. The wind kept on through the night, commencing to lull at 8 a.m. At 10 a.m. one could see an arch of clear sky to the S.W. and W., White Island, the Bluff, and the Western Mountains clearly defined. The wind had fallen very light and we were able to do some camp work, digging out sledges and making the ponies more comfortable. At 11 a low dark cloud crept over the southern horizon and there could be no doubt the wind was coming upon us again. At

1 p.m. the drift was all about us once more and the sun obscured. One began to feel that fortune was altogether too hard on us – but now as I write the wind has fallen again to a gentle breeze, the sun is bright, and the whole southern horizon clear. A good sign is the freedom of the Bluff from cloud. One feels that we ought to have a little respite for the next week, and now we must do everything possible to tend and protect our ponies. All looks promising for the night march.

Wednesday, February 8. – No. 7 Camp. Bearings: Lat. 78° 13'; Mt Terror N. 3 W.; Erebus 23½ Terror 2nd peak from south; Pk. 2 White Island 74 Terror; Castle Rk. 43 Terror. Night march just completed. 10 miles, 200 yards. The ponies were much shaken by the blizzard. One supposes they did not sleep – all look listless and two or three are visibly thinner than before. But the worst case by far is Forde's little pony; he was reduced to a weight little exceeding 400 lbs. on his sledge and caved in altogether on the second part of the march. The load was reduced to 200 lbs., and finally Forde pulled this in, leading the pony. The poor thing is a miserable scarecrow and never ought to have been brought – it is the same pony that did so badly in the ship. Today it is very fine and bright. We are giving a good deal of extra food to the animals, and my hope is that they will soon pick up again – but they cannot stand more blizzards in their present state. I'm afraid we shall not get very far, but at all hazards we must keep the greater number of the ponies alive. The dogs are in fine form – the blizzard has only been a pleasant rest *for them.*

Memo. – Left No. 7 Camp. 2 bales of fodder.

Thursday, February 9. – No. 8 Camp. Made good 11 miles. Good night march; surface excellent, but we are carrying very light loads with the exception of one or two ponies. Forde's poor 'Misery' is improving slightly. It is very keen on its feed. Its fate is much in doubt. Keohane's 'Jimmy Pigg' is less lame than yesterday. In fact there is a general buck-up all round.

It was a coldish march with light head wind and temperature 5° or 6° below zero, but it was warm in the sun all yesterday and promises to be warm again today. If such weather would hold there would be nothing to fear for the ponies. We have come to the conclusion that the principal cause of their discomfort is the comparative thinness of their coats.

We get the well-remembered glorious views of the Western Mountains, but now very distant. No crevasses today. I shall be surprised if we pass outside all sign of them.

One begins to see how things ought to be worked next year if the ponies hold out. Ponies and dogs are losing their snow blindness.

Friday, February 10. – No. 9 Camp. 12 miles 200 yards. Cold march, very chilly wind, overcast sky, difficult to see surface or course.

Noticed sledges, ponies, &c., cast shadows all round.

Surface very good and animals did splendidly.

We came over some undulations during the early part of the march, but the last part appeared quite flat. I think I remember observing the same fact on our former trip.

The wind veers and backs from S. to W. and even to N., coming in gusts. The sastrugi are distinctly S.S.W. There isn't a shadow of doubt that the prevailing wind is along the coast, taking the curve of the deep bay south of the Bluff.

The question now is: shall we by going due southward keep this hard surface? If so, we should have little difficulty in reaching the Beardmore Glacier next year.

We turn out of our sleeping-bags about 9 p.m. Somewhere about 1–1.30 I shout to the Soldier 'How are things?' There is a response suggesting readiness, and soon after figures are busy amongst sledges and ponies. It is chilling work for the fingers and not too warm for the feet. The rugs come off the animals, the harness is put on, tents and camp equipment are loaded on the sledges, nosebags filled for the next halt; one by one the animals are taken off the picketing rope and yoked to the sledge. Oates watches his animal warily, reluctant to keep such a nervous creature standing in the traces. If one is prompt one feels impatient and fretful whilst watching one's more tardy fellows. Wilson and Meares hang about ready to help with odds and ends. Still we wait: the picketing lines must be gathered up, a few pony putties need adjustment, a party has been slow striking their tent. With numbed fingers on our horse's bridle and the animal striving to turn its head from the wind one feels resentful. At last all is ready. One says 'All right, Bowers, go ahead,' and Birdie leads his big animal forward, starting, as he continues, at a steady pace. The horses have got cold and at the word they are off, the Soldier's and one or two others with a rush. Finnesko give poor foothold on the slippery sastrugi, and for a minute or two drivers have some difficulty in maintaining the pace on their feet. Movement is warming, and in ten minutes the column has settled itself to steady marching.

The pace is still brisk, the light bad, and at intervals one or another of us suddenly steps on a slippery patch and falls prone. These are the only real incidents of the march – for the rest it passes with a steady tramp and slight variation of formation. The weaker ponies drop a bit but not far, so that they are soon up in line again when the first halt is made. We have come to a single halt in each half march. Last night it was too cold to stop long and a very few minutes found us on the go again.

As the end of the half march approaches I get out my whistle. Then at a shrill blast Bowers wheels slightly to the left, his tent mates lead still farther out to get the distance for the picket lines; Oates and I stop behind Bowers and Evans, the two other sledges of our squad behind the two other of Bowers's. So we are drawn up in camp formation. The picket lines are run across at right angles to the line of advance and secured to the two sledges at each end. In a few minutes ponies are on the lines covered, tents up again and cookers going.

Meanwhile the dog drivers, after a long cold wait at the old camp, have packed the last sledge and come trotting along our tracks. They try to time their arrival in the new camp immediately after our own and generally succeed well. The mid-march halt runs into an hour to an hour and a half, and at the end we pack up and tramp forth again. We generally make our final camp about 8 o'clock, and within an hour and a half most of us are in our sleeping-bags. Such is at present the daily routine. At the long halt we do our best for our animals by building snow walls and improving their rugs, &c.

Saturday, February 11. – No. 10 Camp. Bearings: Lat. 78° 47'. Bluff S. 79 W.; Left extreme Bluff 65°; Bluff A White Island near Sound, 11 miles. Covered 6 and 5 miles between halts. The surface has got a good deal softer. In the next two marches we should know more certainly, but it looks as though the conditions to the south will not be so good as those we have had hitherto.

Blossom, E. Evans's pony, has very small hoofs and found the going very bad. It is less a question of load than one of walking, and there is no doubt that some form of snow-shoe would help greatly. The question is, what form?

All the ponies were a little done when we stopped, but the weather is favourable for a good rest; there is no doubt this night marching is the best policy.

Even the dogs found the surface more difficult today, but they are pulling very well. Meares has deposed Osman in favour of Rabchick, as the former was getting either very disobedient or very deaf. The change appears excellent. Rabchick leads most obediently.

Mem. for next year. A stout male bamboo shod with a spike to sound for crevasses.

Sunday, February 12. – No. 11 Camp. 10 miles. Depôt one Bale of Fodder. Variation 150 E. South True = N. 30 E. by compass. The surface is getting decidedly worse. The ponies sink quite deep every now and again. We marched 6¼ miles before lunch, Blossom dropping considerably behind. He lagged more on the second march and we halted at 9 miles. Evans said he might be dragged for another mile and we went on for that distance and camped.

The sky was overcast: very dark and snowy looking in the south – very difficult to steer a course. Mt Discovery is in line with the south end of the Bluff from the camp and we are near the 79th parallel. We must get exact bearings, for this is to be called the 'Bluff Camp' and should play an important part in the future. Bearings: Bluff 36° 13'; Black Island Rht. Ex. I have decided to send E. Evans, Forde, and Keohane back with the three weakest ponies, which they have been leading. The remaining five ponies, which have been improving in condition, will go on for a few days at least, and we must see how near we can come to the 80th parallel.

Tonight we have been making all the necessary arrangements for this plan. Cherry-Garrard is to come into our tent.

Monday, February 13. – No. 12 Camp. 9 miles 150 yds. The wind got up from the south with drift before we started yesterday – all appearance of a blizzard. But we got away at 12.30 and marched through drift for 7 miles. It was exceedingly cold at first. Just at starting the sky cleared in the wonderfully rapid fashion usual in these regions. We saw that our camp had the southern edge of the base rock of the Bluff in line with Mt Discovery, and White Island well clear of the eastern slope of Mt Erebus. A fairly easy alignment to pick up.

At lunch time the sky lightened up and the drift temporarily ceased. I thought we were going to get in a good march, but on starting again the drift came thicker than ever and soon the course grew wild. We went on for 2 miles and then I decided to camp. So here we are with a full blizzard blowing. I told Wilson I should camp if it grew thick, and hope he and Meares have stopped where they were. They saw Evans start back from No. 11 Camp before leaving. I trust they have got in something of a march before stopping. This continuous bad weather is exceedingly trying, but our own ponies are quite comfortable this time, I'm glad to say. We have built them extensive snow walls behind which they seem to get quite comfortable shelter. We are five in a tent yet fairly comfortable.

Our ponies' coats are certainly getting thicker and I see no reason why we shouldn't get to the 80th parallel if only the weather would give us a chance.

Bowers is wonderful. Throughout the night he has worn no head-gear but a common green felt hat kept on with a chin stay and affording no cover whatever for the ears. His face and ears remain bright red. The rest of us were glad to have thick Balaclavas and wind helmets. I have never seen anyone so unaffected by the cold. Tonight he remained outside a full hour after the rest of us had got into the tent. He was simply pottering about the camp doing small jobs to the sledges, &c. Cherry-Garrard is remarkable because of his eyes. He can only see through glasses and has to wrestle with all sorts of inconveniences in consequence. Yet one could never guess it – for he manages somehow to do more than his share of the work.

Tuesday, February 14. – 13 Camp. 7 miles 650 yards. A disappointing day: the weather had cleared, the night was fine though cold, temperature well below zero with a keen S.W. breeze. Soon after the start we struck very bad surface conditions. The ponies sank lower than their hocks frequently and the soft patches of snow left by the blizzard lay in sandy heaps, making great friction for the runners. We struggled on, but found Gran with Weary Willy dropping to the rear. I consulted Oates as to distance and he cheerfully proposed 15 miles for the day! This piqued me somewhat and I marched till the sledge-meter showed 6½ miles. By this time Weary Willy had dropped about three-quarters of a mile and the dog teams were approaching. Suddenly we heard much barking in the distance, and later it was evident that something had gone wrong. Oates and I then hurried back. I met Meares, who told me the dogs of his team had got out of hand and attacked Weary Willy when they saw him fall. Finally they had been beaten off and W.W. was being led without his sledge. W.W. had been much bitten, but luckily I think not seriously: he appears to have made a gallant fight, and bit and shook some of the dogs with his teeth. Gran did his best, breaking his ski stick. Meares broke his dog stick – one way and another the dogs must have had a rocky time, yet they seem to bear charmed lives when their blood is up, as apparently not one of them has been injured.

After lunch four of us went back and dragged up the load. It taught us the nature of the surface more than many hours of pony leading!! The incident is deplorable and the blame widespread. I find W.W.'s load was much heavier than that of the other ponies.

I blame myself for not supervising these matters more effectively and for allowing W.W. to get so far behind.

We started off again after lunch, but when we had done two-thirds of a mile, W.W.'s condition made it advisable to halt. He has been given a hot feed, a large snow wall, and some extra sacking – the day promises to be quiet and warm for him, and one can only hope that these measures will put him right again. But the whole thing is very annoying.

Memo. – Arrangements for ponies.

1. Hot bran or oat mashes.
2. Clippers for breaking wires of bales.
3. Pickets for horses.
4. Lighter ponies to take 10 ft. sledges?

The surface is so crusty and friable that the question of snow-shoes again becomes of great importance.

All the sastrugi are from S.W. by S. to S.W. and all the wind that we have experienced in this region – there cannot be a doubt that the wind sweeps up the coast at all seasons.

A point has arisen as to the deposition. David* called the crusts seasonal. This must be wrong; they mark blizzards, but after each blizzard fresh crusts are formed only over the patchy heaps left by the blizzard. A blizzard seems to leave heaps which cover anything from one-sixth to one-third of the whole surface – such heaps presumably turn hollows into mounds with fresh hollows between – these are filled in turn by ensuing blizzards. If this is so, the only way to get at the seasonal deposition would be to average the heaps deposited and multiply this by the number of blizzards in the year.

Monday, February 15. – 14 Camp. 7 miles 775 yards. The surface was wretched today, the two drawbacks of yesterday (the thin crusts which let the ponies through and the sandy heaps which hang on the runners) if anything exaggerated.

Bowers's pony refused work at intervals for the first time. His hind legs sink very deep. Weary Willy is decidedly better. The Soldier takes a gloomy view of everything, but I've come to see that this is a characteristic of him. In spite of it he pays every attention to the weaker horses.

We had frequent halts on the march, but managed 4 miles before lunch and 3½ after.

The temperature was −15° at the lunch camp. It was cold sitting in the tent waiting for the ponies to rest. The thermometer is now −7°, but there is a bright sun and no wind, which makes the air feel quite comfortable: one's socks and finnesko dry well. Our provision allowance is working out very well. In fact all is well with us except the condition of the ponies. The more I see of the matter the more certain I am that we must save all the ponies to get better value out of them next year. It would have been ridiculous to have worked some out this year as the Soldier wished. Even now I feel we went too far with the first three.

One thing is certain. A good snow-shoe would be worth its weight in gold on this surface, and if we can get something really practical we ought to greatly increase our distances next year.

* Professor T. Edgeworth David, C.M.G., F.R.S., of Sydney University, who was the geologist to Shackleton's party.

Memo. Storage of biscuit next year, lashing cases on sledges.
  Look into sledge-meter.
  Picket lines for ponies.
  Food tanks to be size required.
  Two sledges altered to take steel runners.
  Stowage of pony food. Enough sacks for ready bags.

Thursday, February 16. – 6 miles 1450 yards. 15 Camp. The surface a good deal better, but the ponies running out. Three of the five could go on without difficulty. Bowers's pony might go on a bit, but Weary Willy is a good deal done up, and to push him further would be to risk him unduly, so tomorrow we turn. The temperature on the march tonight fell to −21° with a brisk S.W. breeze. Bowers started out as usual in his small felt hat, ears uncovered. Luckily I called a halt after a mile and looked at him. His ears were quite white. Cherry and I nursed them back whilst the patient seemed to feel nothing but intense surprise and disgust at the mere fact of possessing such unruly organs. Oates's nose gave great trouble. I got frost-bitten on the cheek lightly, as also did Cherry-Garrard.

Tried to march in light woollen mits to great discomfort.

Friday, February 17. – Camp 15. Lat. 79° 28½' S. It clouded over yesterday – the temperature rose and some snow fell. Wind from the south, cold and biting, as we turned out. We started to build the depôt. I had intended to go on half a march and return to same camp, leaving Weary Willy to rest, but under the circumstances did not like to take risk.

Stores left in depôt:

	Lat. 79° 29'. Depôt.
245 lbs.	7 weeks' full provision bags for 1 unit
12 lbs.	2 days' provision bags for 1 unit
8 lbs.	8 weeks' tea
31 lbs.	6 weeks' extra butter
176 lbs.	lbs. biscuit (7 weeks' full biscuit)
85 lbs.	8½ gallons oil (12 weeks' oil for 1 unit)
850 lbs.	5 sacks of oats
424 lbs.	4 bales of fodder
250 lbs.	tank of dog biscuit
100 lbs.	2 cases of biscuit
2181	

> 1 skein white line
> 1 set breast harness
> 2 12 ft. sledges
> 2 pair ski, 1 pair ski sticks
> 1 *minimum thermometer**
> 1 tin Rowntree cocoa
> 1 tin matches

With packing we have landed considerably over a ton of stuff. It is a pity we couldn't get to 80°, but as it is we shall have a good leg up for next year and can at least feed the ponies full up to this point.

Our Camp 15 is very well marked, I think. Besides the flag-staff and black flag we have piled biscuit boxes, filled and empty, to act as reflectors – secured tea tins to the sledges, which are planted upright in the snow. The depôt cairn is more than 6 ft. above the surface, very solid and large; then there are the pony protection walls; altogether it should show up for many miles.

I forgot to mention that looking back on the 15th we saw a cairn built on a camp 12½ miles behind – it was miraged up.

It seems as though some of our party will find spring journeys pretty trying. Oates's nose is always on the point of being frost-bitten; Meares has a refractory toe which gives him much trouble – this is the worst prospect for summit work. I have been wondering how I shall stick the summit again, this cold spell gives ideas. I think I shall be all right, but one must be prepared for a pretty good doing.

* see the entry for Chapter Sixteen, *Wednesday November 15*

CHAPTER SIX

Adventure and peril

Saturday, February 18. – Camp 12. North 22 miles 1996 yards.
I scattered some oats 50 yards east of depôt.* The minimum
thermometer showed −16° when we left camp: *inform Simpson*!

The ponies started off well, Gran leading my pony with Weary
Willy behind, the Soldier leading his with Cherry's behind, and
Bowers steering course as before with a light sledge.†

We started half an hour later, soon overtook the ponies, and
luckily picked up a small bag of oats which they had dropped. We
went on for 10¾ miles and stopped for lunch. After lunch to
our astonishment the ponies appeared, going strong. They were
making for a camp some miles farther on, and meant to remain
there. I'm very glad to have seen them making the pace so well.
They don't propose to stop for lunch at all but to march right
through 10 or 12 miles a day. I think they will have little difficulty
in increasing this distance.

For the dogs the surface has been bad, and one or another of us
on either sledge has been running a good part of the time. But we
have covered 23 miles: three marches out. We have four days'
food for them and ought to get in very easily.

As we camp late the temperature is evidently very low and there
is a low drift. Conditions are beginning to be severe on the Barrier
and I shall be glad to get the ponies into more comfortable
quarters.

Sunday, February 19. – Started 10 p.m. Camped 6.30. Nearly 26
miles to our credit. The dogs went very well and the surface became

---

* This was done in order to measure on the next visit the results of wind and snow.
† Scott, Wilson, Meares and Cherry-Garrard now went back swiftly with the dog
teams, to look after the return parties at Safety Camp. Having found all satisfactory, Scott left Wilson and Meares there with the dogs, and marched back with
the rest to Corner Camp, taking more stores to the depôt and hoping to meet
Bowers's rearguard party.

excellent after the first 5 or 6 miles. At the Bluff Camp, No. 11, we picked up Evans's track and found that he must have made excellent progress. No. 10 Camp was much snowed up: I should imagine our light blizzard was severely felt along this part of the route. We must look out tomorrow for signs of Evans being 'held up'.

The old tracks show better here than on the softer surface. During this journey both ponies and dogs have had what under ordinary circumstances would have been a good allowance of food, yet both are desperately hungry. Both eat their own excrement. With the ponies it does not seem so horrid, as there must be a good deal of grain, &c., which is not fully digested. It is the worst side of dog driving. All the rest is diverting. The way in which they keep up a steady jog trot for hour after hour is wonderful. Their legs seem steel springs, fatigue unknown – for at the end of a tiring march any unusual incident will arouse them to full vigour. Osman has been restored to leadership. It is curious how these leaders come on and go off, all except old Stareek, who remains as steady as ever.

We are all acting like seasoned sledge travellers now, such is the force of example. Our tent is up and cooker going in the shortest time after halt, and we are able to break camp in exceptionally good time. Cherry-Garrard is cook. He is excellent, and is quickly learning all the tips for looking after himself and his gear.

What a difference such care makes is apparent now, but was more so when he joined the tent with all his foot-gear iced up, whilst Wilson and I nearly always have dry socks and finnesko to put on. This is only a point amongst many in which experience gives comfort. Every minute spent in keeping one's gear dry and free of snow is very well repaid.

Monday, February 20. – 29 miles. Lunch. Excellent run on hard wind-swept surface – *covered nearly seventeen miles.* Very cold at starting and during march. Suddenly wind changed and temperature rose so that at the moment of stopping for final halt it appeared quite warm, almost sultry. On stopping found we had covered 29 miles, some 35 statute miles. The dogs are weary but by no means played out – during the last part of the journey they trotted steadily with a wonderfully tireless rhythm. I have been off the sledge a good deal and trotting for a good many miles, so should sleep well. E. Evans has left a bale of forage at Camp 8 and has not taken on the one which he might have taken from the depôt – facts which show that his ponies must have been going strong. I hope to find them safe and sound the day after tomorrow.

We had the most wonderfully beautiful sky effects on the march with the sun circling low on the southern horizon. Bright pink clouds hovered overhead on a deep grey-blue background. Gleams of bright sunlit mountains appeared through the stratus.

Here it is most difficult to predict what is going to happen. Sometimes the southern sky looks dark and ominous, but within half an hour all has changed – the land comes and goes as the veil of stratus lifts and falls. It seems as though weather is made here rather than dependent on conditions elsewhere. It is all very interesting.

Tuesday, February 21. – New Camp about 12 miles from Safety Camp. 15½ miles. We made a start as usual about 10 p.m. The light was good at first, but rapidly grew worse till we could see little of the surface. The dogs showed signs of wearying. About an hour and a half after starting we came on mistily outlined pressure ridges. We were running by the sledges. Suddenly Wilson shouted 'Hold on to the sledge', and I saw him slip a leg into a crevasse. I jumped to the sledge, but saw nothing. Five minutes after, as the teams were trotting side by side, the middle dogs of our team disappeared. In a moment the whole team were sinking – two by two we lost sight of them, each pair struggling for foothold. Osman the leader exerted all his great strength and kept a foothold – it was wonderful to see him. The sledge stopped and we leapt aside. The situation was clear in another moment.

We had been actually travelling along the bridge of a crevasse, the sledge had stopped on it, whilst the dogs hung in their harness in the abyss, suspended between the sledge and the leading dog. Why the sledge and ourselves didn't follow the dogs we shall never know. I think a fraction of a pound of added weight must have taken us down. As soon as we grasped the position, we hauled the sledge clear of the bridge and anchored it. Then we peered into the depths of the crack. The dogs were howling dismally, suspended in all sorts of fantastic positions and evidently terribly frightened. Two had dropped out of their harness, and we could see them indistinctly on a snow bridge far below. The rope at either end of the chain had bitten deep into the snow at the side of the crevasse, and with the weight below, it was impossible to move it. By this time Wilson and Cherry-Garrard, who had seen the accident, had come to our assistance. At first things looked very bad for our poor team, and I saw little prospect of rescuing them. I had luckily inquired about the Alpine rope before starting the march, and now Cherry-Garrard hurriedly brought this most essential aid. It takes one a little time to make plans under such sudden circumstances, and for some minutes our efforts were rather futile. We could get not an inch on the main trace of the sledge or on the leading rope, which was binding Osman to the snow with a throttling pressure. Then thought became clearer. We unloaded our sledge, putting in safety our sleeping-bags with the tent and cooker. Choking sounds from Osman made it clear that the pressure on him must soon be relieved. I seized the lashing off Meares's sleeping-bag, passed the tent poles across the crevasse, and with Meares managed to get a few inches on the leading line; this freed Osman, whose harness was immediately cut.

Then securing the Alpine rope to the main trace we tried to haul up together. One dog came up and was unlashed, but by this time the rope had cut so far back at the edge that it was useless to attempt to get more of it. But we could now unbend the sledge and do that for which we should have aimed from the first, namely, run the sledge across the gap and work from it. We managed to do this, our fingers constantly numbed. Wilson held on to the anchored trace whilst the rest of us laboured at the leader end. The leading rope was very small and I was fearful of its breaking, so Meares was lowered down a foot or two to secure the Alpine rope to the leading end of the trace; this done, the work of rescue proceeded in better order. Two by two we hauled the animals up to the sledge and one by one cut them out of their harness. Strangely the last dogs were the most difficult, as they were close under the lip of the gap, bound in by the snow-covered rope. Finally, with a gasp we got the last poor creature on to firm snow. We had recovered eleven of the thirteen.

Then I wondered if the last two could not be got, and we paid down the Alpine rope to see if it was long enough to reach the snow bridge on which they were coiled. The rope is 90 feet, and the amount remaining showed that the depth of the bridge was about 65 feet. I made a bowline and the others lowered me down.

The bridge was firm and I got hold of both dogs, which were hauled up in turn to the surface. Then I heard dim shouts and howls above. Some of the rescued animals had wandered to the second sledge, and a big fight was in progress. All my rope-tenders had to leave to separate the combatants; but they soon returned, and with some effort I was hauled to the surface.

All is well that ends well, and certainly this was a most surprisingly happy ending to a very serious episode. We felt we must have refreshment, so camped and had a meal, congratulating ourselves on a really miraculous escape. If the sledge had gone down Meares and I must have been badly injured, if not killed outright. The dogs are wonderful, but have had a terrible shaking – three of them are passing blood and have more or less serious internal injuries. Many were held up by a thin thong round the stomach, writhing madly to get free. One dog better placed in its harness stretched its legs full before and behind and just managed to claw either side of the gap – it had continued attempts to climb throughout, giving vent to terrified howls. Two of the animals hanging together had been fighting at intervals when they swung into any position which allowed them to bite one another. The crevasse for the time being was an inferno, and the time must have been all too terribly long for the wretched creatures. It was twenty minutes past three when we had completed the rescue work, and the accident must have happened before one-thirty. Some of the animals must have been dangling for over an hour. I had a good opportunity of examining the crack.

The section seemed such as I have shown. It narrowed towards the east and widened slightly towards the west. In this direction there were curious curved splinters; below the snow bridge on which I stood the opening continued, but narrowing, so that I think one could not have fallen many more feet without being wedged. Twice I have owed safety to a snow bridge, and it seems to me that the chance of finding some obstruction or some saving fault in the crevasse is a good one, but I am far from thinking that such a chance can be relied upon, and it would be an awful situation to fall beyond the limits of the Alpine rope.[13a]

We went on after lunch, and very soon got into soft snow and regular surface where crevasses are most unlikely to occur. We have pushed on with difficulty, for the dogs are badly cooked and the surface tries them. We are all pretty done, but luckily the weather favours us. A sharp storm from the south has been succeeded by ideal sunshine which is flooding the tent as I write. It is the calmest, warmest day we have had since we started sledging. We are only about 12 miles from Safety Camp, and I trust we shall push on without accident tomorrow, but I am anxious about some of the dogs. We shall be lucky indeed if all recover.

My companions today were excellent; Wilson and Cherry-Garrard if anything the most intelligently and readily helpful.

I begin to think that there is no avoiding the line of cracks running from the Bluff to Cape Crozier, but my hope is that the danger does not extend beyond a mile or two, and that the cracks are narrower on the pony road to Corner Camp. If eight ponies can cross without accident I do not think there can be great danger. Certainly we must rigidly adhere to this course on all future journeys. We must try and plot out the danger line.* I begin to be a little anxious about the returning ponies.

I rather think the dogs are being underfed; they have weakened badly in the last few days – more than such work ought to entail. Now they are absolutely ravenous.

Meares has very dry feet. Whilst we others perspire freely and our skin remains pink and soft his gets horny and scaly. He amused us greatly tonight by scraping them. The sound suggested the whittling of a hard wood block and the action was curiously like an attempt to shape the feet to fit the finnesko!

Summary of marches made on the depôt journey

Distances in geographical miles. Variation 152 E .

			m.	yds.	
Safety	No. 3 to 4	E.	4	2000	
	4 to 5	⎧ S. 64 E.	4	500 ⎫	
		⎨ S. 77 E.	1	312 ⎬ 9.359	
		⎩ S. 60 E.	3	1575 ⎭	
	5 to 6	S. 48 E.	10	270	Var. 149½ E.

* The party had made a short cut where in going out with the ponies they had made an elbaw, and so had passed within this 'danger line'.

			m.	yds.
Corner	6 to 7	S.	10	145
	7 to 8	S.	?11	198
	8 to 9	S.	12	325
	9 to 10	S.	11	118
Bluff Camp	10 to 11	S.	10	226
	11 to 12	S.	9	150
	12 to 13	S.	7	650
	13 to 14	S.	7	Bowers 775
	14 to 15	S.	8	118
			111	610
Return				
17th–18th	15 to 12	N.	22	1994
18th–19th	12 to 10/9	N.	48	1825
19th–29th lunch	8 Camp	N.	65	1720
19th–20th	7 Camp	N.	77	1820
20th–21st		N. 30–35 W.	93	950
21st–22nd	Safety Camp	N. & W.	107	1125

Wednesday, February 22. – Safety Camp. Got away at 10 again: surface fairly heavy: dogs going badly.

The dogs are as thin as rakes; they are ravenous and very tired. I feel this should not be, and that it is evident that they are underfed. The ration must be increased next year and we *must* have some properly thought out diet. The biscuit alone is not good enough. Meares is excellent to a point, but ignorant of the conditions here. One thing is certain, the dogs will never continue to drag heavy loads with men sitting on the sledges; we must all learn to run with the teams and the Russian custom must be dropped. Meares, I think, rather imagined himself racing to the Pole and back on a dog sledge. This journey has opened his eyes a good deal.

We reached Safety Camp (dist. 14 miles) at 4.30 a.m.; found E. Evans and his party in excellent health, but, alas! with only *one* pony. As far as I can gather Forde's pony only got 4 miles back from the Bluff Camp; then a blizzard came on, and in spite of the most tender care from Forde the pony sank under it. Evans says that Forde spent hours with the animal trying to keep it going, feeding it, walking it about; at last he returned to the tent to say that the poor creature had fallen; they all tried to get it on its feet again but their efforts were useless. It couldn't stand, and soon after it died.

Then the party marched some 10 miles, but the blizzard had had a bad effect on Blossom – it seemed to have shrivelled him up, and now he was terribly emaciated. After this march he could scarcely move. Evans describes his efforts as pathetic; he got on 100 yards, then stopped with legs outstretched and nose to the ground. They rested him, fed him well, covered him with rugs; but again all efforts were unavailing. The last stages came with painful detail. So Blossom is also left on the Southern Road.

The last pony, James Pigg, as he is called, has thriven amazingly – of course great care has been taken with him and he is now getting full feed and very light work, so he ought to do well. The loss is severe; but they were the two oldest ponies of our team and the two which Oates thought of least use.

Atkinson and Crean have departed, leaving no trace – not even a note.

Crean had carried up a good deal of fodder, and some seal meat was found buried.

After a few hours' sleep we are off for Hut Point.

There are certain points in night marching, if only for the glorious light effects which the coming night exhibits.

Wednesday, February 22. – 10 p.m. Safety Camp. Turned out at 11 this morning after 4 hours' sleep.

Wilson, Meares, Evans, Cherry-Garrard, and I went to Hut Point. Found a great enigma. The hut was cleared and habitable – but no one was there. A pencil line on the wall said that a bag containing a mail was inside, but no bag could be found. We puzzled much, then finally decided on the true solution, viz. that Atkinson and Crean had gone towards Safety Camp as we went to Hut Point – later we saw their sledge track leading round on the sea ice. Then we returned towards Safety Camp and endured a very bad hour in which we could see the two bell tents but not the domed. It was an enormous relief to find the dome securely planted, as the ice round Cape Armitage is evidently very weak; I have never seen such enormous water holes off it.

But every incident of the day pales before the startling contents of the mail bag which Atkinson gave me – a letter from Campbell setting out his doings and the finding of *Amundsen* established in the Bay of Whales.

One thing only fixes itself definitely in my mind. The proper, as well as the wiser, course for us is to proceed exactly as though this had not happened. To go forward and do our best for the honour of the country without fear or panic.

There is no doubt that Amundsen's plan is a very serious menace to ours. He has a shorter distance to the Pole by 60 miles – I never thought he could have got so many dogs safely to the ice. His plan for running them seems excellent. But above and beyond all he can start his journey early in the season – an impossible condition with ponies.

The ice is still in at the Glacier Tongue: a very late date – it looks as though it will not break right back this season, but off Cape Armitage it is so thin that I doubt if the ponies could safely be walked round.

Thursday, February 23. – Spent the day preparing sledges, &c., for party to meet Bowers at Corner Camp. It was blowing and drifting and generally uncomfortable. Wilson and Meares killed three seals for the dogs.

Friday, February 24. – Roused out at 6. Started marching at 9. Self, Crean, and Cherry-Garrard, one sledge and tent; E. Evans, Atkinson, Forde, second sledge and tent; Keohane leading his pony. We pulled on ski in the forenoon; the second sledge couldn't keep up, so we changed about for half the march. In the afternoon we pulled on foot. On the whole I thought the labour greater on foot, so did Crean, showing the advantage of experience.

There is no doubt that very long days' work could be done by men in hard condition on ski.

The hanging back of the second sledge was mainly a question of condition, but to some extent due to the sledge. We have a 10 ft., whilst the other party has a 12 ft.; the former is a distinct advantage in this case.

It has been a horrid day. We woke to find a thick covering of sticky ice crystals on everything – a frost rime. I cleared my ski before breakfast and found more on afterwards. There was the suggestion of an early frosty morning at home – such a morning as develops into a beautiful sunshiny day; but in our case, alas! such hopes were shattered: it was almost damp, with temperature near zero and a terribly bad light for travelling. In the afternoon Erebus and Terror showed up for a while. Now it is drifting hard with every sign of a blizzard – a beastly night. This marching is going to be very good for our condition and I shall certainly keep people at it.

Saturday, February 25. – Fine bright day – easy marching – covered 9 miles and a bit yesterday and the same today. Should reach Corner Camp before lunch tomorrow.

Turned out at 3 a.m. and saw a short black line on the horizon towards White Island. Thought it an odd place for a rock exposure and then observed movement in it. Walked 1½ miles towards it and made certain that it was Oates, Bowers, and the ponies. They seemed to be going very fast and evidently did not see our camp. Today we have come on their tracks, and I fear there are only four ponies left.

James Pigg, our own pony, limits the length of our marches. The men haulers could go on much longer, and we all like pulling on ski. Everyone must be practised in this.

Sunday, February 26. – Marched on Corner Camp, but second main party found going very hard and eventually got off their ski and pulled on foot. James Pigg also found the surface bad, so we camped and had lunch after doing 3 miles.

Except for our tent the camp routine is slack. Shall have to tell people that we are out on business, not picnicking. It was another 3 miles to depôt after lunch. Found signs of Bowers's party having camped there and glad to see five pony walls. Left six full weeks' provision: 1 bag of oats, ¼ of a bale of fodder. Then Cherry-Garrard, Crean, and I started for home, leaving the others to bring the pony by slow stages. We covered 6¼ miles in direct line, then had some tea and marched another 8. We must be less than 10 miles from Safety Camp. Pitched tent at 10 p.m., very dark for cooking.

Monday, February 27. – Awoke to find it blowing a howling blizzard – absolutely confined to tent at present – to step outside is to be covered with drift in a minute. We have managed to get our cooking things inside and have had a meal. Very anxious about

the ponies – am wondering where they can be. The return party*
has had two days and may have got them into some shelter – but
more probably they were not expecting this blow – I wasn't. The
wind is blowing force 8 or 9; heavy gusts straining the tent; the
temperature is evidently quite low. This is poor luck.

Tuesday, February 28. – Safety Camp. Packed up at 6 a.m. and
marched into Safety Camp. Found everyone very cold and
depressed. Wilson and Meares had had continuous bad weather
since we left, Bowers and Oates since their arrival. The blizzard
had raged for two days. The animals looked in a sorry condition
but all were alive. The wind blew keen and cold from the east.
There could be no advantage in waiting here, and soon all arrangements were made for a general shift to Hut Point. Packing took a
long time. The snowfall had been prodigious, and parts of the
sledges were 3 or 4 feet under drift. About 4 o'clock the two dog
teams got safely away. Then the pony party prepared to go. As the
clothes were stripped from the ponies the ravages of the blizzard
became evident. The animals without exception were terribly
emaciated, and Weary Willy was in a pitiable condition.

The plan was for the ponies to follow the dog tracks, our small
party to start last and get in front of the ponies on the sea ice. I was
very anxious about the sea ice passage owing to the spread of the
water holes.

The ponies started, but Weary Willy, tethered last without a
load, immediately fell down. We tried to get him up and he made
efforts, but was too exhausted.

Then we rapidly reorganised. Cherry-Garrard and Crean went
on whilst Oates and Gran stayed with me. We made desperate
efforts to save the poor creature, got him once more on his legs
and gave him a hot oat mash. Then after a wait of an hour Oates
led him off, and we packed the sledge and followed on ski; 500
yards away from the camp the poor creature fell again and I felt it
was the last effort. We camped, built a snow wall round him, and
did all we possibly could to get him on his feet. Every effort was
fruitless, though the poor thing made pitiful struggles. Towards
midnight we propped him up as comfortably as we could and
went to bed.

* Bowers, Oates, and Gran, with the five ponies. The two days had after all
brought them to Safety Camp.

Wednesday, March 1, a.m. – Our pony died in the night. It is hard to have got him back so far only for this. It is clear that these blizzards are terrible for the poor animals. Their coats are not good, but even with the best of coats it is certain they would lose condition badly if caught in one, and we cannot afford to lose condition at the beginning of a journey. It makes a late start *necessary for next year.*

Well, we have done our best and bought our experience at a heavy cost. Now every effort must be bent on saving the remaining animals, and it will be good luck if we get four back to Cape Evans, or even three. Jimmy Pigg may have fared badly; Bowers's big pony is in a bad way after that frightful blizzard. I cannot remember such a bad storm in February or March: the temperature was −7°.

Bowers incident

I note the events of the night of March 1 whilst they are yet fresh in my memory.

Thursday, March 2, a.m. – The events of the past 48 hours bid fair to wreck the expedition, and the only one comfort is the miraculous avoidance of loss of life. We turned out early yesterday, Oates, Gran, and I, after the dismal night of our pony's death, and pulled towards the forage depôt* on ski. As we approached, the sky looked black and lowering, and mirage effects of huge broken floes loomed out ahead. At first I thought it one of the strange optical illusions common in this region – but as we neared the depôt all doubt was dispelled. The sea was full of broken pieces of Barrier edge. My thoughts flew to the ponies and dogs, and fearful anxieties assailed my mind. We turned to follow the sea edge and suddenly discovered a working crack. We dashed over this and slackened pace again after a quarter of a mile. Then again cracks appeared ahead and we increased pace as much as possible, not slackening again till we were in line between the Safety Camp and Castle Rock. Meanwhile my first thought was to warn E. Evans. We set up tent, and Gran went to the depôt with a note as Oates and I disconsolately thought out the situation. I thought to myself that if either party had reached safety either on the Barrier or at Hut Point they would immediately

* This was at a point on the Barrier, ½ mile from the edge, in a S.S.E. direction from Hut Point.

have sent a warning messenger to Safety Camp. By this time the messenger should have been with us. Some half-hour passed, and suddenly with a 'Thank God!' I made certain that two specks in the direction of Pram Point were human beings. I hastened towards them and found they were Wilson and Meares, who had led the homeward way with the dog teams. They were astonished to see me – they said they feared the ponies were adrift on the sea ice – they had seen them with glasses from Observation Hill. They thought I was with them. They had hastened out without breakfast: we made them cocoa and discussed the gloomiest situation. Just after cocoa Wilson discovered a figure making rapidly for the depôt from the west. Gran was sent off again to intercept. It proved to be Crean – he was exhausted and a little incoherent. The ponies had camped at 2.30 a.m. on the sea ice well beyond the seal crack on the previous night. In the middle of the night . . .

Friday, March 3, a.m. – I was interrupted when writing yesterday and continue my story this morning . . . In the middle of the night at 4.30 Bowers got out of the tent and discovered the ice had broken all round him: a crack ran under the picketing line, and one pony had disappeared. They had packed with great haste and commenced jumping the ponies from floe to floe, then dragging the loads over after – the three men must have worked splendidly and fearlessly. At length they had worked their way to heavier floes lying near the Barrier edge, and at one time thought they could get up, but soon discovered that there were gaps everywhere off the high Barrier face. In this dilemma Crean volunteering was sent off to try to reach me. The sea was like a cauldron at the time of the break up, and killer whales were putting their heads up on all sides. Luckily they did not frighten the ponies.

He travelled a great distance over the sea ice, leaping from floe to floe, and at last found a thick floe from which with help of ski stick he could climb the Barrier face. It was a desperate venture, but luckily successful.

As soon as I had digested Crean's news I sent Gran back to Hut Point with Wilson and Meares and started with my sledge, Crean, and Oates for the scene of the mishap. We stopped at Safety Camp to load some provisions and oil and then, marching carefully round, approached the ice edge. To my joy I caught sight of the lost party. We got our Alpine rope and with its help dragged the two men to the surface. I pitched camp at a safe distance from the edge and then we all started salvage work. The ice had ceased to drift and lay close and quiet against the Barrier edge. We got the men at 5.30 p.m. and all the sledges and effects on to the Barrier by 4 a.m. As we were getting up the last loads the ice showed signs of drifting off, and we saw it was hopeless to try and move the ponies. The three poor beasts had to be left on their floe for the moment, well fed. None of our party had had sleep the previous night and all were dog tired. I decided we must rest, but turned everyone out at 8.30 yesterday morning. Before breakfast we discovered the ponies had drifted away. We had tried to anchor their floe with the Alpine rope, but the anchors had drawn. It was a sad moment. At breakfast we decided to pack and follow the Barrier edge: this was the position when I last wrote, but the interruption came when Bowers, who had taken the binoculars, announced that he could see the ponies about a mile to the N.W. We packed and went on at once. We found it easy enough to get down to the poor animals and decided to rush them for a last chance of life. Then there was an unfortunate mistake: I went along the Barrier edge and discovered what I thought and what proved to be a practicable way to land a pony, but the others meanwhile, a little overwrought, tried to leap Punch across a gap. The poor beast fell in; eventually we had to kill him – it was awful. I recalled all hands and pointed out my road. Bowers and Oates went out on it with a sledge and worked their way to the remaining ponies, and started back with them on the same track. Meanwhile Cherry and I dug a road at the Barrier edge. We saved one pony; for a time I thought we should get both, but Bowers's poor animal slipped at a jump and plunged into the water: we dragged him out on some brash ice – killer whales all about us in an intense state of excitement. The poor animal couldn't rise, and the only merciful thing was to kill it. These incidents were too terrible.

At 5 p.m. we sadly broke our temporary camp and marched back to the one I had first pitched. Even here it seemed unsafe, so I walked nearly two miles to discover cracks: I could find none, and we turned in about midnight.

So here we are ready to start our sad journey to Hut Point. Everything out of joint with the loss of the ponies, but mercifully with all the party alive and well.

Saturday, March 4, a.m. – We had a terrible pull at the start yesterday, taking four hours to cover some three miles to march on the line between Safety Camp and Fodder Depôt. From there Bowers went to Safety Camp and found my notes to Evans had been taken. We dragged on after lunch to the place where my tent had been pitched when Wilson first met me and where we had left our ski and other loads. All these had gone. We found sledge tracks leading in towards the land and at length marks of a pony's hoofs. We followed these and some ski tracks right into the land, coming at length to the highest of the Pram Point ridges. I decided to camp here, and as we unpacked I saw four figures approaching. They proved to be Evans and his party. They had ascended towards Castle Rock on Friday and found a good camp site on top of the Ridge. They were in good condition. It was a relief to hear they had found a good road up. They went back to their camp later, dragging one of our sledges and a light load. Atkinson is to go to Hut Point this morning to tell Wilson about us. The rest ought to meet us and help us up the hill – just off to march up the hill, hoping to avoid trouble with the pony.[14]

Sunday, March 5, a.m. – Marched up the hill to Evans's Camp under Castle Rock. Evans's party came to meet us and helped us up with the loads – it was a steep, stiff pull; the pony was led up by Oates. As we camped for lunch Atkinson and Gran appeared, the former having been to Hut Point to carry news of the relief. I sent Gran on to Safety Camp to fetch some sugar and chocolate, left Evans, Oates, and Keohane in camp, and marched on with remaining six to Hut Point. It was calm at Evans's Camp, but blowing hard on the hill and harder at Hut Point. Found the hut in comparative order and slept there.

CHAPTER SEVEN

At Discovery Hut

Monday, March 6, a.m. – Roused the hands at 7.30. Wilson, Bowers, Garrard, and I went out to Castle Rock. We met Evans just short of his camp and found the loads had been dragged up the hill. Oates and Keohane had gone back to lead on the ponies. At the top of the ridge we harnessed men and ponies to the sledges and made rapid progress on a good surface towards the hut. The weather grew very thick towards the end of the march, with all signs of a blizzard. We unharnessed the ponies at the top of Ski slope – Wilson guided them down from rock patch to rock patch; the remainder of us got down a sledge and necessaries over the slope. It is a ticklish business to get the sledge along the ice foot, which is now all blue ice ending in a drop to the sea. One has to be certain that the party has good foothold. All reached the hut in safety. The ponies have admirably comfortable quarters under the verandah.

After some cocoa we fetched in the rest of the dogs from the Gap and another sledge from the hill. It had ceased to snow and the wind had gone down slightly. Turned in with much relief to have all hands and the animals safely housed.

Tuesday, March 7, a.m. – Yesterday went over to Pram Point with Wilson. We found that the corner of sea ice in Pram Point Bay had not gone out – it was crowded with seals. We killed a young one and carried a good deal of the meat and some of the blubber back with us.

Meanwhile the remainder of the party had made some progress towards making the hut more comfortable. In the afternoon we all set to in earnest and by supper time had wrought wonders.

We have made a large L-shaped inner apartment with packing cases, the intervals stopped with felt. An empty kerosene tin and some firebricks have been made into an excellent little stove, which has been connected to the old stove-pipe. The solider fare of our meals is either stewed or fried on this stove whilst the tea or cocoa is being prepared on a primus.

The temperature of the hut is low, of course, but in every other respect we are absolutely comfortable. There is an unlimited quantity of biscuit, and our discovery at Pram Point means an unlimited supply of seal meat. We have heaps of cocoa, coffee, and tea, and a sufficiency of sugar and salt. In addition a small store of luxuries, chocolate, raisins, lentils, oatmeal, sardines, and jams, which will serve to vary the fare. One way and another we shall manage to be very comfortable during our stay here, and already we can regard it as a temporary home.

Thursday, March 9, a.m. – Yesterday and today very busy about the hut and overcoming difficulties fast. The stove threatened to exhaust our store of firewood. We have redesigned it so that it takes only a few chips of wood to light it and then continues to give great heat with blubber alone. Today there are to be further improvements to regulate the draught and increase the cooking range. We have further housed-in the living quarters with our old *Discovery* winter awning, and begin already to retain the heat which is generated inside. We are beginning to eat blubber and find biscuits fried in it to be delicious.

We really have everything necessary for our comfort and only need a little more experience to make the best of our resources. The weather has been wonderfully, perhaps ominously, fine during the last few days. The sea has frozen over and broken up several times already. The warm sun has given a grand opportunity to dry all gear.

Yesterday morning Bowers went with a party to pick up the stores rescued from the floe last week. E. Evans volunteered to join the party with Meares, Keohane, Atkinson, and Gran. They started from the hut about 10 a.m; we helped them up the hill, and at 7.30 I saw them reach the camp containing the gear, some 12 miles away. I don't expect them in till tomorrow night.

It is splendid to see the way in which everyone is learning the ropes, and the resource which is being shown. Wilson as usual leads in the making of useful suggestions and in generally providing for our wants. He is a tower of strength in checking the ill-usage of clothes – what I have come to regard as the greatest danger with Englishmen.

Friday, March 10, a.m. – Went yesterday to Castle Rock with Wilson to see what chance there might be of getting to Cape Evans.* The day was bright and it was quite warm walking in the sun. There is no doubt the route to Cape Evans lies over the worst corner of Erebus. From this distance the whole mountain side looks a mass of crevasses, but a route might be found at a level of 3,000 or 4,000 ft.

The hut is getting warmer and more comfortable. We have very excellent nights; it is cold only in the early morning. The outside temperatures range from 8° or so in the day to 2° at night. Today there is a strong S.E. wind with drift. We are going to fetch more blubber for the stove.

Saturday, March 11, a.m. – Went yesterday morning to Pram Point to fetch in blubber – wind very strong to Gap but very little on Pram Point side.

In the evening went half-way to Castle Rock; strong bitter cold wind on summit. Could not see the sledge party, but after supper they arrived, having had very hard pulling. They had had no wind at all till they approached the hut. Their temperatures had fallen to −10° and −15°, but with bright clear sunshine in the daytime. They had thoroughly enjoyed their trip and the pulling on ski.

Life in the hut is much improved, but if things go too fast there will be all too little to think about and give occupation in the hut.

It is astonishing how the miscellaneous assortment of articles remaining in and about the hut have been put to useful purpose.

This deserves description.[15]

Monday, March 13, a.m. – The weather grew bad on Saturday night and we had a mild blizzard yesterday. The wind went to the south and increased in force last night, and this morning there was quite a heavy sea breaking over the ice foot. The spray came almost up to the dogs. It reminds us of the gale in which we drove ashore in the *Discovery*. We have had some trouble with our blubber stove and got the hut very full of smoke on Saturday night. As a result we are all as black as sweeps and our various garments are covered with oily soot. We look a fearful gang of ruffians. The blizzard has delayed our plans and everyone's attention is bent on the stove, the cooking, and the various

* i.e. by land, now that the sea ice was out.

internal arrangements. Nothing is done without a great amount of advice received from all quarters, and consequently things are pretty well done. The hut has a pungent odour of blubber and blubber smoke. We have grown accustomed to it, but imagine that ourselves and our clothes will be given a wide berth when we return to Cape Evans.

Wednesday, March 15, a.m. – It was blowing continuously from the south throughout Sunday, Monday, and Tuesday – I never remember such a persistent southerly wind.

Both Monday and Tuesday I went up Crater Hill. I feared that our floe at Pram Point would go, but yesterday it still remained, though the cracks are getting more open. We should be in a hole if it went.*

As I came down the hill yesterday I saw a strange figure advancing and found it belonged to Griffith Taylor. He and his party had returned safely. They were very full of their adventures. The main part of their work seems to be rediscovery of many facts which were noted but perhaps passed over too lightly in the *Discovery* – but it is certain that the lessons taught by the physiographical and ice features will now be thoroughly explained. A very interesting fact lies in the continuous bright sunshiny weather which the party enjoyed during the first four weeks of their work. They seem to have avoided all our stormy winds and blizzards.

But I must leave Griffith Taylor to tell his own story, which will certainly be a lengthy one. The party gives Evans [P.O.] a very high character.

Today we have a large seal-killing party. I hope to get in a good fortnight's allowance of blubber as well as meat, and pray that our floe will remain.

Friday, March 17, a.m. – We killed eleven seals at Pram Point on Wednesday, had lunch on the Point, and carried some half-ton of the blubber and meat back to camp – it was a stiff pull up the hill.

Yesterday the last Corner Party started: E. Evans, Wright, Crean, and Forde in one team; Bowers, Oates, Cherry-Garrard, and Atkinson in the other. It was very sporting of Wright to join in after only a day's rest. He is evidently a splendid puller.

Debenham has become principal cook, and evidently enjoys the task.

* Because the seals would cease to come up.

Taylor is full of good spirits and anecdote, an addition to the party.

Yesterday after a beautifully fine morning we got a strong northerly wind which blew till the middle of the night, crowding the young ice up the Strait. Then the wind suddenly shifted to the south, and I thought we were in for a blizzard; but this morning the wind has gone to the S.E. – the stratus cloud formed by the north wind is dissipating, and the damp snow deposited in the night is drifting. It looks like a fine evening.

Steadily we are increasing the comforts of the hut. The stove has been improved out of all recognition; with extra stove-pipes we get no back draughts, no smoke inside, whilst the economy of fuel is much increased.

Insulation inside and out is the subject we are now attacking.

The young ice is going to and fro, but the sea refuses to freeze over so far – except in the region of Pram Point, where a bay has remained for some four days holding some pieces of Barrier in its grip. These pieces have come from the edge of the Barrier and some are crumbling already, showing a deep and rapid surface deposit of snow and therefore the probability that they are drifted sea ice not more than a year or two old, the depth of the drift being due to proximity to an old Barrier edge.

I have just taken to pyjama trousers and shall don an extra shirt – I have been astonished at the warmth which I have felt throughout in light clothing. So far I have had nothing more than a singlet and jersey under pyjama jacket and a single pair of drawers under wind trousers. A hole in the drawers of ancient date means that one place has had no covering but the wind trousers, yet I have never felt cold about the body.

In spite of all little activities I am impatient of our wait here. But I shall be impatient also in the main hut. It is ill to sit still and contemplate the ruin which has assailed our transport. The scheme of advance must be very different from that which I first contemplated. The Pole is a very long way off, alas!

Bit by bit I am losing all faith in the dogs – I'm afraid they will never go the pace we look for.

Saturday, *March* 18, a.m. – Still blowing and drifting. It seems as though there can be no peace at this spot till the sea is properly frozen over. It blew very hard from the S.E. yesterday – I could

scarcely walk against the wind. In the night it fell calm; the moon
shone brightly at midnight. Then the sky became overcast and the
temperature rose to +11°. Now the wind is coming in spurts from
the south – all indications of a blizzard.

With the north wind of Friday the ice must have pressed up
on Hut Point. A considerable floe of pressed up young ice is
grounded under the point, and this morning we found a seal on
this. Just as the party started out to kill it, it slid off into the water –
it had evidently finished its sleep – but it is encouraging to have
had a chance to capture a seal so close to the hut.

Monday, March 20. – On Saturday night it blew hard from the
south, thick overhead, low stratus and drift. The sea spray again
came over the ice foot and flung up almost to the dogs; by Sunday
morning the wind had veered to the S.E., and all yesterday it blew
with great violence and temperature down to –11° and –12°.

We were confined to the hut and its immediate environs. Last
night the wind dropped, and for a few hours this morning we had
light airs only, the temperature rising to –2°.

The continuous bad weather is very serious for the dogs. We have
strained every nerve to get them comfortable, but the changes of
wind made it impossible to afford shelter in all directions. Some five
or six dogs are running loose, but we dare not allow the stronger
animals such liberty. They suffer much from the cold, but they
don't get worse.

The small white dog which fell into the crevasse on our home
journey died yesterday. Under the best circumstances I doubt if it
could have lived, as there had evidently been internal injury and an
external sore had grown gangrenous. Three other animals are in a
poor way, but may pull through with luck.

We had a stroke of luck today. The young ice pressed up off Hut
Point has remained fast – a small convenient platform jutting out
from the point. We found two seals on it today and killed them –
thus getting a good supply of meat for the dogs and some more
blubber for our fire. Other seals came up as the first two were
being skinned, so that one may now hope to keep up all future
supplies on this side of the ridge.

As I write the wind is blowing up again and looks like returning
to the south. The only comfort is that these strong cold winds with
no sun must go far to cool the waters of the Sound.

The continuous bad weather is trying to the spirits, but we are fairly comfortable in the hut and only suffer from lack of exercise to work off the heavy meals our appetites demand.

Tuesday, March 21. – The wind returned to the south at 8 last night. It gradually increased in force until 2 a.m., when it was blowing from the S.S.W., force 9 to 10. The sea was breaking constantly and heavily on the ice foot. The spray carried right over the Point – covering all things and raining on the roof of the hut. Poor Vince's cross, some 30 feet above the water, was enveloped in it.

Of course the dogs had a very poor time, and we went and released two or three, getting covered in spray during the operation – our wind clothes very wet.

This is the third gale from the south since our arrival here. Any one of these would have rendered the Bay impossible for a ship, and therefore it is extraordinary that we should have entirely escaped such a blow when the *Discovery* was in it in 1902.

The effects of this gale are evident and show that it is a most unusual occurrence. The rippled snow surface of the ice foot is furrowed in all directions and covered with briny deposit – a condition we have never seen before. The ice foot at the S.W. corner of the bay is broken down, bare rock appearing for the first time.

The sledges, magnetic huts, and in fact every exposed object on the Point are thickly covered with brine. Our seal floe has gone, so it is goodbye to seals on this side for some time.

The dogs are the main sufferers by this continuance of phenomenally terrible weather. At least four are in a bad state; some six or seven others are by no means fit and well, but oddly enough some ten or a dozen animals are as fit as they can be. Whether constitutionally harder or whether better fitted by nature or chance to protect themselves it is impossible to say – Osman, Czigane, Krisravitsa, Hohol, and some others are in first-rate condition, whilst Lappa is better than he has ever been before.

It is so impossible to keep the dogs comfortable in the traces and so laborious to be continually attempting it, that we have decided to let the majority run loose. It will be wonderful if we can avoid one or two murders, but on the other hand probably more would die if we kept them in leash.

We shall try and keep the quarrelsome dogs chained up.

The main trouble that seems to come on the poor wretches is the icing up of their hindquarters; once the ice gets thoroughly into the coat the hind legs get half paralysed with cold. The hope is that the animals will free themselves of this by running about.

Well, well, fortune is not being very kind to us. This month will have sad memories. Still I suppose things might be worse; the ponies are well housed and are doing exceedingly well, though we have slightly increased their food allowance.

Yesterday afternoon we climbed Observation Hill to see some examples of spheroidal weathering – Wilson knew of them and guided. The geologists state that they indicate a columnar structure, the tops of the columns being weathered out.

The specimens we saw were very perfect. Had some interesting instruction in geology in the evening. I should not regret a stay here with our two geologists if only the weather would allow us to get about.

This morning the wind moderated and went to the S.E.; the sea naturally fell quickly. The temperature this morning was $+17°$; minimum $+11°$. But now the wind is increasing from the S.E. and it is momentarily getting colder.

Thursday, March 23, a.m. – No signs of depôt party, which to-night will have been a week absent. On Tuesday afternoon we went up to the Big Boulder above Ski slope. The geologists were interested, and we others learnt something of olivines, green in crystal form or oxidized to bright red, granites or granulites or quartzites, hornblende and felspars, ferrous and ferric oxides of lava acid, basic, plutonic, igneous, eruptive – schists, basalts, &c. All such things I must get clearer in my mind.*

Tuesday afternoon a cold S.E. wind commenced and blew all night.

Yesterday morning it was calm and I went up Crater Hill. The sea of stratus cloud hung curtain-like over the Strait – blue sky east and south of it and the Western Mountains bathed in sunshine, sharp,

---

* As a step towards 'getting these things clearer' in his mind two spare pages of the diary are filled with neat tables, showing the main classes into which rocks are divided, and their natural subdivisions – the sedimentary, according to mode of deposition, chemical, organic, or aqueous; the metamorphic, according to the kind of rock altered by heat; the igneous, according to their chemical composition.

clear, distinct – a glorious glimpse of grandeur on which the curtain gradually descended. In the morning it looked as though great pieces of Barrier were drifting out. From the hill one found these to be but small fragments which the late gale had dislodged, leaving in places a blue wall very easily distinguished from the general white of the older fractures. The old floe and a good extent of new ice had remained fast in Pram Point Bay. Great numbers of seals up as usual. The temperature was up to +20° at noon. In the afternoon a very chill wind from the east, temperature rapidly dropping till zero in the evening. The Strait obstinately refuses to freeze.

We are scoring another success in the manufacture of blubber lamps, which relieves anxiety as to lighting as the hours of darkness increase.

The young ice in Pram Point Bay is already being pressed up.

Friday, March 24, a.m. – Skuas still about, a few – very shy – very dark in colour after moulting.

Went along Arrival Heights yesterday with very keen over-ridge wind – it was difficult to get shelter. In the evening it fell calm and has remained all night with temperature up to +18°. This morning it is snowing with fairly large flakes.

Yesterday for the first time saw the ice foot on the south side of the bay, a wall some 5 or 6 feet above water and 12 or 14 feet below; the sea bottom quite clear with the white wall resting on it. This must be typical of the ice foot all along the coast, and the wasting of caves at sea level alone gives the idea of an overhanging mass. Very curious and interesting erosion of surface of the ice foot by waves during recent gale.

The depôt party returned yesterday morning. They had thick weather on the outward march and missed the track, finally doing 30 miles between Safety Camp and Corner Camp. They had a hard blow up to force 8 on the night of our gale. Started N.W. and strongest S.S.E.

The sea wants to freeze – a thin coating of ice formed directly the wind dropped; but the high temperature does not tend to thicken it rapidly and the tide makes many an open lead. We have been counting our resources and arranging for another twenty days' stay.

Saturday, March 25, a.m. – We have had two days of surprisingly warm weather, the sky overcast, snow falling, wind only in light airs. Last night the sky was clearing, with a southerly wind, and this morning the sea was open all about us. It is disappointing to find the ice so reluctant to hold; at the same time one supposes that the cooling of the water is proceeding and therefore that each day makes it easier for the ice to form – the sun seems to have lost all power, but I imagine its rays still tend to warm the surface water about the noon hours. It is only a week now to the date which I thought would see us all at Cape Evans.

The warmth of the air has produced a comparatively uncomfortable state of affairs in the hut. The ice on the inner roof is melting fast, dripping on the floor and streaming down the sides. The increasing cold is checking the evil even as I write. Comfort could only be ensured in the hut either by making a clean sweep of all the ceiling ice or by keeping the interior at a critical temperature little above freezing-point.

Sunday, *March* 26, p.m. – Yesterday morning went along Arrival Heights in very cold wind. Afternoon to east side Observation Hill. As afternoon advanced, wind fell. Glorious evening – absolutely calm, smoke ascending straight. Sea frozen over – looked very much like final freezing, but in night wind came from S.E., producing open water all along shore. Wind continued this morning with drift, slackened in afternoon; walked over Gap and back by Crater Heights to Arrival Heights.

Sea east of Cape Armitage pretty well covered with ice; some open pools – sea off shore west of the Cape frozen in pools, open lanes close to shore as far as Castle Rock. Bays either side of Glacier Tongue look fairly well frozen. Hut still dropping water badly.

Held Service in hut this morning, read Litany. *One* skua seen today.

Monday, *March* 27, p.m. – Strong easterly wind on ridge today rushing down over slopes on western side.

Ice holding south from about Hut Point, but cleared ½ to ¾ mile from shore to northward. Cleared in patches also, I am told, on both sides of Glacier Tongue, which is annoying. A regular local wind. The Barrier edge can be seen clearly all along, showing there is little or no drift. Have been out over the Gap for walk. Glad to say majority of people seem anxious to get exercise, but one or two like the fire better.

The dogs are getting fitter each day, and all save one or two have excellent coats. I was very pleased to find one or two of the animals voluntarily accompanying us on our walk. It is good to see them trotting against a strong drift.

Tuesday, March 28. – Slowly but surely the sea is freezing over. The ice holds and thickens south of Hut Point in spite of strong easterly wind and in spite of isolated water holes which obstinately remain open. It is difficult to account for these – one wonders if the air currents shoot downward on such places; but even so it is strange that they do not gradually diminish in extent. A great deal of ice seems to have remained in and about the northern islets, but it is too far to be sure that there is a continuous sheet.

We are building stabling to accommodate four more ponies under the eastern verandah. When this is complete we shall be able to shelter seven animals, and this should be enough for winter and spring operations.

Thursday, March 30. – The ice holds south of Hut Point, though not thickening rapidly – yesterday was calm and the same ice conditions seemed to obtain on both sides of the Glacier Tongue. It looks as though the last part of the road to become safe will be the stretch from Hut Point to Turtle-back Island. Here the sea seems disinclined to freeze even in calm weather. Today there is more strong wind from the east. White horse all along under the ridge.

The period of our stay here seems to promise to lengthen. It is trying – trying – but we can live, which is something. I should not be greatly surprised if we had to wait till May. Several skuas were about the camp yesterday. I have seen none today.

Two rorquals were rising close to Hut Point this morning – although the ice is nowhere thick it was strange to see them making for the open leads and thin places to blow.

Friday, March 31. – I studied the wind blowing along the ridge yesterday and came to the conclusion that a comparatively thin shaft of air was moving along the ridge from Erebus. On either side of the ridge it seemed to pour down from the ridge itself – there was practically no wind on the sea ice off Pram Point, and to the westward of Hut Point the frost smoke was drifting to the N.W. The temperature ranges about zero. It seems to be almost certain that the perpetual wind is due to the open winter. Meanwhile the sea refuses to freeze over.

Wright pointed out the very critical point which zero temperature represents in the freezing of salt water, being the freezing temperature of concentrated brine – a very few degrees above or below zero would make all the difference to the rate of increase of the ice thickness.

Yesterday the ice was 8 inches in places east of Cape Armitage and 6 inches in our Bay: it was said to be fast to the south of the Glacier Tongue well beyond Turtleback Island and to the north out of the Islands, except for a strip of water immediately north of the Tongue.

We are good for another week in pretty well every commodity and shall then have to reduce luxuries. But we have plenty of seal meat, blubber, and biscuit, and can therefore remain for a much longer period if needs be. Meanwhile the days are growing shorter and the weather colder.

Saturday, April 1. – The wind yesterday was blowing across the Ridge from the top down on the sea to the west: very little wind on the eastern slopes and practically none at Pram Point. A seal came up in our Bay and was killed. Taylor found a number of fish frozen into the sea ice – he says there are several in a small area.

The pressure ridges in Pram Point Bay are estimated by Wright to have set up about 3 feet. This ice has been 'in' about ten days. It is now safe to work pretty well anywhere south of Hut Point.

Went to Third Crater (next Castle Rock) yesterday. The ice seems to be holding in the near Bay from a point near Hutton Rocks to Glacier; also in the whole of the North Bay except for a tongue of open water immediately north of the Glacier.

The wind is the same today as yesterday, and the open water apparently not reduced by a square yard. I'm feeling impatient.

Sunday, April 2, a.m. – Went round Cape Armitage to Pram Point on sea ice for first time yesterday afternoon. Ice solid everywhere, except off the Cape, where there are numerous open pools. Can only imagine layers of comparatively warm water brought to the surface by shallows. The ice between the pools is fairly shallow. One Emperor killed off the Cape. Several *skuas* seen – three seals up in our Bay – several off Pram Point in the shelter of Horse Shoe Bay. A great many fish in sea ice – mostly small, but a second species 5 or 6 inches long: imagine they are chased by seals and caught in brashy ice where they are unable to escape. Came back over hill: glorious sunset, brilliant crimson clouds in west.

Returned to find wind dropping, the first time for three days. It turned to north in the evening. Splendid aurora in the night; a bright band of light from S.S.W. to E.N.E. passing within 10° of the zenith with two waving spirals at the summit. This morning sea to north covered with ice. Min. temp. for night −5°, but I think most of the ice was brought in by the wind. Things look more hopeful. Ice now continuous to Cape Evans, but very thin as far as Glacier Tongue; three or four days of calm or light winds should make everything firm.

Wednesday, *April* 5, a.m. − The east wind has continued with a short break on Sunday for five days, increasing in violence and gradually becoming colder and more charged with snow until yesterday, when we had a thick overcast day with falling and driving snow and temperature down to −11°.

Went beyond Castle Rock on Sunday and Monday mornings with Griffith Taylor.

Think the wind fairly local and that the Strait has frozen over to the north, as streams of drift snow and ice crystals (off the cliffs) were building up the ice sheet towards the wind. Monday we could see the approaching white sheet − yesterday it was visibly closer to land, though the wind had not decreased. Walking was little pleasure on either day: yesterday climbed about hills to see all possible. No one else left the hut. In the evening the wind fell and freezing continued during night (min. −17°). This morning there is ice everywhere. I cannot help thinking it has come to stay. In Arrival Bay it is 6 to 7 inches thick, but the new pools beyond have only 1 inch of the regular elastic sludgy new ice. The sky cleared last night, and this morning we have sunshine for the first time for many days. If this weather holds for a day we shall be all right. We are getting towards the end of our luxuries, so that it is quite time we made a move − we are very near the end of the sugar.

The *skuas* seem to have gone, the last was seen on Sunday. These birds were very shy towards the end of their stay, also very dark in plumage; they did not seem hungry, and yet it must have been difficult for them to get food.

The seals are coming up in our Bay − five last night. Luckily the dogs have not yet discovered them or the fact that the sea ice will bear them.

Had an interesting talk with Taylor on agglomerate and basaltic dykes of Castle Rock. The perfection of the small cone craters below Castle Rock seem to support the theory we have come to, that there have been volcanic disturbances since the recession of the greater ice sheet.

It is a great thing having Wright to fog out the ice problems, and he has had a good opportunity of observing many interesting things here. He is keeping notes of ice changes and a keen eye on ice phenomena; we have many discussions.

Yesterday Wilson prepared a fry of seal meat with penguin blubber. It had a flavour like cod-liver oil and was not much appreciated – some ate their share, and I think all would have done so if we had had sledging appetites – shades of *Discovery* days!![16]

This Emperor weighed anything from 88 to 96 lbs., and therefore approximated to or exceeded the record.

The dogs are doing pretty well with one or two exceptions. Deek is the worst, but I begin to think all will pull through.

Thursday, April 6, a.m. – The weather continued fine and clear yesterday – one of the very few fine days we have had since our arrival at the hut.

The sun shone continuously from early morning till it set behind the northern hills about 5 p.m. The sea froze completely, but with only a thin sheet to the north. A fairly strong northerly wind sprang up, causing this thin ice to override and to leave several open leads near the land. In the forenoon I went to the edge of the new ice with Wright. It looked at the limit of safety and we did not venture far. The over-riding is interesting: the edge of one sheet splits as it rises and slides over the other sheet in long tongues which creep onward impressively. Whilst motion lasts there is continuous music, a medley of high-pitched but tuneful notes – one might imagine small birds chirping in a wood. The ice sings, we say.

p.m. – In the afternoon went nearly two miles to the north over the young ice; found it about 3½ inches thick. At supper arranged programme for shift to Cape Evans – men to go on Saturday – dogs Sunday – ponies Monday – all subject to maintenance of good weather of course.

Friday, April 7. – Went north over ice with Atkinson, Bowers, Taylor, Cherry-Garrard; found the thickness nearly 5 inches everywhere except in open water leads, which remain open in many places. As we got away from the land we got on an interesting surface of small pancakes, much capped and pressed up, a sort of mosaic. This is the ice which was built up from lee side of the Strait, spreading across to windward against the strong winds of Monday and Tuesday.

Another point of interest was the manner in which the over-riding ice sheets had scraped the under floes.

Taylor fell in when rather foolishly trying to cross a thinly covered lead – he had a very scared face for a moment or two whilst we hurried to the rescue, but hauled himself out with his ice axe without our help and walked back with Cherry.

The remainder of us went on till abreast of the sulphur cones under Castle Rock, when we made for the shore, and with a little mutual help climbed the cliff and returned by land.

As far as one can see all should be well for our return tomorrow, but the sky is clouding tonight and a change of weather seems imminent. Three successive fine days seem near the limit in this region.

We have picked up quite a number of fish frozen in the ice – the larger ones about the size of a herring and the smaller of a minnow. We imagined both had been driven into the slushy ice by seals, but today Gran found a large fish frozen in the act of swallowing a small one. It looks as though both small and large are caught when one is chasing the other.

We have achieved such great comfort here that one is half sorry to leave – it is a fine healthy existence with many hours spent in the open and generally some interesting object for our walks abroad. The hill climbing gives excellent exercise – we shall miss much of it at Cape Evans. But I am anxious to get back and see that all is well at the latter, as for a long time I have been wondering how our beach has withstood the shocks of northerly winds. The thought that the hut may have been damaged by the sea in one of the heavy storms will not be banished.

A sketch of the life at Hut Point

We gather around the fire seated on packing-cases, with a hunk of bread and butter and a steaming pannikin of tea, and life is well worth living. After lunch we are out and about again; there is little to tempt a long stay indoors, and exercise keeps us all the fitter.

The failing light and approach of supper drives us home again with good appetites about 5 or 6 o'clock, and then the cooks rival one another in preparing succulent dishes of fried seal liver. A single dish may not seem to offer much opportunity of variation, but a lot can be done with a little flour, a handful of raisins, a spoonful of curry powder, or the addition of a little boiled pea meal. Be this as it may, we never tire of our dish and exclamations of satisfaction can be heard every night – or nearly every night; for two nights ago [April 4] Wilson, who has proved a genius in the invention of 'plats', almost ruined his reputation. He proposed to fry the seal liver in penguin blubber, suggesting that the latter could be freed from all rankness. The blubber was obtained and rendered down with great care, the result appeared as delightfully pure fat free from smell; but appearances were deceptive; the 'fry' proved redolent of penguin, a concentrated essence of that peculiar flavour which faintly lingers in the meat and should not be emphasised. Three heroes got through their pannikins, but the rest of us decided to be contented with cocoa and biscuit after tasting the first mouthful.[16] After supper we have an hour or so of smoking and conversation – a cheering, pleasant hour – in which reminiscences are exchanged by a company which has very literally had world-wide experience. There is scarce a country under the sun which one or another of us has not travelled in, so diverse are our origins and occupations. An hour or so after supper we tail off one by one, spread out our sleeping-bags, take off our shoes and creep into comfort, for our reindeer bags are really warm and comfortable now that they have had a chance of drying, and the hut retains some of the heat generated in it. Thanks to the success of the blubber lamps and to a fair supply of candles, we can muster ample light to read for another hour or two, and so tucked up in our furs we study the social and political questions of the past decade.

We muster no less than sixteen. Seven of us pretty well cover the floor of one wing of the L-shaped enclosure, four sleep in the other wing, which also holds the store, whilst the remaining five occupy the annexe and affect to find the colder temperature more salubrious. Everyone can manage eight or nine hours' sleep without a break, and not a few would have little difficulty in sleeping the clock round, which goes to show that our extremely simple life is an exceedingly healthy one, though with faces and hands blackened with smoke, appearances might not lead an outsider to suppose it.

Sunday, April 9, a.m. – On Friday night it grew overcast and the wind went to the south. During the whole of yesterday and last night it blew a moderate blizzard – the temperature at highest +5°, a relatively small amount of drift. On Friday night the ice in the Strait went out from a line meeting the shore ³⁄₄ mile north of Hut Point. A crack off Hut Point and curving to N.W. opened to about 15 or 20 feet, the opening continuing on the north side of the Point. It is strange that the ice thus opened should have remained.

Ice cleared out to the north directly wind commenced – it didn't wait a single instant, showing that our journey over it earlier in the day was a very risky proceeding – the uncertainty of these conditions is beyond words, but there shall be no more of this foolish venturing on young ice. This decision seems to put off the return of the ponies to a comparatively late date.

Yesterday went to the second crater, Arrival Heights, hoping to see the condition of the northerly bays, but could see little or nothing owing to drift. A white line dimly seen on the horizon seemed to indicate that the ice drifted out has not gone far.

Some skuas were seen yesterday, a very late date. The seals disinclined to come on the ice; one can be seen at Cape Armitage this morning, but it is two or three days since there was one up in our Bay. It will certainly be some time before the ponies can be got back.

Monday, April 10, p.m. – Intended to make for Cape Evans this morning. Called hands early, but when we were ready for departure after breakfast, the sky became more overcast and snow began to fall. It continued off and on all day, only clearing as the sun set. It would have been the worst condition possible for our attempt, as we could not have seen more than 100 yards.

Conditions look very unfavourable for the continued freezing of the Strait.

Thursday, April 13. – Started from Hut Point 9 a.m. Tuesday. Party consisted of self, Bowers, P. O. Evans, Taylor, one tent;

Evans, Gran, Crean, Debenham, and Wright, second tent. Left Wilson in charge at Hut Point with Meares, Forde, Keohane, Oates, Atkinson, and Cherry-Garrard. All gave us a pull up the ski slope; it had become a point of honour to take this slope without a 'breather'. I find such an effort trying in the early morning, but had to go through with it.

Weather fine; we marched past Castle Rock, east of it; the snow was soft on the slopes, showing the shelter afforded – continued to traverse the ridge for the first time – found quite good surface much wind-swept – passed both cones on the ridge on the west side. Caught a glimpse of fast ice in the Bays either side of Glacier as expected, but in the near Bay its extent was very small. Evidently we should have to go well along the ridge before descending, and then the problem would be how to get down over the cliffs. On to Hutton Rocks 7½ miles from the start – here it was very icy and windswept, inhospitable – the wind got up and light became bad just at the critical moment, so we camped and had some tea at 2 p.m. A clearance half an hour later allowed us to see a possible descent to the ice cliffs, but between Hutton Rocks and Erebus all the slope was much cracked and crevassed. We chose a clear track to the edge of the cliffs, but could find no low place in these, the lowest part being 24 feet sheer drop. Arriving here the wind increased, the snow drifting off the ridge – we had to decide quickly; I got myself to the edge and made standing places to work the rope; dug away at the cornice, well situated for such work in harness. Got three people lowered by the Alpine rope – E. Evans, Bowers, and Taylor – then sent down the sledges, which went down in fine style, fully packed – then the remainder of the party. For the last three, drove a stake hard down in the snow and used the rope round it, the men being lowered by people below – came down last myself. Quite a neat and speedy bit of work and all done in 20 minutes without serious frostbite – quite pleased with the result.

We found pulling to Glacier Tongue very heavy over the surface of ice covered with salt crystals, and reached Glacier Tongue about 5.30; found a low place and got the sledges up the 6 ft. wall pretty easily. Stiff incline, but easy pulling on hard surface – the light was failing and the surface criss-crossed with innumerable cracks; several of us fell in these with risk of strain, but the north side was well snow-covered and easy, with a good valley leading to a low ice cliff – here a broken piece afforded easy descent. I decided to push on for Cape Evans, so camped for tea at 6. At 6.30 found darkness suddenly arrived; it was very difficult to see anything – we got down on the sea ice, very heavy pulling, but plodded on for some hours; at 10 arrived close under Little Razorback Island, and not being able to see anything ahead, decided to camp and got to sleep at 11.30 in no very comfortable circumstances.

The wind commenced to rise during night. We found a roaring blizzard in the morning. We had many alarms for the safety of the ice on which the camp was pitched. Bowers and Taylor climbed the island; reported wind terrific on the summit – sweeping on either side but comparatively calm immediately to windward and to leeward. Waited all day in hopes of a lull; at 3 I went round the island myself with Bowers, and found a little ice platform close under the weather side; resolved to shift camp here. It took two very cold hours, but we gained great shelter, the cliffs rising almost sheer from the tents. Only now and again a whirling wind current eddied down on the tents, which were well secured, but the noise of the wind sweeping over the rocky ridge above our heads was deafening; we could scarcely hear ourselves speak. Settled down for our second night with little comfort, and slept better, knowing we could not be swept out to sea, but provisions were left only for one more meal.

During the night the wind moderated and we could just see outline of land.

I roused the party at 7 a.m. and we were soon under weigh, with a desperately cold and stiff breeze and frozen clothes; it was very heavy pulling, but the distance only two miles. Arrived off the point about ten and found sea ice continued around it. It was a very great relief to see the hut on rounding it and to hear that all was well.

Another pony, Hackenschmidt, and one dog reported dead, but this certainly is not worse than expected. All the other animals are in good form.

Delighted with everything I see in the hut. Simpson has done wonders, but indeed so has everyone else, and I must leave description to a future occasion.

Friday, April 14. – Good Friday. Peaceful day. Wind continuing 20 to 30 miles per hour.

Had Divine Service.

Saturday, April 15. – Weather continuing thoroughly bad. Wind blowing from 30 to 40 miles an hour all day; drift bad, and tonight snow falling. I am waiting to get back to Hut Point with relief stores. Tonight sent up signal light to inform them there of our safe arrival – an answering flare was shown.

Sunday, April 16. – Same wind as yesterday up to 6 o'clock, when it fell calm with gusts from the north.

Have exercised the ponies today and got my first good look at them. I scarcely like to express the mixed feelings with which I am able to regard this remnant.

Freezing of bays. Cape Evans

March 15. – General young ice formed.

March 19. – Bay cleared except strip inside Inaccessible and Razorback Islands to Corner Turk's Head.

March 20. – Everything cleared.

March 25. – Sea froze over inside Islands for good.

March 28. – Sea frozen as far as seen.

March 30. – Remaining only inside Islands.

April 1. – Limit Cape to Island.

April 6. – Present limit freezing in Strait and in North Bay.

April 9. – Strait cleared except former limit and *some* ice in North Bay likely to remain.

CHAPTER EIGHT

Home impressions and an excursion

Impressions on returning to the Hut, April 13, 1911

In choosing the site of the hut on our Home Beach I had thought of the possibility of northerly winds bringing a swell, but had argued, first, that no heavy northerly swell had ever been recorded in the Sound; secondly, that a strong northerly wind was bound to bring pack which would damp the swell; thirdly, that the locality was excellently protected by the Barne Glacier; and finally, that the beach itself showed no signs of having been swept by the sea, the rock fragments composing it being completely angular.

When the hut was erected and I found that its foundation was only 11 feet above the level of the sea ice, I had a slight misgiving, but reassured myself again by reconsidering the circumstances that afforded shelter to the beach.

The fact that such question had been considered makes it easier to understand the attitude of mind that readmitted doubt in the face of phenomenal conditions.

The event has justified my original arguments, but I must confess a sense of having assumed security without sufficient proof in a case where an error of judgment might have had dire consequences.

It was not until I found all safe at the Home Station that I realised how anxious I had been concerning it. In a normal season no thought of its having been in danger would have occurred to me, but since the loss of the ponies and the breaking of the Glacier Tongue I could not rid myself of the fear that misfortune was in the air and that some abnormal swell had swept the beach; gloomy thoughts of the havoc that might have been wrought by such an event would arise in spite of the sound reasons which had originally led me to choose the site of the hut as a safe one.

The late freezing of the sea, the terrible continuance of wind and the abnormalities to which I have referred had gradually strengthened the profound distrust with which I had been forced to regard our mysterious Antarctic climate until my imagination conjured up many forms of disaster as possibly falling on those from whom I had parted for so long.

We marched towards Cape Evans under the usually miserable conditions which attend the breaking of camp in a cold wind after a heavy blizzard. The outlook was dreary in the grey light of early morning, our clothes were frozen stiff and our fingers, wet and cold in the tent, had been frostbitten in packing the sledges.

A few comforting signs of life appeared as we approached the Cape: some old footprints in the snow, a long silk thread from the meteorologist's balloon; but we saw nothing more as we neared the rocks of the promontory and the many grounded bergs which were scattered off it.

To my surprise the fast ice extended past the Cape and we were able to round it into the North Bay. Here we saw the weather screen on Wind Vane Hill, and a moment later turned a small headland and brought the hut in full view. It was intact – stables, outhouses and all; evidently the sea had left it undisturbed. I breathed a huge sigh of relief. We watched two figures at work near the stables and wondered when they would see us. In a moment or two they did so, and fled inside the hut to carry the news of our arrival. Three minutes later all nine occupants* were streaming over the floe towards us with shouts of welcome. There were eager inquiries as to mutual welfare and it took but a minute to learn the most important events of the quiet station life which had been led since our departure. These under the circumstances might well be considered the deaths of one pony and one dog. The pony was that which had been nicknamed Hackenschmidt from his vicious habit of using both fore and hind legs in attacking those who came near him. He had been obviously of different breed from the other ponies, being of lighter and handsomer shape, suggestive of a strain of Arab blood. From no cause which could be discovered either by the symptoms of his illness or the post-mortem held by Nelson could a reason be found for his death. In

* viz. Simpson, Nelson, Day, Ponting, Lashly, Clissold, Hooper, Anton and Demetri.

spite of the best feeding and every care he had gradually sickened until he was too weak to stand, and in this condition there had been no option but to put him out of misery. Anton considers the death of Hackenschmidt to have been an act of 'cussedness' – the result of a determination to do no work for the Expedition!! Although the loss is serious I remember doubts which I had as to whether this animal could be anything but a source of trouble to us. He had been most difficult to handle all through, showing a vicious, intractable temper. I had foreseen great difficulties with him, especially during the early part of any journey on which he was taken, and this consideration softened the news of his death. The dog had been left behind in a very sick condition, and this loss was not a great surprise.

These items were the worst of the small budget of news that awaited me; for the rest, the hut arrangements had worked out in the most satisfactory manner possible and the scientific routine of observations was in full swing. After our primitive life at Cape Armitage it was wonderful to enter the precincts of our warm, dry Cape Evans home. The interior space seemed palatial, the light resplendent, and the comfort luxurious. It was very good to eat in civilised fashion, to enjoy the first bath for three months, and have contact with clean, dry clothing. Such fleeting hours of comfort (for custom soon banished their delight) are the treasured remembrance of every Polar traveller. They throw into sharpest contrast the hardships of the past and the comforts of the present, and for the time he revels in the unaccustomed physical content-ment that results.

I was not many hours or even minutes in the hut before I was haled round to observe in detail the transformation which had taken place during my absence, and in which a very proper pride was taken by those who had wrought it.

Simpson's Corner was the first visited. Here the eye travelled over numerous shelves laden with a profusion of self-recording instruments, electric batteries and switchboards, whilst the ear caught the ticking of many clocks, the gentle whirr of a motor and occasionally the trembling note of an electric bell. But such sights and sounds conveyed only an impression of the delicate method-ical means by which the daily and hourly variations of our weather conditions were being recorded – a mere glimpse of the intricate arrangements of a first-class meteorological station – the one and only station of that order which has been established in Polar regions. It took me days and even months to realise fully the aims of our meteorologist and the scientific accuracy with which he was achieving them. When I did so to an adequate extent I wrote some description of his work which will be found in the following pages of this volume.* The first impression which I am here describing was more confused; I appreciated only that by going to 'Simpson's Corner' one could ascertain at a glance how hard the wind was blowing and had been blowing, how the barometer was varying, to what degree of cold the thermometer had descended; if one were still more inquisitive he could further inform himself as to the electrical tension of the atmosphere and other matters of like import. That such knowledge could be gleaned without a visit to the open air was an obvious advantage to those who were clothing themselves to face it, whilst the ability to study the variation of a storm without exposure savoured of no light victory of mind over matter.

The dark room stands next to the parasitologist's side of the bench which flanks Sunny Jim's Corner – an involved sentence. To be more exact, the physicists adjust their instruments and write up books at a bench which projects at right angles to the end wall of the hut; the opposite side of this bench is allotted to Atkinson, who is to write with his back to the dark room. Atkinson being still absent his corner was unfurnished, and my attention was next claimed by the occupant of the dark room beyond Atkinson's limit. The art of photography has never been so well housed within the Polar regions and rarely without them. Such a palatial chamber for the development of negatives and prints can only be justified by the quality of the work produced in it, and is only justified in our case by the possession of such an artist as Ponting. He was eager to show me the results of his summer work, and meanwhile my eye took in the neat shelves with their array of cameras, &c., the porcelain sink and automatic water tap, the two acetylene gas burners with their shading screens, and the general obviousness of all conveniences of the photographic art. Here, indeed, was encouragement for the best results, and to the photographer be all praise, for it

* See Chapter 9 and Chapter 11.

is mainly his hand which has executed the designs which his brain conceived. In this may be clearly seen the advantage of a traveller's experience. Ponting has had to fend for himself under primitive conditions in a new land; the result is a 'handy man' with every form of tool and in any circumstances. Thus, when building operations were to the fore and mechanical labour scarce, Ponting returned to the shell of his apartment with only the raw material for completing it. In the shortest possible space of time shelves and tanks were erected, doors hung and windows framed, and all in a workmanlike manner commanding the admiration of all beholders. It was well that speed could be commanded for such work, since the fleeting hours of the summer season had been altogether too few to be spared from the immediate service of photography. Ponting's nervous temperament allowed no waste of time – for him fine weather meant no sleep; he decided that lost opportunities should be as rare as circumstances would permit.

This attitude was now manifested in the many yards of cinematograph film remaining on hand and yet greater number recorded as having been sent back in the ship, in the boxes of negatives lying on the shelves and a well-filled album of prints.

Of the many admirable points in this work perhaps the most notable are Ponting's eye for a picture and the mastery he has acquired of ice subjects; the composition of most of his pictures is extraordinarily good, he seems to know by instinct the exact value of foreground and middle distance and of the introduction of 'life', whilst with more technical skill in the manipulation of screens and exposures he emphasises the subtle shadows of the snow and reproduces its wondrously transparent texture. He is an artist in love with his work, and it was good to hear his enthusiasm for results of the past and plans for the future.

Long before I could gaze my fill at the contents of the dark room I was led to the biologists' cubicle; Nelson and Day had from the first decided to camp together, each having a habit of methodical neatness; both were greatly relieved when the arrangement was approved, and they were freed from the chance of an untidy companion. No attempt had been made to furnish this cubicle before our departure on the autumn journey, but now on my return I found it an example of the best utilisation of space. The prevailing note was neatness; the biologist's micro-scope stood on a neat bench surrounded by enamel dishes, vessels, and books neatly arranged; behind him, when seated, rose two neat bunks with neat, closely curtained drawers for clothing and neat reflecting sconces for candles; overhead was a neat arrangement for drying socks with several nets, neatly bestowed. The carpentering to produce this effect had been of quite a high order, and was in very marked contrast with that exhibited for the hasty erections in other cubicles. The pillars and boarding of the bunks had carefully finished edges and were stained to mahogany brown. Nelson's bench is situated very conveniently under the largest of the hut windows, and had also an acetylene lamp, so that both in summer and winter he has all conveniences for his indoor work.

Day appeared to have been unceasingly busy during my absence. Everyone paid tribute to his mechanical skill and expressed gratitude for the help he had given in adjusting instruments and generally helping forward the scientific work. He was entirely responsible for the heating, lighting, and ventilating arrange-ments, and as all these appear satisfactory he deserved much praise. Particulars concerning these arrangements I shall give later; as a first impression it is sufficient to note that the warmth and lighting of the hut seemed as good as could be desired, whilst for our comfort the air seemed fresh and pure. Day had also to report some progress with the motor sledges, but this matter also I leave for future consideration.

My attention was very naturally turned from the heating arrange-ments to the cooking stove and its custodian, Clissold. I had already heard much of the surpassingly satisfactory meals which his art had produced, and had indeed already a first experience of them. Now I was introduced to the cook's corner with its range and ovens, its pots and pans, its side tables and well-covered shelves. Much was to be gathered therefrom, although a good meal by no means depends only on kitchen conveniences. It was gratifying to learn that the stove had proved itself economical and the patent fuel blocks a most convenient and efficient substitute for coal. Save for the thickness of the furnace cheeks and the size of the oven Clissold declared himself wholly satisfied. He feared that the oven would prove too small to keep up a constant supply of bread for all hands; nevertheless he introduced me to this oven with an air of pride which I soon found to be fully justified. For connected therewith was a contrivance for which he was entirely respons- ible, and which in its ingenuity rivalled any of which the hut could boast. The interior of the oven was so arranged that the 'rising' of the bread completed an electric circuit, thereby ringing a bell and switching on a red lamp. Clissold had realised that the continuous ringing of the bell would not be soothing to the nerves of our party, nor the continuous burning of the lamp calculated to prolong its life, and he had therefore added the clockwork mechanism which automatically broke the circuit after a short interval of time; further, this clockwork mechanism could be made to control the emersion of the same warning signals at intervals of time varied according to the desire of the operator – thus because, when in bed, he would desire a signal at short periods, but if absent from the hut he would wish to know at a glance what had happened when he returned. Judged by any standard it was a remarkably pretty little device, but when I learnt that it had been made from odds and ends, such as a cog-wheel or spring here and a cell or magnet there, begged from other departments, I began to realise that we had a very exceptional cook. Later when I found that Clissold was called in to consult on the ailments of Simpson's motor and that he was capable of constructing a dog sledge out of packing cases, I was less sur- prised, because I knew by this time that he had had considerable training in mechanical work before he turned his attention to pots and pans.

My first impressions include matters to which I was naturally eager to give an early half-hour, namely the housing of our animals. I found herein that praise was as justly due to our Russian boys as to my fellow Englishmen.

Anton with Lashly's help had completed the furnishing of the stables. Neat stalls occupied the whole length of the 'lean-to', the sides so boarded that sprawling legs could not be entangled beneath and the front well covered with tin sheet to defeat the 'cribbers'. I could but sigh again to think of the stalls that must now remain empty, whilst appreciating that there was ample room for the safe harbourage of the ten beasts that remain, be the winter never so cold or the winds so wild.

Later we have been able to give double space to all but two or three of our animals, in which they can lie down if they are so inclined.

The ponies look fairly fit considering the low diet on which they have been kept; their coats were surprisingly long and woolly in contrast with those of the animals I had left at Hut Point. At this time they were being exercised by Lashly, Anton, Demetri, Hooper, and Clissold, and as a rule were ridden, the sea having only recently frozen. The exercise ground had lain on the boulder-strewn sand of the home beach and extending towards the Skua lake; and across these stretches I soon saw barebacked figures dashing at speed, and not a few amusing incidents in which horse and rider parted with abrupt lack of ceremony. I didn't think this quite the most desirable form of exercise for the beasts, but decided to leave matters as they were till our pony manager returned.

Demetri had only five or six dogs left in charge, but these looked fairly fit, all things considered, and it was evident the boy was bent on taking every care of them, for he had not only provided shelters, but had built a small 'lean-to' which would serve as a hospital for any animal whose stomach or coat needed nursing.

Such were in broad outline the impressions I received on my first return to our home station; they were almost wholly pleasant and, as I have shown, in happy contrast with the fears that had assailed me on the homeward route. As the days went by I was able to fill in the detail in equally pleasant fashion, to watch the development of fresh arrangements and the improvement of old ones. Finally, in this way I was brought to realise what an extensive and intricate but eminently satisfactory organisation I had made myself responsible for.

NOTES ON FLYLEAF OF FRESH MS. BOOK

Genus Homo, Species Sapiens!

FLOTSAM

Wm. Barents's house in Novaya Zemlya built 1596. Found by Capt. Carlsen 1871 (275 years later) intact, everything inside as left. What of this hut?

The ocean-girt continent.

Might have seemed almost heroic if any higher end than excessive love of gain and traffic had animated the design.   MILTON

He is not worthy to live at all, who, for fear and danger of death, shunneth his country's service or his own honour, since death is inevitable and the fame of virtue immortal.   Sir Humphrey Gilbert

There is no part of the world that can not be reached by man. When the 'can be' is turned to 'has been' the Geographical Society will have altered its status.

At the whirring loom of time unawed
  I weave the living garment of God.   Goethe

By all means think yourself big but don't think everyone else small.

The man who knows everyone's job isn't much good at his own.

When you are attacked unjustly avoid the appearance of evil, but avoid also the appearance of being too good. A man can't be too good, but he can appear too good.

Monday, April 17. – Started from C. Evans with two 10-ft. sledges.
        Party 1.   Self, Lashly, Day, Demetri.
        Party 2.   Bowers, Nelson, Crean, Hooper.

We left at 8 a.m., taking our personal equipment, a week's provision of sledging food, and butter, oatmeal, flour, lard, chocolate, &c., for the hut.

Two of the ponies hauled the sledges to within a mile of the Glacier Tongue; the wind, which had been north, here suddenly shifted to S.E., very biting. (The wind remained north at C. Evans during the afternoon, the ponies walked back into it.) Sky overcast, very bad light. Found the place to get on the glacier, but then lost the track – crossed more or less direct, getting amongst many cracks. Came down in bay near the open water – stumbled over the edge to an easy drift. More than once on these trips I as leader have suddenly disappeared from the sight of the others, affording some consternation till they got close enough to see what has happened. The pull over sea ice was very heavy and in face of strong wind and drift. Every member of the party was frostbitten about the face, several with very cold feet. Pushed on after repairs. Found drift streaming off the ice cliff, a new cornice formed and our rope buried at both ends. The party getting cold, I decided to camp, have tea, and shift foot gear. Whilst tea was preparing, Bowers and I went south, then north, along the cliffs to find a place to ascend – nearly everywhere ascent seemed impossible in the vicinity of Hutton Rocks or north, but eventually we found an overhanging cornice close to our rope.

After lunch we unloaded a sledge, which, held high on end by four men, just reached the edge of the cornice. Clambering up over backs and up sledge I used an ice-axe to cut steps over the cornice and thus managed to get on top, then cut steps and surmounted the edge of the cornice. Helped Bowers up with the rope; others followed – then the gear was hauled up piecemeal. For Crean, the last man up, we lowered the sledge over the cornice and used a bowline in the other end of the rope on top of it. He came up grinning with delight, and we all thought the ascent rather a cunning piece of work. It was fearfully cold work, but everyone working with rare intelligence, we eventually got everything up and repacked the sledge; glad to get in harness again. Then a heavy pull up a steep slope in wretched light, making detour to left to avoid crevasses. We reached the top and plodded on past the craters as nearly as possible as on the outward route. The party was pretty exhausted and very wet with perspiration. Approaching Castle Rock the weather and light improved. Camped on Barrier Slope north of Castle Rock about 9 p.m. Night cold but calm, −38° during night; slept pretty well.

Tuesday, April 18. – Hut Point. Good moonlight at 7 a.m. – had breakfast. Broke camp very quickly – Lashly splendid at camp work as of old – very heavy pull up to Castle Rock, sweated much. This sweating in cold temperature is a serious drawback. Reached Hut Point 1 p.m. Found all well in excellent spirits – didn't seem to want us much!!

Party reported very bad weather since we left, cold blizzard, then continuous S.W. wind with −20° and below. The open water was right up to Hut Point, wind absolutely preventing all freezing along shore. Wilson reported skua gull seen Monday.

Found party much shorter of blubber than I had expected – they were only just keeping themselves supplied with a seal killed two days before and one as we arrived. Actually less fast ice than when we left!

Wednesday, April 19. – Hut Point. Calm during night, sea froze over at noon, 4½ inches thick off Hut Point, showing how easily the sea will freeze when the chance is given.

Three seals reported on the ice; all hands out after breakfast and the liver and blubber of all three seals were brought in. This relieves one of a little anxiety, leaving a twelve days' stock, in which time other seals ought to be coming up. I am making arrangements to start back tomorrow, but at present it is overcast and wind coming up from the south. This afternoon, all ice frozen last night went out quietly; the sea tried to freeze behind it, but the wind freshened soon. The ponies were exercised yesterday and today; they look pretty fit, but their coats are not so good as those in winter quarters – they want fatty foods.

Am preparing to start tomorrow, satisfied that the *Discovery* Hut is very comfortable and life very liveable in it. The dogs are much the same, all looking pretty fit except Vaida and Rabchick – neither of which seem to get good coats. I am greatly struck with the advantages of experience in Crean and Lashly for all work about camps.

Thursday, April 20. – Hut Point. Everything ready for starting this morning, but of course it 'blizzed'. Weather impossible – much wind and drift from south. Wind turned to S.E. in afternoon – temperatures low. Went for walk to Cape Armitage, but it is really very unpleasant. The wind blowing round the Cape is absolutely blighting, force 7 and temperature below –30°. Sea a black cauldron covered with dark frost smoke. No ice can form in such weather.

Friday, April 21. – Started homeward at 10.30.

Left Meares in charge of station with Demetri to help with dogs, Lashly and Keohane to look out for ponies, Nelson and Day and Forde to get some idea of the life and experience. Homeward party, therefore:

Self	Bowers
Wilson	Oates
Atkinson	Cherry-Garrard
Crean	Hooper

As usual all hands pulled up Ski slope, which we took without a halt. Lashly and Demetri came nearly to Castle Rock – very cold side wind and some frostbites. We reached the last downward slope about 2.30; at the cliff edge found the cornice gone – heavy wind and drift worse than before, if anything. We bustled things, and after tantalising delays with the rope got Bowers and some others on the floe, then lowered the sledges packed; three men, including Crean and myself, slid down last on the Alpine rope – doubled and taken round an ash stave, so that we were able to unreeve the end and recover the rope – we recovered also most of the old Alpine rope, all except a piece buried in snow on the sea ice and dragged down under the slush, just like the *Discovery* boats; I could not have supposed this could happen in so short a time.[17]

By the time all stores were on the floe, with swirling drift about us, everyone was really badly cold – one of those moments for quick action. We harnessed and dashed for the shelter of the cliffs; up tents, and hot tea as quick as possible; after this and some shift of foot gear all were much better. Heavy plod over the sea ice, starting at 4.30 – very bad light on the glacier, and we lost our way as usual, stumbling into many crevasses, but finally descended in the old place; by this time sweating much. Crean reported our sledge pulling much more heavily than the other one. Marched on to Little Razorback Island without halt, our own sledge dragging fearfully. Crean said there was great difference in the sledges, though loads were equal. Bowers politely assented when I voiced this sentiment, but I'm sure he and his party thought it the plea of tired men. However, there was nothing like proof, and he readily assented to change sledges. The difference was really extraordinary; we felt the new sledge a featherweight compared with the old, and set up a great pace for the home quarters regardless of how much we perspired. We arrived at the hut (two miles away) ten minutes ahead of the others, who by this time were quite convinced as to the difference in the sledges.

The difference was only marked when pulling over the salt-covered sea ice; on snow the sledges seemed pretty much the same. It is due to the grain of the wood in the runners and is worth looking into.

We all arrived bathed in sweat – our garments were soaked through, and as we took off our wind clothes showers of ice fell on the floor. The accumulation was almost incredible and shows the whole trouble of sledging in cold weather. It would have been very uncomfortable to have camped in the open under such conditions, and assuredly a winter and spring party cannot afford to get so hot if they wish to retain any semblance of comfort.

Our excellent cook had just the right meal prepared for us – an enormous dish of rice and figs, and cocoa in a bucket! The hut party were all very delighted to see us, and the fittings and comforts of the hut are amazing to the newcomers.

Saturday, April 22. – Cape Evans, Winter Quarters. The sledging season is at an end. It's good to be back in spite of all the losses we have sustained.

Today we enjoy a very exceptional calm. The sea is freezing over of course, but unfortunately our view from Observation Hill is very limited. Oates and the rest are exercising the ponies. I have been sorting my papers and getting ready for the winter work.

CHAPTER NINE

The work and the workers

Sunday, April 23. – Winter Quarters. The last day of the sun and a very glorious view of its golden light over the Barne Glacier. We could not see the sun itself on account of the Glacier, the fine ice cliffs of which were in deep shadow under the rosy rays.

Impression. – The long mild twilight which like a silver clasp unites today with yesterday; when morning and evening sit together hand in hand beneath the starless sky of midnight.

It blew hard last night and most of the young ice has gone as expected. Patches seem to be remaining south of the Glacier Tongue and the Island and off our own bay. In this very queer season it appears as though the final freezing is to be reached by gradual increments to the firmly established ice.

Had Divine Service. Have only seven hymn-books, those brought on shore for our first Service being very stupidly taken back to the ship.

I begin to think we are *too* comfortable in the hut and hope it will not make us slack; but it is good to see everyone in such excellent spirits – so far not a rift in the social arrangements.

Monday, April 24. – A night watchman has been instituted mainly for the purpose of observing the aurora, of which the displays have been feeble so far. The observer is to look round every hour or oftener if there is aught to be seen. He is allowed cocoa and sardines with bread and butter – the cocoa can be made over an acetylene Bunsen burner, part of Simpson's outfit. I took the first turn last night; the remainder of the afterguard follow in rotation. The long night hours give time to finish up a number of small tasks – the hut remains quite warm though the fires are out.

Simpson has been practising with balloons during our absence. This morning he sent one up for trial. The balloon is of silk and has a capacity of 1 cubic metre. It is filled with hydrogen gas, which is made in a special generator. The generation is a simple process. A vessel filled with water has an inverted vessel within it; a pipe is led to the balloon from the latter and a tube of india-rubber is attached which contains calcium hydrate. By tipping the tube the amount of calcium hydrate required can be poured into the generator. As the gas is made it passes into the balloon or is collected in the inner vessel, which acts as a bell jar if the stopcock to the balloon is closed.

The arrangements for utilising the balloon are very pretty.

An instrument weighing only 2¼ oz. and recording the temperature and pressure is attached beneath a small flag and hung 10 to 15 ft. below the balloon with balloon silk thread; this silk thread is of such fine quality that 5 miles of it only weighs 4 ozs., whilst its breaking strain is 1¼ lbs. The lower part of the instrument is again attached to the silk thread, which is cunningly wound on coned bobbins from which the balloon unwinds it without hitch or friction as it ascends.

In order to spare the silk any jerk as the balloon is released two pieces of string united with a slow match carry the strain between the instrument and the balloon until the slow match is consumed.

The balloon takes about a quarter of an hour to inflate; the slow match is then lit, and the balloon released; with a weight of 8 ozs. and a lifting power of 2½ lbs. it rises rapidly. After it is lost to ordinary vision it can be followed with glasses as mile after mile of thread runs out. Theoretically, if strain is put on the silk thread it should break between the instrument and the balloon, leaving the former free to drop, when the thread can be followed up and the instrument with its record recovered.

Today this was tried with a dummy instrument, but the thread broke close to the bobbins. In the afternoon a double thread was tried, and this acted successfully.

Today I allotted the ponies for exercise. Bowers, Cherry-Garrard, Hooper, Clissold, P. O. Evans, and Crean take animals, besides Anton and Oates. I have had to warn people that they will not necessarily lead the ponies which they now tend.

Wilson is very busy making sketches.

Tuesday, April 25. – It was comparatively calm all day yesterday and last night, and there have been light airs only from the south today. The temperature, at first comparatively high at −5°, has gradually fallen to −13°; as a result the Strait has frozen over at last and it looks as though the Hut Point party should be with us before very long. If the blizzards hold off for another three days the crossing should be perfectly safe, but I don't expect Meares to hurry.

Although we had very good sunset effects at Hut Point, Ponting and others were much disappointed with the absence of such effects at Cape Evans. This was probably due to the continual interference of frost smoke; since our return here, and especially yesterday and today, the sky and sea have been glorious in the afternoon.

Ponting has taken some coloured pictures, but the result is not very satisfactory and the plates are much spotted; Wilson is very busy with pencil and brush.

Atkinson is unpacking and setting up his sterilizers and incubators. Wright is wrestling with the electrical instruments. Evans is busy surveying the Cape and its vicinity. Oates is reorganising the stable, making bigger stalls, &c. Cherry-Garrard is building a stone house for taxidermy and with a view to getting hints for making a shelter at Cape Crozier during the winter. Debenham and Taylor are taking advantage of the last of the light to examine the topography of the peninsula. In fact, everyone is extraordinarily busy.

I came back with the impression that we should not find our winter walks so interesting as those at Hut Point, but I'm rapidly altering my opinion; we may miss the hill climbing here, but in every direction there is abundance of interest. Today I walked round the shores of the North Bay examining the kenyte cliffs and great masses of morainic material of the Barne Glacier, then on under the huge blue ice cliffs of the Glacier itself. With the sunset lights, deep shadows, the black islands and white bergs it was all very beautiful.

Simpson and Bowers sent up a balloon today with a double thread and instrument attached; the line was checked at about 3 miles, and soon after the instrument was seen to disengage. The balloon at first went north with a light southerly breeze till it reached 300 or 400 feet, then it turned to the south but did not travel rapidly; when 2 miles of thread had gone it seemed to be going north again or rising straight upward.

In the afternoon Simpson and Bowers went to recover their treasure, but somewhere south of Inaccessible Island they found the thread broken and the light was not good enough to continue the search.

The sides of the galley fire have caved in – there should have been cheeks to prevent this; we got some fireclay cement today and plastered up the sides. I hope this will get over the difficulty, but have some doubt.

Wednesday, April 26. – Calm. Went round Cape Evans – remarkable effects of icicles on the ice foot, formed by spray of southerly gales.

Thursday, April 27. – The fourth day in succession without wind, but overcast. Light snow has fallen during the day – tonight the wind comes from the north.

We should have our party back soon. The temperature remains about $-5°$ and the ice should be getting thicker with rapidity.

Went round the bergs off Cape Evans – they are very beautiful, especially one which is pierced to form a huge arch. It will be interesting to climb around these monsters as the winter proceeds.

Today I have organised a series of lectures for the winter; the people seem keen and it ought to be exceedingly interesting to discuss so many diverse subjects with experts.

We have an extraordinary diversity of talent and training in our people; it would be difficult to imagine a company composed of experiences which differed so completely. We find one hut contains an experience of every country and every clime. What an assemblage of motley knowledge!

Friday, April 28. – Another comparatively calm day – temp. $-12°$, clear sky. Went to ice caves on glacier S. of Cape; these are really very wonderful. Ponting took some photographs with long exposure and Wright got some very fine ice crystals. The Glacier Tongue comes close around a high bluff headland of kenyte; it is much cracked and curiously composed of a broad wedge of white *névé* over blue ice. The faults in the dust strata in these surfaces are very mysterious and should be instructive in the explanation of certain ice problems.

It looks as though the sea had frozen over for good. If no further blizzard clears the Strait it can be said for this season that:

The Bays froze over on March 25.

The Strait froze over on April 22.

The Strait dissipated April 29.

The Strait froze over on April 30.

Later. The Hut Point record of freezing is:

Night 24th–25th Ice forming mid-day 25th, opened with leads.

              26th Ice all out, sound apparently open.

              27th Strait apparently freezing.

    Early 28th Ice over whole Strait.

              29th All ice gone.

              30th Freezing over.

    May 4th Broad lead opened along land to Castle Rock, 300 to 400 yds. wide.

Party intended to start on 11th, if weather fine.

Very fine display of aurora tonight, one of the brightest I have ever seen – over Erebus; it is conceded that a red tinge is seen after the movement of light.

Saturday, April 29. – Went to Inaccessible Island with Wilson. The agglomerates, kenytes, and lavas are much the same as those at Cape Evans. The Island is 540 ft. high, and it is a steep climb to reach the summit over very loose sand and boulders. From the summit one has an excellent view of our surroundings and the ice in the Strait, which seemed to extend far beyond Cape Royds, but had some ominous cracks beyond the Island.

We climbed round the ice foot after descending the hill and found it much broken up on the south side; the sea spray had washed far up on it.

It is curious to find that all the heavy seas come from the south and that it is from this direction that protection is most needed.

There is some curious weathering on the ice blocks on the N. side; also the snow drifts show interesting dirt bands. The island had a good sprinkling of snow, which will all be gone, I expect, tonight. For as we reached the summit we saw a storm approaching from the south; it had blotted out the Bluff, and we watched it covering Black Island, then Hut Point and Castle Rock. By the time we started homeward it was upon us, making a harsh chatter as it struck the high rocks and sweeping along the drift on the floe.

The blow seems to have passed over tonight and the sky is clear again, but I much fear the ice has gone out in the Strait. There is an ominous black look to the westward.

Sunday, April 30. – As I feared last night, the morning light revealed the havoc made in the ice by yesterday's gale. From Wind Vane Hill (66 feet) it appeared that the Strait had not opened beyond the island, but after church I went up the Ramp with Wilson and steadily climbed over the Glacier ice to a height of about 650 feet. From this elevation one could see that a broad belt of sea ice had been pushed bodily to seaward, and it was evident that last night the whole stretch of water from Hut Point to Turtle Island must have been open – so that our poor people at Hut Point are just where they were.

The only comfort is that the Strait is already frozen again; but what is to happen if every blow clears the sea like this?

Had an interesting walk. One can go at least a mile up the glacier slope before coming to crevasses, and it does not appear that these would be serious for a good way farther. The view is magnificent, and on a clear day like this, one still enjoys some hours of daylight, or rather twilight, when it is possible to see everything clearly.

Have had talks of the curious cones which are such a feature of the Ramp – they are certainly partly produced by ice and partly by weathering. The ponds and various forms of ice grains interest us.

Tonight have been naming all the small land features of our vicinity.

Tuesday, May 2. – It was calm yesterday. A balloon was sent up in the morning, but only reached a mile in height before the instrument was detached (by slow match).

In the afternoon went out with Bowers and his pony to pick up instrument, which was close to the shore in the South Bay. Went on past Inaccessible Island. The ice outside the bergs has grown very thick, 14 inches or more, but there were freshly frozen pools beyond the Island.

In the evening Wilson opened the lecture series with a paper on 'Antarctic Flying Birds'. Considering the limits of the subject the discussion was interesting. The most attractive point raised was that of pigmentation. Does the absence of pigment suggest absence of reserve energy? Does it increase the insulating properties of the hair or feathers? Or does the animal clothed in white radiate less of his internal heat? The most interesting example of Polar colouring here is the increased proportion of albinos amongst the giant petrels found in high latitudes.

Today have had our first game of football; a harassing southerly wind sprang up, which helped my own side to the extent of three goals.

This same wind came with a clear sky and jumped up and down in force throughout the afternoon, but has died away tonight. In the afternoon I saw an ominous lead outside the Island which appeared to extend a long way south. I'm much afraid it may go across our pony track from Hut Point. I am getting anxious to have the hut party back, and begin to wonder if the ice to the south will ever hold in permanently now that the Glacier Tongue has gone.

Wednesday, May 3. – Another calm day, very beautiful and clear. Wilson and Bowers took our few dogs for a run in a sledge. Walked myself out over ice in North Bay – there are a good many cracks and pressures with varying thickness of ice, showing how tide and wind shift the thin sheets – the newest leads held young ice of 4 inches.

The temperature remains high, the lowest yesterday −13°; it should be much lower with such calm weather and clear skies. A strange fact is now very commonly noticed: in calm weather there is usually a difference of 4° or 5° between the temperature at the hut and that on Wind Vane Hill (64 feet), the latter being the higher. This shows an inverted temperature.

As I returned from my walk the southern sky seemed to grow darker, and later stratus cloud was undoubtedly spreading up from that direction – this at about 5 p.m. About 7 a moderate north wind sprang up. This seemed to indicate a southerly blow, and at about 9 the wind shifted to that quarter and blew gustily, 25 to 35 m.p.h. One cannot see the result on the Strait, but I fear it means that the ice has gone out again in places. The wind dropped as suddenly as it had arisen soon after midnight.

In the evening Simpson gave us his first meteorological lecture – the subject, 'Coronas, Halos, Rainbows, and Auroras'. He has a remarkable power of exposition and taught me more of these phenomena in the hour than I had learnt by all previous interested inquiries concerning them.

I note one or two points concerning each phenomenon.

Corona. – White to brown inside ring called Aureola – outside are sometimes seen two or three rings of prismatic light in addition. Caused by diffraction of light round drops of water or ice crystals; diameter of rings inversely proportionate to size of drops or crystals – mixed sizes of ditto causes aureola without rings.

Halos. – Caused by refraction and reflection through and from ice crystals. In this connection the hexagonal, tetrahedonal type of crystallisation is first to be noted; then the infinite number of forms in which this can be modified together with result of fractures: two forms predominate, the plate and the needle; these forms falling through air assume definite position – the plate falls horizontally swaying to and fro, the needle turns rapidly about its longer axis, which remains horizontal. Simpson showed excellent experiments to illustrate; consideration of these facts and refraction of light striking crystals clearly leads to explanation of various complicated halo phenomena such as recorded and such as seen by us on the Great Barrier, and draws attention to the critical refraction angles of 32° and 46°, the radius of inner and outer rings, the position of mock suns, contra suns, zenith circles, &c.

Further measurements are needed; for instance, of streamers from mock suns and examination of ice crystals. (Record of ice crystals seen on Barrier Surface.)

Rainbows. – Caused by reflection and refraction from and through *drops of water* – colours vary with size of drops, the smaller the drop the lighter the colours and nearer to the violet end of the spectrum – hence white rainbow as seen on the Barrier, very small drops.

Double Bows. – diameters must be 84° and 100° – again from laws of refraction – colours: inner, red outside; outer, red inside – i.e. reds come together.

Wanted to see more rainbows on Barrier. In this connection a good rainbow was seen to N.W. in February from winter quarters. Reports should note colours and relative width of bands of colour.

Iridescent Clouds. – Not yet understood; observations required, especially angular distance from the sun.

Auroras. – Clearly most frequent and intense in years of maximum sun spots; this argues connection with the sun.

Points noticed requiring confirmation:

Arch: centre of arch in magnetic meridian.

Shafts: take direction of dipping needle.

Bands and Curtains with convolutions – not understood.

Corona: shafts meeting to form.

Notes required on movement and direction of movement – colours seen – supposed red and possibly green rays preceding or accompanying movement. Auroras are sometimes accompanied by magnetic storms, but not always, and *vice versa* – in general significant signs of some connection – possible common dependants on a third factor. The phenomenon further connects itself in form with lines of magnetic force about the earth.

(Curious apparent connection between spectrum of aurora and that of a heavy gas, 'argon'. May be coincidence.)

Two theories enunciated:

Arrhenius. – Bombardments of minute charged particles from the sun gathered into the magnetic field of the earth.

Birkeland. – Bombardment of free negative electrons gathered into the magnetic field of the earth.

It is experimentally shown that minute drops of water are deflected by light.

It is experimentally shown that ions are given off by dried calcium, which the sun contains.

Professor Störmer has collected much material showing connection of the phenomenon with lines of magnetic force.

Thursday, May 4. – From the small height of Wind Vane Hill (64 feet) it was impossible to say if the ice in the Strait had been out after yesterday's wind. The sea was frozen, but after twelve hours' calm it would be in any case. The dark appearance of the ice is noticeable, but this has been the case of late since the light is poor; little snow has fallen or drifted and the ice flowers are very sparse and scattered.

We had an excellent game of football again today – the exercise is delightful and we get very warm. Atkinson is by far the best player, but Hooper, P. O. Evans, and Crean are also quite good. It has been calm all day again. Went over the sea ice beyond the Arch berg; the ice half a mile beyond is only 4 inches. I think this must have been formed since the blow of yesterday, that is, in sixteen hours or less.

Such rapid freezing is a hopeful sign, but the prompt dissipation of the floe under a southerly wind is distinctly the reverse.

I am anxious to get our people back from Hut Point, mainly on account of the two ponies; with so much calm weather there should have been no difficulty for the party in keeping up its supply of blubber; an absence of which is the only circumstance likely to discomfort it.

The new ice over which I walked is extraordinarily slippery and free from efflorescence. I think this must be a further sign of rapid formation.

Friday, May 5. – Another calm day following a quiet night. Once or twice in the night a light northerly wind, soon dying away. The temperature down to −12°. What is the meaning of this comparative warmth? As usual in calms the Wind Vane Hill temperature is 3° or 4° higher. It is delightful to contemplate the amount of work which is being done at the station. No one is idle – all hands are full, and one cannot doubt that the labour will be productive of remarkable result.

I do not think there can be any life quite so demonstrative of character as that which we had on these expeditions. One sees a remarkable reassortment of values. Under ordinary conditions it is so easy to carry a point with a little bounce; self-assertion is a mask which covers many a weakness. As a rule we have neither the time nor the desire to look beneath it, and so it is that commonly we accept people on their own valuation. Here the outward show is nothing, it is the inward purpose that counts. So the 'gods' dwindle and the humble supplant them. Pretence is useless.

One sees Wilson busy with pencil and colour box, rapidly and steadily adding to his portfolio of charming sketches and at intervals filling the gaps in his zoological work of *Discovery* times; withal ready and willing to give advice and assistance to others at all times; his sound judgment appreciated and therefore a constant referee.

Simpson, master of his craft, untiringly attentive to the working of his numerous self-recording instruments, observing all changes with scientific acumen, doing the work of two observers at least and yet ever seeking to correlate an expanded scope. So the current meteorological and magnetic observations are taken as never before by Polar expeditions.

Wright, good-hearted, strong, keen, striving to saturate his mind with the ice problems of this wonderful region. He has taken the electrical work in hand with all its modern interest of association with radio-activity.

Evans, with a clear-minded zeal in his own work, does it with all the success of result which comes from the taking of pains. Therefrom we derive a singularly exact preservation of time – an important consideration to all, but especially necessary for the physical work. Therefrom also, and including more labour, we have an accurate survey of our immediate surroundings and can trust to possess the correctly mapped results of all surveying data obtained. He has Gran for assistant.

Taylor's intellect is omnivorous and versatile – his mind is unceasingly active, his grasp wide. Whatever he writes will be of interest – his pen flows well.

Debenham's is clearer. Here we have a well-trained, sturdy worker, with a quiet meaning that carries conviction; he realises the conceptions of thoroughness and conscientiousness.

To Bowers's practical genius is owed much of the smooth working of our station. He has a natural method in line with which all arrangements fall, so that expenditure is easily and exactly adjusted to supply, and I have the inestimable advantage of knowing the length of time which each of our possessions will last us and the assurance that there can be no waste. Active mind and active body were never more happily blended. It is a restless activity, admitting no idle moments and ever budding into new forms.

So we see the balloon ascending under his guidance and anon he is away over the floe tracking the silk thread which held it. Such a task completed, he is away to exercise his pony, and later out again with the dogs, the last typically self-suggested, because for the moment there is no one else to care for these animals. Now in a similar manner he is spreading thermometer screens to get comparative readings with the home station. He is for the open air, seemingly incapable of realising any discomfort from it, and yet his hours within doors spent with equal profit. For he is intent on tracking the problems of sledging food and clothing to their innermost bearings and is becoming an authority on past records. This will be no small help to me and one which others never could have given.

Adjacent to the physicists' corner of the hut Atkinson is quietly pursuing the subject of parasites. Already he is in a new world. The laying out of the fish trap was his action and the catches are his field of labour. Constantly he comes to ask if I would like to see some new form, and I am taken to see some protozoa or ascidian isolated on the slide plate of his microscope. The fishes themselves are comparatively new to science; it is strange that their parasites should have been under investigation so soon.

Atkinson's bench with its array of microscopes, test-tubes, spirit lamps, &c., is next the dark room in which Ponting spends the greater part of his life. I would describe him as sustained by artistic enthusiasm. This world of ours is a different one to him than it is to the rest of us – he gauges it by its picturesqueness – his joy is to reproduce its pictures artistically, his grief to fail to do so. No attitude could be happier for the work which he has undertaken, and one cannot doubt its productiveness. I would not imply that he is out of sympathy with the works of others, which is far from being the case, but that his energies centre devotedly on the minutiae of his business.

Cherry-Garrard is another of the open-air, self-effacing, quiet workers; his whole heart is in the life, with profound eagerness to help everyone. 'One has caught glimpses of him in tight places; sound all through and pretty hard also.' Indoors he is editing our Polar journal, out of doors he is busy making trial stone huts and blubber stoves, primarily with a view to the winter journey to Cape Crozier, but incidentally these are instructive experiments for any party which may get into difficulty by being cut off from the home station. It is very well to know how best to use the scant resources that Nature provides in these regions. In this connection I have been studying our Arctic library to get details concerning snow-hut building and the implements used for it.

Oates's whole heart is in the ponies. He is really devoted to their care, and I believe will produce them in the best possible form for the sledging season. Opening out the stores, installing a blubber stove, &c., has kept *him* busy, whilst his satellite, Anton, is ever at work in the stables – an excellent little man.

P. O. Evans and Crean are repairing sleeping-bags, covering felt boots, and generally working on sledging kit. In fact there is no one idle, and no one who has the least prospect of idleness.

Saturday, May 6. – Two more days of calm, interrupted with occasional gusts.

Yesterday, Friday evening, Taylor gave an introductory lecture on his remarkably fascinating subject – modern physiography.

These modern physiographers set out to explain the forms of land erosion on broad common-sense lines, heedless of geological support. They must, in consequence, have their special language. River courses, they say, are not temporary – in the main they are archaic. In conjunction with land elevations they have worked through geographical cycles, perhaps many. In each geographical cycle they have advanced from *infantile* V-shaped forms; the courses broaden and deepen, the bank slopes reduce in angle as maturer stages are reached until the level of sea surface is more and more nearly approximated. In *senile* stages the river is a broad sluggish stream flowing over a plain with little inequality of level. The cycle has formed a *Peneplain*. Subsequently, with fresh elevation, a new cycle is commenced. So much for the simple case, but in fact nearly all cases are modified by unequal elevations due to landslips, by variation in hardness of rock, &c. Hence modification in positions of river courses and the fact of different parts of a single river being in different stages of cycle.

Taylor illustrated his explanations with examples: the Red River, Canada – plain flat though elevated, water lies in pools, river flows in 'V' 'infantile' form.

The Rhine Valley – the gorgeous scenery from Mainz down due to infantile form in recently elevated region.

The Russian Plains – examples of 'senility'.

Greater complexity in the Blue Mountains – these are undoubted earth folds; the Nepean River flows through an offshoot of a fold, the valley being made as the fold was elevated – curious valleys made by erosion of hard rock overlying soft.

River *piracy* – *Domestic*, the short-circuiting of a *meander*, such as at Coo in the Ardennes; *Foreign*, such as Shoalhaven River, Australia – stream has captured river.

Landslips have caused the isolation of Lake George and altered the watershed of the whole country to the south.

Later on Taylor will deal with the effects of ice and lead us to the formation of the scenery of our own region, and so we shall have much to discuss.

Sunday, May 7. – Daylight now is very short. One wonders why the Hut Point party does not come. Bowers and Cherry-Garrard have set up a thermometer screen containing maximum thermometers and thermographs on the sea floe about ¾' N.W. of the hut. Another smaller one is to go on top of the Ramp. They took the screen out on one of Day's bicycle-wheel carriages and found it ran very easily over the salty ice where the sledges give so much trouble. This vehicle is not easily turned, but may be very useful before there is much snowfall.

Yesterday a balloon was sent up and reached a very good height (probably 2 to 3 miles) before the instrument disengaged; the balloon went almost straight up and the silk fell in festoons over the rocky part of the Cape, affording a very difficult clue to follow; but whilst Bowers was following it, Atkinson observed the instrument fall a few hundred yards out on the Bay – it was recovered and gives the first important record of upper-air temperature.

Atkinson and Crean put out the fish trap in about 3 fathoms of water off the west beach; both yesterday morning and yesterday evening when the trap was raised it contained over forty fish, whilst this morning and this evening the catches in the same spot have been from twenty to twenty-five. We had fish for breakfast this morning, but an even more satisfactory result of the catches has been revealed by Atkinson's microscope. He had discovered quite a number of new parasites and found work to last quite a long time.

Last night it came to my turn to do night watchman again, so that I shall be glad to have a good sleep tonight.

Yesterday we had a game of football; it is pleasant to mess about, but the light is failing.

Clissold is still producing food novelties; tonight we had galantine of seal – it was *excellent*.

Monday, May 8 – *Tuesday, May* 9. – As one of the series of lectures I gave an outline of my plans for next season on Monday evening. Everyone was interested, naturally. I could not but hint that in my opinion the problem of reaching the Pole can best be solved by relying on the ponies and man haulage. With this sentiment the whole company appeared to be in sympathy. Everyone seems to distrust the dogs when it comes to glacier and summit. I have asked everyone to give thought to the problem, to

freely discuss it, and bring suggestions to my notice. It's going to
be a tough job; that is better realised the more one dives into it.

Today (Tuesday) Debenham has been showing me his photographs taken west. With Wright's and Taylor's these will make an
extremely interesting series – the ice forms especially in the region
of the Koettlitz glacier are unique.

The Strait has been frozen over a week. I cannot understand
why the Hut Point party doesn't return. The weather continues
wonderfully calm though now looking a little unsettled. Perhaps
the unsettled look stops the party, or perhaps it waits for the moon,
which will be bright in a day or two.

Anyway, I wish it would return, and shall not be free from
anxiety till it does.

Cherry-Garrard is experimenting in stone huts and with blubber
fires – all with a view to prolonging the stay at Cape Crozier.

Bowers has placed one thermometer screen on the floe about ¾'
out, and another smaller one above the Ramp. Oddly, the floe
temperature seems to agree with that on Wind Vane Hill, whilst
the hut temperature is always 4° or 5° colder in calm weather. To
complete the records a thermometer is to be placed in South Bay.

Science – the rock foundation of all effort!!

Wednesday, May 10. – It has been blowing from the south 12
to 20 miles per hour since last night; the ice remains fast. The
temperature −12° to −19°. The party does not come. I went well
beyond Inaccessible Island till Hut Point and Castle Rock appeared
beyond Tent Island – that is, well out on the space which was last
seen as open water. The ice is 9 inches thick – not much for eight
or nine days' freezing; but it is very solid – the surface wet but very
slippery. I suppose Meares waits for 12 inches in thickness, or fears
the floe is too slippery for the ponies.

Yet I wish he would come.

I took a thermometer on my walk today; the temperature
was −12° inside Inaccessible Island, but only −8° on the sea ice
outside – the wind seemed less outside. Coming in under lee
of Island and bergs I was reminded of the difficulty of finding
shelter in these regions. The weather side of hills seems to afford
better shelter than the lee side, as I have remarked elsewhere.
May it be in part because all lee sides tend to be filled by drift

snow, blown and weathered rock débris? There was a good lee under one of the bergs; in one corner the ice sloped out over me and on either side, forming a sort of grotto; here the air was absolutely still.

Ponting gave us an interesting lecture on Burmah, illustrated with fine slides. His descriptive language is florid, but shows the artistic temperament. Bowers and Simpson were able to give personal reminiscences of this land of pagodas, and the discussion led to interesting statements on the religion, art, and education of its people, their philosophic idleness, &c. Our lectures are a real success.

Friday, *May* 12. – Yesterday morning was quiet. Played football in the morning; wind got up in the afternoon and evening.

All day it has been blowing hard, 30 to 60 miles an hour; it has never looked very dark overhead, but a watery cirrus has been in evidence for some time, causing well marked paraselene.

I have not been far from the hut, but had a great fear on one occasion that the ice had gone out in the Strait.

The wind is dropping this evening, and I have been up to Wind Vane Hill. I now think the ice has remained fast.

There has been astonishingly little drift with the wind, probably due to the fact that there has been so very little snowfall of late.

Atkinson is pretty certain that he has isolated a very motile bacterium in the snow. It is probably air borne, and though no bacteria have been found in the air, this may be carried in upper currents and brought down by the snow. If correct it is an interesting discovery.

Tonight Debenham gave a geological lecture. It was elementary. He gave little more than the rough origin and classification of rocks with a view to making his further lectures better understood.

Saturday, *May* 13. – The wind dropped about 10 last night. This morning it was calm and clear save for a light misty veil of ice crystals through which the moon shone with scarce clouded brilliancy, surrounded with bright cruciform halo and white paraselene. Mock moons with prismatic patches of colour appeared in the radiant ring, echoes of the main source of light. Wilson has a charming sketch of the phenomenon.

I went to Inaccessible Island, and climbing some way up the steep western face, reassured myself concerning the ice. It was evident that there had been no movement in consequence of yesterday's blow.

In climbing I had to scramble up some pretty steep rock faces and screens, and held on only in anticipation of gaining the top of the Island and an easy descent. Instead of this I came to an impossible overhanging cliff of lava, and was forced to descend as I had come up. It was no easy task, and I was glad to get down with only one slip, when I brought myself up with my ice-axe in the nick of time to prevent a fall over a cliff. This Island is very steep on all sides. .There is only one known place of ascent; it will be interesting to try and find others.

After tea Atkinson came in with the glad tidings that the dog team were returning from Hut Point. We were soon on the floe to welcome the last remnant of our wintering party. Meares reported everything well and the ponies not far behind.

The dogs were unharnessed and tied up to the chains; they are all looking remarkably fit – apparently they have given no trouble at all of late; there have not even been any fights.

Half an hour later Day, Lashly, Nelson, Forde, and Keohane arrived with the two ponies – men and animals in good form.

It is a great comfort to have the men and dogs back, and a greater to contemplate all the ten ponies comfortably stabled for the winter. Everything seems to depend on these animals.

I have not seen the meteorological record brought back, but it appears that the party had had very fine calm weather since we left them, except during the last three days when wind has been very strong. It is curious that we should only have got one day with wind.

I am promised the sea-freezing record tomorrow. Four seals were got on April 22, the day after we left, and others have been killed since, so that there is a plentiful supply of blubber and seal meat at the hut – the rest of the supplies seem to have been pretty well run out. Some more forage had been fetched in from the depôt. A young sea leopard had been killed on the sea ice near Castle Rock three days ago, this being the second only found in the Sound.

It is a strange fact that none of the returning party seem to greatly appreciate the food luxuries they have had since their return. It would have been the same with us had we not had a day or two in tents before our return. It seems more and more certain that a very simple fare is all that is needed here – plenty of seal meat, flour, and fat, with tea, cocoa, and sugar; these are the only real requirements for comfortable existence.

The temperatures at Hut Point have not been as low as I expected. There seems to have been an extraordinary heat wave during the spell of calm recorded since we left – the thermometer registering little below zero until the wind came, when it fell to −20°. Thus as an exception we have had a fall instead of a rise of temperature with wind.

[The exact inventory of stores at Hut Point here recorded has no immediate bearing on the history of the expedition, but may be noted as illustrating the care and thoroughness with which all operations were conducted. Other details as to the carbide consumed in making acetylene gas may be briefly quoted. The first tin was opened on February 1, the second on March 26. The seventh on May 20, the next eight at the average interval of 9½ days.]

Sunday, May 14. – Grey and dull in the morning.

Exercised the ponies and held the usual service. This morning I gave Wright some notes containing speculations on the amount of ice on the Antarctic continent and on the effects of winter movements in the sea ice. I want to get into his head the larger bearing of the problems which our physical investigations involve. He needs two years here to fully realise these things, and with all his intelligence and energy will produce little unless he has that extended experience.

The sky cleared at noon, and this afternoon I walked over the North Bay to the ice cliffs – such a very beautiful afternoon and evening – the scene bathed in moonlight, so bright and pure as to be almost golden, a very wonderful scene. At such times the Bay seems strangely homely, especially when the eye rests on our camp with the hut and lighted windows.

I am very much impressed with the extraordinary and general cordiality of the relations which exist amongst our people. I do not suppose that a statement of the real truth, namely, that there is no friction at all, will be credited – it is so generally thought that the many rubs of such a life as this are quietly and purposely sunk in oblivion. With me there is no need to draw a veil; there is nothing to cover. There are no strained relations in this hut, and nothing more emphatically evident than the universally amicable spirit which is shown on all occasions.

Such a state of affairs would be delightfully surprising under any conditions, but it is much more so when one remembers the diverse assortment of our company.

This theme is worthy of expansion. Tonight Oates, captain in a smart cavalry regiment, has been 'scrapping' over chairs and tables with Debenham, a young Australian student.

It is a triumph to have collected such men.

The temperature has been down to −23°, the lowest yet recorded here – doubtless we shall soon get lower, for I find an extraordinary difference between this season as far as it has gone and those of 1902–3.

CHAPTER TEN

In winter quarters: modern style

Monday, May 15. − The wind has been strong from the north all day − about 30 miles an hour. A bank of stratus cloud about 6000 or 7000 feet (measured by Erebus) has been passing rapidly overhead *towards* the north; it is nothing new to find the overlying layers of air moving in opposite directions, but it is strange that the phenomenon is so persistent. Simpson has frequently remarked as a great feature of weather conditions here the seeming reluctance ot the air to 'mix' − the fact seems to be the explanation of many curious fluctuations of temperature.

Went for a short walk, but it was not pleasant. Wilson gave an interesting lecture on penguins. He explained the primitive characteristics in the arrangement of feathers on wings and body, the absence of primaries and secondaries or bare tracts; the modification of the muscles of the wings and in the structure of the feet (the metatarsal joint). He pointed out (and the subsequent discussion seemed to support him) that these birds probably branched at a very early stage of bird life − coming pretty directly from the lizard bird Archaeopteryx of the Jurassic age. Fossils of giant penguins of Eocene and Miocene ages show that there has been extremely little development since.

He passed on to the classification and habitat of different genera, nest-making habits, eggs, &c. Then to a brief account of the habits of the Emperors and Adélies, which was of course less novel ground for the old hands.

Of special points of interest I recall his explanation of the desirability of embryonic study of the Emperor to throw further light on the development of the species in the loss of teeth, &c.; and Ponting's contribution and observation of adult Adélies teaching their young to swim − this point has been obscure. It has been said that the old birds push the young into the water, and, *per contra*, that they leave them deserted in the rookery – both statements seemed unlikely. It would not be strange if the young Adélie had to learn to swim (it is a well-known requirement of the Northern fur seal – sea bear), but it will be interesting to see in how far the adult birds lay themselves out to instruct their progeny.

During our trip to the ice and sledge journey one of our dogs, Vaida, was especially distinguished for his savage temper and generally uncouth manners. He became a bad wreck with his poor coat at Hut Point, and in this condition I used to massage him; at first the operation was mistrusted and only continued to the accompaniment of much growling, but later he evidently grew to like the warming effect and sidled up to me whenever I came out of the hut, though still with some suspicion. On returning here he seemed to know me at once, and now comes and buries his head in my legs whenever I go out of doors; he allows me to rub him and push him about without the slightest protest and scampers about me as I walk abroad. He is a strange beast – I imagine so unused to kindness that it took him time to appreciate it.

Tuesday, May 16. – The north wind continued all night but dropped this forenoon. Conveniently it became calm at noon and we had a capital game of football. The light is good enough, but not much more than good enough, for this game.

Had some instruction from Wright this morning on the electrical instruments.

Later went into our carbide expenditure with Day: am glad to find it sufficient for two years, but am not making this generally known as there are few things in which economy is less studied than light if regulations allow of waste.

Electrical instruments

For measuring the ordinary potential gradient we have two self-recording quadrant electrometers. The principle of this instrument is the same as that of the old Kelvin instrument; the clockwork attached to it unrolls a strip of paper wound on a roller; at intervals the needle of the instrument is depressed by an electromagnet and makes a dot on the moving paper. The relative position of these dots forms the record. One of our instruments is adjusted to give only 1/10th the refinement of measurement of the other by means of reduction in the length of the quartz fibre. The object of this is to continue the record in snowstorms, &c., when the potential difference of air and earth is very great. The instruments are kept charged with batteries of small Daniels cells. The clocks are controlled by a master clock.

The instrument available for radio-activity measurements is a modified type of the old gold-leaf electroscope. The measurement is made by the mutual repulsion of quartz fibres acting against a spring – the extent of the repulsion is very clearly shown against a scale magnified by a telescope.

The measurements to be made with instrument are various:

The *ionization of the air.* A length of wire charged with 2000 volts (negative) is exposed to the air for several hours. It is then coiled on a frame and its rate of discharge measured by the electroscope.

The *radio-activity of the various rocks* of our neighbourhood; this by direct measurement of the rock.

The *conductivity of the air*, that is, the relative movement of ions in the air; by movement of air past charged surface. Rate of absorption of + and – and ions is measured, the negative ion travelling faster than the positive.

Wednesday, May 17. – For the first time this season we have a rise of temperature with a southerly wind. The wind force has been about 30 since yesterday evening; the air is fairly full of snow and the temperature has risen to –6° from –18°.

I heard one of the dogs barking in the middle of the night, and on inquiry learned that it was one of the 'Serais',* that he seemed to have something wrong with his hind leg, and that he had been put under shelter. This morning the poor brute was found dead.

I'm afraid we can place but little reliance on our dog teams and reflect ruefully on the misplaced confidence with which I regarded the provision of our transport. Well, one must suffer for errors of judgment.

This afternoon Wilson held a post-mortem on the dog; he could find no sufficient cause of death. This is the third animal that has died at winter quarters without apparent cause. Wilson, who is nettled, proposes to examine the brain of this animal tomorrow.

* The white dogs.

Went up the Ramp this morning. There was light enough to see our camp, and it looked homely, as it does from all sides. Somehow we loom larger here than at Cape Armitage. We seem to be more significant. It must be from contrast of size; the larger hills tend to dwarf the petty human element.

Tonight the wind has gone back to the north and is now blowing fresh.

This sudden and continued complete change of direction is new to our experience.

Oates has just given us an excellent little lecture on the management of horses.

He explained his plan of feeding our animals 'soft' during the winter, and hardening them up during the spring. He pointed out that the horse's natural food being grass and hay, he would naturally employ a great number of hours in the day filling a stomach of small capacity with food from which he could derive only a small percentage of nutriment.

Hence it is desirable to feed horses often and light. His present routine is as follows:

Morning. – Chaff.

Noon, after exercise. – Snow. Chaff and either oats or oil-cake alternate days.

Evening, 5 p.m. – Snow. Hot bran mash with oil-cake or boiled oats and chaff; finally a small quantity of hay.

This sort of food should be causing the animals to put on flesh, but is not preparing them for work. In October he proposes to give 'hard' food, all cold, and to increase the exercising hours.

As concerning the food we possess he thinks:

The *chaff* made of young wheat and hay is doubtful; there does not seem to be any grain with it – and would farmers cut young wheat? There does not seem to be any 'fat' in this food, but it is very well for ordinary winter purposes.

N.B. – It seems to me this ought to be inquired into. Bran much discussed, but good because it causes horses to chew the oats with which mixed.

Oil-cake, greasy, producing energy – excellent for horses to work on.

Oats, of which we have two qualities, also very good working food – our white quality much better than the brown.

Our trainer went on to explain the value of training horses, of getting them 'balanced' to pull with less effort. He owns it is very difficult when one is walking horses only for exercise, but thinks something can be done by walking them fast and occasionally making them step backwards.

Oates referred to the deeds that had been done with horses by foreigners in shows and with polo ponies by Englishmen when the animals were trained; it is, he said, a sort of gymnastic training.

The discussion was very instructive and I have only noted the salient points.

Thursday, May 18. – The wind dropped in the night; today it is calm, with slight snowfall. We have had an excellent football match – the only outdoor game possible in this light.

I think our winter routine very good. I suppose every leader of a party has thought that, since he has the power of altering it. On the other hand, routine in this connection must take into consideration the facilities of work and play afforded by the preliminary preparations for the expedition. The winter occupations of most of our party depend on the instruments and implements, the clothing and sledging outfit, provided by forethought, and the routine is adapted to these occupations.

The busy winter routine of our party may therefore be excusably held as a subject for self-congratulation.

Friday, May 19. – Wind from the north in the morning, temperature comparatively high (about –6°). We played football during the noon hour – the game gets better as we improve our football condition and skill.

In the afternoon the wind came from the north, dying away again late at night.

In the evening Wright lectured on 'Ice Problems'. He had a difficult subject and was nervous. He is young and has never done original work; is only beginning to see the importance of his task.

He started on the crystallisation of ice, and explained with very good illustrations the various forms of crystals, the manner of their growth under different conditions and different temperatures. This was instructive. Passing to the freezing of salt water, he was not very clear. Then on to glaciers and their movements, theories for same and observations in these regions.

There was a good deal of disconnected information – silt bands, crevasses were mentioned. Finally he put the problems of larger aspect.

The upshot of the discussion was a decision to devote another evening to the larger problems such as the Great Ice Barrier and the interior ice sheet. I think I will write the paper to be discussed on this occasion.

I note with much satisfaction that the talks on ice problems and the interest shown in them have had the effect of making Wright devote the whole of his time to them. That may mean a great deal, for he is a hard and conscientious worker.

Atkinson has a new hole for his fish trap in 15 fathoms; yesterday morning he got a record catch of forty-three fish, but oddly enough yesterday evening there were only two caught.

Saturday, May 20. – Blowing hard from the south, with some snow and very cold. Few of us went far; Wilson and Bowers went to the top of the Ramp and found the wind there force 6 to 7, temperature −24°; as a consequence they got frostbitten. There was lively cheering when they reappeared in this condition, such is the sympathy which is here displayed for affliction; but with Wilson much of the amusement arises from his peculiarly scant headgear and the confessed jealousy of those of us who cannot face the weather with so little face protection.

The wind dropped at night.

Sunday, May 21. – Observed as usual. It blew from the north in the morning. Had an idea to go to Cape Royds this evening, but it was reported that the open water reached to the Barne Glacier, and last night my own observation seemed to confirm this.

This afternoon I started out for the open water. I found the ice solid off the Barne Glacier tongue, but always ahead of me a dark horizon as though I was within a very short distance of its edge. I held on with this appearance still holding up to C. Barne itself and then past that Cape and half way between it and C. Royds. This was far enough to make it evident that the ice was continuous to C. Royds, and has been so for a long time. Under these circumstances the continual appearance of open water to the north is most extraordinary and quite inexplicable.

Have had some very interesting discussions with Wilson, Wright, and Taylor on the ice formations to the west. How to account for

Point of the Barne Glacier: Anton and sledge

the marine organisms found on the weathered glacier ice north of the Koettlitz Glacier? We have been elaborating a theory under which this ice had once a negative buoyancy due to the morainic material on top and in the lower layers of the ice mass, and had subsequently floated when the greater amount of this material had weathered out.

Have arranged to go to C. Royds tomorrow.

The temperatures have sunk very steadily this year; for a long time they hung about zero, then for a considerable interval remained about $-10°$; now they are down in the -20's, with signs of falling (today $-24°$).

Bowers's meteorological stations have been amusingly named Archibald, Bertram, Clarence – they are entered by the initial letter, but spoken of by full title.

Tonight we had a glorious auroral display – quite the most brilliant I have seen. At one time the sky from N.N.W. to S.S.E. as high as the zenith was massed with arches, band, and curtains, always in rapid movement. The waving curtains were especially fascinating – a wave of bright light would start at one end and run along to the other, or a patch of brighter light would spread as if to reinforce the failing light of the curtain.

Auroral notes

The auroral light is of a paleish green colour, but we now see distinctly a red flush preceding the motion of any bright part.

The green ghostly light seems suddenly to spring to life with rosy blushes. There is infinite suggestion in this phenomenon, and in that lies its charm; the suggestion of life, form, colour, and movement never less than evanescent, mysterious – no reality. It is the language of mystic signs and portents – the inspiration of the gods – wholly spiritual – divine signalling. Remindful of superstition, provocative of imagination. Might not the inhabitants of some other world (Mars) controlling mighty forces thus surround our globe with fiery symbols, a golden writing which we have not the key to decipher?

There is argument on the confession of Ponting's inability to obtain photographs of the aurora. Professor Stormer of Norway seems to have been successful. Simpson made notes of his method, which seems to depend merely on the rapidity of lens and plate. Ponting claims to have greater rapidity in both, yet gets no result even with long exposure. It is not only a question of aurora; the stars are equally reluctant to show themselves on Ponting's plate. Even with five seconds exposure the stars become short lines of light on the plate of a fixed camera. Stormer's stars are points and therefore his exposure must have been short, yet there is detail in some of his pictures which it seems impossible could have been got with a short exposure. It is all very puzzling.

Monday, May 22. – Wilson, Bowers, Atkinson, Evans (P.O.), Clissold, and self went to C. Royds with a 'go cart' carrying our sleeping-bags, a cooker, and a small quantity of provision.

The 'go cart' consists of a framework of steel tubing supported on four bicycle wheels.

The surface of the floes carries 1 to 2 inches of snow, barely covering the salt ice flowers, and for this condition this vehicle of Day's is excellent. The advantage is that it meets the case where the salt crystals form a heavy frictional surface for wood runners. I'm inclined to think that there are great numbers of cases when wheels would be more efficient than runners on the sea ice.

We reached Cape Royds in 2½ hours, killing an Emperor penguin in the bay beyond C. Barne. This bird was in splendid plumage, the breast reflecting the dim northern light like a mirror.

It was fairly dark when we stumbled over the rocks and dropped on to Shackleton's Hut. Clissold started the cooking-range, Wilson and I walked over to the Black beach and round back by Blue Lake.

The temperature was down at −31° and the interior of the hut was very cold.

Tuesday, May 23. – We spent the morning mustering the stores within and without the hut, after a cold night which we passed very comfortably in our bags.

We found a good quantity of flour and Danish butter and a fair amount of paraffin, with smaller supplies of assorted articles – the whole sufficient to afford provision for such a party as ours for about six or eight months if well administered. In case of necessity this would undoubtedly be a very useful reserve to fall back upon. These stores are somewhat scattered, and the hut has a dilapidated, comfortless appearance due to its tenantless condition; but even so it seemed to me much less inviting than our old *Discovery* hut at C. Armitage.

After a cup of cocoa there was nothing to detain us, and we started back, the only useful articles added to our weights being a scrap or two of leather and five hymn-books. Hitherto we have been only able to muster seven copies; this increase will improve our Sunday Services.

Wednesday, May 24. – A quiet day with northerly wind; the temperature rose gradually to zero. Having the night duty, did not go out. The moon has gone and there is little to attract one out of doors.

Atkinson gave us an interesting little discourse on parasitology, with a brief account of the life history of some ecto- and some endo-parasites – Nematodes, Trematodes. He pointed out how that in nearly every case there was a secondary host, how in some cases disease was caused, and in others the presence of the parasite was even helpful. He acknowledged the small progress that had been made in this study. He mentioned ankylostomiasis, blood-sucking worms, Bilhartsia (Trematode) attacking bladder (Egypt), Filaria (round tapeworm), Guinea worm, Trichina (pork), and others, pointing to disease caused.

From worms he went to Protozoa – Trypanosomes, sleeping sickness, host tsetse-fly – showed life history comparatively, propagated in secondary host or encysting in primary host –

similarly malarial germs spread by Anopheles mosquitoes – all very interesting.

In the discussion following Wilson gave some account of the grouse disease worm, and especially of the interest in finding free living species almost identical; also part of the life of disease worm is free living. Here we approached a point pressed by Nelson concerning the degeneration consequent on adoption of the parasitic habit. All parasites seem to have descended from free living beasts. One asks 'what is degeneration?' without receiving a very satisfactory answer. After all, such terms must be empirical.

Thursday, May 25. – It has been blowing from south with heavy gusts and snow, temperature extraordinarily high, –6°. This has been a heavy gale. The weather conditions are certainly very interesting; Simpson has again called attention to the wind in February, March, and April at Cape Evans – the record shows an extraordinary large percentage of gales. It is quite certain that we scarcely got a fraction of the wind on the Barrier and doubtful if we got as much as Hut Point.

Friday, May 26. – A calm and clear day – a nice change from recent weather. It makes an enormous difference to the enjoyment of this life if one is able to get out and stretch one's legs every day. This morning I went up the Ramp. No sign of open water, so that my fears for a broken highway in the coming season are now at rest. In future gales can only be a temporary annoyance – anxiety as to their result is finally allayed.

This afternoon I searched out ski and ski sticks and went for a short run over the floe. The surface is quite good since the recent snowfall and wind. This is satisfactory, as sledging can now be conducted on ordinary lines, and if convenient our parties can pull on ski. The young ice troubles of April and May have passed away. It is curious that circumstances caused us to miss them altogether during our stay in the *Discovery*.

We are living extraordinarily well. At dinner last night we had some excellent thick seal soup, very much like thick hare soup; this was followed by an equally tasty seal steak and kidney pie and a fruit jelly. The smell of frying greeted us on awaking this morning, and at breakfast each of us had two of our nutty little *Notothenia* fish after our bowl of porridge. These little fish have an extraordinarily sweet taste – bread and butter and marmalade finished the meal. At the midday meal we had bread and butter, cheese, and cake, and tonight I smell mutton in the preparation. Under the circumstances it would be difficult to conceive more appetising repasts or a regime which is less likely to produce scorbutic symptoms. I cannot think we shall get scurvy.

Nelson lectured to us tonight, giving a very able little elementary sketch of the objects of the biologist. A fact struck one in his explanation of the rates of elimination. Two of the offspring of two parents alone survive, speaking broadly; this the same of the human species or the 'ling', with 24,000,000 eggs in the roe of each female! He talked much of evolution, adaptation, &c. Mendelism became the most debated point of the discussion; the transmission of characters has a wonderful fascination for the human mind. There was also a point striking deep in the debate on Professor Loeb's experiments with sea urchins; how far had he succeeded in reproducing the species without the male spermatozoa? Not very far, it seemed, when all was said.

A theme for a pen would be the expansion of interest in Polar affairs; compare the interests of a winter spent by the old Arctic voyagers with our own, and look into the causes. The aspect of everything changes as our knowledge expands.

The expansion of human interest in rude surroundings may perhaps best be illustrated by comparisons. It will serve to recall such a simple case as the fact that our ancestors applied the terms horrid, frightful, to mountain crags which in our own day are more justly admired as lofty, grand, and beautiful.

The poetic conception of this natural phenomenon has followed not so much an inherent change of sentiment as the intimacy of wider knowledge and the death of superstitious influence. One is much struck by the importance of realising limits.

Saturday, May 27. – A very unpleasant, cold, windy day. Annoyed with the conditions, so did not go out.

In the evening Bowers gave his lecture on sledging diets. He has shown great courage in undertaking the task, great perseverance in unearthing facts from books, and a considerable practical skill in stringing these together. It is a thankless task to search Polar literature for dietary facts and still more difficult to attach due weight to varying statements. Some authors omit discussion of this important item altogether, others fail to note alterations made in

practice or additions afforded by circumstances, others again forget
to describe the nature of various food stuffs.

Our lecturer was both entertaining and instructive when he dealt
with old-time rations; but he naturally grew weak in approaching
the physiological aspect of the question. He went through with it
manfully and with a touch of humour much appreciated; whereas,
for instance, he deduced facts from 'the equivalent of Mr Joule, a
gentleman whose statements he had no reason to doubt'.

Wilson was the mainstay of the subsequent discussion and put
all doubtful matters in a clearer light. 'Increase your fats (carbo-
hydrate)' is what science seems to say, and practice with conserv-
ativism is inclined to step cautiously in response to this urgence. I
shall, of course, go into the whole question as thoroughly as
available information and experience permits. Meanwhile it is useful
to have had a discussion which aired the popular opinions.

Feeling went deepest on the subject of tea versus cocoa; admitting all that can be said concerning stimulation and reaction, I am
inclined to see much in favour of tea. Why should not one be
mildly stimulated during the marching hours if one can cope with
reaction by profounder rest during the hours of inaction?

Sunday, May 28. – Quite an excitement last night. One of the
ponies (the grey which I led last year and salved from the floe)
either fell or tried to lie down in his stall, his head being lashed up
to the stanchions on either side. In this condition he struggled and
kicked till his body was twisted right round and his attitude
extremely uncomfortable. Very luckily his struggles were heard
almost at once, and his head ropes being cut, Oates got him on his
feet again. He looked a good deal distressed at the time, but is now
quite well again and has been out for his usual exercise.

Held Service as usual.

This afternoon went on ski around the bay and back across.
Little or no wind; sky clear, temperature −25°. It was wonderfully
mild considering the temperature – this sounds paradoxical, but
the sensation of cold does not conform to the thermometer –
it is obviously dependent on the wind and less obviously on the
humidity of the air and the ice crystals floating in it. I cannot very
clearly account for this effect, but as a matter of fact I have certainly
felt colder in still air at −10° than I did today when the thermometer
was down to −25°, other conditions apparently equal.

The amazing circumstance is that by no means can we measure the humidity, or indeed the precipitation or evaporation. I have just been discussing with Simpson the insuperable difficulties that stand in the way of experiment in this direction, since cold air can only hold the smallest quantities of moisture, and saturation covers an extremely small range of temperature.

Monday, *May* 29. – Another beautiful calm day. Went out both before and after the mid-day meal. This morning with Wilson and Bowers towards the thermometer off Inaccessible Island. On the way my companionable dog was heard barking and dimly seen – we went towards him and found that he was worrying a young sea leopard. This is the second found in the Strait this season. We had to secure it as a specimen, but it was sad to have to kill. The long lithe body of this seal makes it almost beautiful in comparison with our stout, bloated Weddells. This poor beast turned swiftly from side to side as we strove to stun it with a blow on the nose. As it turned it gaped its jaws wide, but oddly enough not a sound came forth, not even a hiss.

After lunch a sledge was taken out to secure the prize, which had been photographed by flashlight.

Ponting has been making great advances in flashlight work, and has opened up quite a new field in which artistic results can be obtained in the winter.

Lecture – Japan. Tonight Ponting gave us a charming lecture on Japan with wonderful illustrations of his own. He is happiest in his descriptions of the artistic side of the people, with which he is in fullest sympathy. So he took us to see the flower pageants. The joyful festivals of the cherry blossom, the wistaria, the iris and chrysanthemum, the sombre colours of the beech blossom and the paths about the lotus gardens, where mankind meditated in solemn mood. We had pictures, too, of Nikko and its beauties, of Temples and great Buddhas. Then in more touristy strain of volcanoes and their craters, waterfalls and river gorges, tiny tree-clad islets, that feature of Japan – baths and their bathers, Ainos, and so on. His descriptions were well given and we all of us thoroughly enjoyed our evening.

Tuesday, *May* 30. – Am busy with my physiological investig-ations.* Atkinson reported a sea leopard at the tide crack; it proved

* i.e. in relation to a sledging ration.

to be a crab-eater, young and very active. In curious contrast to the sea leopard of yesterday, in snapping round it uttered considerable noise, a gasping throaty growl.

Went out to the outer berg, where there was quite a collection of people, mostly in connection with Ponting, who had brought camera and flashlight.

It was beautifully calm and comparatively warm. It was good to hear the gay chatter and laughter, and see ponies and their leaders come up out of the gloom to add liveliness to the scene. The sky was extraordinarily clear at noon and to the north very bright.

We have had an exceptionally large tidal range during the last three days – it has upset the tide gauge arrangements and brought a little doubt on the method. Day is going into the question, which we thoroughly discussed today. Tidal measurements will be worse than useless unless we can be sure of the accuracy of our methods. Pools of salt water have formed over the beach floes in consequence of the high tide, and in the chase of the crab-eater today very brilliant flashes of phosphorescent light appeared in these pools. We think it due to a small copepod. I have just found a reference to the same phenomenon in Nordenskiöld's *Vega*. He, and apparently Bellot before him, noted the phenomenon. An interesting instance of bi-polarity.

Another interesting phenomenon observed today was a cirrus cloud lit by sunlight. It was seen by Wilson and Bowers 5° above the northern horizon – the sun is 9° below our horizon, and without refraction we calculate a cloud could be seen which was 12 miles high. Allowing refraction the phenomenon appears very possible.

Wednesday, May 31. – The sky was overcast this morning and the temperature up to −13°. Went out after lunch to 'Land's End'. The surface of snow was sticky for ski, except where drifts were deep. There was an oppressive feel in the air and I got very hot, coming in with head and hands bare.

At 5, from dead calm the wind suddenly sprang up from the south, force 40 miles per hour, and since that it has been blowing a blizzard; wind very gusty, from 20 to 60 miles. I have never known a storm come on so suddenly, and it shows what possibility there is of individuals becoming lost even if they only go a short way from the hut.

Tonight Wilson has given us a very interesting lecture on sketching. He started by explaining his methods of rough sketch and written colour record, and explained its suitability to this climate as opposed to coloured chalks, &c. – a very practical method for cold fingers and one that becomes more accurate with practice in observation. His theme then became the extreme importance of accuracy, his mode of expression and explanation frankly Ruskin-esque. Don't put in meaningless lines – every line should be from observation. So with contrast of light and shade – fine shading, subtle distinction, everything – impossible without care, patience, and trained attention.

He raised a smile by generalising failures in sketches of others of our party which had been brought to him for criticism. He pointed out how much had been put in from preconceived notion. 'He will draw a berg faithfully as it is now and he studies it, but he leaves sea and sky to be put in afterwards, as he thinks they must be like sea and sky everywhere else, and he is content to try and remember how these *should* be done.' Nature's harmonies cannot be guessed at.

He quoted much from Ruskin, leading on a little deeper to 'Composition', paying a hearty tribute to Ponting.

The lecture was delivered in the author's usual modest strain, but unconsciously it was expressive of himself and his whole-hearted thoroughness. He stands very high in the scale of human beings – how high I scarcely knew till the experience of the past few months.

There is no member of our party so universally esteemed; only tonight I realise how patiently and consistently he has given time and attention to help the efforts of the other sketchers, and so it is all through; he has had a hand in almost every lecture given, and has been consulted in almost every effort which has been made towards the solution of the practical or theoretical problems of our Polar world.

The achievement of a great result by patient work is the best possible object-lesson for struggling humanity, for the results of genius, however admirable, can rarely be instructive. The chief of the Scientific Staff sets an example which is more potent than any other factor in maintaining that bond of good fellowship which is the marked and beneficent characteristic of our community.

CHAPTER ELEVEN

To Midwinter Day

Thursday, June 1. – The wind blew hard all night, gusts arising to 72 m.p.h.; the anemometer choked five times – temperature +9°. It is still blowing this morning. Incidentally we have found that these heavy winds react very conveniently on our ventilating system. A fire is always a good ventilator, ensuring the circulation of inside air and the indraught of fresh air; its defect as a ventilator lies in the low level at which it extracts inside air. Our ventilating system utilises the normal fire draught, but also by suitable holes in the funnelling causes the same draught to extract foul air at higher levels. I think this is the first time such a system has been used. It is a bold step to make holes in the funnelling as obviously any uncertainty of draught might fill the hut with smoke. Since this does not happen with us it follows that there is always strong suction through our stovepipes, and this is achieved by their exceptionally large dimensions and by the length of the outer chimney pipe.

With wind this draught is greatly increased and with high winds the draught would be too great for the stoves if it were not for the relief of the ventilating holes.

In these circumstances, therefore, the rate of extraction of air automatically rises, and since high wind is usually accompanied with marked rise of temperature, the rise occurs at the most convenient season, when the interior of the hut would otherwise tend to become oppressively warm. The practical result of the system is that in spite of the numbers of people living in the hut, the cooking, and the smoking, the inside air is nearly always warm, sweet, and fresh.

There is usually a drawback to the best of arrangements, and I have said 'nearly' always. The exceptions in this connection occur when the outside air is calm and warm and the galley fire, as in the early morning, needs to be worked up; it is necessary under these conditions to temporarily close the ventilating holes, and if at this time the cook is intent on preparing our breakfast with a frying-pan we are quickly made aware of his intentions. A combination of this sort is rare and lasts only for a very short time, for directly the fire is aglow the ventilator can be opened again and the relief is almost instantaneous.

This very satisfactory condition of inside air must be a highly important factor in the preservation of health.

I have today regularised the pony 'nicknames'; I must leave it to Drake to pull out the relation to the 'proper' names according to our school contracts!*

The nicknames are as follows:

James Pigg	Keohane
Bones	Crean
Michael	Clissold
Snatcher	Evans (P.O.)
Jehu	
China	
Christopher	Hooper
Victor	Bowers
Snippets (windsucker)	
Nobby	Lashly

Friday, June 2. – The wind still high. The drift ceased at an early hour yesterday; it is difficult to account for the fact. At night the sky cleared; then and this morning we had a fair display of aurora streamers to the N. and a faint arch east. Curiously enough the temperature still remains high, about +7°.

The meteorological conditions are very puzzling.

Saturday, June 3. – The wind dropped last night, but at 4 a.m. suddenly sprang up from a dead calm to 30 miles an hour. Almost instantaneously, certainly within the space of one minute, there was a temperature rise of nine degrees. It is the most extraordinary and interesting example of a rise of temperature with a southerly wind that I can remember. It is certainly difficult to account for unless we imagine that during the calm the surface layer of cold air

* Officially the ponies were named after the several schools which had subscribed for their purchase; but sailors are inveterate nicknamers, and the unofficial humour prevailed. See Note 18.

is extremely thin and that there is a steep inverted gradient. When the wind arose the sky overhead was clearer than I ever remember to have seen it, the constellations brilliant, and the Milky Way like a bright auroral streamer.

The wind has continued all day, making it unpleasant out of doors. I went for a walk over the land; it was dark, the rock very black, very little snow lying; old footprints in the soft, sandy soil were filled with snow, showing quite white on a black ground. Have been digging away at food statistics.

Simpson has just given us a discourse, in the ordinary lectures series, on his instruments. Having already described these instruments, there is little to comment upon; he is excellently lucid in his explanations.

As an analogy to the attempt to make a scientific observation when the condition under consideration is affected by the means employed, he rather quaintly cited the impossibility of discovering the length of trousers by bending over to see!

The following are the instruments described:

	Features
The outside (bimetallic) thermograph	
The inside thermograph (alcohol)	Alcohol in spiral, small lead pipe – float vessel
The electrically recording anemometer	Cam device with contact on wheel; slowing arrangement, inertia of wheel
The Dynes anemometer	Parabola on immersed float
The recording wind vane	Metallic pen
The magnetometer	Horizontal force measured in two directions – vertical force in one – timing arrangement.
The high and low potential apparatus of the balloon thermograph	Spotting arrangement and difference, see *ante*.

Simpson is admirable as a worker, admirable as a scientist, and admirable as a lecturer.

Sunday, June 4. – A calm and beautiful day. The account of this, a typical Sunday, would run as follows. Breakfast. A half-hour or so selecting hymns and preparing for Service whilst the hut is being cleared up. The Service: a hymn; Morning Prayer to the Psalms; another hymn; prayers from Communion Service and Litany; a final hymn and our special prayer. Wilson strikes the note on which the hymn is to start and I try to hit it after with doubtful success! After church the men go out with their ponies.

Today Wilson, Bowers, Cherry-Garrard, Lashly, and I went to start the building of our first 'igloo'. There is a good deal of difference of opinion as to the best implement with which to cut snow blocks. Cherry-Garrard had a knife which I designed and Lashly made, Wilson a saw, and Bowers a large trowel. I'm inclined to think the knife will prove most effective, but the others don't acknowledge it *yet*. As far as one can see at present this knife should have a longer handle and much coarser teeth in the saw edge – perhaps also the blade should be thinner.

We must go on with this hut building till we get good at it. I'm sure it's going to be a useful art.

We only did three courses of blocks when tea-time arrived, and light was not good enough to proceed after tea.

Sunday afternoon for the men means a 'stretch off the land'.

I went over the floe on ski. The best possible surface after the late winds as far as Inaccessible Island. Here, and doubtless in most places along the shore, this, the first week of June, may be noted as the date by which the wet, sticky salt crystals become covered and the surface possible for wood runners. Beyond the island the snow is still very thin, barely covering the ice flowers, and the surface is still bad.

There has been quite a small landslide on the S. side of the Island; seven or eight blocks of rock, one or two tons in weight, have dropped on to the floe, an interesting instance of the possibility of transport by sea ice.

Ponting has been out to the bergs photographing by flashlight. As I passed south of the Island with its whole mass between myself and the photographer I saw the flashes of magnesium light, having all the appearance of lightning. The light illuminated the sky and apparently objects at a great distance from the camera. It is evident that there may be very great possibilities in the use of this light for signalling purposes, and I propose to have some experiments.

N.B. – Magnesium flashlight as signalling apparatus in the summer.

Another crab-eater seal was secured today; he had come up by the bergs.

The Castle Berg, with dog sledge

Monday, June 5. – The wind has been S. all day, sky overcast and air misty with snow crystals. The temperature has gone steadily up and tonight rose to +16°. Everything seems to threaten a blizzard which cometh not. But what is to be made of this extraordinary high temperature heaven only knows. Went for a walk over the rocks and found it very warm and muggy.

Taylor gave us a paper on the Beardmore Glacier. He has taken pains to work up available information; on the ice side he showed the very gradual gradient as compared with the Ferrar. If crevasses are as plentiful as reported, the motion of glacier must be very considerable. There seem to be three badly crevassed parts where the glacier is constricted and the fall is heavier.

Geologically he explained the rocks found and the problems unsolved. The basement rocks, as to the north, appear to be reddish and grey granites and altered slate (possibly bearing fossils). The Cloudmaker appears to be diorite; Mt Buckley sedimentary. The suggested formation is of several layers of coal with sandstone above and below; interesting to find if it is so, and investigate coal.

Wood fossil conifer appears to have come from this – better to get leaves – wrap fossils up for protection.

Mt Dawson described as pinkish limestone, with a wedge of dark rock; this very doubtful! Limestone is of great interest owing to chance of finding Cambrian fossils (Archeocyathus).

He mentioned the interest of finding here, as in Dry Valley, volcanic cones of recent date (later than the recession of the ice). As points to be looked to in Geology and Physiography:

1. Hope Island shape.
2. Character of wall facets.
3. Type of tributary glaciers – cliff or curtain, broken.
4. Do tributaries enter 'at grade'?
5. Lateral gullies pinnacled, &c., shape and size of slope.
6. Do tributaries cut out gullies – empty unoccupied cirques, hangers, &c.
7. Do upland moraines show tesselation?
8. Arrangement of strata, inclusion of.
9. Types of moraines, distance of blocks.
10. Weathering of glaciers. Types of surface. (Thrust mark? Rippled, snow stool, glass house, coral reef, honeycomb, plough-share, bastions, piecrust.)
11. Amount of water silt bands, stratified, or irregular folded or broken.
12. Cross section, of valleys 35° slopes?
13. Weather slopes débris covered, height to which.
14. Nunataks, height of rounded, height of any angle in profile, erratics.
15. Evidence of order in glacier delta.

Debenham in discussion mentioned usefulness of small chips of rock – many chips from several places are more valuable than few larger specimens.

We had an interesting little discussion.

I must enter a protest against the use made of the word 'glaciated' by Geologists and Physiographers.

To them a glaciated land is 'one which appears to have been shaped by former ice action'.

The meaning I attach to the phrase, and one which I believe is more commonly current, is that it describes a land at present wholly or partly covered with ice and snow.

I hold the latter is the obvious meaning and the former results from a piracy committed in very recent times.

The alternative terms descriptive of the different meanings are ice-covered and ice-eroded.

Today I have been helping the Soldier to design pony rugs; the great thing, I think, is to get something which will completely cover the hindquarters.

Tuesday, June 6. – The temperature has been as high as +19° today; the south wind persisted until the evening with clear sky except for fine effects of torn cloud round about the mountain. Tonight the moon has emerged from behind the mountain and sails across the cloudless northern sky; the wind has fallen and the scene is glorious.

It is my birthday, a fact I might easily have forgotten, but my kind people did not. At lunch an immense birthday cake made its appearance and we were photographed assembled about it. Clissold had decorated its sugared top with various devices in chocolate and crystallised fruit, flags and photographs of myself.

After my walk I discovered that great preparations were in progress for a special dinner, and when the hour for that meal arrived we sat down to a sumptuous spread with our sledge banners hung about us. Clissold's especially excellent seal soup, roast mutton and red currant jelly, fruit salad, asparagus and chocolate – such was our menu. For drink we had cider cup, a mystery not yet fathomed, some sherry and a liqueur.

After this luxurious meal everyone was very festive and amiably argumentative. As I write there is a group in the dark room discussing political progress with large discussions – another at one corner of the dinner table airing its views on the origin of matter and the probability of its ultimate discovery, and yet another debating military problems. The scraps that reach me from the various groups sometimes piece together in ludicrous fashion. Perhaps these arguments are practically unprofitable, but they give a great deal of pleasure to the participants. It's delightful to hear the ring of triumph in some voice when the owner imagines he has delivered himself of a well-rounded period or a clinching state-ment concerning the point under discussion. They are boys, all of them, but such excellent good-natured ones; there has been no

sign of sharpness or anger, no jarring note, in all these wordy
contests; all end with a laugh.

Captain Scott's birthday dinner, June 6 1911
left to right: Atkinson, Meares, Cherry-Garrard, Oates (standing),
Taylor, Nelson, Evans, Scott, Wilson, Simpson, Bowers,
Gran (standing), Wright, Debenham, Day

Nelson has offered Taylor a pair of socks to teach him some
geology! This lulls me to sleep!

Wednesday, June 7. – A very beautiful day. In the afternoon went
well out over the floe to the south, looking up Nelson at his
icehole and picking up Bowers at his thermometer. The surface
was polished and beautifully smooth for ski, the scene brightly
illuminated with moonlight, the air still and crisp, and the thermometer at −10°. Perfect conditions for a winter walk.

In the evening I read a paper on 'The Ice Barrier and Inland Ice'.
I have strung together a good many new points and the interest
taken in the discussion was very genuine – so keen, in fact, that we
did not break up till close on midnight. I am keeping this paper,
which makes a very good basis for all future work on these
subjects. (See 'Universitas Antarctica', in Volume Two)

Shelters to iceholes

Time out of number one is coming across rediscoveries. Of such a nature is the building of shelters for iceholes. We knew a good deal about it in the *Discovery*, but unfortunately did not make notes of

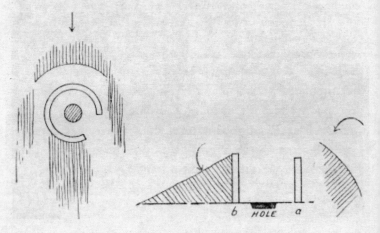

of our experiences. I sketched the above figures for Nelson, and found on going to the hole that the drift accorded with my sketch. The sketches explain themselves. I think wall 'b' should be higher than wall 'a'.

My night on duty. The silent hours passed rapidly and comfortably. To bed 7 a.m.

Thursday, June 8. – Did not turn out till 1 p.m., then with a bad head, an inevitable sequel to a night of vigil. Walked out to and around the bergs, bright moonlight, but clouds rapidly spreading up from south.

Tried the snow knife, which is developing. Debenham and Gran went off to Hut Point this morning; they should return tomorrow.

Friday, June 9. – No wind came with the clouds of yesterday, but the sky has not been clear since they spread over it except for about two hours in the middle of the night when the moonlight was so bright that one might have imagined the day returned.

Otherwise the web of stratus which hangs over us thickens and thins, rises and falls with very bewildering uncertainty. We want

theories for these mysterious weather conditions; meanwhile it is
annoying to lose the advantages of the moonlight.

This morning had some discussion with Nelson and Wright
regarding the action of sea water in melting barrier and sea ice.
The discussion was useful to me in drawing attention to the
equilibrium of layers of sea water.

In the afternoon I went round the Razorback Islands on ski, a
run of 5 or 6 miles; the surface was good but in places still irregular
with the pressures formed when the ice was 'young'.

The snow is astonishingly soft on the south side of both islands.
It is clear that in the heaviest blizzard one could escape the wind
altogether by camping to windward of the larger island. One sees
more and more clearly what shelter is afforded on the weather side
of steep-sided objects.

Passed three seals asleep on the ice. Two others were killed near
the bergs.

Saturday, June 10. – The impending blizzard has come; the wind
came with a burst at 9.30 this morning.

Simpson spent the night turning over a theory to account for the
phenomenon, and delivered himself of
it this morning. It seems a good basis
for the reference of future observations.
He imagines the atmosphere A C in
potential equilibrium with large margin
of stability, i.e. the difference of temperature between A and C being much
less than the adiabatic gradient.

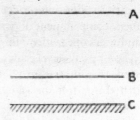

In this condition there is a tendency to cool by radiation
until some critical layer, B, reaches its due point. A stratus cloud
is thus formed at B; from this moment AB continues to cool,
but BC is protected from radiating, whilst heated by radiation
from snow and possibly by release of latent heat due to cloud
formation.

The condition now rapidly approaches unstable equilibrium,
B C tending to rise, A B to descend.

Owing to lack of sun heat the effect will be more rapid in south
than north and therefore the upset will commence first in the
south. After the first start the upset will rapidly spread north,
bringing the blizzard. The facts supporting the theory are the

actual formation of a stratus cloud before a blizzard, the snow and warm temperature of the blizzard and its gusty nature.

It is a pretty starting-point, but, of course, there are weak spots.

Atkinson has found a trypanosome in the fish – it has been stained, photographed and drawn – an interesting discovery having regard to the few species that have been found. A trypanosome is the cause of 'sleeping sickness'.

The blizzard has continued all day with a good deal of drift. I went for a walk, but the conditions were not inviting.

We have begun to consider details of next season's travelling equipment. The crampons, repair of finnesko with sealskin, and an idea for a double tent have been discussed today. P.O. Evans and Lashly are delightfully intelligent in carrying out instructions.

Sunday, June 11. – A fine clear morning, the moon now revolving well aloft and with full face.

For exercise a run on ski to the South Bay in the morning and a dash up the Ramp before dinner. Wind and drift arose in the middle of the day, but it is now nearly calm again.

At our morning service Cherry-Garrard, good fellow, vamped the accompaniment of two hymns; he received encouraging thanks and will cope with all three hymns next Sunday.

Day by day news grows scant in this midwinter season; all events seem to compress into a small record, yet a little reflection shows that this is not the case. For instance, I have had at least three important discussions on weather and ice conditions today, concerning which many notes might be made, and quite a number of small arrangements have been made.

If a diary can be so inadequate here, how difficult must be the task of making a faithful record of a day's events in ordinary civilised life! I think this is why I have found it so difficult to keep a diary at home.

Monday, June 12. – The weather is not kind to us. There has not been much wind today, but the moon has been hid behind stratus cloud. One feels horribly cheated in losing the pleasure of its light. I scarcely know what the Crozier party can do if they don't get better luck next month.

Debenham and Gran have not yet returned; this is their fifth day of absence.

Bowers and Cherry-Garrard went to Cape Royds this afternoon to stay the night. Taylor and Wright walked there and back after breakfast this morning. They returned shortly after lunch.

Went for a short spin on ski this morning and again this afternoon. This evening Evans has given us a lecture on surveying. He was shy and slow, but very painstaking, taking a deal of trouble in preparing pictures, &c.

I took the opportunity to note hurriedly the few points to which I want attention especially directed. No doubt others will occur to me presently. I think I now understand very well how and why the old surveyors (like Belcher) failed in the early Arctic work.

1. Every officer who takes part in the Southern Journey ought to have in his memory the approximate variation of the compass at various stages of the journey and to know how to apply it to obtain a true course from the compass. The variation changes very slowly so that no great effort of memory is required.

2. He ought to know what the true course is to reach one depôt from another.

3. He should be able to take an observation with the theodolite.

4. He should be able to work out a meridian altitude observation.

5. He could advantageously add to his knowledge the ability to work out a longitude observation or an ex-meridian altitude.

6. He should know how to read the sledge-meter.

7. He should note and remember the error of the watch he carries and the rate which is ascertained for it from time to time.

8. He should assist the surveyor by noting the coincidences of objects, the opening out of valleys, the observation of new peaks, &c.[19]

Tuesday, June 13. – A very beautiful day. We revelled in the calm clear moonlight; the temperature has fallen to −26°. The surface of the floe perfect for ski – had a run to South Bay in forenoon and was away on a long circuit around Inaccessible Island in the afternoon. In such weather the cold splendour of the scene is beyond description; everything is satisfying, from the deep purple of the starry sky to the gleaming bergs and the sparkle of the crystals under foot.

Some very brilliant patches of aurora over the southern shoulder of the mountain. Observed an exceedingly bright meteor shoot across the sky to the northward.

On my return found Debenham and Gran back from Cape Armitage. They had intended to start back on Sunday, but were prevented by bad weather; they seemed to have had stronger winds than we.

On arrival at the hut they found poor little 'Mukaka' coiled up outside the door, looking pitifully thin and weak, but with enough energy to bark at them.

This dog was run over and dragged for a long way under the sledge runners whilst we were landing stores in January (the 7th). He has never been worth much since, but remained lively in spite of all the hardships of sledging work. At Hut Point he looked a miserable object, as the hair refused to grow on his hindquarters. It seemed as though he could scarcely continue in such a condition, and when the party came back to Cape Evans he was allowed to run free alongside the sledge.

On the arrival of the party I especially asked after the little animal and was told by Demetri that he had returned, but later it transpired that this was a mistake – that he had been missed on the journey and had not turned up again later as was supposed.

I learned this fact only a few days ago and had quite given up the hope of ever seeing the poor little beast again. It is extraordinary to realise that this poor, lame, half-clad animal has lived for a whole month by himself. He had blood on his mouth when found, implying the capture of a seal, but how he managed to kill it and then get through its skin is beyond comprehension. Hunger drives hard.

Wednesday, June 14. – Storms are giving us little rest. We found a thin stratus over the sky this morning, foreboding ill. The wind came, as usual with a rush, just after lunch. At first there was much drift – now the drift has gone but the gusts run up to 65 m.p.h.

Had a comfortless stroll around the hut; how rapidly things change when one thinks of the delights of yesterday! Paid a visit to Wright's ice cave; the pendulum is installed and will soon be ready for observation. Wright anticipates the possibility of difficulty with ice crystals on the agate planes.

He tells me that he has seen some remarkably interesting examples of the growth of ice crystals on the walls of the cave and has observed the same unaccountable confusion of the size of grains in the ice, showing how little history can be gathered from the structure of ice.

This evening Nelson gave us his second biological lecture, starting with a brief reference to the scientific classification of the organism into Kingdom, Phylum, Group, Class, Order, Genus, Species; he stated the justification of a biologist in such an expedition, as being 'to determine the condition under which organic substances exist in the sea'.

He proceeded to draw divisions between the bottom organisms without power of motion, benthon, the nekton motile life in mid-water, and the plankton or floating life. Then he led very prettily on to the importance of the tiny vegetable organisms as the basis of all life.

In the killer whale may be found a seal, in the seal a fish, in the fish a smaller fish, in the smaller fish a copepod, and in the copepod a diatom. If this be regular feeding throughout, the diatom or vegetable is essentially the base of all.

Light is the essential of vegetable growth or metabolism, and light quickly vanishes in depth of water, so that all ocean life must ultimately depend on the phyto-plankton. To discover the conditions of this life is therefore to go to the root of matters.

At this point came an interlude – descriptive of the various biological implements in use in the ship and on shore: the otter trawl, the Agassiz trawl, the 'D' net, and the ordinary dredger.

A word or two on the using of 'D' nets and then explanation of sieves for classifying the bottom, its nature causing variation in the organisms living on it.

From this he took us amongst the tow-nets with their beautiful silk fabrics, meshes running 180 to the inch and materials costing 2 guineas the yard – to the German tow-nets for quantitative measurements, the object of the latter and its doubtful accuracy, young fish trawls.

From this to the chemical composition of sea water, the total salt about 3.5 per cent, but variable: the proportions of the various salts do not appear to differ, thus the chlorine test detects the salinity quantitatively. Physically plankton life must depend on this salinity and also on temperature, pressure, light, and movement.

(If plankton only inhabits surface waters, then density, temperatures, &c., of surface waters must be the important factors. Why should biologists strive for deeper layers? Why should not deep sea life be maintained by dead vegetable matter?)

Here again the lecturer branched off into descriptions of water bottles, deep sea thermometers, and current-meters, the which I think have already received some notice in this Diary. To what depth light may extend is the difficult problem, and we had some speculation, especially in the debate on this question. Simpson suggested that laboratory experiment should easily determine. Atkinson suggested growth of bacteria on a scratched plate. The idea seems to be that vegetable life cannot exist without red rays, which probably do not extend beyond 7 feet or so. Against this is an extraordinary recovery of *Holosphera Viridis* by German expedition from 2000 fathoms; this seems to have been confirmed. Bowers caused much amusement by demanding to know 'if the pycnogs (pycnogonids) were more nearly related to the arachnids (spiders) or crustaceans'. As a matter of fact a very sensible question, but it caused amusement because of its sudden display of long names. Nelson is an exceedingly capable lecturer; he makes his subject very clear and is never too technical.

Thursday, June 15. – Keen cold wind – overcast sky till 5.30 p.m. Spent an idle day.

Jimmy Pigg had an attack of colic in the stable this afternoon. He was taken out and doctored on the floe, which seemed to improve matters, but on return to the stable he was off his feed.

This evening the Soldier tells me he has eaten his food, so I hope all will be well again.

Friday, June 16. – Overcast again – little wind but also little moonlight. Jimmy Pigg quite recovered.

Went round the bergs in the afternoon. A great deal of ice has fallen from the irregular ones, showing that a great deal of weathering of bergs goes on during the winter and hence that the life of a berg is very limited, even if it remains in the high latitudes.

Tonight Debenham lectured on volcanoes. His matter is very good, but his voice a little monotonous, so that there were signs of slumber in the audience, but all woke up for a warm and amusing discussion succeeding the lecture.

The lecturer first showed a world chart showing distribution of volcanoes, showing general tendency of eruptive explosions to occur in lines. After following these lines in other parts of the world he showed difficulty of finding symmetrical linear distribution near McMurdo Sound. He pointed out incidentally the important inference which could be drawn from the discovery of altered sandstone in the Erebus region. He went to the shapes of volcanoes –

The massive type formed by very fluid lavas – Mauna Loa (Hawaii), Vesuvius, examples.

The more perfect cones formed by ash talus – Fujiama, Discovery.

The explosive type with parasitic cones – Erebus, Morning, Etna.

Fissure eruption – historic only in Iceland, but best prehistoric examples Deccan (India) and Oregon (U.S.).

There is small ground for supposing relation between adjacent volcanoes – activity in one is rarely accompanied by activity in the other. It seems most likely that vent tubes are entirely separate.

Products of volcanoes. – The lecturer mentioned the escape of quantities of free hydrogen – there was some discussion on this point afterwards; that water is broken up is easily understood, but what becomes of the oxygen? Simpson suggests the presence of much oxidizable material.

CO_2 as a noxious gas also mentioned and discussed – causes mythical 'upas' tree – sulphurous fumes attend final stages.

Practically little or no heat escapes through sides of a volcano.

There was argument over physical conditions influencing explosions – especially as to barometric influence. There was a good deal of disjointed information on lavas, ropy or rapid flowing and viscous – also on spatter cones and caverns.

In all cases lavas cool slowly – heat has been found close to the surface after 87 years. On Etna there is lava over ice. The lecturer finally reviewed the volcanicity of our own neighbourhood. He described various vents of Erebus, thinks Castle Rock a 'plug' – here some discussion – Observation Hill part of old volcano, nothing in common with Crater Hill. Inaccessible Island seems to have no connection with Erebus.

Finally we had a few words on the origin of volcanicity and afterwards some discussion on an old point – the relation to the sea. Why are volcanoes close to sea? Debenham thinks not cause and effect, but two effects resulting from same cause.

Great argument as to whether effect of barometric changes on Erebus vapour can be observed. Not much was said about the theory of volcanoes, but Debenham touched on American theories – the melting out from internal magma.

There was nothing much to catch hold of throughout, but discussion of such a subject sorts one's ideas.

Saturday, June 17. – Northerly wind, temperature changeable, dropping to −16°.

Wind doubtful in the afternoon. Moon still obscured – it is very trying. Feeling dull in spirit today.

Sunday, June 18. – Another blizzard – the weather is distressing. It ought to settle down soon, but unfortunately the moon is passing.

Held the usual Morning Service. Hymns not quite successful today.

Tonight Atkinson has taken the usual monthly measurement. I don't think there has been much change.

Monday, June 19. – A pleasant change to find the air calm and the sky clear – temperature down to −28°. At 1.30 the moon vanished behind the western mountains, after which, in spite of the clear sky, it was very dark on the floe. Went out on ski across the bay, then round about the cape, and so home, facing a keen northerly wind on return.

Atkinson is making a new fish-trap hole; from one cause and another, the breaking of the trap, and the freezing of the hole, no catch has been made for some time. I don't think we shall get good catches during the dark season, but Atkinson's own requirements are small, and the fish, though nice enough, are not such a luxury as to be greatly missed from our 'menu'.

Our daily routine has possessed a settled regularity for a long time. Clissold is up about 7 a.m. to start the breakfast. At 7.30 Hooper starts sweeping the floor and setting the table. Between 8 and 8.30 the men are out and about, fetching ice for melting, &c. Anton is off to feed the ponies, Demetri to see the dogs; Hooper bursts on the slumberers with repeated announcements of the time, usually a quarter of an hour ahead of the clock. There is a stretching of limbs and an interchange of morning greetings, garnished with sleepy humour. Wilson and Bowers meet in a state of nature beside a washing basin filled with snow and proceed to rub glistening limbs with this chilling substance. A little later with less hardihood some others may be seen making the most of a meagre allowance of water. Soon after 8.30 I manage to drag myself from a very comfortable bed and make my toilet with a bare pint of water. By about ten minutes to 9 my clothes are on, my bed is made, and I sit down to my bowl of porridge; most of the others are gathered about the table by this time, but there are a few laggards who run the nine o'clock rule very close. The rule is instituted to prevent delay in the day's work, and it has needed a little pressure to keep one or two up to its observance. By 9.20 breakfast is finished, and before the half-hour has struck the table has been cleared. From 9.30 to 1.30 the men are steadily employed on a programme of preparation for sledging, which seems likely to occupy the greater part of the winter. The repair of sleeping-bags and the alteration of tents have already been done, but there are many other tasks uncompleted or not yet begun, such as the manufacture of provision bags, crampons, sealskin soles, pony clothes, &c.

Hooper has another good sweep up the hut after breakfast, washes the mess traps, and generally tidies things. I think it a good thing that in these matters the officers need not wait on themselves; it gives long unbroken days of scientific work and must, therefore, be an economy of brain in the long run.

We meet for our mid-day meal at 1.30 or 1.45, and spend a very cheerful half-hour over it. Afterwards the ponies are exercised, weather permitting; this employs all the men and a few of the officers for an hour or more – the rest of us generally take exercise in some form at the same time. After this the officers go on steadily with their work, whilst the men do odd jobs to while away the time. The evening meal, our dinner, comes at 6.30, and is finished within the hour. Afterwards people read, write, or play games, or occasionally finish some piece of work. The gramophone is usually started by some kindly disposed person, and on three nights of the week the lectures to which I have referred are given. These lectures still command full audiences and lively discussions.

At 11 p.m. the acetylene lights are put out, and those who wish to remain up or to read in bed must depend on candle-light. The majority of candles are extinguished by midnight, and the night watchman alone remains awake to keep his vigil by the light of an oil lamp.

Day after day passes in this fashion. It is not a very active life perhaps, but certainly not an idle one. Few of us sleep more than eight hours out of the twenty-four.

On Saturday afternoon or Sunday morning some extra bathing takes place; chins are shaven, and perhaps clean garments donned. Such signs, with the regular Service on Sunday, mark the passage of the weeks.

Tonight Day has given us a lecture on his motor sledge. He seems very hopeful of success, but I fear is rather more sanguine in temperament than his sledge is reliable in action. I wish I could have more confidence in his preparations, as he is certainly a delightful companion.

Tuesday, June 20. – Last night the temperature fell to −36°, the lowest we have had this year. On the Ramp the minimum was −31°, not the first indication of a reversed temperature gradient. We have had a calm day, as is usual with a low thermometer.

It was very beautiful out of doors this morning; as the crescent moon was sinking in the west, Erebus showed a heavy vapour cloud, showing that the quantity is affected by temperature rather than pressure.

I'm glad to have had a good run on ski.

The Cape Crozier Party are preparing for departure, and heads have been put together to provide as much comfort as the strenuous circumstances will permit. I came across a hint as to the value  of a double tent in Sverdrup's book, *New Land*, and (P.O.) Evans has made a lining for one of the tents; it is secured on the inner side of the poles and provides an air space inside the tent. I think it is going to be a great success, and that it will go far to obviate the necessity of considering the question of snow huts – though we shall continue our efforts in this direction also.

Another new departure is the decision to carry eiderdown sleeping-bags inside the reindeer ones.

With such an arrangement the early part of the journey is bound to be comfortable, but when the bags get iced difficulties are pretty certain to arise.

Day has been devoting his energies to the creation of a blubber stove, much assisted of course by the experience gained at Hut Point.

The blubber is placed in an annular vessel, A. The oil from it passes through a pipe, B, and spreads out on the surface of a plate, C, with a containing flange; *d d* are raised points which serve as heat conductors; *e e* is a tin chimney for flame with air holes at its base.

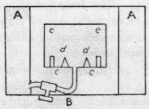

To start the stove the plate C must be warmed with spirit lamp or primus, but when the blubber oil is well alight its heat is quite sufficient to melt the blubber in A and keep up the oil supply – the heat gradually rises until the oil issues from B in a vaporised condition, when, of course, the heat given off by the stove is intense.

This stove was got going this morning in five minutes in the outer temperature with the blubber hard frozen. It will make a great difference to the Crozier Party if they can manage to build a hut, and the experience gained will be everything for the Western Party in the summer. With a satisfactory blubber stove it would never be necessary to carry fuel on a coast journey, and we shall deserve well of posterity if we can perfect one.

The Crozier journey is to be made to serve a good many trial ends. As I have already mentioned, each man is to go on a different food scale, with a view to determining the desirable proportion of fats and carbohydrates. Wilson is also to try the effect of a double wind-proof suit instead of extra woollen clothing.

If two suits of wind-proof will keep one as warm in the spring as a single suit does in the summer, it is evident that we can face the summit of Victoria Land with a very slight increase of weight.

I think the new crampons, which will also be tried on this journey, are going to be a great success. We have returned to the last *Discovery* type with improvements; the magnalium sole plates of our own crampons are retained but shod with ½-inch steel spikes; these plates are riveted through canvas to an inner leather sole, and the canvas is brought up on all sides to form a covering to the 'finnesko' over which it is laced – they are less than half the weight of an ordinary ski boot, go on very easily, and secure very neatly.

Midwinter Day, the turn of the season, is very close; it will be good to have light for the more active preparations for the coming year.

Wednesday, June 21. – The temperature low again, falling to −36°. A curious hazy look in the sky, very little wind. The cold is bringing some minor troubles with the clockwork instruments in the open – and with the acetylene gas plant no insuperable difficulties. Went for a ski run round the bergs; found it very dark and uninteresting.

The temperature remained low during night and Taylor reported a very fine display of Aurora.

Thursday, June 22. – MIDWINTER. The sun reached its maximum depression at about 2.30 p.m. on the 22nd, Greenwich Mean Time: this is 2.30 a.m. on the 23rd according to the local time of the 180th meridian which we are keeping. Dinner tonight is therefore the meal which is nearest the sun's critical change of course, and has been observed with all the festivity customary at Xmas at home.

At tea we broached an enormous Buszard cake, with much gratitude to its provider, Cherry-Garrard. In preparation for the evening our 'Union Jacks' and sledge flags were hung about the large table, which itself was laid with glass and a plentiful supply of champagne bottles instead of the customary mugs and enamel limejuice jugs. At seven o'clock we sat down to an extravagant bill of fare as compared with our usual simple diet.

Beginning on seal soup, by common consent the best decoction that our cook produces, we went on to roast beef with Yorkshire pudding, fried potatoes and Brussels sprouts. Then followed a flaming plum-pudding and excellent mince pies, and thereafter a dainty savoury of anchovy and cod's roe. A wondrous attractive meal even in so far as judged by our simple lights, but with its garnishments a positive feast, for withal the table was strewn with dishes of burnt almonds, crystallised fruits, chocolates and such toothsome kickshaws, whilst the unstinted supply of champagne which accompanied the courses was succeeded by a noble array of liqueur bottles from which choice could be made in the drinking of toasts.

I screwed myself up to a little speech which drew attention to the nature of the celebration as a half-way mark not only in our winter but in the plans of the Expedition as originally published. (I fear there are some who don't realise how rapidly time passes and who have barely begun work which by this time ought to be in full swing.)

We had come through a summer season and half a winter, and had before us half a winter and a second summer. We ought to know how we stood in every respect; we did know how we stood in regard to stores and transport, and I especially thanked the officer in charge of stores and the custodians of the animals. I said that as regards the future, chance must play a part, but that experience showed me that it would have been impossible to have chosen people more fitted to support me in the enterprise to the South than those who were to start in that direction in the spring. I thanked them all for having put their shoulders to the wheel and given me this confidence.

We drank to the Success of the Expedition.

Then everyone was called on to speak, starting on my left and working round the table; the result was very characteristic of the various individuals – one seemed to know so well the style of utterance to which each would commit himself.

Needless to say, all were entirely modest and brief; unexpectedly, all had exceedingly kind things to say of me – in fact I was obliged to request the omission of compliments at an early stage. Nevertheless it was gratifying to have a really genuine recognition of my attitude towards the scientific workers of the Expedition, and I felt very warmly towards all these kind, good fellows for expressing it.

If good will and happy fellowship count towards success, very surely shall we deserve to succeed. It was matter for comment, much applauded, that there had not been a single disagreement between any two members of our party from the beginning. By the end of dinner a very cheerful spirit prevailed, and the room was cleared for Ponting and his lantern, whilst the gramophone gave forth its most lively airs.

When the table was upended, its legs removed, and chairs arranged in rows, we had quite a roomy lecture hall. Ponting had cleverly chosen this opportunity to display a series of slides made from his own local negatives. I have never so fully realised his work as on seeing these beautiful pictures; they so easily outclass anything of their kind previously taken in these regions. Our audience cheered vociferously.

After this show the table was restored for snapdragon, and a brew of milk punch was prepared in which we drank the health of Campbell's Party and of our good friends in the *Terra Nova*. Then the table was again removed and a set of lancers formed.

By this time the effect of stimulating liquid refreshment on men so long accustomed to a simple life became apparent. Our biologist had retired to bed, the silent Soldier bubbled with humour and insisted on dancing with Anton. Evans, P.O., was imparting confidences in heavy whispers. 'Pat' Keohane had grown intensely Irish and desirous of political argument, whilst Clissold sat with a constant expansive smile and punctuated the babble of conversation with an occasional 'Whoop' of delight or disjointed witticism. Other bright-eyed individuals merely reached the capacity to enjoy that which under ordinary circumstances might have passed without evoking a smile.

In the midst of the revelry Bowers suddenly appeared, followed by some satellites bearing an enormous Christmas Tree whose branches bore flaming candles, gaudy crackers, and little presents for all. The presents, I learnt, had been prepared with kindly thought by Miss Souper (Mrs Wilson's sister) and the tree had been made by Bowers of pieces of stick and string with coloured paper to clothe its branches; the whole erection was remarkably creditable and the distribution of the presents caused much amusement.

Whilst revelry was the order of the day within our hut, the elements without seemed desirous of celebrating the occasion with equal emphasis and greater decorum. The eastern sky was massed with swaying auroral light, the most vivid and beautiful display that I had ever seen – fold on fold the arches and curtains of vibrating luminosity rose and spread across the sky, to slowly fade and yet again spring to glowing life.

The brighter light seemed to flow, now to mass itself in wreathing folds in one quarter, from which lustrous streamers shot upward, and anon to run in waves through the system of some dimmer figure as if to infuse new life within it.

It is impossible to witness such a beautiful phenomenon without a sense of awe, and yet this sentiment is not inspired by its brilliancy but rather by its delicacy in light and colour, its transparency, and above all by its tremulous evanescence of form. There is no glittering splendour to dazzle the eye, as has been too often described; rather the appeal is to the imagination by the suggestion of something wholly spiritual, something instinct with a fluttering ethereal life, serenely confident yet restlessly mobile.

One wonders why history does not tell us of 'aurora' worshippers, so easily could the phenomenon be considered the manifestation of 'god' or 'demon'. To the little silent group which stood at gaze before such enchantment it seemed profane to return to the mental and physical atmosphere of our house. Finally when I stepped within, I was glad to find that there had been a general movement bedwards, and in the next half-hour the last of the roysterers had succumbed to slumber.

Thus, except for a few bad heads in the morning, ended the High Festival of Midwinter.

There is little to be said for the artificial uplifting of animal spirits, yet few could take great exception to so rare an outburst in a long run of quiet days.

After all we celebrated the birth of a season which for weal or woe must be numbered amongst the greatest in our lives.

CHAPTER TWELVE

Awaiting the Crozier party

Friday, June 23 – Saturday, June 24. – Two quiet, uneventful days and a complete return to routine.

Sunday, June 25. – I find I have made no mention of Cherry-Garrard's first number of the revived *South Polar Times*, presented to me on Midwinter Day.

It is a very good little volume, bound by Day in a really charming cover of carved venesta wood and sealskin. The contributors are anonymous, but I have succeeded in guessing the identity of the greater number.

The Editor has taken a statistical paper of my own on the plans for the Southern Journey and a well-written serious article on the Geological History of our region by Taylor. Except for editorial and meteorological notes the rest is conceived in the lighter vein. The verse is mediocre except perhaps for a quaint play of words in an amusing little skit on the sleeping-bag argument; but an article entitled 'Valhalla' appears to me to be altogether on a different level. It purports to describe the arrival of some of our party at the gates proverbially guarded by St Peter; the humour is really delicious and nowhere at all forced. In the jokes of a small community it is rare to recognise one which would appeal to an outsider, but some of the happier witticisms of this article seem to me fit for wider circulation than our journal enjoys at present. Above all there is distinct literary merit in it – a polish which leaves you unable to suggest the betterment of a word anywhere,

I unhesitatingly attribute this effort to Taylor, but Wilson and Garrard make Meares responsible for it. If they are right I shall have to own that my judgment of attributes is very much at fault. I must find out.*

* Captain Scott's judgment was not at fault.

A quiet day. Read Church Service as usual; in afternoon walked up the Ramp with Wilson to have a quiet talk before he departs. I wanted to get his ideas as to the scientific work done.

We agreed as to the exceptionally happy organisation of our party.

I took the opportunity to warn Wilson concerning the desirability of complete understanding with Ponting and Taylor with respect to their photographs and records on their return to civilisation.

The weather has been very mysterious of late; on the 23rd and 24th it continuously threatened a blizzard, but now the sky is clearing again with all signs of fine weather.

Monday, June 26. – With a clear sky it was quite twilighty at noon today. Already such signs of day are inspiriting. In the afternoon the wind arose with drift and again the prophets predicted a blizzard. After an hour or two the wind fell and we had a calm, clear evening and night. The blizzards proper seem to be always preceded by an overcast sky in accordance with Simpson's theory.

Taylor gave a most interesting lecture on the physiographic features of the region traversed by his party in the autumn. His mind is very luminous and clear and he treated the subject with a breadth of view which was delightful. The illustrative slides were made from Debenham's photographs, and many of them were quite beautiful. Ponting tells me that Debenham knows quite a lot about photography and goes to work in quite the right way.

The lecture being a précis of Taylor's report there is no need to recapitulate its matter. With the pictures it was startling to realise the very different extent to which tributary glaciers have carved the channels in which they lie. The Canadian Glacier lies dead, but at 'grade' it has cut a very deep channel. The 'double curtain' hangs at an angle of 25°, with practically no channel. Mention was made of the difference of water found in Lake Bonney by me in December 1903 and the Western Party in February 1911. It seems certain that water must go on accumulating in the lake during the two or three summer months, and it is hard to imagine that all can be lost again by the winter's evaporation. If it does, 'evaporation' becomes a matter of primary importance.

There was an excellent picture showing the find of sponges on the Koettlitz Glacier. Heaps of large sponges were found containing corals and some shells, all representative of present-day fauna. How on earth did they get to the place where found? There was a good deal of discussion on the point and no very satisfactory solution offered. Cannot help thinking that there is something in the thought that the glacier may have been weighted down with rubble which finally disengaged itself and allowed the ice to rise. Such speculations are interesting.

Preparations for the start of the Crozier Party are now completed, and the people will have to drag 253 lbs. per man – a big weight.

Day has made an excellent little blubber lamp for lighting; it has an annular wick and talc chimney; a small circular plate over the wick conducts the heat down and raises the temperature of combustion, so that the result is a clear white flame.

We are certainly within measurable distance of using blubber in the most effective way for both heating and lighting, and this is an advance which is of very high importance to the future of Antarctic Exploration.

Tuesday, June 27. – The Crozier Party departed this morning in good spirits – their heavy load was distributed on two 9-feet sledges. Ponting photographed them by flashlight and attempted to get a cinematograph picture by means of a flash candle. But when the candle was ignited it was evident that the light would not be sufficient for the purpose and there was not much surprise when the film proved a failure. The three travellers found they could pull their load fairly easily on the sea ice when the rest of us stood aside for the trial. I'm afraid they will find much more difficulty on the Barrier, but there was nothing now to prevent them starting, and off they went.

With helping contingent I went round the Cape. Taylor and Nelson left at the Razorback Island and report all well. Simpson, Meares, and Gran continued and have not yet returned.

Gran just back on ski; left party at 5¼ miles. Says Meares and Simpson are returning on foot. Reports a bad bit of surface between Tent Island and Glacier Tongue. It was well that the party had assistance to cross this.

This winter travel is a new and bold venture, but the right men have gone to attempt it. All good luck go with them!

Coal consumption

Bowers reports that present consumption (midwinter) = 4 blocks
per day (100 lbs.). An occasional block is required for the absolute
magnetic hut.

He reports 8½ tons used since landing.

This is in excess of 4 blocks per day as follows:

8½ tons in 150 days = 127 lbs. per diem.

= 889 lbs. per week, or nearly 8 cwt.

= 20½ tons per year.

Report August 4.

Used to date = 9 tons = 20,160 lbs.

Say 190 days at 106 lbs. per day.

Coal remaining 20½ tons.

Estimate 8 tons to return of ship.

Total estimate for year, 17 tons. We should have 13 or 14 tons
for next year.

A FRESH MS. BOOK

Quotations on the flyleaf

Where the (Queen's) Law does not carry it is irrational to exact an observance of
other and weaker rules.   RUDYARD KIPLING

Confident of his good intentions but doubtful of his fortitude.

So far as I can venture to offer an opinion on such a matter, the purpose of our
being in existence, the highest object that human beings can set before
themselves is not the pursuit of any such chimera as the annihilation of the
unknown; but it is simply the unwearied endeavour to remove its boundaries a
little further from our little sphere of action.   HUXLEY

Wednesday, June 28. – The temperature has been hovering around
−30° with a clear sky – at midday it was exceptionally light, and
even two hours after noon I was able to pick my way amongst the
boulders of the Ramp. We miss the Crozier Party. Lectures have
ceased during its absence, so that our life is very quiet.

Thursday, June 29. – It seemed rather stuffy in the hut last night –
I found it difficult to sleep, and noticed a good many others in like
case. I found the temperature was only 50°, but that the small
uptake on the stove pipe was closed. I think it would be good to
have a renewal of air at bed time, but don't quite know how to
manage this.

It was calm all night and when I left the hut at 8.30. At 9 the
wind suddenly rose to 40 m.p.h. and at the same moment the

temperature rose 10°. The wind and temperature curves show this sudden simultaneous change more clearly than usual. The curious circumstance is that this blow comes out of a clear sky. This will be disturbing to our theories unless the wind drops again very soon.

The wind fell within an hour almost as suddenly as it had arisen; the temperature followed, only a little more gradually. One may well wonder how such a phenomenon is possible. In the middle of a period of placid calm and out of a clear sky there suddenly rushed upon one this volume of comparatively warm air; it has come and gone like the whirlwind.

Whence comes it and whither goeth?

Went round the bergs after lunch on ski – splendid surface and quite a good light.

We are now getting good records with the tide gauge after a great deal of trouble. Day has given much of his time to the matter, and after a good deal of discussion has pretty well mastered the principles. We brought a self-recording instrument from New Zealand, but this was passed over to Campbell. It has not been an easy matter to manufacture one for our own use. The wire from the bottom weight is led through a tube filled with paraffin as in *Discovery* days, and kept tight by a counterweight after passage through a block on a stanchion rising 6 feet above the floe.

In his first instrument Day arranged for this wire to pass around a pulley, the revolution of which actuated the pen of the recording drum. This should have been successful but for the difficulty of making good mechanical connection between the recorder and the pulley. Backlash caused an unreliable record, and this arrangement had to be abandoned. The motion of the wire was then made to actuate the recorder through a hinged lever, and this arrangement holds, but days and even weeks have been lost in grappling the difficulties of adjustment between the limits of the tide and those of the recording drum; then when all seemed well we found that the floe was not rising uniformly with the water. It is hung up by the beach ice. When we were considering the question of removing the whole apparatus to a more distant point, a fresh crack appeared between it and the shore, and on this 'hinge' the floe seems to be moving more freely.

Friday, June 30, 1911. – The temperature is steadily falling; we are descending the scale of negative thirties and today reached its limit, −39°. Day has manufactured a current vane, a simple arrangement: up to the present he has used this near the Cape. There is little doubt, however, that the water movement is erratic and irregular inside the islands, and I have been anxious to get observations which will indicate the movement in the 'Strait'. I went with him today to find a crack which I thought must run to the north from Inaccessible Island. We discovered it about 2 to 2½ miles out and found it to be an ideal place for such work, a fracture in the ice sheet which is constantly opening and therefore always edged with thin ice. Have told Day that I think a bottle weighted so as to give it a small negative buoyancy, and attached to a fine line, should give as good results as his vane and would be much handier. He now proposes to go one better and put an electric light in the bottle.

We found that our loose dogs had been attacking a seal, and then came across a dead seal which had evidently been worried to death some time ago. It appears Demetri saw more seal further to the north, and this afternoon Meares has killed a large one as well as the one which was worried this morning.

It is good to find the seals so close, but very annoying to find that the dogs have discovered their resting-place.

The long spell of fine weather is very satisfactory.

Saturday, July 1, 1911. – We have designed new ski boots and I think they are going to be a success. My object is to stick to the Huitfeldt binding for sledging if possible. One must wear finnesko on the Barrier, and with finnesko alone a loose binding is necessary. For this we brought 'Finon' bindings, consisting of leather toe straps and thong heel binding. With this arrangement one does not have good control of his ski and stands the chance of a chafe on the 'tendon Achillis'. Owing to the last consideration many had decided to go with toe strap alone as we did in the *Discovery*. This brought into my mind the possibility of using the iron cross bar and snap heel strap of the Huitfeldt on a suitable overshoe.

Evans, P.O., has arisen well to the occasion as a boot maker, and has just completed a pair of shoes which are very nearly what we require.

The soles have two thicknesses of seal skin cured with alum, stiffened at the foot with a layer of venesta board, and raised at the heel on a block of wood. The upper part is large enough to contain a finnesko and is secured by a simple strap. A shoe weighs 13 ozs. against 2 lbs. for a single ski boot – so that shoe and finnesko together are less weight than a boot.

If we can perfect this arrangement it should be of the greatest use to us.

Wright has been swinging the pendulum in his cavern. Prodigious trouble has been taken to keep the time, and this object has been immensely helped by the telephone communication between the cavern, the transit instrument, and the interior of the hut. The timekeeper is perfectly placed. Wright tells me that his ice platform proves to be five times as solid as the fixed piece of masonry used at Potsdam. The only difficulty is the low temperature, which freezes his breath on the glass window of the protecting dome. I feel sure these gravity results are going to be very good.

The temperature has been hanging in the minus thirties all day with calm and clear sky, but this evening a wind has sprung up without rise of temperature. It is now −32°, with a wind of 25 m.p.h. – a pretty stiff condition to face outside!

Sunday, July 2. – There was wind last night, but this morning found a settled calm again, with temperature as usual about −35°. The moon is rising again; it came over the shoulder of Erebus about 5 p.m., in second quarter. It will cross the meridian at night, worse luck, but such days as this will be pleasant even with a low moon; one is very glad to think the Crozier Party are having such a peaceful time.

Sunday routine and nothing much to record.

Monday, July 3. – Another quiet day, the sky more suspicious in appearance. Thin stratus cloud forming and dissipating overhead, curling stratus clouds over Erebus. Wind at Cape Crozier seemed a possibility.

Our people have been far out on the floe. It is cheerful to see the twinkling light of some worker at a water hole or hear the ring of distant voices or swish of ski.

Tuesday, July 4. – A day of blizzard and adventure.

The wind arose last night, and although the temperature advanced a few degrees it remained at a very low point considering the strength of the wind.

This forenoon it was blowing 40 to 45 m.p.h. with a temperature −25° to −28°. No weather to be in the open.

In the afternoon the wind modified slightly. Taylor and Atkinson went up to the Ramp thermometer screen. After this, entirely without my knowledge, two adventurous spirits, Atkinson and Gran, decided to start off over the floe, making respectively for the north and south Bay thermometers, 'Archibald' and 'Clarence'. This was at 5.30; Gran was back by dinner at 6.45, and it was only later that I learned that he had gone no more than 200 or 300 yards from the land and that it had taken him nearly an hour to get back again.

Atkinson's continued absence passed unnoticed until dinner was nearly over at 7.15, although I had heard that the wind had dropped at the beginning of dinner and that it remained very thick all round, with light snow falling.

Although I felt somewhat annoyed, I had no serious anxiety at this time, and as several members came out of the hut I despatched them short distances to shout and show lanterns and arranged to have a paraffin flare lit on Wind Vane Hill.

Evans, P.O., Crean and Keohane, being anxious for a walk, were sent to the north with a lantern. Whilst this desultory search proceeded the wind sprang up again from the south, but with no great force, and meanwhile the sky showed signs of clearing and the moon appeared dimly through the drifting clouds. With such a guide we momentarily looked for the return of our wanderer, and with his continued absence our anxiety grew. At 9.30 Evans, P.O., and his party returned without news of him, and at last there was no denying the possibility of a serious accident. Between 9.30 and 10 proper search parties were organised, and I give the details to show the thoroughness which I thought necessary to meet the gravity of the situation. I had by this time learnt that Atkinson had left with comparatively light clothing and, still worse, with leather ski boots on his feet; fortunately he had wind clothing.

P.O. Evans was away first with Crean, Keohane, and Demetri, a light sledge, a sleeping-bag, and a flask of brandy. His orders were to search the edge of the land and glacier through the sweep of the Bay to the Barne Glacier and to Cape Barne beyond, then to turn east along an open crack and follow it to Inaccessible Island. Evans (Lieut.), with Nelson, Forde, and Hooper, left shortly after, similarly equipped, to follow the shore of the South Bay in similar fashion, then turn out to the Razorback and search there. Next Wright, Gran, and Lashly set out for the bergs to look thoroughly about them and from thence pass round and examine Inaccessible Island. After these parties got away, Meares and Debenham started with a lantern to search to and fro over the surface of our promontory. Simpson and Oates went out in a direct line over the northern floe to the 'Archibald' thermometer, whilst Ponting and Taylor re-examined the tide crack towards the Barne Glacier. Meanwhile Day went to and fro Wind Vane Hill to light at intervals upon its crest bundles of tow well soaked in petrol. At length Clissold and I were left alone in the hut, and as the hours went by I grew ever more alarmed. It was impossible for me to conceive how an able man could have failed to return to the hut before this or by any means found shelter in such clothing in such weather. Atkinson had started for a point a little more than a mile away; at 10.30 he had been five hours away; what conclusion could be drawn? And yet I felt it most difficult to imagine an accident on open floe with no worse pitfall than a shallow crack or steep-sided snow drift. At least I could feel that every spot which was likely to be the scene of such an accident would be searched. Thus 11 o'clock came without change, then 11.30 with its 6 hours of absence. But at 11.45 I heard voices from the Cape, and presently the adventure ended to my extreme relief when Meares and Debenham led our wanderer home. He was badly frostbitten in the hand and less seriously on the face, and though a good deal confused, as men always are on such occasions, he was otherwise well.

His tale is confused, but as far as one can gather he did not go more than a quarter of a mile in the direction of the thermometer screen before he decided to turn back. He then tried to walk with the wind a little on one side on the bearing he had originally observed, and after some time stumbled on an old fish-trap hole, which he knew to be 200 yards from the Cape. He made this 200 yards in the direction he supposed correct, and found nothing. In such a situation had he turned east he must have hit the land somewhere close to the hut and so found his way to it. The fact that he did not, but attempted to wander straight on, is clear evidence of the mental condition caused by that situation. There can be no doubt that in a blizzard a man has not only to safeguard the circulation in his limbs, but must struggle with a sluggishness of brain and an absence of reasoning power which is far more likely to undo him.

In fact Atkinson has really no very clear idea of what happened to him after he missed the Cape. He seems to have wandered aimlessly up wind till he hit an island; he walked all round this; says he couldn't see a yard at this time; fell often into the tide crack; finally stopped under the lee of some rocks; here got his hand frost-bitten owing to difficulty of getting frozen mit on again, finally got it on; started to dig a hole to wait in. Saw something of the moon and left the island; lost the moon and wanted to go back; could find nothing; finally stumbled on another island, perhaps the same one; waited again, again saw the moon, now clearing; shaped some sort of course by it – then saw flare on Cape and came on rapidly – says he shouted to someone on Cape quite close to him, greatly surprised not to get an answer. It is a rambling tale tonight and a half-thawed brain. It is impossible to listen to such a tale without appreciating that it has been a close escape or that there would have been no escape had the blizzard continued. The thought that it would return after a short lull was amongst the worst with me during the hours of waiting.

2 a.m. – The search parties have returned and all is well again, but we must have no more of these very unnecessary escapades. Yet it is impossible not to realise that this bit of experience has done more than all the talking I could have ever accomplished to bring home to our people the dangers of a blizzard.

Wednesday, July 5. – Atkinson has a bad hand today, immense blisters on every finger giving them the appearance of sausages. Tonight Ponting has photographed the hand.

As I expected, some amendment of Atkinson's tale as written last night is necessary, partly due to some lack of coherency in the tale as first told and partly a reconsideration of the circumstances by Atkinson himself.

It appears he first hit Inaccessible Island, and got his hand frostbitten before he reached it. It was only on arrival in its lee that he discovered the frostbite. He must have waited there some time, then groped his way to the western end thinking he was near the Ramp. Then wandering away in a swirl of drift to clear some irregularities at the ice foot, he completely lost the island when he could only have been a few yards from it.

He seems in this predicament to have clung to the old idea of walking up wind, and it must be considered wholly providential that on this course he next struck Tent Island. It was round this island that he walked, finally digging himself a shelter on its lee side under the impression that it was Inaccessible Island. When the moon appeared he seems to have judged its bearing well, and as he travelled homeward he was much surprised to see the real Inaccessible Island appear on his left. The distance of Tent Island, 4 to 5 miles, partly accounts for the time he took in returning. Everything goes to confirm the fact that he had a very close shave of being lost altogether.

For some time past some of the ponies have had great irritation of the skin. I felt sure it was due to some parasite, though the Soldier thought the food responsible and changed it.

Today a tiny body louse was revealed under Atkinson's microscope after capture from 'Snatcher's' coat. A dilute solution of carbolic is expected to rid the poor beasts of their pests, but meanwhile one or two of them have rubbed off patches of hair which they can ill afford to spare in this climate. I hope we shall get over the trouble quickly.

The day has been gloriously fine again, with bright moonlight all the afternoon. It was a wondrous sight to see Erebus emerge from soft filmy clouds of mist as though some thin veiling had been withdrawn with infinite delicacy to reveal the pure outline of this moonlit mountain.

Thursday, July 6. – The temperature has taken a plunge – to −46° last night. It is now −45°, with a ten-mile breeze from the south. Frostbiting weather!

Went for a short run on foot this forenoon and a longer one on ski this afternoon. The surface is bad after the recent snowfall. A new pair of sealskin overshoes for ski made by Evans seem to be a complete success. He has modified the shape of the toe to fit the ski irons better. I am very pleased with this arrangement.

I find it exceedingly difficult to settle down to solid work just at present and keep putting off the tasks which I have set myself.

The sun has not yet risen a degree of the eleven degrees below our horizon which it was at noon on Midwinter Day, and yet today there was a distinct red in the northern sky. Perhaps such sunset colours have something to do with this cold snap.

Friday, July 7. – The temperature fell to −49° last night – our record so far, and likely to remain so, one would think. This morning it was fine and calm, temperature −45°. But this afternoon a 30-mile wind sprang up from the S.E., and the temperature only gradually rose to −30°, never passing above that point. I thought it a little too strenuous and so was robbed of my walk.

The dogs' coats are getting pretty thick, and they seem to take matters pretty comfortably. The ponies are better, I think, but I shall be glad when we are sure of having rid them of their pest.

I was the victim of a very curious illusion today. On our small heating stove stands a cylindrical ice melter which keeps up the supply of water necessary for the dark room and other scientific instruments. This iron container naturally becomes warm if it is not fed with ice, and it is generally hung around with socks and mits which require drying. I put my hand on the cylindrical vessel this afternoon and withdrew it sharply with the sensation of heat. To verify the impression I repeated the action two or three times, when it became so strong that I loudly warned the owners of the socks, &c., of the peril of burning to which they were exposed. Upon this Meares said, 'But they filled the melter with ice a few minutes ago,' and then, coming over to feel the surface himself, added, 'Why, it's cold, sir.' And indeed so it was. The slightly damp chilled surface of the iron had conveyed to me the impression of excessive heat.

There is nothing intrinsically new in this observation; it has often been noticed that metal surfaces at low temperatures give a sensation of burning to the bare touch, but none the less it is an interesting variant of the common fact.

Apropos. Atkinson is suffering a good deal from his hand: the frostbite was deeper than I thought; fortunately he can now feel all his fingers, though it was twenty-four hours before sensation returned to one of them.

Monday, July 10. – We have had the worst gale I have ever known in these regions and have not yet done with it. The wind started at about mid-day on Friday, and increasing in violence reached an average of 60 miles for one hour on Saturday, the gusts at this time exceeding 70 m.p.h. This force of wind, although exceptional, has not been without parallel earlier in the year, but the extraordinary feature of this gale was the long continuance of a very cold temperature. On Friday night the thermometer registered −39°. Throughout Saturday and the greater part of Sunday it did not rise above −35°. Late yester-day it was in the minus twenties, and today at length it has risen to zero.

Needless to say no one has been far from the hut. It was my turn for duty on Saturday night, and on the occasions when I had to step out of doors I was struck with the impossibility of enduring such conditions for any length of time. One seemed to be robbed of breath as they burst on one − the fine snow beat in behind the wind guard, and ten paces against the wind were sufficient to reduce one's face to the verge of frostbite. To clear the anemometer vane it is necessary to go to the other end of the hut and climb a ladder. Twice whilst engaged in this task I had literally to lean against the wind with head bent and face averted and so stagger crablike on my course. In those two days of really terrible weather our thoughts often turned to absentees at Cape Crozier with the devout hope that they may be safely housed.

They are certain to have been caught by this gale, but I trust before it reached them they had managed to get up some sort of shelter. Sometimes I have imagined them getting much more wind than we do, yet at others it seems difficult to believe that the Emperor penguins have chosen an excessively wind-swept area for their rookery.

Today with the temperature at zero one can walk about outside without inconvenience in spite of a 50-mile wind. Although I am loath to believe it there must be some measure of acclimatisation, for it is certain we should have felt today's wind severely when we first arrived in McMurdo Sound.

Tuesday, July 11. − Never was such persistent bad weather. Today the temperature is up to +5° to +7°, the wind 40 to 50 m.p.h., the air thick with snow, and the moon a vague blur. This is the fourth day of gale; if one reflects on the quantity of transported air (nearly 4,000 miles) one gets a conception of the transference which such a gale effects and must conclude that potentially warm upper currents are pouring into our Polar area from more temperate sources.

The dogs are very gay and happy in the comparative warmth. I have been going to and fro on the home beach and about the rocky knolls in its environment – in spite of the wind it was very warm. I dug myself a hole in a drift in the shelter of a large boulder and lay down in it, and covered my legs with loose snow. It was so warm that I could have slept very comfortably.

I have been amused and pleased lately in observing the manners and customs of the persons in charge of our stores; quite a number of secret caches exist in which articles of value are hidden from public knowledge so that they may escape use until a real necessity arises. The policy of every storekeeper is to have something up his sleeve for a rainy day. For instance, Evans (P.O.), after thoroughly examining the purpose of some individual who is pleading for a piece of canvas, will admit that he may have a small piece somewhere which could be used for it, when, as a matter of fact, he possesses quite a number of rolls of that material.

Tools, metal material, leather, straps, and dozens of items are administered with the same spirit of jealous guardianship by Day, Lashly, Oates and Meares, while our main storekeeper Bowers even affects to bemoan imaginary shortages. Such parsimony is the best guarantee that we are prepared to face any serious call.

Wednesday, July 12. – All night and today wild gusts of wind shaking the hut; long, ragged, twisted wind-cloud in the middle heights. A watery moon shining through a filmy cirro-stratus – the outlook wonderfully desolate with its ghostly illumination and patchy clouds of flying snow drift. It would be hardly possible for a tearing, raging wind to make itself more visible. At Wind Vane Hill the anemometer has registered 68 miles between 9 and 10 a.m. – a record. The gusts at the hut frequently exceed 70 m.p.h. – luckily the temperature is up to +5°, so that there is no hardship for the workers outside.

Thursday, July 13. – The wind continued to blow throughout the night, with squalls of even greater violence than before; a new record was created by a gust of 77 m.p.h. shown by the anemometer.

The snow is so hard blown that only the fiercest gusts raise the drifting particles – it is interesting to note the balance of nature whereby one evil is eliminated by the excess of another.

For an hour after lunch yesterday the gale showed signs of moderation and the ponies had a short walk over the floe. Out for exercise at this time I was obliged to lean against the wind, my light overall clothes flapping wildly and almost dragged from me; later when the wind rose again it was quite an effort to stagger back to the hut against it.

This morning the gale still rages, but the sky is much clearer; the only definite clouds are those which hang to the southward of Erebus summit, but the moon, though bright, still exhibits a watery appearance, showing that there is still a thin stratus above us.

The work goes on very steadily – the men are making crampons and ski boots of the new style. Evans is constructing plans of the Dry Valley and Koettlitz Glacier with the help of the Western Party. The physicists are busy always, Meares is making dog harness, Oates ridding the ponies of their parasites, and Ponting printing from his negatives.

Science cannot be served by 'dilettante' methods, but demands a mind spurred by ambition or the satisfaction of ideals.

Our most popular game for evening recreation is chess; so many players have developed that our two sets of chessmen are inadequate.

Friday, July 14. – We have had a horrible fright and are not even yet out of the wood.

At noon yesterday one of the best ponies, 'Bones', suddenly went off his feed – soon after it was evident that he was distressed and there could be no doubt that he was suffering from colic. Oates called my attention to it, but we were neither much alarmed, remembering the speedy recovery of 'Jimmy Pigg' under similar circumstances. Later the pony was sent out for exercise with Crean. I passed him twice and seemed to gather that things were well, but Crean afterwards told me that he had had considerable trouble. Every few minutes the poor beast had been seized with a spasm of pain, had first dashed forward as though to escape it and then endeavoured to lie down. Crean had had much difficulty in keeping him in, and on his legs, for he is a powerful beast. When he returned to the stable he was evidently worse, and Oates and Anton patiently dragged a sack to and fro under his stomach. Every now and again he attempted to lie down, and Oates eventually thought it was wiser to let him do so. Once down, his head gradually drooped until he lay at length, every now and again twitching very horribly with the pain and from time to time raising his head and even scrambling to his legs when it grew intense. I don't think I ever realised before how pathetic a horse could be under such conditions; no sound escapes him, his misery can only be indicated by those distressing spasms and by dumb movements of the head turned with a patient expression always suggestive of appeal. Although alarmed by this time, remembering the care with which the animals are being fed I could not picture anything but a passing indisposition. But as hour after hour passed without improvement, it was impossible not to realise that the poor beast was dangerously ill. Oates administered an opium pill and later on a second, sacks were heated in the oven and placed on the poor beast; beyond this nothing could be done except to watch – Oates and Crean never left the patient. As the evening wore on I visited the stable again and again, but only to hear the same tale – no improvement. Towards midnight I felt very downcast. It is so very certain that we cannot afford to lose a single pony – the margin of safety has already been far over-stepped, we are reduced to face the circumstance that we must keep all the animals alive or greatly risk failure.

So far everything has gone so well with them that my fears of a loss had been lulled in a growing hope that all would be well – therefore at midnight, when poor 'Bones' had continued in pain for twelve hours and showed little sign of improvement, I felt my fleeting sense of security rudely shattered.

It was shortly after midnight when I was told that the animal seemed a little easier. At 2.30 I was again in the stable and found the improvement had been maintained; the horse still lay on its side with outstretched head, but the spasms had ceased, its eye looked less distressed, and its ears pricked to occasional noises. As I stood looking it suddenly raised its head and rose without effort to its legs; then in a moment, as though some bad dream had passed, it began to nose at some hay and at its neighbour. Within three minutes it had drunk a bucket of water and had started to feed.

I went to bed at 3 with much relief. At noon today the immediate cause of the trouble and an indication that there is still risk were disclosed in a small ball of semi-fermented hay covered with mucus and containing tape worms; so far not very serious, but unfortunately attached to this mass was a strip of the lining of the intestine.

Atkinson, from a humanly comparative point of view, does not think this is serious if great care is taken with the food for a week or so, and so one can hope for the best.

Meanwhile we have had much discussion as to the first cause of the difficulty. The circumstances possibly contributing are as follows: fermentation of the hay, insufficiency of water, over-heated stable, a chill from exercise after the gale – I think all these may have had a bearing on the case. It can scarcely be coincidence that the two ponies which have suffered so far are those which are nearest the stove end of the stable. In future the stove will be used more sparingly; a large ventilating hole is to be made near it and an allowance of water is to be added to the snow hitherto given to the animals. In the food line we can only exercise such precautions as are possible, but one way or another we ought to be able to prevent any more danger of this description.

Saturday, July 15. – There was strong wind with snow this morning and the wind remained keen and cold in the afternoon, but tonight it has fallen calm with a promising clear sky outlook. Have been up the Ramp, clambering about in my sealskin over-shoes, which seem extraordinarily satisfactory.

Oates thinks a good few of the ponies have got worms and we are considering means of ridding them. 'Bones' seems to be getting on well, though not yet quite so buckish as he was before his trouble. A good big ventilator has been fitted in the stable. It is not easy to get over the alarm of Thursday night – the situation is altogether too critical.

Sunday, July 16. – Another slight alarm this morning. The pony 'China' went off his feed at breakfast time and lay down twice. He was up and well again in half an hour; but what on earth is it that is disturbing these poor beasts?

Usual Sunday routine. Quiet day except for a good deal of wind off and on. The Crozier Party must be having a wretched time.

Monday, July 17. The weather still very unsettled – the wind comes up with a rush to fade in an hour or two. Clouds chase over the sky in similar fashion: the moon has dipped during daylight hours, and so one way and another there is little to attract one out of doors.

Yet we are only nine days off the 'light value' of the day when we left off football – I hope we shall be able to recommence the game in that time.

I am glad that the light is coming, for more than one reason. The gale and consequent inaction not only affected the ponies, Ponting is not very fit as a consequence – his nervous temperament is of the quality to take this wintering experience badly – Atkinson has some difficulty in persuading him to take exercise – he managed only by dragging him out to his own work, digging holes in the ice. Taylor is another backslider in the exercise line and is not looking well. If we can get these people to run about at football all will be well. Anyway, the return of the light should cure all ailments physical and mental.

Tuesday, July 18. – A very brilliant red sky at noon today and enough light to see one's way about.

This fleeting hour of light is very pleasant, but of course dependent on a clear sky, very rare. Went round the outer berg in the afternoon; it was all I could do to keep up with 'Snatcher' on the homeward round – speaking well for his walking powers.

Wednesday, July 19. – Again calm and pleasant. The temperature is gradually falling down to −35°. Went out to the old working crack* north of Inaccessible Island – Nelson and Evans had had great difficulty in rescuing their sounding sledge, which had been left near here before the gale. The course of events is not very clear, but it looks as though the gale pressed up the crack, raising broken pieces of the thin ice formed after recent opening movements. These raised pieces had become nuclei of heavy snow drifts, which in turn weighing down the floe had allowed water to flow in over the sledge level. It is surprising to find such a big disturbance from what appears to be a simple cause. This crack is now joined, and the contraction is taking on a new one which has opened much nearer to us and seems to run to C. Barne.

We have noticed a very curious appearance of heavenly bodies when setting in a north-westerly direction. About the time of midwinter the moon observed in this position appeared in a much distorted shape of blood-red colour. It might have been a red flare or distant bonfire, but could not have been guessed for the moon.

---

* i.e. a crack which leaves the ice free to move with the movements of the sea beneath.

Yesterday the planet Venus appeared under similar circumstances as a ship's side-light or Japanese lantern. In both cases there was a flickering in the light and a change of colour from deep orange yellow to blood-red, but the latter was dominant.

Thursday, July 20, Friday 21, Saturday 22. – There is very little to record – the horses are going on well, all are in good form, at least for the moment. They drink a good deal of water in the morning.

Saturday, July 22, continued. – This and the better ventilation of the stable make for improvement we think – perhaps the increase of salt allowance is also beneficial.

Today we have another raging blizzard – the wind running up to 72 m.p.h. in gusts – one way and another the Crozier Party must have had a pretty poor time.* I am thankful to remember that the light will be coming on apace now.

Monday, July 24. – The blizzard continued throughout yesterday (Sunday), in the evening reaching a record force of 82 m.p.h. The vane of our anemometer is somewhat sheltered: Simpson finds the hill readings 20 per cent, higher. Hence in such gusts as this the free wind must reach nearly 100 m.p.h. – a hurricane force. Today Nelson found that his sounding sledge had been turned over. We passed a quiet Sunday with the usual Service to break the week-day routine. During my night watch last night I could observe the rapid falling of the wind, which on dying away left a still atmosphere almost oppressively warm at +7°. The temperature has remained comparatively high today. I went to see the crack at which soundings were taken a week ago; then it was several feet open with thin ice between – now it is pressed up into a sharp ridge 3 to 4 feet high: the edge pressed up shows an 18-inch thickness – this is of course an effect of the warm weather.

Tuesday, July 25, Wednesday, July 26. – There is really very little to be recorded in these days, life proceeds very calmly if somewhat monotonously. Everyone seems fit, there is no sign of depression. To all outward appearance the ponies are in better form than they have ever been; the same may be said of the dogs with one or two exceptions.

The light comes on apace. Today (Wednesday) it was very beautiful at noon: the air was very clear and the detail of the

---

* This was the gale that tore away the roofing of their hut, and left them with only their sleeping-bags for shelter. See 'Narrative of the Northern Party', in Volume Two..

Western Mountains was revealed in infinitely delicate contrasts of light.

Thursday, July 27, Friday, July 28. – Calmer days: the sky rosier: the light visibly advancing. We have never suffered from low spirits, so that the presence of day raises us above a normal cheerfulness to the realm of high spirits.

The light, merry humour of our company has never been eclipsed, the good-natured, kindly chaff has never ceased since those early days of enthusiasm which inspired them – they have survived the winter days of stress and already renew themselves with the coming of spring. If pessimistic moments had foreseen the growth of rifts in the bond forged by these amenities, they stand prophetically falsified; there is no longer room for doubt that we shall come to our work with a unity of purpose and a disposition for mutual support which have never been equalled in these paths of activity. Such a spirit should tide us [over] all minor difficulties. It is a good omen.

Saturday, July 29, Sunday, July 30. – Two quiet days, temperature low in the minus thirties – an occasional rush of wind lasting for but a few minutes.

One of our best sledge dogs, 'Julick', has disappeared. I'm afraid he's been set on by the others at some distant spot and we shall see nothing more but his stiffened carcass when the light returns. Meares thinks the others would not have attacked him and imagines he has fallen into the water in some seal hole or crack. In either case I'm afraid we must be resigned to another loss. It's an awful nuisance.

Gran went to C. Royds today. I asked him to report on the open water, and so he went on past the Cape. As far as I can gather he got half-way to C. Bird before he came to thin ice; for at least 5 or 6 miles past C. Royds the ice is old and covered with wind-swept snow. This is very unexpected. In the *Discovery* first year the ice continually broke back to the Glacier Tongue: in the second year it must have gone out to C. Royds very early in the spring if it did not go out in the winter, and in the *Nimrod* year it was rarely fast beyond C. Royds. It is very strange, especially as this has been the windiest year recorded so far. Simpson says the average has exceeded 20 m.p.h. since the instruments were set up, and this figure has for comparison 9 and 12 m.p.h. for the two *Discovery* years. There remains a possibility that we have chosen an especially wind-swept spot for our station. Yet I can scarcely believe that there is generally more wind here than at Hut Point.

I was out for two hours this morning – it was amazingly pleasant to be able to see the inequalities of one's path, and the familiar landmarks bathed in violet light. An hour after noon the northern sky was intensely red.

Monday, July 31. – It was overcast today and the light not quite so good, but this is the last day of another month, and August means the sun.

One begins to wonder what the Crozier Party is doing. It has been away five weeks.

The ponies are getting buckish. Chinaman squeals and kicks in the stable, Nobby kicks without squealing, but with even more purpose – last night he knocked down a part of his stall. The noise of these animals is rather trying at night – one imagines all sorts of dreadful things happening, but when the watchman visits the stables its occupants blink at him with a sleepy air as though the disturbance could not possibly have been there!

There was a glorious northern sky today; the horizon was clear and the flood of red light illuminated the under side of the broken stratus cloud above, producing very beautiful bands of violet light. Simpson predicts a blizzard within twenty-four hours – we are interested to watch results.

Tuesday, August 1. – The month has opened with a very beautiful day. This morning I took a circuitous walk over our land 'estate', winding to and fro in gulleys filled with smooth ice patches or loose sandy soil, with a twofold object. I thought I might find the remains of poor Julick – in this I was unsuccessful; but I wished further to test our new crampons, and with these I am immensely pleased – they possess every virtue in a footwear designed for marching over smooth ice – lightness, warmth, comfort, and ease in the putting on and off.

The light was especially good today; the sun was directly reflected by a single twisted iridescent cloud in the north, a brilliant and most beautiful object. The air was still, and it was very pleasant to hear the crisp sounds of our workers abroad. The tones of voices, the swish of ski, or the chipping of an ice pick carry two or three miles on such days – more than once today we could hear the notes of some blithe singer – happily signalling the coming of the spring and the sun.

This afternoon as I sit in the hut I find it worthy of record that two telephones are in use: the one keeping time for Wright who works at the transit instrument, and the other bringing messages from Nelson at his ice hole three-quarters of a mile away. This last connection is made with a bare aluminium wire and earth return, and shows that we should have little difficulty in completing our circuit to Hut Point as is contemplated.

Account of the Winter Journey *

Wednesday, August 2. – The Crozier Party returned last night after enduring for five weeks the hardest conditions on record. They looked more weather-worn than anyone I have yet seen. Their faces were scarred and wrinkled, their eyes dull, their hands whitened and creased with the constant exposure to damp and cold, yet the scars of frostbite were very few and this evil had never seriously assailed them. The main part of their afflictions arose, and very obviously arose, from sheer lack of sleep, and today after a night's rest our travellers are very different in appearance and mental capacity.

The story of a very wonderful performance must be told by the actors. It is for me now to give but an outline of the journey and to note more particularly the effects of the strain which they have imposed on themselves and the lessons which their experiences teach for our future guidance.

Wilson is very thin, but this morning very much his keen, wiry self – Bowers is quite himself today. Cherry-Garrard is slightly puffy in the face and still looks worn. It is evident that he has suffered most severely – but Wilson tells me that his spirit never wavered for a moment. Bowers has come through best, all things considered, and I believe he is the hardest traveller that ever undertook a Polar journey, as well as one of the most undaunted; more by hint than direct statement I gather his value to the party, his untiring energy and the astonishing physique which enables him to continue to work under conditions which are absolutely paralysing to others. Never was such a sturdy, active, undefeatable little man.

* For the full account of this journey, see Volume Two (page 455).

So far as one can gather, the story of this journey in brief is much as follows: the party reached the Barrier two days after leaving C. Evans, still pulling their full load of 250 lbs. per man; the snow surface then changed completely and grew worse and worse as they advanced. For one day they struggled on as before, covering 4 miles, but from this onward they were forced to relay, and found the half load heavier than the whole one had been on the sea ice. Meanwhile the temperature had been falling, and now for more than a week the thermometer fell below −60°. On one night the minimum showed −71°, and on the next −77°, 109° of frost. Although in this truly fearful cold the air was comparatively still, every now and again little puffs of wind came eddying across the snow plain with blighting effect. No civilised being has ever encountered such conditions before with only a tent of thin canvas to rely on for shelter. We have been looking up the records today and find that Amundsen on a journey to the N. magnetic pole in March encountered temperatures similar in degree and recorded a minimum of 79°; but he was with Esquimaux who built him an igloo shelter nightly; he had a good measure of daylight; the temperatures given are probably 'unscreened' from radiation, and finally, he turned homeward and regained his ship after five days' absence. Our party went outward and remained absent for *five weeks*.

It took the best part of a fortnight to cross the coldest region, and then rounding C. Mackay they entered the wind-swept area. Blizzard followed blizzard, the sky was constantly overcast and they staggered on in a light which was little better than complete darkness; sometimes they found themselves high on the slopes of Terror on the left of their track, and sometimes diving into the pressure ridges on the right amidst crevasses and confused ice disturbance. Reaching the foothills near C. Crozier, they ascended 800 feet, then packed their belongings over a moraine ridge and started to build a hut. It took three days to build the stone walls and complete the roof with the canvas brought for the purpose. Then at last they could attend to the object of the journey.

The scant twilight at midday was so short that they must start in the dark and be prepared for the risk of missing their way in returning without light. On the first day in which they set forth under these conditions it took them two hours to reach the pressure ridges, and to clamber over them roped together occupied nearly the same time; finally they reached a place above the rookery where they could hear the birds squawking, but from which they were quite unable to find a way down. The poor light was failing and they returned to camp. Starting again on the following day they wound their way through frightful ice disturbances under the high basalt cliffs; in places the rock overhung, and at one spot they had to creep through a small channel hollowed in the ice. At last they reached the sea ice, but now the light was so far spent they were obliged to rush everything. Instead of the 2000 or 3000 nesting birds which had been seen here in *Discovery* days, they could now only count about 100; they hastily killed and skinned three to get blubber for their stove, and collecting six eggs, three of which alone survived, they dashed for camp.

It is possible the birds are deserting this rookery, but it is also possible that this early date found only a small minority of the birds which will be collected at a later one. The eggs, which have not yet been examined, should throw light on this point. Wilson observed yet another proof of the strength of the nursing instinct in these birds. In searching for eggs both he and Bowers picked up rounded pieces of ice which these ridiculous creatures had been cherishing with fond hope.

The light had failed entirely by the time the party were clear of the pressure ridges on their return, and it was only by good luck they regained their camp.

That night a blizzard commenced, increasing in fury from moment to moment. They now found that the place chosen for the hut for shelter was worse than useless. They had far better have built it in the open, for the fierce wind, instead of striking them directly, was deflected on to them in furious whirling gusts. Heavy blocks of snow and rock placed on the roof were whirled away and the canvas ballooned up, tearing and straining at its securings – its disappearance could only be a question of time. They had erected their tent with some valuables inside close to the hut; it had been well spread and more than amply secured with snow and boulders, but one terrific gust tore it up and whirled it away. Inside the hut they waited for the roof to vanish, wondering what they could do if it went, and vainly endeavouring to make it secure. After fourteen hours it went, as they were trying to pin down one corner. The smother of snow was on them, and they could only dive for their sleeping-bags with a gasp. Bowers put his head out once and said, 'We're all right,' in as near his ordinary tones as he could compass. The others replied 'Yes, we're all right,' and all were silent for a night and half a day whilst the wind howled on; the snow entered every chink and crevice of the sleeping-bags, and the occupants shivered and wondered how it would all end.

This gale was the same (July 23) in which we registered our maximum wind force, and it seems probable that it fell on C. Crozier even more violently than on us.

The wind fell at noon the following day; the forlorn travellers crept from their icy nests, made shift to spread their floorcloth overhead, and lit their primus. They tasted their first food for forty-eight hours and began to plan a means to build a shelter on the homeward route. They decided that they must dig a large pit nightly and cover it as best they could with their floorcloth. But now fortune befriended them; a search to the north revealed the tent lying amongst boulders a quarter of a mile away, and, strange to relate, practically uninjured, a fine testimonial for the material used in its construction. On the following day they started homeward, and immediately another blizzard fell on them, holding them prisoners for two days. By this time the miserable condition of their effects was beyond description. The sleeping-bags were far too stiff to be rolled up, in fact they were so hard frozen that attempts to bend them actually split the skins; the eiderdown bags inside Wilson's and C.-G.'s reindeer covers served but to fitfully stop the gaps made by such rents. All socks, finnesko, and mits had long been coated with ice; placed in breast pockets or inside vests at night they did not even show signs of thawing, much less of drying. It sometimes took C.-G. three-quarters of an hour to get into his sleeping-bag, so flat did it freeze and so difficult was it to open. It is scarcely possible to realise the horrible discomforts of the forlorn travellers as they plodded back across the Barrier with the temperature again constantly below −60°. In this fashion they reached Hut Point and on the following night our home quarters.

Wilson is disappointed at seeing so little of the penguins, but to me and to everyone who has remained here the result of this effort is the appeal it makes to our imagination as one of the most gallant stories in Polar History. That men should wander forth in the depth of a Polar night to face the most dismal cold and the fiercest gales in darkness is something new; that they should have persisted in this effort in spite of every adversity for five full weeks is heroic. It makes a tale for our generation which I hope may not be lost in the telling.

Moreover the material results are by no means despicable. We shall know now when that extraordinary bird the Emperor penguin lays its eggs, and under what conditions; but even if our information remains meagre concerning its embryology, our party has shown the nature of the conditions which exist on the Great Barrier in winter. Hitherto we have only imagined their severity; now we have proof, and a positive light is thrown on the local climatology of our Strait.

Experience of sledging rations and equipment

For our future sledge work several points have been most satis-factorily settled. The party went on a very simple food ration in different and extreme proportions; they took pemmican, butter, biscuit, and tea only. After a short experience they found that Wilson, who had arranged for the greatest quantity of fat, had too much of it, and C.-G., who had gone for biscuit, had more than he could eat. A middle course was struck which gave a general proportion agreeable to all, and at the same time suited the total quantities of the various articles carried. In this way we have arrived at a simple and suitable ration for the inland plateau. The only change suggested is the addition of cocoa for the evening meal. The party contented themselves with hot water, deeming that tea might rob them of their slender chance of sleep.

On sleeping-bags little new can be said – the eiderdown bag may be a useful addition for a short time on a spring journey, but they soon get iced up.

Bowers did not use an eiderdown bag throughout, and in some miraculous manner he managed to turn his reindeer bag two or three times during the journey. The following are the weights of sleeping-bags before and after:

Weight:	Starting	Final
Wilson, reindeer and eiderdown	17	40
Bowers, reindeer only	17	33
C.-Garrard, reindeer and eiderdown	18	45

This gives some idea of the ice collected.

The double tent has been reported an immense success. It weighed about 35 lbs. at starting and 60 lbs. on return: the ice mainly collected on the inner tent.

The crampons are much praised, except by Bowers, who has an eccentric attachment to our older form. We have discovered a hundred details of clothes, mits, and footwear: there seems no solution to the difficulties which attach to these articles in extreme cold; all Wilson can say, speaking broadly, is 'the gear is excellent, excellent.' One continues to wonder as to the possibilities of fur clothing as made by the Esquimaux, with a sneaking feeling that it may outclass our more civilised garb. For us this can only be a matter of speculation, as it would have been quite impossible to have obtained such articles. With the exception of this radically different alternative, I feel sure we are as near perfection as experience can direct.

At any rate we can now hold that our system of clothing has come through a severer test than any other, fur included.

Effect of Journey. – Wilson lost 3½ lbs.; Bowers lost 2½ lbs.; C.-Garrard lost 1 lb.

CHAPTER THIRTEEN

The return of the sun

Thursday, August 3. – We have had such a long spell of fine clear weather without especially low temperatures that one can scarcely grumble at the change which we found on waking this morning, when the canopy of stratus cloud spread over us and the wind came in those fitful gusts which promise a gale. All day the wind force has been slowly increasing, whilst the temperature has risen to −15°, but there is no snow falling or drifting as yet. The steam cloud of Erebus was streaming away to the N.W. this morning; now it is hidden.

Our expectations have been falsified so often that we feel ourselves wholly incapable as weather prophets – therefore one scarce dares to predict a blizzard even in face of such disturbance as exists. A paper handed to Simpson by David,* and purporting to contain a description of approaching signs, together with the cause and effect of our blizzards, proves equally hopeless. We have not obtained a single scrap of evidence to verify its statements, and a great number of our observations definitely contradict them. The plain fact is that no two of our storms have been heralded by the same signs.

The low Barrier temperatures experienced by the Crozier Party has naturally led to speculation on the situation of Amundsen and his Norwegians. If his thermometers continuously show temperatures below −60°, the party will have a pretty bad winter and it is difficult to see how he will keep his dogs alive. I should feel anxious if Campbell was in that quarter.†

Saturday, August 5. – The sky has continued to wear a disturbed appearance, but so far nothing has come of it. A good deal of light

---

* Prof. T. Edgeworth David, of Sydney University, who accompanied Shackleton's expedition as geologist.
† See Volume Two, Dr. Simpson's Meteorological Report.

snow has been falling today; a brisk northerly breeze is drifting it along, giving a very strange yet beautiful effect in the north, where the strong red twilight filters through the haze.

The Crozier Party tell a good story of Bowers, who on their return journey with their recovered tent fitted what he called a 'tent downhaul' and secured it round his sleeping-bag and himself. If the tent went again, he determined to go with it.

Our lecture programme has been renewed. Last night Simpson gave a capital lecture on general meteorology. He started on the general question of insolation, giving various tables to show proportion of sun's heat received at the polar and equatorial regions. Broadly, in latitude 80° one would expect about 22 per cent. of the heat received at a spot on the equator.

He dealt with the temperature question by showing interesting tabular comparisons between northern and southern temperatures at given latitudes. So far as these tables go they show the South Polar summer to be 15° colder than the North Polar, but the South Polar winter 3° warmer than the North Polar, but of course this last figure would be completely altered if the observer were to winter on the Barrier. I fancy Amundsen will not concede those 3°!!

From temperatures our lecturer turned to pressures and the upward turn of the gradient in high southern latitudes, as shown by the *Discovery* Expedition. This bears of course on the theory which places an anticyclone in the South Polar region. Lockyer's theories came under discussion; a good many facts appear to support them. The westerly winds of the Roaring Forties are generally understood to be a succession of cyclones. Lockyer's hypothesis supposes that there are some eight or ten cyclones continually revolving at a rate of about 10° of longitude a day, and he imagines them to extend from the 40th parallel to beyond the 60th, thus giving the strong westerly winds in the forties and easterly and southerly in 60° to 70°. Beyond 70° there appears to be generally an irregular outpouring of cold air from the Polar area, with an easterly component significant of anticyclone conditions.

Simpson evolved a new blizzard theory on this. He supposes the surface air intensely cooled over the continental and Barrier areas, and the edge of this cold region lapped by warmer air from the southern limits of Lockyer's cyclones. This would produce a condition of unstable equilibrium, with great potentiality for movement. Since, as we have found, volumes of cold air at different temperatures are very loath to mix, the condition could not be relieved by any gradual process, but continues until the stream is released by some minor cause, when, the ball once started, a huge disturbance results. It seems to be generally held that warm air is passing polewards from the equator continuously at the high levels. It is this potentially warm air which, mixed by the disturbance with the cold air of the interior, gives to our winds so high a temperature.

Such is this theory – like its predecessor it is put up for cockshies, and doubtless by our balloon work or by some other observations it will be upset or modified. Meanwhile it is well to keep one's mind alive with such problems, which mark the road of advance.

Sunday, August 6. – Sunday with its usual routine. Hymn singing has become a point on which we begin to take some pride to ourselves. With our full attendance of singers we now get a grand volume of sound.

The day started overcast. Chalky is an excellent adjective to describe the appearance of our outlook when the light is much diffused and shadows poor; the scene is dull and flat.

In the afternoon the sky cleared, the moon over Erebus gave a straw colour to the dissipating clouds. This evening the air is full of ice crystals and a stratus forms again. This alternation of clouded and clear skies has been the routine for some time now and is accompanied by an absence of wind which is delightfully novel.

The blood of the Crozier Party, tested by Atkinson, shows a very slight increase of acidity – such was to be expected, and it is pleasing to note that there is no sign of scurvy. If the preserved foods had tended to promote the disease, the length of time and severity of conditions would certainly have brought it out. I think we should be safe on the long journey.

I have had several little chats with Wilson on the happenings of the journey. He says there is no doubt Cherry-Garrard felt the conditions most severely, though he was not only without complaint, but continuously anxious to help others.

Apropos, we both conclude that it is the younger people that have the worst time; Gran, our youngest member (23), is a very clear example, and now Cherry-Garrard at 26.

Wilson (39) says he never felt cold less than he does now; I suppose that between 30 and 40 is the best all-round age. Bowers is a wonder of course. He is 29. When past the forties it is encouraging to remember that Peary was 52!!

Thursday, August 10. – There has been very little to record of late and my pen has been busy on past records.

The weather has been moderately good and as before wholly incomprehensible. Wind has come from a clear sky and from a clouded one; we had a small blow on Tuesday but it never reached gale force; it came without warning, and every sign which we have regarded as a warning has proved a bogey. The fact is, one must always be prepared for wind and never expect it.

The daylight advances in strides. Day has fitted an extra sash to our window and the light admitted for the first time through triple glass. With this device little ice collects inside.

The ponies are very fit but inclined to be troublesome: the quiet beasts develop tricks without rhyme or reason. Chinaman still kicks and squeals at night. Anton's theory is that he does it to warm himself, and perhaps there is something in it. When eating snow he habitually takes too large a mouthful and swallows it; it is comic to watch him, because when the snow chills his inside he shuffles about with all four legs and wears a most fretful, aggrieved expression: but no sooner has the snow melted than he seizes another mouthful. Other ponies take small mouthfuls or melt a large one on their tongues – this act also produces an amusing expression. Victor and Snippets are confirmed wind-suckers. They are at it all the time when the manger board is in place, but it is taken down immediately after feeding time, and then they can only seek vainly for something to catch hold of with their teeth. 'Bones' has taken to kicking at night for no imaginable reason. He hammers away at the back of his stall merrily; we have covered the boards with several layers of sacking, so that the noise is cured, if not the habit. The annoying part of these tricks is that they hold the possibility of damage to the pony. I am glad to say all the lice have disappeared; the final conquest was effected with a very simple remedy – the infected ponies were washed with water in which tobacco had been steeped. Oates had seen this decoction used effectively with troop horses. The result is the greater relief, since we had run out of all the chemicals which had been used for the same purpose.

I have now definitely told off the ponies for the Southern Journey, and the new masters will take charge on September 1. They will continually exercise the animals so as to get to know them as well as possible. The arrangement has many obvious advantages. The following is the order:

Bowers: Victor	Evans (P.O.): Snatcher
Wilson: Nobby	Crean: Bones
Atkinson: Jehu	Keohane: Jimmy Pigg
Wright: Chinaman	Oates: Christopher
Cherry-Garrard: Michael	Myself & Oates: Snippets

The first balloon of the season was sent up yesterday by Bowers and Simpson. It rose on a southerly wind, but remained in it for 100 feet or less, then for 300 or 400 feet it went straight up, and after that directly south over Razorback Island. Everything seemed to go well, the thread, on being held, tightened and then fell slack as it should do. It was followed for two miles or more running in a straight line for Razorback, but within a few hundred yards of the Island it came to an end. The searchers went round the Island to try and recover the clue, but without result. Almost identically the same thing happened after the last ascent made, and we are much puzzled to find the cause.

The continued proximity of the south-moving air currents above is very interesting.

The Crozier Party are not right yet; their feet are exceedingly sore, and there are other indications of strain. I must almost except Bowers, who, whatever his feelings, went off as gaily as usual on the search for the balloon.

Saw a very beautiful effect on my afternoon walk yesterday: the full moon was shining brightly from a quarter exactly opposite to the fading twilight and the icebergs were lit on one side by the yellow lunar light and on the other by the paler white daylight. The first seemed to be gilded, while the diffused light of day gave to the other a deep, cold, greenish-blue colour – the contrast was strikingly beautiful.

Friday, *August* 11. – The long-expected blizzard came in the night; it is still blowing hard with drift.

Yesterday evening Oates gave his second lecture on 'Horse Management'. He was brief and a good deal to the point. 'Not born but made' was his verdict on the good manager of animals.

'The horse has no reasoning power at all, but an excellent memory'; sights and sounds recall circumstances under which they were previously seen or heard. It is no use shouting at a horse: ten to one he will associate the noise with some form of trouble, and getting excited, will set out to make it. It is ridiculous for the rider of a bucking horse to shout 'Whoa!' – 'I know,' said the Soldier, 'because I have done it.' Also it is to be remembered that loud talk to one horse may disturb other horses. The great thing is to be firm and quiet.

A horse's memory, explained the Soldier, warns it of events to come. He gave instances of hunters and racehorses which go off their feed and show great excitement in other ways before events for which they are prepared; for this reason every effort should be made to keep the animals quiet in camp. Rugs should be put on directly after a halt and not removed till the last moment before a march.

After a few hints on leading, the lecturer talked of possible improvements in our wintering arrangements. A loose box for each animal would be an advantage, and a small amount of litter on which he could lie down. Some of our ponies lie down, but rarely for more than 10 minutes – the Soldier thinks they find the ground too cold. He thinks it would be wise to clip animals before the winter set in. He is in doubt as to the advisability of grooming. He passed to the improvements preparing for the coming journey – the nose bags, picketing lines, and rugs. He proposes to bandage the legs of all ponies. Finally he dealt with the difficult subjects of snow blindness and soft surfaces: for the first he suggested dyeing the forelocks, which have now grown quite long. Oates indulges a pleasant conceit in finishing his discourses with a merry tale. Last night's tale evoked shouts of laughter, but, alas! it is quite unprintable! Our discussion hinged altogether on the final subjects of the lecture as concerning snow blindness – the dyed forelocks seem inadequate, and the best suggestion seems the addition of a sun bonnet rather than blinkers, or, better still, a peak over the eyes attached to the headstall. I doubt if this question will be difficult to settle, but the snow-shoe problem is much more serious. This has been much in our minds of late, and Petty Officer Evans has been making trial shoes for Snatcher on vague ideas of our remembrance of the shoes worn for lawn-mowing.

Besides the problem of the form of the shoes comes the question of the means of attachment. All sorts of suggestions were made last night as to both points, and the discussion cleared the air a good deal. I think that with slight modification our present pony snow-shoes made on the grating or racquet principle may prove best after all. The only drawback is that they are made for very soft snow and unnecessarily large for the Barrier; this would make them liable to be strained on hard patches. The alternative seems to be to perfect the principle of the lawn-mowing shoe, which is little more than a stiff bag over the hoof.

Perhaps we shall come to both kinds: the first for the quiet animals and the last for the more excitable. I am confident the matter is of first importance.

Monday, August 14. − Since the comparatively short storm of Friday, in which we had a temperature of −30° with a 50 m.p.h. wind, we have had two delightfully calm days, and today there is every promise of the completion of a third. On such days the light is quite good for three to four hours at midday and has a cheering effect on man and beast.

The ponies are so pleased that they seize the slightest opportunity to part company with their leaders and gallop off with tail and heels flung high. The dogs are equally festive and are getting more exercise than could be given in the dark. The two Esquimaux dogs have been taken in hand by Clissold, as I have noted before. He now takes them out with a leader borrowed from Meares, usually little 'Noogis'. On Saturday the sledge capsized at the tide crack; Clissold was left on the snow whilst the team disappeared in the distance. Noogis returned later, having eaten through his harness, and the others were eventually found some two miles away, 'foul' of an ice hummock. Yesterday Clissold took the same team to Cape Royds; they brought back a load of 100 lbs. a dog in about two hours. It would have been a good performance for the best dogs in the time, and considering that Meares pronounced these two dogs useless, Clissold deserved a great deal of credit.

Yesterday we had a really successful balloon ascent: the balloon ran out four miles of thread before it was released, and the instrument fell without a parachute. The searchers followed the clue about 2½ miles to the north, when it turned and came back parallel to itself, and only about 30 yards distant from it. The instrument was found undamaged and with the record properly scratched.

Nelson has been out a good deal more of late. He has got a good little run of serial temperatures with water samples, and however meagre his results, they may be counted as exceedingly accurate; his methods include the great scientific care which is now considered necessary for this work, and one realises that he is one of the few people who have been trained in it. Yesterday he got his first net haul from the bottom, with the assistance of Atkinson and Cherry-Garrard.

Atkinson has some personal interest in the work. He has been getting remarkable results himself and has discovered a host of new parasites in the seals; he has been trying to correlate these with like discoveries in the fishes, in hope of working out complete life histories in both primary and secondary hosts.

But the joint hosts of the fishes may be the mollusca or other creatures on which they feed, and hence the new fields for Atkinson in Nelson's catches. There is a relative simplicity in the round of life in its higher forms in these regions that would seem especially hopeful for the parasitologist.

My afternoon walk has become a great pleasure; everything is beautiful in this half light and the northern sky grows redder as the light wanes.

Tuesday, August 15. – The instrument recovered from the balloon shows an ascent of 2½ miles, and the temperature at that height only 5° or 6° C. below that at the surface. If, as one must suppose, this layer extends over the Barrier, it would there be at a considerably higher temperature than the surface. Simpson has imagined a very cold surface layer on the Barrier.

The acetylene has suddenly failed, and I find myself at this moment *writing by daylight* for the first time.

The first addition to our colony came last night, when 'Lassie' produced six or seven puppies – we are keeping the family very quiet and as warm as possible in the stable.

It is very pleasant to note the excellent relations which our young Russians have established with other folk; they both work very hard, Anton having most to do. Demetri is the more intelligent and begins to talk English fairly well. Both are on the best terms with their messmates, and it was amusing last night to see little Anton jamming a felt hat over P. O. Evans's head in high good humour.

Wright lectured on 'Radium' last night.

The transformation of the radio-active elements suggestive of the transmutation of metals was perhaps the most interesting idea suggested, but the discussion ranged mainly round the effect which the discovery of radioactivity has had on physics and chemistry in its bearing on the origin of matter, on geology as bearing on the internal heat of the earth, and on medicine in its curative powers. The geologists and doctors admitted little virtue to it, but of course the physicists boomed their own wares, which enlivened the debate.

Thursday, August 17. – The weather has been extremely kind to us of late; we haven't a single grumble against it. The temperature hovers pretty constantly at about $-35°$, there is very little wind and the sky is clear and bright. In such weather one sees well for more than three hours before and after noon, the landscape unfolds itself, and the sky colours are always delicate and beautiful. At noon today there was bright sunlight on the tops of the Western Peaks and on the summit and steam of Erebus – of late the vapour cloud of Erebus has been exceptionally heavy and fantastic in form.

The balloon has become a daily institution. Yesterday the instrument was recovered in triumph, but today the threads carried the searchers in amongst the icebergs and soared aloft over their crests – anon the clue was recovered beyond, and led towards Tent Island, then towards Inaccessible, then back to the bergs. Never was such an elusive thread. Darkness descended with the searchers on a strong scent for the Razorbacks: Bowers returned full of hope.

The wretched Lassie has killed every one of her litter. She is mother for the first time, and possibly that accounts for it. When the poor little mites were alive she constantly left them, and when taken back she either trod on them or lay on them, till not one was left alive. It is extremely annoying.

As the daylight comes, people are busier than ever. It does one good to see so much work going on.

Friday, August 18. – Atkinson lectured on 'Scurvy' last night. He spoke clearly and slowly, but the disease is anything but precise.

He gave a little summary of its history afloat and the remedies long in use in Navy.

He described the symptoms with some detail. Mental depression, debility, syncope, petechiae, livid patches, spongy gums, lesions, swellings, and so on to things that are worse. He passed to some of the theories held and remedies tried in accordance with them. Ralph came nearest the truth in discovering decrease of chlorine and alkalinity of urine. Sir Almroth Wright has hit the truth, he thinks, in finding increased acidity of blood – acid intoxication – by methods only possible in recent years.

This acid condition is due to two salts, sodium hydrogen carbonate and sodium hydrogen phosphate; these cause the symptoms observed and infiltration of fat in organs, leading to feebleness of heart action. The method of securing and testing serum of patient was described (titration, a colorimetric method of measuring the percentage of substances in solution), and the test by litmus paper of normal or super-normal solution. In this test the ordinary healthy man shows normal 30 to 50: the scurvy patient normal 90.

Lactate of sodium increases alkalinity of blood, but only within narrow limits, and is the only chemical remedy suggested.

So far for diagnosis, but it does not bring us much closer to the cause, preventives, or remedies. Practically we are much as we were before, but the lecturer proceeded to deal with the practical side.

In brief, he holds the first cause to be tainted food, but secondary or contributory causes may be even more potent in developing the disease. Damp, cold, over-exertion, bad air, bad light, in fact any condition exceptional to normal healthy existence. Remedies are merely to change these conditions for the better. Dietetically, fresh vegetables are the best curatives – the lecturer was doubtful of fresh meat, but admitted its possibility in Polar climate; lime juice only useful if regularly taken. He discussed lightly the relative values of vegetable stuffs, doubtful of those containing abundance of phosphates such as lentils. He touched theory again in continuing the cause of acidity to bacterial action – and the possibility of infection in epidemic form. Wilson is evidently slow to accept the 'acid intoxication' theory; his attitude is rather 'non proven'. His remarks were extremely sound and practical as usual. He proved the value of fresh meat in Polar regions.

Scurvy seems very far away from us this time, yet after our *Discovery* experience, one feels that no trouble can be too great or precaution too small to be adopted to keep it at bay. Therefore such an evening as last was well spent.

It is certain we shall not have the disease here, but one cannot foresee equally certain avoidance in the southern journey to come. All one can do is to take every possible precaution.

Ran over to Tent Island this afternoon and climbed to the top – I have not been there since 1903. Was struck with great amount of loose sand; it seemed to get smaller in grain from S. to N. Fine view from top of island: one specially notices the gap left by the breaking up of the Glacier Tongue.

The distance to the top of the island and back is between 7 and 8 statute miles, and the run in this weather is fine healthy exercise. Standing on the island today with a glorious view of mountains, islands, and glaciers, I thought how very different must be the outlook of the Norwegians. A dreary white plain of Barrier behind and an uninviting stretch of sea ice in front. With no landmarks, nothing to guide if the light fails, it is probable that they venture but a very short distance from their hut.

The prospects of such a situation do not smile on us.

The weather remains fine – this is the sixth day without wind.

Sunday, August 20. – The long-expected blizzard came yesterday – a good honest blow, the drift vanishing long before the wind. This and the rise of temperature (to +2°) has smoothed and polished all ice or snow surfaces. A few days ago I could walk anywhere in my soft finnesko with sealskin soles; today it needed great caution to prevent tumbles. I think there has been a good deal of ablation.

The sky is clear today, but the wind still strong though warm. I went along the shore of the North Bay and climbed to the glacier over one of the drifted faults in the ice face. It is steep and slippery, but by this way one can arrive above the Ramp without touching rock and thus avoid cutting soft footwear.

The ice problems in our neighbourhood become more fascinating and elusive as one re-examines them by the returning light; some will be solved.

Monday, August 21. – Weights and measurements last evening. We have remained surprisingly constant. There seems to have been improvement in lung power and grip as shown by spirometer and dynamometer, but weights have altered very little. I have gone up nearly 3 lbs. in winter, but the increase has occurred during the last month, when I have been taking more exercise. Certainly there is every reason to be satisfied with the general state of health.

The ponies are becoming a handful. Three of the four exercised today so far have run away – Christopher and Snippets broke away from Oates and Victor from Bowers. Nothing but high spirits, there is no vice in these animals; but I fear we are going to have trouble with sledges and snow-shoes. At present the Soldier dare not issue oats or the animals would become quite unmanageable. Bran is running low; he wishes he had more of it.

Tuesday, August 22. – I am renewing study of glacier problems; the face of the ice cliff 300 yards east of the homestead is full of enigmas. Yesterday evening Ponting gave us a lecture on his Indian travels. He is very frank in acknowledging his debt to guide-books for information, nevertheless he tells his story well and his slides are wonderful. In personal reminiscence he is distinctly dramatic – he thrilled us a good deal last night with a vivid description of a sunrise in the sacred city of Benares. In the first dim light the waiting, praying multitude of bathers, the wonderful ritual and its incessant performance; then, as the sun approaches, the hush – the effect of thousands of worshippers waiting in silence – a silence to be felt. Finally, as the first rays appear, the swelling roar of a single word from tens of thousands of throats: 'Ambah!' It was artistic to follow this picture of life with the gruesome horrors of the ghat. This impressionist style of lecturing is very attractive and must essentially cover a great deal of ground. So we saw Jeypore, Udaipore, Darjeeling, and a confusing number of places – temples, monuments, and tombs in profusion, with remarkable pictures of the wonderful Taj Mahal – horses, elephants, alligators, wild boars, and flamingoes – warriors, fakirs, and nautch girls – an impression here and an impression there.

It is worth remembering how attractive this style can be – in lecturing one is inclined to give too much attention to connecting links which join one episode to another. A lecture need not be a connected story; perhaps it is better it should not be.

It was my night on duty last night and I watched the oncoming of a blizzard with exceptional beginnings. The sky became very gradually overcast between 1 and 4 a.m. About 2.30 the temperature rose on a steep grade from −20° to −3°; the barometer was falling, rapidly for these regions. Soon after 4 the wind came with a rush, but without snow or drift. For a time it was more gusty than has ever yet been recorded even in this region. In one gust the wind rose from 4 to 68 m.p.h. and fell again to 20 m.p.h. within a minute; another reached 80 m.p.h., but not from such a low point of origin. The effect in the hut was curious; for a space all would be quiet, then a shattering blast would descend with a clatter and rattle past ventilator and chimneys, so sudden, so threatening, that it was comforting to remember the solid structure of our building. The suction of such a gust is so heavy that even the heavy snow-covered roof of the stable, completely sheltered on the lee side of the main building, is violently shaken − one could well imagine the plight of our adventurers at C. Crozier when their roof was destroyed. The snow which came at 6 lessened the gustiness and brought the ordinary phenomena of a blizzard. It is blowing hard today, with broken windy clouds and roving bodies of drift. A wild day for the return of the sun. Had it been fine today we should have seen the sun for the first time; yesterday it shone on the lower foothills to the west, but today we see nothing but gilded drift clouds. Yet it is grand to have daylight rushing at one.

Wednesday, August 23. − We toasted the sun in champagne last night, coupling Victor Campbell's name as his birthday coincides. The return of the sun could not be appreciated as we have not had a glimpse of it, and the taste of the champagne went wholly unappreciated; it was a very mild revel. Meanwhile the gale continues. Its full force broke last night with an average of nearly 70 m.p.h. for some hours: the temperature has been up to +10° and the snowfall heavy. At seven this morning the air was thicker with whirling drift than it has ever been.

It seems as though the violence of the storms which succeed our rare spells of fine weather is in proportion to the duration of the spells.

Thursday, August 24. − Another night and day of furious wind and drift, and still no sign of the end. The temperature has been as high as +16°. Now and again the snow ceases and then the drift rapidly diminishes, but such an interval is soon followed by fresh clouds of snow. It is quite warm outside, one can go about with head uncovered – which leads me to suppose that one does get hardened to cold to some extent – for I suppose one would not wish to remain uncovered in a storm in England if the temperature showed 16 degrees of frost. This is the third day of confinement to the hut: it grows tedious, but there is no help, as it is too thick to see more than a few yards out of doors.

Friday, August 25. – The gale continued all night and it blows hard this morning, but the sky is clear, the drift has ceased, and the few whale-back clouds about Erebus carry a promise of improving conditions.

Last night there was an intensely black cloud low on the northern horizon – but for earlier experience of the winter one would have sworn to it as a water sky; but I think the phenomenon is due to the shadow of retreating drift clouds. This morning the sky is clear to the north, so that the sea ice cannot have broken out in the Sound.

During snowy gales it is almost necessary to dress oneself in wind clothes if one ventures outside for the briefest periods – exposed woollen or cloth materials become heavy with powdery crystals in a minute or two, and when brought into the warmth of the hut are soon wringing wet. Where there is no drift it is quicker and easier to slip on an overcoat.

It is not often I have a sentimental attachment for articles of clothing, but I must confess an affection for my veteran uniform overcoat, inspired by its persistent utility. I find that it is twenty-three years of age and can testify to its strenuous existence. It has been spared neither rain, wind, nor salt sea spray, tropic heat nor Arctic cold; it has outlived many sets of buttons, from their glittering gilded youth to green old age, and it supports its four-stripe shoulder straps as gaily as the single lace ring of the early days which proclaimed it the possession of a humble sub-lieutenant. Withal it is still a very long way from the fate of the 'one-horse shay'.

Taylor gave us his final physiographical lecture last night. It was completely illustrated with slides made from our own negatives, Ponting's Alpine work, and the choicest illustrations of certain scientific books. The preparation of the slides had involved a good deal of work for Ponting as well as for the lecturer, The lecture dealt with ice erosion, and the pictures made it easy to follow the comparison of our own mountain forms and glacial contours with those that have received so much attention elsewhere. Noticeable differences are the absence of moraine material on the lower surfaces of our glaciers, their relatively insignificant movement, their steep sides, &c. . . . It is difficult to convey the bearing of the difference or similarity of various features common to the pictures under comparison without their aid. It is sufficient to note that the points to which the lecturer called attention were pretty obvious and that the lecture was exceedingly instructive. The origin of 'cirques' or 'cwms', of which we have remarkably fine examples, is still a little mysterious – one notes also the requirement of observation which might throw light on the erosion of previous ages.

After Taylor's effort Ponting showed a number of very beautiful slides of Alpine scenery – not a few are triumphs of the photographer's art. As a wind-up Ponting took a flashlight photograph of our hut converted into a lecture hall: a certain amount of faking will be required, but I think this is very allowable under the circumstances.

Oates tells me that one of the ponies, 'Snippets', will eat blubber! the possible uses of such an animal are remarkable!

The gravel on the north side of the hut against which the stable is built has been slowly but surely worn down, leaving gaps under the boarding. Through these gaps and our floor we get an unpleasantly strong stable effluvium, especially when the wind is strong. We are trying to stuff the holes up, but have not had much success so far.

Saturday, August 26. – A dying wind and clear sky yesterday, and almost calm today. The noon sun is cut off by the long low foot slope of Erebus which runs to Cape Royds. Went up the Ramp at noon yesterday and found no advantage – one should go over the floe to get the earliest sight, and yesterday afternoon Evans caught a last glimpse of the upper limb from that situation, whilst Simpson saw the same from Wind Vane Hill.

The ponies are very buckish and can scarcely be held in at exercise; it seems certain that they feel the return of daylight. They were out in morning and afternoon yesterday. Oates and Anton took out Christopher and Snippets rather later. Both ponies broke away within 50 yards of the stable and galloped away over the floe. It was nearly an hour before they could be rounded up. Such escapades are the result of high spirits; there is no vice in the animals.

We have had comparatively little aurora of late, but last night was an exception; there was a good display at 3 a.m.

p.m. – Just before lunch the sunshine could be seen gilding the floe, and Ponting and I walked out to the bergs. The nearest one has been overturned and is easily climbed. From the top we could see the sun clear over the rugged outline of C. Barne. It was glorious to stand bathed in brilliant sunshine once more. We felt very young, sang and cheered – we were reminded of a bright frosty morning in England – everything sparkled and the air had the same crisp feel. There is little new to be said of the return of the sun in Polar regions, yet it is such a very real and important event that one cannot pass it in silence. It changes the outlook on life of every individual, foul weather is robbed of its terrors; if it is stormy today it will be fine tomorrow or the next day, and each day's delay will mean a brighter outlook when the sky is clear.

Climbed the Ramp in the afternoon, the shouts and songs of men and the neighing of horses borne to my ears as I clambered over its kopjes.

We are now pretty well convinced that the Ramp is a moraine resting on a platform of ice.

The sun rested on the sunshine recorder for a few minutes, but made no visible impression. We did not get our first record in the *Discovery* until September. It is surprising that so little heat should be associated with such a flood of light.

Sunday, August 27. – Overcast sky and chill south-easterly wind. Sunday routine, no one very active. Had a run to South Bay over 'Domain'.

Monday, August 28. – Ponting and Gran went round the bergs late last night. On returning they saw a dog coming over the floe from the north. The animal rushed towards and leapt about them with every sign of intense joy. Then they realised that it was our long-lost Julick.

His mane was crusted with blood and he smelt strongly of seal blubber – his stomach was full, but the sharpness of backbone showed that this condition had only been temporary.

By daylight he looks very fit and strong, and he is evidently very pleased to be home again.

We are absolutely at a loss to account for his adventures. It is exactly a month since he was missed – what on earth can have happened to him all this time? One would give a great deal to hear his tale. Everything is against the theory that he was a wilful absentee – his previous habits and his joy at getting back. If he wished to get back, he cannot have been lost anywhere in the neighbourhood, for, as Meares says, the barking of the station dogs can be heard at least 7 or 8 miles away in calm weather, besides which there are tracks everywhere and unmistakeable landmarks to guide man or beast. I cannot but think the animal has been cut off, but this can only have happened by his being carried away on broken sea ice, and as far as we know the open water has never been nearer than 10 or 12 miles at the least. It is another enigma.

On Saturday last a balloon was sent up. The thread was found broken a mile away. Bowers and Simpson walked many miles in search of the instrument, but could find no trace of it. The theory now propounded is that if there is strong differential movement in air currents, the thread is not strong enough to stand the strain as the balloon passes from one current to another. It is amazing, and forces the employment of a new system. It is now proposed to discard the thread and attach the instrument to a flag and staff, which it is hoped will plant itself in the snow on falling.

The sun is shining into the hut windows – already sunbeams rest on the opposite walls.

I have mentioned the curious cones which are the conspicuous feature of our Ramp scenery – they stand from 8 to 20 feet in height, some irregular, but a number quite perfectly conical in outline. Today Taylor and Gran took pick and crowbar and started to dig into one of the smaller ones. After removing a certain amount of loose rubble they came on solid rock, kenyte, having two or three irregular cracks traversing the exposed surface. It was only with great trouble they removed one or two of the smallest fragments severed by these cracks. There was no sign of ice. This gives a great 'leg up' to the 'débris' cone theory.

Demetri and Clissold took two small teams of dogs to Cape Royds today. They found some dog footprints near the hut, but think these were not made by Julick. Demetri points far to the west as the scene of that animal's adventures. Parties from C. Royds always bring a number of illustrated papers which must have been brought down by the *Nimrod* on her last visit. The ostensible object is to provide amusement for our Russian companions, but as a matter of fact everyone finds them interesting.

Tuesday, August 29. – I find that the card of the sunshine recorder showed an hour and a half's burn yesterday and was very faintly marked on Saturday; already, therefore, the sun has given us warmth, even if it can only be measured instrumentally.

Last night Meares told us of his adventures in and about Lolo land, a wild Central Asian country nominally tributary to Lhassa. He had no pictures and very makeshift maps, yet he held us really entranced for nearly two hours by the sheer interest of his adventures. The spirit of the wanderer is in Meares's blood: he has no happiness but in the wild places of the earth. I have never met so extreme a type. Even now he is looking forward to getting away by himself to Hut Point, tired already of our scant measure of civilisation.

He has keen natural powers of observation for all practical facts and a quite prodigious memory for such things, but a lack of scientific training causes the acceptance of exaggerated appearances, which so often present themselves to travellers when unfamiliar objects are first seen. With all deduction on this account the lecture was extraordinarily interesting. Meares lost his companion and leader, poor Brook, on the expedition which he described to us. The party started up the Yangtse, travelling from Shanghai to Hankow and thence to Ichang by steamer – then by houseboat towed by coolies through wonderful gorges and one dangerous rapid to Chunking and Chengtu. In those parts the travellers always took the three principal rooms of the inn they patronised, the cost 150 cash, something less than fourpence – oranges 20 a penny – the coolies with 100 lb. loads would cover 30 to 40 miles a day – salt is got in bores sunk with bamboos to nearly a mile in depth; it takes two or three generations to sink a bore. The lecturer described the Chinese frontier town Quanchin, its people, its products, chiefly medicinal musk pods from musk deer. Here also the wonderful ancient damming of the river, and a temple to the constructor, who wrote, twenty centuries ago, 'dig out your ditches, but keep your banks low.' On we were taken along mountain trails over high snow-filled passes and across rivers on bamboo bridges to Wassoo, a timber centre from which great rafts of lumber are shot down the river, over fearsome rapids, freighted with Chinamen. 'They generally come through all right,' said the lecturer.

Higher up the river (Min) live the peaceful Ching Ming people, an ancient aboriginal stock, and beyond these the wild tribes, the Lolo themselves. They made doubtful friends with a chief preparing for war. Meares described a feast given to them in a barbaric hall hung with skins and weapons, the men clad in buckskin dyed red, and bristling with arms; barbaric dishes, barbaric music. Then the hunt for new animals; the Chinese Tarkin, the parti-coloured bear, blue mountain sheep, the golden-haired monkey, and talk of new fruits and flowers and a host of little-known birds.

More adventures among the wild tribes of the mountains; the white lamas, the black lamas and phallic worship. Curious prehistoric caves with ancient terra-cotta figures resembling only others found in Japan and supplying a curious link. A feudal system running with well oiled wheels, the happiest of communities. A separation (temporary) from Brook, who wrote in his diary that tribes were very friendly and seemed anxious to help him, and was killed on the day following – the truth hard to gather – the recovery of his body, &c.

As he left the country the Nepaulese ambassador arrives, returning from Pekin with large escort and bound for Lhassa: the ambassador half demented: and Meares, who speaks many languages, is begged by ambassador and escort to accompany the party. He is obliged to miss this chance of a lifetime.

This is the meagrest outline of the tale which Meares adorned with a hundred incidental facts – for instance, he told us of the Lolo trade in green waxfly – the insect is propagated seasonally by thousands of Chinese who subsist on the sale of the wax produced, but all insects die between seasons. At the commencement of each season there is a market to which the wild hill Lolos bring countless tiny bamboo boxes, each containing a male and female insect, the breeding of which is their share in the industry.

We are all adventurers here, I suppose, and wild doings in wild countries appeal to us as nothing else could do. It is good to know that there remain wild corners of this dreadfully civilised world.

We have had a bright fine day. This morning a balloon was sent up without thread and with the flag device to which I have alluded. It went slowly but steadily to the north and so over the Barne Glacier. It was difficult to follow with glasses frequently clouding with the breath, but we saw the instrument detached when the slow match burned out. I'm afraid there is no doubt it fell on the glacier and there is little hope of recovering it. We have now decided to use a thread again, but to send the bobbin up with the balloon, so that it unwinds from that end and there will be no friction where it touches the snow or rock.

This investigation of upper air conditions is proving a very difficult matter, but we are not beaten yet.

Wednesday, August 30. – Fine bright day. The thread of the balloon sent up today broke very short off through some fault in the cage holding the bobbin. By good luck the instrument was found in the North Bay, and held a record.

This is the fifth record showing a constant inversion of temperature for a few hundred feet and then a gradual fall, so that the temperature of the surface is not reached again for 2000 or 3000 feet. The establishment of this fact repays much of the trouble caused by the ascents.

Thursday, August 31. – Went round about the Domain and Ramp with Wilson. We are now pretty well decided as to certain matters that puzzled us at first. The Ramp is undoubtedly a moraine supported on the decaying end of the glacier. A great deal of the underlying ice is exposed, but we had doubts as to whether this ice was not the result of winter drifting and summer thawing. We have a little difference of opinion as to whether this morainic material has been brought down in surface layers or pushed up from the bottom ice layers, as in Alpine glaciers. There is no doubt that the glacier is retreating with comparative rapidity, and this leads us to account for the various ice slabs about the hut as remains of the glacier, but a puzzling fact confronts this proposition in the discovery of penguin feathers in the lower strata of ice in both ice caves. The shifting of levels in the morainic material would account for the drying up of some lakes and the terrace formations in others, whilst curious trenches in the ground are obviously due to cracks in the ice beneath. We are now quite convinced that the queer cones on the Ramp are merely the result of the weathering of big blocks of agglomerate. As weathering results they appear unique. We have not yet a satisfactory explanation of the broad roadway faults that traverse every small eminence in our immediate region. They must originate from the unequal weathering of lava flows, but it is difficult to imagine the process. The dip of the lavas on our Cape corresponds with that of the lavas of Inaccessible Island, and points to an eruptive centre to the south and not towards Erebus. Here is food for reflection for the geologists.

The wind blew quite hard from the N.N.W. on Wednesday night, fell calm in the day, and came from the S.E. with snow as we started to return from our walk; there was a full blizzard by the time we reached the hut.

CHAPTER FOURTEEN

Preparations: the Spring Journey

Friday, September 1. – A very windy night, dropping to gusts in morning, preceding beautifully calm, bright day. If September holds as good as August we shall not have cause of complaint. Meares and Demetri started for Hut Point just before noon. The dogs were in fine form. Demetri's team came over the hummocky tide crack at full gallop, depositing the driver on the snow. Luckily some of us were standing on the floe. I made a dash at the bow of the sledge as it dashed past and happily landed on top; Atkinson grasped at the same object, but fell, and was dragged merrily over the ice. The weight reduced the pace, and others soon came up and stopped the team. Demetri was very crestfallen. He is extremely active and it's the first time he's been unseated.

There is no real reason for Meares's departure yet awhile, but he chose to go and probably hopes to train the animals better when he has them by themselves. As things are, this seems like throwing out the advance guard for the summer campaign.

I have been working very hard at sledging figures with Bowers's able assistance. The scheme develops itself in the light of these figures, and I feel that our organisation will not be found wanting, yet there is an immense amount of detail, and every arrangement has to be more than usually elastic to admit of extreme possibilities of the full success or complete failure of the motors.

I think our plan will carry us through without the motors (though in that case nothing else must fail), and will take full advantage of such help as the motors may give. Our spring travelling is to be limited order. E. Evans, Gran, and Forde will go out to find and re-mark 'Corner Camp'. Meares will then carry out as much fodder as possible with the dogs. Simpson, Bowers, and I are going to stretch our legs across to the Western Mountains. There is no choice but to keep the rest at home to exercise the ponies. It's not going to be a light task to keep all these frisky little beasts in order, as their food is increased. Today the change in masters has taken place: by the new arrangement

> Wilson takes Nobby
> Cherry-Garrard takes Michael
> Wright takes Chinaman
> Atkinson takes Jehu.

The newcomers seem very pleased with their animals, though they are by no means the pick of the bunch.

Sunday, September 3. – The weather still remains fine, the temperature down in the minus thirties. All going well and everyone in splendid spirits. Last night Bowers lectured on Polar clothing. He had worked the subject up from our Polar library with critical and humorous ability, and since his recent journey he must be considered as entitled to an authoritative opinion of his own. The points in our clothing problems are too technical and too frequently discussed to need special notice at present, but as a result of a new study of Arctic precedents it is satisfactory to find it becomes more and more evident that our equipment is the best that has been devised for the purpose, always excepting the possible alternative of skins for spring journeys, an alternative we have no power to adopt. In spite of this we are making minor improvements all the time.

Sunday, September 10. – A whole week since the last entry in my diary. I feel very negligent of duty, but my whole time has been occupied in making detailed plans for the Southern journey. These are finished at last, I am glad to say; every figure has been checked by Bowers, who has been an enormous help to me. If the motors are successful, we shall have no difficulty in getting to the Glacier, and if they fail, we shall still get there with any ordinary degree of good fortune. To work three units of four men from that point onwards requires no small provision, but with the proper provision it should take a good deal to stop the attainment of our object. I have tried to take every reasonable possibility of misfortune into consideration, and to so organise the parties as to be prepared to meet them. I fear to be too sanguine, yet taking everything into consideration I feel that our chances ought to be good. The animals are in splendid form. Day by day the ponies get fitter as their exercise increases, and the stronger, harder food toughens their muscles. They are very different animals from those which we took south last year, and with another month of training I feel there is not one of them but will make light of the loads we shall ask them to draw. But we cannot spare any of the ten, and so there must always be anxiety of the disablement of one or more before their work is done.

E. R. Evans, Forde, and Gran left early on Saturday for Corner Camp. I hope they will have no difficulty in finding it. Meares and Demetri came back from Hut Point the same afternoon – the dogs are wonderfully fit and strong, but Meares reports no seals up in the region, and as he went to make seal pemmican, there was little object in his staying. I leave him to come and go as he pleases, merely setting out the work he has to do in the simplest form. I want him to take fourteen bags of forage (130 lbs. each) to Corner Camp before the end of October and to be ready to start for his supporting work soon after the pony party – a light task for his healthy teams. Of hopeful signs for the future none are more remarkable than the health and spirit of our people. It would be impossible to imagine a more vigorous community, and there does not seem to be a single weak spot in the twelve good men and true who are chosen for the Southern advance. All are now experienced sledge travellers, knit together with a bond of friendship that has never been equalled under such circumstances. Thanks to these people, and more especially to Bowers and Petty Officer Evans, there is not a single detail of our equipment which is not arranged with the utmost care and in accordance with the tests of experience.

It is good to have arrived at a point where one can run over facts and figures again and again without detecting a flaw or foreseeing a difficulty.

I do not count on the motors – that is a strong point in our case – but should they work well our earlier task of reaching the Glacier will be made quite easy. Apart from such help I am anxious that these machines should enjoy some measure of success and justify the time, money, and thought which have been given to their construction. I am still very confident of the possibility of motor traction, whilst realising that reliance cannot be placed on it in its present untried evolutionary state – it is satisfactory to add that my own view is the most cautious one held in our party. Day is quite convinced he will go a long way and is prepared to accept much heavier weights than I have given him. Lashly's opinion is perhaps more doubtful, but on the whole hopeful. Clissold is to make the fourth man of the motor party. I have already mentioned his mechanical capabilities. He has had a great deal of experience with motors, and Day is delighted to have his assistance.

We had two lectures last week – the first from Debenham dealing with General Geology and having special reference to the structures of our region. It cleared up a good many points in my mind concerning the gneissic base rocks, the Beacon sandstone, and the dolerite intrusions. I think we shall be in a position to make fairly good field observations when we reach the southern land.

The scientific people have taken keen interest in making their lectures interesting, and the custom has grown of illustrating them with lantern slides made from our own photographs, from books, or from drawings of the lecturer. The custom adds to the interest of the subject, but robs the reporter of notes. The second weekly lecture was given by Ponting. His store of pictures seems unending and has been an immense source of entertainment to us during the winter. His lectures appeal to all and are fully attended. This time we had pictures of the Great Wall and other stupendous monuments of North China. Ponting always manages to work in detail concerning the manners and customs of the peoples in the countries of his travels; on Friday he told us of Chinese farms and industries, of hawking and other sports, most curious of all, of the pretty amusement of flying pigeons with aeolian whistling pipes attached to their tail feathers.

Ponting would have been a great asset to our party if only on account of his lectures, but his value as pictorial recorder of events becomes daily more apparent. No expedition has ever been illustrated so extensively, and the only difficulty will be to select from the countless subjects that have been recorded by his camera – and yet not a single subject is treated with haste; the first picture is rarely counted good enough, and in some cases five or six plates are exposed before our very critical artist is satisfied.

This way of going to work would perhaps be more striking if it were not common to all our workers here; a very demon of unrest seems to stir them to effort, and there is now not a single man who is not striving his utmost to get good results in his own particular department. It is a really satisfactory state of affairs all round. If the Southern journey comes off, nothing, not even priority at the Pole, can prevent the Expedition ranking as one of the most important that ever entered the Polar regions.

On Friday Cherry-Garrard produced the second volume of the *S. P. T.* on the whole an improvement on the first. Poor Cherry perspired over the editorial, and it bears the signs of labour – the letterpress otherwise is in the lighter strain: Taylor again the most important contributor, but now at rather too great a length; Nelson has supplied a very humorous trifle; the illustrations are quite delightful, the highwater mark of Wilson's ability. The humour is local, of course, but I've come to the conclusion that there can be no other form of popular journal.

The weather has not been good of late, but not sufficiently bad to interfere with exercise, &c.

Thursday, September 14. – Another interregnum. I have been exceedingly busy finishing up the Southern plans, getting instruction in photographing, and preparing for our jaunt to the west. I held forth on the 'Southern Plans' yesterday; everyone was enthusiastic, and the feeling is general that our arrangements are calculated to make the best of our resources. Although people have given a good deal of thought to various branches of the subject, there was not a suggestion offered for improvement. The scheme seems to have earned full confidence: it remains to play the game out.

The last lectures of the season have been given. On Monday Nelson gave us an interesting little résumé of biological questions, tracing the evolutionary development of forms from the simplest single-cell animals.

Tonight Wright tackled 'The Constitution of Matter' with the latest ideas from the Cavendish Laboratory: it was a tough subject, yet one carries away ideas of the trend of the work of the great physicists, of the ends they achieve and the means they employ. Wright is inclined to explain matter as velocity; Simpson claims to be with J. J. Thomson in stressing the fact that gravity is not explained.

These lectures have been a real amusement and one would be sorry enough that they should end, were it not for so good a reason.

I am determined to make some better show of our photographic work on the Southern trip than has yet been accomplished – with Ponting as a teacher it should be easy. He is prepared to take any pains to ensure good results, not only with his own work but with that of others – showing indeed what a very good chap he is.

Today I have been trying a colour screen – it is an extraordinary addition to one's powers.

Tomorrow Bowers, Simpson, Petty Officer Evans, and I are off to the west. I want to have another look at the Ferrar Glacier, to measure the stakes put out by Wright last year, to bring my sledging impressions up to date (one loses details of technique very easily), and finally to see what we can do with our cameras. I haven't decided how long we shall stay away or precisely where we shall go; such vague arrangements have an attractive side.

We have had a fine week, but the temperature remains low in the twenties, and today has dropped to $-35°$. I shouldn't wonder if we get a cold snap.

Sunday, October 1. – Returned on Thursday from a remarkably pleasant and instructive little spring journey, after an absence of thirteen days from September 15. We covered 152 geographical miles by sledge-meter (175 statute miles) in 10 marching days. It took us 2½ days to reach Butter Point (28½ miles geog.), carrying a part of the Western Party stores which brought our load to 180 lbs. a man. Everything very comfortable; double tent great asset. The 16th: a most glorious day till 4 p.m., then cold southerly wind. We captured many frostbites. Surface only fairly good; a good many heaps of loose snow which brought sledge up standing. There seems a good deal more snow this side of the Strait; query, less wind.

Bowers insists on doing all camp work; he is a positive wonder. I never met such a sledge traveller.

The sastrugi all across the strait have been across, the main S. by E. and the other E.S.E., but these are a great study here; the hard snow is striated with long wavy lines crossed with lighter wavy lines. It gives a sort of herringbone effect.

After depositing this extra load we proceeded up the Ferrar Glacier; curious low ice foot on left, no tide crack, sea ice very thinly covered with snow. We are getting delightfully fit. Bowers

treasure all round, Evans much the same. Simpson learning fast.
Find the camp life suits me well except the turning out at night!
Three times last night. We were trying nose nips and face guards,
marching head to wind all day.

We reached Cathedral Rocks on the 19th. Here we found the
stakes placed by Wright across the glacier, and spent the remainder
of the day and the whole of the 20th in plotting their position
accurately. (Very cold wind down glacier increasing. In spite of
this Bowers wrestled with theodolite. He is really wonderful. I
have never seen anyone who could go on so long with bare
fingers. My own fingers went every few moments.) We saw that
there had been movement and roughly measured it as about 30
feet. (The old Ferrar Glacier is more lively than we thought.) After
plotting the figures it turns out that the movement varies from
24 to 32 feet at different stakes – this is 7½ months. This is an
extremely important observation, the first made on the movement
of the coastal glaciers; it is more than I expected to find, but small
enough to show that the idea of comparative stagnation was
correct. Bowers and I exposed a number of plates and films in the
glacier which have turned out very well, auguring well for the
management of the camera on the Southern journey.

On the 21st we came down the glacier and camped at the
northern end of the foot. (There appeared to be a storm in the
Strait; cumulus cloud over Erebus and the whalebacks. Very
stormy look over Lister occasionally and drift from peaks; but all
smiling in our Happy Valley. Evidently this is a very favoured
spot.) From thence we jogged up the coast on the following days,
dipping into New Harbour and climbing the moraine, taking
angles and collecting rock specimens. At Cape Bernacchi we
found a quantity of pure quartz *in situ*, and in it veins of copper
ore. I got a specimen with two or three large lumps of copper
included. This is the first find of minerals suggestive of the
possibility of working.

The next day we sighted a long, low ice wall, and took it at first
for a long glacier tongue stretching seaward from the land. As we
approached we saw a dark mark on it. Suddenly it dawned on us
that the tongue was detached from the land, and we turned
towards it half recognising familiar features. As we got close we
saw similarity to our old Erebus Glacier Tongue, and finally

caught sight of a flag on it, and suddenly realised that it might be the piece broken off our old Erebus Glacier Tongue. Sure enough it was; we camped near the outer end, and climbing on to it soon found the depôt of fodder left by Campbell and the line of stakes planted to guide our ponies in the autumn. So here firmly anchored was the huge piece broken from the Glacier Tongue in March, a huge tract about 2 miles long, which has turned through half a circle, so that the old western end is now towards the east. Considering the many cracks in the ice mass it is most astonishing that it should have remained intact throughout its sea voyage.

At one time it was suggested that the hut should be placed on this Tongue. What an adventurous voyage the occupants would have had! The Tongue which was 5 miles south of C. Evans is now 40 miles W.N.W. of it.

From the Glacier Tongue we still pushed north. We reached Dunlop Island on the 24th just before the fog descended on us, and got a view along the stretch of coast to the north which turns at this point.

Dunlop Island has undoubtedly been under the sea. We found regular terrace beaches with rounded water-worn stones all over it; its height is 65 feet. After visiting the island it was easy for us to trace the same terrace formation on the coast; in one place we found water-worn stones over 100 feet above sea-level. Nearly all these stones are erratic and, unlike ordinary beach pebbles, the under sides which lie buried have remained angular.

Unlike the region of the Ferrar Glacier and New Harbour, the coast to the north of C. Bernacchi runs on in a succession of rounded bays fringed with low ice walls. At the headlands and in irregular spots the gneissic base rock and portions of moraines lie exposed, offering a succession of interesting spots for a visit in search of geological specimens. Behind this fringe there is a long undulating plateau of snow rounding down to the coast; behind this again are a succession of mountain ranges with deep-cut valleys between. As far as we went, these valleys seem to radiate from the region of the summit reached at the head of the Ferrar Glacier.

As one approaches the coast, the 'tablecloth' of snow in the foreground cuts off more and more of the inland peaks, and even at a distance it is impossible to get a good view of the inland valleys. To explore these over the ice cap is one of the objects of the Western Party.

So far, I never imagined a spring journey could be so pleasant.

On the afternoon of the 24th we turned back, and covering nearly eleven miles, camped inside the Glacier Tongue. After noon on the 25th we made a direct course for C. Evans, and in the evening camped well out in the Sound. Bowers got angles from our lunch camp and I took a photographic panorama, which is a good deal over-exposed.

We only got 2½ miles on the 26th when a heavy blizzard descended on us. We went on against it, the first time I have ever attempted to march into a blizzard; it was quite possible, but progress very slow owing to wind resistance. Decided to camp after we had done two miles. Quite a job getting up the tent, but we managed to do so, and get everything inside clear of snow with the help of much sweeping.

With care and extra fuel we have managed to get through the snowy part of the blizzard with less accumulation of snow than I ever remember, and so everywhere all-round experience is helping us. It continued to blow hard throughout the 27th, and the 28th proved the most unpleasant day of the trip. We started facing a very keen, frostbiting wind. Although this slowly increased in force, we pushed doggedly on, halting now and again to bring our frozen features round. It was 2 o'clock before we could find a decent site for a lunch camp under a pressure ridge. The fatigue of the prolonged march told on Simpson, whose whole face was frostbitten at one time – it is still much blistered. It came on to drift as we sat in our tent, and again we were weather-bound. At 3 the drift ceased, and we marched on, wind as bad as ever; then I saw an ominous yellow fuzzy appearance on the southern ridges of Erebus, and knew that another snowstorm approached. Foolishly hoping it would pass us by I kept on until Inaccessible Island was suddenly blotted out. Then we rushed for a camp site, but the blizzard was on us. In the driving snow we found it impossible to set up the inner tent, and were obliged to unbend it. It was a long job getting the outer tent set, but thanks to P.O. Evans and Bowers it was done at last. We had to risk frostbitten fingers and hang on to the tent with all our energy: got it secured inch by inch, and not such a bad speed all things considered. We had some cocoa and waited. At 9 p.m. the snow drift again took off, and we were now so snowed up, we decided to push on in spite of the wind.

We arrived in at 1.15 a.m., pretty well done. The wind never let up for an instant; the temperature remained about −16°, and the 21 statute miles which we marched in the day must be remembered amongst the most strenuous in my memory.

Except for the last few days, we enjoyed a degree of comfort which I had not imagined possible on a spring journey. The temperature was not particularly high, at the mouth of the Ferrar it was −40°, and it varied between −15° and −40° throughout. Of course this is much higher than it would be on the Barrier, but it does not in itself promise much comfort. The amelioration of such conditions we owe to experience. We used one-third more than the summer allowance of fuel. This, with our double tent, allowed a cosy hour after breakfast and supper in which we could dry our socks, &c., and put them on in comfort. We shifted our footgear immediately after the camp was pitched, and by this means kept our feet glowingly warm throughout the night. Nearly all the time we carried our sleeping-bags open on the sledges. Although the sun does not appear to have much effect, I believe this device is of great benefit even in the coldest weather − certainly by this means our bags were kept much freer of moisture than they would have been had they been rolled up in the daytime. The inner tent gets a good deal of ice on it, and I don't see any easy way to prevent this.

The journey enables me to advise the Geological Party on their best route to Granite Harbour: this is along the shore, where for the main part the protection of a chain of grounded bergs has preserved the ice from all pressure. Outside these, and occasionally reaching to the headlands, there is a good deal of pressed up ice of this season, together with the latest of the old broken pack. Travelling through this is difficult, as we found on our return journey. Beyond this belt we passed through irregular patches where the ice, freezing at later intervals in the season, has been much screwed. The whole shows the general tendency of the ice to pack along the coast.

The objects of our little journey were satisfactorily accomplished, but the greatest source of pleasure to me is to realise that I have such men as Bowers and P.O. Evans for the Southern journey. I do not think that harder men or better sledge travellers ever took the trail. Bowers is a little wonder. I realised all that he must have done for the C. Crozier Party in their far severer experience.

In spite of the late hour of our return everyone was soon afoot, and I learned the news at once. E. R. Evans, Gran, and Forde had returned from the Corner Camp journey the day after we left. They were away six nights, four spent on the Barrier under very severe conditions – the minimum for one night registered −73°.

I am glad to find that Corner Camp showed up well; in fact, in more than one place remains of last year's pony walls were seen. This removes all anxiety as to the chance of finding the One Ton Camp.

On this journey Forde got his hand badly frostbitten. I am annoyed at this, as it argues want of care; moreover there is a good chance that the tip of one of the fingers will be lost, and if this happens or if the hand is slow in recovery, Forde cannot take part in the Western Party. I have no one to replace him.

E. R. Evans looks remarkably well, as also Gran.

The ponies look very well and all are reported to be very buckish.

Wednesday, October 3. – We have had a very bad weather spell. Friday, the day after we returned, was gloriously fine – it might have been a December day, and an inexperienced visitor might have wondered why on earth we had not started to the South. Saturday supplied a reason; the wind blew cold and cheerless; on Sunday it grew worse, with very thick snow, which continued to fall and drift throughout the whole of Monday. The hut is more drifted up than it has ever been, huge piles of snow behind every heap of boxes, &c., all our paths a foot higher; yet in spite of this the rocks are rather freer of snow. This is due to melting, which is now quite considerable. Wilson tells me the first signs of thaw were seen on the 17th.

Yesterday the weather gradually improved, and today has been fine and warm again. One fine day in eight is the record immediately previous to this morning.

E. R. Evans, Debenham, and Gran set off to the Turk's Head on Friday morning, Evans to take angles and Debenham to geologise; they have been in their tent pretty well all the time since, but have managed to get through some work. Gran returned last night for more provisions and set off again this morning, Taylor going with him for the day. Debenham has just returned for food. He is immensely pleased at having discovered a huge slicken-sided fault in the lavas of the Turk's Head. This appears to be an unusual occurrence in volcanic rocks, and argues that they are of considerable age. He has taken a heap of photographs and is greatly pleased with all his geological observations. He is building up much evidence to show volcanic disturbance independent of Erebus and perhaps prior to its first upheaval.

Meares has been at Hut Point for more than a week; seals seem to be plentiful there now. Demetri was back with letters on Friday and left on Sunday. He is an excellent boy, full of intelligence.

Ponting has been doing some wonderfully fine cinematograph work. My incursion into photography has brought me in close touch with him and I realise what a very good fellow he is; no pains are too great for him to take to help and instruct others, whilst his enthusiasm for his own work is unlimited.

His results are wonderfully good, and if he is able to carry out the whole of his programme, we shall have a cinematograph and photographic record which will be absolutely new in expedition-ary work.

A very serious bit of news today. Atkinson says that Jehu is still too weak to pull a load. The pony was bad on the ship and almost died after swimming ashore from the ship – he was one of the ponies returned by Campbell. He has been improving the whole of the winter and Oates has been surprised at the apparent recovery; he looks well and feeds well, though a very weedily built animal compared with the others. I had not expected him to last long, but it will be a bad blow if he fails at the start. I'm afraid there is much pony trouble in store for us.

Oates is having great trouble with Christopher, who didn't at all appreciate being harnessed on Sunday, and again today he broke away and galloped off over the floe.

On such occasions Oates trudges manfully after him, rounds him up to within a few hundred yards of the stable and approaches cautiously; the animal looks at him for a minute or two and canters off over the floe again. When Christopher and indeed both of them have had enough of the game, the pony calmly stops at the stable door. If not too late he is then put into the sledge, but this can only be done by tying up one of his forelegs; when harnessed and after he has hopped along on three legs for a few paces, he is again allowed to use the fourth. He is going to be a trial, but he is a good strong pony and should do yeoman service.

Day is increasingly hopeful about the motors. He is an ingenious person and has been turning up new rollers out of a baulk of oak supplied by Meares, and with Simpson's small motor as a lathe. The motors *may* save the situation. I have been busy drawing up instructions and making arrangements for the ship, shore station, and sledge parties in the coming season. There is still much work to be done and much, far too much, writing before me.

Time simply flies and the sun steadily climbs the heavens. Breakfast, lunch, and supper are now all enjoyed by sunlight, whilst the night is no longer dark.

NOTES AT END OF VOLUME

When they after their headstrong manner, conclude that it is their duty to rush on their journey all weathers . . .   *Pilgrim's Progress*

> Has any grasped the low grey mist which stands
> Ghostlike at eve above the sheeted lands.'

A bad attack of integrity!!

> Who is man and what his place,
> Anxious asks the heart perplext,
> In the recklessness of space,
> Worlds with worlds thus intermixt,
> What has he, this atom creature,
> In the infinitude of nature?   F. T. PALGRAVE

It is a good lesson – though it may be a hard one – for a man who has dreamed of a special (literary) fame and of making for himself a rank among the world's dignitaries by such means, to slip aside out of the narrow circle in which his claims are recognised, and to find how utterly devoid of significance beyond that circle is all he achieves and all he aims at.

He might fail from want of skill or strength, but deep in his sombre soul he vowed that it should never be from want of heart.

Every durable bond between human beings is founded in or heightened by some element of competition.   R. L. STEVENSON

All natural talk is a festival of ostentation.   R. L. STEVENSON

No human being ever spoke of scenery for two minutes together, which makes me suspect we have too much of it in literature. The weather is regarded as the very nadir and scoff of conversational topics.   R. L. STEVENSON

The last weeks at Cape Evans

Friday, October 6. – With the rise of temperature there has been a slight thaw in the hut; the drips come down the walls and one has found my diary, as its pages show. The drips are already decreasing, and if they represent the whole accumulation of winter moisture it is extraordinarily little, and speaks highly for the design of the hut. There cannot be very much more or the stains would be more significant.

Yesterday I had a good look at Jehu and became convinced that he is useless; he is much too weak to pull a load, and three weeks can make no difference. It is necessary to face the facts and I've decided to leave him behind – we must do with nine ponies. Chinaman is rather a doubtful quantity and James Pigg is not a tower of strength, but the other seven are in fine form and must bear the brunt of the work somehow.

If we suffer more loss we shall depend on the motor, and then! . . . well, one must face the bad as well as the good.

It is some comfort to know that six of the animals at least are in splendid condition – Victor, Snippets, Christopher, Nobby, Bones are as fit as ponies could well be and are naturally strong, well-shaped beasts, whilst little Michael, though not so shapely, is as strong as he will ever be.

Today Wilson, Oates, Cherry-Garrard, and Crean have gone to Hut Point with their ponies, Oates getting off with Christopher after some difficulty. At 5 o'clock the Hut Point telephone bell suddenly rang (the line was laid by Meares some time ago, but hitherto there has been no communication). In a minute or two we heard a voice, and behold! communication was established. I had quite a talk with Meares and afterwards with Oates. Not a very wonderful fact, perhaps, but it seems wonderful in this primitive land to be talking to one's fellow beings 15 miles away. Oates told me that the ponies had arrived in fine order, Christopher a little done, but carrying the heaviest load.

If we can keep the telephone going it will be a great boon, especially to Meares later in the season.

The weather is extraordinarily unsettled; the last two days have been fairly fine, but every now and again we get a burst of wind with drift, and tonight it is overcast and very gloomy in appearance.

The photography craze is in full swing. Ponting's mastery is ever more impressive, and his pupils improve day by day; nearly all of us have produced good negatives. Debenham and Wright are the most promising, but Taylor, Bowers and I are also getting the hang of the tricky exposures.

Saturday, October 7. – As though to contradict the suggestion of incompetence, friend 'Jehu' pulled with a will this morning – he covered 3½ miles without a stop, the surface being much worse than it was two days ago. He was not at all distressed when he stopped. If he goes on like this he comes into practical politics again, and I am arranging to give 10-feet sledges to him and Chinaman instead of 12-feet. Probably they will not do much, but if they go on as at present we shall get something out of them.

Long and cheerful conversations with Hut Point and of course an opportunity for the exchange of witticisms. We are told it was blowing and drifting at Hut Point last night, whereas here it was calm and snowing; the wind only reached us this afternoon.

Sunday, October 8. – A very beautiful day. Everyone out and about after Service, all ponies going well. Went to Pressure Ridge with Ponting and took a number of photographs.

So far good, but the afternoon has brought much worry. About five a telephone message from Nelson's igloo reported that Clissold had fallen from a berg and hurt his back. Bowers organised a sledge party in three minutes, and fortunately Atkinson was on the spot and able to join it. I posted out over the land and found Ponting much distressed and Clissold practically insensible. At this moment the Hut Point ponies were approaching and I ran over to intercept one in case of necessity. But the man party was on the spot first, and after putting the patient in a sleeping-bag, quickly brought him home to the hut. It appears that Clissold was acting as Ponting's 'model' and that the two had been climbing about the berg to get pictures. As far as I can make out Ponting did his best to keep Clissold in safety by lending him his crampons and ice axe, but the latter seems to have missed his footing after one of his 'poses'; he slid over a rounded surface of ice for some 12 feet, then dropped 6 feet on to a sharp angle in the wall of the berg.

He must have struck his back and his head; the latter is contused and he is certainly suffering from slight concussion. He complained of his back before he grew unconscious and groaned a good deal when moved in the hut. He came to about an hour after getting to the hut, and was evidently in a good deal of pain; neither Atkinson nor Wilson thinks there is anything very serious, but he has not yet been properly examined and has had a fearful shock at the least. I still feel very anxious. Tonight Atkinson has injected morphia and will watch by his patient.

Troubles rarely come singly, and it occurred to me after Clissold had been brought in that Taylor, who had been bicycling to the Turk's Head, was overdue. We were relieved to hear that with glasses two figures could be seen approaching in South Bay, but at supper Wright appeared very hot and said that Taylor was exhausted in South Bay – he wanted brandy and hot drink. I thought it best to despatch another relief party, but before they were well round the point Taylor was seen coming over the land. He was fearfully done. He must have pressed on towards his objective long after his reason should have warned him that it was time to turn; with this and a good deal of anxiety about Clissold, the day terminates very unpleasantly.

Tuesday, October 10. – Still anxious about Clissold. He has passed two fairly good nights but is barely able to move. He is unnaturally irritable, but I am told this is a symptom of concussion. This morning he asked for food, which is a good sign, and he was anxious to know if his sledging gear was being got ready. In order not to disappoint him he was assured that all would be ready, but there is scarce a slender chance that he can fill his place in the programme.

Meares came from Hut Point yesterday at the front end of a blizzard. Half an hour after his arrival it was as thick as a hedge. He reports another loss – Deek, one of the best pulling dogs, developed the same symptoms which have so unaccountably robbed us before, spent a night in pain, and died in the morning.

Wilson thinks the cause is a worm which gets into the blood and thence to the brain. It is trying, but I am past despondency. Things must take their course.

Forde's fingers improve, but not very rapidly; it is hard to have two sick men after all the care which has been taken.

The weather is very poor – I had hoped for better things this month. So far we have had more days with wind and drift than without. It interferes badly with the ponies' exercise.

Friday, *October* 13. – The past three days have seen a marked improvement in both our invalids. Clissold's inside has been got into working order after a good deal of difficulty; he improves rapidly in spirits as well as towards immunity from pain. The fiction of his preparation to join the motor sledge party is still kept up, but Atkinson says there is not the smallest chance of his being ready. I shall have to be satisfied if he practically recovers by the time we leave with the ponies.

Forde's hand took a turn for the better two days ago and he maintains this progress. Atkinson thinks he will be ready to start in ten days' time, but the hand must be carefully nursed till the weather becomes really summery.

The weather has continued bad till today, which has been perfectly beautiful. A fine warm sun all day – so warm that one could sit about outside in the afternoon, and photographic work was a real pleasure.

The ponies have been behaving well, with exceptions. Victor is now quite easy to manage, thanks to Bowers's patience. Chinaman goes along very steadily and is not going to be the crock we expected. He has a slow pace which may be troublesome, but when the weather is fine that won't matter if he can get along steadily.

The most troublesome animal is Christopher. He is only a source of amusement as long as there is no accident, but I am always a little anxious that he will kick or bite someone. The curious thing is that he is quiet enough to handle for walking or riding exercise or in the stable, but as soon as a sledge comes into the programme he is seized with a very demon of viciousness, and bites and kicks with every intent to do injury. It seems to be getting harder rather than easier to get him into the traces; the last two turns, he has had to be thrown, as he is unmanageable even on three legs. Oates, Bowers, and Anton gather round the beast and lash up one foreleg, then with his head held on both sides Oates gathers back the traces; quick as lightning the little beast flashes round with heels flying aloft. This goes on till some degree of exhaustion gives the men a better chance. But, as I have mentioned, during the last two days the period has been so prolonged that Oates has had to hasten matters by tying a short line to the other foreleg and throwing the beast when he lashes out. Even when on his knees he continues to struggle, and one of those nimble hind legs may fly out at any time. Once in the sledge and started on three legs all is well and the fourth leg can be released. At least, all has been well until today, when quite a comedy was enacted. He was going along quietly with Oates when a dog frightened him: he flung up his head, twitched the rope out of Oates's hands and dashed away. It was not a question of blind fright, as immediately after gaining freedom he set about most systematically to get rid of his load. At first he gave sudden twists, and in this manner succeeded in dislodging two bales of hay; then he caught sight of other sledges and dashed for them. They could scarcely get out of his way in time; the fell intention was evident all through, to dash his load against some other pony and sledge and so free himself of it. He ran for Bowers two or three times with this design, then made for Keohane, never going off far and dashing inward with teeth bared and heels flying all over the place. By this time people were gathering round, and first one and then another succeeded in clambering on to the sledge as it flew by, till Oates, Bowers, Nelson, and Atkinson were all sitting on it. He tried to rid himself of this human burden as he had of the hay bales, and succeeded in dislodging Atkinson with violence, but the remainder dug their heels into the snow and finally the little brute was tired out. Even then he tried to savage anyone approaching his leading line, and it was some time before Oates could get hold of it. Such is the tale of Christopher. I am exceedingly glad there are not other ponies like him. These capers promise trouble, but I think a little soft snow on the Barrier may effectually cure them.

E. R. Evans and Gran return tonight. We received notice of their departure from Hut Point through the telephone, which also informed us that Meares had departed for his first trip to Corner

Camp. Evans says he carried eight bags of forage and that the dogs went away at a great pace.

In spite of the weather Evans has managed to complete his survey to Hut Point. He has evidently been very careful with it and has therefore done a very useful bit of work.

Sunday, October 15. – Both of our invalids progress favourably. Clissold has had two good nights without the aid of drugs and has recovered his good spirits; pains have departed from his back.

The weather is very decidedly warmer and for the past three days has been fine. The thermometer stands but a degree or two below zero and the air feels delightfully mild. Everything of importance is now ready for our start and the ponies improve daily.

Clissold's work of cooking has fallen on Hooper and Lashly, and it is satisfactory to find that the various dishes and bread bakings maintain their excellence. It is splendid to have people who refuse to recognise difficulties.

Tuesday, October 17. – Things not going very well; with ponies all pretty well. Animals are improving in form rapidly, even Jehu, though I have ceased to count on that animal. Tonight the motors were to be taken on to the floe. The drifts make the road very uneven, and the first and best motor overrode its chain; the chain was replaced and the machine proceeded, but just short of the floe was thrust to a steep inclination by a ridge, and the chain again overrode the sprockets; this time by ill fortune Day slipped at the critical moment and without intention jammed the throttle full on. The engine brought up, but there was an ominous trickle of oil under the back axle, and investigation showed that the axle casing (aluminium) had split. The casing has been stripped and brought into the hut; we may be able to do something to it, but time presses. It all goes to show that we want more experience and workshops.

I am secretly convinced that we shall not get much help from the motors, yet nothing has ever happened to them that was unavoidable. A little more care and foresight would make them splendid allies. The trouble is that if they fail, no one will ever believe this.

Meares got back from Corner Camp at 8 a.m. Sunday morning – he got through on the telephone to report in the afternoon. He must have made the pace, which is promising for the dogs. Sixty geographical miles in two days and a night is good going – about as good as can be.

I have had to tell Clissold that he cannot go out with the Motor Party, to his great disappointment. He improves very steadily, however, and I trust will be fit before we leave with the ponies. Hooper replaces him with the motors. I am kept very busy writing and preparing details.

We have had two days of northerly wind, a very unusual occurrence; yesterday it was blowing S.E., force 8, temp. −16°, whilst here the wind was north, force 4, temp. −6°. This continued for some hours − a curious meteorological combination. We are pretty certain of a southerly blizzard to follow, I should think.

Wednesday , *October* 18. − The southerly blizzard has burst on us. The air is thick with snow.

A close investigation of the motor axle case shows that repair is possible. It looks as though a good strong job could be made of it. Yesterday Taylor and Debenham went to Cape Royds with the object of staying a night or two.

Sunday, *October* 22. − The motor axle case was completed by Thursday morning, and, as far as one can see, Day made a very excellent job of it. Since that the Motor Party has been steadily preparing for its departure. Today everything is ready. The loads are ranged on the sea ice, the motors are having a trial run, and, all remaining well with the weather, the party will get away tomorrow.

Meares and Demetri came down on Thursday through the last of the blizzard. At one time they were running without sight of the leading dogs − they did not see Tent Island at all, but burst into sunshine and comparative calm a mile from the station. Another of the best of the dogs, 'Czigane', was smitten with the unaccountable sickness; he was given laxative medicine and appears to be a little better, but we are still anxious. If he really has the disease, whatever it may be, the rally is probably only temporary and the end will be swift.

The teams left on Friday afternoon, Czigane included; today Meares telephones that he is setting out for his second journey to Corner Camp without him. On the whole the weather continues wretchedly bad; the ponies could not be exercised either on Thursday or Friday; they were very fresh yesterday and today in consequence. When unexercised, their allowance of oats has to be cut down. This is annoying, as just at present they ought to be doing a moderate amount of work and getting into condition on full rations.

The temperature is up to zero about; this probably means about −20° on the Barrier. I wonder how the motors will face the drop if and when they encounter it. Day and Lashly are both hopeful of the machines, and they really ought to do something after all the trouble that has been taken.

The wretched state of the weather has prevented the transport of emergency stores to Hut Point. These stores are for the returning depôts and to provision the *Discovery* hut in case the *Terra Nova* does not arrive. The most important stores have been taken to the Glacier Tongue by the ponies today.

In the transport department, in spite of all the care I have taken to make the details of my plan clear by lucid explanation, I find that Bowers is the only man on whom I can thoroughly rely to carry out the work without mistake, with its arrays of figures. For the practical consistent work of pony training Oates is especially capable, and his heart is very much in the business.

'*October, 1911.* − I don't know what to think of Amundsen's chances. If he gets to the Pole, it must be before we do, as he is bound to travel fast with dogs and pretty certain to start early. On this account I decided at a very early date to act exactly as I should have done had he not existed. Any attempt to race must have wrecked my plan, besides which it doesn't appear the sort of thing one is out for.

'Possibly you will have heard something before this reaches you. Oh! and there are all sorts of possibilities. In any case you can rely on my not doing or saying anything foolish − only I'm afraid you must be prepared for the chance of finding our venture much belittled.

'After all, it is the work that counts, not the applause that follows.

'Words must always fail me when I talk of Bill Wilson. I believe he really is the finest character I ever met − the closer one gets to him, the more there is to admire. Every quality is so solid and dependable; cannot you imagine how that counts down here? Whatever the matter, one knows Bill will be sound, shrewdly practical, intensely loyal and quite unselfish. Add to this a wider knowledge of persons and things than is at first guessable, a quiet vein of humour and really consummate tact, and you have some idea of his values. I think he is the most popular member of the party, and that is saying much.

'Bowers is all and more than I ever expected of him. He is a positive treasure, absolutely trustworthy and prodigiously energetic. He is about the hardest man amongst us, and that is saying a good deal – nothing seems to hurt his tough little body and certainly no hardship daunts his spirit. I shall have a hundred little tales to tell you of his indefatigable zeal, his unselfishness, and his inextinguishable good humour. He surprises always, for his intelligence is of quite a high order and his memory for details most exceptional. You can imagine him, as he is, an indispensable assistant to me in every detail concerning the management and organisation of our sledging work and a delightful companion on the march.

'One of the greatest successes is Wright. He is very thorough and absolutely ready for anything. Like Bowers he has taken to sledging like a duck to water, and although he hasn't had such severe testing, I believe he would stand it pretty nearly as well. Nothing ever seems to worry him, and I can't imagine he ever complained of anything in his life.

'I don't think I will give such long descriptions of the others, though most of them deserve equally high praise. Taken all round they are a perfectly excellent lot.

'The Soldier is very popular with all – a delightfully humorous cheery old pessimist striving with the ponies night and day and bringing woeful accounts of their small ailments into the hut.

'X . . . has a positive passion for helping others – it is extraordinary what pains he will take to do a kind thing unobtrusively.

'One sees the need of having one's heart in one's work. Results can only be got down here by a man desperately eager to get them.

'Y . . . works hard at his own work, taking extraordinary pains with it, but with an astonishing lack of initiative he makes not the smallest effort to grasp the work of others; it is a sort of character which plants itself in a corner and *will* stop there.

'The men are equally fine. Edgar Evans has proved a useful member of our party; he looks after our sledges and sledge equipment with a care of management and a fertility of resource which is truly astonishing – on "trek" he is just as sound and hard as ever and has an inexhaustible store of anecdote.

'Crean is perfectly happy, ready to do anything and go anywhere, the harder the work, the better. Evans and Crean are great friends. Lashly is his old self in every respect, hard working to the limit, quiet, abstemious, and determined. You see altogether I have a good set of people with me, and it will go hard if we don't achieve something.

'The study of individual character is a pleasant pastime in such a mixed community of thoroughly nice people, and the study of relationships and interactions is fascinating – men of the most diverse upbringing and experience are really pals with one another, and the subjects which would be delicate ground of discussion between acquaintances are just those which are most freely used for jest. For instance, the Soldier is never tired of girding at Australia, its people and institutions, and the Australians retaliate by attacking the hide-bound prejudices of the British army. I have never seen a temper lost in these discussions. So as I sit here I am very satisfied with these things. I think that it would have been difficult to better the organisation of the party – every man has his work and is especially adapted for it; there is no gap and no overlap – it is all that I desired, and the same might be said of the men selected to do the work.'

It promised to be very fine today, but the wind has already sprung up and clouds are gathering again. There was a very beautiful curved 'banner' cloud south of Erebus this morning, perhaps a warning of what is to come.

Another accident! At one o'clock 'Snatcher', one of the three ponies laying the depôt, arrived with single trace and dangling sledge in a welter of sweat. Forty minutes after P. O. Evans, his driver, came in almost as hot; simultaneously Wilson arrived with Nobby and a tale of events not complete. He said that after the loads were removed Bowers had been holding the three ponies, who appeared to be quiet; suddenly one had tossed his head and all three had stampeded – Snatcher making for home, Nobby for the Western Mountains, Victor, with Bowers still hanging to him, in an indefinite direction. Running for two miles, he eventually rounded up Nobby west of Tent Island and brought him in.[20] Half an hour after Wilson's return, Bowers came in with Victor distressed, bleeding at the nose, from which a considerable fragment hung semi-detached. Bowers himself was covered with blood and supplied the missing link – the cause of the incident. It appears that the ponies were fairly quiet when Victor tossed his head and caught his nostril in the trace hook on the hame of Snatcher's harness. The hook tore skin and flesh and of course the animal got out of hand. Bowers hung to him, but couldn't possibly keep hold of the other two as well. Victor had bled a good deal, and the blood congealing on the detached skin not only gave the wound a dismal appearance but greatly Increased its irritation. I don't know how Bowers managed to hang on to the frightened animal; I don't believe anyone else would have done so. On the way back the dangling weight on the poor creature's nose would get on the swing and make him increasingly restive; it was necessary to stop him repeatedly. Since his return the piece of skin has been snipped off and proves the wound not so serious as it looked. The animal is still trembling, but quite on his feed, which is a good sign. I don't know why our Sundays should always bring these excitements.

Two lessons arise. Firstly, however quiet the animals appear, they must not be left by their drivers – no chance must be taken; secondly, the hooks on the hames of the harness must be altered in shape.

I suppose such incidents as this were to be expected, one cannot have ponies very fresh and vigorous and expect them to behave like lambs, but I shall be glad when we are off and can know more definitely what resources we can count on.

Another trying incident has occurred. We have avoided football this season especially to keep clear of accidents, but on Friday afternoon a match was got up for the cinematograph and Debenham developed a football knee (an old hurt, I have since learnt, or he should not have played). Wilson thinks it will be a week before he is fit to travel, so here we have the Western Party on our hands and wasting the precious hours for that period. The only single compensation is that it gives Forde's hand a better chance. If this waiting were to continue it looks as though we should become a regular party of 'crocks'. Clissold was out of the hut for the first time today; he is better but still suffers in his back.

The start of the motor sledges

Tuesday October 24. – Two fine days for a wonder. Yesterday the motors seemed ready to start and we all went out on the floe to give them a 'send off'. But the inevitable little defects cropped up, and the machines only got as far as the Cape. A change made by Day in the exhaust arrangements had neglected the heating jackets of the carburetters: one float valve was bent and one clutch troublesome. Day and Lashly spent the afternoon making good these defects in a satisfactory mariner.

This morning the engines were set going again, and shortly after 10 a.m. a fresh start was made. At first there were a good many stops, but on the whole the engines seemed to be improving all the time. They are not by any means working up to full power yet, and so the pace is very slow. The weights seem to me a good deal heavier than we bargained for. Day sets his motor going, climbs off the car, and walks alongside with an occasional finger on the throttle. Lashly hasn't yet quite got hold of the nice adjustments of his control levers, but I hope will have done so after a day's practice.

The only alarming incident was the slipping of the chains when Day tried to start on some ice very thinly covered with snow. The starting effort on such heavily laden sledges is very heavy, but I thought the grip of the pattens and studs would have been good enough on any surface. Looking at the place afterwards I found that the studs had grooved the ice.

Now as I write at 12.30 the machines are about a mile out in the South Bay; both can be seen still under weigh, progressing steadily if slowly.

I find myself immensely eager that these tractors should succeed, even though they may not be of great help to our southern advance. A small measure of success will be enough to show their possibilities, their ability to revolutionise Polar transport. Seeing the machines at work today, and remembering that every defect so far shown is purely mechanical, it is impossible not to be convinced of their value. But the trifling mechanical defects and lack of experience show the risk of cutting out trials. A season of experiment with a small workshop at hand may be all that stands between success and failure.

At any rate before we start we shall certainly know if the worst has happened, or if some measure of success attends this unique effort.

The ponies are in fine form. Victor, practically recovered from his wound, has been rushing round with a sledge at a great rate. Even Jehu has been buckish, kicking up his heels and gambolling awkwardly. The invalids progress, Clissold a little alarmed about his back, but without cause.

Atkinson and Keohane have turned cooks, and do the job splendidly.

This morning Meares announced his return from Corner Camp, so that all stores are now out there. The run occupied the same time as the first, when the routine was: first day 17 miles out; second day 13 out, and 13 home; early third day run in. If only one could trust the dogs to keep going like this it would be splendid. On the whole things look hopeful.

1 p.m. – motors reported off Razorback Island, nearly 3 miles out – come, come!

Thursday, October 26. – Couldn't see the motors yesterday till I walked well out on the South Bay, when I discovered them with glasses off the Glacier Tongue. There had been a strong wind in the forenoon, but it seemed to me they ought to have got further – annoyingly the telephone gave no news from Hut Point, evidently something was wrong. After dinner Simpson and Gran started for Hut Point.

This morning Simpson has just rung up. He says the motors are in difficulties with the surface. The trouble is just that which I noted as alarming on Monday – the chains slip on the very light snow covering of hard ice. The engines are working well, and all goes well when the machines get on to snow.

I have organised a party of eight men including myself, and we are just off to see what can be done to help.

Friday, October 27. – We were away by 10.30 yesterday. Walked to the Glacier Tongue with gloomy forebodings; but for one gust a beautifully bright inspiriting day. Seals were about and were frequently mistaken for the motors. As we approached the Glacier Tongue, however, and became more alive to such mistakes, we realised that the motors were not in sight. At first I thought they must have sought better surface on the other side of the Tongue, but this theory was soon demolished and we were puzzled to know what had happened. At length walking onward they were descried far away over the floe towards Hut Point; soon after we saw good firm tracks over a snow surface, a pleasant change from the double tracks and slippery places we had seen on the bare ice. Our spirits went up at once, for it was not only evident that the machines were going, but that they were negotiating a very rough surface without difficulty. We marched on and overtook them about 2½ miles from Hut Point, passing Simpson and Gran returning to Cape Evans. From the motors we learnt that things were going pretty well. The engines were working well when once in tune, but the cylinders, especially the two after ones, tended to get too hot, whilst the fan or wind playing on the carburetter tended to make it too cold. The trouble was to get a balance between the two, and this is effected by starting up the engines, then stopping and covering them and allowing the heat to spread by conductivity – of course, a rather clumsy device. We camped ahead of the motors as they camped for lunch. Directly after, Lashly brought his machine along on low gear and without difficulty ran it on to Cape Armitage. Meanwhile Day was having trouble with some bad surface; we had offered help and been refused, and with E. Evans alone his difficulties grew, whilst the wind sprang up and the snow started to drift. We had walked into the hut and found Meares, but now we all came out again. I sent for Lashly and Hooper and went back to help Day along. We had exasperating delays and false starts for an hour and then suddenly the machine tuned up, and off she went faster than one could walk, reaching Cape Armitage without further hitch. It was blizzing by this time; a fine sight to see the motor forging away through the mist as the snow flew by. We all went back to the hut; Meares and Demetri have been busy, the hut is tidy and comfortable and a splendid brick fireplace had just been built with a brand new stove-pipe leading from it directly upward through the roof. This is really a most creditable bit of work. Instead of the ramshackle temporary structures of last season we have now a solid permanent fireplace which should last for many a year. We spent a most comfortable night.

This morning we were away over the floe about 9 a.m. I was anxious to see how the motors started up and agreeably surprised to find that neither driver took more than 20 to 30 minutes to get his machine going, in spite of the difficulties of working a blow lamp in a keen cold wind.

Lashly got away very soon, made a short run of about ½ mile, and then after a short halt to cool, a long non-stop for quite 3 miles. The Barrier, five geographical miles from Cape Armitage, now looked very close, but Lashly had overdone matters a bit, run out of lubricant and got his engine too hot. The next run yielded a little over a mile, and he was forced to stop within a few hundred yards of the snow slope leading to the Barrier and wait for more lubricant, as well as for the heat balance in his engine to be restored.

This motor was going on second gear, and this gives a nice easy walking speed, 2½ to 3 miles an hour; it would be a splendid rate of progress if it was not necessary to halt for cooling. This is the old motor which was used in Norway; the other machine has modified gears.*

Meanwhile Day had had the usual balancing trouble and had dropped to a speck, but towards the end of our second run it was evident he had overcome these and was coming along at a fine speed. One soon saw that the men beside the sledges were running. To make a long story short, he stopped to hand over lubricating oil, started at a gallop again, and dashed up the slope without a hitch on his top speed – the first man to run a motor on the Great Barrier! There was great cheering from all assembled, but the motor party was not wasting time on jubilation. On dashed the motor, and it and the running men beside it soon grew small in the distance. We went back to help Lashly, who had restarted his engine. If not so dashingly, on account of his slower speed, he also now took the slope without hitch and got a last handshake as he clattered forward. His engine was not working so well as the other, but I think mainly owing to the first overheating and a want of adjustment resulting therefrom.

Thus the motors left us, travelling on the best surface they have yet encountered – hard windswept snow without sastrugi – a surface which Meares reports to extend to Corner Camp at least.

* This form of motor traction had been tested on several occasions; in 1908 at Lauteret in the Alps, with Dr Charcot the Polar explorer: in 1909 and again 1910 in Norway. After each trial the sledges were brought back and improved.

Providing there is no serious accident, the engine troubles will gradually be got over; of that I feel pretty confident. Every day will see improvement as it has done to date, every day the men will get greater confidence with larger experience of the machines and the conditions. But it is not easy to foretell the extent of the result of older and earlier troubles with the rollers. The new rollers turned up by Day are already splitting, and one of Lashly's chains is in a bad way; it may be possible to make temporary repairs good enough to cope with the improved surface, but it seems probable that Lashly's car will not get very far.

It is already evident that had the rollers been metal-cased and the runners metal-covered, they would now be as good as new. I cannot think why we had not the sense to have this done. As things are I am satisfied we have the right men to deal with the difficulties of the situation.

The motor programme is not of vital importance to our plan and it is possible the machines will do little to help us, but already they have vindicated themselves. Even the seamen, who have remained very sceptical of them, have been profoundly impressed. Evans said, 'Lord, sir, I reckon if them things can go on like that you wouldn't want nothing else' – but like everything else of a novel nature, it is the actual sight of them at work that is impressive, and nothing short of a hundred miles over the Barrier will carry conviction to outsiders.

Parting with the motors, we made haste back to Hut Point and had tea there. My feet had got very sore with the unaccustomed soft foot-gear and crinkly surface, but we decided to get back to Cape Evans. We came along in splendid weather, and after stopping for a cup of tea at Razorback, reached the hut at 9 p.m., averaging 3½ stat. miles an hour. During the day we walked 26½ stat. miles, not a bad day's work considering condition, but I'm afraid my feet are going to suffer for it.

Saturday, October 28. – My feet sore and one 'tendon Achillis' strained (synovitis); shall be right in a day or so, however. Last night tremendous row in the stables. Christopher and Chinaman discovered fighting. Gran nearly got kicked. These ponies are getting above themselves with their high feeding. Oates says that Snippets is still lame and has one leg a little 'heated'; not a pleasant item of news. Debenham is progressing, but not very fast; the

Western Party will leave after us, of that there is no doubt now. It is trying that they should be wasting the season in this way. All things considered, I shall be glad to get away and put our fortune to the test.

Monday, October 30. – We had another beautiful day yesterday, and one began to feel that the summer really had come; but today, after a fine morning, we have a return to blizzard conditions. It is blowing a howling gale as I write. Yesterday Wilson, Crean, P.O. Evans, and I donned our sledging kit and camped by the bergs for the benefit of Ponting and his cinematograph; he got a series of films which should be about the most interesting of all his collection. I imagine nothing will take so well as these scenes of camp life.

On our return we found Meares had returned; he and the dogs well. He told us that (Lieut.) Evans had come into Hut Point on Saturday to fetch a personal bag left behind there. Evans reported that Lashly's motor had broken down near Safety Camp; they found the big end smashed up in one cylinder and traced it to a faulty casting; they luckily had spare parts, and Day and Lashly worked all night on repairs in a temperature of −25°. By the morning repairs were completed and they had a satisfactory trial run, dragging on loads with both motors. Then Evans found out his loss and returned on ski, whilst, as I gather, the motors proceeded; I don't quite know how, but I suppose they ran one on at a time. On account of this accident and because some of our hardest worked people were badly hit by the two days' absence helping the machines, I have decided to start on Wednesday instead of tomorrow. If the blizzard should blow out, Atkinson and Keohane will set off tomorrow for Hut Point, so that we may see how far Jehu is to be counted on.

Tuesday, October 31. – The blizzard has blown itself out this morning, and this afternoon it has cleared; the sun is shining and the wind dropping. Meares and Ponting are just off to Hut Point. Atkinson and Keohane will probably leave in an hour or so as arranged, and if the weather holds, we shall all get off tomorrow. So here end the entries in this diary with the first chapter of our History. The future is in the lap of the gods; I can think of nothing left undone to deserve success.

CHAPTER SIXTEEN

Southern Journey: the Barrier stage

November 1. – Last night we heard that Jehu had reached Hut Point in about 5½ hours. This morning we got away in detachments – Michael, Nobby, Chinaman were first to get away about 11 a.m. The little devil Christopher was harnessed with the usual difficulty and started in kicking mood, Oates holding on for all he was worth.

Bones ambled off gently with Crean, and I led Snippets in his wake. Ten minutes after P. O. Evans and Snatcher passed at the usual full speed.

The wind blew very strong at the Razorback and the sky was threatening – the ponies hate the wind. A mile south of this island Bowers and Victor passed me, leaving me where I best wished to be – at the tail of the line.

About this place I saw that one of the animals ahead had stopped and was obstinately refusing to go forward again. I had a great fear it was Chinaman, the unknown quantity, but to my relief found it was my old friend 'Nobby' in obstinate mood. As he is very strong and fit the matter was soon adjusted with a little persuasion from Anton behind. Poor little Anton found it difficult to keep the pace with short legs.

Snatcher soon led the party and covered the distance in four hours. Evans said he could see no difference at the end from the start – the little animal simply romped in. Bones and Christopher arrived almost equally fresh, in fact the latter had been bucking and kicking the whole way. For the present there is no end to his devilment, and the great consideration is how to safeguard Oates. Some quiet ponies should always be near him, a difficult matter to arrange with such varying rates of walking. A little later I came up to a batch, Bowers, Wilson, Cherry, and Wright, and was happy to see Chinaman going very strong. He is not fast, but very steady, and I think should go a long way.

Victor and Michael forged ahead again, and the remaining three of us came in after taking a little under five hours to cover the distance.

We were none too soon, as the weather had been steadily getting worse, and soon after our arrival it was blowing a gale.

Thursday, November 2. – Hut Point. The march teaches a good deal as to the paces of the ponies. It reminded me of a regatta or a somewhat disorganised fleet with ships of very unequal speed. The plan of further advance has now been evolved. We shall start in three parties – the very slow ponies, the medium-paced, and the fliers. Snatcher starting last will probably overtake the leading unit. All this requires a good deal of arranging. We have decided to begin night marching, and shall get away after supper, I hope. The weather is hourly improving, but at this season that does not count for much. At present our ponies are very comfortably stabled. Michael, Chinaman and James Pigg are actually in the hut. Chinaman kept us alive last night by stamping on the floor. Meares and Demetri are here with the dog team, and Ponting with a great photographic outfit. I fear he won't get much chance to get results.

Friday, November 3. – Camp 1. A keen wind with some drift at Hut Point, but we sailed away in detachments. Atkinson's party, Jehu, Chinaman and Jimmy Pigg led off at eight. Just before ten Wilson, Cherry-Garrard and I left. Our ponies marched steadily and well together over the sea ice. The wind dropped a good deal, but the temperature with it, so that the little remaining was very cutting. We found Atkinson at Safety Camp. He had lunched and was just ready to march out again; he reports Chinaman and Jehu tired. Ponting arrived soon after we had camped with Demetri and a small dog team. The cinematograph was up in time to catch the flying rearguard which came along in fine form, Snatcher leading and being stopped every now and again – a wonderful little beast. Christopher had given the usual trouble when harnessed, but was evidently subdued by the Barrier Surface. However, it was not thought advisable to halt him, and so the party fled through in the wake of the advance guard.

After lunch we packed up and marched on steadily as before. I don't like these midnight lunches, but for man the march that follows is pleasant when, as today, the wind falls and the sun steadily increases its heat. The two parties in front of us camped

5 miles beyond Safety Camp, and we reached their camp some half or three-quarters of an hour later. All the ponies are tethered in good order, but most of them are tired – Chinaman and Jehu *very tired*. Nearly all are inclined to be off feed, but this is very temporary, I think. We have built walls, but there is no wind and the sun gets warmer every minute.

Mirage. – Very marked waving effect to east. Small objects greatly exaggerated and showing as dark vertical lines.

1 p.m. – Feeding time. Woke the party, and Oates served out the rations – all ponies feeding well. It is a sweltering day, the air breathless, the glare intense – one loses sight of the fact that the temperature is low ($+22°$) – one's mind seeks comparison in hot sunlit streets and scorching pavements, yet six hours ago my thumb was frostbitten. All the inconveniences of frozen footwear and damp clothes and sleeping-bags have vanished entirely.

A petrol tin is near the camp and a note stating that the motor passed at 9 p.m. 28th, going strong – they have 4 to 5 days' lead and should surely keep it.

'Bones has eaten Christopher's goggles.'

This announcement by Crean, meaning that Bones had demolished the protecting fringe on Christopher's bridle. These fringes promise very well – Christopher without his is blinking in the hot sun.

Saturday, November 4. – Camp 2. Led march – started in what I think will now become the settled order. Atkinson went at 8, ours at 10, Bowers, Oates and Co. at 11.15. Just after starting picked up cheerful note and saw cheerful notices saying all well with motors, both going excellently. Day wrote 'Hope to meet in 80° 30' (Lat.).' Poor chap, within 2 miles he must have had to sing a different tale. It appears they had a bad grind on the morning of the 29th. I suppose the surface was bad and everything seemed to be going wrong. They 'dumped' a good deal of petrol and lubricant. Worse was to follow. Some 4 miles out we met a tin pathetically inscribed, 'Big end Day's motor No. 2 cylinder broken.' Half a mile beyond, as I expected, we found the motor, its tracking sledges and all. Notes from E. Evans and Day told the tale. The only spare had been used for Lashly's machine, and it would have taken a long time to strip Day's engine so that it could run on three cylinders. They had decided to abandon it and push on with the other alone.

They had taken the six bags of forage and some odds and ends, besides their petrol and lubricant. So the dream of great help from the machines is at an end! The track of the remaining motor goes steadily forward, but now, of course, I shall expect to see it every hour of the march.

The ponies did pretty well – a cruel soft surface most of the time, but light loads, of course. Jehu is better than I expected to find him, Chinaman not so well. They are bad crocks both of them.

It was pretty cold during the night, −7° when we camped, with a crisp breeze blowing. The ponies don't like it, but now, as I write, the sun is shining through a white haze, the wind has dropped, and the picketing line is comfortable for the poor beasts.

This, 1 p.m., is the feeding hour – the animals are not yet on feed, but they are coming on.

The wind vane left here in the spring shows a predominance of wind from the S.W. quarter. Maximum scratching, about S.W. by W.

Sunday, November 5. – Camp 3. 'Corner Camp'. We came over the last lap of the first journey in good order – ponies doing well in soft surface, but, of course, lightly loaded. Tonight will show what we can do with the heavier weights. A very troubled note from E . Evans (with motor) written on morning of 2nd, saying maximum speed was about 7 miles per day. They have taken on nine bags of forage, but there are three black dots to the south which we can only imagine are the deserted motor with its loaded sledges. The men have gone on as a supporting party, as directed. It is a disappointment. I had hoped better of the machines once they got away on the Barrier Surface.

The appetites of the ponies are very fanciful. They do not like the oil cake, but for the moment seem to take to some fodder left here. However, they are off that again today. It is a sad pity they won't eat well now, because later on one can imagine how ravenous they will become. Chinaman and Jehu will not go far I fear.

Monday, November 6. – Camp 4. We started in the usual order, arranging so that full loads should be carried if the black dots to the south prove to be the motor. On arrival at these we found our fears confirmed. A note from Evans stated a recurrence of the old trouble. The big end of No. 1 cylinder had cracked, the machine otherwise in good order. Evidently the engines are not fitted for working in this climate, a fact that should be certainly capable of correction. One thing is proved; the system of propulsion is altogether satisfactory. The motor party has proceeded as a man-hauling party as arranged.

With their full loads the ponies did splendidly, even Jehu and Chinaman with loads over 450 lbs. stepped out well and have finished as fit as when they started. Atkinson and Wright both think that these animals are improving.

The better ponies made nothing of their loads, and my own Snippets had over 700 lbs., sledge included. Of course, the surface is greatly improved; it is that over which we came well last year. We are all much cheered by this performance. It shows a hardening up of ponies which have been well trained; even Oates is pleased!

As we came to camp a blizzard threatened, and we built snow walls. One hour after our arrival the wind was pretty strong, but there was not much snow. This state of affairs has continued, but the ponies seem very comfortable. Their new rugs cover them well and the sheltering walls are as high as the animals, so that the wind is practically unfelt behind them. This protection is a direct result of our experience of last year, and it is good to feel that we reaped some reward for that disastrous journey. I am writing late in the day and the wind is still strong. I fear we shall not be able to go on tonight. Christopher gave great trouble again last night – the four men had great difficulty in getting him into his sledge; this is a nuisance which I fear must be endured for some time to come.

The temperature, +5°, is lower than I like in a blizzard. It feels chilly in the tent, but the ponies don't seem to mind the wind much.

The incidence of this blizzard had certain characters worthy of note –

Before we started from Corner Camp there was a heavy collection of cloud about Cape Crozier and Mount Terror, and a black line of stratus low on the western slopes of Erebus. With us the sun was shining and it was particularly warm and pleasant. Shortly after we started mist formed about us, waxing and waning in density; a slight southerly breeze sprang up, cumulo-stratus cloud formed overhead with a rather windy appearance (radial E. and W.).

At the first halt (5 miles S.) Atkinson called my attention to a curious phenomenon. Across the face of the low sun the strata of mist could be seen rising rapidly, lines of shadow appearing to be travelling upwards against the light. Presumably this was sun-warmed air. The accumulation of this gradually overspread the sky with a layer of stratus, which, however, never seemed to be very dense; the position of the sun could always be seen. Two or three hours later the wind steadily increased in force, with the usual gusty characteristic. A noticeable fact was that the sky was clear and blue above the southern horizon, and the clouds seemed to be closing down on this from time to time. At intervals since, it has lifted, showing quite an expanse of clear sky. The general appearance is that the disturbance is created by conditions about us, and is rather spreading from north to south than coming up with the wind, and this seems rather typical. On the other hand, this is not a bad snow blizzard; although the wind holds, the land, obscured last night, is now quite clear and the Bluff has no mantle.

[Added in another hand, probably dictated:

Before we felt any air moving, during our a.m. march and the greater part of the previous march, there was dark cloud over Ross Sea off the Barrier, which continued over the Eastern Barrier to the S.E. as a heavy stratus, with here and there an appearance of wind. At the same time, due south of us, dark lines of stratus were appearing, miraged on the horizon, and while we were camping after our a.m. march, these were obscured by banks of white fog (or drift?), and the wind increasing the whole time. My general impression was that the storm came up from the south, but swept round over the eastern part of the Barrier before it became general and included the western part where we were.]

Tuesday, November 7. – Camp 4. The blizzard has continued throughout last night and up to this time of writing, late in the afternoon. Starting mildly, with broken clouds, little snow, and gleams of sunshine, it grew in intensity until this forenoon, when there was heavy snowfall and the sky overspread with low nimbus cloud. In the early afternoon the snow and wind took off, and the wind is dropping now, but the sky looks very lowering and unsettled.

Last night the sky was so broken that I made certain the end of the blow had come. Towards morning the sky overhead and far to

the north was quite clear. More cloud obscured the sun to the
south and low heavy banks hung over Ross Island. All seemed
hopeful, except that I noted with misgiving that the mantle on the
Bluff was beginning to form. Two hours later the whole sky was
overcast and the blizzard had fully developed.

This Tuesday evening it remains overcast, but one cannot
see that the clouds are travelling fast. The Bluff mantle is a wide
low bank of stratus not particularly windy in appearance; the
wind is falling, but the sky still looks lowering to the south and
there is a general appearance of unrest. The temperature has been
+10° all day.

The ponies, which had been so comparatively comfortable in
the earlier stages, were hit as usual when the snow began to fall.

We have done everything possible to shelter and protect them,
but there seems no way of keeping them comfortable when the
snow is thick and driving fast. We men are snug and comfortable
enough, but it is very evil to lie here and know that the weather
is steadily sapping the strength of the beasts on which so much
depends. It requires much philosophy to be cheerful on such
occasions.

In the midst of the drift this forenoon the dog party came up and
camped about a quarter of a mile to leeward. Meares has played
too much for safety in catching us so soon, but it is satisfactory to
find the dogs will pull the loads and can be driven to face such a
wind as we have had. It shows that they ought to be able to help us
a good deal.

The tents and sledges are badly drifted up, and the drifts behind
the pony walls have been dug out several times. I shall be glad
indeed to be on the march again, and oh! for a little sun. The
ponies are all quite warm when covered by their rugs. Some of
the fine drift snow finds its way under the rugs, and especially
under the broad belly straps; this melts and makes the coat wet if
allowed to remain. It is not easy to understand at first why the
blizzard should have such a withering effect on the poor beasts.
I think it is mainly due to the exceeding fineness of the snow
particles, which, like finely divided powder, penetrate the hair of
the coat and lodge in the inner warmths. Here it melts, and as
water carries off the animal heat. Also, no doubt, it harasses the
animals by the bombardment of the fine flying particles on tender

places such as nostrils, eyes, and to lesser extent ears. In this way it continually bothers them, preventing rest. Of all things the most important for horses is that conditions should be placid whilst they stand tethered.

Wednesday, November 8. – Camp 5. Wind with overcast threatening sky continued to a late hour last night. The question of starting was open for a long time, and many were unfavourable. I decided we must go, and soon after midnight the advance guard got away. To my surprise, when the rugs were stripped from the 'crocks' they appeared quite fresh and fit. Both Jehu and Chinaman had a skittish little run. When their heads were loose Chinaman indulged in a playful buck. All three started with their loads at a brisk pace. It was a great relief to find that they had not suffered at all from the blizzard. They went out six geographical miles, and our section going at a good round pace found them encamped as usual. After they had gone, we waited for the rearguard to come up and joined with them. For the next 5 miles the bunch of seven kept together in fine style, and with wind dropping, sun gaining in power, and ponies going well, the march was a real pleasure. One gained confidence every moment in the animals; they brought along their heavy loads without a hint of tiredness. All take the patches of soft snow with an easy stride, not bothering themselves at all. The majority halt now and again to get a mouthful of snow, but little Christopher goes through with a non-stop run. He gives as much trouble as ever at the start, showing all sorts of ingenious tricks to escape his harness. Yesterday when brought to his knees and held, he lay down, but this served no end, for before he jumped to his feet and dashed off the traces had been fixed and he was in for the 13 miles of steady work. Oates holds like grim death to his bridle until the first freshness is worn off, and this is no little time, for even after 10 miles he seized a slight opportunity to kick up. Some four miles from this camp P. O. Evans loosed Snatcher's bridle momentarily. The little beast was off at a canter at once and on slippery snow; it was all Evans could do to hold to the bridle. As it was he dashed across the line, somewhat to its danger.

Six hundred yards from this camp there was a bale of forage. Bowers stopped and loaded it on his sledge, bringing his weights to nearly 800 lbs. His pony Victor stepped out again as though nothing had been added. Such incidents are very inspiriting. Of course, the surface is very good; the animals rarely sink to the fetlock joint, and for a good part of the time are borne up on hard snow patches without sinking at all. In passing I mention that there are practically no places where ponies sink to their hocks as described by Shackleton. On the only occasion last year when our ponies sank to their hocks in one soft patch, they were unable to get their loads on at all. The feathering of the fetlock joint is borne up on the snow crust and its upward bend is indicative of the depth of the hole made by the hoof; one sees that an extra inch makes a tremendous difference.

We are picking up last year's cairns with great ease, and all show up very distinctly. This is extremely satisfactory for the home-ward march. What with pony walls, camp sites and cairns, our track should be easily followed the whole way. Everyone is as fit as can be. It was wonderfully warm as we camped this morning at 11 o'clock; the wind has dropped completely and the sun shines gloriously. Men and ponies revel in such weather. One devoutly hopes for a good spell of it as we recede from the windy northern region. The dogs came up soon after we had camped, travelling easily.

Thursday, November 9. – Camp 6. Sticking to programme, we are going a little over the 10 miles (geo.) nightly. Atkinson started his party at 11 and went on for 7 miles to escape a cold little night breeze which quickly dropped. He was some time at his lunch camp, so that starting to join the rearguard we came in together the last 2 miles. The experience showed that the slow advance guard ponies are forced out of their pace by joining with the others, whilst the fast rearguard is reduced in speed. Obviously it is not an advantage to be together, yet all the ponies are doing well. An amusing incident happened when Wright left his pony to examine his sledge-meter. Chinaman evidently didn't like being left behind and set off at a canter to rejoin the main body. Wright's long legs barely carried him fast enough to stop this playful stampede, but the ridiculous sight was due to the fact that old Jehu caught the infection and set off at a sprawling canter in Chinaman's wake. As this is the pony we thought scarcely capable of a single march at start, one is agreeably surprised to find him still displaying such commendable spirit. Christopher is troublesome as ever at the start; I fear that signs of tameness will only indicate absence of strength. The dogs followed us so easily over the 10 miles that Meares thought of going on again, but finally decided that the present easy work is best.

Things look hopeful. The weather is beautiful – temp. +12°, with a bright sun. Some stratus cloud about Discovery and over White Island. The sastrugi about here are very various in direction and the surface a good deal ploughed up, showing that the Bluff influences the wind direction even out as far as this camp. The surface is hard; I take it about as good as we shall get.

There is an annoying little southerly wind blowing now, and this serves to show the beauty of our snow walls. The ponies are standing under their lee in the bright sun as comfortable as can possibly be.

Friday, November 10. – Camp 7. A very horrid march. A strong head wind during the first part – 5 miles (geo.) – then a snowstorm. Wright leading found steering so difficult after three miles (geo.) that the party decided to camp. Luckily just before camping he rediscovered Evans's track (motor party) so that, given decent weather, we shall be able to follow this. The ponies did excellently as usual, but the surface is good distinctly. The wind has dropped and the weather is clearing now that we have camped. It is disappointing to miss even 1½ miles.

Christopher was started today by a ruse. He was harnessed behind his wall and was in the sledge before he realised. Then he tried to bolt, but Titus hung on.

Saturday, November 11. – Camp 8. It cleared somewhat just before the start of our march, but the snow which had fallen in the day remained soft and flocculent on the surface. Added to this we entered on an area of soft crust between a few scattered hard sastrugi. In pits between these in places the snow lay in sandy heaps. A worse set of conditions for the ponies could scarcely be imagined. Nevertheless they came through pretty well, the strong ones excellently, but the crocks had had enough at 9½ miles. Such a surface makes one anxious in spite of the rapidity with which changes take place. I expected these marches to be a little difficult, but not near so bad as today's. It is snowing again as we camp, with a slight north-easterly breeze. It is difficult to make out what is happening to the weather – it is all part of the general warming up, but I wish the sky would clear. In spite of the surface, the dogs ran up from the camp before last, over 20 miles, in the night. They are working splendidly so far.

Sunday, November 12. – Camp 9. Our marches are uniformly horrid just at present. The surface remains wretched, not quite so heavy as yesterday, perhaps, but very near it at times. Five miles out the advance party came straight and true on our last year's Bluff depôt marked with a flagstaff. Here following I found a note from E. Evans, cheerful in tone, dated 7 a.m. 7th inst. He is, therefore, the best part of five days ahead of us, which is good. Atkinson camped a mile beyond this cairn and had a very gloomy account of Chinaman. Said he couldn't last more than a mile or two. The weather was horrid, overcast, gloomy, snowy. One's spirits became very low. However, the crocks set off again, the rearguard came up, passed us in camp, and then on the march about 3 miles on, so that they camped about the same time. The Soldier thinks Chinaman will last for a good many days yet, which is an extraordinary confession of hope for him. The rest of the animals are as well as can be expected – Jehu rather better. These weather appearances change every minute. When we camped there was a chill northerly breeze, a black sky, and light falling snow. Now the sky is clearing and the sun shining an hour later. The temperature remains about +10° in the daytime.

Monday, November 13. – Camp 10. Another horrid march in a terrible light, surface very bad. Ponies came through all well, but they are being tried hard by the surface conditions. We followed tracks most of the way, neither party seeing the other except towards camping time. The crocks did well, all things considered; Jehu is doing extremely well for him. As we camped the sun came out and the cold chilly conditions of the march passed away, leaving everything peaceful, calm, and pleasant. We shall be in a better position to know how we stand when we get to One Ton Camp, now only 17 or 18 miles, but I am anxious about these beasts – very anxious, they are not the ponies they ought to have been, and if they pull through well, all the thanks will be due to Oates. I trust the weather and surface conditions will improve; both are rank bad at present.

3 p.m. – It has been snowing consistently for some hours, adding to the soft surface accumulation inch upon inch. What can such

weather mean? Arguing it out, it is clearly necessary to derive this superfluity of deposition from some outside source such as the open sea. The wind and spread of cloud from the N.E. and the exceptionally warm temperature seem to point to this. If this should come as an exception, our luck will be truly awful. The camp is very silent and cheerless, signs that things are going awry. The temperature in the middle of our tent this morning when the sun was shining on it was 50°! Outside +10°.

Tuesday, November 14. – Camp 11. The surface little improved, but a slightly better and much more cheerful march. The sun shone out midway, and although obscured for a time, it is now quite bright again. Now it is thoroughly warm, the air breathlessly still, and the ponies resting in great comfort. If the snow has finished, the surface deposit, which is three to four inches thick, ought to diminish rapidly. Yet it is painful struggling on through this snow, though the ponies carry it gallantly enough. Christopher has now been harnessed three times without difficulty. After One Ton Camp it ought to be possible to stop him for a midnight halt and so get through the easier on long marches. Nearly 12 statute miles without a stop must be a big strain on the rearguard animals. One Ton Camp is only about 7 miles farther. Meanwhile we passed two of Evans's cairns today and one old cairn of last year, so that we ought to have little difficulty in finding our depôt.

Although we have been passing the black land of the Bluff I have not seen a sign of the land for four days. I had not thought it possible that misty conditions could continue for so long a time in this region; always before we have seen the land repeatedly. Either the whole sky has been clear, or the overhanging cloud has lifted from time to time to show the lower rocks. Had we been dependent on land marks we should have fared ill. Evidently a good system of cairns is the best possible travelling arrangement on this great snow plain. Meares and Demetri up with the dogs as usual very soon after we camped.

This inpouring of warm moist air, which gives rise to this heavy surface deposit at this season, is certainly an interesting meteorological fact, accounting as it does for the very sudden change in Barrier conditions from spring to summer.

Wednesday, November 15. – Camp 12. Found our One Ton Camp without any difficulty [130 geographical miles from Cape

Evans]. About 7 or 8 miles. After 5½ miles to lunch camp, China-man was pretty tired, but went on again in good form after the rest. All the other ponies made nothing of the march, which, however, was over a distinctly better surface. After a discussion we have decided to give the animals a day's rest here, and then to push forward at the rate of 13 geographical miles a day. Oates thinks the ponies will get through, but that they have lost condition quicker than he expected. Considering his usually pessimistic attitude this must be thought a hopeful view. Personally I am much more hopeful. I think that a good many of the beasts are actually in better form than when they started, and that there is no need to be alarmed about the remainder, always excepting the weak ones which we have always regarded with doubt. Well, we must wait and see how things go.

A note from Evans dated the 9th, stating his party has gone on to 80° 30', carrying four boxes of biscuit. He has done something over 30 miles (geo.) in 2½ days – exceedingly good going. I only hope he has built lots of good cairns.

It was a very beautiful day yesterday, bright sun, but as we marched, towards midnight, the sky gradually became overcast; very beautiful *halo rings* formed around the sun. Four separate rings were very distinct. Wilson descried a fifth – the orange colour with blue interspace formed very fine contrasts. We now clearly see the corona ring on the snow surface. The spread of stratus cloud overhead was very remarkable. The sky was clear all around the horizon, but overhead a cumulo-stratus grew early; it seemed to be drifting to the south and later to the east. The broken cumulus slowly changed to a uniform stratus, which seems to be thinning as the sun gains power. There is a very thin, light fall of snow crystals, but the surface deposit seems to be abating the evaporation for the moment, outpacing the light snowfall. The crystals barely exist a moment when they light on our equipment, so that everything on and about the sledges is drying rapidly. When the sky was clear above the horizon we got a good view of very distant land all around to the west; white patches of mountains to the W.S.W. must be 120 miles distant. During the night we saw Discovery and the Royal Society Range, the first view for many days, but we have not seen Erebus for a week, and in that direction the clouds seem ever to concentrate. It is very interesting to watch the weather phenomena of the Barrier, but one prefers the sunshine to days such as this, when everything is blankly white and a sense of oppression is inevitable.

The temperature fell to −15° last night, with a clear sky; it rose to 0° directly the sky covered and is now just +16° to +20°. Most of us are using goggles with glass of light green tint. We find this colour very grateful to the eyes, and as a rule it is possible to see everything through them even more clearly than with naked vision.

The hard sastrugi are now all from the W.S.W. and our cairns are drifted up by winds from that direction; mostly, though, there has evidently been a range of snow-bearing winds round to south. This observation holds from Corner Camp to this camp, showing that apparently all along the coast the wind comes from the land. The minimum thermometer left here shows −73°, rather less than expected; it has been excellently exposed and evidently not at all drifted up with snow at any time. I cannot find the oats I scattered here – rather fear the drift has covered them, but other evidences show that the snow deposit has been very small.

Thursday, November 16. – Camp 12. Resting. A stiff little southerly breeze all day, dropping towards evening. The temperature −15°. Ponies pretty comfortable in rugs and behind good walls. We have reorganised the loads, taking on about 580 lbs. with the stronger ponies, 400-odd with the others.

Friday, November 17. – Camp 13. Atkinson started about 8.30. We came on about 11, the whole of the remainder. The lunch camp was 7½ miles. Atkinson left as we came in. He was an hour before us at the final camp, 13¼ (geo.) miles. On the whole, and considering the weights, the ponies did very well, but the surface was comparatively good. Christopher showed signs of trouble at start, but was coaxed into position for the traces to be hooked. There was some ice on his runner and he had a very heavy drag, therefore a good deal done on arrival; also his load seems heavier and deader than the others. It is early days to wonder whether the little beasts will last; one can only hope they will, but the weakness of breeding and age is showing itself already.

The crocks have done wonderfully, so there is really no saying how long or well the fitter animals may go. We had a horribly cold wind on the march. Temp. −18°, force 3. The sun was shining but seemed to make little difference. It is still shining brightly, temp. 11°. Behind the pony walls it is wonderfully warm and the animals look as snug as possible.

Camp on the march

Saturday, November 18. – Camp 14. The ponies are not pulling well. The surface is, if anything, a little worse than yesterday, but I should think about the sort of thing we shall have to expect henceforward. I had a panic that we were carrying too much food and this morning we have discussed the matter and decided we can leave a sack. We have done the usual 13 miles (geo.) with a few hundred yards to make the 15 statute. The temperature was −21° when we camped last night, now it is −3°. The crocks are going on very wonderfully. Oates gives Chinaman at least three days, and Wright says he may go for a week. This is slightly inspiriting, but how much better would it have been to have had ten really reliable beasts! It's touch and go whether we scrape up to the Glacier; meanwhile we get along somehow. At any rate the bright sunshine makes everything *look* more hopeful.

Sunday, November 19. – Camp 15. We have struck a real bad surface, sledges pulling well over it, but ponies sinking very deep. The result is to about finish Jehu. He was terribly done on getting in tonight. He may go another march, but not more, I think. Considering the surface the other ponies did well. The ponies occasionally sink halfway to the hock, little Michael once or twice almost to the hock itself. Luckily the weather now is glorious for resting the animals, which are very placid and quiet in the brilliant sun. The sastrugi are confused, the underlying hard patches appear as before to have been formed by a W.S.W. wind, but there are some surface waves pointing to a recent south-easterly wind. Have been taking some photographs, Bowers also.

Monday, November 20. – Camp 16. The surface a little better. Sastrugi becoming more and more definite from S.E. Struck a few hard patches which made me hopeful of much better things, but these did not last long. The crocks still go. Jehu seems even a little better than yesterday, and will certainly go another march. Chinaman reported bad the first half march, but bucked up the second. The dogs found the surface heavy. Tomorrow I propose to relieve them of a forage bag. The sky was slightly overcast during the march, with radiating cirro-stratus S.S.W.–N.N.E. Now very clear and bright again. Temp. at night −14°, now +4°. A very slight southerly breeze, from which the walls protect the animals well. I feel sure that the long day's rest in the sun is very good for all of them.

Our ponies marched very steadily last night. They seem to take the soft crusts and difficult plodding surface more easily. The loss of condition is not so rapid as noticed to One Ton Camp, except perhaps in Victor, who is getting to look very gaunt. Nobby seems fitter and stronger than when he started; he alone is ready to go all his feed at any time and as much more as he can get. The rest feed fairly well, but they are getting a very big strong ration. I am beginning to feel more hopeful about them. Christopher kicked the bow of his sledge in towards the end of the march. He must have a lot left in him though.

Tuesday, November 21. – Camp 17. Lat. 80° 35'. The surface decidedly better and the ponies very steady on the march. None seem overtired, and now it is impossible not to take a hopeful view of their prospect of pulling through. (Temp. −14°, night.) The only circumstance to be feared is a reversion to bad surfaces, and that ought not to happen on this course. We marched to the usual lunch camp and saw a large cairn ahead. Two miles beyond we came on the Motor Party in Lat. 80° 32'. We learned that they had been waiting for six days. They all look very fit, but declare themselves to be very hungry. This is interesting as showing conclusively that a ration amply sufficient for the needs of men leading ponies is quite insufficient for men doing hard pulling work; it therefore fully justifies the provision which we have made for the Summit work. Even on that I have little doubt we shall soon get hungry. Day looks very thin, almost gaunt, but fit. The weather is beautiful – long may it so continue! (Temp. +6°, 11 a.m.)

It is decided to take on the Motor Party in advance for three days, then Day and Hooper return. We hope Jehu will last three days; he will then be finished in any case and fed to the dogs. It is amusing to see Meares looking eagerly for the chance of a feed for his animals; he has been expecting it daily. On the other hand, Atkinson and Oates are eager to get the poor animal beyond the point at which Shackleton killed his first beast. Reports on China-man are very favourable, and it really looks as though the ponies are going to do what is hoped of them.

Wednesday, November 22. – Camp 18. Everything much the same. The ponies thinner but not much weaker. The crocks still going along. Jehu is now called 'The Barrier Wonder' and Chinaman 'The Thunderbolt'. Two days more and they will be well past the spot at which Shackleton killed his first animal. Nobby keeps his pre-eminence of condition and has now the heaviest load by some 50 lbs.; most of the others are under 500 lbs. load, and I hope will be eased further yet. The dogs are in good form still, and came up well with their loads this morning (night temp. −1.4°). It looks as though we ought to get through to the Glacier without great difficulty. The weather is glorious and the ponies can make the most of their rest during the warmest hours, but they certainly lose in one way by marching at night. The surface is much easier for the sledges when the sun is warm, and for about three hours before and after midnight the friction noticeably increases. It is just a question whether this extra weight on the loads is compensated by the resting temperature. We are quite steady on the march now, and though not fast yet get through with few stops. The animals seem to be getting accustomed to the steady, heavy plod and take the deep places less fussily. There is rather an increased condition of false crust – that is, a crust which appears firm till the whole weight of the animal is put upon it, when it suddenly gives some three or four inches. This is very trying for the poor beasts. There are also more patches in which the men sink, so that walking is getting more troublesome, but, speaking broadly, the crusts are not comparatively bad and the surface is rather better than it was. If the hot sun continues this should still further improve. One cannot see any reason why the crust should change in the next 100 miles. (Temp. +2°)

The land is visible along the western horizon in patches. Bowers points out a continuous dark band. Is this the dolerite sill?

Thursday, November 23. – Camp 19. Getting along. I think the ponies will get through; we are now 150 geographical miles from the Glacier. But it is still rather touch and go. If one or more ponies were to go rapidly down hill we might be in queer street. The surface is much the same I think; before lunch there seemed to be a marked improvement, and after lunch the ponies marched much better, so that one supposed a betterment of the friction. It is banking up to the south (T. +9°) and I'm afraid we may get a blizzard. I hope to goodness it is not going to stop one marching; forage won't allow that.

Friday, November 24. – Camp 20. There was a cold wind changing from south to S.E. and overcast sky all day yesterday. A gloomy start to our march, but the cloud rapidly lifted, bands of clear sky broke through from east to west, and the remnants of cloud dissipated. Now the sun is very bright and warm. We did the usual march very easily over a fairly good surface, the ponies now quite steady and regular. Since the junction with the Motor Party the procedure has been for the man-hauling people to go forward just ahead of the crocks, the other party following 2 or 3 hours later. Today we closed less than usual, so that the crocks must have been going very well. However, the fiat had already gone forth, and this morning after the march poor old Jehu was led back on the track and shot. After our doubts as to his reaching Hut Point, it is wonderful to think that he has actually got eight marches beyond our last year limit and could have gone more. However, towards the end he was pulling very little, and on the whole it is merciful to have ended his life. Chinaman seems to improve and will certainly last a good many days yet. The rest show no signs of flagging and are only moderately hungry. The surface is tiring for walking, as one sinks two or three inches nearly all the time. I feel we ought to get through now. Day and Hooper leave us tonight.

Saturday, November 25. – Camp 21. The surface during the first march was very heavy owing to a liberal coating of ice crystals; it improved during the second march, becoming quite good towards the end (T. +2°). Now that it is pretty warm at night it is obviously desirable to work towards day marching. We shall start 2 hours later tonight and again tomorrow night.

Last night we bade farewell to Day and Hooper and set out with the new organisation (T. –8°). All started together, the man-haulers, Evans, Lashly, and Atkinson, going ahead with their gear on the 10-ft. sledge. Chinaman and James Pigg next, and the rest some ten minutes behind. We reached the lunch camp together and started therefrom in the same order, the two crocks somewhat behind, but not more than 300 yards at the finish, so we all got into camp very satisfactorily together. The men said the first march was extremely heavy (T. +2°).

The sun has been shining all night, but towards midnight light mist clouds arose, half obscuring the leading parties. Land can be dimly discerned nearly ahead. The ponies are slowly tiring, but we lighten loads again tomorrow by making another depôt. Meares has just come up to report that Jehu made four feeds for the dogs. He cut up very well and had quite a lot of fat on him. Meares says another pony will carry him to the Glacier. This is very good hearing. The men are pulling with ski sticks and say that they are a great assistance. I think of taking them up the Glacier. Jehu has certainly come up trumps after all, and Chinaman bids fair to be even more valuable. Only a few more marches to feel safe in getting to our first goal.

Sunday, November 26. – Camp 22. Lunch camp. Marched here fairly easily, comparatively good surface. Started at 1 a.m. (midnight, local time). We now keep a steady pace of 2 miles an hour, very good going. The sky was slightly overcast at start and between two and three it grew very misty. Before we camped we lost sight of the men-haulers only 300 yards ahead. The sun is piercing the mist. Here in Lat. 81° 35' we are leaving our 'Middle Barrier Depôt', one week for each returning unit as at Mount Hooper.

Camp 22. – Snow began falling during the second march; it is blowing from the W.S.W., force 2 to 3, with snow pattering on the tent, a kind of summery blizzard that reminds one of April showers at home. The ponies came well on the second march and we shall start 2 hours later again tomorrow, i.e. at 3 a.m. (T. +13°) From this it will be a very short step to day routine when the time comes for man-haulage. The sastrugi seem to be gradually coming more to the south and a little more confused; now and again they are crossed with hard westerly sastrugi. The walking is tiring for the men, one's feet sinking 2 or 3 inches at each step. Chinaman and Jimmy Pigg kept up splendidly with the other ponies. It is always rather dismal work walking over the great snow plain when sky and surface merge in one pall of dead whiteness, but it is cheering to be in such good company with everything going on steadily and well. The dogs came up as we camped. Meares says the best surface he has had yet.

Monday, November 27. – Camp 23. (T. +8°, 12 p.m.; +2°, 3 a.m.; +13°, 11 a.m.; +17°, 3 p.m.). Quite the most trying march we have had. The surface very poor at start. The advance party got away in front but made heavy weather of it, and we caught them up several times. This threw the ponies out of their regular work and pro-longed the march. It grew overcast again, although after a summery blizzard all yesterday there was promise of better things. Starting at 3 a.m. we did not get to lunch camp much before 9. The second march was even worse. The advance party started on ski, the leading marks failed altogether, and they had the greatest difficulty in keeping a course. At the midcairn building halt the snow suddenly came down heavily, with a rise of temperature, and the ski became hopelessly clogged (bad *fahrer*, as the Norwegians say). At this time the surface was unspeakably heavy for pulling, but in a few minutes a south wind sprang up and a beneficial result was immediately felt. Pulling on foot, the advance party had even greater difficulty in going straight until the last half mile, when the sky broke slightly. We got off our march, but under the most harassing circumstances and with the animals very tired. It is snowing hard again now, and heaven only knows when it will stop.

If it were not for the surface and bad light, things would not be so bad. There are few sastrugi and little deep snow. For the most part men and ponies sink to a hard crust some 3 or 4 inches beneath the soft upper snow. Tiring for the men, but in itself more even, and therefore less tiring for the animals. Meares just come up and reporting very bad surface. We shall start 1 hour later tomorrow, i.e. at 4 a.m., making 5 hours' delay on the conditions of three days ago. Our forage supply necessitates that we should plug on the 13 (geographical) miles daily under all conditions, so that we can only hope for better things. It is several days since we had a glimpse of land, which makes conditions especially gloomy. A tired animal makes a tired man, I find, and none of us are very bright now after the day's march, though we have had ample sleep of late.

Tuesday, November 28. – Camp 24. The most dismal start imaginable. Thick as a hedge, snow falling and drifting with keen southerly wind. The men pulled out at 3.15 with Chinaman and James Pigg. We followed at 4.20, just catching the party at the lunch camp at 8.30. Things got better half way; the sky showed signs of clearing and the steering improved. Now, at lunch, it is getting thick again. When will the wretched blizzard be over? The walking is better for ponies, worse for men; there is nearly everywhere a hard crust some 3 to 6 inches down. Towards the end of the march we crossed a succession of high hard south-easterly sastrugi, widely dispersed. I don't know what to make of these.

Second march almost as horrid as the first. Wind blowing strong from the south, shifting to S.E. as the snowstorms fell on us, when we could see little or nothing, and the driving snow hit us stingingly in the face. The general impression of all this dirty weather is that it spreads in from the S.E. We started at 4 a.m., and I think I shall stick to that custom for the present. These last few marches have been fought for, but completed without hitch, and, though we camped in a snowstorm, there is a more promising look in the sky, and if only for a time the wind has dropped and the sun shines brightly, dispelling some of the gloomy results of the distressing marching.

Chinaman, 'The Thunderbolt', has been shot tonight. Plucky little chap, he has stuck it out well and leaves the stage but a few days before his fellows. We have only four bags of forage (each one 130 lbs.) left, but these should give seven marches with all the remaining animals, and we are less than 90 miles from the Glacier. Bowers tells me that the barometer was phenomenally low both during this blizzard and the last. This has certainly been the most unexpected and trying summer blizzard yet experienced in this region. I only trust it is over. There is not much to choose between the remaining ponies. Nobby and Bones are the strongest, Victor and Christopher the weakest, but all should get through. The land doesn't show up yet.

Wednesday, November 29. – Camp 25. Lat. 82° 21'. Things much better. The land showed up late yesterday; Mount Markham, a magnificent triple peak, appearing wonderfully close, Cape Lyttelton and Cape Goldie. We did our march in good time, leaving about 4.20, and getting into this camp at 1.15. About 7½ hours on the march. I suppose our speed throughout averages 2 stat. miles an hour.

The land showed hazily on the march, at times looking remarkably near. Sheety white snowy stratus cloud hung about overhead during the first march, but now the sky is clearing, the sun very warm and bright. Land shows up almost ahead now, our pony goal less than 70 miles away. The ponies are tired, but I believe all have five days' work left in them, and some a great deal more. Chinaman made four feeds for the dogs, and I suppose we can count every other pony as a similar asset. It follows that the dogs can be employed, rested, and fed well on the homeward track. We could really get through now with their help and without much delay, yet every consideration makes it desirable to save the men from heavy hauling as long as possible. So I devoutly hope the 70 miles will come in the present order of things. Snippets and Nobby now walk by themselves, following in the tracks well. Both have a continually cunning eye on their driver, ready to stop the moment he pauses. They eat snow every few minutes. It's a relief not having to lead an animal; such trifles annoy one on these marches, the animal's vagaries, his everlasting attempts to eat his head rope, &c. Yet all these animals are very full of character. Some day I must write of them and their individualities.

The men-haulers started 1½ hours before us and got here a good hour ahead, travelling easily throughout. Such is the surface with the sun on it, justifying my decision to work towards day marching. Evans has suggested the word 'glide' for the quality of surface indicated. 'Surface' is more comprehensive, and includes the crusts and liability to sink in them. From this point of view the surface is distinctly bad. The ponies plough deep all the time, and the men most of the time. The sastrugi are rather more clearly S.E.; this would be from winds sweeping along the coast. We have a recurrence of 'sinking crusts' – areas which give way with a report. There has been little of this since we left One Ton Camp until yesterday and today, when it is again very marked. Certainly the open Barrier conditions are different from those near the coast. Altogether things look much better and everyone is in excellent spirits. Meares has been measuring the holes made by ponies' hooves and finds an average of about 8 inches since we left One Ton Camp. He finds many holes a foot deep. This gives a good indication of the nature of the work. In Bowers's tent they had some of Chinaman's undercut in their hoosh yesterday, and say it was excellent. I am cook for the present. Have been discussing pony snow-shoes. I wish to goodness the animals would wear them – it would save them any amount of labour in such surfaces as this.

Thursday, November 30. – Camp 26. A very pleasant day for marching, but a very tiring march for the poor animals, which, with the exception of Nobby, are showing signs of failure all round. We were slower by half an hour or more than yesterday. Except that the loads are light now and there are still eight animals left, things don't look too pleasant, but we should be less than 60 miles from our first point of aim. The surface was much worse today, the ponies sinking to their knees very often. There were a few harder patches towards the end of the march. In spite of the sun there was not much 'glide' on the snow. The dogs are reported as doing very well. They are going to be a great standby, no doubt. The land has been veiled in thin white mist; it appeared at intervals after we camped and I had taken a couple of photographs.

Friday, December 1. – Camp 27. Lat. 82° 47'. The ponies are tiring pretty rapidly. It is a question of days with all except Nobby. Yet they are outlasting the forage, and tonight against some opinion I decided Christopher must go. He has been shot; less regret goes with him than the others, in remembrance of all the trouble he gave at the outset, and the unsatisfactory way he has gone of late. Here we leave a depôt* so that no extra weight is brought on the other ponies; in fact there is a slight diminution. Three more marches ought to carry us through. With the seven crocks and the dog teams we *must* get through I think. The men alone ought not to have heavy loads on the surface, which is extremely trying.

* The Southern Barrier Depôt

Nobby was tried in snow-shoes this morning, and came along splendidly on them for about four miles, then the wretched affairs racked and had to be taken off. There is no doubt that these snow-shoes are *the* thing for ponies, and had ours been able to use them from the beginning they would have been very different in appearance at this moment. I think the sight of the land has helped the animals, but not much. We started in bright warm sunshine and with the mountains wonderfully clear on our right hand, but towards the end of the march clouds worked up from the east and a thin broken cumulo-stratus now overspreads the sky, leaving the land still visible but dull. A fine glacier descends from Mount Longstaff. It has cut very deep and the walls stand at an angle of at least 50°. Otherwise, although there are many cwms on the lower ranges, the mountains themselves seem little carved. They are rounded massive structures. A cliff of light yellow-brown rock appears opposite us, flanked with black or dark brown rock, which also appears under the lighter colour. One would be glad to know what nature of rock these represent. There is a good deal of exposed rock on the next range also.

Saturday, December 2. – Camp 28. Lat. 83°. Started under very bad weather conditions. The stratus spreading over from the S.E. last night meant mischief, and all day we march in falling snow with a horrible light. The ponies went poorly on the first march, when there was little or no wind and a high temperature. They were sinking deep on a wretched surface. I suggested to Oates that he should have a roving commission to watch the animals, but he much preferred to lead one, so I handed over Snippets very willingly and went on ski myself. It was very easy work for me and I took several photographs of the ponies plunging along – the light very strong at 3 (Watkins actinometer). The ponies did much better on the second march, both surface and glide improved; I went ahead and found myself obliged to take a very steady pace to keep the lead, so we arrived in camp in flourishing condition. Sad to have to order Victor's end – poor Bowers feels it. He is in excellent condition and will provide five feeds for the dogs. (Temp. +17°). We must kill now as the forage is so short, but we have reached the 83rd parallel and are practically safe to get through. Tonight the sky is breaking and conditions generally more promising – it is dreadfully dismal work marching through the blank wall of white, and we should have very great difficulty if we had not a party to go ahead and show the course. The dogs are doing splendidly and will take a heavier load from tomorrow. We kill another pony tomorrow night if we get our march off, and shall then have nearly three days' food for the other five. In fact everything looks well if the weather will only give us a chance to see our way to the Glacier. Wild, in his *Diary of Shackleton's Journey*, remarks on December 15, that it is the first day for a month that he could not record splendid weather. With us a fine day has been the exception so far. However, we have not lost a march yet. It was so warm when we camped that the snow melted as it fell, and everything got sopping wet. Oates came into my tent yesterday, exchanging with Cherry-Garrard.

The tents now: Self, Wilson, Oates, and Keohane. Bowers, P. O. Evans, Cherry, and Crean.

Man-haulers: E. R. Evans, Atkinson, Wright, and Lashly. We have all taken to horse meat and are so well fed that hunger isn't thought of.

Sunday, December 3. – Camp 29. Our luck in weather is preposterous. I roused the hands at 2.30 a.m., intending to get away at 5. It was thick and snowy, yet we could have got on; but at breakfast the wind increased, and by 4.30 it was blowing a full gale from the south. The pony wall blew down, huge drifts collected, and the sledges were quickly buried. It was the strongest wind I have known here in summer. At 11 it began to take off. At 12.30 we got up and had lunch and got ready to start. The land appeared, the clouds broke, and by 1.30 we were in bright sunshine. We were off at 2 p.m., the land showing all round, and, but for some cloud to the S.E., everything promising. At 2.15 I saw the south-easterly cloud spreading up; it blotted out the land 30 miles away at 2.30 and was on us before 3. The sun went out, snow fell thickly, and marching conditions became horrible. The wind increased from the S.E., changed to S.W., where it hung for a time, and suddenly shifted to W.N.W. and then N.N.W., from which direction it is now blowing with falling and drifting snow. The changes of conditions are inconceivably rapid, perfectly bewildering. In spite of all these difficulties we have managed to get 11½ miles south and to this camp at 7 p.m. – the conditions of marching simply horrible.

The man-haulers led out 6 miles (geo.) and then camped. I think they had had enough of leading. We passed them, Bowers and I ahead on ski. We steered with compass, the drifting snow across our ski, and occasional glimpse of south-easterly sastrugi under them, till the sun showed dimly for the last hour or so. The whole weather conditions seem thoroughly disturbed, and if they continue so when we are on the Glacier, we shall be very awkwardly placed. It is really time the luck turned in our favour – we have had all too little of it. Every mile seems to have been hardly won under such conditions. The ponies did splendidly and the forage is lasting a little better than expected. Victor was found to have quite a lot of fat on him and the others are pretty certain to have more, so that we should have no difficulty whatever as regards transport if only the weather was kind.

Monday, December 4. – Camp 29, 9 a.m. I roused the party at 6. During the night the wind had changed from N.N.W. to S.S.E.; it was not strong, but the sun was obscured and the sky looked heavy; patches of land could be faintly seen and we thought that at any rate we could get on, but during breakfast the wind suddenly increased in force and afterwards a glance outside was sufficient to show a regular white floury blizzard. We have all been out building fresh walls for the ponies – an uninviting task, but one which greatly adds to the comfort of the animals, who look sleepy and bored, but not at all cold. The dogs came up with us as we camped last night and the man-haulers arrived this morning as we finished the pony wall. So we are all together again. The latter had great difficulty in following our tracks, and say they could not have steered a course without them. It is utterly impossible to push ahead in this weather, and one is at a complete loss to account for it. The barometer rose from 29.4 to 29.9 last night, a phenomenal rise. Evidently there is very great disturbance of atmospheric conditions. Well, one must stick it out, that is all, and hope for better things, but it makes me feel a little bitter to contrast such weather with that experienced by our predecessors.

Camp 30. – The wind fell in the forenoon, at 12.30 the sky began to clear, by 1 the sun shone, by 2 p.m. we were away, and by 8 p.m. camped here with 13 miles to the good. The land was quite clear throughout the march and the features easily recognised.

There are several uncharted glaciers of large dimensions, a confluence of three under Mount Reid. The mountains are rounded in outline, very massive, with small excrescent peaks and undeveloped 'cwms' (T. +18°). The cwms are very fine in the lower foot-hills and the glaciers have carved deep channels between walls at very high angles; one or two peaks on the foot-hills stand bare and almost perpendicular, probably granite; we should know later. Ahead of us is the ice-rounded, boulder-strewn Mount Hope and the gateway to the Glacier. We should reach it easily enough on tomorrow's march if we can compass 12 miles. The ponies marched splendidly today, crossing the deep snow in the undulations without difficulty. They must be in very much better condition than Shackleton's animals, and indeed there isn't a doubt they would go many miles yet if food allowed. The dogs are simply splendid, but came in wanting food, so we had to sacrifice poor little Michael, who, like the rest, had lots of fat on him. All the tents are consuming pony flesh and thoroughly enjoying it. We have only lost 5 or 6 miles on these two wretched days, but the disturbed condition of the weather makes me anxious with regard to the Glacier, where more than anywhere we shall need fine days. One has a horrid feeling that this is a real bad season. However, sufficient for the day is the evil thereof. We are practically through with the first stage of our journey. Looking from the last camp towards the S.S.E., where the farthest land can be seen, it seemed more than probable that a very high latitude could be reached on the Barrier, and if Amundsen journeying that way has a stroke of luck, he may well find his summit journey reduced to 100 miles or so. In any case it is a fascinating direction for next year's work if only fresh transport arrives. The dips between undulations seem to be about 12 to 15 feet. Tonight we get puffs of wind from the gateway, which for the moment looks uninviting.

Four days' delay

Tuesday, December 5. – Camp 30. Noon. We awoke this morning to a raging, howling blizzard. The blows we have had hitherto have lacked the very fine powdery snow – that especial feature of the blizzard. Today we have it fully developed. After a minute or two in the open one is covered from head to foot. The temperature is high, so that what falls or drives against one sticks. The ponies – head, tails, legs, and all parts not protected by their rugs – are covered with ice; the animals are standing deep in snow, the sledges are almost covered, and huge drifts above the tents. We have had breakfast, rebuilt the walls, and are now again in our bags. One cannot see the next tent, let alone the land. What on earth does such weather mean at this time of year? It is more than our share of ill-fortune, I think, but the luck may turn yet. I doubt if any party could travel in such weather even with the wind, certainly no one could travel against it.

Is there some widespread atmospheric disturbance which will be felt everywhere in this region as a bad season, or are we merely the victims of exceptional local conditions? If the latter, there is food for thought in picturing our small party struggling against adversity in one place whilst others go smilingly forward in the sunshine. How great may be the element of luck! No foresight – no procedure – could have prepared us for this state of affairs. Had we been ten times as experienced or certain of our aim we should not have expected such rebuffs.

11 p.m. – It has blown hard all day with quite the greatest snowfall I remember. The drifts about the tents are simply huge. The temperature was +27° this forenoon, and rose to +31° in the afternoon, at which time the snow melted as it fell on anything but the snow, and, as a consequence, there are pools of water on everything, the tents are wet through, also the wind clothes, night boots, &c.; water drips from the tent poles and door, lies on the floor-cloth, soaks the sleeping-bags, and makes everything pretty wretched. If a cold snap follows before we have had time to dry our things, we shall be mighty uncomfortable. Yet after all it would be humorous enough if it were not for the seriousness of delay – we can't afford that, and it's real hard luck that it should come at such a time. The wind shows signs of easing down, but the temperature does not fall and the snow is as wet as ever – not promising signs of abatement.

Keohane's rhyme!

The snow is all melting and everything's afloat,
If this goes on much longer we shall have to turn the
    tent upside down and use it as a boat.

Wednesday, December 6. – Camp 30. Noon. Miserable, utterly miserable. We have camped in the 'Slough of Despond'. The tempest rages with unabated violence. The temperature has gone to $+33°$; everything in the tent is soaking. People returning from the outside look exactly as though they had been in a heavy shower of rain. They drip pools on the floorcloth. The snow is steadily climbing higher about walls, ponies, tents, and sledges. The ponies look utterly desolate. Oh! but this is too crushing, and we are only 12 miles from the Glacier. A hopeless feeling descends on one and is hard to fight off. What immense patience is needed for such occasions!

11 p.m. – At 5 there came signs of a break at last, and now one can see the land, but the sky is still overcast and there is a lot of snow about. The wind also remains fairly strong and the temperature high. It is not pleasant, but if no worse in the morning we can get on at last. We are very, very wet.

Thursday, December 7. – Camp 30. The storm continues and the situation is now serious. One small feed remains for the ponies after today, so that we must either march tomorrow or sacrifice the animals. That is not the worst; with the help of the dogs we could get on, without doubt. The serious part is that we have this morning started our Summit rations – that is to say, the food calculated from the Glacier depôt has been begun. The first supporting party can only go on a fortnight from this date and so forth. The storm shows no sign of abatement and its character is as unpleasant as ever. The promise of last night died away about 3 a.m., when the temperature and wind rose again, and things reverted to the old conditions. I can find no sign of an end, and all of us agree that it is utterly impossible to move. Resignation to misfortune is the only attitude, but not an easy one to adopt. It seems undeserved where plans were well laid and so nearly crowned with a first success. I cannot see that any plan would be altered if it were to do again, the margin for bad weather was ample according to all experience, and this stormy December – our finest month – is a thing that the most cautious organiser might not have been prepared to encounter. It is very evil to lie here in a wet sleeping-bag and think of the pity of it, whilst with no break in the overcast sky things go steadily from bad to worse (T. $+32°$). Meares has a bad attack of snow blindness in one eye. I hope this rest will help him, but he says it has been painful for a long time. There cannot be good cheer in the camp in such weather, but it is ready to break out again. In the brief spell of hope last night one heard laughter.

Midnight. – Little or no improvement. The barometer is rising – perhaps there is hope in that. Surely few situations could be more exasperating than this of forced inactivity when every day and indeed every hour counts. To be here watching the mottled wet green walls of our tent, the glistening wet bamboos, the bedraggled sopping socks and loose articles dangling in the middle, the saddened countenances of my companions – to hear the ever-lasting patter of the falling snow and the ceaseless rattle of the fluttering canvas – to feel the wet clinging dampness of clothes and everything touched, and to know that without there is but a blank wall of white on every side – these are the physical surroundings. Add the stress of sighted failure of our whole plan, and anyone must find the circumstances unenviable. But yet, after all, one can go on striving, endeavouring to find a stimulation in the difficulties that arise.

Friday, December 8. – Camp 30. Hoped against hope for better conditions, to wake to the mournfullest snow and wind as usual. We had breakfast at 10, and at noon the wind dropped. We set about digging out the sledges, no light task. We then shifted our tent sites. All tents had been reduced to the smallest volume by the gradual pressure of snow. The old sites are deep pits with hollowed icy wet centres. The re-setting of the tent has at least given us comfort, especially since the wind has dropped. About 4 the sky showed signs of breaking, the sun and a few patches of land could be dimly discerned. The wind shifted in light airs and a little hope revived. Alas! as I write the sun has disappeared and snow is again falling. Our case is growing desperate. Evans and his man-haulers tried to pull a load this afternoon. They managed to move a sledge with four people on it, pulling in ski. Pulling on foot they sank to the knees. The snow all about us is terribly deep. We tried Nobby and he plunged to his belly in it. Wilson thinks the ponies finished,[21] but Oates thinks they will get another march in spite of the surface, *if it comes tomorrow.* If it should not, we must kill the ponies tomorrow and get on as best we can with the men on ski and the dogs. But one wonders what the dogs can do on such a surface. I much fear they also will prove inadequate. Oh! for fine weather, if only to the Glacier. The temperature remains +33°, and everything is disgustingly wet.

11 p.m. – The wind has gone to the north, the sky is really breaking at last, the sun showing less sparingly, and the land appearing out of the haze. The temperature has fallen to +26°, and the water nuisance is already abating. With so fair a promise of improvement it would be too cruel to have to face bad weather tomorrow. There is good cheer in the camp tonight in the prospect of action. The poor ponies look wistfully for the food of which so very little remains, yet they are not hungry, as recent savings have resulted from food left in their nose-bags. They look wonderfully fit, all things considered. Everything looks more hopeful tonight, but nothing can recall four lost days.

Saturday, December 9. – Camp 31. I turned out two or three times in the night to find the weather slowly improving; at 5.30 we all got up, and at 8 got away with the ponies – a most painful day. The tremendous snowfall of the late storm had made the surface intolerably soft, and after the first hour there was no glide. We pressed on the poor half-rationed animals, but could get none to lead for more than a few minutes; following, the animals would do fairly well. It looked as we could never make headway; the man-haulers were pressed into the service to aid matters. Bowers and Cherry-Garrard went ahead with one 10-foot sledge – thus most painfully we made about a mile. The situation was saved by P.O. Evans, who put the last pair of snowshoes on Snatcher. From this he went on without much pressing, the other ponies followed, and one by one were worn out in the second place. We went on all day without lunch. Three or four miles (T. +23°) found us engulfed in pressures, but free from difficulty except the awful softness of the snow. By 8 p.m. we had reached within a mile or so of the slope ascending to the gap which Shackleton called the Gateway.[22] I had hoped to be through the Gateway with the ponies still in hand at a very much earlier date and, but for the devastating storm, we should have been. It has been a most serious blow to us, but things are not yet desperate, if only the storm has not hopelessly spoilt the surface. The man-haulers are not up yet, in spite of their light load. I think they have stopped for tea, or something, but under ordinary conditions they would have passed us with ease.

At 8 p.m. the ponies were quite done, one and all. They came on painfully slowly a few hundred yards at a time. By this time I was hauling ahead, a ridiculously light load, and yet finding the pulling heavy enough. We camped, and the ponies have been shot.* Poor beasts! they have done wonderfully well considering the terrible circumstances under which they worked, but yet it is hard to have to kill them so early. The dogs are going well in spite of the surface, but here again one cannot get the help one would wish. (T. +19°) I cannot load the animals heavily on such snow. The scenery is most impressive; three huge pillars of granite form the right buttress of the Gateway, and a sharp spur of Mount Hope the left. The land is much more snow-covered than when we saw it before the storm. In spite of some doubt in our outlook, everyone is very cheerful tonight and jokes are flying freely around.

* Camp 31 received the name of Shambles Camp.

CHAPTER SEVENTEEN

On the Beardmore Glacier

Sunday, December 10. – Camp 32.* I was very anxious about getting our loads forward over such an appalling surface, and that we have done so is mainly due to the ski. I roused everyone at 8, but it was noon before all the readjustments of load had been made and we were ready to start. The dogs carried 600 lbs. of our weight besides the depôt (200 lbs.). It was greatly to my surprise when we – my own party – with a 'one, two, three together' started our sledge, and we found it running fairly easily behind us. We did the first mile at a rate of about 2 miles an hour, having previously very carefully scraped and dried our runners. The day was gloriously fine and we were soon perspiring. After the first mile we began to rise, and for some way on a steep slope we held to our ski and kept going. Then the slope got steeper and the surface much worse, and we had to take off our ski. The pulling after this was extraordinarily fatiguing. We sank above our finnesko everywhere, and in places nearly to our knees. The runners of the sledges got coated with a thin film of ice from which we could not free them, and the sledges themselves sank to the crossbars in soft spots. All the time

* While Day and Hooper, of the ex-Motor Party, had turned back on November 24, and Meares and Demetri with the dogs ascended above the Lower Glacier Depôt before returning on December 11, the Southern Party and its supports were organised successively as follows:

December 10, leaving Shambles Camp –
  Sledge 1. Scott, Wilson, Oates, and P.O. Evans.
  Sledge 2. E. Evans, Atkinson, Wright, Lashly.
  Sledge 3. Bowers, Cherry-Garrard, Crean, Keohane.
December 21 at Upper Glacier Depôt –
  Sledge 1. Scott, Wilson, Oates, P.O. Evans.
  Sledge 2. E. Evans, Bowers, Crean, Lashly; while Atkinson, Wright, Cherry-Garrard and Keohane returned.
January 4, 150 miles from the Pole –
  Sledge 1. Scott, Wilson, Oates, Bowers, P.O. Evans; while E. Evans, Crean, and Lashly returned.

Hauling sledge through deep snow

they were literally ploughing the snow. We reached the top of the slope at 5, and started on after tea on the down grade. On this we had to pull almost as hard as on the upward slope, but could just manage to get along on ski. We camped at 9.15, when a heavy wind coming down the glacier suddenly fell on us; but I had decided to camp before, as Evans's party could not keep up, and Wilson told me some very alarming news concerning it. It appears that Atkinson says that Wright is getting played out and Lashly is not so fit as he was owing to the heavy pulling since the blizzard. I have not felt satisfied about this party. The finish of the march today showed clearly that something was wrong. They fell a long way behind, had to take off ski, and took nearly half an hour to come up a few hundred yards. True, the surface was awful and growing worse every moment. It is a very serious business if the men .are going to crack up. As for myself, I never felt fitter and my party can easily hold its own. P.O. Evans, of course, is a tower of strength, but Oates and Wilson are doing splendidly also.

Here where we are camped the snow is worse than I have ever seen it, but we are in a hollow. Every step here one sinks to the knees and the uneven surface is obviously insufficient to support the sledges. Perhaps this wind is a blessing in disguise, already it seems to be hardening the snow. All this soft snow is an after-math of our prolonged storm. Hereabouts Shackleton found hard blue ice. It seems an extraordinary difference in fortune, and at every step S.'s luck becomes more evident. I take the dogs on for half a day tomorrow, then send them home. We have 200 lbs. to add to each sledge load and could easily do it on a reasonable surface, but it looks very much as though we shall be forced to relay if present conditions hold. There is a strong wind down the glacier tonight.

'*Beardmore Glacier.* – Just a tiny note to be taken back by the dogs. Things are not so rosy as they might be, but we keep our spirits up and say the luck must turn. This is only to tell you that I find I can keep up with the rest as well as of old.'

Monday, December 11. – Camp 33. A very good day from one point of view, very bad from another. We started straight out over the glacier and passed through a good deal of disturbance. We pulled on ski and the dogs followed. I cautioned the drivers to keep close to their sledges and we must have passed over a good many crevasses undiscovered by us, thanks to ski, and by the dogs owing to the soft snow. In one only Seaman Evans dropped a leg, ski and all. We built our depôt* before starting, made it very conspicuous, and left a good deal of gear there. The old man-hauling party made heavy weather at first, but when relieved of a little weight and having cleaned their runners and re-adjusted their load they came on in fine style, and, passing us, took the lead. Starting about 11, by 3 o'clock we were clear of the pressure, and I camped the dogs, discharged our loads, and we put them on our sledges. It was a very anxious business when we started after lunch, about 4.30. Could we pull our full loads or not? My own party got away first, and, to my joy, I found we could make fairly good headway. Every now and again the sledge sank in a soft patch, which brought us up, but we learned to treat such occasions with patience. We got sideways to the sledge and hauled it out, Evans (P.O.) getting out of his ski to get better purchase. The great thing is to keep the sledge moving, and for an hour or more there were dozens of critical moments when it all but stopped, and not a few when it brought up altogether. The latter were very trying and tiring. But suddenly the surface grew more uniform and we more

---

* The Lower Glacier Depôt.

accustomed to the game, for after a long stop to let the other parties come up, I started at 6 and ran on till 7, pulling easily without a halt at the rate of about 2 miles an hour. I was very jubilant; all difficulties seemed to be vanishing; but unfortunately our history was not repeated with the other parties. Bowers came up about half an hour after us. They also had done well at the last, and I'm pretty sure they will get on all right. Keohane is the only weak spot, and he only, I think, because blind (temporarily). But Evans's party didn't get up till 10. They started quite well, but got into difficulties, did just the wrong thing by straining again and again, and so, tiring themselves, went from bad to worse. Their ski shoes, too, are out of trim.

Just as I thought we were in for making a great score, this difficulty overtakes us – it is dreadfully trying. The snow around us tonight is terribly soft, one sinks to the knee at every step; it would be impossible to drag sledges on foot and very difficult for dogs. Ski are the thing, and here are my tiresome fellow-countrymen too prejudiced to have prepared themselves for the event. The dogs should get back quite easily; there is food all along the line. The glacier wind sprang up about 7; the morning was very fine and warm. Tonight there is some stratus cloud forming – a hint no more bad weather in sight. A plentiful crop of snow blindness due to incaution – the sufferers E. Evans, Bowers, Keohane, Lashly, Oates in various degrees.

This forenoon Wilson went over to a boulder poised on the glacier. It proved to be a very coarse granite with large crystals of quartz in it. Evidently the rock of which the pillars of the Gateway and other neighbouring hills are formed.

Tuesday, December 12. – Camp 34. We have had a hard day, and during the forenoon it was my team which made the heaviest weather of the work. We got bogged again and again, and, do what we would, the sledge dragged like lead. The others were working hard but nothing to be compared to us. At 2.30 I halted for lunch, pretty well cooked, and there was disclosed the secret of our trouble in a thin film with some hard knots of ice on the runners. Evans's team had been sent off in advance, and we didn't – couldn't! – catch them, but they saw us camp and break camp and followed suit. I really dreaded starting after lunch, but after some trouble to break the sledge out, we went ahead without a hitch, and in a mile or two resumed our leading place with obvious ability to keep it. At 6 I saw the other teams were flagging and so camped at 7, meaning to turn out earlier tomorrow and start a better routine. We have done about 8 or perhaps 9 miles (stat.) – the sledge-meters are hopeless on such a surface.

It is evident that what I expected has occurred. The whole of the lower valley is filled with snow from the recent storm, and if we had not had ski we should be hopelessly bogged. On foot one sinks to the knees, and if pulling on a sledge to half-way between knee and thigh. It would, therefore, be absolutely impossible to advance on foot with our loads. Considering all things, we are getting better on ski. A crust is forming over the soft snow. In a week or so I have little doubt it will be strong enough to support sledges and men. At present it carries neither properly. The sledges get bogged every now and again, sinking to the crossbars. Needless to say, the hauling is terrible when this occurs.

We steered for the Commonwealth Range during the forenoon till we reached about the middle of the glacier. This showed that the unnamed glacier to the S.W. raised great pressure. Observing this, I altered course for the 'Cloudmaker' and later still farther to the west. We must be getting a much better view of the southern side of the main glacier than Shackleton got, and consequently have observed a number of peaks which he did not notice. We are about 5 or 5½ days behind him as a result of the storm, but on this surface our sledges could not be more heavily laden than they are, in fact we have not nearly enough runner surface as it is. Moreover, the sledges are packed too high and therefore capsize too easily. I do not think the glacier can be so broad as S. shows it. Certainly the scenery is not nearly so impressive as that of the Ferrar, but there are interesting features showing up – a distinct banded structure on Mount Elizabeth, which we think may well be a recurrence of the Beacon Sandstone – more banding on the Commonwealth Range. During the three days we have been here the wind has blown down the glacier at night, or rather from the S.W., and it has been calm in the morning – a sort of nightly land-breeze. There is also a very remarkable difference in temperature between day and night. It was +33° when we started, and with our hard work we were literally soaked through with perspiration. It is now +23°. Evans's party kept up much better today; we had their shoes into our tent this morning, and P.O. Evans put them into shape again.

Wednesday, December 13. – Camp 35. A most *damnably* dismal day. We started at eight – the pulling terribly bad, though the glide decidedly good; a new crust in patches, not sufficient to support the ski, but without possibility of hold. Therefore, as the pullers got on the hard patches they slipped back. The sledges plunged into the soft places and stopped dead. Evans's party got away first; we followed, and for some time helped them forward at their stops, but this proved altogether too much for us, so I forged ahead and camped at 1 p.m., as the others were far astern. During lunch I decided to try the 10-feet runners under the crossbars and we spent three hours in securing them. There was no delay on account of the slow progress of the other parties. Evans passed us, and for some time went forward fairly well up a decided slope. The sun was shining on the surface by this time, and the temperature high. Bowers started after Evans, and it was easy to see the really terrible state of affairs with them. They made desperate efforts to get along, but ever got more and more bogged – evidently the glide had vanished. When we got away we soon discovered how awful the surface had become; added to the forenoon difficulties the snow had become wet and sticky. We got our load along, soon passing Bowers, but the toil was simply awful. We were soaked with perspiration and thoroughly breathless with our efforts. Again and again the sledge got one runner on harder snow than the other, canted on its side, and refused to move. At the top of the rise I found Evans reduced to relay work, and Bowers followed his example soon after. We got our whole load through till 7 p.m., camping time, but only with repeated halts and labour which was altogether too strenuous. The other parties certainly cannot get a full load along on the surface, and I much doubt if we could continue to do so, but we must try again tomorrow.

I suppose we have advanced a bare 4 miles today and the aspect of things is very little changed. Our height is now about 1,500 feet; I had pinned my faith on getting better conditions as we rose, but it looks as though matters were getting worse instead of better. As far as the Cloudmaker the valley looks like a huge basin for the lodgement of such snow as this. We can but toil on, but it is woefully disheartening. I am not at all hungry, but pretty thirsty.

(T. +15°) I find our summit ration is even too filling for the present. Two skuas came round the camp at lunch, no doubt attracted by our 'Shambles' camp.

Thursday, December 14. – Camp 36. Indigestion and the soggy condition of my clothes kept me awake for some time last night, and the exceptional exercise gives bad attacks of cramp. Our lips are getting raw and blistered. The eyes of the party are improving, I am glad to say. We are just starting our march with no very hopeful outlook. (T. +13°)

Evening. – (Height about 2000 feet.) Evans's party started first this morning; for an hour they found the hauling stiff, but after that, to my great surprise, they went on easily. Bowers followed without getting over the ground so easily. After the first 200 yards my own party came on with a swing that told me at once that all would be well. We soon caught the others and offered to take on more weight, but Evans's pride wouldn't allow such help. Later in the morning we exchanged sledges with Bowers, pulled theirs easily, whilst they made quite heavy work with ours. I am afraid Cherry-Garrard and Keohane are the weakness of that team, though both put their utmost into the traces. However, we all lunched together after a satisfactory morning's work. In the afternoon we did still better, and camped at 6.30 with a very marked change in the land bearings. We must have come 11 or 12 miles (stat.). We got fearfully hot on the march, sweated through everything and stripped off jerseys. The result is we are pretty cold and clammy now, but escape from the soft snow and a good march compensate every discomfort. At lunch the blue ice was about 2 feet beneath us, now it is barely a foot, so that I suppose we shall soon find it uncovered. Tonight the sky is overcast and wind has been blowing up the glacier. I think there will be another spell of gloomy weather on the Barrier, and the question is whether this part of the glacier escapes. There are crevasses about, one about eighteen inches across outside Bowers's tent, and a narrower one outside our own. I think the soft snow trouble is at an end, and I could wish nothing better than a continuance of the present surface. Towards the end of the march we were pulling our loads with the greatest ease. It is splendid to be getting along and to find some adequate return for the work we are putting into the business.

Friday, December 15. – Camp 37. (Height about 2500. Lat. about 84° 8'.) Got away at 8; marched till 1; the surface improving and snow covering thinner over the blue ice, but the sky overcast and glooming, the clouds ever coming lower, and Evans's is now decidedly the slowest unit, though Bowers's is not much faster. We keep up and overhaul either without difficulty. It was an enormous relief yesterday to get steady going without involuntary stops, but yesterday and this morning, once the sledge was stopped, it was very difficult to start again – the runners got temporarily stuck. This afternoon for the first time we could start by giving one good heave together, and so for the first time we are able to stop to readjust footgear or do any other desirable task. This is a second relief for which we are most grateful.

At the lunch camp the snow covering was less than a foot, and at this it is a bare nine inches; patches of ice and hard névé are showing through in places. I meant to camp at 6.30, but before 5.0 the sky came down on us with falling snow. We could see nothing, and the pulling grew very heavy. At 5.45 there seemed nothing to do but camp – another interrupted march. Our luck is really very bad. We should have done a good march today, as it is we have covered about 11 miles (stat.).

Since supper there are signs of clearing again, but I don't like the look of things; this weather has been working up from the S.E. with all the symptoms of our pony-wrecking storm. Pray heaven we are not going to have this wretched snow in the worst part of the glacier to come. The lower part of this glacier is not very interesting, except from an ice point of view. Except Mount Kyffin, little bare rock is visible, and its structure at this distance is impossible to determine. There are no moraines on the surface of the glacier either. The tributary glaciers are very fine and have cut very deep courses, though they do not enter at grade. The walls of this valley are extraordinarily steep; we count them at least 60° in places. The ice-falls descending over the northern sides are almost continuous one with another, but the southern steep faces are nearly bare; evidently the sun gets a good hold on them. There must be a good deal of melting and rock weathering, the talus heaps are considerable under the southern rock faces. Higher up the valley there is much more bare rock and stratification, which promises to be very interesting, but oh! for fine weather; surely we have had enough of this oppressive gloom.

Saturday, December 16. – Camp 38. A gloomy morning, clearing at noon and ending in a gloriously fine evening. Although constantly anxious in the morning, the light held good for travelling throughout the day, and we have covered 11 miles (stat.), altering the aspect of the glacier greatly. But the travelling has been very hard. We started at 7, lunched at 12.15, and marched on till 6.30 – over ten hours on the march – the limit of time to be squeezed into one day. We began on ski as usual, Evans's team hampering us a bit; the pulling very hard after yesterday's snowfall. In the afternoon we continued on ski till after two hours we struck a peculiarly difficult surface – old hard sastrugi underneath, with pits and high soft sastrugi due to very recent snowfalls. The sledges were so often brought up by this that we decided to take to our feet, and thus made better progress, but for the time with very excessive labour. The crust, brittle, held for a pace or two, then let one down with a bump some 8 or 10 inches. Now and again one's leg went down a crack in the hard ice underneath. We drew up a slope on this surface and discovered a long icefall extending right across our track, I presume the same pressure which caused Shackleton to turn towards the Cloudmaker. We made in for that mountain and soon got on hard, crevassed, undulating ice with quantities of soft snow in the hollows. The disturbance seems to increase, but the snow to diminish as we approach the rocks. We shall look for a moraine and try and follow it up tomorrow. The hills on our left have horizontally stratified rock alternating with snow. The exposed rock is very black; the brownish colour of the Cloud-maker has black horizontal streaks across it. The sides of the glacier north of the Cloudmaker have a curious cutting, the upper part less steep than the lower, suggestive of different conditions of glacier-flow in succeeding ages.

We must push on all we can, for we are now 6 days behind Shackleton, all due to that wretched storm. So far, since we got amongst the disturbances we have not seen such alarming crevasses as I had expected; certainly dogs could have come up as far as this. At present one gets terribly hot and perspiring on the march, and quickly cold when halted, but the sun makes up for all evils. It is very difficult to know what to do about the ski; their weight is considerable and yet under certain circumstances they are extraordinarily useful. Everyone is very satisfied with our summit ration. The party which has been man-hauling for so long say they are far less hungry than they used to be. It is good to think that the majority will keep up this good feeding all through.

Sunday, December 17. – Camp 39, Soon after starting we found ourselves in rather a mess; bad pressure ahead and long waves between us and the land. Blue ice showed on the crests of the waves; very soft snow lay in the hollows. We had to cross the waves in places 30 feet from crest to hollow, and we did it by sitting on the sledge and letting her go. Thus we went down with a rush and our impetus carried us some way up the other side; then followed a fearfully tough drag to rise the next crest. After two hours of this I saw a larger wave, the crest of which continued hard ice up the glacier; we reached this and got excellent travelling for 2 miles on it, then rose on a steep gradient, and so topped the pressure ridge. The smooth ice is again lost and we have patches of hard and soft snow with ice peeping out in places, cracks in all directions, and legs very frequently down. We have done very nearly 5 miles (geo.).

Evening. – (Temp. +12°) Height about 3500 above Barrier. After lunch decided to take the risk of sticking to the centre of the glacier, with good result. We travelled on up the more or less rounded ridge which I had selected in the morning, and camped at 6.30 with 12½ stat. miles made good. This has put Mount Hope in the background and shows us more of the upper reaches. If we can keep up the pace, we gain on Shackleton, and I don't see any reason why we shouldn't, except that more pressure is showing up ahead. For once one can say 'sufficient for the day is the good thereof.' Our luck may be on the turn – I think we deserve it. In spite of the hard work everyone is very fit and very cheerful, feeling well fed and eager for more toil. Eyes are much better except poor Wilson's; he has caught a very bad attack. Remembering his trouble on our last Southern journey, I fear he is in for a very bad time.

We got fearfully hot this morning and marched in singlets, which became wringing wet; thus uncovered the sun gets at one's skin, and then the wind, which makes it horribly uncomfortable.

Our lips are very sore. We cover them with the soft silk plaster which seems about the best thing for the purpose.

I'm inclined to think that the summit trouble will be mostly due to the chill falling on sunburned skins. Even now one feels the cold strike directly one stops. We get fearfully thirsty and chip up ice on the march, as well as drinking a great deal of water on halting. Our fuel only just does it, but that is all we want, and we have a bit in hand for the summit.

The pulling this afternoon was fairly pleasant; at first over hard snow, and then on to pretty rough ice with surface snow-filled cracks, bad for sledges, but ours promised to come through well. We have worn our crampons all day and are delighted with them. P.O. Evans, the inventor of both crampons and ski shoes, is greatly pleased, and certainly we owe him much. The weather is beginning to look dirty again, snow clouds rolling in from the east as usual. I believe it will be overcast tomorrow.

Monday, December 18. – Camp 40. Lunch nearly 4000 feet above Barrier. Overcast and snowing this morning as I expected, land showing on starboard hand, so, though it was gloomy and depressing, we could march, and did. We have done our 8 stat. miles between 8.20 and 1 p.m.; at first fairly good surface; then the ice got very rugged with sword-cut splits. We got on a slope, which made matters worse. I then pulled up to the left, at first without much improvement, but as we topped a rise the surface got much better and things look quite promising for the moment. On our right we have now a pretty good view of the Adams Marshall and Wild Mountains and their very curious horizontal stratification. Wright has found, amongst bits of wind-blown débris, an undoubted bit of sandstone and a bit of black basalt. We must get to know more of the geology before leaving the glacier finally. This morning all our gear was fringed with ice crystals which looked very pretty.

Afternoon. – (Night camp No. 40, about 4500 above Barrier. T. +11°. Lat. about 84° 34'.) After lunch got on some very rough stuff within a few hundred yards of pressure ridge. There seemed no alternative, and we went through with it. Later, the glacier opened out into a broad basin with irregular undulations, and we on to a better surface, but later on again this improvement nearly vanished, so that it has been hard going all day, but we have done a good mileage (over 14 stat.). We are less than five days behind S. now. There was a promise of a clearance about noon, but later more snow clouds drifted over from the east, and now it is snowing again. We have scarcely caught a glimpse of the eastern side of the glacier all day. The western side has not been clear enough to photograph at the halts. It is very annoying, but I suppose we must be thankful when we can get our marches off. Still sweating horribly on the march and very thirsty at the halts.

Tuesday, December 19. – Lunch, rise 650. Dist. 8½ geo. Camp 41. Things are looking up. Started on good surface, soon came to very annoying criss-cross cracks. I fell into two and have bad bruises on knee and thigh, but we got along all the time until we reached an admirable smooth ice surface excellent for travelling. The last mile, névé predominating and therefore the pulling a trifle harder, we have risen into the upper basin of the glacier. Seemingly close about us are the various land masses which adjoin the summit: it looks as though we might have difficulties in the last narrows. We are having a long lunch hour for angles, photographs, and sketches. A slight south-westerly wind came down the glacier as we started, and the sky, which was overcast, has rapidly cleared in consequence.

Night. – Height about 5800. Camp 41. We stepped off this afternoon at the rate of 2 miles or more an hour, with the very satisfactory result of 17 (stat.) miles to the good for the day. It has not been a strain, except perhaps for me with my wounds received early in the day. The wind has kept us cool on the march, which has in consequence been very much pleasanter; we are not wet in our clothes tonight, and have not suffered from the same overpowering thirst as on previous days. (T. +11°) (Min. +5°) Evans and Bowers are busy taking angles; as they have been all day, we shall have material for an excellent chart. Days like this put heart in one.

Wednesday, December 20. – Camp 42. 6500 feet about. Just got off our best half march – 10 miles 1150 yards (geo.), over 12 miles stat. With an afternoon to follow we should do well today; the wind has been coming up the valley. Turning this book* seems to have

---

* In the pocket journal, only one side of each page had been written on. Coming to the end of it, Scott reversed the book, and continued his entries on the empty backs of the pages.

brought luck. We marched on till nearly 7 o'clock after a long lunch halt, and covered 19½ geo. miles, nearly 23 (stat.), rising 800 feet. This morning we came over a considerable extent of hard snow, then got to hard ice with patches of snow: a state of affairs which has continued all day. Pulling the sledges in crampons is no difficulty at all. At lunch Wilson and Bowers walked back 2 miles or so to try and find Bowers's broken sledge-meter, without result. During their absence a fog spread about us, carried up the valleys by easterly wind. We started the afternoon march in this fog very unpleasantly, but later it gradually drifted, and tonight it is very fine and warm. As the fog lifted we saw a huge line of pressure ahead; I steered for a place where the slope looked smoother, and we are camped beneath the spot tonight. We must be ahead of Shackleton's position on the 17th. All day we have been admiring the wonderful banded structure of the rock; tonight it is beautifully clear on Mount Darwin.

I have just told off the people to return tomorrow night: Atkinson, Wright, Cherry-Garrard, and Keohane. All are disappointed – poor Wright rather bitterly, I fear. I dreaded this necessity of choosing – nothing could be more heartrending. I calculated our programme to start from 85° 10' with 12 units of food* and eight men. We ought to be in this position tomorrow night, less one day's food. After all our harassing trouble one cannot but be satisfied with such a prospect.

Thursday, December 21. – Camp 43. Lat. 85° 7'. Long. 163° 4'. Height about 8000 feet. Upper Glacier Depôt. Temp. –2°. We climbed the ice slope this morning and found a very bad surface on top, as far as crevasses were concerned. We all had falls into them, Atkinson and Teddy Evans going down the length of their harness. Evans had rather a shake up. The rotten ice surface continued for a long way, though I wound to and fro towards the land, trying to get on better ground.

At 12 the wind came from the north, bringing the inevitable mist up the valley and covering us just as we were in the worst of places. We camped for lunch, and were obliged to wait two and a half hours for a clearance. Then the sun began to struggle through and we were off. We soon got out of the worst crevasses and on to a long snow slope leading on past Mount Darwin. It was a very long stiff pull

---

* A unit of food means a week's supplies for four men.

up, and I held on till 7.30, when, the other team being some way astern, I camped. We have done a good march, risen to a satisfactory altitude, and reached a good place for our depôt. Tomorrow we start with our fullest summit load, and the first march should show us the possibilities of our achievement. The temperature has dropped below zero, but tonight it is so calm and bright that one feels delightfully warm and comfortable in the tent. Such weather helps greatly in all the sorting arrangements, &c., which are going on tonight. For me it is an immense relief to have the indefatigable little Bowers to see to all detail arrangements of this sort.

We have risen a great height today and I hope it will not be necessary to go down again, but it looks as though we must dip a bit even to go to the south-west.

'*December* 21, 1911. – Lat. 85° S. We are struggling on, considering all things, against odds. The weather is a constant anxiety, otherwise arrangements are working exactly as planned.

'For your own ear also, I am exceedingly fit and can go with the best of them.

'It is a pity the luck doesn't come our way, because every detail of equipment is right.

'I write this sitting in our tent waiting for the fog to clear – an exasperating position as we are in the worst crevassed region. Teddy Evans and Atkinson were down to the length of their harness this morning, and we have all been half-way down. As first man I get first chance, and it's decidedly exciting not knowing which step will give way. Still all this is interesting enough if one could only go on.

'Since writing the above I made a dash for it, got out of the valley out of the fog and away from crevasses. So here we are practically on the summit and up to date in the provision line. We ought to get through.'

CHAPTER EIGHTEEN

The summit journey to the Pole

A FRESH MS. BOOK

On the Flyleaf. – Ages: Self 43, Wilson 39, Evans (P.O.) 37, Oates 32, Bowers 28. Average 36.

Friday, December 22. – Camp 44, about 7100 feet. T. −1°. Bar. 22.3. This, the third stage of our journey, is opening with good promise. We made our depôt this morning, then said an affecting farewell to the returning party, who have taken things very well, dear good fellows as they are.[23]

Then we started with our heavy loads about 9.20, I in some trepidation – quickly dissipated as we went off and up a slope at a smart pace. The second sledge came close behind us, showing that we have weeded the weak spots and made the proper choice for the returning party.

We came along very easily and lunched at 1, when the sledge-meter had to be repaired, and we didn't get off again till 3.20, camping at 6.45. Thus with 7 hours' marching we covered 10½ miles (geo.) (12 stat.).

Obs.: Lat. 85° 13½'; Long. 161° 55'; Var. 175° 46' E.

Tomorrow we march longer hours, about 9 I hope. Every day the loads will lighten, and so we ought to make the requisite progress. I think we have climbed about 250 feet today, but thought it more on the march. We look down on huge pressure ridges to the south and S.E., and in fact all round except in the directon in which we go, S.W. We seem to be travelling more or less parallel to a ridge which extends from Mt Darwin. Ahead of us tonight is a stiffish incline and it looks as though there might be pressure behind it. It is very difficult to judge how matters stand, however, in such a confusion of elevations and depressions. This course doesn't work wonders in change of latitude, but I think it is the right track to clear the pressures – at any rate I shall hold it for the present.

We passed over one or two very broad (30 feet) bridged crevasses with the usual gaping sides; they were running pretty well in N. and S. direction. The weather has been beautifully fine all day as it was last night. (Night Temp. −9°.) This morning there was an hour or so of haze due to clouds from the N. Now it is perfectly clear, and we get a fine view of the mountains behind which Wilson has just been sketching.

Saturday, December 23. − Lunch. Bar. 22.01. Rise 370? Started at 8, steering S.W. Seemed to be rising, and went on well for about 3 hours, then got amongst bad crevasses and hard waves. We pushed on to S.W., but things went from bad to worse, and we had to haul out to the north, then west. West looks clear for the present, but it is not a very satisfactory direction. We have done 8½ (geo.), a good march. (T. −3°. Southerly wind, force 2.)

The comfort is that we are rising. On one slope we got a good view of the land and the pressure ridges to the S.E. They seem to be disposed '*en échelon*' and gave me the idea of shearing cracks. They seemed to lessen as we ascend. It is rather trying having to march so far to the west, but if we keep rising we must come to the end of the disturbance some time.

Saturday night. − Camp 45. T. −3°. Bar. 21.61. ? Rise. Height about 7750. Great vicissitudes of fortune in the afternoon march. Started west up a slope − about the fifth we have mounted in the last two days. On top, another pressure appeared on the left, but less lofty and more snow-covered than that which had troubled us in the morning. There was temptation to try it, and I had been gradually turning in its direction. But I stuck to my principle and turned west up yet another slope. On top of this we got on the most extraordinary surface − narrow crevasses ran in all directions. They were quite invisible, being covered with a thin crust of hardened névé without a sign of a crack in it. We all fell in one after another and sometimes two together. We have had many unexpected falls before, but usually through being unable to mark the run of the surface appearances of cracks, or where such cracks are covered with soft snow. How a hardened crust can form over a crack is a real puzzle − it seems to argue extremely slow movement.

Dead reckoning, 85° 22' 1" S., 159° 31' E.

In the broader crevasses this morning we noticed that it was the lower edge of the bridge which was rotten, whereas in all in the glacier the upper edge was open.

Near the narrow crevasses this afternoon we got about 10 minutes on snow which had a hard crust and loose crystals below. It was like breaking through a glass house at each step, but quite suddenly at 5 p.m. everything changed. The hard surface gave place to regular sastrugi and our horizon levelled in every direction. I hung on to the S.W. till 6 p.m., and then camped with a delightful feeling of security that we had at length reached the summit proper. I am feeling very cheerful about everything tonight. We marched 15 miles (geo.) (over 17 stat.) today, mounting nearly 800 feet and all in about 8½ hours. My determination to keep mounting irrespective of course is fully justified and I shall be indeed surprised if we have any further difficulties with crevasses or steep slopes. To me for the first time our goal seems really in sight. We can pull our loads and pull them much faster and farther than I expected in my most hopeful moments. I only pray for a fair share of good weather. There is a cold wind now as expected, but with good clothes and well fed as we are, we can stick a lot worse than we are getting. I trust this may prove the turning-point in our fortunes for which we have waited so patiently.

Sunday, December 24. – Lunch. Bar. 21.48. ? Rise 160 feet. Christmas Eve. 7½ miles geo. due south, and a rise, I think, more than shown by barometer. This in five hours, on the surface which ought to be a sample of what we shall have in the future. With our present loads it is a fairly heavy plod, but we get over the ground, which is a great thing. A high pressure ridge has appeared on the 'port bow'. It seems isolated, but I shall be glad to lose sight of such disturbances. The wind is continuous from the S.S.E., very searching. We are now marching in our wind blouses and with somewhat more protection on the head.

Bar. 21.41. Camp 46. Rise for day ? about 250 ft. or 300 ft. Hypsometer, 8000 ft.

The first two hours of the afternoon march went very well. Then the sledges hung a bit, and we plodded on and covered something over 14 miles (geo.) in the day. We lost sight of the big pressure ridge, but tonight another smaller one shows fine on the 'port bow', and the surface is alternately very hard and fairly soft; dips and rises all round. It is evident we are skirting more disturbances, and I sincerely hope it will not mean altering course more to the west. 14 miles in 4 hours is not so bad considering the circumstances. The southerly wind is continuous and not at all pleasant in camp, but on the march it keeps us cool. (T. −3°) The only inconvenience is the extent to which our faces get iced up. The temperature hovers about zero.

We have not struck a crevasse all day, which is a good sign. The sun continues to shine in a cloudless sky, the wind rises and falls, and about us is a scene of the wildest desolation, but we are a very cheerful party and tomorrow is Christmas Day, with something extra in the hoosh.

Monday, December 25, CHRISTMAS. – Lunch. Bar. 21.14. Rise 240 feet. The wind was strong last night and this morning; a light snowfall in the night; a good deal of drift, subsiding when we started, but still about a foot high. I thought it might have spoilt the surface, but for the first hour and a half we went along in fine style. Then we started up a rise, and to our annoyance found ourselves amongst crevasses once more – very hard, smooth névé between high ridges at the edge of crevasses, and therefore very difficult to get foothold to pull the sledges. Got our ski sticks out, which improved matters, but we had to tack a good deal and several of us went half down. After half an hour of this I looked round and found the second sledge halted some way in rear – evidently someone had gone into a crevasse. We saw the rescue work going on, but had to wait half an hour for the party to come up, and got mighty cold. It appears that Lashly went down very suddenly, nearly dragging the crew with him. The sledge ran on and jammed the span so that the Alpine rope had to be got out and used to pull Lashly to the surface again. Lashly says the crevasse was 50 feet deep and 8 feet across, in form U, showing that the word 'unfathomable' can rarely be applied. Lashly is 44 today and as hard as nails. His fall has not even disturbed his equanimity.

After topping the crevasse ridge we got on a better surface and came along fairly well, completing over 7 miles (geo.) just before 1 o'clock. We have risen nearly 250 feet this morning; the wind was strong and therefore trying, mainly because it held the sledge; it is a little lighter now.

Night. Camp No. 47. Bar. 21.18. T. −7°. I am so replete that I can scarcely write. After sundry luxuries, such as chocolate and raisins at lunch, we started off well, but soon got amongst crevasses, huge snow-filled roadways running almost in our direction, and across hidden cracks into which we frequently fell. Passing for two miles or so along between two roadways, we came on a huge pit with raised sides. Is this a submerged mountain peak or a swirl in the stream? Getting clear of crevasses and on a slightly down grade, we came along at a swinging pace – splendid. I marched on till nearly 7.30, when we had covered 15 miles (geo.) (17¼ stat.). I knew that supper was to be a 'tightener', and indeed it has been – so much that I must leave description till the morning.

Dead reckoning, Lat. 85° 50' S.; Long. 159° 8' 2" E. Bar. 21.22.

Towards the end of the march we seemed to get into better condition; about us the surface rises and falls on the long slopes of vast mounds or undulations – no very definite system in their disposition. We camped half-way up a long slope.

In the middle of the afternoon we got another fine view of the land. The Dominion Range ends abruptly as observed, then come two straits and two other masses of land. Similarly north of the wild mountains is another strait and another mass of land. The various straits are undoubtedly overflows, and the masses of land mark the inner fringe of the exposed coastal mountains, the general direction of which seems about S.S.E., from which it appears that one could be much closer to the Pole on the Barrier by continuing on it to the S.S.E. We ought to know more of this when Evans's observations are plotted.

I must write a word of our supper last night. We had four courses. The first, pemmican, full whack, with slices of horse meat flavoured with onion and curry powder and thickened with biscuit; then an arrowroot, cocoa and biscuit hoosh sweetened; then a plum-pudding; then cocoa with raisins, and finally a dessert of caramels and ginger. After the feast it was difficult to move. Wilson and I couldn't finish our share of plum-pudding. We have all slept splendidly and feel thoroughly warm – such is the effect of full feeding.

Tuesday, December 26. – Lunch. Bar. 21.11. Four and three-quarter hours, 6¾ miles (geo.). Perhaps a little slow after plum-pudding, but I think we are getting on to the surface which is likely to continue the rest of the way. There are still mild differences of elevation, but generally speaking the plain is flattening out; no doubt we are rising slowly.

Camp 48. Bar. 21.02. The first two hours of the afternoon march went well; then we got on a rough rise and the sledge came badly. Camped at 6.30, sledge coming easier again at the end.

It seems astonishing to be disappointed with a march of 15 (stat.) miles, when I had contemplated doing little more than 10 with full loads.

We are on the 86th parallel. Obs.: 86° 2' S.; 160° 26' E. The temperature has been pretty consistent of late, −10° to −12° at night, −3° in the day. The wind has seemed milder today − it blows anywhere from S.E. to south. I had thought to have done with pressures, but tonight a crevassed slope appears on our right. We shall pass well clear of it, but there may be others. The undulating character of the plain causes a great variety of surface, owing, of course, to the varying angles at which the wind strikes the slopes. We were half an hour late starting this morning, which accounts for some loss of distance, though I should be content to keep up an average of 13' (geo.).

Wednesday, December 27. − Lunch. Bar. 21.02. The wind light this morning and the pulling heavy. Everyone sweated, especially the second team, which had great difficulty in keeping up. We have been going up and down, the up grades very tiring, especially when we get amongst sastrugi which jerk the sledge about, but we have done 7¼ miles (geo.). A very bad accident this morning. Bowers broke the only hypsometer thermometer. We have nothing to check our two aneroids.

Night camp 49. Bar. 20.82. T. −6.3°. We marched off well after lunch on a soft, snowy surface, then came to slippery hard sastrugi and kept a good pace; but I felt this meant something wrong, and on topping a short rise we were once more in the midst of crevasses and disturbances. For an hour it was dreadfully trying − had to pick a road, tumbled into crevasses, and got jerked about abominably. At the summit of the ridge we came to another 'pit' or 'whirl', which seemed the centre of the trouble − is it a submerged mountain peak? During the last hour and a quarter we pulled out on to soft snow again and moved well. Camped at 6.45, having covered 13⅓ miles (geo.). Steering the party is no light task. One cannot allow one's thoughts to wander as others do, and when, as this afternoon, one gets amongst disturbances, I find it is very worrying and tiring. I do trust we shall have no more of them. We have not lost sight of the sun since we came on the summit; we should get an extraordinary record of sunshine. It is monotonous work this; the sledge-meter and theodolite govern the situation.

Thursday, December 28. – Lunch. Bar. 20.77. I start cooking again tomorrow morning. We have had a troublesome day but have completed our 13 miles (geo.). My unit pulled away easy this morning and stretched out for two hours as the second unit made heavy weather. I changed with Evans and found the second sledge heavy – could keep up, but the team was not swinging with me as my own team swings. Then I changed P.O. Evans for Lashly. We seemed to get on better, but at the moment the surface changed and we came up over a rise with hard sastrugi. At the top we camped for lunch. What was the difficulty? One theory was that some members of the second party were stale. Another that all was due to the bad stepping and want of swing; another that the sledge pulled heavy. In the afternoon we exchanged sledges, and at first went off well, but getting into soft snow, we found a terrible drag, the second party coming quite easily with our sledge. So the sledge is the cause of the trouble, and talking it out, I found that all is due to want of care. The runners ran excellently, but the structure has been distorted by bad strapping, bad loading, &c. The party are not done, and I have told them plainly that they must wrestle with the trouble and get it right for themselves. There is no possible reason why they should not get along as easily as we do.

Night camp 50. T. −6°. Bar. 20.66.

Obs.: 86° 27′ 2″ S.; 161° 1′ 15″ E.; Var. 179° 33′ E. Bar. 20.64.

Friday, December 29. – Bar. 20.52. Lunch. Height 9050 about. The worst surface we have struck, very heavy pulling; but we came 6½ miles (geo.). It will be a strain to keep up distances if we get surfaces like this. We seem to be steadily but slowly rising. The satisfactory thing is that the second party now keeps up, as the faults have been discovered; they were due partly to the rigid loading of the sledge and partly to the bad pacing.

Night camp 51. Bar. 20.49. T. −6°. Had another struggle this afternoon and only managed to get 12 miles (geo.). The very hard pulling has occurred on two rises. It appears that the loose snow is blown over the rises and rests in heaps on the north-facing slopes.

It is these heaps that cause our worst troubles. The weather looks a little doubtful, a good deal of cirrus cloud in motion over us, radiating E. and W. The wind shifts from S.E. to S.S.W., rising and falling at intervals; it is annoying on the march as it retards the sledges, but it must help the surface, I think, and so hope for better things tomorrow. The marches are terribly monotonous. One's thoughts wander occasionally to pleasanter scenes and places, but the necessity to keep the course, or some hitch in the surface, quickly brings them back. There have been some hours of very steady plodding today; these are the best part of the business, they mean forgetfulness and advance.

Saturday, December 30. – Bar. 20.42. Lunch. Night camp 52. Bar. 20.36. Rise about 150. A very trying, tiring march, and only 11 miles (geo.) covered. Wind from the south to S.E., not quite so strong as usual; the usual clear sky.

We camped on a rise last night, and it was some time before we reached the top this morning. This took it out of us at the start and the second party dropped. I went on 6½ miles (when the second party was some way astern) and lunched. We came on in the afternoon, the other party still dropping, camped at 6.30 – they at 7.15. We came up another rise with the usual gritty snow towards the end of the march. For us the interval between the two rises, some 8 miles, was steady plodding work which one might keep up for some time. Tomorrow I'm going to march half a day, make a depôt and build the 10-feet sledges. The second party is certainly tiring; it remains to be seen how they will manage with the smaller sledge and lighter load. The surface is certainly much worse than it was 50 miles back. (T. −10°) We have caught up Shackleton's dates. Everything would be cheerful if I could persuade myself that the second party were quite fit to go forward.

Sunday, December 31. – New Year's Eve. 20.17. Height about 9126. T. −10°. Camp 53. Corrected aneroid. The second party depôted its ski and some other weights equivalent to about 100 lbs. I sent them off first; they marched, but not very fast. We followed and did not catch them before they camped by direction at 1.30. By this time we had covered exactly 7 miles (geo.), and we must have risen a good deal. We rose on a steep incline at the beginning of the march, and topped another at the end, showing a distance of about 5 miles between these wretched slopes which give us the hardest pulling, but as a matter of fact, we have been rising all day.

We had a good full brew of tea and then set to work stripping the sledges. That didn't take long, but the process of building up the 10-feet sledges now in operation in the other tent is a long job. Evans (P.O.) and Crean are tackling it, and it is a very remarkable piece of work. Certainly P.O. Evans is the most invaluable asset to our party. To build a sledge under these conditions is a fact for special record. Evans (Lieut.) has just found the latitude – 86° 56' S., so that we are pretty near the 87th parallel aimed at for tonight. We lose half a day, but I hope to make that up by going forward at much better speed.

This is to be called the '3 Degree Depôt', and it holds a week's provision for both units.

There is extraordinarily little mirage up here and the refraction is very small. Except for the seamen we are all sitting in a double tent – the first time we have put up the inner lining to the tent; it seems to make us much snugger.

10 p.m. – The job of rebuilding is taking longer than I expected, but is now almost done. The 10-feet sledges look very handy. We had an extra drink of tea and are now turned into our bags in the double tent (five of us) as warm as toast, and just enough light to write or work with. Did not get to bed till 2 a.m.

Obs.: 86° 55' 47" S.; 165° 5' 48" E.; Var. 175° 40' E. Morning Bar. 20.08.

Monday, January 1, 1912. NEW YEAR'S DAY. – Lunch. Bar. 20.04. Roused hands about 7.30 and got away 9.30, Evans's party going ahead on foot. We followed on ski. Very stupidly we had not seen to our ski shoes beforehand, and it took a good half-hour to get them right; Wilson especially had trouble. When we did get away, to our surprise the sledge pulled very easily, and we made fine progress, rapidly gaining on the foot-haulers.

Night camp 54. Bar. 19.98. Risen about 150 feet. Height about 9600 above Barrier. They camped for lunch at 5½ miles and went on early, completing 11.3 (geo.) by 7.30. We were delayed again at lunch camp, P.O. Evans repairing the tent, and I the cooker. We caught the other party more easily in the afternoon and kept alongside them the last quarter of an hour. It was surprising how easily the sledge pulled; we have scarcely exerted ourselves all day.

We have been rising again all day, but the slopes are less accentuated. I had expected trouble with ski and hard patches, but we found none at all. (T. −14°) The temperature is steadily falling, but it seems to fall with the wind. We are very comfortable in our double tent. Stick of chocolate to celebrate the New Year. The supporting party not in very high spirits, they have not managed matters well for themselves. Prospects seem to get brighter − only 170 miles to go and plenty of food left.

Tuesday, January 2. − T. −17°. Camp 55. Height about 9980. At lunch my aneroid reading over scale 12,250, shifted hand to read 10,250. Proposed to enter heights in future with correction as calculated at end of book (minus 340 feet). The foot party went off early, before 8, and marched till 1. Again from 2.35 to 6.30. We started more than half an hour later on each march and caught the others easy. It's been a plod for the foot people and pretty easy going for us, and we have covered 13 miles (geo.) .

T. −11°: Obs. 87° 20' 8" S.; 160° 40' 53" E.; Var. 180°. The sky is slightly overcast for the first time since we left the glacier; the sun can be seen already through the veil of stratus, and blue sky round the horizon. The sastrugi have all been from the S.E. today, and likewise the wind, which has been pretty light. I hope the clouds do not mean wind or bad surface. The latter became poor towards the end of the afternoon. We have not risen much today, and the plain seems to be flattening out. Irregularities are best seen by sastrugi. A *skua gull* visited us on the march this afternoon − it was evidently curious, kept alighting on the snow ahead, and fluttering a few yards as we approached. It seemed to have had little food − an extraordinary visitor considering our distance from the sea.

Wednesday, January 3. − Height: Lunch, 10,110; Night, 10,180. Camp 56. T. −17°. Minimum −18.5°. Within 150 miles of our goal. Last night I decided to reorganise, and this morning told off Teddy Evans, Lashly, and Crean to return. They are disappointed, but take it well. Bowers is to come into our tent, and we proceed as a five-man unit tomorrow. We have 5½ units of food − practically over a month's allowance for five people − it ought to see us through. We came along well on ski today, but the foot-haulers were slow, and so we only got a trifle over 12 miles (geo.). Very anxious to see how we shall manage tomorrow; if we can march well with the full load we shall be practically safe, I take it. The surface was very bad in patches today and the wind strong.

'Lat. 87° 32'. A last note from a hopeful position. I think it's going to be all right. We have a fine party going forward and arrangements are all going well.'

Thursday, January 4. – T. –17°, Lunch T. –16.5°. We were naturally late getting away this morning, the sledge having to be packed and arrangements completed for separation of parties. It is wonderful to see how neatly everything stows on a little sledge, thanks to P. O. Evans. I was anxious to see how we could pull it, and glad to find we went easy enough. Bowers on foot pulls between, but behind, Wilson and myself; he has to keep his own pace and luckily does not throw us out at all.

The second party had followed us in case of accident, but as soon as I was certain we could get along we stopped and said farewell. Teddy Evans is terribly disappointed but has taken it very well and behaved like a man. Poor old Crean wept and even Lashly was affected. I was glad to find their sledge is a mere nothing to them, and thus, no doubt, they will make a quick journey back.[24] Since leaving them we have marched on till 1.15 and covered 6.2 miles (geo.). With full marching days we ought to have no difficulty in keeping up our average.

Night camp 57. T. –16°. Height 10,280. We started well on the afternoon march, going a good speed for 1½ hours; then we came on a surface covered with loose sandy snow, and the pulling became very heavy. We managed to get off 12½ miles (geo.) by 7 p.m., but it was very heavy work.

In the afternoon the wind died away, and tonight it is flat calm; the sun so warm that in spite of the temperature we can stand about outside in the greatest comfort. It is amusing to stand thus and remember the constant horrors of our situation as they were painted for us: the sun is melting the snow on the ski, &c. The plateau is now very flat, but we are still ascending slowly. The sastrugi are getting more confused, predominant from the S.E. I wonder what is in store for us. At present everything seems to be going with extraordinary smoothness, and one can scarcely believe that obstacles will not present themselves to make our task more difficult. Perhaps the surface will be the element to trouble us.

Friday, January 5. – Camp 58. Height: morning, 10,430; night, 10,320. T. –14.8°. Obs. 87° 57', 159° 13'. Minimum T. –23.5°; T. –21°. A dreadfully trying day. Light wind from the N.N.W. bringing detached cloud and constant fall of ice crystals. The surface, in consequence, as bad as could be after the first hour. We started at 8.15, marched solidly till 1.15, covering 7.4 miles (geo.), and again in the afternoon we plugged on; by 7 p.m. we had done 12½ miles (geo.), the hardest we have yet done on the plateau. The sastrugi seemed to increase as we advance and they have changed direction from S.W. to S. by W. In the afternoon a good deal of confusing cross sastrugi, and tonight a very rough surface with evidences of hard southerly wind. Luckily the sledge shows no signs of capsizing yet. We sigh for a breeze to sweep the hard snow, but tonight the outlook is not promising better things. However, we are very close to the 88th parallel, little more than 120 miles from the Pole, only a march from Shackleton's final camp, and in a general way 'getting on'.

We go little over a mile and a quarter an hour now – it is a big strain as the shadows creep slowly round from our right through ahead to our left. What lots of things we think of on these monotonous marches! What castles one builds now hopefully that the Pole is ours. Bowers took sights today and will take them every third day. We feel the cold very little, the great comfort of our situation is the excellent drying effect of the sun. Our socks and finnesko are almost dry each morning. Cooking for five takes a seriously longer time than cooking for four; perhaps half an hour on the whole day. It is an item I had not considered when re-organising.

Saturday, January 6. – Height 10,470. T. –22.3°. Obstacles arising – last night we got amongst sastrugi – they increased in height this morning and now we are in the midst of a sea of fish-hook waves well remembered from our Northern experience. We took off our ski after the first 1½ hours and pulled on foot. It is terribly heavy in places, and, to add to our trouble, every sastrugus is covered with a beard of sharp branching crystals. We have covered 6½ miles, but we cannot keep up our average if this sort of surface continues. There is no wind.

Camp 59. Lat. 88° 7'. Height 10,430–10,510. Rise of barometer ? T. –22.5°. Minimum –25.8°. Morning. Fearfully hard pull again, and when we had marched about an hour we discovered that a sleeping-bag had fallen off the sledge. We had to go back and carry it on. It cost us over an hour and disorganised our party. We have only covered 10½ miles (geo.) and it's been about the hardest pull we've had. We think of leaving our ski here, mainly because of risk of breakage. Over the sastrugi it is all up and down hill, and the covering of ice crystals prevents the sledge from gliding even on the down-grade. The sastrugi, I fear, have come to stay, and we must be prepared for heavy marching, but in two days I hope to lighten loads with a depôt. We are south of Shackleton's last camp, so, I suppose, have made the most southerly camp.

Sunday, January 7. – Height 10,560. Lunch. Temp. −21.3°. The vicissitudes of this work are bewildering. Last night we decided to leave our ski on account of the sastrugi. This morning we marched out a mile in 40 min. and the sastrugi gradually disappeared. I kept debating the ski question and at this point stopped, and after discussion we went back and fetched the ski; it cost us 1½ hours nearly. Marching again, I found to my horror we could scarcely move the sledge on ski; the first hour was awful owing to the wretched coating of loose sandy snow. However, we persisted, and towards the latter end of our tiring march we began to make better progress, but the work is still awfully heavy. I mean to stick to the ski after this.

Afternoon. Camp 60. T. −23°. Height 10,570. Obs.: Lat. 88° 18' 40" S.; Long. 157° 21' E.; Var. 179° 15' W. Very heavy pulling still, but did 5 miles (geo.) in over four hours.

This is the shortest march we have made on the summit; but there is excuse. Still, there is no doubt if things remained as they are we could not keep up the strain of such marching for long. Things, however, luckily will not remain as they are. Tomorrow we depôt a week's provision, lightening altogether about 100 lbs. This afternoon the welcome southerly wind returned and is now blowing force 2 to 3. I cannot but think it will improve the surface.

The sastrugi are very much diminished, and those from the south seem to be overpowering those from the S.E. Cloud travelled rapidly over from the south this afternoon, and the surface was covered with sandy crystals; these were not so bad as the 'bearded' sastrugi, and oddly enough the wind and drift only gradually obliterate these spiky formations. We have scarcely risen at all today, and the plain looks very flat. It doesn't look as though there were more rises ahead, and one could not wish for a better surface if only the crystal deposit would disappear or harden up. I am awfully glad we have hung on to the ski; hard as the marching is, it is far less tiring on ski. Bowers has a heavy time on foot, but nothing seems to tire him. Evans has a nasty cut on his hand (sledge-making). I hope it won't give trouble. Our food continues to amply satisfy. What luck to have hit on such an excellent ration. We really are an excellently found party.

Monday, January 8. – Camp 60. Noon. T. −19.8°. Min. for night −25°. Our first summit blizzard. We might just have started after breakfast, but the wind seemed obviously on the increase, and so it has proved. The sun has not been obscured, but snow is evidently falling as well as drifting. The sun seems to be getting a little brighter as the wind increases. The whole phenomenon is very like a Barrier blizzard, only there is much less snow, as one would expect, and at present less wind, which is somewhat of a surprise.

Evans's hand was dressed this morning, and the rest ought to be good for it. I am not sure it will not do us all good as we lie so very comfortably, warmly clothed in our comfortable bags, within our double-walled tent. However, we do not want more than a day's delay at most, both on account of lost time and food and the slow accumulation of ice. (Night T. −13.5°) It has grown much thicker during the day, from time to time obscuring the sun for the first time. The temperature is low for a blizzard, but we are very comfortable in our double tent and the cold snow is not sticky and not easily carried into the tent, so that the sleeping-bags remain in good condition. (T. −3°) The glass is rising slightly. I hope we shall be able to start in the morning, but fear that a disturbance of this sort may last longer than our local storms.

It is quite impossible to speak too highly of my companions. Each fulfils his office to the party; Wilson, first as doctor, ever on the lookout to alleviate the small pains and troubles incidental to the work; now as cook, quick, careful and dexterous, ever thinking of some fresh expedient to help the camp life; tough as steel on the traces, never wavering from start to finish.

Evans, a giant worker with a really remarkable head-piece. It is only now I realise how much has been due to him. Our ski shoes and crampons have been absolutely indispensable, and if the original ideas were not his, the details of manufacture and design and the good workmanship are his alone. He is responsible for every sledge, every sledge fitting, tents, sleeping-bags, harness, and when one cannot recall a single expression of dissatisfaction with any one of these items, it shows what an invaluable assistant he has been. Now, besides superintending the putting up of the tent, he thinks out and arranges the packing of the sledge; it is extraordinary how neatly and handily everything is stowed, and how much study has been given to preserving the suppleness and good running qualities of the machine. On the Barrier, before the ponies were killed, he was ever roaming round, correcting faults of stowage.

Little Bowers remains a marvel – he is thoroughly enjoying himself. I leave all the provision arrangement in his hands, and at all times he knows exactly how we stand, or how each returning party should fare. It has been a complicated business to redistribute stores at various stages of re-organisation, but not one single mistake has been made. In addition to the stores, he keeps the most thorough and conscientious meteorological record, and to this he now adds the duty of observer and photographer. Nothing comes amiss to him, and no work is too hard. It is a difficulty to get him into the tent; he seems quite oblivious of the cold, and he lies coiled in his bag writing and working out sights long after the others are asleep.

Of these three it is a matter for thought and congratulation that each is specially suited for his own work, but would not be capable of doing that of the others as well as it is done. Each is invaluable. Oates had his invaluable period with the ponies; now he is a foot slogger and goes hard the whole time, does his share of camp work, and stands the hardship as well as any of us. I would not like to be without him either. So our five people are perhaps as happily selected as it is possible to imagine.

Tuesday, January 9. – Camp 61. RECORD. Lat. 88° 25'. Height 10,270 ft. Bar. risen I think. T. −4°. Still blowing, and drifting when we got to breakfast, but signs of taking off. The wind had gradually shifted from south to E.S.E. After lunch we were able to break camp in a bad light, but on a good surface. We made a very steady afternoon march, covering 6½ miles (geo.). This should place us in Lat. 88° 25', beyond the record of Shackleton's walk. All is new ahead. The barometer has risen since the blizzard, and it looks as though we were on a level plateau, not to rise much further.

Obs.: Long. 159° 17' 45" E.; Var. 179° 55' W.; Min. Temp. −7.2°.

More curiously the temperature continued to rise after the blow and now, at −4°, it seems quite warm. The sun has only shown very indistinctly all the afternoon, although brighter now. Clouds are still drifting over from the east. The marching is growing terribly monotonous, but one cannot grumble as long as the distance can be kept up. It can, I think, if we leave a depôt, but a very annoying thing has happened. Bowers's watch has suddenly dropped 26 minutes; it may have stopped from being frozen outside his pocket, or he may have inadvertently touched the hands. Any way it makes one more chary of leaving stores on this great plain, especially as the blizzard tended to drift up our tracks. We could only just see the back track when we started, but the light was extremely poor.

Wednesday, January 10. – Camp 62. T. −11°. Last depôt 88° 29' S.; 159° 33' E.; Var. 180°. Terrible hard march in the morning; only covered 5.1 miles (geo.). Decided to leave depôt at lunch camp. Built cairn and left one week's food together with sundry articles of clothing. We are down as close as we can go in the latter. We go forward with eighteen days' food. Yesterday I should have said certain to see us through, but now the surface is beyond words, and if it continues we shall have the greatest difficulty to keep our march long enough. The surface is quite covered with sandy snow, and when the sun shines it is terrible. During the early part of the afternoon it was overcast, and we started our lightened sledge with a good swing, but during the last two hours the sun cast shadows again, and the work was distressingly hard. We have covered only 10.8 miles (geo.).

Only 85 miles (geog.) from the Pole, but it's going to be a stiff pull *both ways* apparently; still we do make progress, which is something. Tonight the sky is overcast, the temperature (−11°) much higher than I anticipated; it is very difficult to imagine what is happening to the weather. The sastrugi grow more and more confused, running from S. to E. Very difficult steering in uncertain light and with rapidly moving clouds. The clouds don't seem to come from anywhere, form and disperse without visible reason.

The surface seems to be growing softer. The meteorological conditions seem to point to an area of variable light winds, and that plot will thicken as we advance.

Thursday, January 11. – Lunch. Height 10,540. T. −15.8°. It was heavy pulling from the beginning today, but for the first two and a half hours we could keep the sledge moving; then the sun came out (it had been overcast and snowing with light south-easterly breeze) and the rest of the forenoon was agonising. I never had such pulling; all the time the sledge rasps and creaks. We have covered 6 miles, but at fearful cost to ourselves.

Night camp 63. Height 10,530. Temp. −16.3°. Minimum −25.8°. Another hard grind in the afternoon and five miles added. About 74 miles from the Pole – can we keep this up for seven days? It takes it out of us like anything. None of us ever had such hard work before. Cloud has been coming and going overhead all day, drifting from the S.E., but continually altering shape. Snow crystals falling all the time; a very light S. breeze at start soon dying away. The sun so bright and warm tonight that it is almost impossible to imagine a minus temperature. The snow seems to get softer as we advance; the sastrugi, though sometimes high and undercut, are not hard – no crusts, except yesterday the surface subsided once, as on the Barrier. It seems pretty certain there is no steady wind here. Our chance still holds good if we can put the work in, but it's a terribly trying time.

Friday, January 12. – Camp 64. T. −17.5°. Lat. 88° 57'. Another heavy march with snow getting softer all the time. Sun very bright, calm at start; first two hours terribly slow. Lunch, 4¾ hours, 5.6 miles geo.; Sight Lat. 88° 52'. Afternoon, 4 hours, 5.1 miles – total 10.7.

In the afternoon we seemed to be going better; clouds spread over from the west with light chill wind and for a few brief minutes we tasted the delight of having the sledge following free. Alas! in a few minutes it was worse than ever, in spite of the sun's eclipse. However, the short experience was salutary. I had got to fear that we were weakening badly in our pulling; those few minutes showed me that we only want a good surface to get along as merrily as of old. With the surface as it is, one gets horribly sick of the monotony and can easily imagine oneself getting played out, were it not that at the lunch and night camps one so quickly forgets all one's troubles and bucks up for a fresh effort. It is an effort to keep up the double figures, but if we can do so for another four marches we ought to get through. It is going to be a close thing.

At camping tonight everyone was chilled and we guessed a cold snap, but to our surprise the actual temperature was higher than last night, when we could dawdle in the sun. It is most unaccountable why we should suddenly feel the cold in this manner; partly the exhaustion of the march, but partly some damp quality in the air, I think. Little Bowers is wonderful; in spite of my protest he would take sights after we had camped tonight, after marching in the soft snow all day where we have been comparatively restful on ski.

Night position. – Lat. 88° 57' 25" S.; Long. 160° 21' E.; Var. 179° 49' W. Minimum T. −23.5°.

Only 63 miles (geo.) from the Pole tonight. We ought to do the trick, but oh! for a better surface. It is quite evident this is a comparatively windless area. The sastrugi are few and far between, and all soft. I should imagine occasional blizzards sweep up from the S.E., but none with violence. We leave deep tracks in the snow, which is soft as deep as you like to dig down.

Saturday, January 13. – Lunch. Height 10,390. Barometer low ? Lunch Lat. 89° 3' 18". Started on some soft snow, very heavy dragging and went slow. We could have supposed nothing but that such conditions would last from now onward, but to our surprise, after two hours we came on a sea of sastrugi, all lying from S. to E., predominant E.S.E. Have had a cold little wind from S.E. and S.S.E., where the sky is overcast. Have done 5.6 miles and are now over the 89th parallel.

Night camp 65. – Height 10,270. T. −22.5°, Minimum −23.5°. Lat. 89° 9' S. very nearly. We started very well in the afternoon. Thought we were going to make a real good march, but after the first two hours surface crystals became as sandy as ever. Still we did 5.6 miles geo., giving over 11 for the day. Well, another day with double figures and a bit over. The chance holds.

It looks as though we were descending slightly; sastrugi remain as in forenoon. It is wearisome work this tugging and straining to advance a light sledge. Still, we get along. I did manage to get my thoughts off the work for a time today, which is very restful.

We should be in a poor way without our ski, though Bowers manages to struggle through the soft snow without tiring his short legs.

Only 51 miles from the Pole tonight. If we don't get to it we shall be d—d close. There is a little southerly breeze tonight; I devoutly hope it may increase in force. The alternation of soft snow and sastrugi seems to suggest that the coastal mountains are not so very far away.

Sunday, January 14. – Camp 66. Lunch T. −18°, Night T. −15°. Sun showing mistily through overcast sky all day. Light southerly wind with very low drift. In consequence the surface was a little better, and we came along very steadily 6.3 miles in the morning and 5.5 in the afternoon, but the steering was awfully difficult and trying; very often I could see nothing, and Bowers in my shadow directed me. Under such circumstances it is an immense help to be pulling on ski. Tonight it is looking very thick. The sun can barely be distinguished, the temperature has risen, and there are serious indications of a blizzard. I trust they will not come to anything; there are practically no signs of heavy wind here, so that even if it blows a little we may be able to march. Meanwhile we are less than 40 miles from the Pole.

Again we noticed the cold; at lunch today (Obs.: Lat. 89° 20' 53" S.) all our feet were cold, but this was mainly due to the bald state of our finnesko. I put some grease under the bare skin and found it made all the difference. Oates seems to be feeling the cold and fatigue more than the rest of us, but we are all very fit. It is a critical time, but we ought to pull through. The barometer has fallen very considerably and we cannot tell whether due to ascent of plateau or change of weather. Oh! for a few fine days! So close it seems and only the weather to baulk us.

Monday, January 15. – Lunch camp, Height 9950. Last depôt. During the night the air cleared entirely and the sun shone in a perfectly clear sky. The light wind had dropped and the temperature fallen to −25°, minimum −27°. I guessed this meant a hard pull, and guessed right. The surface was terrible, but for 4¾ hours yielded 6 miles (geo.). We were all pretty well done at camping, and here we leave our last depôt – only four days' food and a sundry or two. The load is now very light, but I fear that the friction will not be greatly reduced.

Night, January 15. – Height 9920. T. –25°. The sledge came surprisingly lightly after lunch – something from loss of weight, something, I think, from stowage, and, most of all perhaps, as a result of tea. Anyhow we made a capital afternoon march of 6.3 miles, bringing the total for the day to over 12 (12.3). The sastrugi again very confused, but mostly S.E. quadrant; the heaviest now almost east, so that the sledge continually bumps over ridges. The wind is from the W.N.W. and chilly, but the weather remains fine and there are no sastrugi from that direction.

Camp 67. Lunch obs.: Lat. 89° 26' 57"; Lat. dead reckoning, 89° 33' 15" S.; Long. 160° 56' 45" E.; Var. 179° E.

It is wonderful to think that two long marches would land us at the Pole. We left our depôt today with nine days' provisions, so that it ought to be a certain thing now, and the only appalling possibility the sight of the Norwegian flag forestalling ours. Little Bowers continues his indefatigable efforts to get good sights, and it is wonderful how he works them up in his sleeping-bag in our congested tent. (Minimum for night –27.5°) Only 27 miles from the Pole. We *ought* to do it now.

Tuesday, January 16. – Camp 68. Height 9760. T. –23.5°. The worst has happened, or nearly the worst. We marched well in the morning and covered 7½ miles. Noon sight showed us in Lat. 89° 42' S., and we started off in high spirits in the afternoon, feeling that tomorrow would see us at our destination. About the second hour of the march Bowers's sharp eyes detected what he thought was a cairn; he was uneasy about it, but argued that it must be a sastrugus. Half an hour later he detected a black speck ahead. Soon we knew that this could not be a natural snow feature. We marched on, found that it was a black flag tied to a sledge bearer; near by the remains of a camp; sledge tracks and ski tracks going and coming and the clear trace of dogs' paws – many dogs. This told us the whole story. The Norwegians have forestalled us and are first at the Pole. It is a terrible disappointment, and I am very sorry for my loyal companions. Many thoughts come and much discussion have we had. Tomorrow we must march on to the Pole and then hasten home with all the speed we can compass. All the day dreams must go; it will be a wearisome return. We are descending in altitudes – certainly also the Norwegians found an easy way up.

Wednesday, January 17. – Camp 69. T. –22° at start. Night –21°. The Pole. Yes, but under very different circumstances from those expected. We have had a horrible day – add to our disappointment a head wind 4 to 5, with a temperature –22°, and companions labouring on with cold feet and hands.

We started at 7.30, none of us having slept much after the shock of our discovery. We followed the Norwegian sledge tracks for some way; as far as we make out there are only two men. In about three miles we passed two small cairns. Then the weather overcast, and the tracks being increasingly drifted up and obviously going too far to the west, we decided to make straight for the Pole according to our calculations. At 12.30 Evans had such cold hands we camped for lunch – an excellent 'weekend' one. We had marched 7.4 miles. Lat. sight gave 89° 53' 37". We started out and did 6½ miles due south. Tonight little Bowers is laying himself out to get sights in terrible difficult circumstances; the wind is blowing hard, T. –21°, and there is that curious damp, cold feeling in the air which chills one to the bone in no time. We have been descending again, I think, but there looks to be a rise ahead; otherwise there is very little that is different from the awful monotony of past days. Great God! this is an awful place and terrible enough for us to have laboured to it without the reward of priority. Well, it is something to have got here, and the wind may be our friend tomorrow. We have had a fat Polar hoosh in spite of our chagrin, and feel comfortable inside – added a small stick of chocolate and the queer taste of a cigarette brought by Wilson. Now for the run home and a desperate struggle. I wonder if we can do it.

Thursday morning, January 18. – Decided after summing up all observations that we were 3.5 miles away from the Pole – one mile beyond it and 3 to the right. More or less in this direction Bowers saw a cairn or tent.

We have just arrived at this tent, 2 miles from our camp, therefore about 1½ miles from the Pole. In the tent we find a record of five Norwegians having been here, as follows:

Roald Amundsen	Sverre H. Hassel
Olav Olavson Bjaaland	Oscar Wisting
Hilmer Hanssen	16 Dec. 1911

The tent is fine – a small compact affair supported by a single bamboo. A note from Amundsen, which I keep, asks me to forward a letter to King Haakon!

The following articles have been left in the tent: 3 half bags of reindeer containing a miscellaneous assortment of mits and sleeping socks, very various in description, a sextant, a Norwegian artificial horizon and a hypsometer without boiling-point thermometers, a sextant and hypsometer of English make.

The Polar party at the South Pole

Left a note to say I had visited the tent with companions. Bowers photographing and Wilson sketching. Since lunch we have marched 6.2 miles S.S.E. by compass (i.e. northwards). Sights at lunch gave us ½ to ¾ of a mile from the Pole, so we call it the Pole Camp. (Temp. Lunch −21°) We built a cairn, put up our poor slighted Union Jack, and photographed ourselves – mighty cold work all of it – less than ½ a mile south we saw stuck up an old underrunner of a sledge. This we commandeered as a yard for a floorcloth sail. I imagine it was intended to mark the exact spot of the Pole as near as the Norwegians could fix it. (Height 9500.) A note attached talked of the tent as being 2 miles from the Pole. Wilson keeps the note. There is no doubt that our predecessors have made thoroughly sure of their mark and fully carried out their programme. I think the Pole is about 9500 feet in height; this is remarkable, considering that in Lat. 88° we were about 10,500.

We carried the Union Jack about ¼ of a mile north with us and left it on a piece of stick as near as we could fix it. I fancy the Norwegians arrived at the pole on the 15th Dec. and left on the 17th, ahead of a date quoted by me in London as ideal, viz. Dec. 22. It looks as though the Norwegian party expected colder weather on the summit than they got; it could scarcely be otherwise from Shackleton's account. Well, we have turned our back now on the goal of our ambition and must face our 800 miles of solid dragging – and goodbye to most of the day-dreams!

CHAPTER NINETEEN

The return from the Pole

Friday, January 19. – Lunch 8.1 miles, T. −22.6°. Early in the march we picked up a Norwegian cairn and our outward tracks. We followed these to the ominous black flag which has first apprised us of our predecessors' success. We have picked this flag up, using the staff for our sail, and are now camped about 1½ miles further back on our tracks. So that is the last of the Norwegians for the present. The surface undulates considerably about this latitude; it was more evident today than when we were outward bound.

Night camp R.2.* Height 9700. T. −18.5°, Minimum −25.6°. Came along well this afternoon for three hours, then a rather dreary finish for the last 1½. Weather very curious, snow clouds, looking very dense and spoiling the light, pass overhead from the S., dropping very minute crystals; between showers the sun shows and the wind goes to the S.W. The fine crystals absolutely spoil the surface; we had heavy dragging during the last hour in spite of the light load and a full sail. Our old tracks are drifted up, deep in places, and toothed sastrugi have formed over them. It looks as though this sandy snow was drifted about like sand from place to place. How account for the present state of our three day old tracks and the month old ones of the Norwegians?

It is warmer and pleasanter marching with the wind, but I'm not sure we don't feel the cold more when we stop and camp than we did on the outward march. We pick up our cairns easily, and ought to do so right through, I think; but, of course, one will be a bit anxious till the Three Degree Depôt is reached.† I'm afraid the return journey is going to be dreadfully tiring and monotonous.

* A number preceded by R. marks the camps on the return journey.

† Still over 150 miles away. They had marched 7 miles on the homeward track the first afternoon, 18 the second day.

Saturday, January 20. – Lunch camp, 9810. We have come along very well this morning, although the surface was terrible bad – 9.3 miles in 5 hours 20 m. This has brought us to our Southern Depôt, and we pick up 4 days' food. We carry on 7 days from tonight with 55 miles to go to the Half Degree Depôt made on January 10. The same sort of weather and a little more wind, sail drawing well.

Night Camp R.3. 9860. Temp. −18°. It was blowing quite hard and drifting when we started our afternoon march. At first with full sail we went along at a great rate; then we got on to an extraordinary surface, the drifting snow lying in heaps; it clung to the ski, which could only be pushed forward with an effort. The pulling was really awful, but we went steadily on and camped a short way beyond our cairn of the 14th. I'm afraid we are in for a bad pull again tomorrow, luckily the wind holds. I shall be very glad when Bowers gets his ski; I'm afraid he must find these long marches very trying with short legs, but he is an undefeated little sportsman. I think Oates is feeling the cold and fatigue more than most of us. It is blowing pretty hard tonight, but with a good march we have earned one good hoosh and are very comfortable in the tent. It is everything now to keep up a good marching pace; I trust we shall be able to do so and catch the ship. Total march, 18½ miles.

Sunday, January 21. – R.4. 10,010. Temp. blizzard, −18° to −11°, to −14° now. Awoke to a stiff blizzard; air very thick with snow and sun very dim. We decided not to march owing to likelihood of losing track; expected at least a day of lay up, but whilst at lunch there was a sudden clearance and wind dropped to light breeze. We got ready to march, but gear was so iced up we did not get away till 3.45. Marched till 7.40 – a terribly weary four-hour drag; even with helping wind we only did 5½ miles (6¼ statute). The surface bad, horribly bad on new sastrugi, and decidedly rising again in elevation.

We are going to have a pretty hard time this next 100 miles I expect. If it was difficult to drag downhill over this belt, it will probably be a good deal more difficult to drag up. Luckily the tracks are fairly distinct, though we only see our cairns when less than a mile away; 45 miles to the next depôt and 6 days' food in hand – then pick up 7 days' food (T. −22°) and 90 miles to go to the 'Three Degree' Depôt. Once there we ought to be safe, but we ought to have a day or two in hand on arrival and may have difficulty with following the tracks. However, if we can get a rating sight for our watches tomorrow we should be independent of the tracks at a pinch.

Monday, January 22. – 10,000. Temp. –21°. I think about the most tiring march we have had; solid pulling the whole way, in spite of the light sledge and some little helping wind at first. Then in the last part of the afternoon the sun came out, and almost immediately we had the whole surface covered with soft snow.

We got away sharp at 8 and marched a solid 9 hours, and thus we have covered 14.5 miles (geo.) but, by Jove! it has been a grind. We are just about on the 89th parallel. Tonight Bowers got a rating sight. I'm afraid we have passed out of the wind area. We are within 2½ miles of the 64th camp cairn, 30 miles from our depôt, and with 5 days' food in hand. Ski boots are beginning to show signs of wear; I trust we shall have no giving out of ski or boots, since there are yet so many miles to go. I thought we were climbing today, but the barometer gives no change.

Tuesday, January 23. – Lowest Minimum last night –30°, Temp. at start –28°. Lunch height 10,100. Temp. with wind 6 to 7, –19°. Little wind and heavy marching at start. Then wind increased and we did 8.7 miles by lunch, when it was practically blowing a blizzard. The old tracks show so remarkably well that we can follow them without much difficulty – a great piece of luck.

In the afternoon we had to reorganise. Could carry a whole sail. Bowers hung on to the sledge, Evans and Oates had to lengthen out. We came along at a great rate and should have got within an easy march of our depôt had not Wilson suddenly discovered that Evans's nose was frostbitten – it was white and hard. We thought it best to camp at 6.45. Got the tent up with some difficulty, and now pretty cosy after good hoosh.

There is no doubt Evans is a good deal run down – his fingers are badly blistered and his nose is rather seriously congested with frequent frost bites. He is very much annoyed with himself, which is not a good sign. I think Wilson, Bowers and I are as fit as possible under the circumstances. Oates gets cold feet. One way and another, I shall be glad to get off the summit! We are only about 13 miles from our 'Degree and half' Depôt and should get there tomorrow. The weather seems to be breaking up. Pray God we have something of a track to follow to the Three Degree Depôt – once we pick that up we ought to be right.

Wednesday, January 24. – Lunch Temp. –8°. Things beginning to look a little serious. A strong wind at the start has developed into a full blizzard at lunch, and we have had to get into our sleeping-bags. It was a bad march, but we covered 7 miles. At first Evans, and then Wilson went ahead to scout for tracks. Bowers guided the sledge alone for the first hour, then both Oates and he remained alongside it; they had a fearful time trying to make the pace between the soft patches. At 12.30 the sun coming ahead made it impossible to see the tracks further, and we had to stop. By this time the gale was at its height and we had the dickens of a time getting up the tent, cold fingers all round. We are only 7 miles from our depôt, but I made sure we should be there tonight. This is the second full gale since we left the Pole. I don't like the look of it. Is the weather breaking up? If so, God help us, with the tremendous summit journey and scant food. Wilson and Bowers are my standby. I don't like the easy way in which Oates and Evans get frostbitten.

Thursday, January 25. – Temp. Lunch –11°, Temp. Night –16°. Thank God we found our Half Degree Depôt. After lying in our bags yesterday afternoon and all night, we debated breakfast; decided to have it later and go without lunch. At the time the gale seemed as bad as ever, but during breakfast the sun showed and there was light enough to see the old track. It was a long and terribly cold job digging out our sledge and breaking camp, but we got through and on the march without sail, all pulling. This was about 11, and at about 2.30, to our joy, we saw the red depôt flag. We had lunch and left with 9½ days' provisions, still following the track – marched till 8 and covered over 5 miles, over 12 in the day. Only 89 miles (geogr.) to the next depôt, but it's time we cleared off this plateau. We are not without ailments: Oates suffers from a very cold foot; Evans's fingers and nose are in a bad state, and tonight Wilson is suffering tortures from his eyes. Bowers and I are the only members of the party without troubles just at present. The weather still looks unsettled, and I fear a succession of blizzards at this time of year; the wind is strong from the south, and this afternoon has been very helpful with the full sail. Needless to say I shall sleep much better with our provision

bag full again. The only real anxiety now is the finding of the
Three Degree Depôt. The tracks seem as good as ever so far;
sometimes for 30 or 40 yards we lose them under drifts, but then
they reappear quite clearly raised above the surface. If the light is
good there is not the least difficulty in following. Blizzards are
our bugbear, not only stopping our marches, but the cold damp
air takes it out of us. Bowers got another rating sight tonight – it
was wonderful how he managed to observe in such a horribly
cold wind. He has been on ski today whilst Wilson walked by the
sledge or pulled ahead of it.

Friday, January 26. – Temp. −17°. Height 9700, must be high
barometer. Started late, 8.50 – for no reason, as I called the hands
rather early. We must have fewer delays. There was a good stiff
breeze and plenty of drift, but the tracks held. To our old blizzard
camp of the 7th we got on well, 7 miles. But beyond the camp
we found the tracks completely wiped out. We searched for
some time, then marched on a short way and lunched, the
weather gradually clearing, though the wind holding. Knowing
there were two cairns at four mile intervals, we had little anxiety
till we picked up the first far on our right, then steering right by
a stroke of fortune, and Bowers's sharp eyes caught a glimpse of
the second far on the left. Evidently we made a bad course
outward at this part. There is not a sign of our tracks between
these cairns, but the last, marking our night camp of the 6th, No.
59, is in the belt of hard sastrugi, and I was comforted to see signs
of the track reappearing as we camped. I hope to goodness we can
follow it tomorrow. We marched 16 miles (geo.) today, but made
good only 15.4.

Saturday, January 27. – R.10. Temp. −16° (lunch), −14.3° (evening). Minimum −19°. Height 9900. Barometer low? Called the
hands half an hour late, but we got away in good time. The
forenoon march was over the belt of storm-tossed sastrugi; it
looked like a rough sea. Wilson and I pulled in front on ski, the
remainder on foot. It was very tricky work following the track,
which pretty constantly disappeared, and in fact only showed itself
by faint signs anywhere – a foot or two of raised sledge-track, a
dozen yards of the trail of the sledge-meter wheel, or a spatter of
hard snow-flicks where feet had trodden. Sometimes none of these
were distinct, but one got an impression of lines which guided.

The trouble was that on the outward track one had to shape course constantly to avoid the heaviest mounds, and consequently there were many zig-zags. We lost a good deal over a mile by these halts, in which we unharnessed and went on the search for signs. However, by hook or crook, we managed to stick on the old track. Came on the cairn quite suddenly, marched past it, and camped for lunch at 7 miles. In the afternoon the sastrugi gradually diminished in size and now we are on fairly level ground today, the obstruction practically at an end, and, to our joy, the tracks showing up much plainer again. For the last two hours we had no difficulty at all in following them. There has been a nice helpful southerly breeze all day, a clear sky and comparatively warm temperature. The air is dry again, so that tents and equipment are gradually losing their icy condition imposed by the blizzard conditions of the past week.

Our sleeping-bags are slowly but surely getting wetter and I'm afraid it will take a lot of this weather to put them right. However, we all sleep well enough in them, the hours allowed being now on the short side. We are slowly getting more hungry, and it would be an advantage to have a little more food, especially for lunch. If we get to the next depôt in a few marches (it is now less than 60 miles and we have a full week's food) we ought to be able to open out a little, but we can't look for a real feed till we get to the pony food depôt. A long way to go, and, by Jove, this is tremendous labour.

Sunday, January 28. – Lunch, –20°. Height, night, 10,130. R.11. Supper Temp. –18°. Little wind and heavy going in forenoon. We just ran out 8 miles in 5 hours and added another 8 in 3 hours 40 mins. in the afternoon with a good wind and better surface. It is very difficult to say if we are going up or down hill; the barometer is quite different from outward readings. We are 43 miles from the depôt, with six days' food in hand. We are camped opposite our lunch cairn of the 4th, only half a day's march from the point at which the last supporting party left us.

Three articles were dropped on our outward march – Oates's pipe, Bowers's fur mits, and Evans's night boots. We picked up the boots and mits on the track, and tonight we found the pipe lying placidly in sight on the snow. The sledge tracks were very easy to follow today; they are becoming more and more raised, giving a good line shadow often visible half a mile ahead. If this goes on and the weather holds we shall get our depôt without trouble. I shall indeed be glad to get it on the sledge. We are getting more hungry, there is no doubt. The lunch meal is beginning to seem inadequate. We are pretty thin, especially Evans, but none of us are feeling worked out. I doubt if we could drag heavy loads, but we can keep going well with our light one. We talk of food a good deal more, and shall be glad to open out on it.

Monday, January 29. – R.12. Lunch Temp. –23°. Supper Temp. –25°. Height 10,000. Excellent march of 19½ miles, 10.5 before lunch. Wind helping greatly, considerable drift; tracks for the most part very plain. Some time before lunch we picked up the return track of the supporting party, so that there are now three distinct sledge impressions. We are only 24 miles from our depôt – an easy day and a half. Given a fine day tomorrow we ought to get it without difficulty. The wind and sastrugi are S.S.E. and S.E. If the weather holds we ought to do the rest of the inland ice journey in little over a week. The surface is very much altered since we passed out. The loose snow has been swept into heaps, hard and wind-tossed. The rest has a glazed appearance, the loose drifting snow no doubt acting on it, polishing it like a sand blast. The sledge with our good wind behind runs splendidly on it; it is all soft and sandy beneath the glaze. We are certainly getting hungrier every day. The day after tomorrow we should be able to increase allowances. It is monotonous work, but, thank God, the miles are coming fast at last. We ought not to be delayed much now with the down-grade in front of us.

Tuesday, January 30. – R.13. 9860. Lunch Temp. –25°, Supper Temp. –24.5°. Thank the Lord, another fine march – 19 miles. We have passed the last cairn before the depôt, the track is clear ahead, the weather fair, the wind helpful, the gradient down – with any luck we should pick up our depôt in the middle of the morning march. This is the bright side; the reverse of the medal is serious. Wilson has strained a tendon in his leg; it has given pain all day and is swollen tonight. Of course, he is full of pluck over it, but I don't like the idea of such an accident here. To add to the trouble Evans has dislodged two finger-nails tonight; his hands are really bad, and to my surprise he shows signs of losing heart over it. He hasn't been cheerful since the accident. The wind shifted from

S.E. to S. and back again all day, but luckily it keeps strong. We can get along with bad fingers, but it [will be] a mighty serious thing if Wilson's leg doesn't improve.

Wednesday, January 31. – 9800. Lunch Temp. –20°, Supper Temp. –20°. The day opened fine with a fair breeze; we marched on the depôt,* picked it up, and lunched an hour later. In the afternoon the surface became fearfully bad, the wind dropped to light southerly air. Ill luck that this should happen just when we have only four men to pull. Wilson rested his leg as much as possible by walking quietly beside the sledge; the result has been good, and tonight there is much less inflammation. I hope he will be all right again soon, but it is trying to have an injured limb in the party. I see we had a very heavy surface here on our outward march. There is no doubt we are travelling over undulations, but the inequality of level does not make a great difference to our pace; it is the sandy crystals that hold us up. There has been very great ablation of the surface since we were last here – the sledge tracks stand high. This afternoon we picked up Bowers's ski† – the last thing we have to find on the summit, thank Heaven! Now we have only to go north and so shall welcome strong winds.

Thursday, February 1. – R.15. 9778. Lunch Temp. –20°, Supper Temp. –19.8°. Heavy collar work most of the day. Wind light. Did 8 miles, 4¼ hours. Started well in the afternoon and came down a steep slope in quick time; then the surface turned real bad – sandy drifts – very heavy pulling. Working on past 8 p.m. we just fetched a lunch cairn of December 29, when we were only a week out from the depôt.§ It ought to be easy to get in with a margin, having 8 days' food in hand (full feeding). We have opened out on the ⅐th increase and it makes a lot of difference. Wilson's leg much better. Evans's fingers now very bad, two nails coming off, blisters burst.

Friday, February 2. – 9340. R.16. Temp.: Lunch –19°, Supper –17°. We started well on a strong southerly wind. Soon got to a steep grade, when the sledge overran and upset us one after another. We got off our ski, and pulling on foot reeled off 9 miles

* Three Degree Depôt.

† Left on December 31.

§ The Upper Glacier Depôt, under Mount Darwin, where the first supporting party turned back.

by lunch at 1.30. Started in the afternoon on foot, going very strong. We noticed a curious circumstance towards the end of the forenoon. The tracks were drifted over, but the drifts formed a sort of causeway along which we pulled. In the afternoon we soon came to a steep slope – the same on which we exchanged sledges on December 28. All went well till, in trying to keep the track at the same time as my feet, on a very slippery surface, I came an awful 'purler' on my shoulder. It is horribly sore tonight and another sick person added to our tent – three out of five injured, and the most troublesome surfaces to come. We shall be lucky if we get through without serious injury. Wilson's leg is better, but might easily get bad again, and Evans's fingers.

At the bottom of the slope this afternoon we came on a confused sea of sastrugi. We lost the track. Later, on soft snow, we picked up E. Evans's return track, which we are now following. We have managed to get off 17 miles. The extra food is certainly helping us, but we are getting pretty hungry. The weather is already a trifle warmer, the altitude lower, and only 80 miles or so to Mount Darwin. It is time we were off the summit – pray God another four days will see us pretty well clear of it. Our bags are getting very wet and we ought to have more sleep.

Saturday, February 3. – R.17. Temp.: Lunch –20°; Supper –20°. Height 9040 feet. Started pretty well on foot; came to steep slope with crevasses (few). I went on ski to avoid another fall, and we took the slope gently with our sail, constantly losing the track, but picked up a much weathered cairn on our right. Vexatious delays, searching for tracks, &c., reduced morning march to 8.1 miles. Afternoon, came along a little better, but again lost tracks on hard slope. Tonight we are near camp of December 26, but cannot see cairn. Have decided it is waste of time looking for tracks and cairn, and shall push on due north as fast as we can.

The surface is greatly changed since we passed outward, in most places polished smooth, but with heaps of new toothed sastrugi which are disagreeable obstacles. Evans's fingers are going on as well as can be expected, but it will be long before he will be able to help properly with the work. Wilson's leg much better, and my shoulder also, though it gives bad twinges. The extra food is doing us all good, but we ought to have more sleep. Very few more days on the plateau I hope.

Sunday, February 4. – R.18. 8620 feet. Temp.: Lunch –22°; Supper –23°. Pulled on foot in the morning over good hard surface and covered 9.7 miles. Just before lunch unexpectedly fell into crevasses, Evans and I together – a second fall for Evans, and I camped. After lunch saw disturbance ahead, and what I took for disturbance (land) to the right. We went on ski over hard shiny descending surface. Did very well, especially towards end of march, covering in all 18.1. We have come down some hundreds of feet. Half way in the march the land showed up splendidly, and I decided to make straight for Mt Darwin, which we are rounding. Every sign points to getting away off this plateau. The temperature is 20° lower than when we were here before; the party is not improving in condition, especially Evans, who is becoming rather dull and incapable.* Thank the Lord we have good food at each meal, but we get hungrier in spite of it. Bowers is splendid, full of energy and bustle all the time. I hope we are not going to have trouble with ice-falls.

Monday, February 5. – R.19. Lunch, 8320 ft., Temp. –17°; Supper, 8120 ft., Temp. –17.2°. A good forenoon, few crevasses; we covered 10.2 miles. In the afternoon we soon got into difficulties. We saw the land very clearly, but the difficulty is to get at it. An hour after starting we came on huge pressures and great street crevasses partly open. We had to steer more and more to the west, so that our course was very erratic. Late in the march we turned more to the north and again encountered open crevasses across our track. It is very difficult manoeuvring amongst these and I should not like to do it without ski.

We are camped in a very disturbed region, but the wind has fallen very light here, and our camp is comfortable for the first time for many weeks. We may be anything from 25 to 30 miles from our depôt, but I wish to goodness one could see a way through the disturbances ahead. Our faces are much cut up by all the winds we have had, mine least of all; the others tell me they feel their noses more going with than against wind. Evans's nose is almost as bad as his fingers. He is a good deal crocked up.

Tuesday, February 6. – Lunch 7900; Supper 7210. Temp. –15° [R.20]. We've had a horrid day and not covered good mileage. On turning out found sky overcast; a beastly position amidst crevasses.

* The result of concussion in the morning's fall.

Luckily it cleared just before we started. We went straight for Mt Darwin, but in half an hour found ourselves amongst huge open chasms, unbridged, but not very deep, I think. We turned to the north between two, but to our chagrin they converged into chaotic disturbance. We had to retrace our steps for a mile or so, then struck to the west and got on to a confused sea of sastrugi, pulling very hard; we put up the sail, Evans's nose suffered, Wilson very cold, everything horrid. Camped for lunch in the sastrugi; the only comfort, things looked clearer to the west and we were obviously going downhill. In the afternoon we struggled on, got out of sastrugi and turned over on glazed surface, crossing many crevasses – very easy work on ski. Towards the end of the march we realised the certainty of maintaining a more or less straight course to the depôt, and estimate distance 10 to 15 miles.

Food is low and weather uncertain, so that many hours of the day were anxious; but this evening, though we are not as far advanced as I expected, the outlook is much more promising. Evans is the chief anxiety now; his cuts and wounds suppurate, his nose looks very bad, and altogether he shows considerable signs of being played out. Things may mend for him on the glacier, and his wounds get some respite under warmer conditions. I am indeed glad to think we shall so soon have done with plateau conditions. It took us 27 days to reach the Pole and 21 days back – in all 48 days – nearly 7 weeks in low temperature with almost incessant wind.

End of the Summit Journey

Wednesday, February 7. – Mount Darwin [or Upper Glacier] Depôt, R.21. Height 7100. Lunch Temp. –9°; Supper Temp. [a blank here], A wretched day with satisfactory ending. First panic, certainty that biscuit-box was short. Great doubt as to how this has come about, as we certainly haven't over-issued allowances. Bowers is dreadfully disturbed about it. The shortage is a full day's allowance. We started our march at 8.30, and travelled down slopes and over terraces covered with hard sastrugi – very tiresome work – and the land didn't seem to come any nearer. At lunch the wind increased, and what with hot tea and good food, we started the afternoon in a better frame of mind, and it soon became obvious we were nearing our mark. Soon after 6.30 we saw our depôt easily and camped next it at 7.30.

Found note from E. Evans to say the second return party passed through safely at 2.30 on January 14 – half a day longer between depôts than we have been. The temperature is higher, but there is a cold wind tonight.

Well, we have come through our 7 weeks' ice camp journey and most of us are fit, but I think another week might have had a very bad effect on P. O. Evans, who is going steadily downhill.

It is satisfactory to recall that these facts give absolute proof of both expeditions having reached the Pole and placed the question of priority beyond discussion.

Thursday, February 8. – R.22. Height 6260. Start Temp. –11°; Lunch Temp. –5°; Supper, zero. 9.2 miles. Started from the depôt rather late owing to weighing biscuit, &c., and rearranging matters. Had a beastly morning. Wind very strong and cold. Steered in for Mt Darwin to visit rock. Sent Bowers over, on ski, as Wilson can't wear his at present. He obtained several specimens, all of much the same type, a close-grained granite rock which weathers red. Hence the pink limestone. After he rejoined we skidded downhill pretty fast, leaders on ski, Oates and Wilson on foot alongside sledge – Evans detached. We lunched at 2 well down towards Mt Buckley, the wind half a gale and everybody very cold and cheerless. However, better things were to follow. We decided to steer for the moraine under Mt Buckley and, pulling with crampons, we crossed some very irregular steep slopes with big crevasses and slid down towards the rocks. The moraine was obviously so interesting that when we had advanced some miles and got out of the wind, I decided to camp and spend the rest of the day geologising. It has been extremely interesting. We found ourselves under perpendicular cliffs of Beacon sandstone, weathering rapidly and carrying veritable coal seams. From the last Wilson, with his sharp eyes, has picked several plant impressions, the last a piece of coal with beautifully traced leaves in layers, also some excellently preserved impressions of thick stems, showing cellular structure. In one place we saw the cast of small waves in the sand. Tonight Bill has got a specimen of limestone with archeocyathus – the trouble is one cannot imagine where the stone comes from; it is evidently rare, as few specimens occur in the moraine. There is a good deal of pure white quartz. Altogether we have had a most interesting afternoon, and the relief of being out of the wind and in a warmer temperature is inexpressible. I hope and trust we shall all buck up again now that the conditions are more favourable. We have been in shadow all the afternoon, but the sun has just reached us, a little obscured by night haze. A lot could be written on the delight of setting foot on rock after 14 weeks of snow and ice and nearly 7 out of sight of aught else. It is like going ashore after a sea voyage. We deserve a little good bright weather after all our trials, and hope to get a chance to dry our sleeping-bags and generally make our gear more comfortable.

Friday, February 9. – R.23. Height 5,210 ft. Lunch Temp. +10°; Supper Temp. +12.5°. About 13 miles. Kept along the edge of moraine to the end of Mt Buckley. Stopped and geologised. Wilson got great find of vegetable impression in piece of limestone. Too tired to write geological notes. We all felt very slack this morning, partly rise of temperature, partly reaction, no doubt. Ought to have kept close in to glacier north of Mt Buckley, but in bad light the descent looked steep and we kept out. Eventually we got amongst bad ice pressure and had to come down over an ice-fall. The crevasses were much firmer than expected and we got down with some difficulty, found our night camp of December 20, and lunched an hour after. Did pretty well in the afternoon, marching 3¾ hours; the sledge-meter is unshipped, so cannot tell distance traversed. Very warm on march and we are all pretty tired. Tonight it is wonderfully calm and warm, though it has been overcast all the afternoon. It is remarkable to be able to stand outside the tent and sun oneself. Our food satisfies now, but we must march to keep on the full ration, and we want rest, yet we shall pull through all right, D.V. We are by no means worn out.

Saturday, February 10. – R.24. Lunch Temp. +12°; Supper Temp. +10°. Got off a good morning march in spite of keeping too far east and getting in rough, cracked ice. Had a splendid night's sleep, showing great change in all faces, so didn't get away till 10 a.m. Lunched just before 3. After lunch the land began to be obscured. We held a course for 2½ hours with difficulty, then the sun dis-appeared, and snow drove in our faces with northerly wind – very warm and impossible to steer, so camped. After supper, still very thick all round, but sun showing and less snow falling. The fallen snow crystals are quite feathery like thistle-down. We have two full days' food left, and though our position is uncertain, we are certainly within two outward marches from the middle glacier depôt. However, if the weather doesn't clear by tomorrow, we must either march blindly on or reduce food. It is very trying. Another night to make up arrears of sleep. The ice crystals that first fell this afternoon were very large. Now the sky is clearer overhead, the temperature has fallen slightly, and the crystals are minute.

Sunday, February 11. – R.25. Lunch Temp. −6.5°; Supper −3.5°. The worst day we have had during the trip and greatly owing to our own fault. We started on a wretched surface with light S.W. wind, sail set, and pulling on ski – horrible light, which made everything look fantastic. As we went on light got worse, and suddenly we found ourselves in pressure. Then came the fatal decision to steer east. We went on for 6 hours, hoping to do a good distance, which in fact I suppose we did, but for the last hour or two we pressed on into a regular trap, Getting on to a good surface we did not reduce our lunch meal, and thought all going well, but half an hour after lunch we got into the worst ice mess I have ever been in. For three hours we plunged on on ski, first thinking we were too much to the right, then too much to the left; meanwhile the disturbance got worse and my spirits received a very rude shock. There were times when it seemed almost impossible to find a way out of the awful turmoil in which we found ourselves. At length, arguing that there must be a way on our left, we plunged in that direction. It got worse, harder, more icy and crevassed. We could not manage our ski and pulled on foot, falling into crevasses every minute – most luckily no bad accident. At length we saw a smoother slope towards the land, pushed for it, but knew it was a woefully long way from us. The turmoil changed in character, irregular crevassed surface giving way to huge chasms, closely packed and most difficult to cross. It was very heavy work, but we had grown desperate. We won through at 10 p.m. and I write after 12 hours on the march. I *think* we are on or about the right track now, but we are still a good number of miles from the depôt, so we reduced rations tonight. We had three pemmican meals left and decided to make them into four. Tomorrow's lunch must serve for two if we do not make big progress. It was a test of our endurance on the march and our fitness with small supper. We have come through well. A good wind has come down the glacier which is clearing the sky and surface. Pray God the wind holds tomorrow. Short sleep tonight and off first thing, I hope.

Monday, February 12. – R. 26. In a very critical situation. All went well in the forenoon, and we did a good long march over a fair surface. Two hours before lunch we were cheered by the sight of our night camp of the 18th December, the day after we made our depôt – this showed we were on the right track. In the afternoon, refreshed by tea, we went forward, confident of covering the remaining distance, but by a fatal chance we kept too far to the left, and then we struck uphill and, tired and despondent, arrived in a horrid maze of crevasses and fissures. Divided councils caused our course to be erratic after this, and finally, at 9 p.m. we landed in the worst place of all. After discussion we decided to camp, and here we are, after a very short supper and one meal only remaining in the food bag; the depôt doubtful in locality. We *must* get there tomorrow. Meanwhile we are cheerful with an effort. It's a tight place, but luckily we've been well fed up to the present. Pray God we have fine weather tomorrow.

[At this point the bearings of the mid-glacier depôt are given, but need not be quoted.]

Tuesday, February 13. – Camp R.27, beside Cloudmaker. Temp. –10°. Last night we all slept well in spite of our grave anxieties. For my part these were increased by my visits outside the tent, when I saw the sky gradually closing over and snow beginning to fall. By our ordinary time for getting up it was dense all around us. We could see nothing, and we could only remain in our sleeping-bags.

At 8.30 I dimly made out the land of the Cloudmaker. At 9 we got up, deciding to have tea, and with one biscuit, no pemmican, so as to leave our scanty remaining meal for eventualities. We started marching, and at first had to wind our way through an awful turmoil of broken ice, but in about an hour we hit an old moraine track, brown with dirt. Here the surface was much smoother and improved rapidly. The fog still hung over all and we went on for an hour, checking our bearings. Then the whole plain got smoother and we turned outward a little. Evans raised our hopes with a shout of depôt ahead, but it proved to be a shadow on the ice. Then suddenly Wilson saw the actual depôt flag. It was an immense relief, and we were soon in possession of our 3½ days' food. The. relief to all is inexpressible; needless to say, we camped and had a meal.

Marching in the afternoon, I kept more to the left, and closed the mountain till we fell on the stone moraines. Here Wilson detached himself and made a collection, whilst we pulled the sledge on. We camped late, abreast the lower end of the mountain, and had nearly our usual satisfying supper. Yesterday was the worst experience of the trip and gave a horrid feeling of insecurity. Now we are right, but we must march. In future food must be worked so that we do not run so short if the weather fails us. We mustn't get into a hole like this again. Greatly relieved to find that both the other parties got through safely. Evans seems to have got mixed up with pressures like ourselves. It promises to be a very fine day tomorrow. The valley is gradually clearing. Bowers has had a very bad attack of snow blindness, and Wilson another almost as bad. Evans has no power to assist with camping work.

Wednesday, February 14. – Lunch Temp. o°; Supper Temp. +1°. A fine day with wind on and off down the glacier, and we have done a fairly good march. We started a little late and pulled on down the moraine. At first I thought of going right, but soon, luckily, changed my mind and decided to follow the curving lines of the moraines. This course has brought us well out on the glacier. Started on crampons; one hour after, hoisted sail; the combined efforts produced only slow speed, partly due to the sandy snowdrifts similar to those on summit, partly to our torn sledge runners. At lunch these were scraped and sand-papered. After lunch we got on snow, with ice only occasionally showing through. A poor start, but the gradient and wind improving, we did 6½ miles before night camp.

There is no getting away from the fact that we are not pulling strong. Probably none of us: Wilson's leg still troubles him and he doesn't like to trust himself on ski; but the worst case is Evans, who is giving us serious anxiety. This morning he suddenly disclosed a huge blister on his foot. It delayed us on the march, when he had to have his crampon readjusted. Sometimes I fear he is going from bad to worse, but I trust he will pick up again when we come to steady work on ski like this afternoon. He is hungry and so is Wilson. We can't risk opening out our food again, and as cook at present I am serving something under full allowance. We are inclined to get slack and slow with our camping arrangements, and small delays increase. I have talked of the matter tonight and hope for improvement. We cannot do distance without the hours. The next depôt* some 30 miles away and nearly 3 days' food in hand.

Thursday, February 15. – R.29. Lunch Temp. +10°; Supper Temp. +4°. 13.5 miles. Again we are running short of provision. We don't know our distance from the depôt, but imagine about 20 miles. Heavy march – did 13¾ (geo.). We are pulling for food and not very strong evidently. In the afternoon it was overcast; land blotted out for a considerable interval. We have reduced food, also sleep; feeling rather done. Trust 1½ days or 2 at most will see us at depôt.

Friday, February 16. – 12.5 m. Lunch Temp. +6.1°; Supper Temp. +7°. A rather trying position. Evans has nearly broken down in brain, we think. He is absolutely changed from his normal self-reliant self. This morning and this afternoon he stopped the march on some trivial excuse. We are on short rations with not very short food; spin out till tomorrow night. We cannot be more than 10 or 12 miles from the depôt, but the weather is all against us. After lunch we were enveloped in a snow sheet, land just looming. Memory should hold the events of a very troublesome march with more troubles ahead. Perhaps all will be well if we can get to our depôt tomorrow fairly early, but it is anxious work with the sick man. But it's no use meeting troubles half way, and our sleep is all too short to write more.

Saturday, February 17. – A very terrible day. Evans looked a little better after a good sleep, and declared, as he always did, that he was quite well. He started in his place on the traces, but half an hour later worked his ski shoes adrift, and had to leave the sledge. The surface was awful, the soft recently fallen snow clogging the ski and runners at every step, the sledge groaning, the sky overcast, and the land hazy. We stopped after about one hour, and Evans came up again, but very slowly. Half an hour later he dropped out again on the same plea. He asked Bowers to lend him a piece of string. I cautioned him to come on as quickly as he could, and he answered cheerfully as I thought. We had to push on, and the

* The Lower Glacier Depôt.

remainder of us were forced to pull very hard, sweating heavily. Abreast the Monument Rock we stopped, and seeing Evans a long way astern, I camped for lunch. There was no alarm at first, and we prepared tea and our own meal, consuming the latter. After lunch, and Evans still not appearing, we looked out, to see him still afar off. By this time we were alarmed, and all four started back on ski. I was first to reach the poor man and shocked at his appearance; he was on his knees with clothing disarranged, hands uncovered and frostbitten, and a wild look in his eyes. Asked what was the matter, he replied with a slow speech that he didn't know, but thought he must have fainted. We got him on his feet, but after two or three steps he sank down again. He showed every sign of complete collapse. Wilson, Bowers, and I went back for the sledge, whilst Oates remained with him. When we returned he was practically unconscious, and when we got him into the tent quite comatose. He died quietly at 12.30 a.m. On discussing the symptoms we think he began to get weaker just before we reached the Pole, and that his downward path was accelerated first by the shock of his frostbitten fingers, and later by falls during rough travelling on the glacier, further by his loss of all confidence in himself. Wilson thinks it certain he must have injured his brain by a fall. It is a terrible thing to lose a companion in this way, but calm reflection shows that there could not have been a better ending to the terrible anxieties of the past week. Discussion of the situation at lunch yesterday shows us what a desperate pass we were in with a sick man on our hands at such a distance from home.

At 1 a.m. we packed up and came down over the pressure ridges, finding our depôt easily.

NOTE. As to the geological specimens brought back from the Beardmore Glacier, one word may be added here. The time spent in collecting, the labour endured in dragging the additional 35 lbs. to the last camp, were a heavy price to pay. But if the cost was great, the scientific value was great also. The fossils they contain, often so inconspicuous that it is a wonder they were discerned by the collectors, prove to be the most valuable obtained by the Expedition, and promise to solve completely the questions of the age and past history of this portion of the Antarctic Continent.

CHAPTER TWENTY

The last march[25]

Sunday, February 18. – R.32. Temp. –5.5°. At Shambles Camp. We gave ourselves 5 hours' sleep at the lower glacier depôt after the horrible night, and came on at about 3 today to this camp, coming fairly easily over the divide. Here with plenty of horsemeat we have had a fine supper, to be followed by others such, and so continue a more plentiful era if we can keep good marches up. New life seems to come with greater food almost immediately, but I am anxious about the Barrier surfaces.

Monday, February 19. – Lunch T. –16°. It was late (past noon) before we got away today, as I gave nearly 8 hours sleep, and much camp work was done shifting sledges* and fitting up new one with mast, &c., packing horsemeat and personal effects. The surface was every bit as bad as I expected, the sun shining brightly on it and its covering of soft loose sandy snow. We have come out about 2' on the old tracks. Perhaps lucky to have a fine day for this and our camp work, but we shall want wind or change of sliding conditions to do anything on such a surface as we have got. I fear there will not be much change for the next 3 or 4 days.

R.33. Temp. –17°. We have struggled out 4.6 miles in a short day over a really terrible surface – it has been like pulling over desert sand, not the least glide in the world. If this goes on we shall have a bad time, but I sincerely trust it is only the result of this windless area close to the coast and that, as we are making steadily outwards, we shall shortly escape it. It is perhaps premature to be anxious about covering distance. In all other respects things are improving. We have our sleeping-bags spread on the sledge and they are drying, but, above all, we have our full measure of food again. Tonight we had a sort of stew fry of pemmican and horseflesh, and voted it the best hoosh we had ever had on a sledge

* Sledges were left at the chief depôts to replace damaged ones.

journey. The absence of poor Evans is a help to the commissariat, but if he had been here in a fit state we might have got along faster. I wonder what is in store for us, with some little alarm at the lateness of the season.

Monday, February 20. – R.34. Lunch Temp. –13°; Supper Temp. –15°. Same terrible surface; four hours' hard plodding in morning brought us to our Desolation Camp, where we had the four-day blizzard. We looked for more pony meat, but found none. After lunch we took to ski with some improvement of comfort. Total mileage for day 7 – the ski tracks pretty plain and easily followed this afternoon. We have left another cairn behind. Terribly slow progress, but we hope for better things as we clear the land. There is a tendency to cloud over in the S.E. tonight, which may turn to our advantage. At present our sledge and ski leave deeply ploughed tracks which can be seen winding for miles behind. It is distressing, but as usual trials are forgotten when we camp, and good food is our lot. Pray God we get better travelling as we are not so fit as we were, and the season is advancing apace.

Tuesday, February 21. – R.35. Lunch Temp. +9½°; Supper Temp. –11°. Gloomy and overcast when we started; a good deal warmer. The marching almost as bad as yesterday. Heavy toil all day, inspiring gloomiest thoughts at times. Rays of comfort when we picked up tracks and cairns. At lunch we seemed to have missed the way, but an hour or two after we passed the last pony walls, and since, we struck a tent ring, ending the march actually on our old pony-tracks. There is a critical spot here with a long stretch between cairns. If we can tide that over we get on the regular cairn route, and with luck should stick to it; but everything depends on the weather. We never won a march of 8½ miles with greater difficulty, but we can't go on like this. We are drawing away from the land and perhaps may get better things in a day or two. I devoutly hope so.

Wednesday, February 22. – R.36. Supper Temp. –2°. There is little doubt we are in for a rotten critical time going home, and the lateness of the season may make it really serious. Shortly after starting today the wind grew very fresh from the S.E. with strong surface drift. We lost the faint track immediately, though covering ground fairly rapidly. Lunch came without sight of the cairn we had hoped to pass. In the afternoon, Bowers being sure we were too far to the west, steered out. Result, we have passed another pony camp without seeing it. Looking at the map tonight there is no doubt we are too far to the east. With clear weather we ought to be able to correct the mistake, but will the weather get clear? It's a gloomy position, more especially as one sees the same difficulty recurring even when we have corrected this error. The wind is dying down tonight and the sky clearing in the south, which is hopeful. Meanwhile it is satisfactory to note that such untoward events fail to damp the spirit of the party. Tonight we had a pony hoosh so excellent and filling that one feels really strong and vigorous again.

Thursday, February 23. – R.37. Lunch Temp. −9.8°; Supper Temp. −12°. Started in sunshine, wind almost dropped. Luckily Bowers took a round of angles and with help of the chart we fogged out that we must be inside rather than outside tracks. The data were so meagre that it seemed a great responsibility to march out and we were none of us happy about it. But just as we decided to lunch, Bowers's wonderful sharp eyes detected an old double lunch cairn, the theodolite telescope confirmed it, and our spirits rose accordingly. This afternoon we marched on and picked up another cairn; then on and camped only 2½ miles from the depôt. We cannot see it, but, given fine weather, we cannot miss it. We are, therefore, extraordinarily relieved. Covered 8.2 miles in 7 hours, showing we can do 10 to 12 on this surface. Things are again looking up, as we are on the regular line of cairns, with no gaps right home, I hope.

Friday, February 24. – Lunch. Beautiful day – too beautiful – an hour after starting loose ice crystals spoiling surface. Saw depôt and reached it middle forenoon. Found store in order except shortage oil [26] – shall have to be very saving with fuel – otherwise have ten full days' provision from tonight and shall have less than 70 miles to go. Note from Meares who passed through December 15, saying surface bad; from Atkinson, after fine marching (2¼ days from pony depôt), reporting Keohane better after sickness. Short note from Evans, not very cheerful, saying surface bad, temperature high. Think he must have been a little anxious.[*] It is an immense relief to have picked up this depôt and, for the time, anxieties are thrust aside. There is no doubt we have been

---

[*] It will be remembered that he was already stricken with scurvy.

rising steadily since leaving the Shambles Camp. The coastal Barrier descends except where glaciers press out. Undulation still, but flattening out. Surface soft on top, curiously hard below. Great difference now between night and day temperatures. Quite warm as I write in tent. We are on tracks with half-march cairn ahead; have covered 4½ miles. Poor Wilson has a fearful attack snow-blindness consequent on yesterday's efforts. Wish we had more fuel.

Night camp R.38. Temp. −17°. A little despondent again. We had a really terrible surface this afternoon and only covered 4 miles. We are on the track just beyond a lunch cairn. It really will be a bad business if we are to have this plodding all through. I don't know what to think, but the rapid closing of the season is ominous. It is great luck having the horsemeat to add to our ration. Tonight we have had a real fine 'hoosh'. It is a race between the season and hard conditions and our fitness and good food.

Saturday, February 25. − Lunch Temp. −12°. Managed just 6 miles this morning. Started somewhat despondent; not relieved when pulling seemed to show no improvement. Bit by bit surface grew better, less sastrugi, more glide, slight following wind for a time. Then we began to travel a little faster. But the pulling is still *very* hard; undulations disappearing but inequalities remain.

Twenty-six Camp walls about 2 miles ahead, all tracks in sight − Evans's track very conspicuous. This is something in favour, but the pulling is tiring us, though we are getting into better ski drawing again. Bowers hasn't quite the trick and is a little hurt at my criticisms, but I never doubted his heart. Very much easier − write diary at lunch − excellent meal − now one pannikin very strong tea − four biscuits and butter.

Hope for better things this afternoon, but no improvement apparent. Oh! for a little wind − E. Evans evidently had plenty.

R.39. Temp. −20°. Better march in afternoon. Day yields 11.4 miles − the first double figure of steady dragging for a long time, but it meant and will mean hard work if we can't get a wind to help us. Evans evidently had a strong wind here, S.E. I should think. The temperature goes very low at night now when the sky is clear as at present. As a matter of fact this is wonderfully fine weather − the only drawback the spoiling of the surface and absence of wind. We see all tracks very plain, but the pony-walls have evidently been badly drifted up. Some kind people had substituted a cairn at last camp.[27] The old cairns do not seem to have suffered much.

Sunday, February 26. – Lunch Temp. –17°. Sky overcast at start, but able see tracks and cairn distinct at long distance. Did a little better, 6½ miles to date. Bowers and Wilson now in front. Find great relief pulling behind with no necessity to keep attention on track. Very cold nights now and cold feet starting march, as day footgear doesn't dry at all. We are doing well on our food, but we ought to have yet more. I hope the next depôt, now only 50 miles, will find us with enough surplus to open out. The fuel shortage still an anxiety.

R.40. Temp. –21°. Nine hours' solid marching has given us 11½ miles. Only 43 miles from the next depôt. Wonderfully fine weather but cold, very cold. Nothing dries and we get our feet cold too often. We want more food yet and especially more fat. Fuel is woefully short. We can scarcely hope to get a better surface at this season, but I wish we could have some help from the wind, though it might shake us up badly if the temp. didn't rise.

Monday, February 27. –Desperately cold last night: –33° when we got up, with –37° minimum. Some suffering from cold feet, but all got good rest. We must open out on food soon. But we have done 7 miles this morning and hope for some 5 this afternoon. Overcast sky and good surface till now, when sun shows again. It is good to be marching the cairns up, but there is still much to be anxious about. We talk of little but food, except after meals. Land disappearing in satisfactory manner. Pray God we have no further set-backs. We are naturally always discussing possibility of meeting dogs, where and when, &c. It is a critical position. We may find ourselves in safety at next depôt, but there is a horrid element of doubt.

Camp R.41. Temp. –32°. Still fine clear weather but very cold – absolutely calm tonight. We have got off an excellent march for these days (12.2) and are much earlier than usual in our bags. 31 miles to depôt, 3 days' fuel at a pinch, and 6 days' food. Things begin to look a little better; we can open out a little on food from tomorrow night, I think.

Very curious surface – soft recent sastrugi which sink underfoot, and between, a sort of flaky crust with large crystals beneath.

Tuesday, February 28. – Lunch. Thermometer went below –40° last night; it was desperately cold for us, but we had a fair night. I decided to slightly increase food; the effect is undoubtedly good. Started marching in –32° with a slight north-westerly breeze blighting. Many cold feet this morning; long time over foot gear, but we are earlier. Shall camp earlier and get the chance of a good night, if not the reality. Things must be critical till we reach the depôt, and the more I think of matters, the more I anticipate their remaining so after that event. Only 24½ miles from the depôt. The sun shines brightly, but there is little warmth in it. There is no doubt the middle of the Barrier is a pretty awful locality.

Camp 42. Splendid pony hoosh sent us to bed and sleep happily after a horrid day, wind continuing; did 11½ miles. Temp. not quite so low, but expect we are in for cold night (Temp. –27°).

Wednesday, February 29. – Lunch. Cold night. Minimum Temp. –37.5°; –30° with north-west wind, force 4, when we got up. Frightfully cold starting; luckily Bowers and Oates in their last new finnesko; keeping my old ones for present. Expected awful march and for first hour got it. Then things improved and we camped after 5½ hours marching close to lunch camp – 22½. Next camp is our depôt and it is exactly 13 miles. It ought not to take more than 1½ days; we pray for another fine one. The oil will just about spin out in that event, and we arrive 3 clear days' food in hand. The increase of ration has had an enormously beneficial result. Mountains now looking small. Wind still very light from west – cannot understand this wind.

Thursday, March 1. – Lunch. Very cold last night – minimum –41.5°. Cold start to march, too, as usual now. Got away at 8 and have marched within sight of depôt; flag something under 3 miles away. We did 11½ yesterday and marched 6 this morning. Heavy dragging yesterday and very heavy this morning. Apart from sledging considerations the weather is wonderful. Cloudless days and nights and the wind trifling. Worse luck, the light airs come from the north and keep us horribly cold. For this lunch hour the exception has come. There is a bright and comparatively warm sun. All our gear is out drying.

Friday, March 2. – Lunch. Misfortunes rarely come singly. We marched to the [Middle Barrier] depôt fairly easily yesterday afternoon, and since that have suffered three distinct blows which have placed us in a bad position. First we found a shortage of oil; with most rigid economy it can scarce carry us to the next depôt on this surface [71 miles away]. Second, Titus Oates disclosed his feet, the toes showing very bad indeed, evidently bitten by the late temperatures. The third blow came in the night, when the wind, which we had hailed with some joy, brought dark overcast weather. It fell below −40° in the night, and this morning it took 1½ hours to get our foot gear on, but we got away before eight. We lost cairn and tracks together and made as steady as we could N. by W., but have seen nothing. Worse was to come – the surface is simply awful. In spite of strong wind and full sail we have only done 5½ miles. We are in a very queer street since there is no doubt we cannot do the extra marches and feel the cold horribly.

Saturday, March 3. – Lunch. We picked up the track again yesterday, finding ourselves to the eastward. Did close on 10 miles and things looked a trifle better; but this morning the outlook is blacker than ever. Started well and with good breeze; for an hour made good headway; then the surface grew awful beyond words. The wind drew forward; every circumstance was against us. After 4¼ hours things so bad that we camped, having covered 4½ miles. [R.46] One cannot consider this a fault of our own – certainly we were pulling hard this morning – it was more than three parts surface which held us back – the wind at strongest, powerless to move the sledge. When the light is good it is easy to see the reason. The surface, lately a very good hard one, is coated with a thin layer of woolly crystals, formed by radiation no doubt. These are too firmly fixed to be removed by the wind and cause impossible friction on the runners. God help us, we can't keep up this pulling, that is certain. Amongst ourselves we are unendingly cheerful, but what each man feels in his heart I can only guess. Putting on foot gear in the morning is getting slower and slower, therefore every day more dangerous.

Sunday, March 4. – Lunch. Things looking very black indeed. As usual we forgot our trouble last night, got into our bags, slept splendidly on good hoosh, woke and had another, and started marching. Sun shining brightly, tracks clear, but surface covered with sandy frost-rime. All the morning we had to pull with all our strength, and in 4½ hours we covered 3½ miles. Last night it was overcast and thick, surface bad; this morning sun shining and surface as bad as ever. One has little to hope for except perhaps strong dry wind – an unlikely contingency at this time of year. Under the immediate surface crystals is a hard sastrugi surface, which must have been excellent for pulling a week or two ago. We are about 42 miles from the next depôt and have a week's food, but only about 3 to 4 days' fuel – we are as economical of the latter as one can possibly be, and we cannot afford to save food and pull as we are pulling. We are in a very tight place indeed, but none of us despondent *yet*, or at least we preserve every semblance of good cheer, but one's heart sinks as the sledge stops dead at some sastrugi behind which the surface sand lies thickly heaped. For the moment the temperature is on the −20° – an improvement which makes us much more comfortable, but a colder snap is bound to come again soon. I fear that Oates at least will weather such an event very poorly. Providence to our aid! We can expect little from man now except the possibility of extra food at the next depôt. It will be real bad if we get there and find the same shortage of oil. Shall we get there? Such a short distance it would have appeared to us on the summit! I don't know what I should do if Wilson and Bowers weren't so determinedly cheerful over things.

Monday, March 5. – Lunch. Regret to say going from bad to worse. We got a slant of wind yesterday afternoon, and going on 5 hours we converted our wretched morning run of 3½ miles into something over 9. We went to bed on a cup of cocoa and pemmican solid with the chill off. (R.47) The result is telling on all, but mainly on Oates, whose feet are in a wretched condition. One swelled up tremendously last night and he is very lame this morning. We started march on tea and pemmican as last night – we pretend to prefer the pemmican this way. Marched for 5 hours this morning over a slightly better surface covered with high moundy sastrugi. Sledge capsized twice; we pulled on foot, covering about 5½ miles. We are two pony marches and 4 miles about from our depôt. Our fuel dreadfully low and the poor Soldier nearly done. It is pathetic enough because we can do nothing for him; more hot food might do a little, but only a little, I fear. We none of us expected these terribly low temperatures, and of the rest of us Wilson is feeling them most; mainly, I fear, from his self-sacrificing devotion in doctoring Oates's feet. We cannot help each other, each has enough to do to take care of himself. We get cold on the march when the trudging is heavy, and the wind pierces our worn garments. The others, all of them, are unendingly cheerful when in the tent. We mean to see the game through with a proper spirit, but it's tough work to be pulling harder than we ever pulled in our lives for long hours, and to feel that the progress is so slow. One can only say 'God help us!' and plod on our weary way, cold and very miserable, though outwardly cheerful. We talk of all sorts of subjects in the tent, not much of food now, since we decided to take the risk of running a full ration. We simply couldn't go hungry at this time.

Tuesday, March 6. – Lunch. We did a little better with help of wind yesterday afternoon, finishing 9½ miles for the day, and 27 miles from depôt. [R.48] But this morning things have been awful. It was warm in the night and for the first time during the journey I overslept myself by more than an hour; then we were slow with foot gear; then, pulling with all our might (for our lives) we could scarcely advance at rate of a mile an hour; then it grew thick and three times we had to get out of harness to search for tracks. The result is something less than 3½ miles for the forenoon. The sun is shining now and the wind gone. Poor Oates is unable to pull, sits on the sledge when we are track-searching – he is wonderfully plucky, as his feet must be giving him great pain. He makes no complaint, but his spirits only come up in spurts now, and he grows more silent in the tent. We are making a spirit lamp to try and replace the primus when our oil is exhausted. It will be a very poor substitute and we've not got much spirit. If we could have kept up our 9-mile days we might have got within reasonable distance of the depôt before running out, but nothing but a strong wind and good surface can help us now, and though we had quite a good breeze this morning, the sledge came as heavy as lead. If we were all fit I should have hopes of getting through, but the poor Soldier has become a terrible hindrance, though he does his utmost and suffers much I fear.

Wednesday, March 7. – A little worse I fear. One of Oates's feet very bad this morning; he is wonderfully brave. We still talk of what we will do together at home.

We only made 6½ miles yesterday. [R.49] This morning in 4½ hours we did just over 4 miles. We are 16 from our depôt. If we only find the correct proportion of food there and this surface continues, we may get to the next depôt [Mt Hooper, 72 miles farther] but not to One Ton Camp. We hope against hope that the dogs have been to Mt Hooper: then we might pull through. If there is a shortage of oil again we can have little hope. One feels that for poor Oates the crisis is near, but none of us are improving, though we are wonderfully fit considering the really excessive work we are doing. We are only kept going by good food. No wind this morning till a chill northerly air came ahead. Sun bright and cairns showing up well. I should like to keep the track to the end.

Thursday, March 8. – Lunch. Worse and worse in morning; poor Oates's left foot can never last out, and time over foot gear something awful. Have to wait in night foot gear for nearly an hour before I start changing, and then am generally first to be ready. Wilson's feet giving trouble now, but this mainly because he gives so much help to others. We did 4½ miles this morning and are now 8½ miles from the depôt – a ridiculously small distance to feel in difficulties, yet on this surface we know we cannot equal half our old marches, and that for that effort we expend nearly double the energy. The great question is, What shall we find at the depôt? If the dogs have visited it we may get along a good distance, but if there is another short allowance of fuel, God help us indeed. We are in a very bad way, I fear, in any case.

Saturday, March 10. – Things steadily downhill. Oates's foot worse. He has rare pluck and must know that he can never get through. He asked Wilson if he had a chance this morning, and of course Bill had to say he didn't know. In point of fact he has none. Apart from him, if he went under now, I doubt whether we could get through. With great care we might have a dog's chance, but no more. The weather conditions are awful, and our gear gets steadily more icy and difficult to manage. At the same time of course poor Titus is the greatest handicap. He keeps us waiting in the morning until we have partly lost the warming effect of our good breakfast, when the only wise policy is to be up and away at once; again at lunch. Poor chap! it is too pathetic to watch him; one cannot but try to cheer him up.

Yesterday we marched up the depôt, Mt Hooper. Cold comfort. Shortage on our allowance all round. I don't know that anyone is to blame. The dogs which would have been our salvation have evidently failed.* Meares had a bad trip home I suppose.

This morning it was calm when we breakfasted, but the wind came from the W.N.W. as we broke camp. It rapidly grew in strength. After travelling for half an hour I saw that none of us could go on facing such conditions. We were forced to camp and are spending the rest of the day in a comfortless blizzard camp, wind quite foul. [R. 52.]

Sunday, March 11. – Titus Oates is very near the end, one feels. What we or he will do, God only knows. We discussed the matter after breakfast; he is a brave fine fellow and understands the situation, but he practically asked for advice. Nothing could be said but to urge him to march as long as he could. One satisfactory result to the discussion; I practically ordered Wilson to hand over the means of ending our troubles to us, so that any one of us may know how to do so. Wilson had no choice between doing so and our ransacking the medicine case. We have 30 opium tabloids apiece and he is left with a tube of morphine. So far the tragical side of our story. [R.53]

The sky completely overcast when we started this morning. We could see nothing, lost the tracks, and doubtless have been swaying a good deal since – 3.1 miles for the forenoon – terribly heavy dragging – expected it. Know that 6 miles is about the limit of our endurance now, if we get no help from wind or surfaces. We have 7 days' food and should be about 55 miles from One Ton Camp tonight, 6 x 7 = 42, leaving us 13 miles short of our distance, even if things get no worse. Meanwhile the season rapidly advances.

---

* For the last six days the dogs had been waiting at One Ton Camp under Cherry-Garrard and Demetri. The supporting party had come out as arranged on the chance of hurrying the Pole travellers back over the last stages of their journey in time to catch the ship. Scott had dated his probable return to Hut Point anywhere between mid-March and early April. Calculating from the speed of the other return parties, Dr Atkinson looked for him to reach One Ton Camp between March 3 and 10. Here Cherry-Garrard met four days of blizzard; then there remained little more than enough dog food to bring the teams home. He could either push south one more march and back, at imminent risk of missing Scott on the way, or stay two days at the Camp where Scott was bound to come, if he came at all. His wise decision, his hardships and endurance are recounted by Dr Atkinson in Volume Two, 'The Last Year at Cape Evans'.

Monday, March 12. – We did 6.9 miles yesterday, under our necessary average. Things are left much the same, Oates not pulling much, and now with hands as well as feet pretty well useless. We did 4 miles this morning in 4 hours 20 min. – we may hope for 3 this afternoon, 7 x 6 = 42. We shall be 47 miles from the depôt. I doubt if we can possibly do it. The surface remains awful, the cold intense, and our physical condition running down. God help us! Not a breath of favourable wind for more than a week, and apparently liable to head winds at any moment.

Wednesday, March 14. – No doubt about the going downhill, but everything going wrong for us. Yesterday we woke to a strong northerly wind with temp. −37°. Couldn't face it, so remained in camp [R. 54] till 2, then did 5¼ miles. Wanted to march later, but party feeling the cold badly as the breeze (N.) never took off entirely, and as the sun sank the temp. fell. Long time getting supper in dark. [R. 55.]

This morning started with southerly breeze, set sail and passed another cairn at good speed; half-way, however, the wind shifted to W. by S. or W.S.W., blew through our wind clothes and into our mits. Poor Wilson horribly cold, could [not] get off ski for some time. Bowers and I practically made camp, and when we got into the tent at last we were all deadly cold. Then temp. now midday down −43° and the wind strong. We must go on, but now the making of every camp must be more difficult and dangerous. It must be near the end, but a pretty merciful end. Poor Oates got it again in the foot. I shudder to think what it will be like tomorrow. It is only with greatest pains rest of us keep off frostbites. No idea there could be temperatures like this at this time of year with such winds. Truly awful outside the tent. Must fight it out to the last biscuit, but can't reduce rations.

Friday, March 16 *or Saturday* 17. – Lost track of dates, but think the last correct. Tragedy all along the line. At lunch, the day before yesterday, poor Titus Oates said he couldn't go on; he proposed we should leave him in his sleeping-bag. That we could not do, and we induced him to come on, on the afternoon march. In spite of its awful nature for him he struggled on and we made a few miles. At night he was worse and we knew the end had come.

Should this be found I want these facts recorded. Oates's last thoughts were of his Mother, but immediately before he took pride in thinking that his regiment would be pleased with the bold way in which he met his death. We can testify to his bravery. He has borne intense suffering for weeks without complaint, and to the very last was able and willing to discuss outside subjects. He did not – would not – give up hope till the very end. He was a brave soul. This was the end. He slept through the night before last, hoping not to wake; but he woke in the morning – yesterday. It was blowing a blizzard. He said, 'I am just going outside and may be some time.' He went out into the blizzard and we have not seen him since.

I take this opportunity of saying that we have stuck to our sick companions to the last. In case of Edgar Evans, when absolutely out of food and he lay insensible, the safety of the remainder seemed to demand his abandonment, but Providence mercifully removed him at this critical moment. He died a natural death, and we did not leave him till two hours after his death. We knew that poor Oates was walking to his death, but though we tried to dissuade him, we knew it was the act of a brave man and an English gentleman. We all hope to meet the end with a similar spirit, and assuredly the end is not far.

I can only write at lunch and then only occasionally. The cold is intense, –40° at midday. My companions are unendingly cheerful, but we are all on the verge of serious frostbites, and though we constantly talk of fetching through I don't think any one of us believes it in his heart.

We are cold on the march now, and at all times except meals. Yesterday we had to lay up for a blizzard and today we move dreadfully slowly. We are at No. 14 pony camp, only two pony marches from One Ton Depôt. We leave here our theodolite, a camera, and Oates's sleeping-bags. Diaries, &c., and geological specimens carried at Wilson's special request, will be found with us or on our sledge.

Sunday, March 18. – Today, lunch, we are 21 miles from the depôt. Ill fortune presses, but better may come. We have had more wind and drift from ahead yesterday; had to stop marching; wind N.W., force 4, temp. –35°. No human being could face it, and we are worn out *nearly*.

My right foot has gone, nearly all the toes – two days ago I was proud possessor of best feet. These are the steps of my downfall. Like an ass I mixed a small spoonful of curry powder with my melted pemmican – it gave me violent indigestion. I lay awake and in pain all night; woke and felt done on the march; foot went and I didn't know it. A very small measure of neglect and have a foot which is not pleasant to contemplate. Bowers takes first place in condition, but there is not much to choose after all. The others are still confident of getting through – or pretend to be – I don't know! We have the last *half* fill of oil in our primus and a very small quantity of spirit – this alone between us and thirst. The wind is fair for the moment, and that is perhaps a fact to help. The mileage would have seemed ridiculously small on our outward journey.

Monday, March 19. – Lunch. We camped with difficulty last night and were dreadfully cold till after our supper of cold pemmican and biscuit and a half a pannikin of cocoa cooked over the spirit. Then, contrary to expectation, we got warm and all slept well. Today we started in the usual dragging manner. Sledge dreadfully heavy. We are 15½ miles from the depôt and ought to get there in three days. What progress! We have two days' food but barely a day's fuel. All our feet are getting bad – Wilson's best, my right foot worst, left all right. There is no chance to nurse one's feet till we can get hot food into us. Amputation is the least I can hope for now, but will the trouble spread? That is the serious question. The weather doesn't give us a chance – the wind from N. to N.W. and −40° temp. today.

Wednesday, March 21. – Got within 11 miles of depôt Monday night;[*] had to lay up all yesterday in severe blizzard.[27] Today forlorn hope, Wilson and Bowers going to depôt for fuel.

Thursday, March 22 *and* 23. – Blizzard bad as ever – Wilson and Bowers unable to start – tomorrow last chance – no fuel and only one or two of food left – must be near the end. Have decided it shall be natural – we shall march for the depôt with or without our effects and die in our tracks.

Thursday, March 29. – Since the 21st we have had a continuous gale from W.S.W. and S.W. We had fuel to make two cups of tea apiece and bare food for two days on the 20th. Every day we

* The 60th camp from the Pole.

have been ready to start for our depôt *11 miles* away, but outside the door of the tent it remains a scene of whirling drift. I do not think we can hope for any better things now. We shall stick it out to the end, but we are getting weaker, of course, and the end cannot be far.

It seems a pity, but I do not think I can write more.

R. SCOTT

For God's sake look after our people.

* * *

Wilson and Bowers were found in the attitude of sleep, their sleeping-bags closed over their heads as they would naturally close them.

Scott died later. He had thrown back the flaps of his sleeping-bag and opened his coat. The little wallet containing the three notebooks was under his shoulders and his arm flung across Wilson. So they were found eight months later.

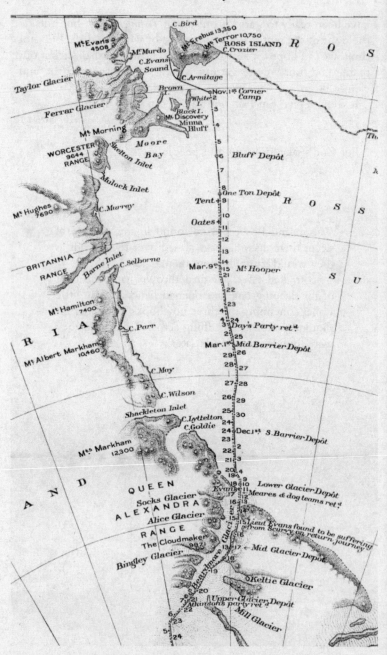

Main Southern Journey: Cape Evans to Queen Alexandra Range

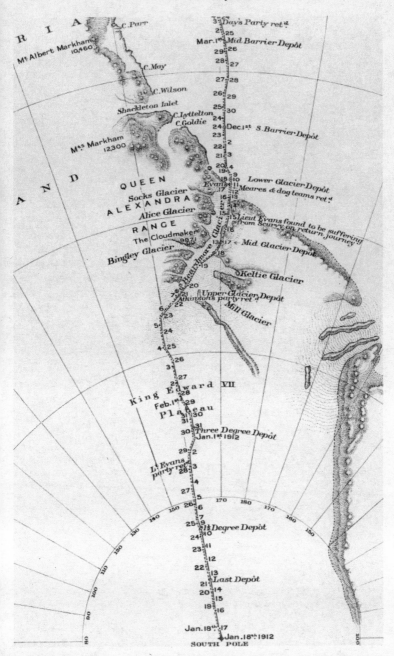

Main Southern Journey: Queen Alexandra Range to the South Pole

FAREWELL LETTERS

With the diaries in the tent were found the following letters.

To Mrs E. A. Wilson

MY DEAR MRS WILSON,

If this letter reaches you Bill and I will have gone out together.
We are very near it now and I should like you to know how
splendid he was at the end – everlastingly cheerful and ready
to sacrifice himself for others, never a word of blame to me for
leading him into this mess. He is not suffering, luckily, at least
only minor discomforts.

His eyes have a comfortable blue look of hope and his mind
is peaceful with the satisfaction of his faith in regarding himself as part of the great scheme of the Almighty. I can do
no more to comfort you than to tell you that he died as he
lived, a brave, true man – the best of comrades and staunchest
of friends.

My whole heart goes out to you in pity,

Yours,

R. SCOTT

To Mrs Bowers

MY DEAR MRS BOWERS,

I am afraid this will reach you after one of the heaviest blows of
your life.

I write when we are very near the end of our journey, and I
am finishing it in company with two gallant, noble gentlemen.
One of these is your son. He had come to be one of my closest
and soundest friends, and I appreciate his wonderful upright
nature, his ability and energy. As the troubles have thickened his
dauntless spirit ever shone brighter and he has remained cheerful, hopeful, and indomitable to the end.

The ways of Providence are inscrutable, but there must be some reason why such a young, vigorous and promising life is taken.

My whole heart goes out in pity for you.

Yours,

R. Scott

To the end he has talked of you and his sisters. One sees what a happy home he must have had and perhaps it is well to look back on nothing but happiness.

He remains unselfish, self-reliant and splendidly hopeful to the end, believing in God's mercy to you.

To Sir J. M. Barrie

MY DEAR BARRIE,

We are pegging out in a very comfortless spot. Hoping this letter may be found and sent to you, I write a word of farewell . . . More practically I want you to help my widow and my boy – your godson. We are showing that Englishmen can still die with a bold spirit, fighting it out to the end. It will be known that we have accomplished our object in reaching the Pole, and that we have done everything possible, even to sacrificing ourselves in order to save sick companions. I think this makes an example for Englishmen of the future, and that the country ought to help those who are left behind to mourn us. I leave my poor girl and your godson, Wilson leaves a widow, and Edgar Evans also a widow in humble circumstances. Do what you can to get their claims recognised. Goodbye. I am not at all afraid of the end, but sad to miss many a humble pleasure which I had planned for the future on our long marches. I may not have proved a great explorer, but we have done the greatest march ever made and come very near to great success. Goodbye, my dear friend,

Yours ever,

R. Scott

We are in a desperate state, feet frozen, &c. No fuel and a long way from food, but it would do your heart good to be in our tent, to hear our songs and the cheery conversation as to what we will do when we get to Hut Point.

Later. – We are very near the end, but have not and will not lose our good cheer. We have four days of storm in our tent and nowhere's food or fuel . . . We did intend to finish ourselves when things proved like this, but we have decided to die naturally in the track.

As a dying man, my dear friend, be good to my wife and child. Give the boy a chance in life if the State won't do it. He ought to have good stuff in him . . . I never met a man in my life whom I admired and loved more than you, but I never could show you how much your friendship meant to me, for you had much to give and I nothing.

To the Right Hon. Sir Edgar Speyer, Bart.
                              Dated March 16, 1912. Lat. 79.5°

MY DEAR SIR EDGAR,
I hope this may reach you. I fear we must go and that it leaves the Expedition in a bad muddle. But we have been to the Pole and we shall die like gentlemen. I regret only for the women we leave behind.

I thank you a thousand times for your help and support and your generous kindness. If this diary is found it will show how we stuck by dying companions and fought the thing out well to the end. I think this will show that the Spirit of pluck and the power to endure has not passed out of our race . . .

Wilson, the best fellow that ever stepped, has sacrificed himself again and again to the sick men of the party . . .

I write to many friends hoping the letters will reach them some time after we are found next year.

We very nearly came through, and it's a pity to have missed it, but lately I have felt that we have overshot our mark. No one is to blame and I hope no attempt will be made to suggest that we have lacked support.

Goodbye to you and your dear kind wife.
                              Yours ever sincerely,
                                    R. SCOTT

To Vice-Admiral Sir Francis Charles Bridgeman, K.C.F.O., K.C.B.

MY DEAR SIR FRANCIS,
I fear we have slipped up; a close shave; I am writing a few letters
which I hope will be delivered some day. I want to thank you
for the friendship you gave me of late years, and to tell you how
extraordinarily pleasant I found it to serve under you. I want to
tell you that I was not too old for this job. It was the younger
men that went under first . . . After all we are setting a good
example to our countrymen, if not by getting into a tight place,
by facing it like men when we were there. We could have come
through had we neglected the sick. Goodbye, and goodbye to
dear Lady Bridgeman.

Yours ever,
R. SCOTT

Excuse writing – it is –40, and has been for nigh a month.

To Vice-Admiral Sir George le Clerc Egerton, K.C.B.

MY DEAR SIR GEORGE,
I fear we have shot our bolt – but we have been to Pole and
done the longest journey on record.

I hope these letters may find their destination some day.

Subsidiary reasons of our failure to return are due to the
sickness of different members of the party, but the real thing that
has stopped us is the awful weather and unexpected cold towards
the end of the journey.

This traverse of the Barrier has been quite three times as severe
as any experience we had on the summit.

There is no accounting for it, but the result has thrown out my
calculations, and here we are little more than 100 miles from the
base and petering out.

Goodbye. Please see my widow is looked after as far as Admiralty is concerned.

R. SCOTT

My kindest regards to Lady Egerton. I can never forget all your
kindness.

To Mr J. J. Kinsey – Christchurch

March 24th, 1912

MY DEAR KINSEY,

I'm afraid we are pretty well done – four days of blizzard just as we were getting to the last depôt. My thoughts have been with you often. You have been a brick. You will pull the expedition through, I'm sure.

My thoughts are for my wife and boy. Will you do what you can for them if the country won't.

I want the boy to have a good chance in the world, but you know the circumstances well enough.

If I knew the wife and boy were in safe keeping I should have little regret in leaving the world, for I feel that the country need not be ashamed of us – our journey has been the biggest on record, and nothing but the most exceptional hard luck at the end would have caused us to fail to return. We have been to the S. pole as we set out. God bless you and dear Mrs Kinsey. It is good to remember you and your kindness.

Your friend,

R. SCOTT

Letters to his Mother, his Wife, his Brother-in-law (Sir William Ellison Macartney), Admiral Sir Lewis Beaumont, and Mr and Mrs Reginald Smith were also found, from which come the following extracts.

The Great God has called me and I feel it will add a fearful blow to the heavy ones that have fallen on you in life. But take comfort in that I die at peace with the world and myself – not afraid.

Indeed it has been most singularly unfortunate, for the risks I have taken never seemed excessive.

. . . I want to tell you that we have missed getting through by a narrow margin which was justifiably within the risk of such a journey . . . After all, we have given our lives for our country – we have actually made the longest journey on record, and we have been the first Englishmen at the South Pole.

You must understand that it is too cold to write much.

. . . It's a pity the luck doesn't come our way, because every detail of equipment is right.

I shall not have suffered any pain, but leave the world fresh from harness and full of good health and vigour.

Since writing the above we got to within 11 miles of our depôt, with one hot meal and two days' cold food. We should have got through but have been held for *four* days by a frightful storm. I think the best chance has gone. We have decided not to kill ourselves, but to fight to the last for that depôt, but in the fighting there is a painless end.

Make the boy interested in natural history if you can; it is better than games; they encourage it at some schools. I know you will keep him in the open air.

Above all, he must guard and you must guard him against indolence. Make him a strenuous man. I had to force myself into being strenuous as you know – had always an inclination to be idle.

There is a piece of the Union Jack I put up at the South Pole in my private kit bag, together with Amundsen's black flag and other trifles. Send a small piece of the Union Jack to the King and a small piece to Queen Alexandra.

What lots and lots I could tell you of this journey. How much better has it been than lounging in too great comfort at home. What tales you would have for the boy. But what a price to pay.

Tell Sir Clements I thought much of him and never regretted his putting me in command of the *Discovery*.

MESSAGE TO THE PUBLIC

The causes of the disaster are not due to faulty organisation, but to misfortune in all risks which had to be undertaken.

1. The loss of pony transport in March 1911 obliged me to start later than I had intended, and obliged the limits of stuff transported to be narrowed.

2. The weather throughout the outward journey, and especially the long gale in 83° S., stopped us.

3. The soft snow in lower reaches of glacier again reduced pace.

We fought these untoward events with a will and conquered, but it cut into our provision reserve.

Every detail of our food supplies, clothing and depôts made on the interior ice-sheet and over that long stretch of 700 miles to the Pole and back, worked out to perfection. The advance party would have returned to the glacier in fine form and with surplus of food, but for the astonishing failure of the man whom we had least expected to fail. Edgar Evans was thought the strongest man of the party.

The Beardmore Glacier is not difficult in fine weather, but on our return we did not get a single completely fine day; this with a sick companion enormously increased our anxieties.

As I have said elsewhere we got into frightfully rough ice and Edgar Evans received a concussion of the brain – he died a natural death, but left us a shaken party with the season unduly advanced.

But all the facts above enumerated were as nothing to the surprise which awaited us on the Barrier. I maintain that our arrangements for returning were quite adequate, and that no one in the world would have expected the temperatures and surfaces which we encountered at this time of the year. On the summit in lat. 85° 86° we had −20°, −30°. On the Barrier in lat. 82°, 10,000 feet lower, we had −30° in the day, −47° at night pretty regularly, with continuous head wind during our day marches. It is clear that these circumstances come on very suddenly, and our wreck is certainly due to this sudden advent of severe weather, which does not seem to have any satisfactory cause. I do not think human beings ever came through such a month as we have come through, and we should have got through in spite of the weather but for the sickening of a second companion, Captain Oates, and a shortage of fuel in our depôts for which I cannot account, and finally, but for the storm which has fallen on us within 11 miles of the depôt at which we hoped to secure our final supplies. Surely misfortune could scarcely have exceeded this last blow. We arrived within 11 miles of our old One Ton Camp with fuel for one last meal and food for two days. For four days we have been unable to leave the tent – the gale howling about as. We are weak, writing is difficult, but for my own sake I do not regret this journey, which has shown that Englishmen can endure hardships, help one another, and meet death with as great a fortitude as ever in the past. We took risks, we knew we took them; things have come out against us, and therefore we have no cause for complaint, but bow to the will of Providence, determined still to do our best to the last. But if we have been willing to give our lives to this enterprise, which is for the honour of our country, I appeal to our countrymen to see that those who depend on us are properly cared for.

Had we lived, I should have had a tale to tell of the hardihood, endurance, and courage of my companions which would have stirred the heart of every Englishman. These rough notes and our dead bodies must tell the tale, but surely, surely, a great rich country like ours will see that those who are dependent on us are properly provided for.

R. SCOTT

APPENDIX: NOTES

Note 1. – Dogs. These included thirty-three sledging dogs and a collie bitch, 'Lassie'. The thirty-three, all Siberian dogs excepting the Esquimaux 'Peary' and 'Borup', were collected by Mr Meares, who drove them across Siberia to Vladivostok with the help of the dog-driver Demetri Gerof, whom he had engaged for the expedition. From Vladivostok, where he was joined by Lieutenant Wilfred Bruce, he brought them by steamer to Sydney, and thence to Lyttelton.

The dogs were the gift of various schools, as shown by the following list.

DOGS PRESENTED BY SCHOOLS, ETC.

School's, &c. name for dog	Russian name of dog	Translation, description or nickname of dog	Name of School, &c., that presented dog
Beaumont	Kumgai	Isle off Vladivostok	Beaumont College
Bengeo	Mannike Noogis	Little Leader	Bengeo, Herts
Bluecoat	Giliak	Indian tribe	Christ's Hospital
Bristol	Lappa Uki	Lop Ears	Grammar, Bristol
Bromsgrove	'Peary'	'Peary'	Bromsgrove School (cost of transport)
Colston's	Bullet	Bullet	Colston's School
Danum	Rabchick	Grouse	Doncaster Grammar
Derby I	Suka	Lassie	Girls' Secondary School, Derby
Derby II	Silni	Stocky	Secondary Technical School, Derby
Devon	Jolti	Yellowboy	Devonshire House Branch, Navy League
Duns	Brodiaga	Robber	Berwickshire High School
Falcon	Seri	Grey	High School, Winchester
Felsted	Visoli	Jollyboy	Felsted School
Glebe	Pestry	Piebald	Glebe House School

School's, &c. name for dog	Russian name of dog	Translation, description or nickname of dog	Name of School, &c., that presented dog
Grassendale	Suhoi II	Lanky	Grassendale School
Hal	Krisravitsa	Beauty	Colchester Royal Grammar School
Hampstead	Ishak	Jackass	South Hampstead High School (Girls)
Hughie	Gerachi	Ginger	Master H. Gethin Lewis
Ilkley	Wolk	Wolf	Ilkley Grammar
Innie	Suhoi I	Lanky	Liverpool Institute
Jersey	Bear	Bear	Victoria College, Jersey
John Bright	Seri Uki	Grey Ears	Bootham
Laleham	Biela Noogis	White Leader	Laleham
Leighton	Pudil	Poodle	Leighton Park, Reading
Lyon	Tresor	Treasure	Lower School of J. Lyon
Mac	Deek I	Wild One	Wells House
Manor	Colonel	Colonel	Manor House
Mount	Vesoi	One Eye	Mount, York
Mundella	Bulli	Bullet	Mundella Secondary
Oakfield	Ruggiola Sabaka	'Gun Dog' (Hound)	Oakfield School, Rugby
Oldham	Vaida	Christian name	Hulme Grammar School, Oldham
Perse	Vaska	Lady's name	Perse Grammar
Poacher	Malchick Chorney Stareek	Black Old Man	Grammar School, Lincoln
Price Llewelyn	Hohol	Little Russian	Intermediate, Llandudno Wells
Radlyn	Czigane	Gipsy	Radlyn, Harrogate
Richmond	Osman	Christian name	Richmond, Yorks
Regent	Marakas Seri	Grey	Regent Street Polytechnic
Steyne	Petichka	Little Bird	Steyne, Worthing
Sir Andrew	Deek II	Wild One	Sir Andrew Judd's Commercial School
Somerset	Churnie Kesoi	One eye	A Somerset School
Tiger	Mukáka	Monkey	Bournemouth School
Tom	Stareek	Old Man	Woodbridge
Tuar Golleniai	Julik	Scamp	Intermediate School, Cardiff
Vic	Glinie	Long Nose	Modern, Southport
Whitgift	Mamuke Rabchick	Little Grouse	Whitgift Grammar
Winston	Borup	Borup	Winston Higher Grade School (cost transport)
	Meduate	Lion	N.Z. Girls' School

Note 2. – Those who are named in these opening pages were all keen supporters of the Expedition. Sir George Clifford, Bart., and Messrs. Arthur and George Rhodes were friends from Christchurch. Mr M. J. Miller, Mayor of Lyttelton, was a master shipwright and contractor, who took great interest in both the *Discovery* and the *Terra Nova*, and stopped the leak in the latter vessel which had been so troublesome on the voyage out. Mr Anderson belonged to the firm of John Anderson & Sons, engineers, who own Lyttelton Foundry. Mr Kinsey was the trusted friend and representative who acted as the representative of Captain Scott in New Zealand during his absence in the South. Mr Wyatt was business manager to the Expedition.

Note 3. – Dr Wilson writes: I must say I enjoyed it all from beginning to end, and as one bunk became unbearable after another, owing to the wet, and the comments became more and more to the point as people searched out dry spots here and there to finish the night in oilskins and greatcoats on the cabin or wardroom seats, I thought things were becoming interesting.

Some of the staff were like dead men with sea-sickness. Even so Cherry-Garrard and Wright and Day turned out with the rest of us and alternately worked and were sick.

I have no sea-sickness on these ships myself under any conditions, so I enjoyed it all, and as I have the run of the bridge and can ask as many questions as I choose, I knew all that was going on.

All Friday and Friday night we worked in two parties, two hours on and two hours off; it was heavy work filling and handing up huge buckets of water as fast as they could be given from one to the other from the very bottom of the stokehold to the upper deck, up little metal ladders all the way. One was of course wet through the whole time in a sweater and trousers and sea boots, and every two hours one took these off and hurried in for a rest in a greatcoat, to turn out again in two hours and put on the same cold sopping clothes, and so on until 4 a.m. on Saturday, when we had baled out between four and five tons of water and had so lowered it that it was once more possible to light fires and try the engines and the steam pump again and to clear the valves and the inlet which was once more within reach. The fires had been put out at 11.40 a.m. and were then out for twenty-two hours while we baled. It was a weird night's work with the howling gale and the darkness and the immense seas running over the ship every few minutes and no engines and no sail, and we all in the engine-room, black as ink with engine-room oil and bilge water, singing chanties as we passed up slopping buckets full of bilge, each man above slopping a little over the heads of all below him; wet through to the skin, so much so that some of the party worked altogether naked like Chinese coolies; and the rush of the wave backwards and forwards at the bottom grew hourly less in the dim light of a couple of engine-room oil lamps whose light just made the darkness visible, the ship all the time rolling like a sodden lifeless log, her lee gunwale under water every time.

December 3. We were all at work till 4 a.m. and then were all told off to sleep till 8 a.m. At 9.30 a.m. we were all on to the main hand pump, and, lo and behold! it worked, and we pumped and pumped till 12.30, when the ship was once more only as full of bilge water as she always is and the position was practically solved.

There was one thrilling moment in the midst of the worst hour on Friday when we were realising that the fires must be drawn, and when every pump had failed to act, and when the bulwarks began to go to pieces and the petrol cases were all afloat and going overboard, and the word was suddenly passed in a shout from the hands at work in the waist of the ship trying to save petrol cases that smoke was coming up through the seams in the after hold. As this was full of coal and patent fuel and was next the engine-room, and as it had not been opened for the airing, it required to get rid of gas on account of the flood of water on deck making it impossible to open the hatchways; the possibility of a fire there was patent to everyone and it could not possibly have been dealt with in any way short of opening the hatches and flooding the ship, when she must have foundered. It was therefore a thrilling moment or two until it was discovered that the smoke was really steam, arising from the bilge at the bottom having risen to the heated coal.

Note 4. – *December* 26. We watched two or three immense blue whales at fairly short distance; this is *Balaenoptera Sibbaldi*. One sees first a small dark hump appear and then immediately a jet of grey fog squirted upwards fifteen to eighteen feet, gradually spreading as it rises vertically into the frosty air. I have been nearly in these blows once or twice and had the moisture in my face with a sickening smell of shrimpy oil. Then the bump elongates and up rolls an immense blue-grey or blackish grey round back with a faint ridge along the top, on which presently appears a small hook-like dorsal fin, and then the whole sinks and disappears. [Dr Wilson's Journal]

Note 5. – *December* 18. Watered ship at a tumbled floe. Sea ice when pressed up into large hummocks gradually loses all its salt. Even when sea water freezes it squeezes out the great bulk of its salt as a solid, but the sea water gets into it by soaking again, and yet when held out of the water, as it is in a hummock, the salt all drains out and the melted ice is blue and quite good for drinking, engines, &c. [Dr Wilson's Journal]

Note 6. – It may be added that in contradistinction to the nick-names of Skipper conferred upon Evans, and Mate on Campbell, Scott himself was known among the afterguard as The Owner.

Note 7. – (Penguins) They have lost none of their attractiveness, and are most comical and interesting; as curious as ever, they will always come up at a trot when we sing to them, and you may often see a group of explorers on the poop singing 'For she's got bells on her fingers and rings on her toes, elephants to ride upon wherever she goes', and so on at the top of their voices to an admiring group of Adélie penguins. Meares is the greatest attraction; he has a full voice which is musical but always very flat. He declares that 'God save the King' will always send them to the water, and certainly it is often successful. [Dr Wilson's Journal]

Note 8. – We were to examine the possibilities of landing, but the swell was so heavy in its break among the floating blocks of ice along the actual beach and ice foot that a landing was out of the question. We should have broken up the boat and have all been in the water together. But I assure you it was tantalising to me, for there about 6 feet above us on a small dirty piece of the old bay ice about ten feet square one living Emperor penguin chick was standing disconsolately stranded, and close by stood one faithful old Emperor parent asleep. This young Emperor was still in the down, a most interesting fact in the bird's life history at which we had rightly guessed, but which no one had actually observed before. It was in a stage never yet seen or collected, for the wings were already quite clean of down and feathered as in the adult, also a line down the breast was shed of down, and part of the head. This bird would have been a treasure to me, but we could not risk life for it, so it had to remain where it was. It was a curious fact that with as much clean ice to live on as they could have wished for, these destitute derelicts of a flourishing colony now gone north to sea on floating bay ice should have preferred to remain standing on the only piece of bay ice left, a piece about ten feet square and now pressed up six feet above water level, evidently wondering why it was so long in starting north with the general exodus which must have taken place just a month ago. The whole incident was most interesting and full of suggestion as to the slow working of the brain of these queer people. Another point was most weird to see, that on the *under* side of this very dirty piece of sea ice, which was about two feet thick and which hung over the water as a sort of cave, we could see the legs and lower halves of dead Emperor chicks hanging through, and even in one place a dead adult. I hope to make a picture of the whole quaint incident, for it was a corner crammed full of Imperial history in the light of what we already knew, and it would otherwise have been about as unintelligible as any group of animate or inanimate nature could possibly have been. As it is, it throws more light on the life history of this strangely primitive bird. . . .

We were joking in the boat as we rowed under these cliffs and saying it would be a short-lived amusement to see the overhanging cliff part company and fall over us. So we were glad to find that we were rowing back to the ship and already 200 or 300 yards away from the place and in open water when there was a noise like crackling thunder and a huge plunge into the sea and a smother of rock dust like the smoke of an explosion, and we realised that the very thing had happened which we had just been talking about. Altogether it was a very exciting row, for before we got on board we had the pleasure of seeing the ship shoved in so close to these cliffs by a belt of heavy pack ice that to us it appeared a toss-up whether she got out again or got forced in against the rocks. She had no time or room to turn and get clear by backing out through the belt of pack stern first, getting heavy bumps under the counter and on the rudder as she did so, for the ice was heavy and the swell considerable. [Dr Wilson's Journal]

Note 9. – Dr Wilson writes in his Journal: *January* 14. He also told me the plans for our depôt journey on which we shall be starting in about ten days' time. He wants me to be a dog driver with himself, Meares, and Teddie Evans, and this is what I would have chosen had I had a free choice at all. The dogs run in two teams and each team wants two men. It means a lot of running as they are being driven now, but it is the fastest and most interesting work of all, and we go ahead of the whole caravan with lighter loads and at a faster rate; moreover, if any traction except ourselves can reach the top of Beardmore Glacier, it will be the dogs, and the dog drivers are therefore the people who will have the best chance of doing the top piece of the ice cap at 10,000 feet to the Pole. May I be there! About this time next year may I be there or thereabouts! With so many young bloods in the heyday of youth and strength beyond my own I feel there will be a most difficult task in making choice towards the end and a most keen competition – *and* a universal lack of selfishness and self-seeking with a complete absence of any jealous feeling in any single one of the comparatively large number who at present stand a chance of being on the last piece next summer.

It will be an exciting time and the excitement has already begun in the healthiest possible manner. I have never been thrown in with a more unselfish lot of men – each one doing his utmost fair and square in the most cheery manner possible.

As late as October 15 he writes further: 'No one yet knows who will be on the Summit party: it is to depend on condition, and fitness when we get there.' It is told of Scott, while still in New Zealand, that being pressed on the point, he playfully said, 'Well, I should like to have Bill to hold my hand when we get to the Pole'; but the Diary shows how the actual choice was made on the march.

Note 10. – Campbell, Levick, and Priestley set off to the old *Nimrod* hut eight miles away to see if they could find a stove of convenient size for their own hut, as well as any additional paraffin, and in default of the latter, to kill some seals for oil.

Note 11. – The management of stores and transport was finally entrusted to Bowers. Rennick therefore remained with the ship. A story told by Lady Scott illustrates the spirit of these men – the expedition first, personal distinctions nowhere. It was in New Zealand and the very day on which the order had been given for Bowers to exchange with Rennick. In the afternoon Captain Scott and his wife were returning from the ship to the house where they were staying; on the hill they saw the two men coming down with arms on each other's shoulders – a fine testimony to both. 'Upon my word,' exclaimed Scott, 'that shows Rennick in a good light!'

Note 12. – *January* 29. The seals have been giving a lot of trouble, that is just to Meares and myself with our dogs. The whole teams go absolutely crazy when they sight them or get wind of them, and there are literally hundreds along some of the cracks. Occasionally when one pictures oneself quite away from trouble of that kind, an old seal will pop his head up at a blowhole a few yards ahead of the team, and they are all on top of him before one can say 'Knife'! Then one has to rush in with the whip – and every one of the team of eleven jumps over the harness of the dog next to him and the harnesses become a muddle that takes much patience to unravel, not to mention care lest the whole team should get away with the sledge and its load and leave one behind to follow on foot at leisure. I never did get left the whole of this depôt journey, but I was often very near it and several times had only time to seize a strap or a part of the sledge and be dragged along helter-skelter over everything that came in the way till the team got sick of galloping and one could struggle to one's feet again. One gets very wary and wide awake when one has to manage a team of eleven dogs and a sledge load by oneself, but it was a most interesting experience, and I had a delightful leader, 'Stareek' by name – Russian for 'Old Man', and he was the most wise old man. We have to use Russian terms with all our dogs. 'Ki Ki' means go to the right, 'Chui' means go to the left, 'Esh to' means lie down – and the remainder are mostly swear words which mean everything else which one has to say to a dog team. Dog driving like this in the orthodox manner is a very different thing to the beastly dog driving we perpetrated in the *Discovery* days. I got to love all my team and they got to know me well, and my old leader even now, six months after I have had anything to do with him, never fails to come and speak to me whenever he sees me, and he knows me and my voice ever so far off. He is quite a ridiculous 'old man' and quite the nicest, quietest, cleverest old dog I have ever come across. He looks in face as if he knew all the wickedness of all the world and all its cares and as if he were bored to death by them. [Dr Wilson's Journal]

Note 13. – *February* 15. There were also innumerable subsidences of the surface – the breaking of crusts over air spaces under them, large areas of dropping a ¼ inch or so with a hushing sort of noise or muffled report. My leader Stareek, the nicest and wisest old dog in both teams, thought there was a rabbit under the crust every time one gave way close by him and he would jump sideways with both feet on the spot and his nose in the snow. The action was like a flash and never checked the team – it was most amusing. I have another funny little dog, Mukáka, small but very game and a good worker. He is paired with a fat, lazy and very greedy black dog, Nugis by name, and in every march this sprightly little Mukáka will once or twice notice that Nugis is not pulling and will jump over the trace, bite Nugis like a snap, and be back again in his own place before the fat dog knows what has happened. [Dr Wilson's Journal]

Note 13a. – Taking up the story from the point where eleven of the thirteen dogs had been brought to the surface, Mr Cherry-Garrard's Diary records:

This left the two at the bottom. Scott had several times wanted to go down. Bill said to me that he hoped he wouldn't, but now he insisted. We found the Alpine rope would reach, and then lowered Scott down to the platform, sixty feet below. I thought it very plucky. We then hauled the two dogs up on the rope, leaving Scott below. Scott said the dogs were very glad to see him; they had curled up asleep – it was wonderful they had no bones broken.

Then Meares's dogs, which were all wandering about loose, started fighting our team, and we all had to leave Scott and go and separate them, which took some time. They fixed on Noogis (I) badly. We then hauled Scott up: it was all three of us could do – fingers a good deal frost-bitten at the end. That was all the dogs. Scott has just said that at one time he never hoped to get back the thirteen or even half of them. When he was down in the crevasse he wanted to go off exploring, but we dissuaded him. Of course it was a great opportunity. He kept on saying, ' I wonder why this is running the way it is – you expect to find them at right angles.'

Scott found inside crevasse warmer than above, but had no thermometer. It is a great wonder the whole sledge did not drop through: the inside was like the cliff of Dover.

Note 14. – *February* 28. Meares and I led off with a dog team each, and leaving the Barrier we managed to negotiate the first long pressure ridge of the sea ice where the seals all lie, without much trouble – the dogs were running well and fast and we kept on the old tracks, still visible, by which we had come out in January, heading a long way out to make a wide detour round the open water off Cape Armitage, from which a very wide extent of thick black fog, 'frost smoke' as we call it, was rising on our right. This completely obscured our view of the open water, and the only suggestion it gave me was that the thaw pool off the Cape was much bigger than when we passed it in January and that we should probably have to make a detour of three or four miles round it to reach Hut Point instead of one or two. I still thought it was not impossible to reach Hut Point this way, so we went on, but before we had run two miles on the sea ice we noticed that we were coming on to an area broken up by fine threadlike cracks evidently quite fresh, and as I ran along by the sledge I paced them and found they curved regularly at every 30 paces, which could only mean that they were caused by a swell. This suggested to me that the thaw pool off Cape Armitage was even bigger than I thought and that we were getting on to ice which was breaking up, to flow north into it. We stopped to consider, and found that the cracks in the ice we were on were the rise and fall of a swell. Knowing that the ice might remain like this with each piece tight against the next only until the tide turned, I knew that we must get off it at once in case the tide did turn in the next half-hour, when each crack would open up into a wide lead of open water and we should find ourselves on an isolated floe. So we at once turned and went back as fast as possible to the unbroken sea ice. Obviously it was now unsafe to go round to Hut Point by Cape Armitage and we therefore made for the Gap. It was between eight and nine in the evening when we turned, and we soon came in sight of the pony party, led as we thought by Captain Scott. We were within ½ a mile of them when we hurried right across their bows and headed straight for the Gap, making a course more than a right angle off the course we had been on. There was the seals' pressure ridge of sea ice between us and them, but as I could see them quite distinctly I had no doubt they could see us, and we were occupied more than once just then in beating the teams off stray seals, so that we didn't go by either very quickly or very silently. From here we ran into the Gap, where there was some nasty pressed-up ice to cross and large gaps and cracks by the ice foot; but with the Alpine rope and a rush we got first one team over and then the other without mishap on to the land ice, and were then practically at Hut Point. However, expecting that the pony party was following us, we ran our teams up on to level ice, picketed them, and pitched our tent, to remain there for the night, as we had a half-mile of rock to cross to reach the hut and the sledges would have to be carried over this and the dogs led by hand in couples – a very long job. Having done this we returned to the ice foot with a pick and a shovel to improve the road up for horse party, as they would have to come over the same bad ice we had found difficult with the dogs; but they were nowhere to be seen close at hand as we had expected, for they were miles out, as we soon saw, still trying to reach Hut Point by the sea ice round Cape Armitage thaw pool, and on the ice which was showing a working crack at 30 paces. I couldn't understand how Scott could do such a thing, and it was only the next day that I found out that Scott had remained behind and had sent Bowers in charge of this pony party. Bowers, having had no experience of the kind, did not grasp the situation for some time, and as we watched him and his party – or as we thought Captain Scott and his party – of ponies we saw them all suddenly realise that they were getting into trouble and the whole party turned back; but instead of coming back towards the Gap as we had, we saw them go due south towards the Barrier edge and White Island. Then I thought they were all right, for I knew they would get on to safe ice and camp for the night. We therefore had our supper in the tent and were turning in between eleven and twelve when I had a last look to see where they were and found they had camped as it appeared to me on safe Barrier ice, the only safe thing they could have done. They were now about six miles away from us, and it was lucky that I had my Goerz glasses with me so that we could follow their movements. Now as everything looked all right, Meares and I turned in and slept. At 5 a.m. I awoke, and as I felt uneasy about the party I went out and along the Gap to where we could see their camp, and I was horrified to see that the whole of the sea ice was now on the move and that it had broken up for miles further than when we turned in and right back past where they had camped, and that the pony party was now, as we could see, adrift on a floe and separated by open water and a lot of drifting ice from the edge of the fast Barrier ice. We could see with our glasses that they were running the ponies and sledges over as quickly as possible from floe to floe whenever they could, trying to draw nearer to the safe Barrier ice again. The whole Strait was now open water to the N. of Cape Armitage, with the frost smoke rising everywhere from it, and full of pieces of floating ice, all going up N. to Ross Sea.

March 1. Ash Wednesday. The question for us was whether we could do anything to help them. There was no boat anywhere and there was no one to consult with, for everyone was on the floating floe as we believed, except Teddie Evans, Forde, and Keohane, who with one pony were on their way back from Corner Camp. So we searched the Barrier for signs of their tent and then saw that there was a tent at Safety Camp, which meant evidently to us that they had returned. The obvious thing was to join up with them and go round to where the pony party was adrift, and see if we could help them to reach the safe ice. So without waiting for breakfast we went off six miles to this tent. We couldn't go now by the Gap, for the ice by which we had reached land yesterday was now broken up in every direction and all on the move up the Strait. We had no choice now but to cross up by Crater Hill and down by Pram Point and over the pressure ridges and so on to the Barrier and off to Safety Camp. We couldn't possibly take a dog sledge this way, so we walked taking the Alpine rope to cross the pressure ridges, which are full of crevasses.

We got to this tent soon after noon and were astonished to find that not Teddie Evans and his two seamen were here, but that Scott and Oates and Gran were in it and no pony with them. Teddie Evans was still on his way back from Corner Camp and had not arrived. It was now for the first time that we understood how the accident had happened When we had left Safety Camp yesterday with the dogs, the ponies began their march to follow us, but one of the ponies was so weak after the last blizzard and so obviously about to die that Bowers, Cherry-Garrard, and Crean were sent on with the four capable ponies while Scott, Oates, and Gran remained at Safety Camp till the sick pony died, which happened apparently that night. He was dead and buried when we got there. We found that Scott had that morning seen the open water up to the Barrier edge and had been in a dreadful state of mind, thinking that Meares and I, as well as the whole pony party, had gone out into the Strait on floating ice. He was therefore much relieved when we arrived and he learned for the first time where the pony party was trying to get to fast ice again. We were now given some food, which we badly wanted, and while we were eating we saw in the far distance a single man coming hurriedly along the edge of the Barrier ice from the direction of the catastrophe party and towards our camp. Gran went off on ski to meet him, and when he arrived we found it was Crean, who had been sent off by Bowers with a note, unencumbered otherwise, to jump from one piece of floating ice to another until he reached the fast edge of the Barrier in order to let Capt. Scott know what had happened. This he did, of course not knowing that we or anyone else had seen him go adrift, and being unable to leave the ponies and all his loaded sledges himself. Crean had considerable difficulty and ran a pretty good risk in doing this, but succeeded all right. There were now Scott, Oates, Crean, Gran, Meares, and myself here and only three sleeping-bags, so the three first remained to see if they could help Bowers, Cherry-Garrard, and the ponies, while Meares, Gran, and I returned to look after our dogs at Hut Point. Here we had only two sleeping-bags for the three of us, so we had to take turns, and I remained up till 1 o'clock that night while Gran had six hours in my bag. It was a bitterly cold job after a long day. We had been up at 5 with nothing to eat till 1 o'clock, and walked 14 miles. The nights are now almost dark.

March 2. A very bitter wind blowing and it was a cheerless job waiting for six hours to get a sleep in the bag. I walked down from our tent to the hut and watched whales blowing in the semi-darkness out in the black water of the Strait. When we turned out in the morning the pony party was still on floating ice but not any further from the Barrier ice. By a merciful providence the current was taking them rather along the Barrier edge, where they went adrift, instead of straight out to sea. We could do nothing more for them, so we set to our work with the dogs. It was blowing a bitter gale of wind from the S.E. with some drift and we made a number of journeys backwards and forwards between the Gap and the hut, carrying our tent and camp equipment down and preparing a permanent picketing line for the dogs. As the ice had all gone out of the Strait we were quite cut off from any return to Cape Evans until the sea should again freeze over, and this was not likely until the end of April. We rigged up a small fireplace in the hut and found some wood and made a fire for an hour or so at each meal, but as there was no coal and not much wood we felt we must be economical with the fuel, and so also with matches and everything else, in case Bowers should lose his sledge loads, which had most of the supplies for the whole party to last twelve men for two months. The weather had now become too thick for us to distinguish anything in the distance and we remained in ignorance as to the party adrift until Saturday. I had also lent my glasses to Captain Scott. This night I had first go in the bag, and turned out to shiver for eight hours till breakfast. There was literally nothing in the hut that one could cover oneself with to keep warm and we couldn't run to keeping the fire going. It was very cold work. There were heaps of biscuit cases here which we had left in *Discovery* days, and with these we built up a small inner hut to live in.

March 3. Spent the day in transferring dogs in couples from the Gap to the hut. In the afternoon Teddie Evans and Atkinson turned up from over the hills, having returned from their Corner Camp journey with one horse and two seamen, all of which they had left encamped at Castle Rock, three miles off on the hills. They naturally expected to find Scott here and everyone else and had heard nothing of the pony party going adrift, but having found only open water ahead of them they turned back and came to land by Castle Rock slopes. We fed them and I walked half-way back to Castle Rock with them.

March 4. Meares, Gran, and I walked up Ski Slope towards Castle Rock to meet Evans's party and pilot them and the dogs safely to Hut Point, but half-way we met Atkinson, who told us that they had now been joined by Scott and all the catastrophe party, who were safe, but who had lost all the ponies except one – a great blow. However, no lives were lost and the sledge loads and stores were saved, so Meares and I returned to Hut Point to make stables for the only two ponies that now remained, both in wretched condition, of the eight with which we started. [Dr Wilson's Journal]

Note 15. – *March* 12. Thawed out some old magazines and picture papers which were left here by the *Discovery*, and gave us very good reading. [Dr Wilson's Journal]

Note 16. – *April* 4. Fun over a fry I made in my new penguin lard. It was quite a success and tasted like very bad sardine oil. [Dr Wilson's Journal]

Note 17. – *Voyage of the Discovery*, chap. 9. 'The question of the moment is, what has become of our boats? Early in the winter they were hoisted out to give more room for the awning, and were placed in a line about one hundred yards from the ice foot on the sea ice. The earliest gale drifted them up nearly gunwale high, and thus for two months they remained in sight whilst we congratulated ourselves on their security. The last gale brought more snow, and piling it in drifts at various places in the bay, chose to be specially generous with it in the neighbourhood of our boats, so that afterwards they were found to be buried three or four feet beneath the new surface. Although we had noted with interest the manner in which the extra weight of snow in other places was pressing down the surface of the original ice, and were even taking measurements of the effects thus produced, we remained fatuously blind to the risks our boats ran under such conditions. It was from no feeling of anxiety, but rather to provide occupation, that I directed that the snow on top of them should be removed, and it was not until we had dug down to the first boat that the true state of affairs dawned on us. She was found lying in a mass of slushy ice, with which also she was nearly filled. For the moment we had a wild hope that she could be pulled up, but by the time we could rig shears the air temperature .had converted the slush into hardened ice, and she was found to be stuck fast. At present there is no hope of recovering any of the boats: as fast as one could dig out the sodden ice, more sea-water would flow in and freeze . . . The danger is that fresh gales bringing more snow will sink them so far beneath the surface that we shall be unable to recover them at all. Stuck solid in the floe they must go down with it, and every effort must be devoted to preventing the floe from sinking.' As regards the rope, it is a familiar experience that dark objects which absorb heat will melt their way through the snow or ice on which they lie.

Note 18. –

PONIES PRESENTED BY SCHOOLS, ETC.

School's, &c., name of pony	Nickname of pony	Name of school, &c., presenting pony
Floreat Etona	Snippet	Eton College
Christ's Hospital	Hackenschmidt	Christ's Hospital
Westminster	Blossom	Westminster
St Paul's	Michael	St Paul's
Stubbington	Weary Willie	Stubbington House, Fareham
Bedales	Christopher	Bedales, Petersfield
Lydney	Victor	The Institute, Lydney, Gloucester
West Down	Jones	West Down School
Bootham	Snatcher	Bootham
South Hampstead	Bones	South Hampstead High School (Girls)
Altrincham	Chinaman	Seamen's Moss School, Altrincham
Rosemark	Cuts	Captain and Mrs Mark Kerr (H. M. S. *Invincible*)
Invincible	James Pigg	Officers and Ship's Company of H. M. S. *Invincible*
Snooker King	Jehu	J. Foster Stackhouse and friend
Brandon	Punch	The Bristol Savages
Stoker	Blücher	R. Donaldson Hudson, Esq.
Manchester	Nobby	Manchester various
Cardiff	Uncle Bill	Cardiff various
Liverpool	Davy	Liverpool various

SLEEPING-BAGS PRESENTED BY SCHOOLS, ETC.

School's, &c., name of sleeping-bag	Name of traveller using sleeping-bag	Name of school, &c., presenting sleeping-bag
Cowbridge	Commander Evans	Cowbridge
The Wick, Hove	Lieutenant Campbell	The Wick, Hove
Taunton	Seaman Williamson	King's College, Taunton
Bryn Derwen	Seaman Keohane	Bryn Derwen
Grange	Dr Simpson	The Grange, Folkestone
Brighton	Lieutenant Bowers	Brighton Grammar School
Cardigan	Captain Scott	The County School, Cardigan
Carter-Eton	Mr Cherry-Garrard	Mr R. T. Carter, Eton College
Radley	Mr Ponting	Stones Social, Radley
Woodford	Mr Meares	Woodford House
Bramhall	Seaman Abbott	Bramhall Grammar School
Louth	Dr Atkinson	King Edward VI Grammar School, Louth
Twyford I	Seaman Forde	Twyford School
Twyford II	Mr Day	Twyford School
Abbey House	Seaman Dickason	Mr Carvey's House, Abbey House School
Waverley	Mr Wright	Waverley Road, Birmingham
St John's	Seaman Evans	St John's House
Leyton	Ch. Stoker Lashly	Leyton County High School
St Bede's	Seaman Browning	Eastbourne
Sexeys	Dr Wilson	Sexeys School
Worksop	Mr Debenham	Worksop College
Regent	Mr Nelson	Regent Street Polytechnic Secondary School
Trafalgar	Captain Oates	Trafalgar House School, Winchester
Altrincham	Mr Griffith Taylor	Altrincham, various
Invincible	Dr Levick	Ship's Company, H. M. S. *Invincible*
Leeds	Mr Priestley	Leeds Boys' Modern School

SLEDGES PRESENTED BY SCHOOLS, ETC.

(N.B. The name of the pony in parentheses is the name given by the school, &c., that presented the pony)

School's, &c., name of sledge	Description of sledge	Name of school, &c., presenting sledge
Amesbury	Pony: Uncle Bill (Cardiff)	Amesbury, Bickley Hall, Kent
John Bright	Dog sledge	Bootham
Sherborne	Pony: Snippets (Floreat Etona)	Sherborne House School

School's, &c., name of sledge	Description of sledge	Name of school, &c., presenting sledge
Wimbledon	Pony: Blossom (Westminster)	King's College School, Wimbledon
Kelvinside	Northern sledge (man-hauled)	Kelvinside Academy
Pip	Dog sledge	Copthorne
Christ's Hospital	Dog sledge	Christ's Hospital
Hampstead	Dog sledge	University College School, Hampstead
Glasgow	Pony: Snatcher (Bootham)	High School, Glasgow
George Dixon	Pony: Nobby (Manchester)	George Dixon Secondary School
Leys	Pony: Punch (Brandon)	The Leys School, Cambridge
Northampton	Motor sledge, No. 1	Northampton County School
Charterhouse I	Pony: Blücher (Stoker)	Charterhouse
Charterhouse II	Western sledge (man-hauled)	Charterhouse
Regent	Northern sledge (man-hauled)	Regent Street Polytechnic Secondary School
Sidcot	Pony: Hackenschmidt (Christ's Hospital)	Sidcot, Winscombe
Retford	Pony: Michael (St Paul's)	Retford Grammar School
Tottenham	Northern sledge (man-hauled)	Tottenham Grammar School
Cheltenham	Pony: James Pigg (H. M. S. *Invincible*)	The College, Cheltenham
Knight	First Summit sledge (man-hauled)	Sidcot School, Old Boys
Crosby	Pony: Christopher (Bedales)	Crosby Merchant Taylors'
Grange	Pony: Chinaman (Altrincham)	'Grange', Buxton
Altrincham	Pony: Victor (Lydney)	Altrincham (various)
Probus	Pony: Weary Willie (Stubbington)	Probus
Rowntree	Second Summit sledge (man-hauled)	Workmen, Rowntree's Cocoa Works
'Invincible' I	Third Summit sledge (man-hauled)	Officers and Men, H. M. S. *Invincible*
'Invincible' II	Pony: Jehu (Snooker King)	Officers and Men, H. M. S. *Invincible*
Eton	Pony: Bones (South Hampstead)	Eton College
Masonic	Motor sledge, No. 2	Royal Masonic School, Bushey

TENTS PRESENTED BY SCHOOLS, ETC.

Name of tent	Party to which attached	School, &c.,presenting tent
Fitz Roy	Southern Party	Fitz Roy School, Crouch End
Ashdown	Northern Party	Ashdown House, Forest Row, Sussex
Brighton & Hove	Reserve, Cape Evans	Brighton & Hove High School, (Girls)
Bromyard	Reserve, Cape Evans	Grammar, Bromyard
Marlborough	Reserve, Cape Evans	The College, Marlborough
Bristol	Mr Ponting (photo-graphic artist)	Colchester House, Bristol
Croydon	Reserve, Cape Evans	Croydon High School
Broke Hall	Reserve, Cape Evans	Broke Hall, Charterhouse
Pelham	Southern Party	Pelham House, Folkestone
Tollington	Depôt Party	Tollington School, Muswell Hill
St Andrews	Southern Party	St Andrews, Newcastle
Richmond	Dog Party	Richmond School, Yorks
Hymers	Depôt Party	Scientific Society, Hymers College, Hull
King Edward	Depôt Party	King Edward's School
Southport	Cape Crozier Depôt	Southport Physical Training College
Jarrow	Reserve, Cape Evans	Jarrow Secondary School
Grange	Reserve, Cape Evans	The Grange, Buxton
Swindon	Reserve, Cape Evans	Swindon
Sir John Deane	Motor Party	Sir. J. Deane's Grammar School
Llandaff	Reserve, Cape Evans	Llandaff
Castleford	Reserve, Cape Evans	Castleford Secondary School
Hailey	Reserve, Cape Evans	Hailey
Uxbridge	Northern Party	Uxbridge County School
Stubbington	Reserve, Cape Evans	Stubbington House, Fareham

Note 19. – These hints on Polar Surveying fell on willing ears. Members of the afterguard who were not mathematically trained plunged into the very practical study of how to work out observations. Writing home on October 26, 1911, Scott remarks:

' "Cherry" has just come to me with a very anxious face to say that I must not count on his navigating powers. For the moment I didn't know what he was driving at, but then I remembered that some months ago I said that it would be a good thing for all the officers going South to have some knowledge of navigation so that in emergency they would know how to steer a sledge home. It appears that "Cherry" thereupon commenced a serious and arduous course of study of abstruse navigational problems which he found exceedingly tough and now despaired mastering. Of course there is not one chance in a hundred that he will ever have to consider navigation on our journey and in that one chance the problem must be of the simplest nature, but it makes matters much easier for me to have men who take the details of one's work so seriously and who strive so simply and honestly to make it successful.'

And in Wilson's diary for October 23 comes the entry: 'Working at latitude sights – mathematics which I hate – till bedtime. It will be wiser to know a little navigation on the Southern sledge journey.'

Note 20. – Happily I had a biscuit with me and I held it out to him a long way off. Luckily he spotted it and allowed me to come up, and I got hold of his head again. [Dr Wilson's Journal]

Note 21. – *December* 8. I have kept Nobby all my biscuits tonight as he is to try and do a march tomorrow, and then happily he will be shot and all of them, as their food is quite done.

December 9. Nobby had all my biscuits last night and this morning, and by the time we camped I was just ravenously hungry. It was a close cloudy day with no air and we were ploughing along knee deep . . . Thank God the horses are now all done with and we begin the heavy work ourselves. [Dr Wilson's Journal]

Note 22. – *December* 9. The end of the Beardmore Glacier curved across the track of the Southern Party, thrusting itself into the mass of the Barrier with vast pressure and disturbance. So far did this ice disturbance extend, that if the travellers had taken a bee-line to the foot of the glacier itself, they must have begun to steer outwards 200 miles sooner.

The Gateway was a neck or saddle of drifted snow lying in a gap of the mountain rampart which flanked the last curve of the glacier. Under the cliffs on either hand, like a moat beneath the ramparts, lay a yawning ice-cleft or *bergschrund*, formed by the drawing away of the steadily moving Barrier ice from the rocks. Across this moat and leading up to the gap in the ramparts, the Gateway provided a solid causeway. To climb this and descend its reverse face gave the easiest access to the surface of the glacier.

Note 23. – Return of first Southern Party from Lat. 85° 7' S. top of the Beardmore Glacier.

Party: E. L. Atkinson, A. Cherry-Garrard, C. S. Wright, Petty Officer Keohane.

On the morning of December 22, 1911, we made a late start after saying goodbye to the eight going on, and wishing them all good luck and success. The first 11 miles was on the down-grade over the ice-falls, and at a good pace we completed this in about four hours. Lunched, and on, completing nearly 23 miles for the first day. At the end of the second day we got among very bad crevasses through keeping too far to the eastward. This delayed us slightly and we made the depôt on the third day. We reached the Lower Glacier Depôt three and a half days after. The lower part of the glacier was very badly crevassed. These crevasses we had never seen on the way up, as they had been covered with three to four feet of snow. All the bridges of crevasses were concave and very wide; no doubt their normal summer condition. On Christmas Day we made in to the lateral moraine of the Cloudmaker and collected geological specimens. The march across the Barrier was only remarkable for the extremely bad lights we had. For eight consecutive days we only saw an exceedingly dim sun during three hours. Up to One Ton Depôt our marches had averaged 14.1 geographical miles a day. We arrived at Cape Evans on January 28, 1912, after being away for three months. [E.L.A.]

Note 24. – *January* 3. Return of the second supporting party.

Under average conditions, the return party should have well fulfilled Scott's cheery anticipations. Three-man teams had done excellently on previous sledging expeditions, whether in *Discovery* days or as recently as the mid-winter visit to the Emperor penguins' rookery; and the three in this party were seasoned travellers with a skilled navigator to lead them. But a blizzard held them up for three days before reaching the head of the glacier. They had to press on at speed. By the time they reached the foot of the glacier, Lieut. Evans developed symptoms of scurvy. His spring work of surveying and sledging out to Corner Camp and the man-hauling, with Lashly, across the Barrier after the breakdown of the motors, had been successfully accomplished; this sequel to the Glacier and Summit marches was an unexpected blow.

Withal, he continued to pull, while bearing the heavy strain of guiding the course. While the hauling power thus grew less, the leader had to make up for loss of speed by lengthening the working hours. He put his watch on an hour. With the 'turning out' signal thus advanced, the actual marching period reached 12 hours. The situation was saved, and Evans flattered himself on his ingenuity. But the men knew it all the time, and no word said!

At One Ton Camp he was unable to stand without the support of his ski sticks; but with the help of his companions struggled on another 53 miles in four days. Then he could go no farther. His companions, rejecting his suggestion that he be left in his sleeping-bag with a supply of provisions while they pressed on for help, 'cached' everything that could be spared, and pulled him on the sledge with a devotion matching that of their captain years before, when he and Wilson brought their companion Shackleton, ill and helpless, safely home to the *Discovery*. Four days of this pulling, with a southerly wind to help, brought them to Corner Camp; then came a heavy snowfall: the sledge could not travel. It was a critical moment. Next day Crean set out to tramp alone to Hut Point, 34 miles away. Lashly stayed to nurse Lieut. Evans, and most certainly saved his life till help came. Crean reached Hut Point after an exhausting march of 18 hours; how the dog-team went to the rescue is told by Dr Atkinson in the second volume. At the *Discovery* hut Evans was unremittingly tended by Dr Atkinson, and finally sent by sledge to the *Terra Nova*. It is good to record that both Lashly and Crean have received the Albert medal.

Note 25. – At this point begins the last of Scott's notebooks. The record of the Southern Journey is written in pencil in three slim MS. books, some 8 inches long by 5 wide. These little volumes are meant for artists' notebooks, and are made of tough, soft, pliable paper which takes the pencil well. The pages, 96 in number, are perforated so as to be detachable at need.

In the Hut, large quarto MS. books were used for the journals, and some of the rough notes of the earlier expeditions were recast and written out again in them; the little books were carried on the sledge journeys, and contain the day's notes entered very regularly at the lunch halts and in the night camps. But in the last weeks of the Southern Journey, when fuel and light ran short and all grew very weary, it will be seen that Scott made his entries at lunch time alone. They tell not of the morning's run only, but of 'yesterday'.

The notes were written on the right-hand pages, and when the end of the book was reached, it was 'turned' and the blank backs of the leaves now became clean right-hand pages. The first two MS. books are thus entirely filled: the third has only part of its pages used and the 'Message to the Public' is written at the reverse end.

Inside the front cover of No. 1 is a 'ready' table to convert the day's run of geographical miles as recorded on the sledge-meter into statute miles, a list of the depôts and their latitude, and a note of the sledge-meter reading at Corner Camp.

These are followed in the first pages by a list of the outward camps and distances run as noted in the book, with special 'remarks' as to cairns, latitude, and so forth. At the end of the book is a full list of the cairns that marked the track out.

Inside the front cover of No. 2 are similar entries, together with the ages of the Polar party and a note of the error of Scott's watch.

Inside the front cover of No. 3 are the following words: 'Diary can be read by finder to ensure recovering of Records, &c., but Diary should be sent to my widow.' And on the first page:

'Send this diary to my widow.   R. SCOTT'

The word 'wife' had been struck out and 'widow' written in.

Note 26, p. 578. At this, the Barrier stage of the return journey, the Southern Party were in want of more oil than they found at the depôts. Owing partly to the severe conditions, but still more to the delays imposed by their sick comrades, they reached the full limit of time allowed for between depôts. The cold was unexpected, and at the same time the actual amount of oil found at the depôts was less than they had counted on.

Under summer conditions, such as were contemplated, when there was less cold for the men to endure, and less firing needed to melt the snow for cooking, the fullest allowance of oil was 1 gallon to last a unit of four men ten days, or $\frac{1}{40}$ of a gallon a day for each man.

The amount allotted to each unit for the return journey from the South was apparently rather less, being $\frac{2}{3}$ gallon for eight days, or ⅟₄₈ gallon a day for each man. But the eight days were to cover the march from depôt to depôt, averaging on the Barrier some 70–80 miles, which in normal conditions should not take more than six days. Thus there was a substantial margin for delay by bad weather, while if all went well the surplus afforded the fullest marching allowance.

The same proportion for a unit of five men works out at ⅚ of a gallon for the eight-day stage.

Accordingly, for the return of the two supporting parties and the Southern Party, two tins of a gallon each were left at each depôt, each unit of four men being entitled to ⅔ of a gallon, and the units of three and five men in proportion.

The return journey on the Summit had been made at good speed, taking twenty-one days as against twenty-seven going out, the last part of it, from Three Degree to Upper Glacier Depôt, taking nearly eight marches as against ten, showing the first slight slackening as P. O. Evans and Oates began to feel the cold; from Upper Glacier to Lower Glacier Depôt ten marches as against eleven, a stage broken by the Mid-Glacier Depôt of three and a half days' provisions at the sixth march. Here there was little gain, partly owing to the conditions, but more to Evans's gradual collapse.

The worst time came on the Barrier; from Lower Glacier to Southern Barrier Depôt (51 miles), 6½ marches as against 5 (two of which were short marches, so that the 5 might count as an easy 4 in point of distance); from Southern Barrier to Mid Barrier Depôt (82 miles), 6 marches as against 5½; from Mid Barrier to Mt Hooper (70 miles), 8 as against 4¾, while the last remaining 8 marches represent but 4 on the outward journey.

As to the cause of the shortage, the tins of oil at the depôts had been exposed to extreme conditions of heat and cold. The oil was specially volatile, and in the warmth of the sun (for the tins were regularly set in an accessible place on the top of the cairns) tended to become vapour and escape through the stoppers even without damage to the tins. This process was much accelerated by reason that the leather washers about the stoppers had perished in the great cold. Dr Atkinson gives two striking examples of this.

1. Eight one-gallon tins in a wooden case, intended for a depôt at Cape Crozier, had been put out in September 1911. They were

snowed up; and when examined in December 1912 showed three tins full, three empty, one a third full, and one two-thirds full.

2. When the search party reached One Ton Camp in November 1912 they found that some of the food, stacked in a canvas 'tank' at the foot of the cairn, was quite oily from the spontaneous leakage of the tins seven feet above it on the top of the cairn.

The tins at the depôts awaiting the Southern Party had of course been opened and the due amount to be taken measured out by the supporting parties on their way back. However carefully re-stoppered, they were still liable to the unexpected evaporation and leakage already described. Hence, without any manner of doubt, the shortage which struck the Southern Party so hard.

Note 27. – The Fatal Blizzard. Mr Frank Wild, who led one wing of Dr Mawson's Expedition on the northern coast of the Antarctic continent, Queen Mary's Land, many miles to the west of the Ross Sea, writes that 'from March 21 for a period of nine days we were kept in camp by the same blizzard which proved fatal to Scott and his gallant companions.' (*The Times*, June 2, 1913) Blizzards, however, are so local that even when, as in this case, two are nearly contemporaneous, it is not safe to conclude that they are part of the same current of air.

VOLUME TWO

The Barrier Silence

The Silence was deep with a breath like sleep
  As our sledge runners slid on the snow,
And the fateful fall of our fur-clad feet
  Struck mute like a silent blow
On a questioning 'Hush?' as the settling crust
  Shrank shivering over the floe.
And a voice which was thick from a soul that was sick
  Came back from the Barrier – 'Go!
For the secrets hidden are all forbidden
  Till God means man to know.'
And this was the thought that the silence wrought,
  As it scorched and froze us through,
That we were the men God meant should know
  The heart of the Barrier snow,
By the heat of the sun, and the glow
  And the glare from the glistening floe,
As it scorched and froze us through and through
  With the bite of the drifting snow.

These verses were written by Dr Wilson for the *South Polar Times*. It was characteristic of the man that he sent them in typewritten, lest the editor should recognise his hand and judge them on personal rather than literary grounds. Many of their readers confess that they felt in these lines Wilson's own premonition of the event. The version now given is the final form, as it appeared in the *South Polar Times*.

THE WINTER JOURNEY TO CAPE CROZIER

by Dr Edward A. Wilson, Lieut. H. R. Bowers, R.N.,
and Apsley Cherry-Garrard

JUNE 27 1911, TO AUGUST 1 1911

The object of this expedition to the Emperor penguin rookery in the darkness and cold of an Antarctic winter was set forth years before in Dr Wilson's Report of the Zoology of the *Discovery* Voyage. It was to secure eggs at such a stage as could furnish a series of early embryos by which alone the particular points of interest in the development of the bird could be worked out; for it seemed probable 'that we have in the Emperor penguin the nearest approach to a primitive form not only of a penguin, but of a bird.' These points could not be investigated in the deserted eggs and chicks which had been obtained in *Discovery* days. Such a journey 'entailed the risks of sledge travelling in midwinter with an almost total absence of light', for the Emperor is singular in nesting at the coldest season of the year, and 'the party would have to be on the scene at any rate early in July . . . It would at any time require that a party of three at least, with full camp equipment, should traverse about a hundred miles of the Barrier surface and should, by moon-light, cross over with rope and axe the immense pressure ridges which form a chaos of crevasses at Cape Crozier . . . which have taken a party as much as two hours of careful work to cross by daylight.'

Furthermore, it afforded an opportunity of obtaining an exact knowledge of the winter conditions on the Barrier at its western end, and throughout its dangers and difficulties Bowers kept a most remarkable meteorological record (given at the end of this volume), the substance of which is embodied in this Report. The three travellers also experimented with their sledging rations, each for some time taking a different proportion of pemmican and biscuit, the results of which were used in order to make up the rations for future use.

The journey was planned to last six weeks, with a stay of several days near the rookery, but was shortened by the extreme cold and consequent consumption of their store of fuel, and the tempest which drove the party back from Cape Crozier.

To the report written by Dr Wilson various notes and details are added in square brackets from Mr Cherry-Garrard's diary. This diary, be it said, was never written for publication. It was a private record, for private remembrance. It tells of incidents and impressions in their personal bearing, and so telling, incidentally preserves the fuller human colouring that has been sedulously stripped away from Dr Wilson's objective record, written with a more strictly scientific outlook.

Such notes have a manifold value. Every personality receives its own impression of the same incidents, recalls a different aspect, throws sidelights from a different angle. The young traveller records for himself a fresh and vivid personal impression, undiminished by reshaping into the perhaps necessary reticence of an official report. Not least, also, he gives us details about his chief which Dr Wilson could not or would not have set down.

His own share in the expedition is the more remarkable because, short-sighted as he was, he could not wear his spectacles under such conditions.

With the help of these notes, the reader can fill in somewhat of those lights and shades which the official report, addressed to a Polar explorer, needed not to add. Now that the other two comrades in the adventure are no more, Mr Cherry-Garrard has been prevailed upon to let his diary be used as it is used here. Let him be assured that his chief fear is groundless – the fear that in allowing such very personal jottings to be quoted, he should be imagined to magnify his own share in the expedition, instead of insisting, as he would have insisted in a public report, on the wonderful work of his friends: the strength, the steadfastness, and the serenity with which they carried it through. There was never an angry word from beginning to end, even in the most trying times. These unpremeditated notes help to make Wilson and Bowers stand out in their true colours.

*　　*　　*

Tuesday, June 27, 1911. – Leaving the hut at Cape Evans shortly before 11 a.m., Bowers, Cherry-Garrard and I started for our first march, accompanied by Simpson, Meares, Griffith Taylor, Nelson and Gran, who all helped us to drag our two sledges, and by a number of others who came to see us round the Cape.

We made for the western extremity of Big Razorback Island, and halted when it had just closed and covered the Little Razorback. We were then not 100 yards from the actual end of the rock and the sledge-meter read 3 miles 700 yards. Nelson and Taylor left us here and we continued with the other three.

We could now just distinguish the rock patches of Castle Rock and Harbour Heights and we made in a bit to pass as close as possible to the end of Glacier Tongue, where pressure lines were said to be less numerous in the sea ice than farther out. It was so dark, however, that we never saw the end of this Glacier Tongue, and we only knew we had passed it when the lower two-thirds of the Turk's Head Cliffs were suddenly cut off.

We then ran into some very difficult hummocky sea ice with steep-cut drifts, and our rear sledge capsized. It was too dark to avoid them, so Meares, Simpson and Gran remained with us and helped us until we had cleared them. We were then about three-quarters of a mile beyond Glacier Tongue and the sledge-meter read 5 m. 250 yds.

The wind, light southerly airs alternating with calm all the forenoon, now began to blow with some force from the east, and the sky became more and more overcast in the south [a half blizzard, in fact]; so we persuaded the three helpers to return from here. After this we had very little trouble with rough ice, and though the loads (about 250 lbs. each) were heavy enough to make us slow, we had a good surface to go on.

We camped for lunch at 2.30 p.m., having made six and one-third miles from Cape Evans. The double tent was easy to pitch, and we began a routine of brushing down the inside, after removing all the contents, every time we broke camp. This routine we continued the whole way to Cape Crozier, and it made a great difference to the collection of ice on the upper two-thirds of the tent. It was the duty of the cook for the day to see to this, and we were each of us cook for one day in turn. The lower third of the tent skirt lining gradually got more and more iced up by trickles from above during the running of the primus, and nothing short of melting it out would have enabled us to keep it clear of ice. We gave up the brushing-down routine on the journey home from Cape Crozier, for we had to burn oil so sparingly that we tied up the ventilator permanently and kept in all the steam and heat we could, to thaw out our finnesko, which we hung in the roof at night. We were so iced up as to our clothes and sleeping-bags that nothing outside made any difference, and the omission of brushing down saved time in getting off.

After lunch we got away at 4 p.m. and made for what we believed to be Hut Point, but in the dark we got a good deal too close in towards Castle Rock, much more than was necessary. Our pace was slow owing to the weights, but the surface was not bad. It was chiefly crusty rough sea ice, salt to the taste still; or it had an inch or two of white crusty snow on the rough, darker sea ice, alternating with broader drifts of hard windswept snow, making long, low mounds over which the sledges ran easily. These seemed here to result from an E.N.E. wind coming from the neck on the promontory, the wind which we caught just after passing the Glacier Tongue, and again off the ridge along Castle Rock, where it blew to force 5, up to 8 p.m., when we camped for the night, having made 9¾ miles from Cape Evans. [Setting this tent in dark is difficult, but not too bad even in that wind. Bill warns me seriously against running risk of frostbite. I find no specs very hard in setting tent – must be sure not to let any inability arising from this get on my nerves – 41 more days we hope.] Castle Rock was here nearly abeam. The wind dropped soon after and we had a clear starlit night.

The temperature for the day ranged from −14.5° to −15°, and the minimum temperature for the night was −26°.

Wednesday, June 28, 1911. – Turned out at 7.30 a.m. The going became very heavy with the two sledges, and we made very little more than a mile an hour over a surface which was all rough, rubbly salt sea ice with no snow on it. Bowers thinks that we were on definitely younger ice than that which we were on farther out yesterday and on our return. He thinks there was a large open lead along the shore which was the last to freeze up, and that this resulted from off-shore winds.

We reached Hut Point at 1.30 p.m., having crossed three or four cracks and lines of pressure chiefly radiating from Hut Point itself.

The sledge-meter showed 13 m. 1500 yds., but we had not come in a direct line from Cape Evans. We lunched in the hut and had no difficulty with the door, as there was hardly any snowdrift against it.

After lunch we made better going to Cape Armitage, though there was still no snow here on the rough, rubbly ice, but it was not so bad as what we had been on during the forenoon, where the sea ice was still salt and crunchy, with humps everywhere, formed from the old weathered ice and salt flowers, none bigger than one's fist, allowing the feet to crush between them every step at a different angle. After Cape Armitage the surface became hard and snow-covered; and with the best going we met with the whole journey for a short two miles, we quickly reached the edge of the Barrier, finding a good slope of snowdrift where we struck it, and having no difficulty in drawing our sledges up one at a time. There was a snow-covered crack as usual at the top of the drift, not a working crack, and invisible until broken into.

Unfortunately, both in going out and in coming back, we reached the Barrier edge in too bad a light to see whether these snowdrifts were quite continuous all along the edge, but from the fact that they were so at the two different points at which we struck the edge in the dark, I think it is probable that the slope is now continuous pretty well everywhere. We rose about 12 ft. off the sea ice.

Coming down the snow slope off the Barrier was a stream of very cold air which we felt first when we were only a few yards from the foot, and lost very soon after reaching the top. [Got both hands bitten going up Barrier – all ten fingers.]

It was now 6.30 p.m., and we camped at 7, the last half-hour on the Barrier surface being uphill, and very heavy compared with the easy going on the snow-covered sea ice from Cape Armitage. There was no doubt as to the existence of this slope up; we confirmed it on our return, and I take it to be a proof that the Barrier at this point has in recent years broken back at any rate half a mile or a mile farther than it did this year – for the previous broken edges can be supposed to fill up successively in this way and so to produce a gradient without steps.

We had nothing but light variable airs all day with a clear sky. The temp. ranged from −24.5° in the morning by Castle Rock to −26.5° at Hut Point and −47° at the edge of the Barrier.

Thursday, June 29, 1911. – We spent a cold night with temp. down to −56.5° [Frightful cold last night – bad night. Bill has hardly slept for two nights – clothes beginning to get bad], and it was −49° when we turned out at 9 a.m.; but the day was fine and calm on the whole, with occasional light easterly airs only.

Curtains of aurora covered a great part of the sky to the east both morning and evening, and it was one of the chief pleasures of our journey out that we were facing east, where almost all the aurora occurred, and so we could watch its changes as we marched, almost the whole time. Nine-tenths of the aurora we saw was in the east and S.E. of the sky, often well up to the zenith, but always starting from below the Barrier horizon. We never saw any that appeared close at hand.

The temp. remained at −50° all day, and Cherry and I both felt the cold of the snow very much in our feet on the march, he getting his big toes blistered by frostbite, and I my heel and the sole of my foot. A good many of Cherry's finger-tips also went last night at the edge of the Barrier and are bulbous today; but he takes them as a matter of course and says nothing, and he never once allowed them to interfere with his usefulness.

The surface today was firm, generally; hard and windswept in some places, and soft and sandy in others. The sledges today went heaviest on the harder areas for some reason, which was quite exceptional. I think there was a fixed deposit of gritty crystals on the apparently smooth surface. Always after this it was the soft sandy drifts which held us up more than anything else.

We made two or three long sloping gradients today in our march going eastward. These also we confirmed on our return journey, when we recrossed three long low waves on about the same line, and I believe them to be the continuation of a series of extensive waves which run out from the point at which the glacier flow from Mt Terra Nova runs into the Barrier. These waves curve gradually south-westward from the south-easterly direction in which they first join the Barrier. Hodgson and I followed up and roughly charted one of this group of waves in our journey in 1903 when we were examining the tide crack along the south side of Ross Island. They are very long and definite disturbances, and in our march were taken so diagonally that they seemed much longer. The difference of surface was quite noticeable, harder on the ridge summits and softer in the hollows. We have never met with anything like a crevasse on them.

Friday, June 30, 1911. – The surface today proved too heavy for us – we were unable to drag both sledges together, so we relayed one at a time, by daylight from 11 a.m. to 3 p.m. – and by candle-lamp from 4.30 p.m. to 7.45 p.m. We made only 3¼ miles in the day. The surface was soft and sandy, and though always crusted, always let one through an inch or two, as well as the sledge runners.

Heavy subsidences were continual all day, and the surface seemed to give way more when we were on the edges of the softer sandy patches. They were not extensive as a rule as far as one could judge, but they were exceptionally frequent – much more so than I have known them in the summer. There was no reason to think they dropped more than ¼ to ½ inch. The temp. today ranged from −55° in the morning to −61.6° at lunch and −66° on camping for the night. We had calm weather all day, and some aurora to watch in the E. and from N.E. to S. during the march.

[*June* 30. – Relaying all day – surface awful. It does not look as if we could pull this off. Last night was record sledging temperature −75° on sledge, −69° under sledge.* I was in big bag and most of night shivered till back seemed to break, then warm for half minute and then on again the same thing: turned right over, froze in and got a little sleep. Feet liable to go. One big toe went and I don't know for how long.]

Saturday, July 1, 1911. – We turned out at 7.30 a.m. No dawn was visible, but at 10.45 a.m., when we got away, we were able to relay by daylight, and continued so until 3 p.m. After lunch we relayed by candle lamp from 4.15 p.m. to 7.45 p.m. The surface was like sand, and so heavy that we could only slowly move one sledge along. Subsidences very frequent all day. We made only 2¼ miles in all. [Bill and Birdie very unselfish and helpful – impossible to wear glasses and so I am handicapped.]

Between 5 p.m. and 7 p.m. there was a very fine aurora, large beams making very extensive curtains from E. to S. up to an altitude of 45°, and with characteristic black sky beneath the arches. The colour was a very orange yellow.

* Wilson gives this under July 1 for the night of June 30. For the lowest temperature met, see under July 6.

Erebus smoke has been difficult to see, no long stream of smoke, but very small puffs apparently going eastward each day.

The min. temp. last night was −69°, and today we had −66.6° in the morning and −60.5° at 10 p.m. Light south-easterly airs and north-easterly airs during the march, at these temperatures, forced us all to adjust our noseguards.

Note. − All the temperatures and weather notes in this Report are taken directly from Bowers's record. Bowers also made himself responsible for the sledge-meter records, and for notes on the condition of the ice on Ross Sea when we were at Cape Crozier. He also kept full notes of the aurorae, and did so much generally throughout the journey and with so much persistence notwithstanding the difficulties that beset us, that this Report must be considered as much his as mine. He has moreover read it all through and has materially helped me in making it complete. What I think of him and of Cherry-Garrard as companions for a sledge journey of this kind I have already made known to you, sir, in conversation. It would be impossible to say too much about either of them. I think their patience and persistence from beginning to end was what made five weeks of discomfort not only bearable but much more than pleasant. I have added this note since his revision of the Report.

Sunday, July 2, 1911. − Min. temp. for the night was −65.2°, and this notwithstanding a breeze of force 3 from the S.S.E. with slight drift. The temp. during the day ranged from −60° to −65° with calm, and light airs which again made us adjust nose nips. After their use this day and yesterday, however, they were unnecessary, and some of us never again used them.

A fog bank formed along the Promontory ridge during the afternoon, but rose, and later dispersed to the westward. We all noticed that our frozen fur mits thawed out on our hands while it lasted.

Sunday, July 2, 1911 (*continued*). − We were again relaying today by daylight from 11 a.m. to 3 p.m., and by moonlight instead of candle-lamp from 4.30 to 8 p.m. This was the first we had seen of the new moon. As it passed exactly behind the summit of Erebus it gave us an extraordinary picture of an eruption.

We had a fine aurora in the south low on the horizon as a low curtain and arch, with a very striking orange colour all over.

We made only 2½ miles in the day. [A terrible day. I felt absolutely done up at lunch – three frostbitten toes on one foot – and heel and one toe on the other – burning oil is all that keeps us going now – better night however. We are getting into the swing of doing everything slowly and in mits.

I have pricked six or seven blisters on fingers tonight.]

Monday, July 3, 1911. – The min. temp. for the night was –65°. The weather was calm to begin with and clear, but became gradually overcast all round, starting with a few curve-backed storm clouds over Terror. After lunch however the sky cleared again completely, and we were able to relay by moonlight in the afternoon. We had made only 1½ miles by daylight in the forenoon march, and in the whole day only 2½ miles.

The temp. ranged from –52° to –58.2°.

We had a magnificent display of auroral curtains between 7.30 p.m. and 8 p.m., during which four-fifths of the eastern half of the sky was covered by waving curtains right up to the zenith, where they were all swinging round from left to right in foreshortened, swaying curtains forming a rapidly moving whirl, constantly altering its formation. Some of the lower curtains were very brilliant and showed bands of orange and green and again orange fading into lemon yellow upwards. Bowers noted it as follows: 'Remarkably brilliant aurora working from the N.E. to the zenith and spreading over two-thirds of the sky. Curtain form in interwoven arcs, curtains being propelled along as if by wind; the whole finally forming a vast mushroom overhead and moving towards the S.E. Colours, lemon yellow, green and orange.'

It was such a striking display that we all three halted and lay on our backs for a long time watching its evolutions.

Our sleeping-bags are beginning to show the effect of these low temperatures notwithstanding every care to keep them and our clothing dry. We left Cape Evans with three reindeer-skin bags for use to begin with, and a down bag each as a reserve lining. Cherry's fur bag was a very large one, much too large for warmth at these temperatures. My own was a good fit for warmth, but became so small when wet and frozen up that it broke in every direction. Bowers's bag was the right size for him, but also broke in more than one place later on when wet and frozen. All were as good as could be wished as regards the skins. Cherry has been so cold in his large bag with the hair inside that today he has turned it to hair outside, and bent his down bag as a lining to decrease the space.

Bowers's bag, begun with hair outside, is still so in use. My own, begun with hair inside, is still so in use. All are already rather wet and stiff when frozen, but we sleep in them well enough, and have no difficulty in rolling them up and unrolling them at night. [Bill having cold bad nights – feels it a bit I think – I have been half falling asleep at halts, Birdie ditto – surface a little better – foreshortening the mountains. Clothes for day have been so stiff we have to stop in position we just stand in when we get out of tent.]

Tuesday, July 4, 1911. – The min. temp. for the night was −65.4°, but on turning out at 7.20 a.m. we found the sky completely overcast and snow falling, with occasional gusts from E.N.E. to S. and S.S.E. At 9.30 a.m. the temp. had risen to −27.5°, with a wind force of 4 from the N.E.

Nothing was visible anywhere by which to make a course, so we had breakfast and turned in again. We were warm and comfortable all day, but though there were signs of clearing by night time we had to do without a march.

The min. temp. for the day was −44.5°, and during the following night −54.6°.

Everything was obscured round Erebus and Terror by clouds, though later it became possible to see Terror Point, and we knew that we were still out of the direct path of the southerly blizzards which sweep round Cape Crozier.

This lie-in has saturated our clothing through, and our Burberries stiffen outside the tent so much that it becomes almost difficult to get in again through the door. Our feet so far have been almost constantly warm, except on the march when plodding slowly on soft snow. We had then to keep a watchful eye on them to avoid getting frostbitten toes or heels. I regretted having left my puttees behind, as the additional wrapping round the ankles would have been a great protection to the feet.

We are using oil in the double tent now, after cooking is done, to dry and thaw out socks and finnesko before putting them on in the morning. It has seemed to us an almost necessary precaution at these temperatures unless one is prepared to take the damp socks into the sleeping-bag every night, and this with so many weeks ahead of us we are loath to do, as we are trying our best to keep the bags dry in many ways – for instance, we kept our pyjama trousers and pyjama jackets only for night wear to begin with, until they became so wet and stiff that in order to wear them at all they had to be kept on permanently. From the day of the blizzard incident at Cape Crozier back to Cape Evans, neither Bowers nor I made use of our jackets, however, at all – they were stowed away, stiff, in the tank, and so returned home.

Wednesday, July 5, 1911. – At 3 a.m. the whole sky was clearing and at 7 a.m. we turned out. The surface was now worse than we had as yet experienced, and we moved dreadfully slowly with one sledge load at a time. In 7½ hours hauling we only made 1½ miles good.

The min. temp. last night was −54.6°, and by the evening the temp. had dropped to −61.1°. We were then surrounded by a white fog, but could see Erebus and Terror. The cirro-stratus gave a white-looking sky in the moonlight and a fair halo with mock moons and vertical beams and a particularly well-defined mock moon beneath on the horizon.

All day we had been hauling up hill, and we hoped it was Terror Point we were crossing. Settlements of the crust occurred regularly again at short intervals. The surface still shows no sign of windcut sastrugi, and though much of it is wind-hardened and smooth, it appears to be the result of variable winds of no great force, and it is also covered to a very great extent by deep sheets of soft snow, on which the sledges hang up exactly as though they were going over sand. There is no surface marking on this snow except marks resembling horses' hoofs, with edges that have a peculiar planed-off appearance.

Whether harder or softer, the whole surface is crusted and lets one's feet in for a couple of inches, spoiling one's pull on the sticky-runnered sledges.

Thursday, July 6, 1911. – Again a calm day and clear, though a heavy bank of fog lies over the pressure ridges ahead of us, and over the seaward area to the east.

We had relay work again on a very heavy surface, which, however, improved slightly in the afternoon. But the result of 7½ hours' hauling was a forward move of 1½ miles only.

The min. temp. for the night had been −75.3°. At starting in the morning it was −70.2° and at noon - 76.8°. At 5.15 p.m., when we camped for lunch, it was −77° exactly, and at midnight it had risen again to −69°, when there was some low-lying white fog and mist to the N. and N.N.W. The butter, when stabbed with a knife, 'flew' like very brittle toffee. Our paraffin at these temperatures was perfectly easy to pour, though there was just a trace of opalescent milkiness in its appearance.

Friday, July 7, 1911. − We got away late, at noon, in a thick white fog, in which it was impossible to see where we were going. We still had to relay, though the surface had distinctly improved. There was no sign of wind sastrugi yet.

After lunch, which we finished about 6.30 p.m., we got an indistinct view of the mountains, and saw we were beginning to close Mt Terra Nova with Mt Terror, but the fog came down again at once, and at 9.45 p.m. we camped, as we were unable to guess at all what direction we had been making. We only made one and two-thirds miles good in the day.

The min. temp. for the night from 12 to 2 p.m. had been −75.8°. At 2 p.m. it was −58.3°, and at 7 p.m. had risen to −55.4°, a change which we felt as a grateful one both in our hands and feet on the march. [There is something after all rather good in doing something never done before − these temperatures must be world's record.]

Saturday, July 8, 1911. − A day of white fog and high moonlight but without a trace of landmark to guide us. We relayed as usual, four hours in the forenoon, for 1¼ miles, and three hours in the afternoon for one mile only. We were on a better surface, either more windswept or else improved by the rise in temperature, but still deep and soft to walk in, though often with harder crusted areas. Here and there were really hard and slippery windswept snow surfaces occurring under a covering of some inches of quite soft snow, showing the peculiar planed-off appearance which was always associated with horse-shoe impressions and very heavy dragging. We made our course today by compass.

The min. temp. for the night was −59.8° and at 10.30 a.m. −52.3°, with south-easterly airs, and −47° at 7.15 p.m.

Sunday, July 9, 1911. − Dense mist, and white fog [the fourth day of fog], and snow falling all day, made relaying impossible, but we found we could manage the two sledges together again on the improving surface.

Our chief difficulty was to avoid gradually and unwittingly mounting the slopes of Mt Terror to our left, where there are any number of crevassed patches of ice, and running into the pressure ridges on our right. Between these two lay an area of more or less level land ice which was safe going – but in two or three places I knew it was necessary to cross long snow capes running across our path from Mt Terror – and here, if one wished to avoid very long uphill drags one had to approach the pressure ridges fairly closely – a thing quite easy with daylight, but affording us constant trouble in the dark and fog which hampered us all along this part of our journey.

Today no landmarks were visible at all. We made a little over one mile in the forenoon and ¾ mile more in the afternoon. It was a great relief to have done so without relaying. The moon was invisible [only a glow where she is] and everything was obscured by fog, but the surface was improving every hour. In the afternoon we ran into crevassed ground, after having suspected we were pulling the sledges up and down several rises of moderate gradient. As we expected this, however, before reaching the second long snow cape, we went on. The surface was again hard and icy in places, with sometimes six inches of snow loose upon it. Our feet went through this snow and slipped upon the ivory-hard surface underneath. This was often near the top of the ridges. In the hollows the surface was deep and soft and crusted. One could judge much of the nature of the surface, and of the chance of finding crevasses, by the sound and by the feel of one's feet on the snow, without seeing anything at all of the surface one was covering. Occasionally the moonlit fog allowed an edge to be lit up here and there, but the surface is so extraordinarily uniform and featureless that we believe we are still well out of the windswept line of southerly blizzard and still in an area of eddying winds, heavy snowfall, and constant fogs formed by the meeting of cold Barrier air with the warmer, moister air which comes up from the sea ice, and especially from the innumerable fissures of the pressure ridges. We called this Fog Bay.

The moon had again become visible almost overhead, but nothing else, until just as we found ourselves going up a longer rise and a steeper one than usual we saw a grey, irregular, mountainous-looking horizon confronting us close ahead. So here we unhitched from the sledges, and tying our lanyards together into a central knot, we walked up about 50 yards of icy slope interspersed with cracks, and having reached the top found we had another similar broken and irregular horizon ahead of us and another on our left. These were obviously the pressure ridges, and when we stood still we could hear a creaking and groaning of the ice underneath and around us, which convinced us, and later led us to think that the tidal action of the coast here was taken up in part at any rate by the pressure ridges without forming any definite tide crack.

This excursion from our sledges gave us, as we thought, our right direction for the safer land ice, but on turning ourselves with them in that direction, we found we were still running into the same crevassed mounds and ridges, so, finding a hollow with deeper snow in it, we camped for the night, and decided to wait until we could see exactly where we had got to.

The absence of a well-marked tide crack – which had rather puzzled us in the *Discovery* days – in the crossing of land-ice slopes such as Terror Point (Cape McKay) and the 'second snowcape', both of which come straight down from Terror and run into the pressure ridges, was a question which we had in our minds all these days. We assuredly did cross several small cracks on these slopes which had the appearance of a certain amount of working, but their breadth was a matter of a couple of inches only, and if tidal they must take up only an insignificant frac-tion of the movement. They are so small that they may easily have been obscured by snowfall in the old days. Bowers is convinced they are to be considered tidal cracks. I am not so sure myself, and hope to have a better view of them by daylight before deciding whether there is anything to take up tidal movement besides the pressure ridges, which seem to me more than sufficient.

This day the temp. ranged from −36.7° up to −27°, with light airs northerly and southerly.

Some hours after midnight it began to blow and to snow more heavily.

The min. temp. for the night was −24.5° up to noon the next day.

Monday, July 10, 1911. – By noon a blizzard was blowing from the S.S.W., of force 6 to 8, and the air was as thick as could be with snow. This continued all day, and we lay wet and warm in our bags, listening to the periodic movements of the ice pressure, apparently tidal to some extent, beneath and about us.

Tuesday, July 11, 1911. The temp. at 10 a.m. went up to +7.8° ['a rise of over 80°' from the record minimum], and at 8 p.m. was still +6.8°, with a minimum for the day of +3.2°. The wind came from S.W., force 5 to 9, and very squally. This continued all day with a very considerable snowfall which packed our tent in 1½ to 2 feet all round, as well as all our sledge gear. Cherry is still in his down bag inside the reindeer with fur outside. Bowers still as he started, with fur outside. I turned my bag yesterday from fur inside to fur outside. The rise in temperature and the long lie-in during this blizzard have steamed us and our clothes into a very sodden wet condition, and one wondered what a return to low temperatures would effect.

We have been discussing our respective rations, and they have been somewhat revised as follows.

On July 6 Cherry felt the need for more food, and would have chosen fat, either butter or pemmican, had he not been experimenting on a large biscuit allowance. So he increased his biscuits to twelve a day, and found that it did away to some extent with his desire for more food and fat. But he occasionally had heartburn, and has certainly felt the cold more than Bowers and I have, and has had more frostbite in hands, feet, and face than we have.

I have altogether failed to eat anything approaching my allowance of 8 ozs. of butter a day. The most I have managed has been about 2 or 3 ozs.

Bowers has also found it impossible to eat his extra allowance of pemmican for lunch.

So yesterday – that is, a fortnight out – we decided that Cherry and I should both alter our dietary, he to take 4 ozs. a day of my butter and I to take two of his biscuits, i.e. 4 ozs., in exchange.

This brought Cherry's diet and mine to the same. Bowers continued his diet, taking his extra pemmican when he felt it possible – but this became increasingly less frequent and all the way home he went without it.

Cherry's diet and mine was now, *per diem*:

Pemmican	12 ozs.
Biscuit	16 ozs.
Butter	4 ozs. (we rarely eat more than 2 ozs.)

Bowers's diet was now:

Pemmican	12 ozs.
Biscuit	16 ozs.
Extra pemmican	4 ozs. (rarely eaten)

Our daily routine was, for breakfast, to have first tea, then pemmican and biscuit; for lunch, tea and biscuit (and butter for Cherry and myself); for supper, hot water and pemmican and biscuit.

We none of us missed sugar or cocoa, or any of the other foods we have been used to on sledge journeys, and we all found we were amply satisfied on this diet. Cocoa would have been pleasanter at night than plain hot water, but the hot water with biscuit soaked in it was very good.

We still carry out the brush routine every time we break camp, to clear away all the rime formed on the inner tent lining. The outer tent is extraordinarily free from frost – and remained so to the day we returned to Cape Evans. The lower skirts of the inner tent, however, are solid with ice.

Towards evening the wind abated considerably, and parts of Mt Terror came into view, but during the night the wind came on again with much snow and violent gusts, increasing at times to force 10. We were unable to march. The min. temp. for the night was −7.6°.

Wednesday, July 12, 1911. – We were compelled to remain in our bags again all day. Wind from S.W., force 10, and squally up to force 9 all the afternoon, with much drift. Temp. up to +2.9° again in the morning. Towards night there were lulls, and at 3 a.m. the wind ceased. Bowers turned his bag from hair outside to hair inside, his first change since starting.

Thursday, July 13, 1911. – After digging out our sledges and tent, which were pretty deeply buried in drift, we had a really good day's march, making 7½ miles in 7½ hours with both sledges. [Seems a marvellous run] During our march, in our effort to avoid the pressure ridges on our right, we got imperceptibly somehow too high up on to the slopes of Terror and were held up by a very wide crevasse with an unsafe-looking sunken lid, which we caught sight of in a momentary break of moonlight just in time to avoid it. We turned down its side and found it was one of a number that marked a low mound in the land ice slopes. We made out east again to get once more into the safety limit of land ice on the flat, which seemed very narrow in the dark.

We camped about 8 p.m. Min. temp. for last night was −22.2° and by the evening the temperature had dropped to −28.6°, but there was still a lot of cirro-stratus about, which the blizzard doesn't seem to have cleared away. There were also windy-looking clouds about, with lunar coronae and occasional halos. During the daylight there was a very striking rosy glow all over the northern sky even up to the summit of Mt Terror. The whole sky was a rich rosy purple, due to a thin cirro-stratus or alti-stratus I think.

The new surface was very flat, and very windswept, but not cut into sastrugi at all. Most of the new areas are low, flat, soft drifts, or low mounds, slightly rounded at the top and of large area. The softer areas have still the shaved or planed-off appearance with none but the horse-hoof shaped impressions on the surface.

Friday, July 14, 1911. – We made five and one-third miles in all today by a good morning march, but an afternoon march cut short by a complete loss of all light. After lunch we once more found we had overdone our easting and had run again into one of the higher pressure ridges. We turned north from it and encountered more crevasses, but by zig-zagging and sounding in advance on a longer trace we succeeded in getting clear of them. We had the Knoll before us at the time while there was light enough to see it. Our moonlight was, however, all but spent, so much of it had been lost in fogs and blizzard and bad weather. We were making for rather east of the Knoll today in our endeavour to keep within the flat area of land ice. Sastrugi were increasing rapidly here, and we were now entering the true path of the southerly blizzard.

The min. temp. for the night had been −35°. At 8.30 a.m. it was −17.4°, and in the afternoon and evening it was −24.6°. [The experiences so lightly passed over in the official account were sufficiently thrilling in themselves. The other diary records:

Rather a hair-raising day − very bad night − by hard slogging 2¾ miles this morning − then on in thick gloom which suddenly lifted and we found ourselves under a huge great mountain of pressure ridge looking black in shadow – we went on bending to left when Bill fell and put his arm into a crevasse – we went over this and another and some time after got somewhere up to left, and both Bill and I put a foot into a crevasse – we sounded all about and everywhere was hollow, and so we ran the sledge down over it and all was well. My nerves were about on edge at end of day.]

At the Knoll

Saturday, July 15, 1911. – The min. temp. for the night was −34.5°, but at 10.30 a.m. it was −19.2°, with a breeze of force 3 from the S.S.W. We got a clear view this morning, however, and could see the moraine shelf facing the Knoll, where we had decided to build our stone hut. We had a short, steep, uphill three miles' pull over very hard and deep-cut sastrugi to this spot, and then, rounding the lower end of the moraine, we found ourselves in the Knoll gap and pitched our last outward camp in a large open smooth snow hollow, hard and windswept as to surface, but in places not cut up by sastrugi. This camp lay about 150 yards below the ridge where we proposed to build our stone hut. [Here we are after a real slog – 700 feet up, camped on very hard snow with our hut site chosen off to W. on some moraine – we have been discussing what to call the hut which we hope to build under a big boulder on the slope, walling one side of it – Terra Igloo I expect. It seems too good to be true – 19 days out, this is our 15th camp – four days' blizzard. Surely seldom has anyone been so wet – our bags hardly possible to get into – our wind-clothes just frozen boxes. Birdie's patent balaclava is like iron – it is wonderful how our cares have vanished.] We had originally intended building on the Adélie penguin rookery, but so much of our time has been taken up in getting here, and our oil was already so short, that we decided to build as close as we could to our work with the Emperor penguins, and take the chance of doing so in the blizzard area. In the Adélie penguin rookery we should have been out of the blizzards, but five miles from our principal work. We hoped, however, to find something of a lee for our hut, and to put up with the blizzards.

On the ridge top above the snow hollow where we were camped was a low, rough mass of rock *in situ* with a quantity of loose rock masses of erratics of various kinds, some granite, some hard basalt, and some crumbly volcanic lava lying around. There was also a lot of rough gravel and plenty of hard snow which could be cut into paving-stone slabs. So here we had all the material we wanted, and as the corner under the rock *in situ* [which, it was hoped, would make a large part of one of the walls] was too solidly iced up with ice and gravel to clear out, we chose a spot [a moderately level piece of moraine] some 6 or 8 yards on the lee side of the actual ridge, a position which we thought would be out of the wind's force itself, but which we eventually found was all the more dangerous for that reason, as it was right in the spot where the upward suction was to be at its greatest. At lunch time, 4.15 p.m., we still had a southerly wind of force 4, with the temp. at −13°, and this wind we found to be due to a more or less constant flow of cold air down from the slopes of Terror.

We had a magnificent outlook from this spot where we were building our hut. To the east we looked out over the Great Barrier with the whole range of pressure ridges laid out at our feet, about 800 feet below [looking as if giants had been ploughing up with ploughs which made furrows 40 or 50 feet high]. To the north and N.E. we had the Knoll, and beyond it a clear open view over the ice of the Ross Sea. And to the south we looked along the path we had come along the slopes of Terror, stretching away towards the Bluff, while on our right these slopes climbed up to the summit of Mt Terror, which was plainly visible against the sky.

We saw that Ross Sea was completely frozen over. No open leads were to be seen, but much of the ice appeared to be young and thin, with little snow on it. These and the following notes on the ice of Ross Sea were kept by Bowers.

I began the use of my eiderdown bag today inside the reindeer bag with the fur outside, and after this made no change till the day we reached Cape Evans again.

Sunday, July 16, 1911. – Today looking over Ross Sea we saw a cloud of frost smoke drifting eastward along the Cape Crozier cliffs, evidently from an open lead along the coast. Otherwise the sea was covered by an unbroken sheet of ice.

The temp. varied today between −20.8° and −28.5°, and we again had the south-westerly breeze of force 3 to 5 coming down our snow slope from Mt Terror. The weather was clear in the morning, but became hazy with cirro-stratus and fog soon after noon from the south.

We worked at the stone hut all the daylight and as long as we could see by the waning moonlight, and while Cherry built up the walls, Bowers and I collected rocks and piled up the outside of the walls with snow slabs and gravel. We had a pick and a shovel to work with.

[It was quite a question what it was to be called: in his Diary Bill called it 'Oriana Hut', and the ridge the Oriana ridge: we discussed 'Terra Igloo', 'Bleak House', 'The House on the Hill'.

Birdie gathered rocks from over the hill; nothing was too big for him. Bill did the banking up outside. The stones were good; the snow, however, was blown so hard as to be practically ice: a pick made little impression upon it, and the only way was to chip out big blocks gradually by the small shovel.

There was now little moonlight or daylight, but for the next two days we used both to their utmost, being up at all times by day and night, and often working on when there was great difficulty to see anything: one day Birdie was digging with the hurricane lamp by his side.]

The hut was placed so as to escape the force of the southerly wind under the moraine ridge. We were about 800 feet above sea level. Our method of construction was to build four walls of solid rock, leaving a small gap for a door in the lee end. The weather wall was highest, and the breadth of the hut was 7½ to 8 ft., so that the 9-foot sledge rested across from wall to wall as a cross rafter to support the canvas roof. The two side walls were built up to the height of the weather wall at the weather end, but were not so high by a couple of feet at the door end. The length of the hut was about 10 ft.

Against the outer side of the rock-walls were laid large slabs of hard snow like paving stones, each having its icy windswept surface outside. Between the slabs of snow and the rock walls we shovelled moraine gravel. Over all this fell the canvas roof, anchored by lanyards to heavy rocks all round, and battened down to its outer side again by a double banking of ice slabs and gravel; finally, every crevice was packed in by hand with soft snow until the whole wall was uniformly tight all round. The work took us all the light we had of three days to finish. The canvas roof was made so ample in size that it came right down to the ground on the weather side and more than half-way down all the other sides. This, we thought, could not fail to make the walls tight when packed in and over as explained above, but it completely failed to keep out either snow drift or gravel dust when the wind began to blow in earnest later on, for both drift and dust poured in through every crack between the stones of the weather walls and lee walls without shifting any of the more bulky packing at all.

Monday, July 17, 1911. – We continued with the hut and spent the whole of available daylight and moonlight in getting on with the walls, which were all but finished for placing the roof and door. For this we want a calm if possible.

We began work today in a light air, but it was blowing again with force 3 from the S.W. from noon onwards, and the temp. all day varied between −19.5° and −23.3°. The sky was overcast. [Birdie was very disappointed that we could not finish the whole thing that day, but there was a lot to do yet, and we were tired out. We turned out early the next day to try and get the roof on, but it was blowing hard. (*Tuesday,* 18th) When we got to the top we did some digging, &c., but it was quite impossible to try and get the roof on, and we had to leave it. We realised this day that it blew much harder at the top of the slope than where our tent was pitched. It was bitterly cold up there that morning.]

Over Ross Sea are now two open leads of water like broad irregular streets extending from the Cape Crozier cliffs away to the N.E. and lying more or less parallel to one another.

Tuesday, July 18, 1911. – No leads or open water were visible today over Ross Sea. The temp., −26.5° to −27.3°, with S.S.W. wind of force 4 to 5 all day, made work almost impossible at the hut. We got everything ready for placing and fixing the roof, but couldn't do it in the wind. We left the work at noon and turned in to spend a very cold night, a thing which we generally found was the consequence of not having done any hard work or marching during the day. [During this time our bags were getting worse and worse, but were still very possible, and we always looked forward to the days of the 'Stone Age' when the blubber stove should be going and we were to dry everything. When we arrived we had begun our fifth out of six tins of oil, and we were economising oil as much as possible, often only having two hot meals a day.

It was curious how the estimate of how much oil was necessary to our return, diminished as our stock decreased: at first we said we must have at least two gallons to go back with: then about Terror Point a tin and two full primus lamps; until it came down to one full gallon tin, and this is what we actually did use.]

Wednesday, July 19, 1911. – As it was a fine, calm day we decided to use it in an effort to reach the Emperor rookery and get some blubber, as our last can of oil but one was already running low and we had determined to keep the last can untouched for the journey home. We started down at 9.30 a.m., just as dawn appeared on the horizon in the east. We took an empty sledge, with a couple of ice axes, Alpine rope, harnesses, and skinning tools. We had about a mile to go down snow slopes to the edge of the first pressure ridge, and our intention was to keep close in under the land ice cliffs which are very much more extensive now than they were ten years ago. Then we hoped to get in under the actual rock cliffs which had always been the best way down to the rookery in the *Discovery* days. But somehow we got down by a slope which led us into a valley between the first two pressure ridges, and we found it impossible to get back in under the land ice cliffs. Nor had we then seen any other way down from the land ice except by the slope we followed. The rest was apparently all ice cliff about 80 to 100 ft. high. We tried again and again to work our way in to the left where the land ice cliffs joined the rock cliffs, but though we made considerable headway now and then along snow slopes and drift ridges by crossing the least tumbled parts of the intervening pressure lines, we yet came time after time to impossible places [with too great a drop], and had to turn back and try another way. [Bill led on a length of Alpine rope on the toggle of the sledge. Birdie was in his harness on the toggle, and I was in my harness on the rear of the sledge. Two or three times we tried to get down the ice slopes to the comparatively level road under the cliff, but it was always too great a drop. In that dim light every proportion was distorted, and some of the places we actually did manage to negotiate with ice axes and Alpine rope looked absolute precipices, and there were always crevasses at the bottom if you slipped. This day I went into various crevasses at least six times, once when we were close to the sea going right in to my waist, rolling out and then down a steep slope until brought up by Birdie and Bill on the rope.] We tried one possible opening after another, and all led to further impasses until the daylight was two-thirds gone, and we found ourselves faced in a large snow hollow by a chaotic pile of ice blocks and snowdrifts standing almost vertically in our path and all round us, to a height of some sixty feet, and completely stopping all chance of progress forward [a great *cul-de-sac* which probably formed the end of the two ridges, where they butted on to the sea ice]. Here we had the mortification of hearing the cries of Emperor penguins echoed to us by the rock cliffs on our left. We were still, however, out of sight of the rookery and we had still a quarter of a mile of chaotic pressure to cross [to be caught in the night there was a horrible idea], so we reluctantly gave up the attempt for the day and with great caution and much difficulty owing to the failing light retraced the steps it had taken us about three hours to make. We had been roped together the whole time and had used the sledge continually over soft and rotten-looking snow bridges. It was dark by the time we reached safe ground after clambering about five hours to no purpose. [Birdie was very good at picking the tracks up again. At last we lost them altogether and settled we must go ahead. As a matter of fact we picked them up again, and by then were out of the worst; but we were glad to see the tent again.]

During the day a light southerly breeze had been blowing with a clear sky. The temp. had varied from −30° with south-westerly wind of force 2 at 4 p.m. to −37°, which had been the minimum in the early morning between 3 a.m. and 9.30 a.m.

There was again some frost smoke over the sea ice under the Cape Cliffs and a small shining open lead of water in the offing.

Thursday, July 20, 1911. – We turned out at 3 a.m. in order to get our hut roof fixed on and made safe in calm weather, and we had decided to make another attempt when day came at 9.30 a.m. to reach the Emperor rookery and get the blubber which we now really began to need. We got the roof on the hut and made it all safe. [Little did we think what that roof had in store for us as we packed it in with snow blocks, stretching it over our second 8-ft. sledge which we put athwartships in the middle of the wall. The windward end came right down to the ground, and we tied it down securely to rocks before packing it in. To do this we had a good two feet or more of slack all round, and in every case we tied it to rocks by lanyards at intervals of every two feet. The door was the difficulty, and for the present we left the cloth arching over the stones, forming a kind of portico. The whole was well packed over with slabs of hard snow, but there was no soft snow with which to fill up the gaps between the blocks.] We then had breakfast and got away in good time for the pressure ridges before day broke. We had the same equipment as yesterday, and crampons of the new canvas pattern which Cherry and I found most reliable and comfortable, though Bowers preferred the old pattern used at Hut Point. Going down today we made for a different and rather narrow slope leading much more directly down to the foot of the land ice cliffs. We had missed it yesterday in the bad light when walking along the cliff tops looking for a way down, but we had seen it from below [at a place where there was a break in the big ice cliff] and had decided to try for it today. It took us down the right direction [twice we crept up to the edge of the cliff with no success, but the third time we found the ridge down], and we got down directly in under the old land ice cliffs which still cover the more southern portions of the basalt cliffs of the Knoll. These ice cliffs are a monument to what wind can do; they are more than a hundred feet high in places and are deeply scooped out into vast grooved and concave hollows as though by a colossal gouge. By following along the foot of these weather-worn and dirty-banded old relics of glaciation one comes by a series of slides and climbs and scrambles to quite recent exposures of dark rock cliffs which were not exposed when I was here ten years ago.

Then, passing along the foot of these, one comes to more and loftier ice cliffs and more and still loftier rock cliffs, and along the very foot of these, in among rock débris and snow drifts and frozen thaw pools, and boulders which have fallen into the trough, we had to walk and climb and slide and crawl in the direction of the sea ice rookery. [We got along till finally we climbed along the top of a snow ridge with a razor-back edge. On our right was a drop of great depth with crevasses at the bottom: on our left was a smaller drop, also crevassed. We crawled along: it was exciting work in the half darkness. At the end was a series of slopes full of crevasses, and finally we got right in under the rock on to moraine.] At one spot we appeared again to have come to an impasse, for one of the largest and most chaotic pressure ridges had actually come up against the rock face of the Crozier cliffs, but we found a man-hole in the space between the ice and the rock which was big enough, and only just big enough, for us to crawl through one by one. [Bill disappeared into the hole, and we followed and managed to wriggle through, working ourselves over a gully the other side by jamming our bodies against one side with our legs against the cliff on the other. In another place we got up another hole between two jams of pressure, rather like an enlarged rabbit-hole. The place was strewn with fallen ice blocks and rocks, and if one fell on us we should have finished, also if the Barrier had just then chosen to give a squeeze.] We had to leave the sledge here. Once past this we were in an enclosed snow pit with an almost vertical wall which required about fifteen steps to be cut to get out of it. From here we had again a series of drift troughs between the rock cliffs and the pressure ridges until at last we got out on to the actual ice foot, overhanging the sea ice by a small overhanging cliff of 10 or 12 feet. This was the lowest point of the ice foot and there was no snow drift running down from it on to the sea ice anywhere. This rather suggests that even this bay ice was not at all old as yet – possibly not even a month old. Farther on round the foot of the Crozier rock cliffs the ice foot cliff was very considerably higher, 20 to 30 feet.

The light was rapidly failing when we at last reached the sea ice, and we had to be very quick in doing what we had to do here. We saw there was no seal in sight. We saw also that there were only about 100 Emperor penguins instead of a couple of thousand as in 1902 and 1903. They were all standing in one compact group under the ice cliffs of the Barrier a few hundred yards from where we had emerged. We decided to get three penguin skins with their blubber and a few eggs. We therefore left Cherry on the ice foot with the Alpine rope to help us up again from the sea ice. Bowers and I jumped down and went off to the Emperors. We saw at once that some of them were crouching with eggs on their feet, as they tried to shuffle away with them without losing their hold. As we hustled them, however, a good many eggs were dropped and left lying on the ice, or were picked up again by the unemployed birds that saw and took their opportunity to seize an egg. We collected six eggs and killed and skinned three birds, and went back to the ice foot where Cherry was waiting to help us up with the rope.

We passed the eggs and skins up, and then by climbing on Bowers's back I also got up; but no amount of combined pulling would lift Bowers, as the rope only cut and jammed into the overhanging cliff of ice. He, however, hunted round till he found a place where he helped himself up by cutting steps while we hauled at the same time. It took a little time, but at last we were all up, and at once started back by the way we had come in a very failing light. Bowers had unfortunately got one leg into a crack in the sea ice, and his crampon, finnesko and socks became frozen into a solid mass. Had we been able to bring the sledge along to this point the ice foot would have given us no difficulty at all, but we had left it behind at the manhole. [A whole procession of Emperors came round just as they were coming back from the floe.]

The small number of Emperor penguins collected here at this time is surprising. There were not more than 100 birds, and without forcing all of them to abandon their eggs it was impossible to guess how many had laid or were incubating. It looked to me as though every fourth or fifth bird had an egg, but this is only a guess and may be quite wrong, though I am certain that there were more birds without eggs than with eggs. Why there should be so few birds here this July, when there were so many more here in September and October ten years ago, is difficult to understand. The examination of the three eggs we have brought back with us may throw some light on the question. They may have only just begun to lay, and these may have been the earliest arrivals. Others may yet arrive in numbers and lay this year.

Another possible explanation is that the ice has not remained in, and that the rookery has been dissipated lately; and some support is lent to this possibility by the absence of all snowdrifts on to the sea ice from the ice foot.

I see no way of deciding this question except by another visit to the rookery – either this year in September or October – or next year, preferably in August. The most valuable work probably could be done in August, and a visit would be much facilitated if by any possibility some supply of oil and food could be left at the Adélie penguin rookery by the ship during the coming summer. But I am not blind to the difficulties there may be in her doing this.

A very interesting fact we saw at the rookery this time was that these birds are so anxious to incubate an egg that they will incubate a rounded lump of ice instead, just as before we noticed them incubate a dead and frozen chick, if they were unable to secure a living one. Both Bowers and I, in the failing light, mistook these rounded dirty lumps of ice for eggs, and picked them up as eggs before we realised what they were. One of them I distinctly saw dropped by a bird, and it was roughly egg-shaped and of the right size – hard, dirty and semi-translucent ice. Another was, as I thought, a deformed egg, and as such I picked it up. It was shaped thus.

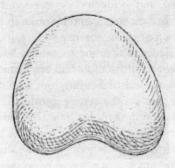

Ice 'nest-egg' mistaken for a deformed egg.

I also saw one of the birds return and tuck one of these ice 'nest-eggs' on to its feet, under the abdominal flap. I had a real egg in my hand, so I put it down on the ice close to this bird, and the bird at once left the lump of ice and shuffled to the real egg and pushed it in under its flap on to the feet. It apparently knew the difference, and it shows how strong is the desire to brood over something.

The three birds that we killed and skinned were very thickly blubbered, and the oil we got from them burnt very well indeed – and much more fiercely than the seal oil. There was about ¼ inch of pure fat under the skin. The birds were in excellent plumage. Bowers noticed there was very little soiled sea ice where they were standing, which also supports the idea of a very recent arrival, or recent freezing of the bay ice, or both.

There was another small group of Emperors wandering by the ice foot down which we came, but none of them had eggs. We saw no others.

The sea was frozen over as far as the horizon. There was a little evidence of pressure in cracks of the sea ice in the bay. Our visit was a very hurried one, unfortunately, owing to the shortness of the light and the risk of getting benighted in the pressure ridges. Subsequent events unfortunately made another visit impossible.

[We legged it back as hard as we could go, two eggs each in our fur mits; Birdie with two skins tied on behind, and myself with one. We were roped up, and climbing the ridges and getting through the holes was very difficult. In one place where there was a steep rubble and snow slope down I left the ice-axe half-way up; in another it was too dark to see our former ice-axe footsteps, and I could see nothing, and so just let myself go and trusted to luck. Bill said with infinite patience, 'Cherry, you must learn how to use an ice-axe.' For the rest of the trip my windclothes were in rags.

We found the sledge, and none too soon. We had four eggs left, more or less whole. Both mine had burst in my mits: the first I emptied out, the second I left in my mit to put in the cooker; it never got there, but on the return journey I had my mits far more easily thawed out than Birdie's (Bill had none), and I believe the grease in the egg did them good. When we got into the hollows under the ridge where we had to cross, it was too dark to do anything but feel our way – which we did over many crevasses, found the ridge and crept over it. Higher up we could see more, but to follow our tracks soon became impossible, and we plugged straight ahead and luckily found the slope down which we had come.

It began to blow, and as we were going up the slope to the tent, blew up to 4; it was such a bad light that we missed our way entirely and got right up above our knoll, and only found it after a good deal of search; meanwhile the weather was getting thick.]

On returning to the stone hut we flenced one of the penguin skins and cooked our supper on the blubber stove, which burnt furiously. I was incapacitated for the time being by a sputter of the hot oil catching me in one eye. We slept in the hut for the first time.

[We moved into the igloo and began a wretched night. The wind was coming in all round. It began to drift, and the drift came in by a back draught under the door and covered everything – bags, socks, and all our gear. Bill started up the blubber stove with

the blubber ready in it. The first thing it did was to spurt a blob of
boiling blubber into his eye: for the rest of the night he lay, quite
unable to stifle his groans, in obviously very great pain – and he
told us afterwards that he thought his eye was gone. We managed
to cook a meal somehow, and Birdie got the stove going afterwards; but it was quite useless to try and warm the place. The wind
was working in through the cracks in the snow blocks which we
had used for baulking outside, and there was no possibility of
stopping these cracks. I got out and cut up a triangular piece
outside the door so as to get the roof cloth in under the stones, and
then packed it down as best I could with snow and so blocked
most of the drift coming in. Bill said the next evening, 'At any
rate things look better tonight – I think we reached bedrock last
night' – as a matter of fact we hadn't by some long way. The igloo
was naturally very cold, and it blizzed all that night, blowing 6.

The greater part of the next day the wind had fallen, and we got
all the drift we could find from the last night – it wasn't much –
and packed in the sides of the igloo.]

The temperature today had not been below −28.3°. There had
been a southerly wind all day which we had felt at all the more
exposed parts of the way down to the sea ice and in the hollows
under the cliffs. It gradually freshened in the afternoon and stratus
came up from the south. At 8 p.m. it was blowing force 6 from the
S.S.W., but the sky was clear to the N.E.

Friday, July 21, 1911. – Our first night in the hut was comfortable enough, though the breeze freshened during the night and
increased to force 8, but fell to 5 in the morning. The only thing
we did not quite like was the tendency the wind had to lift the
canvas roof off its supporting sledge so we piled large slabs of icy
snow on the canvas top to steady it down and prevent this.

The temp. ranged from −20.4° to −23.7°, and though the wind
dropped to light airs the weather looked thick and unsettled, with
stratus moving up rapidly from the south.

We spent the whole of our daylight in packing our hut with soft
snow, until not a crack or a crevice remained visible anywhere on
the outside.

Then we brought up our tent from the hollow below, and
pitched it, for the sake of convenience, under the lee end of our
hut, quite close to the door. My idea in doing this was to get more

efficient heat for drying socks and other gear than was possible in the hut. The large open canvas roof of the hut allowed all the heat to escape at once, but in the double tent the intense heat of the blubber stove dried anything hung in the apex in a very short time.

We cooked our supper in the tent, nearly stifling ourselves with the smoke, but the heating effect was immense. [The blubber stove heated the oil so much that we expected every minute that the whole would flare up. It took a lot of primus to start it. We took our finnesko in to try and dry them there with the rest of the gear when we left. Bill and I, however, took our private bags back into the igloo. After dinner we flenced one of the Emperor skins as hard as we could and boiled down the blubber in the inner cooker – very good stuff – nearly filling the stove up.] We then moved to the hut to sleep, believing it to be as safe and as comfortable as it could be made until we got some covering for the roof, such as sealskins. When we turned in there was practically no wind at all, but the sky was overcast. When I turned out three or four hours later there was still no wind; but it came on to blow suddenly soon after 3 a.m., and blew heavily from the S. with little drift at first.

Saturday, July 22, 1911. – By 6.30 a.m. it was blowing force 9 to 10 from the S.S.W., with heavy drift and wind in strong gusts, and when Bowers turned out he found the tent had disappeared, legs, lining, cover and all, leaving the cooker and all the gear we had left in it overnight on the ground. The drift was now very thick and there was nothing to be done but to collect the gear, which Bowers and Cherry did and passed it in to me in the hut. Very little of the gear was lost. All our finnesko were there and were recovered, as well as a quantity of smaller gear. The only losses were the two flat parts of the cooker, which we never found afterwards.

[We were woken up by Birdie shouting through the door, 'Bill, Bill, the tent has gone.' I got out, helped Birdie, and passed the gear which had been in the tent into the igloo, where Bill took it. It was impossible to stand against the wind: Birdie was blown right over; each time we got something it was a fight to get the three or four yards to the igloo door: if the wind had started us down the slope nothing would have stopped us. The place where the tent had been was littered with gear. When we came to reckon up afterwards we had everything except the bottom piece of the cooker and the top of the outer cooker. The former was left on the top of the cooker, the latter was in its groove. We never regained them. The most wonderful thing of all was that all our finnesko were lying where they were left, which happened to be on the ground in the part of the tent which was under the lee of the igloo. Also Birdie's private bag was there, and a tin of sweets.

Birdie brought two tins of sweets away with him as a luxury, for we had no sugar in our ration: one we had on our arrival at the Knoll; this was the second, of which we knew nothing, and which was for Bill's birthday, the next day. We started eating them on Saturday, however, and the tin came in useful to Bill afterwards.

The roar of the wind in the igloo sounded just like the rush of an express train through a tunnel. As it topped the rise it sucked our roof cloth upwards, letting it down with tremendous bangs. We could only talk in shouts, and began to get seriously alarmed about our roof.]

Inside the hut we were now being buried by fine snow drift, which was coming through the cracks of the walls in fine spouts, especially through the weather wall and over the door in the lee wall. We tried to plug the inlets with socks, but as fast as we closed one the drift came in by another, and heaps of soft drift gradually piled up to 6 and 8 inches on everything. It seems that the strong wind blowing over the roof of the hut sucked it upwards and tried hard to lift it off, producing so much suction into the interior of the hut that the fine drift came in everywhere notwithstanding our day spent in packing every crack and cranny. When there was no more snow drift to come in, fine black moraine dust came in and blackened everything like coal dust. The canvas roof, upon which we had put heavy slabs of icy snow, was lifted clean off and was stretched upwards and outwards like a tight dome and as taut as a drum. There was no chafe or friction anywhere except along the lee end wall top, and there we plugged every space between the canvas and the wall stones with pyjama jackets, fur mits, socks, &c. So long as the ice slabs remained on the top, moreover, there was no flapping and everything seemed fairly secure. Our only fear was that to allow of the admission of so much drift and dust through the weather wall there must have been openings in our packing — and we thought it possible that by degrees the upward tension might draw the canvas roof out. We could not be quite certain that the ice-slabs were not being eaten away. This, however, proved not to be our danger; the slabs remained sound to the end and the canvas buried in the walls did not draw anywhere at all, even for an inch.

The storm continued unabated all day, and we decided to cook a meal on the blubber stove. We felt a great satisfaction in having three penguin skins to cook with for some days, so that we could last out any length of blizzard without coming to our last can of oil.

We got the blubber stove going once or twice, but it insisted on suddenly going out for no apparent reason. And before we had boiled any water, in trying to restart it with the spirit lamp provided for the purpose, the feed-pipe suddenly dropped off, unsoldered, rendering the whole stove useless. [That was the end of the stove; very lucky it ended when it did, for it was obviously a most dangerous thing.] We therefore poured the melted oil into tins and lamps for the journey home in case our candles ran out, and for drying or thawing out socks and mits.

We then considered matters in the light of a shortage of oil and absence of tent. We decided first to go as long as we could without a hot meal so long as the blizzard kept us inactive. We also saw that we could not afford to start our last can of oil with the vague chance of getting a seal and improvising a blubber stove and so staying on here. We still had a fill of oil in our fifth can. As for the tent, we believed we should at any rate find part of it, if only the legs, and we saw no impossibility in improvising a tent cover of some sort from the canvas roof of our hut, even if the tent and lining were both lost.

Lying in our bags in the hut we were very wet, and got wetter from the fine drift every time we moved in or out of them. Everything was buried in a pile of soft, fine drift. But we were not cold. We finished our breakfast on the primus when the blubber stove gave out, and this was our last meal for a good many hours as it happened. [At intervals during the next 24 hours Birdie, who was absolutely magnificent, was up and about, stopping up every crevice where wind or drift was working in with socks, mits, and anything handy. A drift hole was especially bad in the middle of the windward wall, drifting us all up lightly, and putting a lot in

Birdie's corner. The only possible thing to do for the roof would have been lashings over it outside, and in that wind that was out of the question. Our position, with the tent gone, was bad.]

We could not understand quite how the tent had been blown away, for we had taken extra precautions in setting it, and had got as nearly perfect a spread as possible. Moreover, it was in the lee of the hut, and we had buried the valance not only with heaps of snow, but with 4 or 5 rocks on the snow in each bay, and to make things quite secure, the last thing before turning in Bowers and I had hoisted the heavy canvas tank, full of gear, almost more than one could lift alone, on to the weather skirt.

We could only think that the same sucking action which lifted our roof also lifted the tent, or that it was twisted off its legs by getting caught sideways by a squall which came partly round the end of the hut corner. Anyhow, as it was gone, we decided to take the earliest opportunity of any light to go and look for it.

Other things happened before this opportunity arrived.

Sunday, July 23, 1911. – Bowers estimated the wind at force 11 and noted it as blowing with almost continuous storm force, with very slight lulls followed by squalls of great violence.

About noon the canvas roof of the hut was carried away, and the storm continued unabated all day, but latterly without much drift.

It happened that this was my birthday – and we spent it lying in our bags without a roof or a meal, wishing the wind would drop, while the snow drifted over us.

The roof went as follows. We saw, as soon as light showed through the canvas in the early morning, that the snow blocks on the top had all been blown off, and that the upward strain was now as bad as ever, with a greater tendency to flap at the lee end wall. And where the canvas was fixed in over the door it began to work on the heavy stones which held it down, jerking and shaking them so that it threatened to throw them down. Bowers was trying all he could to jam them tight with pyjama jackets and bamboos, and in this I was helping him when the canvas suddenly ripped, and in a moment I saw about six rents all along the lee wall top, and in another moment we were under the open sky with the greater part of the roof flapped to shreds. The noise was terrific, and rocks began to tumble in off the walls on to Bowers and Cherry, happily without hurting them, and in a smother of drift Bowers and I bolted into our bags, and in them the three of us lay listening to the flap of the ragged ends of canvas over our heads, which sounded like a volley of pistol shots going on for hour after hour. As we lay there I think we were all revolving plans for making a tent now to get back to Hut Point with, out of the floorcloth on which we lay – the only piece of canvas now left us, except for the pieces still firmly embedded in the hut walls. We were all warm enough, though wet, as we had carried a great deal of snow into the bags with us, and every time we looked out more drift which was accumulating over us would fall in. I hoped myself that this would not prove to be one of the five- or eight-day blizzards which we had experienced at Cape Crozier in days gone by.

Monday, July 24, 1911. – The storm continued unabated until midnight, and then dropped to force 9 with squalls interspersed by short lulls. At 6.30 a.m. the wind had dropped to force 2. At 10 a.m. it was about force 3, and we awaited the moment when there would be light enough for us to look for our tent. Meanwhile Bowers suggested an *al fresco* meal under the floorcloth as we sat in our bags. We lit the primus and got the cooker going and had a good hot meal, the first for 48 hours, the tent floorcloth resting on our heads.

As it was still dark when we had finished we lay in our bags again for a bit. Daylight appeared, and we at once turned out, and it was by no means reassuring to find that the weather in the south still looked as bad and thick as it possibly could. We therefore lost no time at all in getting away down wind to look for the tent. Everywhere we found shreds of green canvas roof the size of a pocket-handkerchief, but not a sign of the tent, until a loud shout from Bowers, who had gone more east to the top of a ridge than Cherry and I, told us he had seen it. He hurried down, and slid about a hundred yards down a hard snow slope, sitting in his haste, and there we joined him where he had found the whole tent hardly damaged at all, a quarter of a mile from where we had pitched it. One of the poles had been twisted right out of the cap, and the lower stops of the tent lining had all carried away more or less, but the tent itself was intact and untorn.

We brought it back, pitched it in the old spot in the snow hollow below our hut, and then brought down our bags and cooker and all essential gear, momentarily expecting the weather to break on us again. It looked as thick as could be and close at hand in the south.

We discussed the position, and came to the conclusion that as our oil had now run down to one can only, and as we couldn't afford to spend time trying to fix up an improvised blubber stove in a roofless hut, we ought to return to Cape Evans.

It was disappointing to have seen so very little of the Emperor penguins, but it seemed to me unavoidable, and that we had attempted too difficult an undertaking without light in the winter.

I had also some doubt as to whether our bags were not already in such a state as might make them quite unusable should we meet with really low temperatures again in our journey home.

I therefore decided to start for Hut Point the next day. To this end we sorted out all our gear, and made a depôt in a corner of the stone hut of all that we could usefully leave there for use on a future occasion. This depôt I fixed up finally with Cherry the next morning while Bowers packed up the sledge at our tent. We put rocks on our depôt and the nine-foot sledge, and the pick, with a matchbox containing a note tied to the handle, where it could not be missed. We also fixed up bamboos round the walls to attract attention to the spot.

[Mr Cherry-Garrard's account of this episode must be quoted in full:

All that day and night it *blew* 11, with absolutely no real lull; what the wind was in the gusts we shall never know – it was something appalling. We quite lost count of time, but Sunday morning it was just the same. This was Bill's birthday.

About now we began to realise that the roof must go. The stones holding the door end (leeward) of the roof began to work: drift was coming in, and the place where I had slit up the roof to fold it in over the door was obviously weak: the foodbags did something to remedy this. Bill told us he thought that to turn over, flaps under, would give us our best chance. We could do nothing, and lay in our bags until Birdie told us that the roof was flapping more: he was out of his bag trying to hold the rocks firm, and I and Bill were sitting up in ours pressing against them with a bamboo. Suddenly the roof went – first, I believe, over the door, splitting into seven or eight strips along the leeward end, and then ripping into hundreds of pieces in about half a minute.

We got into our bags as best we could. I remember trying to get Bill into his, as he was farther out than I was; he wouldn't let me – 'Please get into your bag, Cherry.' Both Birdie's hands went in getting back to his. We turned our bags over, flaps under, as much as possible, and were gradually drifted up.

It was a most appalling position. I knew that Peary had once come through a blizzard lying in the open in his bag in the summer. I had no idea that human beings could do so in winter in the state in which we were already. I wondered whether it was really worth trying to keep warm. I confess that I considered that we were now come to the end. If we got out of the blizzard and had, as we decided, to try and get back by digging ourselves into the snow for the night, I meant to ask Bill to let us have enough morphia to deaden the pain when, as I think still it must have come, the cold became too much to live. With a steep icy slope below us, ending in an ice-cliff which itself led into the pressure, I don't know whether any of us had much hope of finding the tent – though afterwards as the wind went down we said we had. Without the tent I think we must have died.

I suppose at times all through this blizzard we must have dozed – I remember waking once after this to hear Bill singing hymns – every now and then I could hear a little, and Bill says Birdie was doing the same: I chimed in a bit, but not very much. Early Monday morning there were decided lulls in the wind, and the blizzard had practically blown itself out. Before daylight, while it was still blowing, we turned out and went down the slope to try and find the tent. We could see nothing, and were forced to return. It was now 48 hours since we had had a meal, and we managed about the weirdest meal ever eaten N. or South. We got the floorcloth under the heads of our bags, then got into our bags and drew the floorcloth over our heads and got the primus going in this shelter, and the cooker held by hand over the primus. In time we got both tea and pemmican – the blubber left in the cooker burnt and gave the tea a burnt taste – none of us will ever forget that meal. I enjoyed it as much as such a meal ever could be enjoyed, and that burnt taste will always bring back that memory.

A little glow of light began to come up and we turned out to have a further search for the tent. Birdie went off before Bill and me. I dragged my eiderdown out on my feet all sopping wet; it was impossible to get it back, and I let it freeze – it was soon just like a rock. I followed Bill down the slope when we heard a shout on our right and made for it with hope. We got on a slope, slipped, and went sliding down, quite unable to stop ourselves, and came to Birdie with the tent, outer lining still on the bamboos. We were so thankful we said nothing. The tent was over the ridge to the N.E. of the igloo at the bottom of the steep slope about half of a mile away. I believe that it blew away because part of it was in the wind, and part in the lee of the igloo.

It looked as if it would start blowing again at any moment and was getting thick, and we hurried back with the tent, slithering up and down, and pitched it where we had pitched it on our arrival. Never was tent so firmly dug in, by Bill, while Birdie and I got our gear, such as we could find, down from the igloo. Luckily the wind from the S. and the back-draught from the N. had blown everything inwards when the roof went, and we managed to find or dig out almost everything except Bill's fur mits. These were packed into a hole in rocks to prevent drift coming in. We had a meal in the tent; searched for the parts of the cooker down the slope, but only found a track of small bits of roof cloth. We were very weak. We packed the tank ready for a start back in the morning and turned in, utterly worn out. It was only −12° that night, but my left big toe was frostbitten in my bag, which I was trying to use without an eiderdown lining.]

Tuesday, July 25, 1911. –There was a stiff cold breeze of force 4 and temp. −15.3° which came down our slope from S.S.W., with thick weather and heavy clouds moving up from the Barrier in the south. We quickly finished all our final arrangements and got away down into the gut by the pressure ridges, where we found ourselves pulling against a gale rapidly freshening from the S.W. [My job, writes Cherry-Garrard, was to balance the sledge behind: I was so utterly done I don't believe I could have pulled effectively. Birdie was much the strongest of us. The strain and want of sleep was getting me in the neck, and Bill looked very bad.]

This wind became so strong after we had gone a mile that we camped, much against our inclinations, in amongst ice-hard, wind-swept sastrugi [our hands going one after the other], and the gale continued and freshened to force 9 and lasted all night. Bowers here determined that the tent should not go off alone, and arranged a line by which he fastened the cap of the tent to himself as he lay in his bag. The temp. during the day was from $-15.3°$ to $-17°$, and the whole sky was overcast.

Bowers today turned his bag to hair outside. Cherry had a sound sleep in his bag, which he badly wanted.

[I, writes C.-G., was feeling as if I should crack, and accepted Birdie's eiderdown, which he had not used and had for many days been asking me to use. It was wonderfully self-sacrificing of him, more than I can write. I felt a brute to take it, but I was getting useless, unless I got some sleep, which my big bag would not allow. The day we got down to the Emperors I felt so done that I did not much care whether I went down a crevasse or not. We had gone through a great deal since then. Bill and Birdie kept on assuring me that I was doing more than my share of the work, but I think that I was getting more and more weak. Birdie kept wonderfully strong: he slept most of the night; the difficulty was for him to get into his bag without going to sleep. He kept the meteorological log untiringly, but some of these nights he had to give it up for the time because he could not keep awake. He used to fall asleep with his pannikin in his hand and let it fall, and once he had the lighted primus.

Bill's bag was getting hopeless: it was really too small for an eiderdown and was splitting all over the place – great long holes. He never consciously slept for nights – he did sleep a bit, for we heard him. Except for this night and the next, when Birdie's eiderdown was fairly dry, I never consciously slept; except that I used to wake for five or six nights running with the same night-mare – that we were drifted up and that Bill and Birdie were passing the gear into my bag, cutting it open to do so – or some other variation, I did not know that I had been asleep at all.]

All our bags were by this time so saturated with water that they froze too stiff to bend with safety, so from now onwards to Cape Evans we never rolled them up, but packed them one on the other full length, like coffins, on the sledge. Even so, they were breaking or broken in several places in the efforts we made to get into them in the evenings. We always took the precaution to stow our personal kit bags and sleeping fur boots and socks in such parts as would give us an entry to start getting in by. They were all very uncomfortable and our whole journey home was done on a very limited allowance of conscious sleep, while one or other of the party almost invariably dozed off and had a sleep over the cooker in the comparative comfort of sitting on a bag instead of lying inside it.

Wednesday, July 26, 1911. – We got in only half a day's march, as the wind continued until nearly all the daylight had gone. Leaving at about 2 p.m., we made 4½ miles in 3½ hours, and once more found ourselves on a very suspicious surface in the darkness, where we several times stepped into rotten lidded crevasses in smooth, wind-swept ice. We continued, however, feeling our way along by keeping always off hard ice-slopes and on the crustier deeper snow which characterises the hollows of the pressure ridges, which I believed we had once more fouled in the dark. We had no light, and no landmarks to guide us, except vague and indistinct silhouetted slopes ahead, which were always altering and whose distance and character it was impossible to judge. We never knew whether we were approaching a steep slope at close quarters or a long slope of Terror, miles away, and eventually we travelled on by the ear, and by the feel of the snow under our feet, for both the sound and the touch told one much of the chances of crevasses or of safe going. We continued thus in the dark in the hope that we were at any rate in the right direction.

The sky cleared when the wind fell, and the temperature dropped from −21.5° at 11 a.m. to −45° at 9 p.m. We then made our night camp amongst the pressure ridges off the Terror moraine, on snow that felt soft and deep enough to be safe in what we believed to be one of the hollows [and when we camped after getting into a bunch of crevasses and being completely lost, 'At any rate,' Bill said, as we camped that night, 'I think we are well clear of the pressure.' There were pressure pops all night, just as though someone was whacking an empty tank.]

Thursday, July 27, 1911. – We got away with the coming of daylight and found that our suspicions overnight had been true. We were right in amongst the larger pressure ridges and had come for a considerable distance between two of them without actually crossing any but very insignificant ones. Ahead of us was a safe and clear road to the open Barrier to the south, but we wanted to go to the S.W. And as the pressure ridges were invariably crevassed on the summits we hoped that by continuing along this valley we might find some low spot where we could cross the ridge on our right, and again get on the safer land ice. We, however, found no such dip, and after some time decided we must cross the ridge on our right [an enormous pressure ridge, blotting out the moraine and half Terror, rising like a great hill]. In doing so we managed to negotiate several rottenly bridged narrow crevasses [both Bill and I putting a leg down] and one broad one which we only discovered when we were all on it with the sledge, and then Bowers dropped suddenly into one and hung up in his harness out of sight and out of reach from the surface. It was a crevasse I had just put my foot in, but Bowers went in even as I shouted a warning. We were too close to one another in our harness and the sledge followed us and bridged the crevasse. I had hold of Bowers's harness, while Cherry lowered a bowline on the end of the Alpine rope into which Bowers got his foot, and then by alternately hauling on one and the other we got him up again. After this, for the next few days while we were on doubtful ground, I went ahead with 12 or 15 feet of rope on my trace, and so was able to give good warning and to change the course easily if I found we were getting on to bad ground.

[C.-G. gives a fuller account.

Just over the top Birdie went right down a crevasse, which was about wide enough to take him – he went down slowly, his head disappearing quite slowly – and he went down till his head was four feet below the surface, a little of his harness catching up on something. Bill went for his harness, I went for the bow of the sledge. Bill told me to get the Alpine rope and Birdie directed from below what we could do: we could not possibly haul him up as he was, for the sides of the crevasse were soft and he could not help himself. I put a bowline on the Alpine rope, and lying down over him gave him the loop, which he got under his leg. We then pulled him up inch by inch: first by drawing up his leg he could give one some slack, then raising himself on his leg he could give Bill some slack on the harness, and so we gradually got him up. It was a near go for Birdie: the crevasse was probably about 100 feet deep, and did not narrow as it went down.

It was a wonderful piece of presence of mind that Birdie in such a position could direct us how to get him up – by a way which, as far as we know, he invented on the spur of the moment, a way which we have used since on the Beardmore.

In front of us we could see another ridge, and we did not know how many lay beyond that. Things looked pretty bad. Bill took a long lead on the Alpine rope and we got down our present difficulty all right. From this moment our luck changed and everything went for us to the end. This method of the leader being on a long trace in front we all agreed to be very useful. When we went out on the sea ice the whole experience was over in a few days and Hut Point was always in sight – and there was daylight. I always had the feeling that the whole series of events had been brought about by an extraordinary run of accidents, and after a certain stage it was quite beyond our power to guide the course of events. When, on the way to C. Crozier, the moon suddenly came out of the cloud to show us a great crevasse which would have taken us all with our sledge without any difficulty, I felt that we were not to go under on this trip after such a deliverance. When we lost our tent – and there was a very great balance of probability, to me, that we should never find it again – and were lying out the blizzard in our bags, I believe we were face to face with a long fight against cold which we could not have survived. I cannot put down in writing how helpless I believe we were to help ourselves, and how we were brought out of a very terrible series of experiences.

When we started back I had a feeling that things might change for the better – and this day I had a distinct idea that we were to have one more bad experience and that after that we could hope for better things. Bill, I know, has much the same feeling about a divine providence which was looking after us.]

We then got on well and soon reached safe land ice, having sounded for and found all the cracks in our path in time to avoid or cross them safely.

We next got on to a very long upward incline, and made good going till we had to camp, having covered 7¼ miles in the day.

The temp. varied from −45° to −47° during the day, but the weather was calm and clear enough later on for us to see something of where we were going.

Friday, July 28, 1911. – We were away before daylight and found ourselves still on the upward slope of a very long gradient facing a gentle breeze, which as usual was flowing down the slope. The Bastion Crater was on our right with the Conical Hill surmounting it, a landmark visible from Observation Hill.

We went on and on up this slope until at last we found ourselves in a calm on the divide with a magnificent view of the Western Range, Mt Discovery and the Hut Point Peninsula and all the other familiar landmarks showing very clearly in the dim daylight. [I cannot describe what a relief the light was to us.] We then knew we were over Terror Point and almost out of the blizzard area. The surface all up this slope was good going, hard but smooth, hardened however by variable winds of no great force, with but few areas of the softer sandy drifts which are the heavy ones to drag over.

Across the divide we went downhill with the air-stream on our backs, and very soon we were once more on the old softer crusty surface of the Barrier itself, with trifling sastrugi and heavier pulling, a surface into which the sledge runners and the feet sank a couple of inches. Subsidences again began and soon became frequent. Bright fine weather, and Terror peak visible all day, as well as Erebus from the time when we first caught sight of it over Terror slope. One of the features of Erebus during the whole of this march was the outstanding old Northern Crater, which stood out boldly against the skyline part of the way down the slope. We lost it, however, at the end of today's march.

Bowers turned his bag again today from fur outside to fur inside, and so it remained till we reached Cape Evans.

The temperature ranged from $-47.2°$ in the morning to $-38°$ in the evening. At our lunch camp it was $-40.3°$. We made 6¾ miles in the day.

We were now travelling with a view to getting in all the daylight we could and at the same time with a view to reducing our nights to the shortest possible, for we got but little sleep and were often uncomfortably cold all night. We therefore turned out generally at 5.30 a.m., lunched at 2.30 p.m., and camped at 6 p.m., to turn in between 9 p.m. and 10 p.m.

[Though our sledge, which we called the Pantechnicon, was a mountain, and of a considerable weight, we started to do good marches. We dare not roll up our bags since the blizzard in case they should break. For two nights I got a fair sleep in the new eiderdown, nights which would have been nightmares under ordinary circumstances, but which now put some new life into me.

Bill was now having the worst nights – never sleeping as far as he knew. We were not much better. My new eiderdown was already sopping and as hard as iron: I never thawed out the greater part of my big bag. Even Birdie began to shiver in his bag. Sometimes we would have done a great deal not to stop marching and turn in: but we had to turn in each night for six or seven hours, rising about 5 a.m.]

Our hands gave us more pain with cold than any other part, and this we all found to be the case. In the bags the hands, and half-mits and any other covering we liked to use, got soaking wet, and the skin sodden like washerwomen's hands. The result, on turning out, was that they were ready to freeze at once, and even the tying of the tent door became a real difficulty, the more so as the tie had become stiff as wire. Another difficulty in the bags was the freezing of the lanyards after one had tied them inside the bag. Nothing would loosen them save thawing, in one's already painfully cold hands, and this was often awkward if one wished to turn out quickly. I believe the only satisfactory covering for the hands in these conditions would be a bag of dry saennegras, but we had only sufficient for our feet and it was not tried.

Our feet gave us very little trouble indeed, except on the march, when they were often too cold for safety during slow and heavy plodding in soft snow. We always changed our footgear before eating our supper, and to this we attribute the fact that we seldom had cold feet at night, even at the worst.

Saturday, July 29, 1911. – We got away before daylight and marched a good soft plod all day, making 6½ miles. Subsidences were frequent, and at lunch the whole tent and contents, myself included, as I was cook for the day, dropped suddenly with a perceptible bump, and with so long and loud a reverberation all round that we all stood and listened for some minutes. Cherry said it started when his foot went through some snow under the top crust, not when he was digging through this crust. The central subsidence set off innumerable others all round and these others in continually widening circles, and the noise took quite two or three minutes to die away.

We had no wind today, calm and southerly airs only, and a temp. ranging from −42° a.m. to −45.3° p.m.

There was an aurora all night, and at 3 a.m. Bowers noted a brilliant variegated curtain, altitude 30° to 60°, extending from the N.E. to about S.S.W., with much motion in the rays, and with orange and green well defined.

Sunday, July 30, 1911. – We had a day of perfect weather and good travelling and covered 7½ miles. The amount of daylight during this and the preceding two days has been surprisingly great, and enabled us to see a tremendous amount of detail in the hills and snow slopes of the promontory on our right, all of which looked very much nearer than they actually were. The dawn on the eastern horizon was also exceptionally fine in colour, almost pure carmine in a very broad band, changing imperceptibly, but without any intermediate orange or yellow, into green and blue above. The peaks of the Western Range all caught pink lights reflected from the sky, and these shone up against the greyer pink foreglow behind them. None of them caught the actual sunlight yet.

The temp. was low, −55.3° in the morning, −63.2° to −61.8° in the afternoon, and on to the evening, with light easterly and north-easterly airs from time to time. [*Apropos* of the cold: we now got low temperatures once more, but −60° now hardly called for comment; in fact some nights of −60° we never even inquired the temperature.]

Once we saw a drift swirl suddenly spring into the air about 100 ft. high and sweep along the surface for a long way before it disappeared.

After lunch we had interesting views of the formation and dispersal of fog banks which formed from time to time all along the Hut Point promontory. There appeared to be a line along which the cold Barrier air met the warmer sea ice air of the north side. Fog resulted, which gradually rose and spread, and blotted out all the land ahead of us, and then as rapidly dispersed to the south, leaving the whole sky and air as clear and bright as before. This happened again and again with no formation of cloud south of the ridge.

Eventually, however, the northerly wind came over, rising, and forming a complete overcast beneath which one could see the Western and Southern Mountains and horizon all perfectly clear.

We saw today and yesterday, hanging round the summits of Erebus and Terror, some very unusually delicate spider-web-like cirrus cloudlets, coloured dark reddish, and looking like tangled thread or like unravelled silk – they were slight and thin, but very well defined, and they changed very slowly.

Monday, July 31, 1911. – We turned out soon after 5 a.m. and had calm clear weather again ahead of us, though Terror was apparently again in trouble, for it was covered in a cap cloud.

We had good going and had covered 5½ miles in 5½ hours by the time we reached the edge of the Barrier about 1½ miles off the Pram Point ridges.

The surface of the Barrier during this march had today become very much harder and more windswept. It was not cut into sastrugi, but polished into low, flatly rounded areas, with only occasional drifts of sandy snow, which dragged heavily and allowed the feet to sink in through a thin crust. The difference this walking on a hard surface made to the warmth of our feet was very noticeable, notwithstanding that the temperature was still −57°.

At the Barrier edge we simply ran down a drift slope on to the sea ice, which had only a few inches of snow covering, six inches at the most as noted by Bowers, and hard and wind-swept. Here again we felt the flow of cold air pouring from the Barrier on to the sea ice, so we camped about 100 yards away to be out of it and had lunch. The temp. here was −43°. The sledge-meter now showed 38 miles from our camp in the Knoll gap at Cape Crozier. From this point to Hut Point was 3 miles, and it was again an excellent hardened smooth snow surface all the way to Cape Armitage, and rather the same rough, crunchy sea ice, with very few snow-covered patches, from Cape Armitage to Hut Point.

By the time we reached the hut the sky had become completely overcast and the temp. had gone up to −27°. It was still quite calm, and the sky cleared again during the night. We camped at the hut. [The last day we had been using our oil to warm ourselves, since we had a half-tin left, having used the first half very sparingly. Birdie made a bottom for the cooker out of an empty biscuit-tin, which was most successful. We cooked on Bill's bag in the middle, generally one of us steadying the cooker with his hands.

It used to be quite a common experience to spill some water or hoosh on to our bags as they lay on the floor-cloth. This did not worry us, since it was practically impossible for our bags to be wetter than they were.

During the last four days Birdie quite often fell asleep as he was marching; I do not know that Bill ever did this. I never did so till the last day, when for about an hour I was falling asleep constantly as we marched along – waking when I came up against Bill or Birdie.]

Tuesday, August 1, 1911. – In the hut we pitched the dome tent and lit a primus to warm it while we cooked our supper. We had thus a much more comfortable night than the blubber stove could have given us.

[The hut struck us as fairly warm; we could almost feel it getting warmer as we went round C. Armitage. We managed to haul the sledge up the ice foot. We pitched the dome tent in the place where Crean used to sleep and got both primus going in it – for there was plenty of oil there, and we got it really warm, and drank cocoa without sugar so thick that next morning we were gorged with it. We were very happy, falling asleep between each mouthful. After some hours of this we discussed several schemes of not getting into our bags at all, but settled it was best to do so.]

We had three hours in our bags and turned out at 3 a.m., hoping to make an early start to get into Cape Evans before dinner-time. But a strong easterly wind got up and prevented our start, so we continued to doze in the tent as we sat there, in preference to being in our bags.

At 9.30 a.m. the wind dropped, and we got away at 11, but met with a very cold breeze off the land on rounding Hut Point. We walked out of it, however, in a mile or so by getting into the open, and then made a straight course all the way for Cape Evans, deciding not to camp for lunch until we had passed the broken ice off the end of Glacier Tongue by daylight. This took us 5½ hours, and we camped at 4.30 p.m., exactly 8 miles from Hut Point.

The surface was varied, and we were a mile or so farther out all the way on this our return journey than on our outward journey, so it differed rather from the surface we had then.

After leaving Hut Point we had very rough, rubbly sea ice with no snow worth mentioning for two or three miles. What indications there were of wind came from the land and showed north-easterly winds off shore. Their direction, however, very gradually altered till we were crossing them exactly at right angles, indicating due easterly winds from the ridge. Later still and farther on towards the Glacier Tongue and Cape Evans the indications gradually turned to show south-easterly winds. These are the winds which seem chiefly to affect the surface of the strait ice during the winter, and as we got on towards the Glacier Tongue the snow-covering became increasingly greater, as well as the evidence of stronger easterly winds. Extensive flatly rounded, hard-surfaced drifts became more abundant and afforded excellent going, so that when we were about 6 miles from Hut Point we were doing about 2 miles an hour. After this, and especially during the 8th mile from Hut Point, we met with a lot of hummocky cracks where the ice had been pressed up into long ridges and subsequently had been drifted up, forming very difficult sastrugi and providing much trouble for a sledge. We still had sufficient daylight, and after lunch, moonlight, to negotiate these, though it was easy to see how much trouble they might give one in the dark, as they did on our way out.

All the day we were watching the changes in some iridescent clouds which hung low on the northern horizon. The edges were brilliant with pale yellow sunlight, while inside this was a broad band of orange yellow, and inside this again a narrow band of grey surrounding a large and vivid patch of emerald green. There was no trace of the violet and rose pink which characterises the opalescent cirrus clouds one sees later on when the sun is higher in the sky.

On the actual horizon was a band of rich red with purple streaks of cloud on it, giving it a very unusual magenta colour.

After lunch we had good moonlight and a good wind-swept, snow-covered surface – and though there were more of these pressure ridges abreast of Tent Island we had plenty of light to negotiate them.

We had had no wind today. The temp. had ranged from −27.3° at Hut Point to −31° off Glacier Tongue.

Off Inaccessible Island at 9.30 p.m. we were met by a northerly breeze of force 3, which continued until our arrival at Cape Evans. [I well remember when we got into the hut here, and we were very keen to get in without any fuss. We got right up to the door before anyone saw us, and then I simply could not get out of my harness.

As we came round the Point, Bill asked us to spread out if anyone came out of the Hut, to show we were all there – a very useful idea.]

This was the thirty-sixth day of our absence.

E. A. WILSON

So ends the official Report of the Cape Crozier Party, simple and reticent to the last. But again the reader, eager for more colour, will welcome the fuller description of the last march home, the welcome at Cape Evans, and general impressions of travel, which we owe to Mr Cherry-Garrard's pen.

We just pulled for all we were worth and did nearly two miles an hour; for two miles a baddish salt surface, then big, undulating, hard sastrugi and good going. Several times I fell asleep as we were marching. We had done eight miles by 4 p.m. and were past Glacier Tongue. Then half a mile of bad pressure ice running from Glacier Tongue to Tent Island, and then rather worse going past Inaccessible, where we met a strong northerly wind. Up to now the light from the moon had been good, but now the light was worse and we were very done. At last we rounded the Cape and gradually pulled in and right up to the door, without disturbing anything. As we were getting out of our harness, always a big business in our frozen state, Hooper came out, suddenly said 'By Jove!' and rushed back, and then there was pandemonium.

It was 9.30 p.m., and a good many had turned out of their beds. Everybody hung on to some part of us and got our clothes off: mine next morning weighed 24 lbs. As they heard our story or bits of it they became more and more astonished. We were set down to cocoa and bread and butter and jam: we did not want anything else. Scott I heard say, 'But, look here, you know, this is the hardest journey that has ever been made.' They told us afterwards that we had a look in our faces as if we were at our last gasp, a look which had quite gone next morning. Ponting said he had seen the same look on some Russian prisoners' faces at Mukden. I just tumbled into my dry, warm blankets. I expect it was as near an approach to bliss as a man can get on this earth.

Sleeping-bags. [written August 3, 1912] – The life of a man on such a journey as this depends mainly upon the life of his sleeping-bag. We all three of us took eiderdown linings. Bill's bag proved really too small to take his eiderdown, and on the return journey his bag split down the seams to an alarming extent, letting in the cold air. Latterly in this journey it was by no means an uncommon experience for us to take over an hour in getting into our bags. One night I especially remember when Bill had practically given up all hope of getting his head into his. He finally cut off the flaps of his eiderdown, and with Birdie on one side and myself on the other we managed to lever the lid of the head of the bag open and gradually he got his head into it. I made a great mistake in taking a 'large-sized' bag – though it was a small one. What a man really wants is a large 'middle-sized' bag. The last fortnight, whenever the temperature was very low, I never thawed out the parts of my bag which were not pressing tight up against my body. I have forgotten what Bill's and Birdie's bags weighed when we got in. Mine (bag and eiderdown) was 45 lbs., personal gear 10 lbs. When we started that bag was about 18 lbs.: *the accumulation of ice was therefore 27 lbs.*

Birdie's bag just fitted him beautifully, though perhaps it would have been a little small with an eiderdown inside. As I understand from Atkinson, Birdie had undoubtedly a greater heat supply than other men ordinarily have. He never had serious trouble with his feet, while ours were constantly frostbitten. He slept I should be afraid to say how much longer than we did, even in the last days. It was a pleasure to lie awake, practically at any rate all night, and hear his snores. Largely owing to the arrangement of toggles, also not having shipped his eiderdown bag, but mainly due to his extraordinary energy, he many times turned his bag during the journey, and thus he got rid of a lot of the moisture in his bag, which came out as snow or actual knobs of ice. When we did turn our bags, the only way was directly we turned out, and even then you had to be quick before the bag froze. Getting out of the tent at night, it was quite a race to get back to your bag, before it began to get hard again. Of course this was in the lowest temperatures.

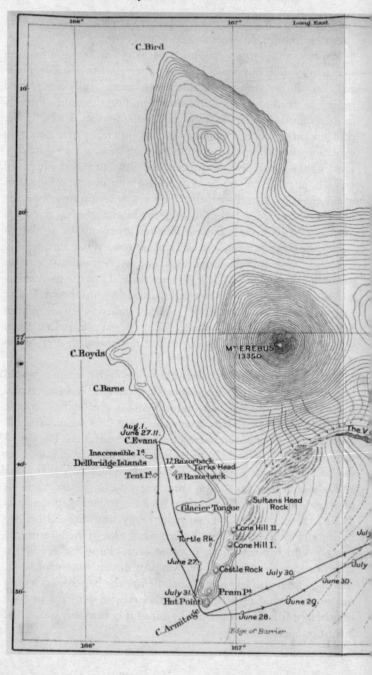

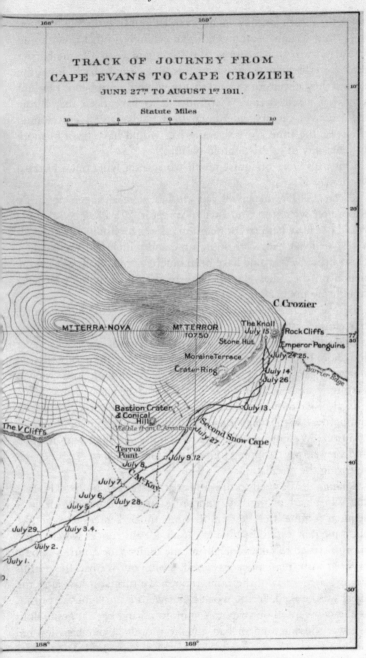

TRACK OF JOURNEY FROM
CAPE EVANS TO CAPE CROZIER
JUNE 27TH TO AUGUST 1ST 1911.

Statute Miles

C Crozier

The Knoll
July 15
Rock Cliffs

MT TERRA-NOVA
MT TERROR
10750
Stone Hut
Emperor Penguins
July 24-25.

MoraineTerrace
July 14
Crater Ring
July 26

Barrier Edge

Bastion Crater
& Conical
Hill
Visible from C.Armitage
July 13

Second Snow Cape
July 27

The V Cliffs

Terror
Point
July 8.
July 9.12.

C. M. Kay.
July 7.
July 6.
July 28.
July 5.

July 29.
July 3.4.

July 2.
July 1.

On the return journey we never rolled our bags up, but let them freeze out straight – arranging them carefully so that they should freeze in the best shape for getting into them again. On the Barrier they were literally as hard as boards, but coming back down the Sound they never got so hard that they would not bend. I cannot say what a self-sacrifice I consider it to have been that Birdie handed over his dry eiderdown to me when we were coming back. At the time a dry sleeping-bag would have been of more value to any of us than untold wealth.

Our bags were of course much worse after lying out a blizzard in them.

Clothes. – The details of our clothes were all taken down by Scott after we got in, and I will not repeat. We all agreed that we could not have bettered our clothing. I was foolish in starting with a vest which I had worn some time and which had stretched. A close-fitting vest would have been much warmer. As it was, on the march on the stillest day there seemed to be a draught blowing straight up my back.

Before we had been many days in these very cold temperatures our clothes used to freeze so stiff in a few seconds after stepping outside the tent, that from our waists upwards we could never move our body or heads from that position until they were thawed out again at the next meal. We therefore got into the way of getting frozen in a position which would be most comfortable. Our arms we moved with a good deal of straining, and getting into our harness was always a long job, all three doing one set of harness at a time. We got into the way of doing everything with mits on and very slowly, stopping immediately our hands were going, and restoring the circulation.

Routine. – We used to turn in for at least seven hours. This was the worst part of the day, and breakfast to me became in consequence quite the best meal. Sometimes I used to feel like shouting that it must be time to get up. Getting under weigh in the morning used to take generally a little under four hours, 3½ hours as far as I can remember was good. Going out we had the primus going a large part of the time, though we turned it low after the meal was cooked. In the worst times we used to light the primus while we were in our bags in the morning and keep it going until we were just getting or had got the mouth of our bags levered open in the evening. We also tried getting the primus into our bags to thaw them out, but it was not very successful. Cooking coming back was a much longer process, since we had to hold the cooker up, having lost its proper stand and the top of the outer cooker – though Birdie's substitute was very good.

After breakfast we would be pretty warm, and having loaded the sledge the next job was to get a bearing on to some star or the moon if anything was visible. This meant lighting matches, always a big business. To light the candle in the tent we used sometimes to have to try three or even four boxes before one would light. Steering was very haphazard generally.

Then into our harness – and then four hours' march or relaying, if possible. The possibility depended on whether our feet got too cold, but the difficulty was to know when they were frostbitten.

Relaying was at first by naked candle – later by hurricane lamp – following back our tracks in the snow for the second sledge. We never could decide which was the heavier. We camped for lunch if possible before we got too cold, since this was always a cold job.

We cooked alternately day by day. The worst part was lighting up. The weekly bag was very cold to handle. Generally (often) we had to take off our finnesko or one of them to examine our feet and nurse them back if they were gone.

Then four hours' march more if possible.

Footgear on as soon as possible on camping. Our night footgear was very good.

It is also difficult already, after two nights' rest, with a dozen men all round anticipating your every wish, and with the new comfortable life of the hut all round you, to realise completely how bad the last few weeks have been, how at times one hardly cared whether we got through or not, so long as (I speak for myself) if I was to go under it would not take very long. Although our weights are not very different, I am only 1 lb., and Bill and Birdie 3½ lbs., lighter than when we started, we were very done when we got in, falling asleep on the march, and unable to get into our finnesko or eat our meals without falling asleep. Although we were doing good marches up to the end, we were pulling slow and weak, and the cold was getting at us in a way in which it had never touched us before. Our fingers were positive agony immediately we took them out of our mits, and to undo a lashing took a very long time. The night we got in Scott said he thought it was the hardest journey which had ever been made. Bill says it was infinitely worse than the Southern Journey in 1902–3.

I would like to put it on record that Captain Scott considered this journey to be the hardest which had ever been done. This was a well-considered judgment.

A. Cherry-Garrard

NARRATIVE OF THE NORTHERN PARTY BETWEEN JANUARY 25, 1911, AND JANUARY 18, 1913
by Commander Victor L. A. Campbell, R.N.

Members of the Northern Party
Lieut. Victor L. A. Campbell, R.N.
Surgeon G. Murray Levick, R.N.
Raymond E. Priestley (Geologist)
Petty Officer G. P. Abbott, R.N.
Petty Officer F. V. Browning, R.N.
Seaman H. Dickason, R.N.

Wednesday, January 25, 1911. – We said goodbye to Captain Scott and the Southern Depôt Party, and at 9 the following morning left Glacier Tongue for Butter Point, to land the Western Geological Party. A light southerly wind had cleared the loose ice out of the bay, and we had no difficulty in getting the ship alongside the ice foot, so that by 6 the same evening we had landed the party, laid out a depôt, and left on our cruise to the eastward, where I hoped to effect a landing, if not on King Edward's Land itself, at least in some inlet near the eastern end of the Barrier.

I had received the following instructions from Captain Scott, and they explain our subsequent movements:

Winter Quarters, Cape Evans
23 January, 1911

Instructions to Leader of Eastern Party
Directions as to the landing of your party are contained in the instructions to the Commanding Officer of the *Terra Nova* handed to you herewith.

Whilst I hope that you may be able to land in King Edward's Land, I fully realise the possibility of the conditions being unfavourable and the difficulty of the task which has been set you.

I do not think you should attempt a landing unless the Ship can remain in security near you for at least three days, unless all your stores can be placed in a position of safety in a shorter time.

The Ship will give you all possible help in erecting your hut, &c., but I hope you will not find it necessary to keep her by you for any length of time.

Should you succeed in landing, the object you will hold in view is to discover the nature and extent of King Edward's Land. The possibilities of your situation are so various that it must be left to you entirely to determine how this object may best be achieved.

In this connexion it remains only to say that you should be at your winter station and ready to embark on February 1, 1912.

If the Ship should not arrive by February 15, and your circumstances permit, you should commence to retreat across the Barrier, keeping at first near the edge in order to see the Ship should she pass.

It would be a wise precaution to lay out a depôt in this direction at an earlier date, and I trust that a further depôt will be provided in some inlet as you go east in the Ship.

When I hear that you have been safely landed in King Edward's Land I shall take steps to ensure that a third depôt is laid out. This will be placed by the Western Party one mile from the Barrier Edge and thirty miles from Cape Crozier.

You will of course travel light on such a journey, and remember that fresh food can be obtained at Cape Crozier. A sledge sail should help you.

From Cape Crozier you should make for Hut Point, where shelter and food will be found pending the freezing over of the bays to the north.

Should you be unable to land in the region of King Edward's Land you will be at liberty to go to the region of Robertson Bay after communicating with Cape Evans.

I think it very possible that a suitable wintering spot may be found in the vicinity of Smith's Inlet, but the Ship must be handled with care as I have reason to believe that the pack sometimes presses on this coast.

Should you be landed in or near Robertson Bay you will not expect to be relieved until March in the following year, but you should be in readiness to embark on February 25.

The main object of your exploration in this region would naturally be the coast westward of Cape North.

Should the Ship have not returned by March 25 it will be necessary for you to prepare for a second winter.

In no case would it be advisable for you to attempt to retreat along the coast. Seals and penguins should be plentiful and possibly some useful stores may remain at Cape Adare, but the existence of stores should not be regarded as more than a possibility.

In conclusion I wish you all possible good luck, feeling assured that you will deserve it.

(Signed) R. SCOTT

By 9 a.m. on the 27th we were off Cape Crozier and commenced our survey of the Barrier to see what changes had taken place since 1901.

About 9 a.m. on January 30 we passed an inlet opening N. by W., 1100 yards long, 250 wide, having perpendicular sides about 90 feet high.

This evening about seven we saw a large piece of the Barrier break off. We were at the time within 900 yards of the cliff, when we heard a noise like thunder and saw a cloud of spray rise up about half a mile ahead of us. The cloud of spray completely hid the Barrier at that place, and as this cleared we saw that a large piece had broken off, while débris of ice was forced out across our bows, making us alter course to avoid it.

January 31. – While steaming up a bay this afternoon another large piece of the Barrier broke away. It must have been five miles away, but we heard the noise like a peal of thunder and through our glasses saw a cloud of spray hanging over the place like a fog.

Soon after 3 p.m. we were up at the head of the bay, when we found new ice had formed. The Barrier here runs down nearly to the water's edge, and were it only farther to the eastward would not be a bad place to winter.

A number of Sibbald whales were blowing in the bay, and on the ice we saw several seals, and some Emperor penguins. Time and coal were precious; so we did not wait, but turned, and steamed out of the bay.

On getting outside we found a strong S.E. wind, and as we had the current against us as well, we decided not to work along the

Barrier, but to shape course direct for Cape Colbeck, in which case we could carry fore and aft sail. We encountered strong S.E. wind but no pack, until 3 o'clock on the morning of the 2nd, when we made heavy pack with a number of small bergs in it right ahead.

The sea was breaking heavily on the pack edge, so we altered course to the southward, and after a few hours' steaming against a nasty head sea we got round it. About eight o'clock the wind fell, and shortly afterwards we sighted what was apparently ice-covered land on the starboard bow – soundings gave 208 fathoms. The day was lovely, and we had a good view of the land, which proved to be Cape Colbeck, a long convex ice dome without a rock showing. Sextant angles made the summit 750 feet high, while the ice face averaged 100 feet. Some heavy pack and a large number of bergs were lying off the cliff, but working our way slowly through we found open water under the cliff. Our prospects were now bright; open water ahead and a perfect day. However, in the afternoon our hopes were blighted; about 10 miles east of Cape Colbeck we came on a line of solid unbroken pack, into which a number of bergs were frozen, stretching from the ice cliffs of King Edward's Land out to the N.W. as far as we could see from the crow's nest. We steamed up to the edge of the ice, stopped, and sounded, getting bottom at 169 fathoms.

Several seals, one of which looked like a sea leopard, and some Adélie and Emperor penguins were on the ice, while large flocks of Antarctic petrels were flying about everywhere.

The ice cliffs, stretching as far as we could see, gave us no hope of finding a landing-place.

There is evidence of a great deal of pressure here and the upper edge of the cliff near us, 100 feet high, showed a pressure ridge, where evidently a large berg had been forced against it.

At 5.0 p.m. we reluctantly turned and retraced our steps, the only chance of a landing-place being Balloon Bight or some inlet at the east end of the Barrier. Soundings off Cape Colbeck gave us 89 fathoms. During the night we sailed as close as possible to the ice face but passed nothing but high cliffs. About 3 o'clock on the morning of the 3rd a strong S.E. wind sprang up, bringing a low mist, but not thick enough to prevent us keeping close to the coast. Soon after the cliff dipped a little and appeared on both bows, showing we were running into a bay; this was the place where I had had great hopes of effecting a landing, but we were unable to do so.

It was interesting to note that while the eastern side of the bay was clean cut, the western side was much weather-worn and honeycombed with caves, evidently worn by the strong westerly current which sweeps along the Barrier. We saw two narrow inlets opening N.E. but not wide enough to trust the ship in; moreover, as they open in this direction they are more liable to be blocked by any loose ice drifting in.

In the afternoon the weather cleared and we were able to get sights, showing we were still to the eastward of Balloon Bight. By 9 a.m. we were off the place where Balloon Bight should have been, and our sights put us south of the old Barrier edge. There was no doubt about it; Balloon Bight had gone. By midnight we were off Shackleton's Bay of Whales. On rounding the eastern point our surprise can be imagined when we saw a ship, which I recognised as the *Fram*, made fast alongside the sea ice.

Standing in, we made fast a little way ahead of her and hoisted our colours, she answering with the Norwegian ensign. There was no doubt it was Captain Amundsen.

Pennell and I immediately went on board and saw Lieutenant Neilsen, who was in command. He told us Amundsen was up at the camp about three miles in, over the sea ice, but would be down about 9 o'clock, and accordingly soon after 9 I returned on board and saw Amundsen, who told me his plans. He had been here since January 4, after a good passage, having been held only four days in the pack. He had intended wintering at Balloon Bight, but on finding that had gone, had fixed on the Bay of Whales as the best place.

He asked me to come up and see his camp, so Pennell, Levick and I went up, and found he had erected his hut on the Barrier, about 3 miles from the coast. The camp presented a very workmanlike appearance, with a good-sized hut containing a kitchen and living-room with a double tier of bunks round the walls, while outside several tents were up and 116 fine Greenland dogs picketed round.

His party, besides himself, consisted of Johansen, who was with Dr Nansen in his famous sledge journey of '97, and seven others.

After coffee and a walk round the camp Amundsen and two others returned with us and had lunch in the *Terra Nova*.

We left early in the afternoon, and after sounding and dredging in the bay, proceeded west along the Barrier, of which there still remained nearly 100 miles we had not seen.

Outside the bay we were unlucky enough to pick up a S.W. wind, but with clear weather we kept close along the Barrier edge to long. 170° W., where we had left it on our way east, without seeing any inlet or possible place to land. This was a great disappointment to us all, but there was nothing for it but to return to McMurdo Sound to communicate with the main party and then try and effect a landing in the vicinity of Smith's Inlet or as far to the westward as possible on the north coast of Victoria Land, and if possible to explore the unknown coast west of Cape North.

We therefore made the best of our way to Cape Evans, and in spite of a moderate S.W. gale arrived on the evening of the 8th.

Here I decided to land the two ponies, as they would be very little use to us on the mountainous coast of Victoria Land, and in view of the Norwegian expedition I felt the Southern Party would require all the transport available.

After landing the ponies we steamed up to the sea ice by Glacier Tongue, and from there, taking Priestley and Abbott, I went with letters to leave at Hut Point, where the Depôt Party would call on their way back. The surface was good and we got back to the ship about 3 a.m., and then proceeded to water ship at Glacier Tongue. While watering ship an accident occurred which might have been serious. The ship was secured alongside, and Abbott was just stepping ashore when a large piece of ice broke away with him on it and fell between the ship and the ice edge. Luckily he was not hurt, and was soon pulled on board again, none the worse, except for a ducking.

By 8 o'clock in the evening of the 9th we were all ready, and proceeded north with a fair S.E. wind, but thick snow.

During the afternoon of February 12th the wind freshened into a gale with heavy snow, and not wanting to close Cape Adare in such thick weather we hove to under main lower topsail with Cape Adare bearing N.W., distant 20 miles.

During the night the wind increased, and continued blowing a very heavy gale until the evening of the 15th. In spite of the very heavy sea the ship was fairly dry, but being so light we took a lot of ice water, washing away the bulwarks we had repaired since the previous gale.

The coal question was becoming serious; if this went on much longer it looked as if we should not be able to land, as Pennell had to keep enough coal to get back to New Zealand.

On the evening of the 15th the wind eased a little, and by 10 a.m. on the 16th we raised steam and shaped course for Cape Adare, which was now 110 miles to the S.W. It came on to blow hard again from the S.E. in the afternoon, but we were able nearly to lay our course under lower topsails; the snow squalls were very thick, but luckily not much ice was sighted. Late in the afternoon the weather cleared and we sighted the mountainous coast of Victoria Land. During the night we got among a lot of weathered bergs and loose pack, which had the effect of smoothing the sea.

At 4 a.m. on the 17th we were within about 2 miles of the coast just east of Smith's Inlet.

The land here was heavily glaciated, hardly a rock showing, except some high cliffs and the Lyall Islands to the westward.

Heavy pack lay to the west of us, so we had to work along to the eastward, where the sea was fairly clear of ice.

Some large floes lay close in under the cliffs, grinding up against them in the heavy swell that was running. I was very much disappointed at seeing no piedmont to work along on the western sledge journey. The cliffs were several hundred feet high except where the glaciers ran down, the front of these being from 50 to 180 feet high.

We worked along to the eastward, keeping as close as we could, and keeping a good lookout for a possible landing.

The scenery was magnificent. In the afternoon we entered Robertson Bay and found we had a strong tide with us, which was fortunate as the wind had freshened again from the S.S.E. The scenery here was even wilder, the Admiralty Range towering over our heads and so steep that, except in the valleys, no snow or ice was able to lodge, and bare rock showed everywhere.

Large glaciers filled all the valleys, but the gradient was so steep that they were heavily crevassed from top to bottom.

By 5 o'clock we were off the Dugdale Glacier, which runs out in three long tongues, in places only 10 feet high.

It appeared to have altered considerably since Borchgrevink's time, as he charts only one long tongue. It was not a good place for wintering, the surface being crevassed and the sides too steep to be climbed; the ice tongue would have been a good place to lie alongside and land stores, but as some of this broke away and drifted out to sea a week later, it was as well we did not try.

After having a look at Duke of York Island we steamed up to the head of the bay, but with no better success. So about midnight we turned and made for Ridley Beach, a triangular beach on the west side of Cape Adare, the place where the Southern Cross Party wintered in 1900.

I was very much against wintering here, as until the ice forms in Robertson Bay one is quite cut off from any sledging operations on the mainland, for the cliffs of the peninsula descend sheer into the sea.

Pennell, however, had only just enough coal as it was to get back to New Zealand, so at 3 a.m. on the 18th we anchored off the south shore of the beach and commenced landing stores. A cold, wet job it was. A lot of loose ice round the shore and a surf made it difficult for the boats to get in; the water shoaled some way out, which meant wading backwards and forwards with the stores, while several times the boats broached to as they touched and half swamped. We worked from 3 a.m. till midnight, and started again at 4 a.m. on Sunday.

The way everyone behaved was splendid, Davies the carpenter in particular working at the hut for 48 hours on end. Communication with the ship was twice cut off by heavy pack setting into the bay.

By 4 a.m. Monday everything was landed, the ship party re-embarked, and the ship proceeded north, while we of the shore party, who were all dead tired, turned in for a few hours' sleep. One of Borchgrevink's huts was standing, but was half full of snow; the other one had no roof and had evidently been used as a nesting place by generations of penguins. After clearing out the snow of the former we had quite comfortable quarters while we built our own hut. With the exception of the 21st, when we had a mild blizzard, we had fine weather for building the hut, for which we were very thankful, as that, and carrying up all the stores, proved a long job for a small party. We used to start work every morning at 6, and knock off between 8 and 9 every evening, by which time we were pretty tired.

By an oversight only two hammers had been landed, so four unfortunates had to use Priestley's geological hammers. These are heavy, square-headed implements, designed to chip, and judging by our mangled fingers the man who made them knew his business. We had rather a shock on Friday, when on examining the fifteen carcases of frozen mutton left by the ship we found them to be covered with green mould.

They must have been in this condition on board, as we buried them in the ice as soon as they were landed; anyhow we had to condemn them, to the great delight of the skua gulls; but penguins and seals are plentiful, so we shall not be short of fresh meat.

While at work on the Saturday we heard a loud report up at the head of the bay, and through our glasses we could see that a large piece of the Dugdale Glacier tongue had broken off.

By working late Saturday night we had the outside of the hut ready and the guys set up, so on Sunday we had a wash and change of clothes, church in the forenoon and a day off, which gave us an opportunity for a look round.

The view is magnificent: to the southward we see the Admiralty Range of mountains, with Mts Sabine, Minto, and Adam rising to over 10,000 feet; away to the west the mountains are not so high, but completely snow-covered, and slope gradually down to Cape North; behind us are the black basalt cliffs of the Cape Adare Peninsula, and in one place there is quite an easy way to the top. When we landed we found Borchgrevink's hut inhabited by a solitary moulting penguin. He was very indignant at being turned out and stood all day at the door scolding us. He also did showman to the crowds of sightseers who came to watch us. I am afraid many of the sightseers got knocked on the head and put in the ice-house. It is brutal work, for they are such friendly little beasts, and take such an interest in us; but they and the seals are our only fresh meat.

Sunday, March 5. – We have put in a good week's work, thanks to fine weather. The hut was ready and we moved in last night, and celebrated the occasion with a great house-warming. We have also had time to put up the meteorological screen and dig a beautiful ice-house in a small stranded berg on the south shore. Unfortunately, the day after the larder was filled a big surf came rolling in and the berg began to break up. We had only just time to rescue the forty penguins with which we had stocked it, and carry the little corpses to a near ice-house built of empty cases filled with ice and well out of reach of the sea. The whole beach we are on is a penguin rookery in summer, and has been so for generations. We are constantly reminded of it – in fact so forcibly is this so inside the hut, that before putting down the floor Levick dressed the ground with bleaching-powder. He did this so thoroughly, and inhaled so much of the gas, that he had to retire to his bunk blind in both eyes, with a bad sore throat and all the symptoms of a heavy cold in his head.

This afternoon Abbott, Priestley, Levick, and I climbed to the top of Cape Adare, and certainly the view over the bay was lovely, the east side of the peninsula descending in a sheer cliff to the Ross Sea. We collected some fine bits of quartz and erratic boulders about 1000 feet up, and Levick got some good photographs of the Admiralty Range. On the way down I found some green alga on the rocks.

Monday, March 6. – We set to work on the coal and stores and carried everything up to the hut, stacking them on the weather side.

We have now settled down into a regular routine; we turn out at 7 a.m., have breakfast at 8 a.m., dinner at 1 p.m., and supper at 7 p.m.

The weather is fairly fine, the temperature keeping between 18° and 20° F., but with a cold east wind. Loose pack sets into the bay with the flood and drifts out with the ebb tide.

March 9. – We had a most magnificent surf breaking on the western shore over a fringe of grounded pack, throwing spray and bits of ice 30 or 40 feet into the air.

On the 11th and 12th we had our first blizzard with heavy drift, and the hut shook a little, but nothing gave way. The remaining penguins began gathering in parties on the sea shore, which looked as though they were going to leave us for the winter; we had now 120 penguins and 4 seals in the ice-house, which should be sufficient for the winter. All manner of bergs drift past our beach, and it is interesting to note the difference in the buoyancy between the two types of berg – the glacier-formed iceberg and the barrier berg composed chiefly or wholly of névé. In one instance a glacier berg about 70 or 80 feet high grounded off our beach in 36 fathoms, and a few days after a barrier berg of similar height drifted past well inside the former.

March 19. – A week of snow and drift, with very little sun.

This morning about seven o'clock it came on to blow from the S.E., with lots of drift. Our anemometer registered wind at 84 miles an hour and then broke; some of the squalls after this must have been of hurricane force. The dome tent which I had up for magnetic observations was blown away, and we never saw a sign of it again. The wind eased in the evening, but blew a gale all night.

A very big sea was breaking on the south shore, the spray being carried right across the peninsula, coating our hut with ice. During the heavier squalls it was impossible to stand. The hut shook a great deal, but beyond a few things being shaken off the shelves no damage was done.

The following day was lovely, and we had a fine aurora in the evening. An arc of yellow stretched from N.W. to N.E., while a green and red curtain extended from the N.W. horizon to the zenith.

On March 27 we launched the 'pram', which is a Norwegian skiff, and tried trawling off the south shore, but did not do very well, our total catch being one sea louse, one sea slug, and one spider; certainly the fishermen, Priestley, Browning, and Dickason, had plenty of difficulties to contend with, as the sea ice was forming so fast that they were compelled to spend most of their time breaking a passage through it.

March 30. – We had another wonderful aurora display this evening. It was like a great curtain of light shaken by a wind, the lower edges being a red colour.

April 9. – The last week has been calm and snowy, and young ice is forming very quickly on the south shore, but on the north shore where there is more swell the sea keeps fairly open. The whole shore since the last gale is piled with enormous blocks of ice, 15 to 20 feet square, and as many of them are glacier ice we find them most useful for our drinking water.

One of the problems of our spring journey along the coast is how we are going to get back if the ice goes out, or even get over the big lanes that are sure to open in the spring, so I have decided to build two kayaks, by making canvas boats to fit round the sledges; these can be carried on the sledges when travelling over the ice and the sledge fitted in them when crossing open water.

April 17. – The first kayak was finished last Thursday and the canvas dressed with hot blubber, but owing to a week of winds we had not been able to try her until today. She proved a great success. I made the first cruise in her along the north shore, using a bamboo as a paddle; she was not at all crank and carried me easily. We will build another, so that by lashing the two together we should have a very seaworthy craft.

May 2. – A lovely day, and as the second kayak was ready we tried her. I have given her more freeboard than the last, and she is, if anything, more seaworthy.

The temperature, which had been steadily dropping all last month, is now at about – 7° F., very pleasant in calm weather, but in the winds most of us have had our faces frostbitten.

It is wonderful how quickly the time is passing. I suppose it is our regular routine, and the fact of all having plenty to do.

Levick is photographer, microbiologist, and stores officer. His medical duties have been nil, with the exception of stopping one of my teeth, a most successful operation; but as he had been flensing a seal a few days before, his fingers tasted strongly of blubber!

Priestley's geology keeps him wandering on the top or on the slopes of Cape Adare, and he certainly gets more exercise than any of us.

He is also meteorologist, and when he does have any spare moments is out with the trawl or fish trap.

I am doing a survey of Cape Adare and the magnetic observations.

Abbott is carpenter and has the building of the kayaks.

Browning is assistant meteorologist and his special care is the acetylene gas plant, a thankless task, as any escape of gas or bad light brings a certain amount of criticism.

Dickason has proved himself a most excellent cook and baker, while the 'galley' is a model of neatness.

The following was our daily routine during the winter:

At 7 a.m. we turned out, one hand going down to the ice foot to get ice for cooking purposes. A number of empty cases were kept full of ice in the 'lean to' outside the hut for use during blizzards when we could not get down to the ice foot. Breakfast was at 8 a.m., and consisted of porridge, seal steak or bacon, and tea. After breakfast we would turn to at our various jobs and worked till 1 p.m., when we had a cold lunch, bread and cheese and sometimes sardines, then work again until 4 p.m., when we had tea. After tea we cleared up decks, and then the rest of the day everyone had to himself.

Dinner was at 7 p.m., and was usually seal or penguin, pudding, and dessert. After dinner hardly a night passed without a gramophone concert.

Saturday morning was devoted to a good soap-and-water scrub of the whole hut, everyone piling their belongings on their beds, Saturday afternoon being 'make and mend'.

Sunday breakfast was at 9 a.m. to give the cook a lie-in, and every week church was held at 10.30 a.m.

In fine weather Sunday was a great day for a long walk, either over the sea ice or up Cape Adare.

During the week everyone had a washing day, when he had a bath and washed his clothes, clothes lines being rigged across the hut.

Of the two huts left by Sir George Newnes's expedition in 1899, one hut was standing in fairly good condition, the other was roofless. The former we repaired, and it made a very good workshop, while the latter, after clearing out and roofing with a tarpaulin, we turned into a store house. Taking it all round we were a very happy and contented little community, but as a wintering station Cape Adare is not good, being cut off from the mainland until June, when the sea ice can be trusted not to go out in a blizzard.

The sea ice has been forming in Robertson Bay for the last week, and now we are able to walk several miles to the southward. To the northward of our beach is a lot of open water, owing to the strong tidal streams off Cape Adare.

On May 5 began our longest and hardest blow, lasting with occasional lulls until the 14th. The morning was overcast, with a cold southerly wind, and when I was out for a walk with Levick we both got our noses frostbitten. In the evening a strong gale blew with drift, and between 1 and 4 a.m. on the 6th the squalls were of hurricane force.

The hut shook and creaked, but stood up to it all right, though some of the ruberoid on the roof was ripped off, a heavy ladder blown some way to leeward, and the outer wall of our porch, made of cases and boards, blown in. In the forenoon the wind eased a little and we were able to get out and secure what we could. The squalls were still so fierce it was impossible to stand in them, and one had to 'heave to' on hands and knees until they passed.

All the sea ice had gone out, although it was over 2 feet thick, and on the 8th the gale freshened again, and during the night the squalls were as hard as any we had had, stones and pebbles rattling against the hut. On the 9th it eased a little, but blew a whole gale until Saturday 13th, when the wind dropped. The peninsula had been swept bare of snow, but the beach and huts were covered with frozen spray. On the 19th the sun left us, but the weather improved, being clear and cold, while the temperature dropped to below zero F. By May 28 the sea ice seemed pretty solid all round us, the temperature being −30° F., and we walked out to the 'Sisters', two pillar rocks lying off Cape Adare. The ice here showed heavy pressure. There are a good number of bergs frozen in to the northward of us.

Now the winter cold had set in we were obliged to rig our second stove in the hut, finding it impossible to keep the temperature of the hut above −25° F.

On June 1 we had a twenty-four hours' blizzard, but I am thankful to say the sea ice held, except off the north shore, where it was driven out for about 100 yards along the beach.

June 11. − We have had a week of the most glorious calm and clear weather, the temperature today being −25° F.

We have been out to most of the neighbouring bergs, and one in Robertson Bay has the most wonderful caves. Levick got some very good photographs of these with flashlight. Unfortunately Priestley, who was working the flash, got his face badly burnt.

We have felt the want of an alarm clock, as in such a small party it seems undesirable that anyone should have to remain awake the whole night to take the 2−4 a.m. observations, but Browning has come to the rescue with a wonderful contrivance. It consists of a bamboo spring held back by a piece of cotton rove through a candle which is marked off in hours. The other end of the cotton is attached to the trigger of the gramophone, and whoever takes the midnight observations winds the gramophone, 'sets' the cotton, lights the candle, and turns the trumpet towards

Priestley, who has to turn out for the 2 a.m., and then turns in himself. At ten minutes to two the candle burns the thread and releases the bamboo spring, which being attached to the trigger starts the gramophone in the sleeper's ear, and he turns out and stops the tune. This arrangement works beautifully, and can be timed to five minutes.

Other things we should have brought are fencing masks and foils. As it is, Abbott has manufactured some helmets out of old flour-tins and also some bamboo sabres, and there have been desperate encounters out on the snow.

The prismatic skies we get during the day now are perfectly lovely, and last night we had, I think, the best coloured aurora we have seen. It was a great curtain across the northern sky, the colours being red, green, and yellow.

This spell of fine weather continued until June 18, when the glaciers were obscured with drift, and we could hear the rumbling of pressure on the other side of Cape Adare, a sure sign of wind, although with us it was still quite calm.

We counted twenty-six seals along the tide crack today, whereas for some weeks before we had not seen any.

June 19. – Last night about 8 it came on to blow a full gale, with heavy drift and squalls of hurricane force. The hut worked a good deal and some of the outer planking was ripped off. It was my turn for the midnight rounds, and I got my nose rather badly frost-bitten, so today it is one big blister.

On the morning of the 20th the wind went down and we were able to repair the hut. The sea ice stood the blizzard well, but again it had been forced back about a hundred yards from the north shore.

On June 22 we celebrated Midwinter Day with the usual festivities.

July 10. – The days are already a little lighter, and we are making ready our sledging equipment, for on the 28th of this month I propose making an expedition into Robertson Bay for a week to see what sort of surface to expect up the coast, the pressure all round our beach and Cape Adare being very bad.

We have seen several Antarctic petrels, and it is hard to account for these birds down here in the middle of winter, unless there is open water a little north of us.

July 29. – Priestley, Abbott, and I left the hut for our short expedition into Robertson Bay.

Taking provisions for a fortnight, we left about 8 a.m., when it was beginning to get light. The surface was appalling, and in spite of our light sledge (400 lbs.) it took us three days to reach Duke of York Island, a distance of 22 miles by the route we took to avoid the bad pressure. The salt-flecked smooth ice, being very sticky, was much heavier going even than the pressure ice.

We spent a day at Duke of York Island collecting, and started back at daybreak, August 2. During the day the weather looked so threatening I made for the cliffs just south of Warning Glacier to get some shelter in case of a blizzard. We got some heavy squalls and drift in the afternoon, which nearly made us camp, but keeping on we reached land about 5.30, camping between two high pressure ridges under the cliffs. The noise of the wind in the bay was terrific, and we were thankful to have got some shelter. After supper we turned in, and being tired after our hard pull were soon asleep. I was awakened about 9 p.m. by a tremendous din, and found the lee skirting of the tent had blown out from under the heavy ice blocks we had piled on it, and the tent poles were bending under the weight of wind. We just had time to roll out of our bags and hang on to the skirting or the tent would have gone. Taking advantage of a lull we got out and piled more ice on the skirting, but even that was not enough, and we spent a miserable night hanging on to the skirting of the tent. The blizzard dropped by noon the next day, and by one o'clock we were off again, camping at 5.30, when it was too dark to go on.

Starting again just before daybreak on the 4th, we reached the hut the same evening. The temperatures we experienced were not low, the lowest being −26.8 F.

The chief result of this journey was to show that we must expect very bad travelling surfaces up the coast and that I must alter my original plan, which was to start about August 20 with two units of three. I now saw that it would take a party of four to get along over the pressure ice we must expect, so I decided to take Priestley, Abbott, and Dickason with six weeks' provisions and do without a supporting party, leaving Levick and Browning to carry on the work at Cape Adare.

August 8. – Levick, Priestley, Browning, and Dickason left this morning for Warning Glacier to do geology. We had depôted our outfit about 10 miles down the coast, only packing our sleeping-bags, so they were able to go without a sledge, taking their sleeping-bags on their backs. I remained at the hut with Abbott, who was laid up with water on the knee, and I was kept busy by the combined duties of cook and bottle-washer, meteorologist, etc.

August 10. – Levick's party returned at 4 p.m., bringing in all our equipment. They had had overcast weather and high temper-atures, and Levick had only been able to get six photographs, which were not good.

August 16. – We woke up this morning to find the ice had gone out in the night. This was a bitter disappointment and a blow to all my hopes of a western journey over the sea ice – the only comfort is that it came when it did, as had it come a fortnight later, we should have gone out with it. Yesterday a strong blizzard began to blow from the S.E., with lots of drift, and the gale continued very hard all day. About 8 p.m. it lulled a little, only to come on again with redoubled violence between 10 p.m. and midnight.

The squalls were terrific, harder than anything we had yet ex-perienced, shaking the hut so that several things fell off the shelves. The roof of our store house was torn off, and the two gable ends which took all six of us to lift were slung about 20 yards away.

This morning the water extended from our beach to the coast of the mainland a little west of the Dugdale Glacier, and as far as we could see to the westward.

Three Antarctic and two snowy petrels, attracted no doubt by the open water, were flying about the beach.

On the 17th, Levick, Priestley, and I climbed Cape Adare to see the ice conditions in the Ross Sea after the gale. Large stretches of open water lay to the S.E. and east, while small pools and lanes were very numerous on the northern horizon, and a heavy bank of fog or mist seemed to indicate a lot of open water there. To the S.W. across Robertson Bay the open water appeared to reach right up to the cliffs of the mainland, but the day was not very clear, and it was hard to make out distinctly if there was a strip of fast ice along the coast.

August 21. – A lovely clear day. We went up Cape Adare again to see the ice conditions to the westward. Owing to the young ice over the open water it was hard to make out if there was an ice foot along the cliffs of the mainland. If the ice remains in I shall go into Robertson Bay early in September to see if the coast journey is feasible, for our only other alternative is to find glaciers leading on to the plateau.

To get a better idea of the gradient of these I climbed about 2500 feet up the slopes of Cape Adare, and the result was not very encouraging. I doubt if the glaciers in Robertson Bay lead directly to the plateau, as the Admiralty Range rises in a series of unbroken ridges of bare rock from the sea to apparently far inland.

Altogether the outlook made me wish more than ever that the ship had had sufficient coal to take us back to Wood Bay.

The spell of fine weather lasted till the 30th, allowing thin ice to form over the open water, except in some pools near Cape Adare which the current seemed to keep open. The night of the 30th a blizzard began, with heavy drift, some of the squalls being very heavy indeed, but it moderated towards the morning. The new ice had not gone out, but a large sheet of open water was visible to the north, while along the northern horizon an open water sky was visible. A decided swell along the beach makes me certain open water is not far distant.

September 7. – September came in with blizzards which prevented our getting away as early as we wished. Yesterday and today, however, we have been getting sledges and outfit over the bad pressure ice which lies to the southward of the beach.

We are taking a 12-ft. and a 10-ft. sledge, the latter being on iron runners, as no wooden runners would stand the sharp edges of the pressure ice for long. We also find the iron runners, in spite of the 40 lbs. extra weight, run much better over the salt-flecked ice. Once over the pressure we packed the 12-ft. sledge and secured it on the 10-ft.

Our total weight including sledges amounts to 1163 lbs.

The sledging ration we are taking is based on Shackleton's ration adapted for coast sledging.

We are convoying Levick and Browning as far as Warning Glacier, where the former is going to take photographs.

September 22. – On this journey the surfaces were so bad that we only managed to reach Cape Barrow, the western limit of Robertson Bay.

After our return we experienced a spell of bad weather until the 22nd, when it cleared, so Levick started off again for Warning Glacier to get the photographs he had been unable to take before.

Priestley, Browning, and Dickason went with him, and the party took provisions for a week.

September 27. – Levick and his party returned today and reported bad weather and blizzards nearly the whole time. They managed, however, to get a few photographs. I am arranging to start on our western journey October 1. Levick and Browning will come as far as Cape Wood to take photographs.

October 3. – Weather-bound until today, when, the weather clearing in the afternoon, we transported our sledges and gear over the pressure ice lying round the beach and left them three miles south.

October 4. – A fine morning, so after a 5.30 breakfast we started away with our sleeping-bags on our backs, and picking up our sledges made pretty good progress over salt-flecked ice with occasional belts of pressure.

To show the superiority of our iron runners over salt-flecked ice, I may mention that two of us pulled the iron-runner sledge weighing 1000 lbs. and kept ahead of Levick's sledge with only 200 lbs. and four men in the traces. About 12 miles out we came to a lot of pressure, so I took my party, consisting of Priestley, Abbott, and Dickason, and steered for Relay Bay, telling Levick and Browning to go their own pace and make the best of their way to the cave.

We camped that night in the middle of Relay Bay and after supper pulled the iron-runner sledge and depôt to a cave discovered on the north side of Point Penelope on a former journey, where we left it, as this sledge is no use in deep snow. We found Levick had just arrived all right, so picking up our ski and a few things we had left there, we returned to camp. The temperature remains −15° F.

A lovely morning with the temperature −21° F.; we were on the march by 8.30 over a fairly good surface.

In the afternoon we got into deep snow again and had to put on ski; we had fitted each ski with a detachable strip of sealskin which made pulling on them much easier. We camped that night 4 miles south of Cape Wood, after picking up our 12-ft. sledge and depôt at Birthday Point. Temperature −28° F.

October 6. – The morning was overcast but warmer, the temperature being –3° F. Today we reached a little bay north of Cape Barrow.

After supper we heard an extraordinary noise like a ship's siren, which I suppose must have been a seal, but none of us had heard anything like it before. During the night we were awakened by an avalanche falling near us, but we were not near enough to the cliff to be in danger.

October 7. – We made a depôt in Siren Bay, leaving one sledge and taking on the 12-ft. sledge and four weeks' provisions. We had an early lunch and started. By keeping some way from the coast we got into fairly good surface, but I noticed round some of the pressure ridges pools of very new ice, while some large areas of flat ice appeared to have been recently flooded, the ice being dark and slushy.

We camped at 6.30, having done five miles since noon. In clearing away the snow for the tent we found the ice brownish in colour and quite salt. While we were turning in, Priestley, who was in his bag, heard a seal gnawing the ice just under his head and remarked to me that it seemed very close, so I sung out to Abbott to take an ice-axe and test the ice. After a few blows he was through and reported the ice only eight inches thick and very soft and sodden.

We turned out and tried several places, with the same result.

Then Priestley and I went about a quarter of a mile towards the land and tried again, with no better result. Finally we found a small patch where the ice was about 15 inches thick and we shifted camp.

Things looked serious, for the season was becoming advanced and the summer thaw approaching, while we had to advance along a straight coast line with steep cliffs as far as we could see. After talking over the situation with Priestley we decided that unless we could find thicker ice near the land we should have to turn, as this ice might break up any time.

It was a bitter disappointment, for I had expected at least to be able to get beyond Cape North this way. It came on to blow with drift in the night, but fortunately the wind did not last, and to our delight on turning out we found the sun breaking through.

After breakfast, taking ski and a spade, I went in towards the land, trying a lot of places and always finding thin sodden ice; in places the under layers of snow were so wet and soft it seemed as though the ice was depressed below the surface of the sea.

After taking a round of angles we returned, making Siren Bay the same night. On our way back we sounded the ice several times, finding thin ice until we reached the tide crack at the mouth of the bay.

October 9 and 10. – We went north along the coast on ski, collecting and examining the face of the glacier, but we found no place where it was possible to climb up. The snow along the coast was very soft and deep, making progress difficult even on ski. We saw a good number of snow and Antarctic petrels circling about the cliffs as if they nested here.

October 11. – The temperature when we turned out was −22.8° F.

Our only chance of doing anything now was to try and get up on one of the glaciers, and although we had seen no accessible place on our outward march, we decided to follow round each bay and examine the coast closely. Today we returned to Birthday Point.

October 12. – A fine morning; I got a round of angles while Priestley went round the bay on ski. We saw a seal near the camp which had just given birth.

Our noses are frostbitten and sunburnt and are a curious sight. They have swollen very much; Abbott's is the worst, being one great blister. I had an attack of snow blindness in the afternoon.

October 13. – Temperature −1° F., weather thick, with snow. We pulled out after breakfast and made for Sphinx Rock, where we camped at 1.30, just in time, as it came on to blow hard, with heavy drift. We saw several seals up along the side crack.

October 14. – Weather-bound all day in the tent, blowing a blizzard, with heavy drift, impossible to see five yards.

October 15. – The wind dropped in the morning, but the weather remained overcast. Priestley went collecting and taking photographs, while the rest of us took one sledge half-way over to Point Penelope, as our load was very big after picking up the depôts.

October 16. – Weather overcast and snowing, but much warmer; we went round the bay collecting. It is impossible to get on to any of the glaciers from the sea ice, as they are all wall-faced.

October 17. – After getting some photographs of icebergs we started for Point Penelope. The forenoon was fine, but during our halt for lunch a heavy bank of cloud worked up from the N., and soon after resuming our march a S.E. wind sprang up, bringing snow and drift. The weather got so bad we had to leave one sledge about a mile out, and got into camp in the cave with the others just as the blizzard came on. In the cave we were as snug as could be, and finding some seal meat Levick had left, put it in the hoosh and had a great feed.

October 19. – Temperature zero. Weather very thick. We laid out a depôt off the Dugdale ice tongue which will do for our next trip into Robertson Bay.

October 20. – Weather very thick; land on the other side of the bay being obscured, we had to shape course by compass to Cape Adare. Starting about 9, we pulled through the fog, getting into rather troublesome pack, till one o'clock, when we halted for lunch. During lunch the fog lifted, and by climbing a berg I was able to see a lead of smooth ice about half a mile to the northward. Getting on to this we made good progress, arriving back at the hut at 5 p.m. A good many seals were up, and about two miles from home we came on the first party of penguins.

After our return from this second coast trip the sea ice became too rotten to be trustworthy, even in Robertson Bay, while to the north of the beach, where the sweep of the current was exceptionally strong, the various open water patches which had been present since August rapidly widened and coalesced, and in December the ice both east and west of the cape broke out with great rapidity.

Our work, therefore, was now restricted to the immediate confines of the beach and the peninsula of Cape Adare, and this time was principally occupied in taking routine observations and adding to our biological collections.

Amongst the specimens collected at this time were several fine sea leopards, which I was fortunate enough to shoot near the rookery. As most of them were shot in the water, we had some difficulty in securing the bodies, and it was here that our kayaks were very useful.

We could carry these light and yet seaworthy craft down to the ice foot and launch them, and from them slip a noose round the body as it lay on the bottom in two or three fathoms of water. The line was then passed ashore and the united strength of the party just sufficed to land the quarry.

After Christmas a permanent camp was established on Cape Adare and we were divided into three watches, one of which was always stationed on top of the cape to look out for the ship. During one of these watches Priestley and Dickason walked ten miles south along the cape, to find out whether, in the event of the ship not picking us up, it was possible for us to make our way south this way. They report the cape to reach a height of 4200 feet at its highest point, and from there they were able to get a good view of Warning Glacier and consider that it would be impossible to make an extended journey in this direction.

On the morning of January 4 Browning sighted the ship and signalled us on the beach below by hoisting a flag as arranged, and two days later all our gear was aboard and we were on our way to try our fortune two or three hundred miles farther south along the coast.

January 8, 1912. p.m. – This evening Pennell and I from the crow's nest saw open water behind the heavy pack we had been working through all day. I had given up hope of being able to land at Evans Coves, and talking it over with Pennell had just decided to come down in the ship and pick up Debenham first, when we saw the open water, and by 9 the same evening we were secured alongside the sea ice about 1½ miles from the piedmont, north of Evans Coves. It was a lovely evening, and with the help of the ship's people we soon had our outfit on the piedmont by a big moraine, where we had arranged to make our depôt, and be picked up by the ship on February 18.

Our stores were six weeks' sledging rations, one 12-ft. sledge (Priestley, Dickason, and myself), and one 10-ft. sledge (Levick, Abbott, and Browning). In addition to this I landed a depôt consisting of seven boxes of biscuits, one box of cocoa (24 tins), one box of chocolate (36 lbs.), one box of sugar (56 lbs.), 4 weekly bags of pemmican (14 lbs. each), 2 weekly bags of raisins, 2 cheeses, 1 bag of onions, 14 tins of oil, a little spare clothing, a spare sleeping-bag, and a spare tent and poles. Also my small primus stove, and two spare sledges, one of which was fitted with iron runners. By midnight we were camped, and saw the last of the ship steaming out of the bay.

January 9. – Turned out at 6 a.m., but we did not get away until 10.30, shaping course N.W. for some foothills between us and Mt Melbourne. Hard rough ice and a strong S.W. breeze made our sledges skid and did the runners no good. Crossed many thaw pools and channels covered with thin ice, through which we broke. After about an hour's pulling, however, we got on to a snow surface, which was better going. We camped early to try and repair the sledge-meter. Got a good round of angles after hoosh. Night calm but overcast. Lengthened the traces as we may expect crevasses.

January 10. – Overslept ourselves, not turning out until 7. It was 9 o'clock before we were under way. Our course lay over the piedmont ice, close under the northern foothills which lay between us and Mt Melbourne. Some way ahead it looked as if a glacier from Mt Melbourne came out on the piedmont, thereby giving us a road to the north. Soon after starting snow began to fall, and that, combined with a slight up-grade, made our sledges very heavy. About noon we rounded a point (Cape Mossyface), on which we found a quantity of lichen, and came on to a smooth glacier, of easy gradient, and snow-covered, which I hoped came from Mt Melbourne; but the weather was so thick with snow we could see nothing, so camped for lunch in the hope of its clearing, as I had no wish to pull the heavy sledges up a *cul-de-sac*. This evening so much snow fell that we had to remain in camp, being unable to see ten yards. Snowing all night.

January 11. Still snowing as hard as ever at 5.30 a.m., but by 7.30 the clouds began to break, and by 9 we were on the march. Snow very soft and deep, making pulling very heavy, so that we had to relay. All six of us had difficulty in getting one sledge along. We then all put on ski, and were able to get along better as we broke a regular trail along which the sledge ran.

The snow and mist cleared away about 10 a.m., giving us a magnificent view up a large glacier, the main body of which seemed to flow past the west slope of Mt Melbourne. A few miles south of Mt Melbourne and on the west side of the main glacier, a tributary glacier, which we named from its shape the Boomerang, flows in. In the afternoon a S.W. wind improved the surface and each team was able to manage its own sledge. A lovely night, but all hands very tired.

January 12. – Woke at 3 a.m. to find strong wind, with drift. The snow ceased a little while we had breakfast, only to come down harder than ever afterwards, and as Dickason and I were suffering from snow-blindness we did not march till 3, when the wind eased. Camped at the entrance of the Boomerang Glacier, which I think may be a possible way through to Wood Bay.

January 13. – Turned out at 6. A lovely morning, so leaving camp standing we went a little way up the Boomerang Glacier to see if it would be possible to get the sledges up. The route looked feasible but probably difficult for sledges, so I decided to try the main glacier first. Returning to camp about 1 o'clock we pulled north, camping for the night north of the Boomerang and under some steep ice slopes.

January 14. – Another fine day. Dickason and I were snow-blind, so the others climbed the ice slope to see if they could find a way for the sledge. They returned to camp about 3.30, and said that after climbing several ice undulations, more or less crevassed, they came to a steep ice slope leading to a rocky ridge.

Owing to the nails having come out of Browning's boots he kept losing his balance and nearly dragging the party down with him, and as there were several large crevasses at the bottom of the slope, Priestley very wisely decided to return. The icefalls we see from our present camp apparently connect with the ridge. It was worth going on to see, however, so we got under weigh and marched till 7 p.m., when we camped at the foot of the first ice falls on snow, the weather having come over very thick in the afternoon.

January 15. – Still and very thick when we turned out at 6 a.m., so there was nothing for it but to turn in again after breakfast. The Antarctic teaches one patience if nothing else.

We are fairly sheltered, but can hear the wind roaring in the crags on the side of the glacier, and the snow and drift are so thick that we can only see a few yards. Occasionally in the lulls we can see the blue icefalls looming up through the drift, and then everything shuts down again.

The conditions remained the same until breakfast on January 19, when it began to clear from the southward. We started away after breakfast with the surface awful, and the snow so deep I doubt if we should have got the sledges along at all if we had not had ski, which enabled us to break a trail. As soon as it was clear to the northward, Priestley and I climbed the slopes on our left on ski, leaving the remainder halted at the bottom. The view from the ridge was not promising. The icefalls reached right up to the ridge, a mass of seracs and crevasses as far as we could see, and I decided to return and try the Boomerang Glacier, which lay a few miles south of us. The sun now came out, and in the deep sticky surface it took all six of us to pull one sledge. We had to relay all the way, and it was six o'clock before we reached the N. lateral moraine of the Boomerang Glacier, where we camped.

January 20. – After breakfast we divided into two parties. I, taking Levick and Dickason, climbed the mountain on the N. side of the glacier. Priestley, taking Abbott and Browning, went up the glacier on the moraine, where Priestley wanted to collect.

At the first possible place my party left the glacier, and, after about an hour's climb, came out on a snow field, where we roped up and ploughed through deep snow lying over ice, along the foot of a steep slope, which we attempted to climb by cutting steps in order to reach a rocky spur several hundred feet above us. Half-way up, however, we had to retrace our steps, the snow being inclined to avalanche, and continue our way along the foot of the slope for about an hour, when we were able to get on another rocky spur and climb.

Some of the granite boulders were hollowed out in a wonderful way by the action of sand-carrying wind. We crawled right inside some, and found room for five or six men.

The view from where we were was very fine in every direction but N.W., where a higher ridge bounded our horizon. Looking down on the Mt Melbourne neck we had first proposed crossing, I saw, to my surprise, that the flat ice on top of the neck was heavily crevassed.

We got back to camp about 6.30, and found the others had not yet arrived. They turned up a little before 9, all very tired. Priestley reported very heavy going, soft snow up to their thighs, which completely hid the crevasses, and they dropped down a good many.

They reached a height of 3680 feet above the camp, but could not see whether the glacier would form a good route over into Wood Bay.

As far as they went it would be possible to get sledges, but progress would be very slow indeed, so considering our limited time we decided to work along more to the westward in the hope of finding a larger and easier glacier. Even if unsuccessful we should be breaking new ground, and Priestley could put in some good collecting from the different moraines, while I surveyed.

January 21. – A fine morning, but wind in the mountains. After getting a round of angles, we started, my party crossing the Boomerang Glacier and working down the west side of the Melbourne Glacier, while I sent Levick's party back the way we came, down the east side of the Melbourne Glacier, with orders to collect from the different exposures, and join us at the S.W. entrance of the main glacier.

The surface was better, and we camped that evening on the south moraine of the Boomerang and well down the Melbourne Glacier.

We had been unable to wear our glasses yesterday climbing, and were now paying the penalty, for we were all snow-blind, so we dressed each other's eyes with Hemisine, and turned in very sorry for ourselves.

January 22. – Only one eye among the three of us, and that belongs to Dickason. He tells me that it is a lovely morning, and that he can see to cook hoosh. After hoosh our last hope goes and we do no more cooking that day. We have all had snow-blindness before, but never anything like so bad as this, and are in great pain. Priestley's eyes and mine are quite closed up, and I think Dickason's are nearly as bad.

January 23. – Eyes better, but still very painful. Started after breakfast. Surface a little soft, but good pulling on ski.

After 6 p.m. the surface got so bad, owing to undercut sastrugi, that we had to relay half our load at a time, and even then had frequent upsets. We camped at 9.30 p.m. about 1 mile E. of a cape we named Cape 'Sastrugi'.

January 24. – A fine morning, but no sign of Levick's party, so after getting a true bearing and round of angles, I joined Priestley and Dickason collecting, on Cape Sastrugi. I made some sketches. This piedmont we are on extends west to the Mt Nansen Range, and seems quite flat, except where glaciers run in, where there are undulations and crevasses.

January 25. – Overcast. Levick has not turned up yet, which is very annoying. It is useless going to look for him, as the undulations at the mouth of the Melbourne Glacier would completely hide a party, unless both happened on the same route. Collecting today on some moraines south of us, Priestley fell through a snow bridge of a crevasse up to his arms. He was not roped at the time, so it was lucky he did not go through altogether.

January 26. – A clear morning, but blowing hard, with drift. Climbed the hills to the N.W., taking the theodolite and sketchbook, and got a true bearing and good round of angles.

I also made out the truant party calmly camped on the east side of the Melbourne Glacier. So returning to camp we packed food for eighteen days, and depôted the remainder, together with the specimens, and a note to Levick telling him my proposed plans, which were to try the two glaciers which came in at the N.W. corner of the piedmont, for a route into Wood Bay, and directing him not to attempt them unless he caught me up, but to photograph and collect on the shores of the piedmont.

January 27. – Overcast. Tops of mountains obscured. Strong wind in squalls. Started after breakfast, and with our light load made good progress. We made a big sweep round Cape Sastrugi to try and avoid the crevasses, but without success.

The afternoon was hot and muggy, and when we camped that night we were wet with perspiration. After supper I went out with Priestley to collect, and the sun being hot I took off my vest, and, turning it inside out, put it over my sweater, where it dried beautifully. I remarked to Priestley at the time that this ought to bring me luck, and sure enough, immediately afterwards I found a sandstone rock containing fossil wood, the best specimen as yet secured by the party.

January 28. – Blowing hard from the N.W., with drift, but clear sky. The temperature being warm, the drift made everything very wet. After breakfast Priestley hunted for fossils, while I got another round of angles. We then marched, edging over to the northern moraines, on which we camped that night.

January 29. – A beautiful day, but no sign of the other party. After breakfast we started, and crossing moraine, steered for what we called 'Corner Glacier', a small steep glacier whose course lay more on our route for Wood Bay. The going was easy, and we camped that evening on the north lateral moraine, which lies at the foot of a steep scree descending from the mountains. The moraine was a very large one, with a number of conical heaps and with lakes in all the little valleys. The noise of running water from a lot of streams sounded very odd after the usual Antarctic silence. Occasionally an enormous boulder would come crashing down from the heights above, making jumps of from 50 to 100 feet at a time.

January 30. – Another fine morning, so after breakfast we started for the south end of 'Black Ridge', from which place we could get a view up the Priestley Glacier. Arriving there about 1 o'clock we found we were cut off from the moraine by a barranca from 40 to 50 feet deep. The glacier itself seemed an important one, judging by the disturbance it made in the piedmont where it flowed in, large undulations and big crevasses extending many miles out.

Although not so steep as Corner Glacier, it was much more crevassed, but what decided us to try Corner Glacier was that the Priestley Glacier curved from a S.W. direction, which would have taken us off our course. Accordingly, after I had secured a round of angles, we steered for the foot of the icefalls of the Corner Glacier, getting there about 5 p.m. After hoosh we left camp standing and climbed the glacier, which proved a very easy job, as, although steep and broken, the seracs are worn smooth and many of the crevasses filled in, which looks as if there was very little movement now.

Arriving at the top of the first icefall we found ourselves on rather a steep broken surface, the valley running in a north-westerly direction for a few miles, where it was fed by several steep glaciers or ice cascades from the heights. It would have been interesting to follow this glacier up, but the route was quite impossible for a sledge and we returned to camp footsore and disappointed.

January 31. – Fog, snow, and then drift kept us in our tent till one o'clock, when, the snow easing up a little, we marched for the moraines of the Priestley Glacier. I had now given up all hope of getting through to Wood Bay this year, our time being too short to get over by the Boomerang Glacier, which I consider the only practicable route for a sledge, so we turned our attention to the Priestley Glacier, on whose moraines Priestley hoped to find some more fossil wood.

We camped about 6 on the southern moraine. While so doing Dickason caught sight of Levick and his party heading for the Corner Glacier. After some difficulty we managed to attract their attention and they pulled over and camped near us, Levick had apparently misunderstood my instructions, and waited for me at Cape Mossyface, then seeing his mistake he headed for Cape Sastrugi across the mouth of the Melbourne Glacier and crossed a maze of crevasses. He says, 'Getting under way about 10, we marched till 12.30 over fairly good surface. After that we got into a perfect network of crevasses. They were mostly snow-bridged, and had we not had ski on we could never have got over, as we could break holes in them in places with our ice-axes. It was 7.30 before we found a place where there was a small space sufficiently free from crevasses to enable us to camp. One of the snow bridges we had to cross broke under the weight of the sledge, but only just under the bows. Had she gone down altogether the result might have been serious. After that we relayed, taking half our load at a time.'

February 1. – We decided to put in the rest of our time collecting from the moraines and foot-hills north of where we had landed, as we knew we should have no time to get far enough up the Boomerang to survey any new ground. During the day I found one large piece of sandstone with the impression of part of a fossil tree.

February 2. – We spent the forenoon breaking up a big boulder, a longer job than we expected, as the lower half was embedded in the frozen soil. After digging it out and rolling it over, Priestley split it open. Inside we found a beautiful specimen of wood. Levick photographed it before we proceeded to break it up, as we knew we could never get it out whole.

February 3. – The weather, which had been perfect up till now, changed, and we woke to find it overcast, with a cold N.W. wind blowing.

We started away after breakfast and made good way, passing Cape Sastrugi before we camped.

February 4. – Fine day. We crossed the Campbell Glacier. The surface was very good for pulling on ski, but too soft without.

We camped tonight about 6 miles off the main depôt. My eyes rather bad.

February 5. – Priestley and Dickason went over to collect on Lichen Island, while Levick and Abbott did the slopes north of us.

Priestley found an extraordinary quantity of lichens on the island.

February 6. – Fine morning, but a strange southwesterly wind.

Getting under way after breakfast, we reached the main depôt about 3 o'clock, and found to our surprise Debenham's party had never landed, our letters to him being still in the 'post box' we had fixed up.

February 7. – The wind, which had fallen yesterday evening, freshened up between 1 and 2 a.m., and, when we turned out, was blowing a whole gale, but with a clear sky. An ex-meridian altitude gave the latitude of this place 74° 55' S. In the afternoon Levick, Priestley, Dickason, and I climbed to the top of what we afterwards called Inexpressible Island to see if we could make out the Nansen Moraine, which Priestley wanted to visit. I told him to take Abbott and Dickason tomorrow, while I carry the theodolite up here and get a round of angles.

February 8. – Both parties started directly after breakfast; Priestley, taking Abbott and Dickason and a week's provisions, went round west of the island, keeping on the piedmont ice, and I climbed the island with the theodolite, taking Levick and Browning with me.

It was a clear day but blowing a regular gale from the west, the wind from the plateau feeling very cold – an unpleasant day for theodolite work. By aneroid I made the height of the island 1320 feet. We returned to camp about 7 p.m.

February 9. – It came on to blow very hard in the morning, and we had to secure the tents with big stones on the skirting, the snow being all blown off. In the evening Browning got two penguins for the pot.

February 10. – Still blowing very hard, too hard in fact to set up the theodolite. Priestley and party pulled in about 2 p.m. He said they had had a gale of wind the whole time, the wind only dropping for two hours. The moraine we saw from the top of the island appears to be the Priestley Glacier moraine. They found some sandstone with fossil wood inclusions, but not such good specimens as we got inland.

In the afternoon Priestley and I found a lot of shells, worm casts, and sponge spicules in little holes on the piedmont.

February 11. – The wind dropped after breakfast, so Priestley, Dickason, and I sledged over to the hills north of us and camped by a lake on the southern slopes. Levick, Abbott, and Browning, leaving their camp standing, examined Evans Coves on the S. Island. They found a small penguin rookery and a large number of seals on the ice foot.

They also found a large number of old dead seals on the beach, one or two of the largest measuring 12 feet in length.

February 12. – Heavy snow, wind, and drift all day. Levick and his party pulled in about 3 p.m. and camped near us.

February 13. – Snowing all night, and although it eased this morning, it kept on all day, stopping our survey completely. In the evening we killed three penguins for food. Levick and party returned to the main depôt.

February 14 *and* 15. – Priestley and I spent the two days collecting and surveying. On the night of the 15th it began to snow, and, a strong plateau wind getting up, we spent the 16th in our tent, the drift being too thick to do anything.

February 17. – Still blowing hard, with drift, but clear overhead. In the afternoon we packed up, and pulled over to the main depôt, as the ship was due the following day. We camped late in the evening in our old place under the moraine. Blowing a heavy gale all night.

February 18 *to* 29. – Most of this time while we were waiting for the *Terra Nova* the wind blew with uninterrupted violence and the tents suffered considerably. Our own tent split near the cap, but after several failures we managed to tie a lashing round the top and so saved the split from spreading to the body of the canvas.

Levick's tent also split near the opening, and Abbott was obliged to sew the rent up in spite of the coldness of the blizzard.

On February 24 the blizzard lulled for a short time and we were enabled to get a little exercise, but the whole of this time was occupied with a not too cheerful discussion about food.

Our sledging provisions were due to give out on the 27th and it was necessary to reserve at least half of the depôt food for the sledge journey down the coast in the spring which would become inevitable should the ship not relieve us. It was therefore necessary to reduce the ration at once, and I asked Priestley to take charge of all food from now on till the time we were relieved or relieved ourselves.

We decided to reduce the biscuit to half ration and cut out everything else for the time being except seal meat and a small portion of pemmican for flavouring. This same day we were fortunate enough to kill a small crab-eater seal. I tasted a small piece of raw blubber and rather liked it, while Abbott and Browning declared that it had a very strong flavour of melon.

It was some time, however, before the blubber was added to our diet as a regular ration. During this short period of calm several times one or other of the party thought they saw smoke off the end of the Drygalski, but there seems no doubt that what they saw was only what is known as frost smoke, the vapour from the leads of open water on pack ice, though the ship certainly was at one time within 25 miles of us.

On the 27th further discomfort was added to our condition as the gale was accompanied by blinding drift, so that we had all the unpleasantness of a barrier blizzard with no adequate shelter; for the tents were threadbare and torn in several places. The snow was soon so thick that the sledge was completely buried with drift and the tent three-quarters hidden.

During most of this fortnight we were living on one meal a day, and on this day we were unable even to get this, so that by the 29th, when the wind eased for a day or two, we were in no wise in a condition to look forward with equanimity to the chance of a winter without sufficient food or decent shelter; in fact so weak were we that a walk of a mile or two tired us far more than a hard day's sledging had done a month before.

Perhaps the worst feature in our present position, however, is the absence of any news from our comrades, and the fear which is naturally growing within us lest the ship should have got into some trouble during this heavy weather.

February 29. – The wind dropped in the morning, and we had our first fine day since the 15th. In the afternoon we pulled over and camped on the island south of the moraine, which we have named Inexpressible Island. In the evening after hoosh we climbed 'Lookout' Hill, and saw what we thought was smoke on the horizon, and under it a small black speck. Unfortunately, it turned out to be only an iceberg with a cloud behind it, showing dark under a snow-squall.

Soon after the wind and snow recommenced.

March 1. – The weather cleared at 10 a.m. I had decided to start killing seals for the winter today if there was no sign of the ship, so after seeing no sign of anything from Look-out Hill, we killed and cut up two seals and eighteen penguins.

There are very few of the former up, and seals hate wind, so we must pray for fine weather to stock our larder, as the animals seldom leave the water in the winter.

March 2 *to* 4. – It came on to blow hard in the night of the 1st, and continued blowing steadily for the next three days.

The gale reached its height on the 3rd, when the tent split and we had to shift camp on to a snowdrift, where we could raise a bit of a snow wall. These last three days we have been lying in our wet bags, watching the tent poles bend and quiver as each squall strikes the tent, and speculating as to what can have happened to the ship.

We also feel having only two biscuits a day and an insufficient supply of seal meat. We are hungry both for news of the Southern Party and for more food.

March 5 *to* 15. – The conditions are gradually but surely becoming more unbearable, and we cannot hope for improvement until we are settled in some permanent home for the winter. The tents we are living in at present are more threadbare than ever, and are pierced with innumerable holes both large and small, so that during the whole time we are inside them we are living in a young gale.

Today, March 15, is the last that I expect the ship, and from now on I shall conclude something has happened and that she is not coming.

For some days we have been preparing in every way possible for the winter, and our position may be summed up as follows: we landed, besides our sledging rations, six boxes of biscuits with 45 lbs. in each box. The sledging biscuits were finished on March 1, and of the others we have to keep two boxes intact for our journey down the coast.

We have also enough cocoa to give us a mug of very thin cocoa five nights of the week; enough tea for a mug of equally thin tea once a week; and the remaining day we must reboil the tea leaves or drink hot water *solus*. Our only luxuries are a very small amount of chocolate and sugar, sufficient to give us a stick of chocolate every Saturday and every other Wednesday, and eight lumps of sugar every Sunday. A bag of raisins we are keeping to allow twenty-five raisins per man on birthdays and red-letter days, and I can see that one of Priestley's difficulties in the future is going to be preventing each man from having a birthday once a month. We have decided to open up neither the chocolate nor the sugar till we are settled in our winter quarters, and, at present, breakfast and supper each consist of a mug of weak seal hoosh and one of weak cocoa, with one biscuit.

To eke out these provisions we have eleven seals and 120 penguins already killed, but to get through the whole winter, even on half rations, we shall require several more seals, and the infrequency of their appearance is causing us all great anxiety.

The wind is incessant, but although strong and very cold, it at least has the merit of being usually free from drift, so that on most days we can work even if under very disadvantageous conditions.

There is plenty of work for all hands, for besides collecting the seals and penguins we have had to carry over our equipment, such as it is, and the provisions from our depôt at Hell's Gate to the site of the snow cave on Inexpressible Island, while three or four of us are usually at work there with pick and shovel.

We have selected a hard drift under the lee of a small hill and have commenced burrowing into it, using two short-handled ice-axes of Priestley's. It is slow work, but after a few hours we had a sheltered place to work in and made better progress.

We have also been experimenting on a blubber reading-lamp and are, I think, on a fair way to success.

March 16. – Blowing hard all day, very cold. Our bags and all gear are covered with drift. The outlook is not very cheerful. We are evidently in for a winter here, under very hard conditions. When we can be out and working things are not so bad, but lying in our bags covered with drift, with nothing to do but speculate as to what has happened to the ship, is depressing. We are using salt water in our hoosh and some bleached and decayed sea-weed from a raised beach, which we try to imagine is like cabbage. Priestley says he would not object to fresh seaweed, but cannot induce himself to include prehistoric seaweed in our regular ration.

March 17. Still blowing, but clear, so after breakfast we struck camp, and started carrying our gear to the hut. The distance is only 1 mile, but over a chaos of big boulders which are the cause of many falls. Our boots have given out and finnesko would not last a day on such surface. Before we had got all our gear over, it came on to blow harder than ever, the squalls bringing small pebbles along with them, and we were several times taken off our feet and blown down.

Luckily no one was damaged, although we all got pretty well frostbitten. It was a great relief to get into our finished hut out of the wind.

We were all dead tired, and turned in directly after hoosh.

March 18. – Our first night in the hut was cold, as we have no door yet and no insulation; in fact, it will take at least two days' more work to make it big enough for us, but it is a shelter from the wind, which we can hear roaring outside. We spent the day chipping away at the ice walls and floor. As a matter of fact our 'hut' is only a cave dug into the snow drift, and our roof is of hard snow about 3 feet thick, while the walls and floor are of ice. As snow is a better insulator than ice, we shall line the walls with snow blocks and pack the space between the snow and ice with seaweed. The floor will be of a layer of small pebbles on the ice, with seaweed on top of that; then our tent cloths are spread on the seaweed.

March 19. – A very heavy gale is blowing, but this no longer interferes with our work, and the hut has grown to quite a respectable size.

Our craving for biscuit is growing awful. We do not like this meat diet. In the afternoon the wind moderated a little, but the squalls were still heavy. About 6 p.m. we heard voices outside, and Levick and his party arrived without sleeping-bags and all pretty well frostbitten. They had had a bad time, their tent poles having been broken in a squall, and their tent blown to rags. They had piled rocks on the rest of their gear and then came over to look for us. After reviving them with hoosh, we spent a most uncomfortable night, sleeping two in each bag.

Levick was my partner. My bag was, luckily, a good one, and nothing split, but I should not care to repeat the experience.

March 20. – Luckily the weather had improved enough for Levick's party to get their bags and gear over. The rest of us worked at the hut.

March 21. – A cold wind, but fine. Priestley, Levick, and Dickason worked at the hut, while Abbott, Browning, and I went over to the main depôt to bring some more gear over. On the way over we saw a seal come up several times and try to get on the ice foot. Leaving Browning to watch the seal, Abbott and I went over for the load, and on our way to our great joy we saw Browning cutting up the seal. But a still greater treat was in store for us. The seal's stomach was full of fish, thirty-six of which were nearly whole. We took these up to the hut, fried them in blubber, and found them excellent. In future we shall always look for fish as soon as we kill a seal.

March 22. – Spent the day bringing up what stores we had left, while some worked at the hut, which is already beginning to look more habitable. The weather is clear and cold, but these strong plateau winds continue, and we get our noses frostbitten every time we go out. My nose is one great blister.

The sea was freezing over in the bay, but the wind kept the ice from forming permanently.

March 23. – We put in another good day's work at the hut. Abbott and I killed and cut up a seal. We have now 13.

March 24, 25, 26. – Blowing a gale, with drift. We worked at insulating the hut.

March 27. – It lulled a little in the forenoon, so three of us managed to get as far as the ice foot to bring up blubber, which we pack on our backs, and which, in spite of being frozen, makes our clothes in an awful mess.

In fact we are saturated to the skin with blubber, and our clothes in consequence feel very cold.

When we kill a seal, we cut out the heart, liver, and kidneys; then cut the meat up into convenient joints and the blubber and skin into pieces about 2 feet square, which we can carry up on our backs and flense in the hut. We also preserve the head, as besides its meat it contains the greatest delicacy of all, the brain. The gale came on harder than ever in the afternoon.

Browning and I are suffering from dysentery.

March 29 *to April* 5. – High wind and bitterly cold. We all get frostbitten constantly while working at the hut, and most of us are suffering from dysentery.

April 5. – A great improvement in the weather, and we got on well with the hut. We also carried up a lot of our things from the depôt. In the evening just as we were stopping work I saw three seals up on the ice, so we turned out again and killed and butchered them. This makes sixteen seals, and if we can march early should put us out of danger with regard to food. To celebrate the occasion Priestley allowed us an extra biscuit each.

April 7. – Northerly gales and drift since the 5th. The way from the hut to the ice foot is strewn with huge boulders, and it is a difficult job walking over these in a gale of wind without a load, while when one is staggering up under a load of meat or blubber, it is particularly maddening. When a squall catches you, over you go between two boulders, with your legs in the air and the load of blubber holding you down firmly. Our boots are all giving out with this rough walking, and we dare not use our finnesko, but must keep them for spring sledging. Our feet are getting very frequently frostbitten and are beginning to feel as if the circulation might become permanently injured.

April 9. Warmer today. We saw a small seal on a floe but were unable to reach him. The bay remains open still. On the still days a thin film of ice forms, but blows out as soon as the wind comes up. In these early days, before we had perfected our cooking and messing arrangements, a great part of our day was taken up with cooking and preparing the food, but later on we got used to the ways of a blubber stove, and things went more smoothly. We had landed all our spare paraffin from the ship, and this gave us enough oil to use the primus for breakfast, provided we melted the ice over the blubber fire the day before. The blubber stove was made of an old oil-tin cut down. In this we put some old seal-bones taken from the carcases we found on the beach. A piece of blubber skewered on to a marline spike and held over the flame dripped oil on the bones and fed the fire. In this way we could cook hoosh nearly as quickly as we could on the primus. Of course the stove took several weeks of experimenting before it reached this satisfactory state. With certain winds we were nearly choked with a black oily smoke that hurt our eyes and brought on much the same symptoms as accompany snow-blindness.

We take it in turns to be cook and messman, working in pairs; Abbott and I, Levick and Browning, Priestley and Dickason, and thus each has one day on in three. The duties of the cooks are to turn out at 7 and cook and serve out the breakfast, the others remaining in their bags for the meal. Then we all have a siesta till 10.30, when we turn out for the day's work. The cook starts the blubber stove and melts blubber for the lamps. The messman takes an ice-axe and chips frozen seal meat in the passage by the light of a blubber lamp. A cold job this and trying to the temper, as scraps of meat fly in all directions and have to be carefully collected afterwards. The remainder carry up the meat and blubber or look for seals. By 5 p.m. all except the cooks are in their bags, and we have supper. After supper the cooks melt ice for the morning, prepare breakfast, and clear up. Our rations at this time were as follows: breakfast, 1 mug of penguin and seal hoosh and 1 biscuit. Supper 1½ mugs of seal, 1 biscuit and ¾ pint of thin cocoa, tea, or hot water. We were always hungry on this, and to swell the hoosh we used occasionally to try putting in seaweed, but most of it had deteriorated owing to the heat of the sun and the attentions of the penguins.

The cocoa we could only afford to have five days a week and then very thin, but as we had a little tea we had weak tea on Sunday and reboiled the leaves for Monday. As already stated we had a little chocolate (2 ounces per man a week), and 8 lumps of sugar every Sunday. Our tobacco soon ran out, even with the most rigid economy, and we were reduced to smoking the much-boiled tea and wood shavings – a poor substitute. About the middle of this month we found we were getting through our seal meat too fast, so had to come down to half the above ration, and it was not until the middle of July, when we got some more seals, that we were able to go back to the old ration.

There is no doubt that during this period we were all miserably hungry, even directly after the meals. Towards the end of June we had to cut down still more, and have only one biscuit per day, and after July to stop the biscuit ration altogether until September, when we started one biscuit a day again. By this means we were able to save enough biscuits for a month at half ration for our journey down the coast. I am sure seals have never been so thoroughly eaten as ours were. There was absolutely no waste. The brain was our greatest luxury; then the liver, kidneys, and heart, which we used to save for Sundays. The bones, after we had picked all the meat off them, we put on one side, so that if the worst came to the worst we could pound them up for soup. The best of the undercut was saved for sledging. After our experience in March, when we got thirty-nine fish out of a seal's stomach, we always cut them open directly we killed them in the hope of finding more, but we never again found anything fit to eat. One of our greatest troubles was a lack of variety in the flavouring of our meals. Two attempts were made by Levick to relieve this want from the medicine chest, but both were failures. Once we dissolved several ginger tabloids in the hoosh without any effect at all, and on the historic occasion when we used a mustard plaster, there was a general decision that the correct term would have been linseed plaster, as the mustard could not be tasted at all and the flavour of linseed was most distinct.

For lighting purposes the blubber lamps we made were very satisfactory. We had some little tins, which had contained 'Oxo'. These, filled with melted blubber and a strand of rope for a wick, gave quite a good light. A tin bridge was pierced to hold the wick and laid across the top of the Oxo tin. We luckily had one or two books – *David Copperfield*, *The Life of R. L. Stevenson*, and *Simon the Jester* being the favourites – and after hoosh Levick used to read a chapter of one of them. Saturday evenings, we each had a stick of chocolate, and usually had a concert, and Sunday evening at supper twelve lumps of sugar were served out and we had church, which consisted of my reading a chapter of the Bible, followed by hymns. We had no hymn-book, but Priestley remembered several hymns, while Abbott, Browning, and Dickason had all been, at some time or other, in a choir, and were responsible for one or two of the better-known psalms. When our library was exhausted we started lectures, Levick's on anatomy being especially interesting.

April 12. – A calm day. Priestley and I went over to the main depôt to get some oil we had left there on the sledges, and in the afternoon I went into the cove south of us to look for seals. I saw one lying on some new ice, but I could not reach him. I found an old penguin egg. It was four months old if it had been laid this year, so I brought it back on the chance of its having been frozen all the time, but no such luck. It was hopelessly bad.

April 13–17. – Strong westerly wind, bitterly cold.

April 20. – The same wind continues, but slightly warmer. A large piece had calved off the Drygalski ice tongue. I think this northern face must be altering very fast, as its appearance does not tally with the last survey.

April 23. – Another calm day. Browning and Dickason saw two seals on floes, but were unable to reach them. The sea is still open. On calm days a thin film of ice forms, but disappears as soon as the wind gets up. The current also plays an important part, I am sure, as in Arrival Bay, where there is no current, the ice has formed, and is several feet thick, although the winds are just as strong.

April 24, 25, 26. – Blowing a hard blizzard. On the 25th Dickason dropped 'Y' deck watch and broke the glass, but 'R' and 'C' are going strong, and with sticking-plaster and 'new skin' we have mended Y's glass. We are very snug in our den, and hardly hear the wind.

From *April 27 to May* 5 the weather prevented much outside work and we spent most of our time in our bags, or working at the improvement of the long tunnel which led to our home. We are roofing this with sealskins on a framework of bamboos, trusting to the drift to increase the thickness of the roof and so insulate us more thoroughly against the cold. We have also dug out one or two alcoves in which to keep meat, blubber, and miscellaneous stores.

We lost the sun today and shall not get him back till August 12.

May 6. – About three times a week we have to bring up salt water ice for the hoosh, as we have run out of salt. This morning Priestley and I went down for sea ice, and as usual were walking round Look-out Point to see if any seals were up, when coming across the sea ice in Arrival Bay we saw figures. We had often talked of the possibility of the ship being caught in Wood Bay and relieving us from that direction.

We both got rather a thrill on sighting them, though they were so close to the open water as to make it improbable that they should be anything but penguins. Still I ran back to the hut for my glasses, as through the low drift they seemed tall enough to be men.

Abbott followed me down with an ice-axe, since, if they were not men, they were food. They turned out to be four Emperor penguins heading into Arrival Bay, so we jumped the tide crack, all getting wet, and made off to intercept them. We came up with them after a long chase, and bagged the lot, Levick coming up just too late for the kill. They were in fine condition, and it was all we could do to carry them back to the hut, each taking a bird. There is no doubt our low diet is making us rather weak. We had a full hoosh and an extra biscuit in honour of the occasion.

May 7. – A blizzard with heavy drift has been blowing all day, so it was a good job we got the penguins. We have got the roof on the shaft now, but in these blizzards the entrance is buried in snow, and we have a job to keep the shaft clear. Priestley has found his last year's journal, and reads some to us every evening.

From now till the end of the month strong gales again reduced our outside work to a minimum, and most of our energies were directed to improving our domestic routine.

We have now a much better method for cutting up the meat for the hoosh. Until now we had to take the frozen joints and hack them in pieces with an ice-axe. We have now fixed up an empty biscuit tin on a bamboo tripod over the blubber fire. The small pieces of meat we put in this to thaw; the larger joints hang from the bamboo. In this way they thaw sufficiently in the twenty-four hours to cut up with a knife, and we find this cleaner and more economical.

We celebrated two special occasions on this month, my wedding-day on the 10th, and the anniversary, to use a paradox, of the commissioning of the hut on the 17th, and each time the commiss-ariat officer relaxed his hold to the extent of ten raisins each.

Levick is saving his biscuit to see how it feels to go without cereals for a week. He also wants to have one real good feed at the end of the week. His idea is that by eating more blubber he will not feel the want of the biscuits very much.

On May 25 we had an unpleasant experience that might have been serious. Drift had blocked the funnel and shaft so that the smoke from the blubber stove became unbearable and we made up our minds to put it out. As a matter of fact it went out, and we had the greatest difficulty in keeping the lamps alight. This ought to have warned us the air was bad.

In spite of this we lit the primus stove to cook the evening hoosh, though we had the greatest difficulty in making it burn. Just before hoosh was ready it went out, and all the lamps followed suit.

Three matches struck in succession did the same before we realised there was no air. I groped for a spade, and crawling along the shaft drove it through the drift, when a match burned immediately, the primus stove gave us no trouble, and all went well; but it was a lesson to us, and in future I kept a long bamboo stuck through the chimney, and the wind keeping it shaking maintained an air-hole. When I fetched the bamboo it was only about 10 yards from the entrance of the shaft, yet the drift was so smothering and the night so dark, it was with the greatest difficulty I could find it.

Towards the end of the month the shaft was so frequently blocked with snow that we dug it out altogether, and then made a hatch with a sack and some bamboos, the coamings being of snow blocks, and the effect of this was at once to be seen in the improvement of the ventilation.

In spite of frequent frostbites during our few trips outside, they have one good point, for they make us appreciate the shelter of the hut and allow us to forget the dirt and grease of everything.

June 1. – Still blowing hard, but clear. Open water in the bay; but when the moon is in the east we can see the blink of ice in the Ross Sea, so I hope the bay will soon freeze over. We have been discussing our best route down, whether to go round the Drygalski on the sea ice or over the tongue. I do not myself think the ice can be depended on round the Drygalski. It runs out so far into the Ross Sea, and even in winter I believe there is a lot of movement far out.

On the other hand, Professor David speaks of the Drygalski ice tongue as a bad place to cross owing to rough ice, barrancas, and crevasses. I think that unless the sea ice looks very good I shall choose the ice tongue.

June 2. – A still, fine day, and we are able to lay in a good stock of sea ice, blubber, and meat from our depôts.

One of the seal meat depôts being on the south side of the cove, about a mile away, it is only on fine days we can reach it now we get no daylight.

June 7. – The wind came up again on the night of the 2nd, and has been blowing hard ever since. Levick some days ago designed a new stove, which we call the 'Complex' in opposition to our old one, the 'Simplex'. The reason the 'Complex' did not catch on with the rest of us he put down to professional jealousy, but today I came in to find the designer using the old 'Simplex', while a much battered 'Complex' lay outside on the drift, where it remained for the rest of the winter.

June 10. – The last two days have been calm, and with thick snow, but today the old wind came back again, and now it is blowing a gale and the drift is smothering. Levick searched his medicine case for luxuries, and found bottles of ginger, lime juice, and citron tabloids.

The limejuice we keep for sledging, but the two others we serve out from time to time. Our new hatch works well, and although it gets covered up, it keeps the shaft from getting blocked with snow, while the bamboo in the chimney keeps us an air hole.

June 12. – The wind moderated today, and we were able to get out for sea ice and meat, and also a fresh store of bones from the old carcases of seals which we make use of in our blubber stoves.

June 16. – Being Sunday we get twelve lumps of sugar and have two tabloids of ginger each. These chewed up with sugar and a little imagination give us preserved ginger. The weather during the week has been thick with snow when it has not been blowing, but we have given up hoping for good weather, and if we can get a lull every few days to bring up sea ice and blubber, we shall not worry.

June 20. – The wind eased a little today, and I got out for a walk, but soon came in with a frostbitten nose. Our wind clothes are torn and so rotten with blubber that we have to be constantly mending them. The grease makes any snow or drift stick to them, and brushing them when we come in from a walk is a long business. We are feeling very excited about the feast on Midwinter Day, and have been discussing the menu for some time. It will consist of liver hoosh and biscuits, four sticks of chocolate, twenty-five raisins, and a sip of Wincarnis each.

June 22. – Midwinter Day. The weather was seasonable: pitch dark, with wind and a smothering drift outside. We woke up early, and being too impatient to wait longer, turned out, and for breakfast had our first full hoosh. In the evening we had another followed by cocoa with sugar in it, then four citric acid and two ginger tabloids, finishing up the evening with a sing-song and a little tobacco, which had been saved for the occasion. In addition four biscuits and four sticks of chocolate were served out, so that we retired to bed with full stomachs once again, and some of us have even saved a bite or two for tomorrow.

After Midwinter Day time passed more quickly, and the knowledge that every day the sun was approaching us cheered us immensely. During the next month we have to celebrate no less than three birthdays, and each with its accompanying slight increase of ration gives us something to look forward to and so helps to pass the intervening days.

The only occurrence which was worthy of note before the end of June was an unpleasant one involving much extra work.

On June 29 we found our seal carcases nearly buried in salt ice, although they were some 200 yards back from the seaward edge of the icefoot. Evidently the spring tides had been the cause of this, and we had a lot of trouble digging the bodies out.

July 4. – Southerly wind, with snow, noise of pressure at sea and the ice in the bay breaking up. Evidently there is wind coming, and the sea ice which has recently formed will go again like the rest. It is getting rather a serious question as to whether there will be any sea ice for us to get down the coast on. I only hope that to the south of the Drygalski ice tongue, where the south-easterlies are the prevailing winds, we shall find the ice has held. Otherwise it will mean that we shall have to go over the plateau, climbing up by Mount Larsen, and coming down the Ferrar Glacier, and if so we cannot start until November, and the food will be a problem.

We made a terrible discovery in the hoosh tonight: a penguin's flipper. Abbott and I prepared the hoosh. I can remember using a flipper to clean the pot with, and in the dark Abbott cannot have seen it when he filled the pot. However, I assured everyone it was a fairly clean flipper, and certainly the hoosh was a good one.

July 5. – A heavy snowstorm from the S.E., the first one we have had from that quarter since the hut was ready. It blocked the entrance completely. Consequently the air got pretty bad. The primus went out and the lamps burnt dimly until we dug through the drift and let in fresh air. Priestley and I cleared the door, but it was so thick with snow it soon drifted up again. It felt wonderfully warm out and we got quite hot digging. During the night we kept night watch two hours each, the watchman's duty being to keep the entrance from being blocked, as it was useless trying to keep the chimney clear – in fact, snow came down so fast it put the blubber fire out, and the smoke rendered the hut almost untenable, so that we had to cook the evening hoosh with the primus and use most of our precious oil.

July 7. – Blew hard all night, drifting up the outer door completely. We cleared the shaft, but as our chimney was buried in drift, we could get no draught for the blubber fire, so we had to build the chimney up with seal skin and snow blocks. All this time the drift was perfectly blinding, although the stars were showing overhead.

That evening we had another 'no air' scare, the primus going out and lamps burning dimly until we had made air-holes with bamboos. I see we shall have to be careful in these snowstorms.

July 8. – Still blowing hard, but not so much drift. We had an awful job digging out, as the drift over our door was packed quite hard. This storm has added 2 or 3 feet of hard snow to our drift. It has made the hut much warmer, but has buried our outside meat depôt, and Priestley and I have been trying all day to find it without success.

July 10. – A 'Red Letter' day. As I was walking down to Look Out Point I saw a seal up. It was getting late, so I returned for the knives, and taking Abbott and Browning with me, we ran down and found 2 fat seals.

Abbott had only a short-handled ice-axe with him and had a job to stun his seal. He made several mis-hits, and finally, as the seal was making for the edge, he jumped on its back and gave it a blow on the nose that stunned it. Abbott then got out his knife and tried to stick the seal, but the handle was greasy, and his hands cold, and they slipped up the blade, cutting three fingers badly, so that I had to send him back to the hut, where he arrived feeling very faint from loss of blood. It was quite dark when Browning and I finished cutting up the seals. They were in good condition, the blubber being very thick. It was quite late by the time we got back, but we were able to have a big hoosh, and we shall no longer have to be on half-rations of seal meat. We were running things uncomfortably close before. We had six lumps of sugar in honour of the occasion.

July 12. – Abbott's fingers are badly hurt. Levick is afraid the tendons are cut and that he will not be able to bend them again.

Browning and Dickason went for a walk today and killed 2 fat seals they found, so we had another double hoosh. The rest of us spent today and yesterday depôting the meat from the first two seals.

July 13. – A lovely morning. The sky orange and saffron in the north about noon. Spent the day carrying meat up. The wind got back to its old quarter in the afternoon, and came on to blow hard and very cold, punishing us badly as we struggled up with the meat.

The thin ice that had formed over the bay during the last few days blew out. I do not think this bay will ever be safe to travel on, so we shall have to take the Drygalski ice tongue route and march later.

July 20. – It has been blowing since the 14th, but being clear we have been able to get out every day. Today being Priestley's birthday we allowed him to do no work and served out six lumps of sugar, a stick of chocolate, and twenty raisins. A sing-song followed in the evening. Altogether a most successful day.

July 24. – The wind got round to the southward yesterday and came on to blow really hard, and is blowing great guns now.

July 26. – The wind dropped suddenly, after blowing a hard gale since the 24th. Priestley and I got down to our last kill and found the bay ice had broken away to within 3 or 4 feet of the carcases, but none of the meat had gone, for which we were very thankful. In the afternoon it was blowing very hard again, and we all got frostbitten carrying up the meat.

July 31. – After two days of warm snowy weather with a moderate S.E. breeze the wind has again swung to the west and is blowing a gale. Signs and tracks of seals are numerous and we have seen several swimming near the ice foot. I think our lean days are over.

August 3. – It has been blowing the same hard westerly wind, clear and cold. Browning got his hand badly frostbitten getting sea ice. It 'went' right up to the wrist and he was a long time bringing it round.

I walked over to the piedmont in the afternoon to look for some penguins we had depôted there. The bay ice had held well. On the piedmont it was blowing hard, with drift, but evidently a low level wind, as half-way up the hills at an altitude of about 1000 feet lay a thin stratus cloud, above which there was no drift off the hills. The sky was very fine to the north.

August 7. – Today and yesterday have been very warm, the weather overcast, with snow and drift, and our door continually drifting up. Abbott and Browning improved the entrance by building a torpedo-boat hatch out of ski sticks and snow blocks. We felt the increased draught for the blubber stove immediately. The heavy snow of the last month has buried our whole hut about 3 ft. deeper and made it much warmer. Our trouble now is the water that drips from the roof whenever we light the blubber stove. We lost our depôt of sledging meat under the new snow, and although we knew its position to within a few yards it took us a week's digging before we found it.

August 10. – Today we celebrated the return of the sun, but needless to say we did not see him, owing to a heavy gale. We made merry tonight over brain and liver hoosh, two biscuits, six lumps of sugar, and a stick of chocolate, finishing up with sweet cocoa.

We have built up a high chimney, using snow blocks, seal skins, and an old biscuit tin, and we get much less smoke inside now.

August 13. – The wind, which had eased in the early morning, began to freshen about 10. In spite of the gale, Abbott, Browning, and myself started over to the depôt sledge in Arrival Bay. Before we got half-way across the bay the wind and drift came down, shutting out everything; but we kept on and reached the depôt, leaving a note in case a relief party came up. Each of us carried back a load of oil, or of mending material for repairing sledging gear.

On our way back we saw the rays of the sun over the tops of the hills, and this made us feel very cheerful.

August 14. – Blowing hard all night, but eased in the forenoon. Priestley managed to pick the brain out of one of the frozen seal carcases. I walked up the ridge at the back of the hut and had the first view of the sun. He was shining through a pink haze of drift and looked lovely. We stood blinking at each other for some time and then a frozen nose sent me home.

August 15. – Being a fine morning we decided to bring the iron runner sledge over from Arrival Bay. Of course as soon as we started the wind came down on us again, but the drift was not so thick as before. I foolishly did not put on a helmet, and my cheeks, nose, and chin 'went' rather badly, taking a long time to come round, though Priestley and Abbott helped to thaw it out for me. This evening our other sledge is completely buried.

August 20. – My birthday, and as it was my day on as cook, the others relieved me and I spent a lazy day.

It has been blowing for the last two days, with open water, but last night the wind eased for a few hours, and immediately ice formed all over the bay.

Our birthday ration tonight consists of two biscuits, twenty raisins, six lumps of sugar each, strong tea, and liver hoosh. As usual we finished up with a sing-song.

August 28. – The wind dropped last night after blowing hard since the 20th, and we put in a good day carrying blubber and meat up from the ice foot. There was a cold breeze and I got my nose and feet frozen. We are all suffering much from frostbitten feet, as our ski boots are pretty well worn out and their soles are full of holes.

In the evening Abbott came running in for my glasses as he saw something that looked like a sledge party on the piedmont, but as usual this proved a false alarm.

August 31. – Calm and very cold since the 28th. We had our last stick of chocolate till we start sledging, but tomorrow we start one biscuit a day each. We have been all this month without biscuit and have felt none the worse, so evidently a seal meat and blubber diet is healthy enough. Strangely enough we do not get tired of it.

From the top of the hill I could see sea ice on the horizon, but the bay remains open.

September 5. – A very heavy gale has been blowing since the first, keeping all hands inside the hut. We have had an epidemic of enteritis which is hard to account for, as we are eating seal meat that has never seen the sun, but I think the 'oven' or tin we thaw the meat out in may have had something to do with it, so we have condemned it.

It is a great pity getting this a few weeks before starting sledging, as it is making us all so weak.

September 6. – A great improvement in the public health due to Levick's wisely curtailing the hoosh. I have been the least affected, but Browning and Dickason are still very bad. I hope this may be the end of it, as we are still all weak, and for the first time in the winter there has been a general gloom. The weather has been vile, but improved today.

September 11. – The best day we have had yet, bright and clear with a light westerly wind. Priestley and I went over to the depôt moraine to look at the geological specimens and put them round the bamboo mark, but found they had been buried in a drift, and after digging all day had to come away without them. On our way back we dug out the sledges, which had been nearly buried. When we got back we found Abbott and Dickason had been all round the coves after seals, but without success. We are still short of sledging meat, having only five bags of cut-up meat, and we shall require eight. The allowance will be two mugs per day for each man, and each bag contains forty-two mugs, or one week's meat for each tent.

A thin scum of ice formed over the bay, but even if the sea ice did form now I should not trust it for sledging.

September 12. – Overcast and low drift. I am repairing Levick's sleeping-bag and putting a new flap on my own; a slow job when one has to work by the light of a blubber lamp.

September 13. – Browning and Dickason saw a seal with a fish in its mouth, but he would not come up on the ice. These two are still very bad with diarrhoea, and we are giving them fresh-water hoosh to see if that does any good.

September 14. – Browning was very bad in the night. I wish we had a change of diet to give him. He has been ill, off and on, for five months now and has been very cheerful through it all. Priestley and Dickason are also down with enteritis but are not so bad. We have some Oxo and I shall try Browning on this before sledging. The rest of us are feeling fairly fit. At the beginning of this month we started Swedish exercises, and will keep it up until we start sledging, as oar leg muscles have shrunk to nothing. As the hut is not nearly 6 feet high we are obliged to do these exercises and all our other work without standing upright, and this has given rise to what we called the 'Igloo Back', which is caused by the stretching of the ligaments round the spine and is very painful.

September 17. – A fine morning. Priestley and Abbott went over to the moraine depôt to dig for the specimens, while Dickason and I dug out the sledges, which had been buried again. After a hard day's work we got our sledges clear, and brought up the tent poles to shorten and repair for sledging. Getting back late we heard that Priestley had found a seal, which he and Browning killed and cut up. There has been great rejoicing tonight, for this will complete our sledging provisions. We served out an extra biscuit for supper. The fine day has made us all impatient to start.

September 19. – Snowing all day, but we had plenty of work to do in the hut, sewing bags and repairing sledge gear. The sea is freezing over again.

September 20. – Priestley and Abbott went over to the depôt moraine to dig for the precious specimens, the rest of us sewing or cutting up meat for the journey. In the afternoon I walked over and joined Priestley. I found them very disappointed, having been digging all day without success. I thought they were digging too far to the westward, so I tried sinking pits at the east end of the drift, and after about half an hour's work, found the specimens. We carried them all to the moraine and stacked them round the bamboo mark. We got back late and found the others cutting up the last bag of sledging meat.

Served out one biscuit and six lumps of sugar each and had seal's brain in the hoosh.

September 21. – A fine morning; Levick and Abbott dug out the last sledge, but had to come back in the afternoon, as it came on to snow and blow hard. I got noon sights for time and found my watch had kept a fairly even rate, which was satisfactory.

September 24. – We were able to start carrying meat, &c., down to the sledges today as it was fine. The weather the two previous days had been very bad. Browning has had another acute attack of dysentery and we cannot march until he is better.

On my way back from the sledges I saw some fresh guano on the sea ice, and looking about saw an Emperor penguin. I killed it and we carried it up to the hut; I hope it may do Browning good, as the seal meat certainly does not agree with him. We are all ready to start now as soon as he is fit to walk, but it is blowing a gale tonight.

September 27. – Still blowing, but clear. We found two seals up under the lee of some pressure, and killed one for extra meat; the other was the first we have been able to let go since the last autumn.

September 28. – Strong south-west wind and overcast in the morning, clearing and coming out finer in the late noon. Priestley saw six Emperors. We got five of them. I was very glad to get these, as they seem to agree with Browning much better than seal. He has been bad again and is getting pessimistic about himself.

September 29. – Overhauled the sledge runners, scraping and waxing them. We also carried down all the equipment that was ready. We are taking the 12-ft. sledge and the 10-ft., the latter being fitted with iron runners, which will be a great help on sea ice. The weather was overcast, with north-west wind.

September 30. – A calm morning. As Dickason and Browning were both better we abandoned the igloo after breakfast. Carrying down the rest of our gear occupied four of us most of the day, and I left the two sick men in the hut, cleaning the cookers, until the last load.

It came on very thick with snow in the afternoon and it was 6.30 p.m. before we pulled out. Snow drifts made the pulling heavy and by 8.30 we had only pulled a mile, and as we were all pretty tired after our long day's carrying we camped. Dickason was bad in the night, but we are all very cheerful at being on the march again, and the change from the dirt and dark of the igloo will do us all good. Our sledging rations also seemed sumptuous, the daily ration per man being:

2 pannikins of meat	stick of chocolate
¾ pannikin of blubber	8 lumps of sugar
1 pannikin of cocoa	a little pemmican
3 biscuits	

At the commencement of the winter we had some spare wind clothing, sweaters, mits, and underclothing, which we had landed from the ship. This I put on one side for the journey down and only issued it before leaving the igloo. There was not enough of everything to go round, but by making the clothes into lots and drawing for them we all got something. To keep them clean we only changed into them just before leaving the igloo, but the luxury of getting into dry clean clothing after the greasy rags we discarded was indescribable. We had been in the same clothes for nine months, carrying, cooking, and handling blubber, and all our garments were black and soaked through and through with grease. We were fairly well off for paraffin as we had only used the primus to cook our morning hoosh. Dickason's generosity in volunteering to work the primus always had also made a lot of difference, as he handles the stove with more economy than any other of us.

October 1. – We turned out at 5.30 a.m. The morning was still and overcast, but with the sun trying to break through. We got away by 7, but made slow progress, finding the drifts very heavy. My unit consisted of Priestley, Dickason, and myself, with the 12-ft. sledge, and as Levick had the iron runner sledge we had the heavier load. We had to relay most of the day, as Dickason could pull very little and Browning not at all. In fact the latter had to rest constantly, so our progress was slow, and by lunch time we had only made 2½ miles. Our supply of oil would not run to hot lunch, so we had a cold lunch sitting under the lee of the sledge. Before leaving the igloo we had cooked some seal steaks over the blubber fire, but when examined in the light of day these looked so filthy and distasteful, that we discarded them in favour of shreds of raw penguin and seal.

The walking had made both Dickason and Browning much worse, so I had to camp at 6.30 p.m., having only done 5 miles. We are all very tired, but in good spirits at leaving the dirt and squalor of the hut behind. A lovely evening and every appearance of a fine day tomorrow.

October 2. – A fine morning when we turned out at 5.30. The surface was rather better and we did not have to relay, but it was all we could do to move the sledges. About 11 o'clock we got on to a blue ice surface and worked our way through a loose moraine. A bitter wind from the plateau got up about noon, bringing drift that in the squalls was so thick one could not see more than a few yards. The wind was fair, however, and we raced along over the blue ice until we suddenly came to a huge crevasse barring our passage. We proceeded cautiously along its edge to the eastward until we found a place where it was snow-bridged, and then leaving the sledges with Levick and Browning, the rest of us roped up and went across, testing it with our ice-axes as we advanced.

The snow bridge was 175 paces across, and except for one place on the weather side it seemed perfectly safe. I should like to have stayed and examined it, as from its width it had more the appearance of an inlet of the sea ending in a wide crevasse, but the gale was rising and the drifting snow so thick I thought it best to get the sledges across and push on; the surface was good the other side, and with the gale behind us, we raced along, trusting to the wind to steer by, as it was impossible to see where we were going.

The pace was too much for poor Browning, who was very bad again, and we had to camp at 5.30, having done about 8.5 miles. Dickason, I am thankful to say, is better and was able to pull today.

The wind dropped after supper, leaving us a lovely but a very cold evening.

October 3. – A very cold night, the wind getting up again at 3 a.m. and bringing drift. Levick had trouble with his primus and we did not get away till nine a.m. Soft snowdrifts made the going very slow and heavy, until just before noon, when we got on ice again among rocks. These we examined, but found no sandstone. The drift was very thick, and, about 2, getting on undulating broken ice, I thought it advisable to pitch one tent, lunch, and wait for the weather to clear. About 3.30 the wind became rather worse, so we pitched the other tent and camped, the distance covered in the day being 3 miles. Browning looked very bad, but Dickason's condition is still improving.

October 4. – Blowing hard, with blinding drift. We delayed breakfast until 9 a.m., hoping it would clear, but as there was no improvement in the weather we turned in again, and as we were not marching we went on half rations of biscuit. Very cold.

October 5. – Turned out at six to find a slight improvement, so had breakfast; but before we finished the wind and drift came down on us again as bad as ever, so that there was nothing for it but to coil down in our bags and wait. About noon the weather improved and we were off. The surface soon changed for the better and we made good way through some more scattered moraines which came from the Reeves Glacier. We noticed a marked open water sky to our left and front and pulled on till 6 p.m., hoping to make the inlet, as we wanted salt ice for the hoosh, but without attaining our object. It is impossible to pull longer, as the days are still short and we have no candles. We have made about six miles.

October 6. – We turned out at 5.45 to find the weather thick, but blue sky to the northward. We were back on a snow surface again, so we took the precaution of waxing the runners, with good results.

It was warm work pulling through the soft snow and we were glad to stop for lunch. We could make out the edge of the piedmont quite plainly, but could see nothing of the inlet until about 2 p.m., when we saw the mouth of it. A broad open-water lead several miles wide seemed to extend right along the barrier edge, but in the inlet itself the sea was frozen over. The snow was soft and the pulling very heavy, so it was 6 o'clock before we reached camp, on the north side of the inlet, about fifty yards from the cliff. Several seals and penguins were up on the sea ice, while snowdrifts gave us an easy road down from the barrier. The surface of the piedmont was broken by small crevasses here, one running right under the tent. We all enjoyed our salt-water hoosh and turned in very tired. Browning rather better. Dickason quite recovered. A lovely evening. Distance 8.5 miles.

October 7. – A beautiful morning after a comparatively warm night. We were away soon after 8, down the snowdrift slope and over a tide crack 4 ft. wide. The sea ice proved very heavy going, as it was covered with deep crusted snow through which we had a job to move the sledges. We saw rather an amusing incident here. A number of seals were lying along the tide crack, and just after we had crossed we saw one more struggle up on the ice and go to sleep with her tail within a few inches of the tide crack. She had hardly gone to sleep when a head came cautiously up, saw her, dipped down again, then coming cautiously up again, bit her hard. The poor beast squealed, hit at her assailant several times with her tail and wriggled off as fast as she could across the ice, but the practical joker did not follow up the attack.

Beyond a stiff pull in deep snow we had no difficulty in getting our sledges up the snow drift and on the south cliff. Once on top we were troubled with a rather deep crusted snow surface, with long undulations which were fairly hard and good going on the summits, but with deep soft snow in the valleys. Curious conical mounds of blue ice showed up here and there. These are survivals, I imagine, of the seracs and icefalls visible on our right hand where the David Glacier flows down from the mountains, making a big disturbance. To avoid these we had to steer in a south-easterly direction. The day was fine but cold and we were all in good spirits, as even if we could not get down to Cape Evans by the sea ice, we could make certain of getting plenty of food here. Distance about 6 miles.

October 8. – Bright sun but cold westerly wind with low drift when we turned out at 5.30. We were away by 8 and the going was much the same as yesterday, only the ice hummocks were more numerous and the undulations steeper. In the afternoon the sun went behind nimbus haze and the light got very bad indeed, and was the cause of us nearly coming to grief. The snow was very wind-blown and slippery on the top of the undulations, but soft in the hollows, and we had been racing down the slopes to help us through the soft snow. Soon after 4 the light got so bad we could not see where we were stepping, and when well on our way down one of these slopes, I thought I saw a crevasse in front, so swung the sledge, and was going ahead to reconnoitre, when I found we were on the edge of a steep slope about 20 ft. high, which went sheer down into a barranca. We had to get the sledges up the slippery slope again – no easy job – and try round. After about a mile we found a place we could cross, but the delays of roping up to prospect made our day's march small. Dickason is bad again. I suppose it must be the heavy pulling. Distance 6 miles. The weather thick, with slight snow.

October 9. – I turned out to look at the weather at 4 a.m. and found it snowing and so thick I could only just see the other tent.

By 7 it was better though still thick, so after breakfast we started and steered a more easterly course to try and get out of this broken country. The light and surface were vile, while a cold westerly wind did not improve matters. We found ourselves in country just as bad, so steered due south and went straight ahead, but even going as cautiously as we could we nearly repeated yesterday's experience, stopping the sledge just in time on the edge of the cliff and having to work back up the slope and round. The wind had increased to a gale with drift to add to our discomfort. About 4 o'clock, however, the sun came out, the wind eased, and we got into better country. Just before camping, from the top of one of the ridges I got a view of the coast line south of the Drygalski, and the sea ice in Geikie Inlet, so I hope the worst of the Drygalski is past. Dickason is much better, but Browning is very bad again. We camped soon after 6, all very tired. Distance 6 miles.

October 10. – Turned out at 5 a.m. to find a lovely day with bright sun but a cold wind. At 7.30 just after starting a low drift got up and the wind was freshening but bitterly cold – so cold in fact that at lunch-time we only stopped long enough to eat some frozen meat and blubber, and then were off again over these endless undulations that give one the impression of always going up hill. At last on one of the undulations we saw sea ice to the southward, and a few minutes afterwards Dickason pointed to a white mass, looking like a cloud, which I made out to be Mount Erebus. While crossing another long undulation about three-quarters of a mile across, we came to a cliff barring our passage, but by bearing to the east, we found a place where we could cross the big crevasse that lay in front of it by a snow drift. The crevasse was about 10 yards wide, but well bridged. Once on top we saw the sea ice below us and about a mile and a half ahead. The drift, which had been blinding in the squalls, now cleared and we had a good view.

The sea ice seemed fast as far as we could see in all directions, and this was a great relief to us. The Drygalski had not been so formidable as I expected, in spite of the broken ice; we only broke through into a few crevasses, although I have no doubt there are plenty there.

They are well bridged after the winter. We had no trouble in getting down to the sea ice, as hard snow drifts completely hid the south cliff. At 6 p.m. we camped, all tired but very pleased at having the Drygalski behind us and good sea ice in front. We had an extra biscuit and a stick of chocolate to celebrate the occasion. The night was very cold but fine. We have crossed to the westward of David's route.

I think distance about 7 miles.

October 11. – Westerly wind with heavy drift, and very cold. As there was no improvement after breakfast we turned in again. About 2 p.m. a solitary Emperor penguin came and called outside the tent. We went outside and killed and butchered him; his heart and liver are in the hoosh pot as I write this. The remainder of his flesh, which is not bad raw when it is frozen, we cut up into thin strips to eat on the march. It was very cold work cutting him up in the wind.

The sun came out and the wind and drift eased in the evening, so Abbott and I re-packed the sledges, securing the wooden one on top of the iron-runner sledge. We find this the best arrangement for sea ice, although the resultant load is rather top-heavy. It was very cold and we got our hands very badly frostbitten.

October 12. – A cold wind but clear when we turned out at 4.30 a.m.

We were off before 7 over a fair surface. Soon after lunch we had some trouble with pressure ice, resulting in one upset. A lovely evening when we camped that night, Erebus and Melbourne both being in sight. Browning was better but still had bad cramping pains in his stomach. Distance 11 miles.

October 13. – A disappointing day, overcast, light northerly airs, and not much pressure, but a very heavy drag through deep crusted snow. We were all very tired when we camped. Distance 7 miles. We passed a track which at first we thought had been left by a sledge but afterwards proved to be that of a seal.

October 14. – The weather was much the same today as yesterday, but the surface was better. We pulled in shore to avoid heavy pressure which ran across our bows. A haze of snow crystals obscured the land, and this made the journey tedious and we were glad to camp, having done about 10 miles, but not I fear half that on our course. The prevailing ridges run about N.N.E.

October 15. – A fine morning, but cold wind from south. We turned out at 4.45 and for the first two hours made good progress. The sun came out quite hot and the wind dropped in the middle of the day, so that we were able to spend an hour over lunch. The mirage was wonderful, the pressure to the southward being seen inverted in the sky.

We came across more tracks, which I think must be seal. It is curious that we have seen no animals; I can only account for it by presuming that this is old ice with no cracks. Soon after 4 we had to cross pressure ridges, for though we had been dodging them since lunch, they now became so high we had to camp and re-pack sledges. We shall have to relay the sledges tomorrow, taking them over one at a time.

Distance about 10 miles, but not half that on our course. A clear but cold evening.

October 16. – I suppose every now and then we swallow a bit of bad meat, and whether from that reason or some other, I was very bad last night with cramp and pains in the stomach, and this morning I am feeling cold and sick. Levick gave me some medicine that put new life into me. We have had a wearisome day of relaying, with frequent upsets, and have been cutting a path through high and heavy pressure ice, half hidden under a soft snow into which we fell and floundered about.

At 5.30 the light was so bad that I camped. Distance perhaps 3 miles, but it is impossible to gauge accurately with this sort of travelling.

October 17. – Turned out at 5.15 to find snow falling, and by the time we had finished breakfast a southerly gale was blowing, with heavy drift, and it was impossible to march, so we turned in and spent the day in our bags.

October 18. – The wind dropped in the night and the sky cleared about 6, leaving a fine day. We have had another heavy day's work relaying over bad pressure, but yesterday's rest has done us all a lot of good and we went at it quite fresh. We saw the Nordenskiold ice tongue ahead miraged up and looking quite close. About 5 p.m. we came to the end of this infernal pressure, and saw smooth surface between us and the tongue end, and by 6.30 camped on the smooth ice. I had noticed a seal up about a mile west of us as we were relaying over the last of the pressure, so after we had camped I went away on ski to look for him.

After going about 2 miles I struck his tracks and followed them till they disappeared down a hole. Through the seal hole I tried to feel the lower edge of the ice but was unable to do so. I take it therefore that the ice must be at least 3 feet thick. This smooth surface we are on must be due, I think, to the current coming up under the Nordenskiold, causing this part of the sea to freeze over late in the season.

A cold evening with slight snow. Approximate distance 6 miles.

October 19. – A fine morning but colder. We turned out at 3.30, and after breakfast Levick, Abbott, and Browning went to the seal hole while we packed and started the sledges. They were successful this time and caught the seal asleep by the hole, and soon had him cut up and packed on one of the sledges. At 10 we stopped for lunch. The day was lovely for marching, being clear and cold, but the surface was vile; no pressure, but soft sandy snow. We halted for a second lunch of raw seal at 3.30 p.m. Levick, Abbott, and Browning like it, the rest of us do not. We camped at 6.15, all very tired. Distance 9 miles. A lovely evening.

October 20. – A lovely morning, clear, calm, and cold. A stiff pull over a heavy surface brought us to the foot of the cliff of the

Nordenskiold ice tongue. The cliff here is about 50 feet high and very much indented. A few miles to the east a deep bay or inlet ran in to the southward.

A steep snowdrift enabled us to get on the ice tongue, but we had to unpack the sledges and carry most of the gear up, after hauling the sledges up to the top with the Alpine rope, as it was so steep.

We camped on the top at about 5 p.m. Priestley, Levick, and I then roped up and went on to see what the going was like for the next day.

We found long shallow undulations, and as far as we could see no crevasses. We shall cross it a long way inside David's route. Curiously enough, there was hardly any tide crack between the sea ice and the tongue.

Several seals were in sight, but we did not kill any, as I am sure we shall get any amount south of this tongue. The tongue seems to be ice to within 2 feet of the top and the surface is rather a soft snow. Distance 6 miles.

October 21. – Turning out at 5.30 a.m. we depôted all unnecessary gear and started considerably lighter. Should we have to turn back we can always pick this depôt up easily. The day was lovely, but rather warm for pulling, and the surface soft but not bad going. We came across no crevasses and by 3.30 ran down an easy slope to the sea ice. The snow on the latter was rather deep. We lashed the wooden runner sledge on the one with the iron runners and pulled on till about 6, when we camped.

October 22. – A nice morning, but soon after starting a cold southerly wind got up, resulting in several frostbitten noses. We were travelling over pressure well hidden by soft snow. In the afternoon we had some excitement seeing a dark conical object ahead, much the same shape as a tent. As Browning was rather bad, we left him with Dickason and Abbott to rest with the sledges, while Levick, Priestley, and I went on to look at it, but after going about a mile we made it out to be some black grit blown on to a conical piece of ice. On returning to the sledges we pulled in shore to try and get a better surface, but had to camp at 5 p.m. as Browning was so bad. Distance about 6 miles. We are about 1 mile from land, which appears to be low ice-covered foothills.

October 23. – I was bad in the night and did not wake till 6.30. The day was warmer, but I feel very cold and rather weak and slack. The light was bad, but we made fair progress. Passed inside a number of stranded bergs evidently broken off from the piedmont. About 4 p.m. we saw a seal near a stranded berg and we camped early, in order to kill and cut him up. There were tracks of several more near the berg, so I think we are coming to the land of plenty. A brain and liver hoosh did us all good. We are all feeling slack and stale. Distance 6 miles. We had to reduce to two biscuits per day owing to slow progress.

October 24. – A lovely morning, clear and calm with a few clouds over the mountains. While we were packing the sledges Browning went to the seal hole, but there were none up. The surface was heavy crusted snow with belts of pressure. During the day we passed a large number of stranded bergs and any amount of seals up round them, many of them with young.

Our route lay along a piedmont, evidently aground, judging by the steep slopes and crevasses in places. Soon after 4 p.m. we opened out a wide bay which I made out to be Tripp Bay. After this the surface improved. After camping, Levick and Abbott killed and cut up a seal.

There was a curious line of stranded bergs and pressure running parallel to the coast and about two miles off, which looks as if there might be a shoal there. Our distance today about 7 miles.

October 25. – Both Dickason and I had a bad night, and I felt very cold when I turned out at about 5 a.m. We soon got warm, however, for the snowdrifts between the pressure were awful. We made out Tripp Island at the head of the bay in the afternoon. It has been a very tiring day, and as Browning was rather bad we camped at 4.30. Distance 7 miles.

October 26. – A fine morning. We started away after breakfast with both sledges, while Priestley went into the bay on ski to look at Tripp Island and see if Professor David had left his depôt of rocks there. We knew he had depôted the specimens on some island on the coast, but did not know which.

The surface had improved, so the rest of us were able to get the sledges along at a fair pace and it was noon before Priestley caught us up. He had seen nothing of the depôt, but collected some rock specimens himself. By 5 p.m. we were off another little island on the top of which I made out a bamboo with my glasses. We pulled in and camped under the north end. We had a hard struggle over the pack, but within a few hundred yards of land we found a smooth lead up and down the coast. After this we made a point of keeping close to the coast line on our journey, and it certainly paid us, in spite of the extra mileage. After hoosh Priestley and I climbed to the top of the island and collected Professor David's specimens, also some letters his party had left in a tin, addressed to Mrs David, Dr Mawson, Lieutenant Shackleton, and to Commanding Officer, S.Y. *Nimrod*. We brought all these down and packed them on the sledge. When I got back to camp Levick came to me about Browning's condition. He was getting very anxious about him, suspecting organic trouble. I suggested his and Browning's remaining at Granite Harbour with all the gear, while the rest of us pushed on with a light sledge to get provisions from Butter Point, where we knew there would be a small depôt, but Levick thought it best to bring him on, as, if the trouble was organic, the sooner he could be laid up in a hut the better. We shall therefore push on, putting him on the sledge when he gets tired, and to keep his strength up give him one extra biscuit per day. Seal meat seems to be poison to him. Our distance this day was about 8 miles.

October 27. – A fine morning. Temperature warmer. We got away after breakfast, keeping inside Depôt Island and getting beautiful smooth ice nearly clear of snow, which lasted to Cape Ross, where we had to cross bad pressure ridges off the cape. The ridges were so bad we had to cut passages for the sledges with ice axes. We had smooth ice again to Cape Gregory, which is now an island, and we were able to make our way through the strait between Gregory Island and the piedmont; after this we again struck a heavy surface. We were now in Granite Harbour. After pulling 2 miles through the deep snow we camped. Distance about 12 miles. The changes in the face of the piedmont are rather interesting. In 1902 Depôt Island was charted a point by the *Discovery*. By 1909 it had turned into an island and was named accordingly by Professor David. David reported Gregory Point a cape in 1909 and it is now (1912) an island.

We saw rock outcropping from the piedmont at various places, and no doubt these exposures will be points or islands at some near period in the future. Priestley collected specimens everywhere he could. We saw an enormous quantity of seals and young up, so this is evidently a great breeding-place.

October 28. – A fine morning; we made fair progress over a snow surface. We had to make a detour into the bay to avoid pressure. A cold wind sprang up in the afternoon, and my nose, which had got very sunburnt all the morning, promptly froze, and when thawed out was very painful. We camped about 6 p.m. two miles north of Cape Roberts. No seals were up on the south side of the bay. Distance 10 miles. No sign of the ship or of Debenham's party.

October 29. – Turned out at 4.30 a.m. A fine day, but a bank of cloud to the south and a cold westerly wind. A two hours' march brought us to Cape Roberts, where I saw through my glasses a bamboo stuck on the top of the cape. Leaving the sledges, Priestley and I climbed the cape, when we found a record left by the Western Party last year before they were picked up, and giving their movements, while near by was a depôt of provisions they had left behind. We gave such a yell the others ran up the slope at once. It seemed almost too good to be true.

We found two tins of biscuits, one slightly broached, and a small bag each of raisins, tea, cocoa, butter, and lard. There were also clothes, diaries, and specimens from Qranite Harbour. I decided to camp here and have a day off. Dividing the provisions between the two tents, we soon had hoosh going and such a feed of biscuit, butter, and lard as we had not had for 9 months, and we followed this up with sweet, thick cocoa. After this we killed and cut up a seal as we are getting short of meat and there is every prospect of a blizzard coming on.

Levick and Abbott saw a desperate fight between two bull seals today. They gashed each other right through skin and blubber till they were bleeding badly.

We had another hoosh and more biscuit and lard in the evening; then we turned into our bags and, quite torpid with food, discussed our plans on arriving at Cape Evans. We had quite decided we should find no one there, for we believed the whole party had been blown north in the ship, while trying to reach us. Still discussing plans we fell asleep. What with news from the main party and food (although both were a year old) it was the happiest day since we last saw the ship. I awoke in the night, finished my share of the butter and most of my lard, then dozed off again.

October 30. – The blizzard never came off. We turned out to find a beautiful warm morning. After another big feed of biscuits and a brain-and-liver hoosh we started in the highest spirits. The change of diet has done Browning good already. I took all the books, food, specimens, and records of Taylor's party, leaving only the old clothes.

I also left a note saying we were all well. The surface was fairly good with occasional belts of rough pressure ice that delayed us considerably. Taylor's journal speaks of Glacier Tongue having broken away from MacMurdo Sound and grounded on the coast south of Dunlop Island. It will be interesting to see if it is still there. At midday we camped for lunch, and the hot tea and biscuit made a great difference to our marching. This was the first hot lunch we had had and we all appreciated it. Between 5 and 6 the pressure was very bad; not high, but jagged and continuous, bruising our feet. Luckily we had the iron-runner sledge. Wooden runners would have been torn to shreds. Camped at 6.15. Distance 8 miles. Dunlop Island in sight about 3 miles ahead.

October 31. – A lovely morning. The south-west breeze of the night had dropped and the day felt warm. We suffered the same painful surface until within a mile of Dunlop Island, when we reached a smooth surface. We lunched on the north side of Dunlop Island. After lunch we searched it for records, but found nothing. Priestley collected some specimens. Resuming our march we got on to smooth ice between Dunlop Island and the mainland and kept a good surface until we camped at 6.15, half-way across the 'Bay of Sails'. Distance 11 miles: Mt Erebus rising to the height of several thousand feet.

November 1. – 5 a.m. A fine morning with heavy clouds to the south. We had a good surface and made good progress. Priestley collected from Cape Gneiss and Marble Point. We lunched at the latter cape, and at 3.45 we reached Cape Bernacchi, where we collected the remainder of Taylor's depôt, three-quarters of a tin of biscuits, one bag of pemmican, and ditto of sugar, raisins, tea, and cocoa. The pemmican and raisins were most acceptable, as we had finished ours. Priestley collected some specimens and we started away again at 4.30, across pressure towards Butter Point. At 6 p.m. we camped about 1 mile south of Cape Bernacchi with smooth ice ahead.

We are certainly having the most lovely weather, clear, calm, and cold enough to make marching a pleasure. A large number of seals and young up.

November 2. – 5 a.m. A fine morning. Got away early over good snow surface, reaching Butter Point at 2.30. There was a good deal of pressure off the point, so leaving the sledges on the good ice we walked the half-mile to the depôt. We had been seeing a large number of seals and young since Granite Harbour, but just off Butter Point the number was extraordinary.

Getting up to the depôt we found an enormous quantity of stores, also a note from Atkinson saying he had tried to relieve us last April but had found no ice beyond this spot. As there was no further message we were anxious for the safety of this party, as we know how unreliable the autumn ice is. As to what had happened it was hopeless trying to speculate. This had upset all our theories and I had a vague feeling something was wrong.

I therefore decided to leave one tin of biscuits here and get right across the sound as soon as possible. Taking a few luxuries such as chocolate and jam, we went back to the sledges and pulled in a south-east direction until about 7 p.m., when we camped. Distance 14 miles. Weather fine. The latter part of our march we were delayed by pressure ridges running north and south.

November 3. – 5.15 a.m. Weather overcast, surface good, with belts of heavy pressure, the ridges running north and south. Some of the smooth ice had struck me as being rather new ice. At 11.30 our iron-runner sledge broke down hopelessly, one side coming off. We had a hasty lunch, packed the sleeping-bags, records, and a little fresh food on the other sledge, depôted all the remainder, and then started on again. The smooth-ice leads between the pressure were suspiciously dark and greasy-looking, so after going about half a mile we sounded with an ice axe and found we were on thin soft ice, which cannot have been much more than a day or two old. Turning the sledge we went back at a run, not stopping until we got on to better ice by the old sledge. Taking the rest of the food we then started W.S.W. towards the Eskers. Several leads were so new we had to cross them at a run, and it was 7.30 before we found sound ice, with no weak leads between us and the shore, and then I decided to camp.

November 4. – Weather overcast and warm. We turned out at 4.30, and after breakfast Priestley, Abbott, and Dickason went back with the empty sledge to get the remainder of the depôt, and if possible fit on the iron runners, while Levick, Browning, and I went back with packs to get more food. We had a long tramp to Butter Point and back over rough ice, and we had done 18 miles before we got back to camp, Levick and I with a 50-lb. pack and Browning with a smaller one, as he had not quite recovered.

The change in Browning's condition owing to the biscuit is marvellous.

A week ago he could just walk by the sledge on a march of 8 or 10 miles; tonight, although tired, he is none the worse for his 18-mile walk. We found Priestley and his party had already arrived with the rest of the depôt when we got back, and to my great joy he had been able to fit the iron runners on to the 12-ft. sledge.

November 5. – We turned out at 3.30. A lovely morning, with bright sun. After breakfast we started away, steering for the Dailey Islands, but we were forced to make a detour to the west to avoid rotten ice-leads.

The mirage was extraordinary. At one place we thought we saw three men pulling a sledge; Priestley and I walked towards them; they apparently stopped; Priestley started semaphoring while I looked through my glasses. No result. Suddenly they turned and I saw they were Emperor penguins, miraged up in a way that made them look like figures. These leads of bad ice seemed to run into Blue Glacier, but I thought I could see good ice beyond them, so we raced the sledge straight across, getting over without a mishap. Once over we found old ice behind a pressure ridge, and after crossing that struck the Barrier edge, here about 4 feet high, with snowdrifts leading on to it. A large number of seals and Emperor penguins were on the old ice. Here we lunched. The Barrier edge runs out in a tongue, and we had struck it on the north-west corner. We were thus able to steer direct for Hut Point over the tongue. At 5 p.m. we came up to the pinnacled ice lying on the east side of the tongue.

This pinnacled ice is very rough and gritty and is evidently the remains of an old moraine of the Koettlitz Glacier. By skirting to the north of this we found a lane of old sea ice on which we could travel until we had passed it. Enormous crowds of Emperors were here. In one bunch I estimated there were about 300. After travelling about 6 miles on this old ice the pinnacled ice gave out and we were able to head for Hut Point again over the Barrier. I had hoped to get into Hut Point the same night, so camped for hoosh at 6.30. Resuming our march we went on till 1 a.m., when I found we were still 7 miles off. I therefore camped, had some cocoa, and turned in. We had done a good march, twenty-one hours since we turned out, and had we been able to hold a straight course we should have easily got in.

November 6. – Another fine morning. We marched till 1 p.m., when our sledge broke down, the whole runner coming off. As we were only 1 mile from Hut Point, I camped. Priestley, Dickason, and I walked in to look for news and get another sledge, as I was sure some would be there.

As we neared the Point we noticed fresh tracks of mule and dogs.

I pointed them out to Priestley, and said, 'I hope there is nothing wrong with the Pole party, as I do not like the look of these.' He said, 'No more do I.' We ran up to the hut and found a letter from Atkinson to the 'Commanding Officer, *Terra Nova*.' I opened this and learnt the sad news of the loss of the Polar Party. The names of the party were not given, and finding Atkinson in charge of the search party which had started, I was afraid two units, or eight men, were lost. Finding a sledge only slightly damaged I took that back to the camp, getting back there about 5 p.m.

We were all rather tired, so instead of starting straight on to Cape Evans, we had supper and went to sleep. Before turning in we made a depôt of the broken sledge, all rock specimens, clothes, and food, so as to travel light to Cape Evans. I was very anxious to get there as soon as possible, as I thought there was a chance that there might be one or two mules or enough dogs to enable me to follow the search party. It had been a great disappointment for us to have missed them by a week, as we were all anxious to join in the search.

November 7. – 4 a.m. A lovely morning. After a hasty breakfast we were off, arriving at Cape Evans at 5 p.m. We found no one at home, but a letter on the door of the hut gave us all the news and the names of the lost party. Very soon Debenham and Archer returned, giving us a most hearty welcome, and no one can realise what it meant to us to see new faces and to be home after our long winter. Our clothes, letters, &c., had been landed from the ship, and we were able to read our home letters, which we had only time to glance at in the ship in February. Archer provided a sumptuous dinner that night, and we sailed into it in a way that made Debenham hold his breath. A bath and change of clothes completed the transformation.

November 8. – Weather overcast, with a cold south-easterly wind of medium force. I went round with Debenham and was much surprised at the amount of stores. If we were down for another winter there should be no lack. Our clothes had been landed by the ship. There was nothing we wanted except boots, of which I served out one pair to each.

It was hopeless to think of following the search party, the only transport being a few dogs that had been left behind as they were slow or weak. Atkinson's plans were to push on and search to the top of the Beardmore Glacier unless he found traces of the party before, so there was no hope of catching him. I find our party are not so fit as I thought. Most of us have developed swollen ankles and legs (oedema), and when the flesh is pressed in the holes remain there.

From November 8 till the return of the sledge party we were all very busy transcribing our last winter's diaries, developing photographs, and renewing what of our outfit we were unable to replace.

On the 11th Levick, Abbott, and Dickason left for Hut Point, and the next day but one they returned, bringing with them our records and specimens. They had taken all the provisions left on our broken sledge to Hut Point.

November 25. – A mild blizzard. Priestley and Debenham had arranged to start for Cape Royds today, taking Dickason, but decided to wait for better weather.

At 8 p.m. two dog teams with Atkinson, Cherry-Garrard, and Demetri arrived. They had found the remains of the Polar Party 11 miles south of 'One Ton Depôt'. Atkinson brought back all their records and personal gear, which I asked him to take charge of personally.

November 26. – I went with Atkinson to Hut Point with a dog team.

It was a fine, clear day, and leaving Cape Evans at noon we got there about 2 p.m. The surface was good and I walked up to the Gap and saw the rest of the party in camp at ' Safety Camp'.

November 27. – The remainder of the party pulled in about 2 a.m., and it was very pleasant meeting them all again. Atkinson and I left them there and returned to Cape Evans, getting in at 5 a.m. next morning.

November 28. – A fine day. The party with the mules arrived at 1 p.m. Although five mules out of seven were brought back we had to shoot two of them, as they refused all food and were in a very bad condition.

We now settled down to routine work and short sledge journeys on Ross Island, and for geological survey work, Priestley and Debenham taking a party up Mt Erebus.

The ship arrived January 18, just as we were starting to prepare for a third winter.

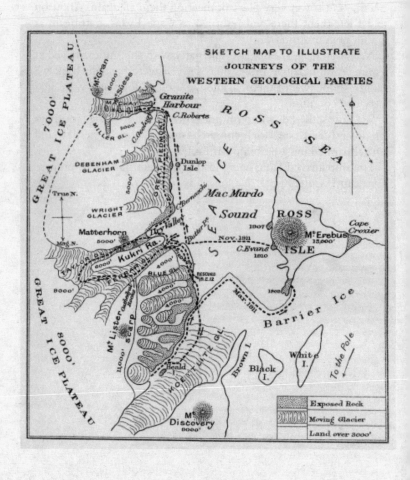

by *Griffith Taylor, B.A., B.Sc., B.E., F.G.S.*

[see also maps on pages 654–57]

CHAPTER I

Koettlitz, Ferrar, and Taylor Glaciers

The following chapters describe the doings of six members of the Expedition during a detailed exploration of the 'Western Mountains' in South Victoria Land. A few words as to the scene of our operations and the personnel of the parties will serve as an introduction to the narrative of the sledge journeys.

As you stand on Cape Evans with your back to the steam cloud of Erebus you see across McMurdo Sound a glorious range of mountains running due north and south and rising to 13,000 feet in the south-west. These are the Western Mountains. Their southern limit is the extinct volcanic cone of Discovery, and far to the north one can follow the same range of snow-clad peaks until it merges with the grey line of the horizon. Beyond this grey line was Granite Harbour (76° 50'), and that marked the northern limit of our survey; while the Koettlitz Glacier (in 78° 20'), which hid the lower slopes of Discovery, was the 'farthest south' reached in our two sledging trips.

On clear days we could see every little cup-shaped valley which roughened the mighty scarp of Lister, so sharply that it seemed impossible that they were seventy miles away. Due west was the valley of the Lower Ferrar Glacier, while the long gleaming snow slope at its mouth was the Butter Point Piedmont – the starting place for all Western exploration, where depôts have been made ever since the butter was left there by the 1902 expedition.

Hidden behind the ranges was the Great Ice Plateau. From this height of 7000 feet descended the great rivers of ice – the Koettlitz,

Ferrar, Taylor, and Mackay Glaciers – with which the following pages are concerned.

Now as to my mates. What is the 'Call to the Wild' which seems to draw men back to the Antarctic? In my opinion it is the association with picked companions, especially chosen for their suitability for the environment, which constitutes the charm of life in the Antarctic. The deserts of Australia or the wilds of Spitzbergen would appeal equally to me with the same companions.

There is a famous old school near Sydney where for many years there were representatives from two families, the Debenhams and Taylors. So that Frank Debenham and myself were old friends and graduates in geology of the same 'varsity. In later years at Cambridge there was an informal club of research students in which Wright of Caius and Taylor of Emmanuel were fellow-members. Debenham's experience as Commissary-General at many a camp in Australia made him invaluable sledging – while Wright was an expert in traversing snow-clad country, for he often spent his vacations from Toronto University surveying in the Canadian backwoods.

Next may I introduce Tryggve Gran, the youngest and yet the most travelled officer in the Expedition except our leader himself. Interested in sport, travel, music, literature, and languages, 'Trigger' never let a day pass without enlivening our march by some of his many adventures.

Of the two petty officers, Edgar Evans coached the first party, all of whom were new chums, in Antarctic sledging. He was one of the *Discovery* men and was an ideal sledge mate; while Forde, another giant of the navy, was sledge master on our Granite Harbour journey.

It is interesting to note that the six men represented six nationalities. Debenham and Wright come from Australia and Canada; Gran is a hardy Norseman; Forde is Irish; Evans came from Cardiff; while I was the only member born in England. If I have dwelt on this question of personnel, it is because it is so important a factor in exploration, and these few words help to explain the unbroken harmony which existed during our six months' sledging.

On January 26, 1911, Captain Scott handed to me the Sledging Orders governing our movements on the first Western Journey.

They give a comprehensive account of what we actually carried out, and I therefore insert them here, omitting only a paragraph concerning Hut Point.

DEAR TAYLOR,

I purpose to disembark a sledge-party of which you will have charge, on the sea ice of McMurdo Sound as near the Ferrar Glacier as possible.

Your companions will be Messrs Debenham, Wright, and Petty Officer Evans.

You will have two sledges with food and equipment for eight weeks.

The object of your journey will be the geological exploration of the region between the Dry Valley and the Koettlitz Glacier.

Your movements must depend to some extent on the breaking of the sea ice. Your best and safest plan appears to be to carry all your provision up the Ferrar Glacier to a point in the medial moraine abreast of Descent Pass, and to make a depôt at that point. With a fortnight's food you could then continue the ascent to the junction of the Dry Valley glacier and descend the Valley of that glacier. On returning to your depôt you will be in a position to observe the extent of open water, and you can either descend the glacier and pass to the east around Butter Point, or climb Descent Pass, descending by the Blue Glacier or by one of the more southerly foothill glaciers, and thus continue the examination of the Koettlitz Glacier area.

On completion of your work you should cross to Hut Point, being careful not to camp too near open water . . .

Wishing you the best of luck,

Yours sincerely,

(sgd.) R. SCOTT

With regard to our equipment only one feature deserves comment. We carried an exceptionally large photographic battery, which was necessitated by the character of the problems which, engaged our attention. For instance, Wright was chiefly interested in the forms of ice-structure which we encountered. The most delicate ice-crystals, which withered at a breath, must needs be photographed *in situ*. There was no possibility of his bringing back specimens for study in the hut during the dark winter months. For similar reasons a somewhat bulky polariscope in which sheets of ice were examined in polarised light formed part of his load, and was vulgarly referred to as 'the Barrel Organ'. He also had charge of the theodolite.

Debenham was engaged on the more usual work of collecting rock specimens and mapping their occurrence in the field. For this purpose another camera was essential, since in general his investigations were carried out on the cliffs at some distance from the rest of us.

The subject which primarily interested myself was the physiographic aspect of the region, or, as it may popularly be described, 'the last chapter in the geological history of Antarctica'. In other words, how has the land surface been affected by the flow of glaciers, by the action of wind, frost, water, and ice? And a second and more interesting question I set myself was, How do the resulting features differ from those observed in more temperate regions, where water plays such an important part and ice erosion is absent?

On January 27 Pennell took us across the Sound in the *Terra Nova* from Glacier Tongue to Butter Point, where we arrived about 4 p.m. We spent some time packing our gear on our two sledges. The total load was arrived at as follows:

	lbs.
Two sledges and steel runners	171
Food for eight weeks	630
Tools, tents, &c	130
Instruments, cameras, &c	65
Four personal bags	50
	1046

We had heavy equipment for four men – averaging about 270 lbs. each – but as we were only proposing to take one sledge for a considerable portion of the journey this was of little importance.

From the coast we had a magnificent view of the lower portion of the Ferrar Glacier. The valley was about four miles wide and extended south-west for thirty miles. Up this we were to journey, ascending 3000 feet in the next few days.

Everyone noticed the grand sweep of the cliffs at the side. The northern face for twenty miles is a marvellous wall-like cliff about 3000 feet high – as straight and smooth as if planed by a giant carpenter. And indeed it is a typical glacial valley, where the lateral spurs, such as break up the continuity of an ordinary *river-cut* valley, are entirely wanting.

We started about 6 p.m. and pulled the sledges about four miles before camping for the night.

I asked Evans to cook for the first week, as he was experienced with the cooker and primus lamp. Debenham's reputation was such that I was sure he would master polar cooking sooner than any of us. So he became cook's-mate and assistant – to rise to chef next week. Wright agreed to take the third week, and I thought by that time I might have learnt enough to improve on my own very modest culinary attainments.

We started on a Friday, and our calendar was reckoned from cook's day to cook's day. There was never any doubt as to which day of the week it was, because each cook was so keen to relinquish his post at the close of his term of office!

While Evans was initiating Debenham in the mysteries of pemmican, Wright and I walked across the sea ice a mile or so to the south and reached a 'lateral tongue' or prolongation of the main glacier. There was a sudden rise of some three feet, and the surface in place of being level and comparatively smooth was carved out into deep irregular bowls with overhanging margins. These were in all probability giant 'sunholes', and their floors were covered with a most beautiful carpet of snow crystals.

Examined closely each crystal was like the segment of a fan strengthened by cross-ribs, and these 'fan-plates' were often half an inch across. The surface as a whole reminded me strongly of the appearance of a coral reef – and it was about as pleasant a sight to us as the latter is to the navigator. Wright was the only one who appreciated their beauty, we others being more concerned with the numerous capsizes caused by this 'coral reef' structure, which characterised the whole of the lower Ferrar Glacier. We returned to the tent, and as usual at starting found it impossible to eat all our pemmican. It seemed much too rich and abundant – alas, how fleeting was this opinion!

Next day, January 28, we sledged several miles up the glacier, but spent all the afternoon examining a beautiful hanging glacier which lay like a great white mantle flung on the northern wall of the Ferrar Valley. To reach this side glacier we had to cross a much weathered portion of the Ferrar's surface. Large dome-covered ponds into which we fell at frequent intervals made one of us remark, 'Just like a promenade on the roof of the Crystal Palace.'

As usual the rock slopes were fringed by a colonnade of gigantic pinnacles thirty feet high separated by narrow crevasses. The sun glistening on the icy minarets and beautiful icicles made a most impressive sight. Beyond this we soon reached the talus or débris slopes below the 'Double Curtain' glacier. A stiff climb up this brought us to the snout of the tributary, and we found that this 'mantle of ice' ended in a vertical face forty feet thick. While Wright and Debenham investigated this region, I climbed up 2500 feet and stood on the shoulder of the Kukri Hills.

A wonderful panorama was spread out before me which was especially striking to the south-west. Here jutted out the three grand gables – like the roof of a Gothic cathedral – which were so appropriately named the Cathedral Rocks. Below this we were to leave our first depôt.

As we returned to the tent some two miles off we came across several parties of Emperor penguins stolidly awaiting the end of their moulting season. They probably totalled one hundred. Only one individual was garbed in new and shining raiment, and him I slew in preparation for a change of diet if our appetite failed on a pemmican regime.

All next day we pulled steadily up the glacier to the west, encouraged by Evans's opinion that we should meet better sledging surfaces higher up the glacier.

On the 30th we had very heavy going up the broad ice undulations and about noon got among the crevasses. We all slipped in at various intervals, but they were quite narrow and gave us no trouble. The snow was a foot thick in many places and alternated with 'glass-roof' ice into which we fell frequently. However, we kept on till 9 p.m., when we reached the big moraine below Cathedral Rocks, and there made our depôt as Captain Scott had advised.

Above our depôt the slope was steeper, but we had only half the load to pull, and towards 6 p.m. on the next evening we reached the top of the lower Ferrar and found ourselves on a small ice plateau about 3200 feet above sea level. We now marched along the grandest geological section it has ever been my good fortune to see. The cliff to the north, 3300 feet high, was capped by yellowish sandstone. Beneath this were two wonderful horizontal sheets of dark lava which had intruded through the granite base so that the rocks looked like a gigantic sandwich composed of alternating yellow, black and red layers. The lower slopes of the red granite were covered by the old lateral moraine, a layer of dark débris left by the Ferrar Glacier when it almost filled the valley we were following.

We pushed on till 9 p.m., descending slightly as we proceeded to the north, and camped on the glacier filling the upper end of the Dry Valley. The exploration of this glacier – which Scott had rapidly traversed in 1903 – was the work before us during the next fortnight. Captain Scott has honoured me by giving it the name of Taylor Glacier.

I kept too near to the Kukri Hills on descending into the Taylor Glacier and we struck an extremely steep slippery surface consisting of clear ice cut into rounded hollows a foot across. This characteristic surface – like giant thumb-marks in a piece of putty – was full of small crevasses, and here the sledge repeatedly 'took charge'. We rolled about all over the place, and someone remarked that we had all the appearance of being drunk and none of the pleasure of it!

To our surprise, after five days' pulling over heavy snow in the Ferrar Glacier, we found no snow in the parallel Taylor Valley, only about 10 miles farther north. After lunching among the scattered blocks of the medial moraine we descended about a thousand feet, the sledge doing its own pulling. Debenham and I went on ahead with slack traces, while Evans and Wright enlivened the valley with what they were pleased to call 'cheerful song'! A strong keen wind was blowing up the valley, but the most remarkable feature of this region prevented it from becoming obnoxious. There was no drift-snow!

Imagine a valley 4 miles wide, 3000 feet deep, and 25 miles long without a patch of snow – and this in the Antarctic in latitude $77\frac{1}{2}°$ S. By this time we could see the 'snout' of the glacier just below us. The slope became too steep for the sledge and at six o'clock we halted to try and find a site for our camp.

Beyond the snout was a wide, bare stony trough, extending many miles to the east. The lower slopes were strewn with reddish granite boulders. Here and there on the upper slopes piles of intensely black fragments – for all the world like coal dumps – marked recent lava flows.

Between the serrated crests of the giant cliffs towering five or six thousand feet above us were cascading rivers of ice. These hanging glaciers spread out in great white lobes over the lower slopes of dark rock, and in some cases the cliffs were so steep that the lower portion of the tributary glacier was fed purely by avalanches falling from the ice fields up above. And, most amazing of all, not a snowdrift in sight. It was warm weather most of the time we spent in Dry Valley – rising sometimes above freezing-point – and everywhere streams were tinkling among the black boulders, so much so that this valley, in spite of its name, was certainly the wettest area I saw in Antarctica!

About a mile back from the end of the glacier we made a permanent camp. We could drag the sledge no further, and I recognised that 'packing' on our backs was the only way to map this snowless region.

Bare ice surrounded us, forty-foot ice cliffs and a wide 'glacier moat' separated us from the steep rock slopes. Nowhere could we find a place to stand easily – while it was impossible to pitch the tent. However, the centre of the glacier was cut up by surface streams into deep gullies whose sunny southern sides were cut into a series of picturesque alcoves. They were most beautiful specimens of Nature's architecture, the steep walls of clear ice being fretted by the sun into a thousand pilasters and niches. We lowered the sledge down 20 feet into one of these Gothic apses, and found ideal conditions for a sheltered camp. We had a strongly running stream – an inch deep – alongside; and though the wind howled along the surface of the glacier nothing was even disturbed in Alcove Camp.

We spent two days mapping the vicinity, and then started our trek to the sea. We packed up the tent, our sleeping-bags, and five days' food. Our method of march was rather amusing. Wright carried his pack in the Canadian method by a 'tump-line' round his forehead. He took the theodolite. P. O. Evans wrapped his goods and the tent round the tent poles and proudly carried them like a standard over his shoulder. Debenham copied the Australian swagsman with a bundle in front nearly balancing the main bulk behind. I found, as usual, that a strap over the right shoulder (as used by the Italian harpist) suited my convenience best. Very reluctantly we left our trusty cooker behind, but Debenham carried his camera and half the food, while I bore the remainder and a veritable goldminer's dish, to try for gold in the gravels of Dry Valley.

We marched down a narrow gap, cut through a great bar of granite, and saw ahead of us quite a large lake, some three miles long. It was of course frozen, but through the thick ice covering we could see water plants, and below the steep cliffs the water seemed very deep. We lunched at the east end of the lake – the first of many cold meals, and like all of them consisting chiefly of biscuit and butter, varied by biscuit without butter. However, we had a cake of chocolate each afternoon and a little cheese.

Hereabouts the wide valley was filled with morainic débris, and we passed close to several of the cliff glaciers. I was much surprised to find that the bed of the valley now commenced to rise, for we knew we were approaching the sea. We continued to ascend and could see no way out of the trough. Immediately ahead was a great rock barrier across the valley and evidently several thousand feet high. However, in the next few miles I counted no less than thirteen dead seals which had somehow come up from the coast, and I felt sure we could easily manage anything they could traverse.

Soon we began to open up a narrow defile down the north side of the valley, but this outlet – a sort of notch one thousand feet deep scored in the bottom of the trough – was apparently barred by a tributary cliff glacier.

It was now nearly six o'clock and my shoulder was aching with my pack. Judging from the readiness of the others to drop their loads, I concluded that they felt the same. But we all had an idea that a few minutes later would give us a view of the sea.

We wondered if we could pass around the snout of this wonderful tributary immediately in front. It opposed a face of ice 40 feet high, but just where it butted into the steep (south) slope of the defile there was a gap. So narrow was this that one could almost touch the ice face on one side and the side of the defile on the other. Through this we carried our packs; through this in the other direction the seals must have laboriously crawled to die far inland.

We could not see the sea, but found the defile occupied by a frozen lake a mile long. There were dry gravelly banks around this lake and here we pitched the tent. We had brought no floor-cloth, but after the wet and icy floor of the 'Alcove' camp – where Wright had slept in a pool of water three inches deep – we found the warm gravel most comfortable. We had our frugal meal, washed down by cold water from the lake adjacent. The latter was distinctly medicinal and had no outlet, so ignoring climatic differences we unanimously christened it Lake Chad.

I was quite worried to know what had become of the broad stony valley which Shackleton's men had seen from the coast in 1908, and wondered if we were side-tracked in some tributary valley. So after dinner P.O.Evans – who was always eager for extra work – accompanied me to the top of the ridge immediately south of the tent. It was a stiff ascent of 1600 feet to a flat bare expanse obviously planed by bygone glaciers. To my surprise I saw that a much larger rounded valley lay immediately north of this ridge, but this 'Round' Valley, unlike the defile, did not connect with the Taylor glacier. To the east some ten miles beyond a broad débris-strewn plain lay the sea, and in the far distance we could see the glaciers on the slopes of Erebus and the pyramid of Beaufort Island.

Early on the 5th Evans and I started for the coast, while Debenham and Wright investigated the rocks and glaciers near the defile. We proceeded S.E., passing several tributary glaciers, and had to cross many streams running across the plain from the southern wall. We reached a suitable station on the eastern slopes of the Kukri Hills and I took a round of angles with the theodolite which linked Dry Valley to Ross Island. We got back at nine o'clock and found that Debenham had collected many interesting minerals from the marble outcrops of the defile.

Next morning Wright and I ascended the Riegel which so nearly barred the valley. We climbed 2400 feet and then walked to the top of the scarp facing up the valley to the west. So tempestuous was the wind that we could not stand against it, much less use the theodolite. At last there came a lull, and almost before we had the theodolite ready the gale had veered to the east – diametrically opposite – and continued to blow almost as fiercely from that quarter. Our apparent fine weather in the west was, I think, largely due to the fact that there was so little snowfall there; in fact, this region would have been an arid desert even in more favoured climes.

After supper I took the prospecting dish and washed for gold in the gravels alongside the lake. There were numerous quartz 'leads' in the slates with which metamorphic and eruptive rocks were associated, while water was abundant in Lake Chad. In spite of these favouring conditions neither Debenham nor myself could get a 'colour'. Only a 'tail' of magnetite in the dish rewarded our perseverance. So we depôted the dish on a boulder in the defile, for we knew that there would be no water available for gold-seeking in the remainder of our journey.

On the 7th we trekked back to Alcove Camp. We lunched below the 'Matterhorn', one of the most striking peaks in the Western Mountains. It appears to be composed of a cluster of dolerite pinnacles surmounting a pyramid of granite. We took careful angles to ascertain its height, which we estimated at 9000 feet. Great was my astonishment when we plotted our results in the hut to find that our peak was a bare 5000 feet. In the absence of trees or houses or any standards for comparison it was absolutely impossible to estimate any height or distance in these icy regions, and we soon learnt to profoundly mistrust our own guesses and to openly disbelieve anyone else's!

The warmth of the last few days had ruined the Alcove as a camp site. We had much difficulty in finding another. But about 100 yards north in the next deep gully was a patch of moraine exactly like a heap of road-metal. We levelled this as well as we could, and slept none the worse for what P.O. Evans called 'a few feathers in the bed'. I draw a veil over our performance at supper, the first hot meal for nearly a week!

Before we left this region Debenham climbed 2500 feet up the south slope and mapped a great wall of basic lava which clung like a black wart on the glaciated shoulder of the valley. On the opposite side, still higher, we could see a beautiful little crater of the same dark rock, which proved conclusively that the volcanic fires had illumined the glacier since ice had filled the trough to the brim.

We made good speed up the glacier and camped again at the west end of the Kukri Hills. After supper Wright and I went over to the great 'glacier moat' which separates the ice from the granite cliffs. I was very anxious to see whether there was any evidence of erosion by the glacier on the cliffs at the foot of the moat.

We carried ice axes and 120 feet of Alpine rope. At the edge of the glacier there was a sharp curve formed by a snow cornice. Carefully peering over the edge, we could see there was a frozen stream about 200 feet below.

Wright lowered me over the edge – which I found was formed of soft snow and projected, like the eaves of a house, about ten feet. Some thirty feet down was a sort of platform and then the steep edge of the great glacier.

Wright paid out the rope and I let myself down to its end, about 80 feet above the moat. I started cutting steps down the remainder, but my ski boots were so worn out I got no grip, and I reached the moat purely by the force of gravity. My instruments were luckily not damaged and I found the depth to be 207 feet, while the moat was 100 feet wide at the bottom. Débris screened the cliff foot and I could see no planation by the ice.

I managed to cut steps up to the rope and reached the platform under the cornice. Wright hauled away manfully, with the natural but unexpected result that the rope cut through the snow cornice and his efforts resulted in my head being enveloped in snow, and there I stopped. I cried 'Lower away', reached the platform again, and crawled along under the cornice, but could see no way out of the *cul-de-sac*. Gloomily I returned to the rope and descended to the moat, arriving in exactly the same manner, save that the skin vanished from the knuckles of my left hand this time! However, after tramping some distance north we found a place where the cornice had broken off, and here I was hauled up, my ice axe finding a tender spot in my leg as I reached 'glacier *firma*'.

Our rest was disturbed all night by a sound like continuous volley-firing. This was due to the cooling temperatures causing the glacier to contract and split.

In the forenoon Wright and P. O. Evans explored the ice falls and moraines near Solitary Rocks while Debenham and I walked towards Knob Head. The direction of the moraines revealed the interesting fact that all the ice from the Plateau was moving into Dry Valley and not into the Lower Ferrar as was previously supposed. The Ferrar and Taylor glaciers are 'apposed' glaciers linked like Siamese twins by the col at Knob Head. Originally they were quite distinct, and they will again be separated when the ice has dwindled a little farther.

That evening we discussed literature. P. O. Evans disliked Dickens and Kipling, whom Debenham and I enjoy thoroughly. He preferred a well-known foreign writer whose name he very sensibly pronounced Dum-ass. Our sledging library was quite extensive, for each of us had devoted a pound of our personal allowance to books. I will give the catalogue, if only as a caution to later explorers. Debenham took my Browning and the 'Autocrat'; Evans had a William le Queux and the *Red Magazine*; Wright had two mathematical books, both in German; I took Debenham's Tennyson and three small German books. The *Red Magazine*, the 'Autocrat', and Browning were most often read; Evans's contribution being an easy winner. Somehow we didn't hanker after German.

On the 10th we descended 1200 feet down a series of undulations and reached our depôt at Cathedral Rocks. The skua gulls had found the carcase of the Emperor and our chance of a variation in the menu had departed with the gulls.

On the 11th Wright and Debenham carried out a very important operation to determine the movement of the Ferrar Glacier. They fixed stakes right across the glacier which were aligned on two prominent peaks. Some six months later Captain Scott remeasured this line and found that very considerable movement, amounting to 30 feet, had taken place during the winter.

Meanwhile P. O. Evans and I prospected for a route up the steep snow slope of Descent Pass. Evans had been with Armitage when he used this route in 1903. We found the conditions very different. Soon we were sinking nearly two feet at every step in soft snow, through which I knew it would be almost impossible to drag the sledges. The slope soon increased to 11°, so that we found some difficulty in progressing even unencumbered. There I first made the acquaintance of the 'Barrier Shudder'. Every now and then a shiver would shake the surface and we could hear the eerie wave of sound expanding like a ripple all around. Sometimes one could see the whole snow surface sinking slightly, and at first the effect was very unpleasant.

We had been roped for two miles and were still ascending. We now began to get among crevasses, though few were visible through the thick sheet of snow. Quite suddenly I slipped in to the thigh, and sounding with the ice axe just in front found two inches of snow over the crevasse and very little more behind me. I was evidently standing in a narrow bridge. At the same time Evans called out that he was over another about 15 feet behind, so that for a few moments things were rather involved. He got back on to firmer ground and hauled me back, and when we saw the surface begin to cave in bodily we decided, in Evans's graphic language, to 'give it a miss'.

We seemed to be in the least impossible part of the pass, and I could see plenty worse ahead. So I decided to abandon this route and continue down the Ferrar to Butter Point and so reach the Koettlitz Glacier via the Piedmont Glacier.

During our absence Wright had also slipped into a crevasse while fixing the stake nearest Cathedral Rocks. We inspanned after lunch and moved down the glacier to our old camp at the mouth of the Ferrar.

The morning of February 13 was bright and clear. We could see no change in the sea ice filling New Harbour where we had crossed it a fortnight before. I therefore headed south-east towards Butter Point. Here we had an experience that might have ended our journey prematurely.

We got along at a good rate for two miles, when Evans drew my attention to something black sticking up in the ice just ahead.

We had noticed an unusual creaking sound, which I put down to ice crystals falling, but this strange object demanded investigation. I ran forward a little, and the black spike was obviously the back fin of a killer whale. The creaking was really a warning that the bay ice was on the move. Meanwhile the ice I was on moved off with a jolt, a mark of attention from the killer which we did not appreciate. However, I jumped the three-foot crack which resulted and we hastened to the fixed ice nearly two miles south. It was a case of '*festina lente*'. We could not drag the heavy sledges more than 2 miles an hour and were continually crossing cracks where the oozy snow and creaking showed how insecure was our passage. Soon after we reached the Butter Point piedmont the whole bay ice moved off in great floes to the northward, so that seven miles of it had broken away since the ship landed us. It is quite impossible to tell whether sea ice is solid or not, for the first cracks are so small and the elevation of the eye so little that the only safe way to traverse sea ice in late summer is to keep off it!

We expected to find the Butter Point piedmont an easy level surface, but of its kind it was the worst I met with down South. All the afternoon we were plugging up an interminable snow slope. Just as one got one's foot braced to draw the sledges through the clinging snow, it would break through a crust and sink nearly to the knee. Then we would meet a few yards of firmer surface and bet whether we could make a dozen steps before the soft 'mullock' started again. Even worse was the jar when you expected deep snow and found a firm crust one inch below the surface. I carried a pedometer, and when we had done 27,500 of these paces I felt we had earned our supper.

Blue Glacier now confronted us. P. O. Evans and I prospected across the snout and were glad to find that though it showed crevasses in places, yet it was so free from snow that we should have no great difficulty in crossing them. They curved round parallel to the coast, and of course lay along the line of our march, so that we came on to them end-on and fell in several times. But by the evening of the 15th we were safely camped in the rugged ice south of the crevassed portion. Evans as usual enlivened us with navy yarns. He illustrated the kindness of the sailorman by a story of a mate of his who started a poultry-farm. To Jack's disgust the ducks in his yard had no belief in altruism and with their broad bills gave the hens no chance. 'So,' said Taff Evans, 'evenchooly he gets a file and trims their bills like the hens, and then everything went all sprowsy!'

If anyone had asked us what we should like sent post haste from civilisation there would have been a unanimous yell of 'Boots!' The rough scrambling over the rocks and jagged ice of the past fortnight and the alternate soaking and freezing they had experienced had ruined mine completely. Deep constrictions formed in the leather across the toe and behind the ankle and raised great blisters, and even boils in Debenham's case. I had no sole on the right foot, but within the next day or so the temperature fell considerably and the thin leather lining froze as hard as steel and so protected my foot. For days a loose boot-nail which had accidentally been pressed sideways into the sole when it was wet clung like a leech!

Each morning we had a painful ceremony when it was necessary to don our frozen boots. Remarks more fervid than polite flew about the tent, and some of us found that quotations from the poet philosopher lubricated the process.

> . . . Gritstone, gritstone a–crumble:
> Clammy squares that sweat, as if the corpse they keep
> Were oozing through

was supposed to be a very potent incantation. We carried no blacking, but this ceremony was called 'Browning the Boots'.

Open water washed the face of the Blue Glacier. Black snaky heads – reminding me of prehistoric plesiosaurs – could be seen darting about amid the brash ice. They were Emperor penguins, which swim with their bodies submerged.

To the south of us stretched the sea ice, which was evidently rotten and ready to move north. Beyond the Blue Glacier on the right stretched a broad fringe of moraine which extended fairly continuously along the north side of the Koettlitz Glacier. Immediately ahead of us was a fifty-foot ice cliff, but some distance to the south we found a lower place and managed with the Alpine rope to lower the sledges down to the sea ice. We crossed the 'pressure ice' – where great cakes had been up-ended to form a frozen rampart – and reached a good sledging surface at last. Near by was a great pool of water containing many seals, where jostling ice pancakes were surging about, so there was obviously no time to lose. We pushed gaily south and camped that night in a little gravelly dell among the moraines.

All night long we could hear the groaning of the sea ice as it ground on the coast: a most melancholy sound, composed of varying notes of which I wrote an analysis in the by no means stilly watches of the night as follows: 'A tiger's growling purr, *plus* the sough and whistle of the wind through a draughty house, with an undercurrent of the creak due to hard breeches rubbing on a new leather saddle.'

On February 17 we arrived at the lower reaches of the Koettlitz Glacier. For the lower twenty-five miles this great ice-river rises but little above sea level. But what a river! South of the Dailey Isles, where it merges with the Great Ice Barrier, it is ten miles wide. A region of icy pinnacles and bastions, of lakes and winding gullies, as if a storm-lashed sea had suddenly been clutched in the grip of King Frost. Most picturesque in appearance, but as a sledging proposition it can only be described as infernal!

Soon after leaving the sea ice we plunged into a maze of 'glass-house' and 'bottle-glass' ice, whose names almost explain themselves. The former were great curved platforms often thirty feet wide, which threw us all together in the middle and then dropped us several feet through the 'glass' into a pool of water beneath. The 'bottle-glass' was due to the sun melting the ice ripples into a thousand spikes and edges which received us when we fell – which happened every few minutes.

Finally we sledged along the 'lower storey' below the glass-house surface – on the floor of the drained lakes; twisting round ice pillars, pulling the sledges under sheets of projecting ice, lifting them over barriers. But it got worse instead of better, and at last I decided to return to 'the land and make our depôt here instead of higher up the Koettlitz, as I had hoped to do. To reach the moraine we had to cross a sort of 'rip' where a strong deep current of water flowed northward. Along this seals used to appear and would stop to study our movements with some interest.

This camp on the moraine marked the end of the third week. We celebrated it by killing a seal, and next day fried his liver. This was also a memorable day because, as someone remarked, I started cooking and we all lived through it!

I cut off a piece of the seal's belly-skin and sewed pieces over my worn-out boots. It wasn't a very neat job, for it was done with a marlin spike and waxed yarn – but as soon as I started walking the soft seal-skin changed to armour-plate, and when ultimately I wanted to remove these 'brogans' I had to break them off with my geological hammer.

We spent two days exploring the very interesting region behind the moraines. Long parallel valleys, each containing a dwindling valley glacier, led towards the scarp below the Royal Society Range. Thirteen thousand feet above us towered Mount Lister, but we rarely saw the crest, for it was buried in clouds for the greater part of our journey.

On the 20th we left one sledge at the depôt and made another attempt to penetrate the fastnesses of the Koettlitz Glacier.

The Koettlitz glacier, with Royal Society Range behind

We had to cut tracks along the bottom of the glasshouse channels, and Debenham and I pulled while Wright and Evans devoted all their energies to lifting the sledge over the obstructions. The sledge dropped two feet and rolled upside down on one occasion, and later Wright went through the roof and was completely lost to sight in one of the glass-houses. By 6 p.m. we must have progressed almost two miles – and this with a light load! A thick snowstorm came up and we camped amid weird surroundings. All round us were ice sculptures of every conceivable shape. There were great wedge-shaped blocks, so fretted by the sun that they looked as if formed of wicker work. We called these 'fascines'. Others resembled giant pedestal-tables with fringes of icicles. Near the tent, displayed on one of these tables, was a great white monster with an armour-plated back, head, legs, and tail complete. We called this halt 'Armadillo Camp' in recognition of the genius of King Frost.

During the next four days we struggled up the middle of the Koettlitz Glacier. It was a strenuous time, but I recall a pleasant noon halt when P. O. Evans earned an honest penny. We saw him playing with the rope which lashed his sleeping-bag. Says Evans, 'I'll show you how to make a clove-hitch with one hand, and I bet you a 1s. 3d. dinner (our usual currency) you can't do it after you've seen me do it six times!' Debenham took the bet, and we all watched Evans closely. Then 'Deb' tried, and to our joy succeeded, for the handy-man was rarely 'done'. But he never turned a hair, and booked the bets that now filled the air. Again Debenham proceeded to try, and failed and Wright and I were equally unsuccessful. Evans made quite a haul, but after saying he had never seen anyone do it by sheer luck before, he proceeded to teach us the dodge; and later Debenham became quite a knot-master under his willing tuition.

'A fine sunny morning, the first for many days. Even this scene of desolation looks cheerful.' Thus my sledge diary for the 21st. But the route did not improve. I wrote: 'We got going on awful stuff – rounded pools of ice, between tables. It got worse and worse, and after many bumps and leaps and falls I decided to prospect. We had done half a mile in the hour . . . We started again about 3 p.m. Awful heavy work over "glass-house" and leaping three-foot chasms, between high fascines and across decomposing rivers of ice.'

About 4.30 we saw a ragged piece of skin projecting from under an ice-table and found that it was part of a large fish. We spent half an hour chipping it out and recovered the dorsal spines, skin, tail, and the vertebrae. These were preserved in a yellow fatty substance smelling like vaseline and quite soft. I made rather a ludicrous mistake here. I carefully preserved a very hard irregular mass coated with this flesh, thinking it was a bone, but later, after we had carried it for days on the sledge, we found that this 'pelvic bone' – as we called it – melted in warm water! No head was found, and in this respect the fish – which was possibly about four feet long – agrees with the four large headless fish found by the *Discovery* Expedition. We had a hot discussion in the hut as to this problem of decapitation, but came to no definite conclusion, for it seemed too far for seals to carry it.

That night we slept at Park Lane Camp. We had been traversing a frozen park, set out in circular beds with winding paths in every direction. The 'flower beds' were represented by elevated masses of ice thirty feet across, exactly like an apple-pie with a raised crust – even to the four cuts made by the housewife across the top! The last two days we had only progressed seven miles, and for five of them we had carried the sledge rather than dragged it.

Next day, however, we found that to the south the glacier was nearly continuous. It had not been dissected by thaw-waters to nearly the same extent, and by 4 p.m. we managed to advance ten miles to the south-west. We camped on a platform of weathered ice, so rotten that it resembled a layer of honeycomb. We found that this honeycomb ice was very common in this part of the Koettlitz.

We tried to find an easier way out of the numerous undulations which now characterised the surface, but unsuccessfully, and so plugged on south-west. We used to 'pully-haul' up one side (i.e. hand over hand) and then toboggan down the other. P. O. Evans was an expert steersman, while we others used to keep the ropes clear. But we had some nasty falls, especially Evans, who got a cut deep in his palm from a piece of 'bottle-glass' ice, in spite of his thick mitts.

At noon we came across a picturesque tunnel in the ice, about three feet wide, seven feet high, and one hundred feet long. It had been cut out by thaw waters which had now drained away.

In and out wound the lanes, forming a regular network through all sorts of picturesque pinnacles. Here was one like a yacht on stocks, there a perfect wedding-cake twelve feet high, again a lady's bonnet, and so on in infinite variety. At close of day we pitched Camp Labyrinth.

On the 24th we emerged from the pinnacles and reached the coast moraines again near Heald Island. Here I decided to make our terminal camp. In a gravelly hollow we pitched the tent and next morning was devoted to a 'make and mend'. All our sleeping-bags and finnesko were wet with the sloppy ice-floors of the last week – for we had not been able to find any snow-drifts on which to camp. They are much warmer and drier than ice.

Behind the tent to the north were slopes about 1000 feet high leading to empty 'hanging' valleys. These radiated from the base of the Lister scarp, which rose in one steep face 10,000 feet to the summit. This face was pitted by gigantic cup valleys or, as they are technically called, cwms, and presented a spectacle which probably could be paralleled nowhere in the world.

Looking southward across the Koettlitz from the mouth of one of these hanging valleys one could see some sort of plan in the icy maze which had so bewildered us. Above Heald Island the valley was filled with the glacial stream in a normal uniform mass, interrupted only by crevasses and falls. But to the east of Heald Island it took the form of a glacier 'delta'. Below the falls the ice descended to the east in a series of broad undulations, a portion of which we had traversed on the 23rd. Long promontories of ice fifty feet high extended from the unbroken glacier mass and probably represented the crests of the undulations. These degenerated at the ends into icebergs and monoliths of ice, and these again had weathered into the bastions and pinnacles. Lower down the thaw waters had etched these into still smaller units, and along the coast just below me the streams had formed a well-defined if narrow avenue of smooth ice, which promised us an easier return.

On these slopes I found an ice-scratched block – the only specimen I had seen in a hundred miles of moraine débris!

I returned to the tent along the margin of the glacier and was amazed to see seal tracks in the fresh snow. We were over twenty miles from the sea and had not seen any possible route for seals on our outward journey. Yet here were two seals – asleep as usual – on the old glacier ice. I disturbed one of them to see what it would do. He sneezed and grunted at me. When I teased him further he began to warble! I heaved a lump of ice at him, whereupon he lolloped twenty yards to a wet patch, lay over on his side, and produced a whole octave of musical notes from his chest, ranging up to a canary-like chirrup. Finally he crawled under a deep ledge, and vigorously butting with his shoulders, opened out a hole and flopped under the avenue ice.

I soon reached camp and found that Wright and Debenham had both met parties of seals. We all thought of the constant stream along the tide crack by our last depôt and came to the conclusion that this was largely fresh water and formed the main drainage of the Upper Koettlitz. By this sub-glacial stream the seals penetrated nearly thirty miles inland up the Koettlitz Glacier.

On the 26th we crossed the glacier to Heald Island – which projected a thousand feet above the glacier and separated it into two streams of ice. While Debenham collected garnets and other interesting minerals, I climbed the island and sketched the topography up the glacier.

In the silts amid the ice we found large sponges and a fungus-like alga. The sponge must have been brought up by the ice from marine waters at some period far back in history. The alga had probably grown in a glacier pond, since drained away.

Next day we marched twelve miles west to explore a large tributary glacier which we could see across the low-level lateral moraine. After crossing two miles of moraine we suddenly came on a steep gully about 100 feet deep, at the bottom of which was a strongly flowing stream. This originated in a lake three-quarters of a mile long, but for a considerable distance flowed under the moraine, and ultimately entered the seals' sub-glacial stream and so reached the sea. Coleridge's lines entered one's mind:

> Where Alph the sacred river ran
> Through caverns measureless to man
> Down to a sunless sea.

So we christened this stream the Alph River.

We marched along the lake and up the gully beyond. Here a tributary entered from a large cave in the moraine wall to the north. The roof of this cave was coated with most beautiful ice crystals, which resembled pine twigs in shape and were about two inches long. Many brownish ice stalactites and stalagmites fringed the walls of the cave, and Wright was lucky in obtaining some beautiful photos of these structures.

At 4 p.m. we reached our goal – the steep face of the Walcott glacier, but as the weather looked stormy we had to retreat immediately. Wright and I compared compass readings here. The needles swung extremely sluggishly, but we found they were reliable to four degrees – which is about eight times the ordinary error. The fact that magnetic south was nearly due north also complicated matters here! We marched back by a different route and discovered a strong outcrop of basic lava about fifty feet thick which was rich in olivine and had caught up fragments of garnet rock in its passage through the earth's crust.

The month of March opened with a bright sunny morning, just suited for our proposed climb up one of the hinterland ranges. We climbed up the slope about eight hundred feet and so reached the level floor of the 'hanging valley' just behind the camp. We marched along this to the north end of the valley towards a prominent peak on the eastern ridge. A stiff climb over snow slopes and rugged granite led to the summit, which we reached at 1 p.m. The aneroid made this 3000 feet above sea level. It was a beautiful day and we could see Erebus, Discovery, Morning, and the Pyramid up the Koettlitz. Lister itself, as usual, was in the clouds, but nearly all below was visible. We could see numerous hinterland ridges reaching from the Lower Koettlitz to the Lister scarp, and satisfied ourselves that no lateral 'Snow Valley' existed below the scarp such as has been indicated in earlier maps.

It was very cold on this hill (which we called Terminus Mountain); and after swinging the theodolite and taking several photographs we hurried back to the tent down Ward Valley.

On March 2 we started our homeward trek; nothing could be worse than our outward track up the middle of the glacier – though we were able to study the changes of the glacier ice and so did not regret it. I therefore decided to hug the coast on our return, though near the depôt the ice was so full of silt from the moraines that we had not seen any feasible route along the coast thereabouts.

For the next few days we followed the course of the sub-glacial Alph river. Some four miles down stream from Terminus Camp a rampart of ice pinnacles commenced, which recalled the monoliths of Stonehenge. These walled off the rough sea of the Koettlitz Glacier from the frozen surface of the 'river'. This broad lane was here a quarter of a mile wide and consisted of a level surface broken up by deep sunken 'paths'. The more elevated areas were preferable for sledging, for the paths occasionally let us through into water. The whole structure was due to the drainage of water away from rivers and lakelets whose surface had frozen.

This splendid track – which we called 'Alph Avenue' – enabled us to proceed with unexpected ease, and each day we halted and explored one of the numerous tributary valleys which characterised the hinterland.

Each valley was of the same type. A great bar of débris – a terminal moraine in fact – some three hundred feet high blocked the mouth of the tributary. Within this was a bare rounded valley extending to the foot of Lister. Some five miles from the coast was the snout of a tributary glacier which had originally deposited the moraine, but now was shrunk back to a mere shadow of its former self.

All along our route were groups of seals, and numerous skua gulls enlivened the surroundings. Coming back from one of our detours I was much amused to see Wright crawling about among the seals in his investigation of the ice – while thirty skuas were anxiously awaiting the demise of this obviously crazy seal!

The summer was over now and we were getting fifty degrees of frost in the nights. The weather was gloomy, the sun rarely appearing till it had sunk below the level of the pall of stratus.

We had an eventful lunch just before reaching our depôt. We pitched the tent and fastened the door to keep out the wind. I was sitting next the door with my precious lumps of sugar on the floorcloth when I noticed that water was creeping into the tent. In a few seconds it was several inches deep. We bolted our raisins, pocketed the lumps of butter and sugar and rushed out with the sleeping-bags. There was a small lake all round us, rapidly rising round sledge and tent. The water was rushing out of a crack one hundred yards below us, probably driven back by a high tide. We had quite a pilgrimage to get our sledge packed again, having to walk round the newly formed bay.

The avenue petered out here, after furnishing us with a magnificent highway for twenty miles. We had some pretty rough work for the next mile or so, but reached our depôt safely on the evening of the 5th. We had a fine feed of seal liver fried in blubber. Debenham was cook and P. O. Evans was frankly sceptical as to the result. He took his whack gingerly, but handsomely acknowledged it tasted much better than in *Discovery* days. We turned over the fry with my bowie knife and found that safety-pins made excellent forks.

On the 6th we started across the head of McMurdo Sound to reach Ross Island. We had now two sledges to pull, but the surface was good and we soon approached the Dailey Isles. We made an interesting discovery here. All around were heaps of large sponges – a foot in diameter – buried in snow and ice. Among the long spicules we found Bryozoa, Brachiopoda, Serpulae, mollusca, and a fine 'solitary' coral.

That evening we climbed West Dailey Isle – a mass of volcanic lava 600 feet high – to try to see the extent of open water. The head of McMurdo Sound is occupied by a broad wedge of pinnacle ice about twelve miles wide at its base. It was necessary either to cross this or go right round it. We had had such heavy work with one light sledge that the latter route seemed the best, even though it was more than twice the distance.

For the next two days we marched north – almost the opposite direction from our destination at Hut Point. At noon-halt we found that Debenham had two toes frostbitten – owing to a tight boot – but with rubbing they came back all right. We camped at the edge of the Pinnacles, which here were over thirty feet high and separated by deep gullies filled with snags, glass-house, and all manner of obstructions.

Next day we moved along the edge of the Pinnacles, which led us towards Butter Point, much to our disgust. During the forenoon we had heard weird 'blowings' on our right, but it was rather a shock to come on a great bay in the Pinnacle ice, where the latter had recently broken off, and to see our friends the killer whales cruising around only 100 yards ahead! We had to turn at once and march willy-nilly into the Pinnacles, so as to put a little distance between ourselves and the recent break of 'Orca Bay'.

Before going many yards into the Pinnacles we came on a 'river' of salt water, fifty feet or so below the general level. Luckily the pancake ice from Orca Bay had jammed in this 'river' and it was strong enough to carry the sledges. We hauled them hand over hand up the further bank.

After lunch we came to a fifteen-foot drop and we had of course to adopt relaying. Either Debenham or myself went ahead as quickly as possible and found a route by climbing pinnacles or bastions. The other three pulled the smaller sledge as indicated by the guide. After a mile or so we all went back and pulled the heavy sledge up to the other.

Next day passed in the same way, but we were cheered by the sight of a patch of smooth surface ahead of us. Though only four miles off it took us nearly two days to reach it. Bad sandy patches delayed us and ruined the runners. On returning with the second sledge we could often see what looked like wisps of yellow tobacco in the lee of the jagged points of ice. These were long filaments of ash torn from our unfortunate runners.

So passed Edgar Evans's birthday, in honour of which we had some superfine chocolates which seemed in some way to bring us in touch with civilisation again.

At noon on the 10th we reached sea ice again beyond the Pinnacles and had good hopes of reaching Hut Point by night, for it was only a little over ten miles away. I wrote in my diary: 'The surface got so much better that we decided to get to Hut Point or bust! About 5 p.m. we decided to bust, for there was five miles of water between us and the hut. So we deviated with what speed we might to the south, gradually veering in the teeth of a young blizzard.'

In the morning we could see frost smoke rising from the water apparently for miles right across our track. In place of reaching the hut in one day we evidently had a long detour to make to get around the open water. We called this place 'Camp Had Again' for obvious reasons, and started off, after digging out the sledges and tent, once more directly away from our objective.

We pulled six miles south before lunch, leaving Hut Point behind us on the left. The end of the great bay seemed in sight now and I felt justified in bearing east a little. We were only half a mile from the water when we came on sledge tracks, and these puzzled us greatly. We thought they must have been made by a depôt party but could see no depôt. I wrote 'It is not possible it has gone out, as undoubtedly some of the Barrier has?'

As a matter of fact these were the tracks of the rescue party who had tried to save the ponies when Bowers, Cherry-Garrard, and Crean went adrift only ten days before. In view of our experiences the next few days I was glad we did not know of this disaster.

A strong drift was blowing when we broke camp, but we could see the sun and had bearings, so we moved round the open water to the north. After two miles we saw something black which turned out to be a fodder depôt. We built it up, for it was nearly invisible, and left a note for the Depôt Party, which was waste labour, for they had all returned a week before.

The wind increased in force, but we kept on till noon, when we came to open water and a great crack in the Barrier. Here the surface rose several feet quite sharply and Wright nearly slipped in as we were crossing. The drift was getting very much worse and we could see nothing a few yards ahead. I felt this was a bad position and turned inland; we pulled about three-quarters of an hour and could not get any farther through the blinding snow. We managed to pitch the tent and then sat down to wait till the blizzard would let us move somewhere less exciting and farther from the breaking edge of the Barrier. Here, however, we stopped all through the next day and until ten on the third day.

It was the worst blizzard I experienced while sledging in the South, and in consequence my sledge diary is rather scrappy. I wrote: 'Finally decided to have an early supper and turn into our wet bags. We lit the primus and let the flame singe our feet to warm them. Talked of Cambridge cakes and teas and other delights. Evans told a cheerful tale of the snow round the tent at Cape Crozier which pinned them in for five days in September 1903! We can't see 100 feet anywhere. The rime is dripping down my neck and covering our bags. Drifts are slipping off the tent. Wind veering somewhat southerly from south-east. Now and again we peep out of the door, but no improvement. Couldn't get on to the shore probably to camp, as the water is evidently exceptionally far to the east . . . Guess we'll shiver it out. The booming of the lid of the biscuit tin outside is like the Inchcape Bell!'

The next day was much the same, but though the blizzard blew as strong as ever, driving the drift in great sheets into the open sound, yet I felt that as we had got through one day and night all right, so we should the next; which is very common if unscientific logic!

On the 14th it lulled a bit by 10 a.m., and as we knew the direction I decided to make for Castle Rock. The blizzard had piled a long snow slope in the lee of our tent, 100 feet to the north-west of the sledges. We dug out the sledges and packed the gear, and then marched out, the wind helping us materially.

I anticipated some trouble from the tide crack next the land which P. O. Evans had crossed in 1903. However, all was lost to view in the mist of drift, though we seemed to be ascending. Nevertheless, we could see Castle Rock at intervals, and steered by that. I thought we must have crossed the tide crack unknowingly, when the sun appeared and showed us we were one-third of the way up the promontory! With its customary irrationality Antarctica had decided to dispense with a tide crack in 1911, though the next expedition will probably find a chasm fifty feet deep where the Barrier presses on Ross Island.

We joyfully had lunch, transferred all necessaries to the big sledge, and pulled up the 1000 feet to Castle Rock, which we reached in two hours. We had a short rest and then proceeded to tackle the last two miles which lay along the crest of the promontory. Here I saw Evans over-cautious for the first time, but I can well understand his feelings. This was March 14, and on the same day in 1903, after a heavy blizzard, he and his mates were in the same spot trying to reach the hut. They went astray in the drift, and poor Vince lost his footing and slipped down Danger Slope into the sea.

However, there was no drift at this height, and we proceeded easily enough past Castle Rock and got on to the broad ridge beyond. After a mile or so we saw four men over toward Crater Heights. A great sight; though it was comic to see them marching in a row in their swollen wind-clothes. Except for their swinging arms, they looked to us just like a row of the Emperor penguins we had seen in New Harbour. They were Wilson, Bowers, Atkinson, and Cherry-Garrard. These told us the news and took charge of our sledge, while I went off and made my report to Captain Scott.

The geological expedition to Granite Harbour

During January, February, and March 1911 the Western Geological Party had investigated the coast and hinterland south of Cape Bernacchi to Mt Discovery. Captain Scott decided that this survey should be continued northward to Granite Harbour and that special attention should be given to the hinterland at this locality, if we could find a track up the ice falls of the Mackay Glacier.

His sledging instructions to me commence as follows:

The objects of your journey have been discussed and need not here be particularised. In general they comprise the geological exploration of the coast of Victoria Land.

Your party will consist of Debenham, Gran, and Forde; and you will cross the Sound on or about October [date not filled in. – G. T.]

You will depart from Butter Point with provision as under:

11 weeks' pemmican
10 gallons oil
18 weeks' remainder food articles
25 lbs. cooking fat

and make along the coast to Granite Harbour. You will leave at Butter Point 2 weeks' provision for your party for use in case you are forced to retreat along the coast late in the season, and for the same eventuality you will depôt a week's provision at Cape Bernacchi.

On arrival in Granite Harbour you will choose a suitable place to depôt the main bulk of your provision.

As the commanding officer of the *Terra Nova* has been referred to the Bluff Headland shown in the photograph on page 154 *Voyage of the Discovery* as the place near which you are likely to be found, it is obviously desirable that your depôt should be in this vicinity.

I approve your plan to employ your time thereafter approximately as follows:

During what remains of the first fortnight of November in exploring north of Granite Harbour.

During the last fortnight of November in exploring south of Granite Harbour.

It was originally intended that we were to have the honour of starting the 'long trails' during the second summer. But owing to an unfortunate accident Debenham injured his knee, and when the time came for our start he was quite unable to leave his bunk. The motor party left and then the Pole party. We had probably a month's sledging on the sea ice ahead of us – and we knew that the ice might break up and float north early in December, so that it became a serious question how long I could delay the start. On the 5th Gran, Forde, and I pulled our heavy sledge beyond the great shear crack (2½ miles) and left it there.

On November 7 Dr Simpson, Debenham, Nelson and myself held a council. We decided that Debenham could not do anything safely for a week. If he tried to hobble along his leg would never improve and it would probably lame him for life. Nelson very kindly volunteered to take Debenham's place and help us across to Butter Point with our sledges. Then we would return by Friday night, when we trusted to find Debenham able to start.

We pushed off at 9.45 with the small sledge, and in about an hour picked up the other, and then our troubles began. We found that we could only just drag the two along at the rate of about one mile an hour. We were all pretty soft after the winter and as usual found the first day or two extra special hard work. Crossing the thicker snow drifts the sledge runners stuck so much that the waistbelt on which one pulled seemed to dislocate one's pelvis!

At one o'clock we were only 4½ miles from the hut. As we were pitching the lunch camp the drift was rising rapidly and before we could get the tent properly fixed a blizzard was upon us. Everything was soon obliterated. At first I thought I could see the Western Mountains 30 miles away, but later found out that I was gazing at a snow 'pressure ridge' about ten yards off!

Let us look round the tent and see how we have profited by the previous season's sledging. In the roof is a larger ventilator. This, strangely enough, keeps us drier – for the steam from the cooker escapes instead of condensing on the bags and tent. By special request our floorcloth is eighteen inches wider, and now our cameras and instruments do not get buried in snow as heretofore. But greatest blessing of all is an ordinary scrubbing-brush. This lies just inside the door where a man may reach in and find it – brush himself free from loose snow outside the tent, then brush his boots when inside the tent, and finally sweep the floorcloth. It was wonderful what a difference this made to our comfort – for previously any little mass of snow first melted on one's body or bag and then froze into a cake of ice which had to be re-melted before one was warm enough to sleep.

Our chance of a rapid journey to Butter Point soon became very slender. The snow drifted nearly to the peak of the tent and drove in the windward side as a great swelling bulge. The sledges were soon covered a foot deep. There we lay 'all that day' and read and talked and snoozed till 7.30 next morning.

On the 8th we had done over 3 miles by lunch time and could see the cracks in the glacier of Butter Point so clearly that it seemed only five miles off. But it was a long twenty!

In the afternoon we did three more stages until we had been on the go for eleven hours. Eight miles seemed a poor result for such an expenditure of energy.

At 4 o'clock on Thursday we were twenty-three miles from the Hut. It was gloomy weather, but the surface had not been so soft and we still hoped to reach Butter Point. However, we saw the sky darkening to south'ard. Gradually Minna Bluff vanished, then Erebus clouded over, Castle Rock disappeared, and we knew that another blizzard was upon us.

This time it lasted 36 hours. Early on Saturday morning I could just see the Western Mountains. The drift covered the door and of course the sledges were buried. We put up a depôt flag and started back at 4.30 a.m. for headquarters. We had now only the sleeping-bags, cooker, tent, and one day's food. But owing to the surface, that 23 miles was stiff going. I thought we should be in by noon, but it took us just twelve hours to reach the dead penguins and refuse which unavoidably characterise the vicinity of Cape Evans.

I note that we immediately rushed the cook, and that the menu consisted of soup, rissoles and fruit tart, of which I had three extra helps and still felt hungry!

Debenham's leg had not improved much, but we decided to start with him on Tuesday (14th) and Nelson (and Anton) again volunteered to help us along, and if necessary they could fetch Debenham back.

It blizzed till 3 p.m. on Tuesday. We could then just see the Western Mountains and it seemed useless to wait longer. There was a great barrier of stranded bergs off the Cape, and in the lee of these several miles of clear ice – swept by the blizzards – appeared. The wind blew so strongly behind us that Debenham was able to ease his leg by sitting on the sledge. We managed six miles before night. Next day we were half-way across the Sound. On Thursday (16th) it was very thick. Large 'fluff-balls' of snow were falling, but there was little wind. I felt justified in pushing off and trying to steer by the compass, for we could only see about 200 yards ahead. Debenham walked behind the sledge with the compass as near S. 65° W. (mag.) as he could keep it. Forde and Nelson glanced back to see his signals, and I tried to sight bits of ice pinnacle in our line ahead. It was eerie work. No sound, no sight, just gray-white mist enveloping us. Behind, Debenham's black figure – in front, a sheet of white with a few dark patches, any of which might be a small lump of ice ten yards off or a huge pressure ridge 200 yards away!

After several miles of this blindfold work, we were wondering how we were getting on – for the compass is by no means reliable so near the magnetic pole. Suddenly we realised Crusoe's sensations more closely than ever before. We were over twenty miles from the hut and there for the first time saw our footprints of the previous week! Nelson offered a reward of his raisins for the man who saw the depôt first, and Anton soon won them. We reached our sledge at 2 p.m. and all six lunched merrily in our tent. Anton enlivened the meal by giving us a Russian groom's opinions on marriage in very broken English.

The passing of this blizzard was a beautiful sight. Gradually the solid billows of gloomy cloud drifted to the north, leaving a brilliant blue sky. The straight edge of the storm nimbus was fringed with mackerel cloud as if a great grey curtain were being drawn away from the glorious snow-clad mountains of the west.

We reached Butter Point on the evening of the 17th. About 300 yards up the snow slope is the depôt which has been used by all the Western Parties since 1903. Here we found the boxes left for us by Captain Scott in September. We dragged up the small sledge and loaded it with meal, cocoa, sugar, and pemmican. Then on the second trip we dragged down 330 lbs. of biscuit.

Then we had a busy time in the two tents opening pemmican and cocoa tins and sorting food. When Forde and Gran repacked the two sledges we had over 1200 lbs. to drag along.

Load of the Western Geological Party

	lbs.
'Tent' sledge	50
'Biscuit' sledge	50
Boots, stove, crampons	40
Sleeping-bags (4)	50
Personal gear (4)	60
Tent, cooker, &c.	35
	285
Theodolite	12
Cameras and plates	30
Repair bag, &c	5
Geological tools, &c.	15
Shovel and ice axes (3)	16
	78
Food, &c. (14 weeks), at 56 lbs. a week, less 4 weeks' pemmican	744
Oil	100
	844
Total	1207

In face of the difficulty we had experienced with five men and a less load I knew we should have a hard task when Nelson and Anton left us.

We left Butter Point on the 18th, and after seeing us well started the 'Convoy Commando' exchanged farewells. We gave them three cheers and Nelson and sturdy little Anton marched steadily across to Cape Royds, thirty miles away. Henceforth for

over three months we were left to our own devices. We were
now really starting, although the relaying to date had almost
totalled a hundred miles, in all of which Nelson's assistance had
been invaluable.

So we moved off, Debenham linking in; for to our great joy his
leg was certainly not worse for its drastic treatment. The sun was
bright and we wore amber or green glasses. Through them the
snow looked like the rippled sand at the mouth of a shallow river.
Forde turned out in an Antarctic Panama with a brim slightly less
than a yard wide. Gran and Debenham had felt hats with ear flaps.
I just tied my felt hat down *à la* coal scuttle until it was too cold,
and then we had to wear our 'balaclava' helmets.

Now we started a fortnight's relaying. Weary work at best, but
when the course lies on sea-ice – which may go out any day – and
your retreat is barred by a vertical ice-barrier thirty feet high, an
anxious time as well.

We now started a regular routine of five stages a day. After
breakfast we packed the sledges and left the 'biscuit' sledge
flagged at our camp. Then pushed on about a mile with the 'tent'
sledge. Flagged that and tramped back to the other. Pulled it to
the 'tent' sledge and then rested five minutes and criticised the
Antarctic generally and the snow surface more particularly! So
that in about two hours we had shifted our half ton a whole mile,
and walked three in doing it. Then on again for another mile
with the tent sledge. Here we pitched the lunch camp. Debenham boiled the tea and got the tent fixed while we three brought
up the lighter biscuit sledge. In the afternoon we managed three
of these stages, Debenham as before having the tent ready when
we brought in the last sledge.

On November 20 we reached Cape Bernacchi. It was an awful
surface. We crossed a layer of loose ice crystals in which one
sometimes sank to the knee. Debenham's knee got a very painful
wrench so that he could do no relaying. However, he started the
plane table survey which he carried on throughout the whole
journey – thus producing by far the most detailed sledge map of
any part of Victoria Land.

We left a depôt of one week's stores here, as ordered by Captain
Scott. We stuck a bright tin on the pole (as well as the flag) which
shows up well when the sun is bright.

The outlook was not promising. Ahead of us was a wide bay filled with screw-pack. This is sea ice which has been jammed haphazard on to the coast. Many of the upturned blocks were eight feet high. Snow had fallen on this surface and filled in some of the hollows, and a more inviting man-trap or leg-breaker it would be difficult to imagine. However, by next day's noon we were through the worst of it. It was such hurried, tiring work that we had no leisure for photography. There was a quaint spoor standing up in relief two inches above the snow and made by an Emperor penguin, of which I should have much liked a stereo-photo.

On the 21st we came up to an old friend. Nearly filling a small bay was a giant berg about two miles long with a black spot near the north-east corner. This was the end of Glacier Tongue which had broken away on March 1 in the big gale and settled down fifty miles or so away on the other side of the Sound.

The fodder depôt had been left on the tongue by Oates in January and served as a useful survey mark. Our best route lay within this mass of transported ice. It was a good omen that there were some twenty seals basking off the cape, for we knew we should have to live largely on seal meat during our stay at Granite Harbour.

As we pulled under the thirty-foot ice cliffs of the broken Tongue we could see remarkable snow folds apparent in some fresh sections – which tend to show that much of it had grown *in situ* (in its former position) from snow cornices and drift rather than from mainland ice.

The mainland shore was now almost wholly covered by the southern portion of the huge piedmont glacier which extends in an unbroken 'Chinese Wall' of ice to Granite Harbour. It was an imposing sight and an ugly one to a sledging party travelling over the sea ice – for as one moves north there are fewer and fewer places where it can be ascended, and its thirty-foot barrier affords a poor lee in time of trouble. This piedmont was moulded over hill and dale in an alternation of icy dimples and pimples, but several rounded domes and ridges projected as Nunatakker – or *Nunakoller* as I prefer to term these *smoothed* rock outcrops, for *tak* means a peak.

The next morning (22nd) we had to cross a bay about six miles wide. As we lugged our heavy sledge close to the numerous seals they would raise their heads and gaze superciliously at us, then roll over on the other side and go off to sleep again; no doubt much preferring their own lot in life.

Returning from the first trip we felt a strong southerly wind. I decided to try our sail as the wind was dead behind us and as there was no drift.

Forde superintended the rigging of our ice-yacht. The mast consisted of four of the tent poles, the other two going across and forming yards. The leather 'bucket' uniting the poles formed a sort of pulley over which the main halyard was passed. Two sheets to the poop (as I suppose the rear of the sledge yacht should be called) kept the sail steady. These terms are probably not used in their strict nautical sense!

We had a great job to start the two sledges – for as usual after waiting a short time the runners froze to the surface. However, Debenham 'broke her out', the sail filled, and when we once got going we found the half-ton quite manageable.

We felt we were progressing at racing speed when we accomplished a mile in forty-five minutes with both sledges, which before had taken two hours. But needless to say we had to pull with all our strength at the same time, though the wind must have almost accounted for one of the sledges. The miles piled up and we did 6½ geographical miles by 7 p.m., instead of 4½ by 9 p.m. as heretofore.

Between two bergs we had to cross a 'working' crack several feet wide. We were much amused at the efforts of a young seal which was baa-ing loudly and trying to climb a huge mountain eight inches high!

We reached Dunlop Island at noon the next day, helped by the wind and sail. There was a strait about a quarter of a mile wide separating it from the mainland cape. This strait consisted of blue glassy ice covered in narrow belts by thin wettish salty snow. This next mile led to the worst language I think I heard on any sledge journey! My journal states: 'The wind drove the whole 1200 lbs. across the ice, while our combined efforts, almost bursting blood vessels, were needed to cross five yards of the thin snow. When we were on the snow – where you could grip – the sledge was on ice and needed no pulling. When we were on ice the sledge was on detestable sticky stuff and wouldn't budge. We had a merry time and cursed the glassy ice and its mate.'

From Dunlop Island as far north as we could see stretched an icy barrier, the furthest visible promontory of the piedmont being almost due north, though the maps of this coast showed a well-marked bend to the west.

Unfortunately the wind changed in direction, and after it had nearly blown the sledge over I decided to 'down sail' and steer nearer the coast.

We reached a spot where it was possible to climb up the ice. Here by the tide crack we pitched our tent. Gran and I climbed up 200 feet, crossing a few rather large crevasses. We could see no open water within ten miles.

On the 24th we got off at 9.30. I decided to try one sledge first and tack on the other if all went well. There was no wind and it was very hot. We could only just drag one sledge along and had only managed to get a mile northward by 1 p.m. Debenham had wrenched his knee, I sprained a leg muscle, and our progress was practically nil. So I decided to pitch the tent and go in for night marching, when the temperature would be below freezing-point and the surface harden a little. A queer state of affairs! I wrote: 'It was too hot to keep inside the sleeping-bags so I lay outside without a coat, in one pair of socks and finneskoes till about 6 when Praise Be it got cooler!'

Night marching commenced about 9 p.m. The surface was much better and as usual was best when a sort of 'pancake patchwork' of ice projected above the soft snow. We were never able to use the sail again and had to relay practically all the remainder of our journey.

To the east appeared a brown island about 100 feet high and a quarter of a mile long. We hoped this had been missed by previous explorers, and while Debenham and I took angles with the plane table and theodolite the other two made a detour to examine our 'find'. Unfortunately it turned out to be a 'silt-berg' – a mass of ice filled with mud and moraine material. Many of the 'doubtful islands' marked on Polar charts no doubt originated in the same way.

We had so far had neither time nor opportunity to examine the geology of the coast we were skirting. It was apparent also that as we proceeded northwards the glaciers had retreated less, and except on the capes no rock was exposed. From our low position we could only see the summits of the 'faceted' walls marking the three great valley glaciers which opened into the Piedmont Glacier. Far away to the east, Erebus was throwing a huge steam banner to the south. Later in the evening, after some premonitory puffs, the banner shifted to the north. We now had an imposing view of the great black 'fang' of the old crater wall, and just behind this the lower dark dome of Terror contrasted strongly with its snow-covered rival Erebus.

It was very warm in the tent (though the air temperature outside was only +18°) and owing to the sun effect on the dark tent water lay in little pools on the cloth valance. Luckily this altered before we started, or the surface would have rivalled seccotine! I finished my day's notes with the remark: 'I don't take very full geological notes for obvious reasons – we only see a piece of rock about every three days!'

I will copy some notes I made on our sledge routine at this time. 'Our first movement, when we try to take 1200 lbs. at one fell swoop, is to "break out" the sledges, so as to free the runners from ice. Then I give a Hipp! cautioning Debenham not to strain hard, and the runners come away grudgingly and you feel as if they were pulling you asunder. Once under way they improve and we can do as much as three-quarters of a mile in an hour, while the sweat rolls off us, groans rend the air, and Forde curses audibly! Gran slips about on the ice and nearly kicks out Forde's patella. I get up steam too much on easy ground till I hear Forde out of time. We come to an ice ridge and there's bound to be soft snow just beyond. You step into this just as the sledges start up the little slope, slip down nearly to the knee, flounder about, and the whole caravan stops! So twisted I my right leg and it twinges all the time, while Gran diagnoses burst veins with great gusto . . . ' How Debenham got through with his disabled knee I don't know. We used to yell out 'Crack' as Gran and I stepped into them first, and so he managed to keep out of some, but he suffered some awful wrenches with gallant fortitude.

On Sunday the 26th we camped amid a cluster of icebergs not far from a low rocky cape.

It was very heavy pulling through the snow which had collected around the bergs. As we reached the screw pack at the cape I wished to photograph the great cubes of sea-ice thrown 20 feet up on to the rocks by previous gales. Gran went ahead, and almost immediately cried out that Granite Harbour was in sight. I hastily climbed up through the granite blocks and there it was; we were right at it! This was Cape Roberts, and it formed the south extremity of the outer part of the harbour. We had arrived three days sooner than the coast charts had led us to expect, and who so joyful as we!

Looking north-west we could see a large and deep bay, some ten miles across, very like New Harbour in appearance. It contained two inner fiord valleys – of which the southern is occupied by the Mackay Glacier and is much the larger. I took several panorama photos with Forde in the foreground collecting skua eggs – or rather trying to, for they had not laid any yet, though many pairs were evidently considering the subject. Their nests – mere hollows two inches deep in the gravel – were ready, but they merely sat about on cold feet, and stretched their wings and squawked at us.

There was a low snow-covered col across the cape and Forde found a feasible track over it which thus avoided the rough screw-pack off the cape. So I agreed to try an 'overland' route with the sledges.

Now arose an interesting question. Where was the Rendezvous Bluff photographed on page 154 in the *Voyage of the Discovery*? After lunch – a midnight feast as we were now marching – we inspanned and made straight for a hanging glacieret we named the 'Spillover'. We did a long march to 'see round the corner'. We crossed several working cracks and reached a small knob of granite beneath frowning ice cliffs. About here a huge bluff rose into view which we decided must be the Discovery Bluff. It looked rather higher than 500 feet and we saw it from another angle, but no other headland seemed at all similar. I wondered if we were in some other bay altogether, for it differed considerably from the *Discovery* position. We returned from First View Point for our other sledge. On our second trip it seemed as if we would never reach the Point, for in our eagerness we had done a two-mile stage. The weather looked thick to south'ard and there was a threatening table-cloth on Erebus. We hauled the sledges over some wide tide cracks and bumpy ice and put up the tent in a little alcove. Here there was not room to spread the poles properly, so the tent flapped under the blizzard. We were safe however on *fixed* ice for the first time for days, even if it was only a yard or so wide!

On leaving View Point we proceeded due west up the south side of Granite Harbour. We saw ahead of us an ice tongue projecting into the bay ice. We had to cross a nasty tide crack quite twenty feet wide, but luckily only a foot or two in the middle was of pulpy ice. Very heavy clouds rolled up from the south and it started to snow, so I decided to camp in the lee of the tongue. We made a good pitch on the ice with splendid snow blocks for the carving from a big drift alongside.

Dates and meals were rather hard to adjust at this time. Midnight would be in the middle of a march, and supper would be celebrated at 8 a.m. However, as night marching was no good for surveying, I decided to go back to day work now we were inside the Harbour. An opportune blizzard kept us to the tent long enough to enable us to straighten out the calendar!

It continued to snow. We cut out breakfast and kept comfortably to our bags all morning. We had lunch normally at 1.30. Our last meal had been a lunch (at midnight) and Gran caused some amusement by demanding the chocolate for the missed meal. During this blizzard I was cook, and trying to increase my culinary skill I wrote down full notes of our menu.

Breakfast. – Pemmican (looking like lumps of block chocolate) is put into the aluminium cup to full measure.

Meanwhile enough snow or ice has been melted in the cooker to cover the bowl of a spoon. The pemmican is added to this. Some water is taken out in another cup and the 'thickers' stirred up in it. The latter consists of three spoonsful of wheat meal or peaflour, with salt and pepper to taste. Debenham had a happy knack with the 'thickers' which made the hoosh slip down in a most comforting and glutinous way. I tried boiling hard and mixing soft and *vice versa*, but finally discovered that the art consisted in dropping the 'thickers' in just as the hoosh boiled and pouring it out 'good and quick'. About twenty minutes over the primus cooked the pemmican hoosh. Then cocoa (or tea) is made by pouring water from the outer cooker into the inner cooker, where a flavour of pemmican is superadded to it. I liked cocoa best for marching, the others preferred tea, so we had alternate days, though the sledging law says 'cocoa'.

With regard to biscuits we were in two camps. At Shackleton's depôt we found a cache of ordinary biscuits and Debenham preferred these, so I agreed to take a small tin along in lieu of an equal weight of sledging biscuits. So that Gran and I had two sledge biscuits each while the 'soft-teeth' ate Shackleton's brand. Forde dropped a cake of chocolate in his cocoa. *Nous autres* preferred to eat it at lunch.

Lunch. – We always had tea; Gran and I liked it weaker and the other two had the last pannikins full. Six lumps of sugar per man were served out, and as many raisins as you could carry out of the bag in your spoon. (N.B. – It had to be a *dry* spoon.) Butter was whacked out if you hadn't had it already. I made mine last lunch and supper by putting a bit by, though sometimes the bit vanished under the hot hoosh if I forgot to take it out of the pannikin. Three biscuits each and a cake of chocolate.

Supper. – Cocoa follows hoosh. We have two biscuits and a cake of chocolate. One spoon was used in our camp for measuring, stirring, tasting, eating soup and tea, &c. – all alternating gaily as different operations employ the cook. I believe other camps followed the rule, 'One man – one spoon – one cup', but we were strictly socialistic. If your tea or hoosh was too hot you stood it on the floor. If you didn't watch it, it might melt its way out of sight – but that was a most infrequent incident. 'Shut-eye' was played to ensure fair division; the cook pointing to the fragments of chocolate or butter and the blind person giving one of our names. The cook has to share out food, stir the hoosh, watch the primus, and generally hop around; so that he has a busy time. This doesn't matter except at supper, when he doesn't get his feet warm in dry socks as soon as the others.

When the snow stopped, Gran and I walked to the root of the ice tongue and climbed up the granite cliffs to the west of it. On the top we found a bare plateau 300 yards wide on which were some large lichens and a small patch of true moss, quite perky at $+15°$ and evidently prepared to grow vigorously if permitted. The tongue was a mile long and exhibited the usual regular waves in its profile.

On the next day we continued west. The clear sheet of ice we had seen ahead of us was now covered with snow and our hopes of easy sledging were not fulfilled. At lunch time the sun was so hot that the surface was not traversable. We halted therefore and Gran and I walked south to a small bay.

There was a wonderful granite cliff with overhanging glacier streams connecting the upper ice with the lower. Probably not long ago a continuous ice sheet covered this 150-feet cliff, but now only comparatively narrow ribbons of ice are left, though these are quite continuous in spite of the steep fall. They were, however, in an unstable position and we heard several avalanches – hence our name for it of Avalanche Bay. Just to the east of these 'ice-ribbons' was a rock outcrop which seemed to me the first spot in the harbour whence the top of the piedmont ice could be reached if the bay ice went out.

After supper we pulled on towards the Discovery Bluff. The surface improved somewhat and we started out for more relay work. We could see Discovery Bluff quite close, and after half a mile I judged we were half-way and went back for the second sledge. Then on again and it never seemed to get any nearer. Instead of half a mile it was two miles. Bringing up the second sledge was a weary grind. As Debenham said when we arrived, 'We were too tired to think!' We got in about midnight and pitched camp on the tide crack. There was a young seal – still in its woolly coat – lamenting its mother's absence with great persistence. 'Baa-aa!' it said, like a cross between a lamb and a very vigorous young bull. This resounded from the granite cliff above us – and occasionally the mother re-echoed it from the tide crack, where she wisely kept. I was glad to see eight seals here – most of which I intended to kill. Gran caught the young one by the tail, which increased the bellows of anguish. It then bolted to the water, in which it swam readily, and we turned in amid a chorus from the seals.

On the 30th we journeyed on round the steep face of the Discovery Bluff and opened up a fine little bay with a regular beach of granite boulders. Here was much lichen and lots of 'knobs' of dried-up moss. I climbed up a few hundred feet and got a good view to the south-west, where a beautiful glacier came into the harbour at such a low angle it seemed to offer a feasible route to the hinterland. Debenham had discovered a nice patch of gravel and a suitable site for our stone kitchen, so we decided to make our headquarters on this point, which we christened

Cape Geology. The beach, in honour of our country and of the mossy verdure, and in memory of our isolation, we named Botany Bay!

We had lunch about 3 p.m. and then we marched off to get the wherewithal for our first seal-hoosh. A seal lay only a quarter of a mile west of the camp. I poleaxed her with an ice axe and we cut her up under Forde's direction. Forde's right hand was still in bandages from the serious frostbite of September and, indeed, his third finger had not recovered by the end of our expedition.

It was rather a sanguinary business, especially for tyros. Gran fairly paddled in blood, and I fear I was little better. We took all the meat we could carry and Debenham had about 40 lbs. of blubber.

By this time about a dozen skuas had assembled. We did not frighten them, for we wished to attract as many as possible and later abstract their eggs. I wrote: 'About six pairs are breeding along the beach here, so we ought to get a dozen "new laid", and save them a world of trouble by killing them also.' (I'm afraid we were not very altruistic!)

Now we set to work at our stone kitchen. All the way from Cape Evans we had dragged a blubber stove strongly made in sheet iron by Bernard Day. The granite hereabouts weathered in long joints and we found a natural hollow about a yard wide and three yards long. The lower walls of the hut were therefore of solid granite about fifteen feet thick – which should ensure freedom from draughts. We broke out blocks from the floor and Gran smashed off a troublesome projection by repeatedly dropping a boulder weighing a hundredweight upon it until it decided to cave in.

At 10 p.m. I made a great discovery. I saw something black floating in a little pool, and closer inspection revealed a cluster of minute insects. The others had almost dropped to sleep and I was much chagrined at the luke-warm reception of my news. 'They'll keep till tomorrow, won't they?' was the tenor of their remarks.

Hitherto only a few odd legs and tails in some moss had been recorded for the Insecta from 77° South. Later Debenham found there were lots under many of the pebbles. Here they clustered in a film of ice. As one turned a pebble to the sun they would thaw out and crawl around for exercise. I got a brush out of the medical chest and spread a sheet of paper with seccotine. Then brushed them off carefully on to the paper and so embalmed several thousand. We also got a few lively little beggars about one quarter the size of the big blue ones. The latter were nearly one millimetre long.

The first of December was my birthday, and I received congratulations. We ran up the sledge flags and our black and red depôt flags in honour of our arrival at our rendezvous. Debenham said he couldn't let me cook on my birthday and kindly offered to prepare the festive board. Meanwhile Gran, Forde, and I brought in our other sledge from two miles back.

Gran presented me with a bottle of prunes and one of Savoy sauce, which he had lugged along from the hut in his personal gear – a present only to be fully appreciated by those whose menu was as limited as ours.

About 5.30 a long streamer of smoke announced that the famous stove was going, and Debenham produced a splendid liver fry, followed by cocoa in very quick time. 'I could have eaten two whacks of the fry easily.' After we were snugly in our bags in the tent, I divided off half a box of fancy chocolates. These were provided by Fry's for just such a contingency, and we passed a resolution that the leader should write and thank Fry's for their gift; for crunching those elaborate chocolates brought one nearer to civilisation than anything we experienced sledging.

Next day was spent in getting meat from another seal and in finishing the hut walls. From our rate of consumption I reckoned that one seal would give us 2½ meals of liver and ten meals of meat, while his blubber would cook about 30 meals.

Debenham and I flensed the seal-skin on a block of ice. This consisted in removing the white tallowy two-inch layer of blubber from the outer leather with sharp knives. It was rather a troublesome task in which we were not assisted by the numerous skua gulls which surrounded us. This skin was one of three we required for the roof of the stone hut.

Gran and Forde worked very energetically on the latter. Gran was so keen at lifting huge blocks of granite that I had to caution him against straining his back. We used a sledge for the roof tree, and sewed the skins together and then pulled them taut by heavy stones hung round the edges. Finally the hut looked quite snug with the smoke pouring out of the chimney (and also it must be confessed out of the front), and the *tout ensemble* was very like an Irish shebeen in Forde's opinion. Gran was reading Jules Verne's *Mysterious Island* this trip, so we named our sample of Polar architecture 'Granite House' from that exciting melodrama.

On the 3rd Gran and I set about placing a letter on the Rendez-vous Bluff as Captain Scott instructed me. We climbed up one of the big couloirs about 500 feet and then got on to a projecting spur, where we fixed a stout bamboo pole in a crack 3 feet deep in the granite – which just admitted the staff. I left a letter for Pennell as to our depôt. We then hurried down the cliff and went out to slay another seal. We had a difficult time trying to pack the hide, blubber, and liver on the sledge. The rounded portions ran about all over the sledge. Gran swears they worked their way up hill and came out of the folds of skin in which we tied them.

I threw some bits of meat into the 'shear crack' while washing the liver, and the water was soon full of amphipods. These are humble relations of the shrimps, and Gran declared his intention of trying for bigger 'fish' here if he could make a hook. However, we never had time to test this food supply.

On the 4th I decided to climb the Bluff. First we skirted low cliffs, below which were large 'joint-channels' in the granite with carpets of thick fungus-like moss. These were green underneath, but the tufts were still black, contracted and dryish. Then over crags to a slope of talus débris in which I found a large frondose lichen about 8 inches across with well-developed branches and pseudo-roots. We got to the top in an hour, and our doubts as to the height were justified. The Rendezvous Bluff was sixteen hundred feet high instead of 500 as we expected!

We got a magnificent view of Granite Harbour and its hinterland.

Far to the east Erebus was wholly visible, while to the west we could see the great ice plateau. Right out to sea was Beaufort Island, and there was no open water near the harbour. Closer was the cluster of fifteen bergs near Cape Roberts and the small tongue of ice where we had camped during the blizzard. But a most amazing discovery was that the whole inner part of the harbour was occupied by a great glacier tongue some five miles long and a mile wide. This projected out to sea from the Mackay icefalls and ended in three splay 'fingers'. It was a hundred feet above the sea ice and crevassed beyond description for the greater part of its length.

Across the harbour was a low plateau about 1000 feet above the sea, formed of black dolerite. Small glaciers hung over the steep cliffs, one being the 'Spillover' mentioned previously. Then looking west came the crevasses of the Mackay icefalls, as impassable and impossible as Dr Wilson had described them. But in the southwest corner was the smaller New Glacier, and I felt sure we could get up that way somehow.

About twelve miles up the glacier was a huge nunatak with a cap of black dolerite rising into three peaks. This cap reminded me of a Chinese junk, but Debenham objected to Junk Mountain and suggested Gondola Mt. It was sad to find out later that Professor David on his journey to the Magnetic Pole had seen and fixed this peak and called it Mount Suess!

As will be seen, we investigated this most interesting rock island in the upper Mackay Glacier fairly thoroughly.

On the 5th, about 4 p.m., we started off with a week's provisions to map the northern coast of the harbour. We had only one sledge and got along in fine style – the first easy sledging we had met – and as it turned out practically the last! We camped at 6.30 at the end of the Mackay Tongue, for we should lose sight of all our survey stations if we went farther.

The sky looked very ugly – the sun dimly glaring through gloomy clouds, while a low thick bank of dark stratus covered the eastern horizon. The barometer fell nearly half an inch in twelve hours, and we were quite expectant of a blizzard, for similar conditions on a smaller scale preceded the blizzard at the piedmont tongue. Our meteorology was quite sound. The first furious blizzard we had experienced now commenced, for the wind force was about 7, while the drift was thick and wetting. I will copy my diary here.

'10 *a.m.* – We have a pretty snug camp on snow one foot thick which you can accommodate to your hip bone, but which it is difficult to stand the primus upon (especially as the cooker base is full of fat, and is now our frying pan at the hut!). It started snowing about midnight and clothed the tent by 3 a.m. I woke to hear the tent flapping and shaking down young avalanches, and it's been going strong ever since.

'2 p.m. – Still blizzing strongly; there have been one or two lulls of a few minutes, but they don't seem to mean much. It is snowing like fury too, pattering on the tent like rain on wooden shingles. If you budge from the tent (Debenham did so to get a note-book) you get very cold because the drift melts and wets you at this high temperature of +23°. We had a meal about 11 a.m., Gran cooking a good pemmican with a large supply of broken biscuit therein. This strong S.E. wind blows practically direct from Cape Roberts on to the tongue on our lee, so I don't much fear it will shift out this ice. Anyhow we can't move and I'm learning to take these blizzes philosophically. Besides, the bags are dry and warm, and when I tire of writing this diary I snooze a bit, and then read Harker's *Petrology* (Debenham's), and then snooze more. Or Poe's *Tales* (too fantastic and Oriental to please me, most of them), or *Martin Chuzzlewit*, or German Grammar. Forde is reading *The Mysterious Island* which Gran has nearly finished at last. Debenham started to work out a latitude but is now "wropped in Morfus". Last night's "hoosh" was an enormous success, 2½ pots of Forde's concentrated seal-hoosh mixed with water and meal made a top-hole hoosh – very tasty and all indigenous!

'6 p.m. – The tent is beastly sloppy. We have just finished our lunch, and if we can't get away, that is our last meal today. Today is a queer camp – the first down here where we have actually been dripped on when no primus is going. We have put the cooker under the tied-up door and it is filling I see. Forde is dressing his hand and Debenham keeping warm very sensibly in his bag.

'*Noon*. – It is now noon and we are still snowed up off the end of the Mackay Tongue. Forty-three hours now and we have not got away. It dripped most of the night, for the temperature was +27° outside and warmer inside. There was a puddle by the door, but Gran's and my bags have absorbed most of that, and Debenham's is wetter. I put on my boots, wind coat, and puttees and dug out the thermometer. The sledge is buried two feet under snow. Debenham's big camera tripod shows above the snow and a bamboo pole – also the top of the shovel – but the rest is clean buried . . . Then I came in and had breakfast.'

We had lunch about 2 and now saw blue sky occasionally to the east. Gradually the whole snow cloud blew over *en masse* to the west, leaving blue sky and a bright sun. We dug out the sledge, nothing of which showed, and tried to start off. We harnessed up alternately so as to beat out a track in the soft snow. The going was awful and the sledge pulled us flat on our faces in the snow – of course wetting us through. However, we managed to do about a mile in 3 hours and pitched camp in the middle of North Bay.

This blizzard is evidently the same which delayed Captain Scott at the foot of the Beardmore, more than 800 miles south of where it trapped us.

On the 8th we had an eventful day. We were about two miles from the coast, the nearest land being the flat glacier-cut shelf which we named the Kar Plateau. 'We loaded up the sledge and found we couldn't move it. It just stuck with the prow covered with soft snow. So we stuck up the flag-pole and "packed" all we could carry on our backs. Gran went first with his very heavy bag (half water) and the tent-poles. He plugged away in great style, but made rather a devious track as different parts of the coast appealed to him. By the time we arrived near the land Gran was manoeuvring with the tent-poles to try and cross the tide-crack. This was a rotten affair. An ice foot 2 feet or more high, separated from us by a couple of feet of open water, was bad enough but nearly forty feet of the floe was soft and mushy, so that through the thick snow you could not tell which was hard ice and which open water. There were seals all over this mushy stuff and we came unexpectedly on their holes nearly buried in snow. Debenham and Forde were looking down one to see the thickness of the mushy ice, when a seal leaped out three feet, and as Forde pathetically put it " nearly frightened a loife out of me, Sorr! " Meanwhile Gran had laid the poles up against the floe and left his bag just behind, when the mush gave way and in he went. He rescued his bag, and clinging to the poles he somehow managed to crawl up the ice foot, but he was pretty wet and soon very cold.

We traversed some distance to the north, Gran on the ice foot and myself on the mush. At every footstep water oozed up, and this doubtful belt was forty feet wide. I managed to get to land, but we could not have got the sledge over. We returned to find Debenham had gone through also. So I determined to make our survey from where we left the sledge and to return immediately thereto.

First, however, we had to get Gran off the ice foot. He threw his bag out towards us and as I went to get it I went in nearly to my waist. Luckily I managed to lean back on to less rotten mush. Then we lashed the bag ropes together and threw them to him. He threw the tent-poles on to the mush and then launched himself spread-eagle on the poles. The whole floe rocked up and down like a jelly, but the poles kept him up and he reached us without further mishap.

This slush – half ice, half snow – was much riskier than broken floe, for there was nothing to grip, and I think Forde voiced our opinions when he said: 'You done a wise thing to give that place a miss!' Gran and I were pretty chilled when we reached our tent, but soon got warm in our bags and slept off any ill effects.

We had an even more difficult time returning. My diary records it as 'hellish'. We managed the two miles with the light sledge in four hours, during which we experienced an interesting anatomical phenomenon – as if our insides were getting driven out of our backs by the drag of the harness!

Next day by evening we reached Camp Geology again. Everything was buried in snow. A tin of biscuits weighing 40 lbs. had been blown six feet off a rock. Granite Hut was half filled with snow and we later found that our flag-pole on the bluff, although of male bamboo two inches thick, was broken into a dozen strands.

December 10 was a Sunday, and we registered our highest temperature of +40°. We expected the warmest day early in January, but it rarely rose above freezing point any more that summer. In the evening Gran and I planted his sea-kale seeds on a patch of mossy soil inside a granite hollow. It seemed a bit wet, but Gran assured us it would be up in a week and eatable in a month! Our mouths watered at the thought of cabbages, though I don't think we others were optimistic.

The ship was due to pick us up in about a month to take us 200 miles north to Terra Nova Bay, and so of course we thought of a sweepstake as to its date of arrival. Unfortunately we couldn't decide on a stake. Money was no use. We should get any food we liked when we got on board. 'Gran suggested the *first bath* for the winner. But this though very sensible didn't catch on, for as we have no clean clothes probably we won't waste time on it!'

The next few days, sledging on the sea ice was impossible, so I decided to survey and collect near our headquarters. I took angles for the latitude and longitude of Cape Geology (obtaining 162° 49') and was able to corroborate our sledge-meter record as to the correct position of Granite Harbour. Debenham and Gran climbed to the highest point of the Rendezvous Bluff and found its height to be 1624 feet. They saw open water off the harbour.

The skuas now commenced to lay. Gran said that he got his first egg from a nest half full of water, and declared that the bird looked much relieved when her uncomfortable charge was removed. Two of the nests which I saw seemed to show faint signs of intelligence on the part of the owners. In place of a mere hole in the wet gravel one had about twenty long feathers arranged round the edge – while the other was improved by the addition of some dried moss which the bird had picked from a foot away. I am afraid this intellectual activity on their part did not preserve their eggs!

We boiled four and I tasted my first Antarctic egg. They are the size of a small hen's egg, brown in colour with black, tawny and buff flecks on them. They have not so much taste as those of the common fowl and the albumen is translucent and bluish. They were very good and I could have managed six, though the Polar record of sixteen was I felt sure beyond my attainment.

The movement of the Mackay Tongue was an interesting problem. The sea ice was puckered into great pressure ridges off Cape Geology by the irresistible outward movement of the glacier. Great diagonal cracks traversed the floe from the same reason. So I decided to try to fix a stake on the Tongue, and with the theodolite we could accurately fix its progress to the east.

The chief difficulty was to get a mark. We had no wood to spare. Stones would sink into the ice. Finally I used the broken end of the signal pole. I tied some sealskin on the top for a flag, and painted it well with blubber soot, of which unlimited quantities coated Granite Hut. Gran and I walked over to the Tongue and marched 200 yards up it quite easily. Then we suddenly came on many deep crevasses masked by snow round which we had to steer carefully.

I sighted south with the theodolite to the tent on Cape Geology and north to a large crack in the granite of the Kar Plateau. These directions were not collinear of course at first, but I moved the theodolite until they were. This took a long time and we had to go back to get round a crevasse before we got it fixed. Returning we had hard work to find a track and got lost amid the parallel crevasses, which had an awkward tendency to join after you had followed them for a few hundred yards. On our return I found it was an excellent station, the stake lying directly in line with the crack in the cliff 5 miles off across the bay.

As a result of the seal-flensing to provide a roof for Granite Hut, I cut myself rather frequently. This was usual and a matter of no moment generally. Seven of these cuts healed up in a few days, but one on my right hand gave rise to much trouble. We carried a medical chest full of pills, and Debenham was sledge doctor and knew as much of medicine as Dr Wilson could get on a sheet of notepaper. He felt an expert at snow-blindness, frost-bites and dyspepsia, but my hand baffled him. However, Gran had served on many vessels in his naval training and at first I had great faith in him. He gravely felt my pulse, and then the arm-pit. 'Do you feel any pain here?' I truthfully said 'No!' 'No blood poisoning in that finger,' says Gran. Next day it was worse, and Gran proceeded to lance it with great gusto, with the result that the thumb and two fingers swelled double normal size. For a week I could not sleep, and I tried all sorts of bandages and most of the pills – as expert opinion favoured frost-bite, rheumatism, or blood-poisoning. Gran remembered aspirin as good for rheumatism – so the patient swallowed two. Then he said he meant salicylate, so I took two of them; and then he cheered us by telling us how a former invalid with whom he had had medical dealings died on his hands!

However, on the 16th we sledged to the head of the harbour to examine the numerous capes and bays and to try and find a path up to the great inland plateau. First of all we made for a low dark cape from which the Mackay Glacier had receded slightly. From our hut it looked just like a black hand stretched out from a snowy cuff so we named it Cuff Cape. We found it a very interesting spot with moraines, rock-striae, perched blocks, and other evidences of past ice action in great profusion.

The next few days we explored and mapped a headland which we called the *Flat Iron* from its resemblance to the sky-scraper of that name. On its southern face was a deep bowl-shaped bay with a little hanging glacier at the back, and possessing a dry gravelly beach. Here in the Devil's Punch Bowl beneath the Devil's Thumb we stayed till December 23.

It was a grand collecting ground. Almost every variety of granite, diorite and gabbro occurred on the Flat Iron. Debenham found a great 'dyke' of marble included in the granites, and containing large specimens of natrolite, pyroxene, and amphibolite. The New Glacier had only just ceased to cascade over the Devil's Ridge into the Punch Bowl, and the condition of this narrow granite ridge exposed after its submergence by a huge glacier was of extreme interest to the physiographer.

There were several pretty little tarns on the slopes, and Gran celebrated Midsummer Day by a dip, in which I would willingly have accompanied him but for my disabled hand.

Towards the end of this trip I began to be able to read my own left-hand writing. Unfortunately no one else has succeeded in doing so, and I find that the meaning of many (no doubt) most valuable notes is now lost to me also!

By Christmas Day we were back at Cape Geology ready to tackle the hinterland. We celebrated the day in a manner worthy of the occasion. Forde rigged up all our sledge-flags: Gran's, which was given to him by Queen Maud of Norway, Debenham's and mine with Australian and Cambridge emblems, while Forde, not to be outdone, cut out a white harp from a linen specimen-bag and sewed it on some green burberry! We had a fine lunch. Twenty-seven skua eggs had been collected, and Forde took the precaution of cracking them first. The first shewed considerable development – but he went into the fry, much to Gran's disgust. Then about four fair ones and then eight bad ones; and finally we had two each – a thirty per cent. success! We opened the Christmas bag; a slice of pudding each, with ginger and caramels. An epicurean feast I warrant you.

A dense sea fog rolled in that night and enveloped everything, and next morning all of us (except Gran, whom nothing harmed) had rheumatic pains. Luckily this wore off later. It was Debenham's birthday, so we finished the box of chocolates, and Gran gave him a long-treasured box of cigarettes.

At noon of the 27th we once more reached the Flat Iron. I was at first of the opinion that the New Glacier would be the easier route, but the others favoured the Flat Iron, and their arguments decided me to try that route. We found it much easier than the glacier would have been. However, it was no joke reaching the snow plateau behind the Flat Iron. We had to climb one thousand feet of rough granite-strewn slopes carrying the sledge and fourteen days' provisions on our backs.

Gran and Forde managed the thirteen-foot sledge, while Debenham and I transported gear, but it took a long time and many traverses to get everything up to our camp on the snow. Luckily my disabled hand did not prevent sledge-hauling or packing, but it was now a long time since I had been able to sketch, photograph, or use the theodolite.

From the camp we could see open water, but it was a long way off; so that I wrote: 'It must go out a mile a day, or Pennell will have trouble to meet us.' I remember we spent that evening discussing a proposed sledge trip in Norway over the little ice-cap of Justedals Brae.

We left our snug gravelly camp after breakfast and pushed off up the great glacier. We were well knotted to the sledge and I went on a longer line so as to prospect for crevasses. It was comforting to think that though I couldn't help to pull anyone else out, the other three would have no difficulty in dragging me up. We zigzagged down from the Flat Iron on to the snow plateau. This was about ten miles wide and seven miles long. It was bounded by the long red ridge of granite ahead of us which we called the Redcliff Nunakol. On the south were the crevasses of the new glacier, while on the north were the icefalls of the Mackay, like a suddenly frozen storm-tossed sea. Gran said this would be called Skauk in Scandinavia, so we adopted that name.

The surface was covered with deep snow and there were many east-west depressions in this, into which we fell occasionally. I am not sure if they were crevasses; they may have been subglacial streams. We heard here the eerie 'Barrier Shudder', as the surface fell in around us, but familiarity made us disregard this.

There was a wonderful series of peaks to the south, rising about 5000 feet high and separated by the snow-filled bowls which are technically called cwms. Mount England was a very prominent object to the south-east, confronting us with a giant wall of granite 4000 feet high. This was seamed by couloirs and gullies, down which small snow avalanches formed white tongues leading to the crevassed slopes of the New glacier below.

Mount England and Minnehaha Ice Falls, Granite Harbour

About four o'clock we deviated to the south so as to camp on the Redcliff Nunakol. We descended a little the last mile and finally crossed a large frozen lake and reached a gravelly point on the *nunakol*. Here we pitched a comfortable camp about 30 feet above the glacier. Alongside was a little waterfall flowing from a marshy flat on which some moss was growing.

We spent December 29 surveying this island in the glacier. It was about 1000 feet above the glacier, but its rounded contours showed that it had been overwhelmed by the ice flood, fairly recently in geological time. About 5 miles farther west was Gondola Mountain (Mount Suess). This was a true nunatak or 'lonely peak'; for it towered 3000 feet above the glacier and its jagged summit had not been planed by the Mackay Glacier at its period of maximum flood.

Forde carried the theodolite up for me, and I managed to sketch the panorama. It extended over sixteen pages of my notebook, and under the circumstances was a work of art; for there was a cold wind blowing, and I hadn't been able to draw for weeks. Many of the boulders had pot holes eroded in them, I think by wind and frost action. I boldly attempted to draw these also, sitting with my boots among them and drawing the latter also to show the scale!

We were confined to the tent by snow all the next day. Debenham and I made a chess-board on the back of his plane-table and cut out card discs for the pieces. After several weeks we began to realise the appearance of the men, and later we played many games while we were waiting on Cape Roberts.

On the last day of 1911 we left this camp and moved west to Gondola Mountain. The glacier was deeply snow-covered, and though we sank in it the sledge pulled pretty well. There must have been plenty of crevasses where the ice stream curved round the end of the *nunakol*, but though we sank in a foot or two at times, yet the snow was so deep we didn't break through anywhere. The sun came out to cheer us, and later in the day we reached a scattered moraine of granite blocks. The ice had been melted here in the previous summer, and we heard the old familiar creaking and splintering of 'glass-house' and 'bottle-glass' which reminded Debenham and myself of our trip up the Koettlitz Glacier.

Finally we came to a sudden ice cliff about 100 feet high, but just not too steep for tobogganing. So we 'let her go' and slid down into the stream-cut gully which fringed the Gondola Ridge.

This was the most interesting locality I saw in Antarctica. On nearer approach the likeness to a gondola disappeared, as the great granite buttress supporting the dolerite capping came into view. I must apologise for comparing this fine mountain to a decayed molar tooth, with three black cusps and a rounded hollow between, but there was a great similarity in shape. To the north of the nunatak was a low ridge about two miles long, composed of granite and separated from the mount by a col or pass which rose but little above the glacier level. All along the eastern slopes were piles of moraine material. Great cones of débris, built up of granite, dolerite and a yellow rock (which we were glad to recognise as Beacon Sandstone), stood out like watch-towers on the morainic rampart.

Towards one of these, like a railway embankment of yellow sand, we directed our way. We carried our gear to the top, smoothed off the site somewhat, and then pitched our camp on mesozoic sandstones – probably the first time this has been done in Victoria Land! Just below was a little lake dammed by the embankment, and when I cut through three inches of ice near a big black boulder, a bountiful supply of water welled up in the hole. On the bank was some dark shale, by far the most promising rock for fossils that we had yet seen. Before the day was over Debenham had found some, and we examined all the shale carefully and obtained many specimens. They were vesicular horny plates shaped like the tiles capping a roof ridge. Some were about two inches long and had a well-marked keel. Others had a beautiful bluish lustre, and there were bits of wood in the shale also. (They are very like the armour-plates of certain mesozoic fish, but they have not yet been submitted to a specialist.)

A heavy cloud-fog descended over us next morning, but in the afternoon cleared off a little. The dark pall shrouded Gondola Mountain, but hung about 3000 feet up for the most part. Gran and I explored the Gondola Ridge behind the tent. Some of the fine-grained boulders were beautifully polished by the friction of the glacier ice. I thought I saw a skua egg here, but it was a piece of mottled sandstone exactly the same size and shape. All the crags were *roche moutonnée*, i.e. rounded by the ancient glacier, the lower eastern face being almost mirror-like in places from the scour of the ice. Here and there we came on large perched blocks, sometimes precariously poised on three or four small pebbles.

During the night we found it rather cold. Consequently I slept with my head right in the bag and awoke rather late from an exciting railway accident! However, nothing was lost thereby, for the heavens still encompassed us. Forde put in some good work with wax ends on my boot, and I searched the shales near the tent and found more 'sarpent critters', as Seaman Evans christened all our fossils.

Debenham made another discovery; this time of some lumps of coal, and we got many specimens later of the same material. All these were in the moraine just north-east of Gondola Nunatak and I was anxious to find their original home. The 3rd was a more promising day, and Gran and I determined to circumnavigate the nunatak if possible. We walked along to the south over the great moraine which fringed the granite ridge. There were some large blocks of granite in this, some twenty feet across. There was of course much of the basic rock (dolerite) also, for we could see that the cap of the nunatak was formed of jointed columns recalling those of Staffa.

On the south-west face of the nunatak we saw a long lenticular mass of yellow sedimentary rock lying above the red granite, but below the black dolerite cap. It was quite inaccessible, being about 1000 feet up, but I have little doubt that the shales and coal were associated with this formation, for the moraine trended exactly in that direction.

Meanwhile Debenham and Forde had reached the central hollow of the nunatak, but had not time to ascend one of the 'cusps'.

On the 4th – leaving Debenham busy with the plane table – we others attacked the nunatak. Gran had his camera, I took the theodolite in a rucksack, and Forde carried the legs. The eastern face of the nunatak consisted of a giant granite bulwark 1800 feet above the ice. Dark dykes had weathered out somewhat, so that it appeared to be pierced for guns. We scrambled up the gap between the bulwarks and the deck of the Gondola and found the latter occupied by two little lakes. From here we separated, Gran making for the north-west cusp while Forde and I chose the south-west peak. The slope was very steep; and consisted of granite and sandstone up to 2000 feet. Then everything was covered by the broken columns of dolerite. I think, however, that hereabouts the sandstone layer was *in situ*, and in view of the paucity of fossiliferous beds in Victoria Land, all such occurrences have an especial interest.

I reached the top about 2 a.m. and found it 3000 feet above the tent. Gran soon appeared on the other peak, which the theodolite made 100 feet lower – much to his disgust!

The view was magnificent. A few feet away was a thousand-feet precipice above the lower talus slopes. Out to sea we could see miles of open water, with floes drifting about therein, but it looked no nearer than a month ago. I guessed it 10 miles east of Cape Roberts (Pennell said the pack ice was nearer 30 miles wide). Some four miles to the south was a gap in the mountain wall where a low-level distributary glacier seemed to flow into the next great valley. The gigantic cliffs at each side were topped by natural forts composed of Beacon sandstones and shales. I have named this interesting glacier the Miller Glacier – while Debenham christened one to the north the Cleveland. He naively explained that his friends must have a large glacier because there were such a lot of them!

To the west, about ten miles away, was the ice plateau descending in ice falls and marked by two (rock) *nunakol*s. There was apparently a fairly easy route to the ice plateau to the south of this *nunakol* – certainly shorter and probably not so crevassed as the route *via* the Ferrar and Taylor glaciers. A very high mountain showed up to the south-west – 10,000 feet I should think, but all our survey angles were so acute that it is difficult to fix their distance exactly. To the north-west was a fine black-capped peak where the glacier left the Plateau. This I called Mount Tryggve Gran.

We were due back at Cape Geology about the 8th, so I felt that this was our western limit. We spent another day surveying the nunatak and collecting more coal and fossils, and left about noon on the 6th for our return to the rendezvous. We reached our Flat Iron Camp without incident and devoted a day to collecting and photography.

One photograph was an epitome of the physiography of the region. I note that it shows 'the ice face, the crevasses, the skauk, young "calved" bergs, low moraines, retreating glacier, high moraines, granite pavements, shear cracks in the bay ice, the ice tongue, the faceted cliffs, cwm valleys, overflow glacierets, hogback ridges, non-glaciated peaks, the old glacier flood floor, and the junction of the granite and the dolerite.' All this on a single ¼-plate negative!

Each day I entered up the meteorological log. The clouds were described also, very often by the word *overcast*. But this afternoon we noticed the sea fog rolling in below us, gradually blotting out the bay, then the ice tongue and the headlands below. I was some distance away from the tent and before I could return the camp was completely hidden. The others also managed to get back safely, but the cold and the high cliffs round the Flat Iron made it a nasty place to be lost in the fog. We could do nothing much that afternoon and I described the weather in one word as *undercast*!

We had a chapter of small accidents while we were transporting our gear down to the sea ice 1000 feet below us. I found on arrival that the cap of the theodolite stand had joggled off. I returned and met Forde. He looked at *his* load and found the handle of the primus pump had disappeared. We spent some time searching, but it was quite useless among the rough granite blocks. Just as we started pulling on the sea ice Debenham missed the sight-ruler, an indispensable part of the plane table. Luckily he found this about a mile back and Forde managed to make some ingenious leather caps that served instead of the other lost articles.

According to orders we now spent the last week surveying the neighbourhood of the rendezvous. The blubber stove was going strong most of the day to melt water or cook supper. We used to light it with paper rubbed in the blubber. The black sooty blubber oil would leak out and melt the ice on the floor of the hut. The soot caked all the cooking utensils, and spread itself liberally over us. Gran could always be relied on to make any special delicacy such as porridge, for which we saved our 'thickers' and a little oatmeal we had. This used to take him about three hours in the cold hut – while we worked out sights or wrote notes snugly in the comparatively clean tent.

Moreover on these occasions Gran enlivened the cape by carolling grand opera. When he felt the cold and soot and smoke rather too much for him *Pagliacci* or *Bertran du Born* would sink to pianissimo. Then we would shout our 'Bravos' and 'Encores' and the northern Caruso would start off again and away flew the skuas. So by degrees a steaming pot of 'good stoof, that will stick to your ribs' was brought to the tent by our hardy Norse mate.

We found Gran's seakale sprouting in their rock garden. No less than twelve dicotyledons! I'm sure they were the first grown under natural (or rather unnatural) conditions in 77° South. Unfortunately they only flourished a week, and even the native mosses did not get green that summer – which made me sure it was a very cold January.

On the 10th there was an addition to our circle. Gran found two skua chicks in one nest and took one as a pet. He tried to feed it, with the result that it nearly died; so he returned it. However, one of the pair of chicks is always killed in the first week or so.

Gran and I went over to the Mackay Ice Tongue to determine accurately the movement of the latter in the past thirty days. We reached the stake without much trouble by prodding for the crevasses and then set about finding its progress to the east. Gran had my Goerz glasses, and lying full length on the snow he observed Debenham. The latter was stationed at the theodolite some two miles off at Cape Geology, and signalled to Gran with a flag as to

which way I was to move. Finally I got just in a line with my
transit of December 14. I measured the distance to the stake and
it was 82 feet! The glacier moves nearly a yard a day. Debenham's
conjecture that the *Discovery* made no mention of this imposing
tongue because it was *not* imposing in 1902! is very likely correct.
It may easily have been several miles shorter when Captain Scott
first saw the Rendezvous Bluff.

The date of our relief now approached. Captain Scott wrote: 'It
will certainly be wise for you to confine your movements to the
region of Granite Harbour during the second week in January . . .
You will of course make every effort to be at the rendezvous at the
proper time, January 15.'

There was nothing further to do near Cape Geology. One of the
most difficult portions of our retreat was the nine miles between
Cape Geology and the mouth of Granite Harbour. I decided –
after consulting the others – to leave for Cape Roberts on the 14th,
for there we should also be in a better position to see the ship,
while if the bay ice 'went out' there was no feasible way out of the
cul-de-sac at Cape Geology.

We packed up all we should require at Terra Nova Bay – where
we were to spend the last four weeks of summer – and left the
600 lbs. of specimens, spare boots, &c., at Cape Geology, where
they could be picked up by the ship.

We moved off at 7.30 on the 14th. We had a very heavy load for
one sledge – 900 lbs. I believe – but I hoped we could pull it
without relaying. The surface was bad, being several inches deep
in new-fallen snow. We took an hour to do the first mile and then
had to cross one of the many wide shear cracks. These were
twenty feet wide and were literally torn in the six-foot bay ice by
the irresistible pressure of the Mackay Tongue. The edges were
ragged – and composed of interlocking promontories. By means of
these and an island jammed between we got our load across safely.
The east was very gloomy and it started to snow. In previous years
this bay had been clear of ice in January – so that I did not want to
be caught in a blizzard on it in the middle of that month. The
surface improved slightly, but we next struck a 30-foot shear crack
filled with mushy snow. A little searching showed us a possible
track. Debenham and I tied together and crossed first and then the
others, and then we judged the sledge might do it. I expect it

would have sunk like a stone if the ice had given way, but we had to get over here or nowhere.

The snow came down thickly now and we plugged ahead, steering by compass for the small piedmont tongue where we had been held up two days on our arrival. Suddenly we seemed to run into a snow slope – and by a mighty expenditure of energy we got the sledge up on to the tongue and were safely on fixed ice for the time.

We soon got the tent pitched, for there was not much wind, and had some tea. I will quote my diary.

'We were all in a cold sweat – for the work is very hard, and yet you don't keep warm. However, we got into our bags and were soon warm, if damp. This blizzard was but temporary, and about 4 p.m. it blew over to the west. I crossed the tongue to see the descent on the other side. It was about five feet down a steep snow slope. Beyond was a narrow shear crack with two seals, but the big crack at the end of the tongue went farther east. We pulled over the glacier and down the slope past the seals without difficulty. Then on a little farther and saw a crack to our right. It seemed only about a foot wide, and I was testing this weak spot with the ski-stick, when the soft snow on which I was standing collapsed and I went into the water. Luckily I grabbed Deb's hand, and Forde and Gran got my harness. I was jerked out like a cork from a bottle and was never so near flying! None saw the others pull, and they all thought I felt very light! We plugged on to the east and came to the main wavy crack – an ugly blighter 30 feet across of mushy water. Luckily this also narrowed at the bend, and after some searching we pulled over him also.

'I was getting jolly tired here. However, we could see our destination at last and so pushed on. A keen wind came up from the south-west and swept over the 100-foot glacier wall to the south, driving snow across our course. We crossed a little crack which Debenham thought was new since the snowfall! To our left were many birds about a mile away and black patches of ominous appearance were showing. Debenham climbed on the sledge and was sure it was open water, and I agreed, but we couldn't do anything and pushed on. I got some relief for my blessed tired legs by marching a longer stride, and we plugged on hoping it would hold firm another hour. However, at long length we began to see details in the never-ending glacier wall on our left – icicles, crevasses and snowdrifts – and at last could make out a feasible slope up on to the cape and felt safe. I had cramp from the pulling and couldn't move for a time.' It was, however, a distinct anti-climax when we got to the top of the cape to see that we had been misled by some queer shadows, that there was firm ice for at least seven miles and no sign of water anywhere! However, our experience at New Harbour made both Debenham and myself realise the risk we were running if the break-up of the ice – now long overdue – had eventuated.

'*Monday, January* 15, 1912; the day on which we were to be relieved. Nary a relief – nor any sign of it, and skuas squawking round us!

'We surveyed our cape expecting to find lots of pools of water, but there is none anywhere. Everything is covered with snow except the big boulders and three patches of gravel – of which we have annexed the largest.'

When we arrived each was inhabited by a pair of skua gulls – which we may call White, Black, and Gray. The Whites had one egg, the Blacks a young chick, and the Grays two eggs. The history of these families was pathetic in the extreme.

We dispossessed the Blacks, and I put young Blackie in a new nest – just as well made as his own – which I scraped out a little distance away. The parents fled squawking and left the chicken cruising about on strong stumpy legs with the head low like an apteryx. All night long it yelled for food, so next day I transferred it to the Whites' nest near the warm egg. Meanwhile Debenham set up the blubber stove on a rock ledge near by, to get to which he crossed the Grays' nest rather frequently. They resented this, but sensibly made the best of a bad job and ate up *their* eggs.

The further history of young Blackie was chronicled by the Sledge Poet:

> 'Lo! A miracle hath happened,'
> said returning Skua-White,
> 'Here's our nest just full of chicken,
> full of howling appetite.'
> Said Skua-White unto his mate,
> 'For fear this should become a habit
> We'd better eat our egg. Besides,
> you may be very sure he'd grab it.'

> So little Blackie reigned supreme
> Until one day when he was fed
> By the kind and humane leader,
> Foster father, foster feeder,
> On rich and tasty lumps of blubber,
> His little tummy stretched like rubber,
> Stretched too much . . . and now *he's* dead.

The skuas are the most quarrelsome birds I know. They would fight for hours over the carcase of a freshly killed seal before they realised there was enough food for ten times as many skuas – and by this time the flesh would be frozen so hard they could make no impression on it. The penguins have their own peculiar propensities, while the seals used to amaze us by their callousness. The day after we reached Cape Roberts we killed a large seal and cut it up while another twenty yards away watched us quite casually and did not budge for hours.

There was nothing much to do on the cape. It was triangular in shape, and about half a mile long. It rose about 50 feet above the sea ice. The broad base of the triangle was covered with snow which gradually merged into the Piedmont Glacier. There was no ice wall here, so that the glacier was presumably stagnant at this corner. The great granite tors of the cape were all flattened, showing that they had been planed off by a former extension of the ice sheet. Debenham spent some time making a detailed plane table survey. I fixed several theodolite stations, but as the days went by our life settled into a monotonous round.

I cut the meals down to two a day. We had plenty of seal meat and biscuit, but all the other stores were approaching their last week.

We used to have supper about 7 p.m. Every other day it consisted of a half ration of pemmican – for though seal meat is not so black as it's painted (and it's very black indeed), yet we had eaten little else for a month, and were all heartily sick of it. Then we turned in and used to yarn or read till about 3 a.m., when we managed to get to sleep. We turned out at noon and had a biscuit and seal lunch. During the afternoon we used to walk over the cape and inspect the cracks in the sea ice. One man was kept fairly busy cutting up seal meat, while the cook coaxed the stove to cook the fry.

Debenham was our only smoker, and certainly found tobacco a great solace. I had brought socks instead of tobacco, and had looked forward to jeering at him when his tobacco and socks gave out. Unfortunately our socks lasted much better this trip as our boots were stronger, and I never used my spare socks!

Gran started a drama – a great 'nature play', full of storms and wrecks with a strong substratum of melodrama. It was called *Tangholman Lighthouse* and we used to urge him to fill it full of incident and cut out the 'nature' part of it. I read *Martin Chuzzlewit* for the nth time and found it, as always, very interesting; while Forde tackled *Incomparable Bellairs* – a book which charmed Gran – but luckily Forde made it last a very long time.

We played chess with our cardboard pieces. I think we were fairly even, though Debenham often tried risky openings, to my advantage. The place of Seaman Evans as Society Entertainer was taken by Gran. His varied adventures in Arctic seas, among the Andes, in Turkey, Venezuela, and other of the less known regions of the earth interested us much. He was, I remember, very anxious to experience the delights of 'station life' as portrayed by Debenham.

January 20 was Gran's birthday. I was sorry I couldn't return his kindly present (of Savoy sauce, &c.), but I told him I would give him a ship during the day. The Sledge Poet contributed the following Birthday Ode dealing with Gran's avowed Nietzschean principles; which is here published – if the Editor thinks fit – with Gran's gracious permission.

ODE TO TRYGGVE
on his 23rd birthday, Cape Roberts
(*chanted at ye Full Pemmican Feast*)

O Tryggve Gran, O Tryggve Gran,
I would thou wert a moral man.
   And yet since we
   (The other three)
Are just as moral as can be,
A *soupçon de diablerie*
Improves our little company.

O Tryggve Gran, a holy calm
Is most essential in a psalm;
But prose should be a thought less calmer
When elevated into drama.

And yet though we
(The other three)
Are critical to a degree,
We wish success some future day
To the first Polar 'Nature Play'.

O Tryggve Gran, thou art a man
Who hath compressed within a span
Of three and twenty years, such deeds
That hearing which, each man's heart bleeds
 Among us three;
 And yet though we
Are kind to every girl we see,
I have no doubt each lovely creature
Would rather help *you* follow Nietzsche!

O Tryggve Gran, you should be dead
A-many years ago – instead
Of which, he saves you oft,
That 'Little Cherub up Aloft'.
 And therefore we
 (The other three)
In this new principle agree
(As with your luck no man can quarrel)
'Twill serve us best to be unmoral!!!

I was just writing the last line of the poem (?) when Gran yelled out 'Ship Ho!' We had seen ships many times already, but he was certain of this, so we turned out, and there under the fang of Erebus we could see some topmasts. Later we could make out three masts and black smoke – so we knew it was the good old *Terra Nova*, and not the *Fram*, which burned smokeless oil fuel.

We set about elevating our flag farther up the glacier. We took it up a long way, nearly to the top as we thought. On our return we saw it was only one quarter of the way up, a good example of the trickiness of snow slopes in this respect. I arranged night-watches to observe any signals or sledge parties, and we turned in hoping to be aboard in twenty-four hours.

[Nay, gentle reader, you are not at the end of my narrative; it was just twenty-four *days* before we were relieved!]

Next day she was in much the same position, about twenty miles away across the screw pack and broken floes. About two miles away a great crack stretched north and south. It was fully eight miles long, and seemed to presage the breaking up of the sea ice.

On the 22nd we could not see the ship. A strong south wind sprang up and the gradually clouding sky seemed to portend a blizzard. 'The stronger the better,' I wrote, 'if it will only drive out this blessed floe.' We took a few photographs. There were two Emperor penguins moulting on each side of our cape, but Debenham reported that they were too frightful to photo! Forde and I had a day with my stereo-camera taking various interesting details around the cape – planed granite blocks, pressure ice in the bay; and then the Emperors, awful as they were, several seal and berg pictures, &c.; but sad to relate all these negatives were smashed when the sledge fell over the glacier cliff.

I did not entertain the idea of trying to reach Pennell across the screw pack. We should get into a more precarious region each mile, and we could not communicate with the ship to ensure her awaiting us. Pennell could send a party, with safety at either end, if he desired. I was, however, very glad later to find that Pennell also considered the pack absolutely impossible for sledging from the ship.

We saw her during the next few days, and then she never showed up again.

On the 27th a blizzard started, which we hoped would move out the ice. It tore our sledge flags badly, so that we brought them down from our distress signal 350 feet up the glacier, leaving only the big depôt flag there.

It was very trying work with the blubber stove, for there was no shelter on the cape. When there was any wind the flames would blow out of the door and give no heat at all. The water did not get tepid in half an hour; whereas on a calm day it would boil in twenty minutes. I spent an hour trying to cook the fry and barely succeeded in melting the fat. We decided that the stove could not be used in high winds, even though it was in a sort of ice cave, and the cook sat in the door to keep the wind out!

Our rations had been cut down by half for a fortnight. Three or four biscuits a day, butter every other day, chocolate one stick; pemmican one-eighth; sugar and tea two-thirds. However, we had plenty of seal meat, and as we were not working we required much less food.

So passed several days. Gran spent all one afternoon making chupatties. The lid of the camera box was his pudding-board. He used the wheat meal 'thickers' for dough, and collared our allowance of raisins. The cakes were cut out with the rim of a cup, and then fried in a mixture of butter, fat, blubber, and soot. Anyhow the result was highly successful, though the inside was somewhat wet and the whole cake I should now consider distinctly heavy!

Each day we started the last bag of something precious. First the pemmican, then the chocolate, then the butter. Only one seal had been visible for some days, and I decreed her doom. She lay on a large piece of ice which was rising and falling with the swell. We reached this across an ice island, surging about in a large pool. In spite of all this movement, no more of the ice moved north as far as we could judge.

On the evening of February 1st I held a council. Captain Scott's instructions read: 'I am of the opinion that the retreat should not be commenced until the bays have refrozen, probably towards the end of March. An attempt to retreat overland might involve you in difficulties – whereas you could build a stone hut, provision it with seal meat and remain in safety in any convenient station on the coast.'

However, he gave me permission to begin the retreat in February if we were not relieved in January, and I began to prepare for this event, for I felt sure we could traverse the piedmont glacier.

Cracks seemed to be spreading on the sea ice even while one was watching it. The surging ice-blocks in the tide-crack, now twenty feet wide, rose several feet. Now and again a huge shock, as of a big rock bumping on another, announced a new crack, while a constant roar, like that of a distant lion, announced the periods of maximum of the swell rolling in from twenty miles away.

On February 3 Debenham, Gran, and I climbed the glacier slope behind our camp to prospect for a path. We roped up and proceeded about three miles southward, keeping well behind the crevasses. These are numerous on the steep seaward slope, but we met with none on the fairly level ground, though we could see them just below us. The surface was not very good, usually two inches deep in snow and occasionally a foot deep. This did not promise easy sledging; but the snow was dry now, and I was going to cut down the weights to a minimum.

We could see open water about twenty miles off, but a huge mass of ice pack was apparent as far north as we could see. There seemed to be a broad belt of pack, at least sixty miles long, which was quite absent in January 1902.

Obviously our exploration of Terra Nova Bay was impossible now, and it looked as if the ship would never reach us at Cape Roberts. With good luck we might cross the piedmont glacier to Cape Bernacchi in a few days, and Pennell might find it easier to reach us there, while we should at any rate be nearer to head-quarters. There was also a week's food there, and we had now only a fortnight's sledging stores left.

On February 4, Gran and I explored the sea ice below the pied-mont for about four miles to the southward. We passed through the fifteen bergs in the little bay, and then got among the screw pack. This was covered with snow and afforded us extremely heavy going, as may be imagined. Near the shore was a perfect network of new cracks with the ice 'working' all the time. Below the glacier wall was a deep tide crack four feet wide, but where some ice blocks had fallen in we managed to get across to fixed ice. As a result of this journey I decided to march first along the sea ice, and then climb up the piedmont at this point.

Next morning I wrote a long letter to Pennell which we all signed. We made a depôt on the highest point of the cape, and fixed a flag alongside with the letter in a little tin match-box. The journal for Captain Scott I left in the food cairn in my ditty-bag. I remorselessly weeded out everyone's gear. We took nothing but what we stood up in, and our notes and the instruments. Luckily most of Debenham's and all Gran's negatives were films, but I had to leave nearly all my plates and my cherished Brown-ing. I knew we had some bad crevassed country to traverse – thirty miles of this – and then I expected thirty miles of coast work, largely over moraine and rock, where we should have to portage the sledge and all our gear on our backs. This would bring us to Butter Point, whence our route was the same as in the previous summer. With a light sledge it was just possible we might be able to raise it if it slipped down a crevasse; and this was quite a probable event, for in traversing along a piedmont glacier the party moves *parallel* to the crevasses. One thus reaches them imperceptibly, and the whole party with its outfit may be marching over a crevasse, whereas in crossing them at right angles this is rarely the case.

We turned our backs finally on Cape Roberts at 11 a.m. on February 5. Our flag waved bravely, and below it was the cairn of stones covering the food left there by Scott's orders. If we had to return it would give us a breathing space; but I never saw the cape again. For many months the flag was left in solitude. The screw pack never broke adrift that winter. In the next spring six desperate men sledging southward, to more endurable – though, as they thought, no less solitary – quarters, here found the first news of the main party. Our depôt possibly saved Petty Officer Browning's life. It certainly gave the Northern Party their first bearable day for many months. Brave old flag – it hangs in Tewkesbury in Priestley's home, and there my old Browning was restored to me after many months!

So we marched on. We were all stiff and out of training, and the sledge did not pull easily, but we reached the tide crack and crossed it much more readily than I expected. After lunch we pulled up the steep slope of the glacier and to our delight found the surface grow harder almost every hour. But other troubles were upon us. So much so that for three days I felt it doubtful if anyone would ever read my diary! However, on the evening of the 8th I wrote up the 5th (and succeeding days) as follows.

'Then quite suddenly we came on huge crevasses all round the shop. Some open – which I took care not to keep too close to, and others bridged. They seemed too wide to do anything with, but after cautioning the others to tread quietly, I prodded across safely, though the ice axe pushed in all its length easily. Then the others followed and the sledge after. Gran fell in at the near edge and saw the straight wall. Several of these were over 20 feet wide, but we had to chance them, and tested them all before the sledge started. Then we marched along between two fairly visible ones and luckily they didn't join. The surface got flatter and they died out gradually, so that we made fair progress. We came to another enclosed snow basin, and I felt sure the seaward slope would be safer. So it was, though Forde went down a small one. We pulled along this up to a sort of col about 8 miles from Cape Roberts, and here, as we were well beyond the mouth of the Big Valley, we camped.

'My only fear now was that bad weather might cover the glacier with soft snow, for I felt that all the big crevasses would be lidded and the little ones could hardly swallow the lot of us.'

'Next morning we made the harness traces longer, so that only one man at a time need cross even a wide crevasse. We had to traverse the mouth of another large valley glacier. Three of these debouched on the piedmont glacier from the Western Mountains, and the pressure from the northernmost (the Debenham Glacier) was responsible for the crevasses of March 5. The second valley glacier was not so large, but we anticipated trouble. We had a stiff pull uphill for three-quarters of a mile, but some of the snow was so hard that the sledge runners made no mark! This was an ideal surface, for one's feet did not slip on it, though occasionally the sledge skidded. We were about 700 feet above the sea here and entered a col just below a huge snow hill.

'Afterwards we were cutting around the hill aforesaid when suddenly appeared many crevasses. So we deviated abruptly and ascended the hill sharply. We encountered three, into one of which I fell, but they were not very wide. The moral of this is: don't go for the break of a hill facing and near the sea, but stick to humdrum grades if possible; if not, still don't go for the break of a hill!'

The somewhat frivolous tone of the above note is evidence that it was written when we had traversed the worst of the piedmont. It was always the case 'down South'. One never got photographs or 'instantaneous pen-pictures' of anything really exciting. It was always a case of 'Get a move on, and get out of this good and quick', so that one's diary lost most where it would have been most interesting.

We were now behind Dunlop Island and about 1250 feet up the piedmont. We were astonished to find that the floe had all broken up to south'ard. Long curved cracks parallel to the coast marked where pieces were continually floating off. We congratulated ourselves on our safe position on the piedmont, for we should have sledged into this without knowing it, had we continued much farther on the sea ice. Small bergs looking just like white yachts dotted the open water, which seemed to extend south to Castle Rock. There was no sign of the *Terra Nova*. We began to think she had come to grief, for Pennell knew we were free to move off on February 1.

After supper Debenham got out his plane table and continued his survey. He was at first much puzzled by the position of his station on the stranded Glacier Tongue to the south-east. He realised soon, however, that it had twisted round, and was even now preparing to continue its journey to the Nirvana of warm northern waters.

We had been blessed with sunshine the last few days. I do not believe we should have managed to dodge the crevasses otherwise, for in dull weather you cannot tell any difference between a ten-foot hollow or a ten-foot hummock when it is only a yard or two away. However, as a result of the sunshine Forde had a bad touch of snow-blindness. Debenham got out the medical chest. He ground up some $ZnSO_4$, picked it up on a paint-brush, and dropped it in the corner of Forde's eye. Later in the night I gave Forde another dose, for the pain is pretty considerable.

The next day my right eye was sore and watering in spite of the amber glasses, and I feared I was to become a patient also. We plugged along over an absolutely level snow plain, where Debenham, without warning, dropped into a crevasse over which I had crossed without puncturing the lid.

In the afternoon my eyes gave out, and I put bandages on the right eye, and gave up the lead to Debenham. It was an astonishing relief to cease from staring at the glaring surface, and either pull along with shut eyes or keep one eye on the gratefully dirty back of Debenham's white woollen jacket!

Debenham led us safely past three huge crevasses, and we halted for a spell among a cluster of smaller ones. That evening we climbed up the snow hill behind Gneiss Point about 1350 feet above the sea, and as we had now passed the third valley glacier, I felt we had finished with the crevasses for the time being. We camped on hard snow and Debenham treated me for snow-blindness.

The zinc sulphate may truthfully be described as an 'eye-opener', but later the cocaine in the mixture calms things down! You are advised 'to keep your face cool', but unfortunately I had to keep my head in the bag to get warm. However, Forde was pretty right next day and my eyes soon stopped aching, though everything appeared double for many hours!

On the 8th we reached the land near Cape Bernacchi. There was a steep ice slope 200 feet high at an angle of 30°. Luckily it was much honeycombed and sun-eaten. We put grummets (rope brakes) on the sledge and managed to get it down by 1.30 p.m. We had a very cheerful lunch, for we knew the depôt was only a few miles south. Then we found an ice-foot all the way along the edge of the rocks and moraine which led us right to the Bernacchi cairn. This was a regular ice pathway about 20 yards wide. It was due to sea-ice which had become cemented to the shore, the tide crack being farther away from the rocks and defining that part of the floe which had lately drifted away to sea.

No one had visited our depôt. New Harbour was full of new broken floe, but a fine ice-foot seemed to promise well for our next march.

We stayed a day at Cape Bernacchi, for I wished to get a good station for the triangulation of this coast. Gran and I took the theodolite to the top of a hill 2900 feet high at the north-east end of Dry Valley. We named this Hjort's Hill in honour of the maker of our trusty primus lamp. As we were climbing this hill Gran swore he could see the ship off Cape Evans through the binoculars. It seemed clear to me also – smoke, cross-trees, hull, and 3 masts, but after an hour or so we decided it was only a miraged crack in the Barne glacier. Our disappointment was very keen, though I am now not so sure that we did not really see the ship, some forty miles away. We could see the twenty-foot débris cones behind the hut quite easily on a clear day.

I wrote the usual letter to Pennell. I had left two in Granite Harbour and two on the piedmont now, though it did not look as if any would ever be read. All through the 10th we skirted New Harbour, finding a fairly feasible ice-foot between the granite-strewn slopes and the open water. We came across a Spratt's biscuit box here – which was evidently left by the 1902 expedition. We saved a considerable detour by crossing the head of the harbour on the sea ice and camped below the Kukri Hills, where I halted rather early to get a round of angles. We were held up here all next day by a snowstorm, which we spent reading and sewing.

On the 12th we rounded the Kukri Hills, and when the ice-foot petered out we were luckily able to continue on the sea ice. We had lunch amid a colony of over forty seals, and then reached the southern side of the Ferrar Glacier, where we camped on a rather wet and muddy heap of 'road metal' moraine.

We were now safely round New Harbour, and curiously enough crossed the sea ice at the mouth of the Ferrar on the same day of the year as when we nearly went out to sea on our first sledge journey. Henceforward we knew our route. We had plenty of food at the Butter Point depôt, which we reached that evening, and knew we could reach the old *Discovery* hut before the end of the month.

This depôt had been blown over and wrecked generally. We took some pemmican, butter, and chocolate, and next day proceeded south along the Butter Point piedmont, leaving another note for Pennell. The surface was much better than the preceding year, but curiously enough we found quite a number of small crevasses. Debenham and Forde fell in together in one of these, and the burly Irishman jammed so tightly, it was quite a business pulling him out of it! In the evening we reached the Strand Moraines. These are great piles of ancient silt, gravel, and erratic blocks which were dropped here by the ancestor of the present Koettlitz Glacier. At the southern end of these moraines – which were several miles long – was quite a large lake. We tobogganed down to this and across to a nice little gravelly delta just made for the tent. We found that the open water reached just to this point, the sound still being frozen to south'ard, though obviously breaking away in great sheets. I wrote that night: 'No *Terra Nova*. We should have been picked up at Evans Coves (Terra Nova Bay) tomorrow.' We had the choice of two routes now. Either to cross the snout of the Blue Glacier, or to take to the sea ice and coast round the latter. We had done the former and knew it would only take a day. The latter might be quicker, though a great calved berg blocked the route about two miles ahead. Debenham preferred the glacier, the other two the sea ice. I made a bet with Gran that we couldn't get the sledge between the calved berg and the glacier without unloading it. This had a rather interesting outcome. I finally decided to keep to land ice on the principle of 'the Devil you know being preferable to the Devil you don't.'

It was annoying to find that the Blue Glacier had so completely changed its complexion in the twelve months. In place of clear blue ice where one could see every crevasse, it was one uniform sheet of smooth snow, and we soon began to fall into the crevasses.

In a very short time we had all been in a couple of times, and it was evidently an unhealthy region for sledging. I deviated to the edge of the glacier to try and lower the sledge on to the sea ice; and we soon got abreast of the calved berg, where we halted a few minutes.

Away to the south-east we could see a blizzard coming up, and I wanted to get a snug camp in the gullies south of the Blue Glacier. We had an argument as to who had won the bet, for there was a high jumble of ice where the calf jammed the parent glacier. The other two decided in my favour, and so we pushed off on the top of the glacier edge to the wished-for camp. Gran was dissatisfied with the court's decision and kept glancing back to the scene under discussion. Just as we were dipping down the slope which cut off all view to northward he yelled out: 'Ship Ho!' – and there she was over the top of the black moraines.

'We turned back good and quick to retraverse the crevasses, for she was four miles off and we were afraid might miss us, as a snowstorm was brewing in the east. She steamed along past the berg and out along the floe. We pulled back hard, crossing crevasses carelessly, but not falling in much, and finally could make out that she had a flag on the gaff, apparently recognising us. We kept along the edge of the glacier till we could find a place to get down. Here was a drop of 30 feet, almost vertical, with a big tide crack and a tide pool at the bottom. Gran went down first, and then I got down half-way. Unluckily, as we were lowering the sledge Forde was pulled over by his harness and fell right on to Gran, who was squashed into the snow while the sledge came down on top of us. It nearly broke in the middle; however, we lugged it over to the ice and set off hot-foot over the two miles of ice. The ship now anchored near the floe and four men came to meet us. They harnessed up and told us the news. We heard that the Southern Party were going very well, that there was no sign of Amundsen, and that there had been no accidents of importance.' Also that they had not been able to communicate with Cape Evans until a week before, and had been unloading stores every available moment before they came over to search for us. And then the world's news at first hearing made us feel safer in the Antarctic. The disruption of China, the Franco-German-English trouble in Morocco, the Italians and Turks in Tripoli, and the great strikes in

England. We had missed an eventful year during our sojourn in the peaceful regions of the South.

It was no easy business reaching the ship. The sea ice was rapidly breaking up, and moving off to the northward in great rectangular fragments. Finally the ship butted a cake of floe towards the fixed ice and held it there long enough to get the sledge over.

Once on board we made a dive for our mail. A pillow-case full for each of us, and all home news satisfactory.

We had been picked up just a month later than the date fixed by Captain Scott. We were now only a few hours' sail from Cape Evans, and looked forward to a change and the comforts of the hut. But the blizzard we had been watching caught us and was succeeded by many others, and not for ten days did we get near the hut. In fact, during the ensuing three weeks there were only three hours in which we could get into touch with headquarters, before we turned our faces to the north.

So ends my narrative. During the six months that we had spent sledging we had mapped a hundred miles of coast and hinterland, our detailed surveys extending in places over thirty miles from the sea. Our general scientific results are briefly described in the final chapters of the book. All our collections were safely brought back to England in the *Terra Nova* in 1913.

What is the best personal result of our sledge journeys? A group of friends who are closer than brothers. Here's luck to my mates – to Debenham, Wright, and Gran!

Map of the region of the Western Journeys: north-western portion

Map of the region of the Western Journeys: north-eastern portion

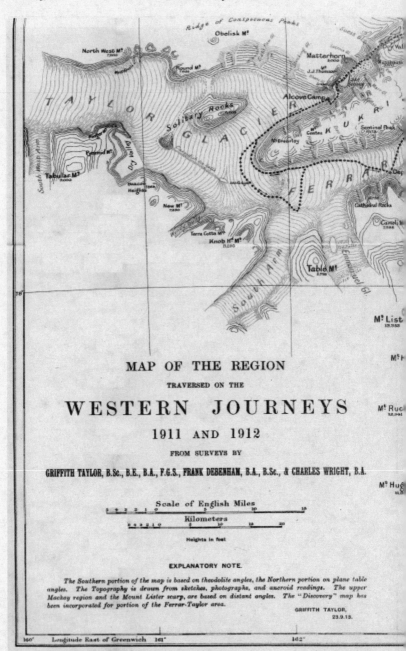

MAP OF THE REGION

TRAVERSED ON THE

WESTERN JOURNEYS

1911 AND 1912

FROM SURVEYS BY

GRIFFITH TAYLOR, B.Sc., B.E., B.A., F.G.S., FRANK DEBENHAM, B.A., B.Sc., & CHARLES WRIGHT, B.A.

Scale of English Miles

Kilometers

Heights in feet

EXPLANATORY NOTE.

The Southern portion of the map is based on theodolite angles, the Northern portion on plane table angles. The Topography is drawn from sketches, photographs, and aneroid readings. The upper Mackay region and the Mount Lister scarp, are based on distant angles. The "Discovery" map has been incorporated for portion of the Ferrar-Taylor area.

GRIFFITH TAYLOR,
23.9.13.

Map of the region of the Western Journeys: south-western portion

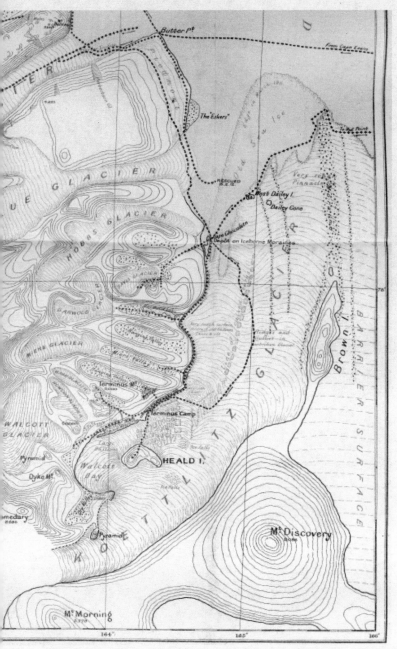

Map of the region of the Western Journeys: south-eastern portion

SPRING DEPÔT JOURNEY

by Commander Edward R. G. R. Evans, R.N.

On September 9, 1911, the depôt party, consisting of Lieutenant Evans, Gran, and Forde, left Cape Evans to dig out the depôts at Safety Camp and Corner Camp. As later on the dog teams were to take out quantities of stores to Corner Camp it was deemed advisable to visit this spot, and if necessary put new flags to mark it, and build up the cairn.

The party started at 8 a.m. on ski, in beautifully fine, clear weather. We saw remarkable earth shadows on the clouds over Erebus.

Nelson came with us to Glacier Tongue, and while we had four men we travelled at 3 miles per hour; directly he left our speed decreased materially.

There is no doubt a four-man team has enormous advantages over one of three. The increase in permanent weights is very slight, consisting only of a sleeping-bag and a small personal bag; the only disadvantage is the difference in the time taken to cook meals. When marching against time the three-man unit saves nearly half an hour a day.

We passed Meares driving home from Hut Point, but he was half a mile inshore and didn't come out on account of the dogs, who are very hard to control if they get near another sledge team.

There was no object in camping for lunch on the sea ice, and we pushed on to Hut Point for lunch. The distance by sledge-meter was 13 miles 300 yards (statute 15 miles 264 yards). We found Meares had left everything at Hut Point in splendid order, and we soon had the blubber stove going and a meal cooked. At 5.15, it being quite fine, we repacked sledge and marched 4 miles out towards Safety Camp. We stopped about 9 p.m., had supper, and turned into our bags.

Our camp was on the sea ice, and we noticed an extraordinary change in the temperature after rounding Cape Armitage; the thermometer at Hut Point showed −21° and on camping it was −42°, with a sharp biting breeze coming away from the Barrier. Minimum temp. −45°.

On the following day we started off in a light easterly wind, temperature −36.5°, and hauled our sledge to Safety Camp, which is distant from Cape Evans 22 miles 452 yards (statute). We dug out the depôt, tallied stores, and then put up a wind recorder of Simpson's.

It was interesting to see how Safety Camp had drifted up during the winter. It took many hours to dig it out, and although this depôt contained, amongst other things, 73 bales of fodder, each of 107 lbs. weight, the snow had completely covered it.

After lunch we took 6 tins of paraffin from here and marched 8 miles 641 yards between 5.30 and 8.30 p.m. At 9 p.m. the thermometer showed 45.2° below zero.

The temperature fell a good deal during the night and we could scarcely sleep. Gran, using an eiderdown bag inside his sleeping-bag, was warmer than the other two of us, but later on our journey the eiderdown bag was like a board and he had very little if any advantage from it.

On September 11, at 7 a.m., the temperature was −58.2°, the minimum for the night being −62.3°.

At 9 a.m. we started off, and marched 5½ miles by sledge-meter (statute 6 miles 530 yards).

We built cairns at every night and lunch camp, and small 'top-hats' whenever we had a halt. Corner Camp is very difficult to find, as landmarks are so often obscured by cloud and drift in this vicinity. One of our objects was to mark the track clearly.

We stopped for lunch at 2; the land was entirely obscured by mist, although the sky was clear overhead. Thermometer at −43°.

The surface in the forenoon though variable was fairly good; we marched another 5¾ miles by our sledge-meter during the after-noon and camped at 8.30, the weather gradually becoming worse, wind from W.S.W., with low drift. By the time our tent was pitched a fair blizzard was on us. Temperature −34.5°.

By 10 p.m. the tent was well drifted up, weather squally, but all snug inside. We had with us the new pattern double tent, which is a horrible thing − it shortens the space down so, and is the most trying thing to spread in a breeze. To quote my diary:

'There is a sharp difference of opinion as to the value of this invention. Naturally the maker, Petty Officer Evans, is very proud of it, but the other seamen hate it. However, we shall give it a good test now, likewise the ski-shoes, which I like immensely if they are the right size; if too big they are trodden down and spoilt very soon, but if too small one's toes get frost-bitten where the shoes pinch.'

Tuesday, September 12, 1911. – Blizzard continued till 8 a.m., when wind decreased to force 5; it however still continued to drift until 10 a.m., when wind dropped to force 3, weather overcast and snowing. Temperature −19°; the minimum for the night being −40°. The wind increased to force 6 with drift at 11 a.m., but by 2 p.m. it was fine enough to make a start, which we did in a biting cold wind. We built a good cairn here, but it was cold work.

We marched this day till 8.30 p.m., when it was very nearly dark and very misty. Surface bad after the blizzard; we covered 7 miles 783 yards (statute). Temperature on camping −46°.

September 13, 1911. – The diary continues: Having shivered in my bag all night, at 5 o'clock I told the others to get up, both of them being awake. We cooked a meal and prepared to scout for Corner Camp. On going out to take the meteorological observations found min. temp. −73.3°. Present temp. −58°. I don't think anyone was surprised, as it was very cold during the night. I got a glimpse of Observation Hill and the sun, and I found the bearing of the former was N. 70 W. instead of N. 68 W., so we struck S.S.W. for a short distance and then saw the flagstaff of Corner Camp. On arriving at the depôt found the whole cairn buried thus:

so dug out all the forenoon and eventually got all stores out and tallied. We left one tin of biscuits here, two bags of treacle, six bags of butter, and six tins of paraffin. We put all biscuit tins and sacks of oats on end on the top of the cairn we built.

The complete tally of stores is:

Sledging biscuits	9 cases	Cocoa	6 bags
Butter	14 bags	Oil	11 cans
Cheese	6 bags	Oats	3 sacks
Tea	2 tins	Sugar	6 bags
Fodder	½ bale	Chocolate	6 bags
Pemmican	6 bags	Raisins	6 bags
Cereals	6 bags	Treacle	2 bags

The cairn is now like this:

We left at 5 p.m. and started to march to Hut Point – non-stop run – as I wished to get my gear nicely dried at C. Evans before going out with Meares on the 20th. We had no wish to remain at Corner Camp, as all the time we were digging it was drifting a little and blowing about 5, temperature −32° – about all we could 'stick'. After striking camp we marched till 10.30 p.m., doing 9.5 miles by sledge-meter. When 4 miles from Corner Camp the wind dropped to a calm. At 10.30 had pemmican and tea, then at midnight started off, and steering by stars kept on a W.N.W. course till about 5 a.m. (September 14), when we had a light breakfast of tea and biscuit. Off again before 6, and continued marching until we came to the edge of the Barrier about 12.45. We did not stop at Safety Camp, but marched straight to Hut Point, arriving at 3 p.m. At the hut we had a meal of tea and chapatties which Forde made. We ate steadily till about 5.30, and then discussed marching to C. Evans. Had we started we might have got in by 3 a.m., but not before; but we had marched all through one night, and besides digging out Corner Camp we had marched 30 miles 40 yds. by sledge-meter, equal to 34.6 stat. miles, which on top of a day's work was good enough for me. We therefore prepared the hut for the night. Turned in about 7 and soon fell asleep. Gran woke Forde and myself about 10 p.m. with cocoa and porridge, both of which were splendid. We then slept till 9 a.m. on the 15th.

September 15, 1912. – Turned out at 9 a.m., cooked a fine breakfast, and then washed all the cooking gear, cleared out the hut, got on our marching gear, and at 2 p.m. started off for C. Evans. We had an easy march on the sea ice and arrived back at 9.25 p.m. Found that the sledge party Capt. Scott is taking W. had left that morning, and that I was not going on my second trip to Corner Camp as the dogs will not start for another month. I found by comparison that my watch had lost two seconds since I left nearly a week ago. Turned in about 11.30 p.m., and was soon snoring.

Marching average	m.	yds.
Sat. Sept. 9, whole day	19	1186
Sun. Sept. 10, half day	8	641
Mon. Sept. 11, whole day	12	1588
Tues. Sept. 12, half day	7	783
Wed. Sept. 13, whole day	3	1786
Thu. Sept. 14, whole day	34	1040
Fri. Sept. 15, half day	15	264
	102	248

Time out of hut, 6½ days. Allow off for two diggings and blizzard 3½ days, equals 5 days' marching.

THE LAST YEAR AT CAPE EVANS

by Surgeon E. L. Atkinson, R. N.

CHAPTER I

In writing the record of the second year I must give all credit to A. Cherry-Garrard. It is entirely from his diaries and from the official diary kept by him that these records are compiled. To make matters clear it would be as well to go over the events after the return of the first Southern Party. It consisted of A. Cherry-Garrard, C. S. Wright, Petty Officer Keohane, and myself. We returned to Cape Evans on January 28, 1912. The orders then given to me by Captain Scott were for myself and Demetri, with two dog teams (if Meares were returning in the ship), to proceed as far south as possible, taking into consideration the times of return of the various parties, and in order to hasten the return of the final party. The dog teams were in no manner a relief expedition and were simply meant to bring the last party home more speedily.

On our return to Cape Evans the ship had not as yet been communicated with. Indeed communication was not established until February 4, owing to bad sea ice intervening.

On February 9 we started landing stores from the ship, and in this all hands were employed.

On February 13, the sea ice having started to break up in the south bay, I judged it advisable to make a start with the two dog teams for Hut Point, 15 miles to the south of Cape Evans, a journey across sea ice. It was from this point that the Barrier could be reached and the return of the Southern Party hastened by the dog teams. The two dog teams, Demetri the Russian boy, and myself were kept at Hut Point by bad weather until February 19. On the night of the 13th the weather began to abate. At 3.30 a.m., while we were in our sleeping-bags, Petty Officer Crean reached the hut and brought in the news of Lieutenant Evans's breakdown beyond Corner Camp. Crean had done a remarkable walk of over 35 statute miles to get what relief he could, leaving Lashly to look after Evans, who was in a very serious state and with only a small supply of food left. Within half an hour of his arrival a very thick blizzard came on and it was impossible to make a start. The blizzard kept on the whole day, and it was not until 4.30 on the afternoon of the 20th that a start was possible. Demetri and I then made a start with both dog teams. The weather was exceedingly thick and we could only see a very short distance. We travelled, with one rest for the dogs, until 4.30 p.m. the next day. Then the weather being too thick to travel we camped, judging that we were somewhere near the camp with Lieutenant Evans and Lashly. During a temporary clearness we saw the flag which Lashly had put up on the sledge about 2 miles away. We found Lashly and Evans within the tent. During the whole of that night and the next day the blizzard continued and it was impossible to travel. The story of Lashly's and Crean's devotion will no doubt be told in another place. Lashly looked after Evans, and his nursing arrangements were splendid.

At 3 a.m. on the morning of the 22nd we made a start, Evans being in his sleeping-bag on the sledge. The teams travelled well, and with only one break 15 miles from Hut Point we reached home and safety for him at midday, after 5 hours' actual travelling. Considering his condition, I judged that if I were able to obtain help from Cape Evans it would be better for me to stay with Lieutenant Evans and for Wright or Cherry-Garrard to take my place with the dog teams and to go south with Demetri.

On February 23 Demetri went to Cape Evans, and that same night Wright, Cherry-Garrard and Davies the carpenter came up to Hut Point. Having regard to his work, it was better that Wright should not take command of the dog teams, and so it was settled that Cherry-Garrard should do this. After due consideration of weights and the probabilities of the date by which the final party could return to certain depôts, it was decided that the dogs should take 24 days' food for themselves and 21 days' food for the two men, carrying in addition two weeks' surplus supplies for the Southern Party complete and certain delicacies which they had asked for. The totals brought the weight carried by each team up to the most economical travelling limit for the time of year. As there was no dog food in any of the depôts except at Corner Camp or along any of the route, it meant that, counting in this supply, 24 days was the limit of their usefulness.

Again, it cannot be too firmly emphasized that the dog teams were meant merely to hasten the return of the Southern Party and by no means as a relief expedition.

The next two days, February 24 and 25, were devoted to giving the dogs a much-needed rest and to making up provisions and dog food. Indeed, owing to bad weather, it would have been imposs-ible to have made a start on these days. The following record of the journey of the two dog teams is taken entirely from Cherry-Garrard's diary.

February 26. – Since it looked fair last night, at 2 a.m. they decided to start. There was a strong wind and a fair amount of drift at the time. The dogs proceeded well to Safety Camp and then on to the biscuit depôt, 15 miles from Hut Point. There they were rested for a short while and finally started at 6 p.m., and reached Corner Camp at 10 p.m. The dogs were working splendidly and together, and completed the distance of 30 geographical miles for the day in thick weather and with a head wind.

On February 27 they again had a head wind and low drift; they made good 10 miles and then camped for tea; proceeding after-wards over a very good surface but with bad light, they completed 18½ miles for the day, seeing but one cairn, which they only made out when it was 20 yards away. They camped in the nick of time, as a blizzard broke upon them and they had great difficulty in getting the tent pitched. The dogs pulled well and were very fit and not done up. It may be noted in passing that the difficulties of camping and breaking camp are enormously increased in bad weather when there is a unit of only two men instead of four.

Next day, February 28, they started at 7.45 p.m. on a beautifully clear day and ran 10 miles up to the time they camped for tea. The surface was good, with very large sastrugi. On one of these, while Demetri was ahead, Cherry-Garrard's sledge upset; he had to unload the sledge partially in order to right it. As it was righted the team took charge. Cherry-Garrard clung to the sledge but lost his driving stick, and it was not until the team had taken him over a mile to the south that they were stopped. The weather was coming on thick, and it was an anxious time as their weekly bag, cooker and tent poles had been left behind. Eventually both teams returned and the sledge was re-packed. A blizzard came on and they were unable to travel until the next afternoon. There was a strong wind and the temperature began falling on this day. They completed 16¾ miles for the day.

February 29 proved a good clear day and they reached the Bluff Depôt in latitude 79° south. The sledge-meters had been giving a great deal of trouble and did not tally; this, with the bad light, increased the difficulty of navigation enormously.

On March 1 they started about mid-day after giving the dogs a good rest, which they needed after their long runs of the previous days. They proceeded for 10 miles without seeing anything. The weather came on thick and they had to camp at 6.30 p.m. It cleared a little later and they made good two more miles. The party on this day saw a snowy petrel. The position of this bird so far south and away from food is remarkable.

On March 2 they had a cold and sleepless night with a low temperature and a blizzard blowing from the north-west. The rate of travel was so quick that the dogs' run was finished early and the two men had to spend an unusually long time in their sleeping-bags, which in this cold weather was bad for them and bad for their gear. About mid-day the weather cleared enough to let them start.

On March 4 they reached One Ton Depôt in the morning, travelling during a clear night and morning. A blizzard came on after their arrival and the temperature had fallen considerably. Cherry-Garrard, owing to the low temperature, found his glasses of no use and had to trust to Demetri to pick out the cairns. Owing to the cold weather and the thin coats of the dogs he rightly decided to give them more food.

On March 5, 6, 7, and 8 they had exceedingly cold weather and blizzard. On none of these days would it have been possible for them to proceed south had they wished to do so. This party had no minimum thermometer, but on most of the nights before the sun had set the temperature had fallen to nearly minus 40°, which probably meant a minimum temperature of between 40° and 50° for the night. The dogs were in bad condition and feeling the cold. Demetri also declared that he felt far from well. These days of bad weather left Cherry-Garrard with the alternative of holding on at the camp or of travelling south for one day and allowing one day to return to the One Ton Depôt. Owing to the difficulties of keeping the right line with dog teams, he very wisely decided to remain at One Ton Depôt, leaving himself with only 8 days' dog food to return on.

Strict injunctions had been given by Captain Scott that the dogs should not be risked in any way.

On March 10 they depôted their two weeks' supply of provisions for the Southern Party, including several smaller delicacies. One Ton was then supplied with sufficient man provisions for a party of five for over a month. On this same day they started their return journey at 8 a.m. after a very cold night. Their gear and sleeping-bags were all iced up and neither of the men in good condition. The dogs at the start went practically wild, Demetri's sledge crossing Cherry-Garrard's and smashing the sledge-meter adrift. They fought as they went in their harness and had no idea of direction. This continued for six or seven miles and then they got better. After this the weather became gradually overcast and navigation became difficult. After camping, they again proceeded slowly by compass, completing 23 miles for the day, but had no idea of their whereabouts at the end.

The next morning, March 11, the weather was so overcast that they could not start. Quoting from his diary: 'Started at 2 p.m. with just a litle patch of blue sky, but we did not know where we were going and stopped at 8 miles in a blizzard. I think we were turning circles most of the time.' During the night and morning of March 12 they had a very heavy blizzard and very low temperature. Demetri declared that he could see the Bluff and that they were right into the land. This meant that they would be amongst the ice pressure and crevasses. They steered east away from this, and the weather clearing slightly, they saw White Island and headed back toward this. The temperature now remained below minus 30 for the whole of the day and the dogs and men began to feel the effects of the low temperature and high winds.

On March 13 they got a point of land to steer upon, realising that they were well to the east of what their position ought to have been. They did 18 miles for the day and camped in a fog. The year was closing in and the time of the travelling day was much decreased. Demetri thought that he saw the flag of Corner Camp to the west and steered for it. Luckily the foot hills cleared and they were able to avoid the ice pressure and crevasses of White Island, for which they had been steering. The total run for the day was about 11 miles.

On March 14 they had a clear day and realised that they were a good deal out of their reckoning. Getting under way they saw what they thought was a cairn; making for it, they found it was a great open crevasse or chasm with pressure on the farther side miraged. They then made out south-east and crossed several big crevasses. Soon after this they saw the motor one mile to the east, and Corner Camp 2 miles beyond that. They ran on past Corner Camp and eventually reached the Biscuit Depôt 15 miles from Hut Point. On this day Demetri nearly fainted and declared that he was completely done. Their main anxiety now was whether the sea ice between the edge of the Barrier and Hut Point still remained in.

On March 15 they were held up all day at the Biscuit Depôt by a blizzard, Demetri's condition causing Cherry-Garrard great alarm.

On March 16, after a night of blizzard, they started at 8 a.m. They reached Hut Point late in the afternoon, meeting there Petty Officer Keohane and myself. Both men were in exceedingly poor condition, Cherry-Garrard's state causing me serious alarm. The dogs were frost-bitten, and miserably thin, while in many cases their harnesses were iced up and frozen to them. They were quite unfit for any further work that season.

Cherry-Garrard under the circumstances and according to his instructions was in my judgment quite right in everything that he did. I am absolutely certain no other officer of the Expedition could have done better.

On February 23, when Demetri went to Cape Evans to try and obtain help, he had a letter from me to Lieutenant Pennell, commanding the *Terra Nova*, conveying my request. After Cherry-Garrard and Demetri had left on the 26th, Lashly, Lieutenant Evans, Wright, and myself were left at Hut Point.

On February 29, the sea ice having gone out to within a quarter of a mile of Hut Point, the ship arrived. Lieutenant Evans in his sleeping-bag was placed on a sledge and removed on board the ship. She returned to Cape Evans, landing Wright and Lashly there, together with some stores. She then proceeded north to Evans Coves to try and pick up Lieutenant Campbell and his party. Lieutenant Evans's condition being still serious I had to accompany him. After several unsuccessful attempts to relieve Campbell, the ship returned to Cape Evans on March 4. Here, Keohane was picked up, and he and I were landed by the ship at Hut Point, Until the arrival of the dog teams on March 16 we occupied ourselves killing seals and laying in a store of meat and blubber before the return of the Southern Party. The ship, meanwhile, had proceeded north on a third attempt to relieve Campbell and his party. Owing to her small coal supply, she could not stay in the Sound later than March 8, and thus she was unable to notify us at the base of her success or failure in this undertaking.

On March 16, Cherry-Garrard and Demetri came in and reported that they had seen no sign of the Polar Party; they also reported the early break of the season, exceedingly low temperatures and the bad weather on the Barrier. The condition of both men was such that it was impossible for them to do any further sledging that season. I told Cherry-Garrard that we should have to make another journey to try and get to the Polar Party; he readily agreed and said that he would be quite ready himself after a few days' rest. The taking of Demetri, owing to his health, was out of the question. On the third day after his return Cherry-Garrard collapsed in the morning, suffering from an over-strained heart; it was a very sad blow to him to realise that he was unable to help during this anxious time, and it was a hard measure to have to tell him that further sledging that year was impossible for him.

Realising that something had to be done, I proposed to Keohane that he should come out alone with me. He was cheerful and willing and proved of the very greatest service during a very trying time.

We discussed fully the probable dates of the return of the party to certain points and the possibility of two men being able to render them material assistance. Owing to the bad light and the time of the year, the probabilities were that they could only be met at depôts.

On March 26 Keohane and I, having eighteen days' food for ourselves and the major portion of a week's ration for the Polar Party, started south. On the first day we made good about nine miles after a very hard pull. The temperature was exceedingly low but the weather fair. Our minimum thermometer failed on this journey, so that there was no accurate record of the temperatures. After a sleepless night we started at 8.30 and made good another nine miles. The day was overcast and there was no point to steer by. The weather continued cold and there was practically no sleep at night in the tent occupied by only two men.

On March 29 it was again overcast, with strong breeze; we made good eleven miles and then, the weather clearing, we realised that we were too far in to White Island amongst the pressure.

On the 30th we made out from White Island, then a few miles south of Corner Camp. We returned to the motor, taking up the sledge left there by Lieutenant Evans, and then on to Corner Camp. Taking into consideration the weather and temperatures and the time of the year, and the hopelessness of finding the party except at any definite point like a depôt, I decided to return from here. We depôted the major portion of a week's provisions to enable them to communicate with Hut Point in case they should reach this point. At this date in my own mind I was morally certain that the party had perished, and in fact on March 29 Captain Scott, 11 miles south of One Ton Depôt, made the last entry in his diary.

A partial blizzard sprang up and we set sail; with this help we made good 8 miles during the two hours of light remaining to us.

On March 31, snow was falling heavily and we got under way in a very bad light. Our condition was bad, as owing to the low temperatures we had got no sleep. We made good to the Biscuit Depôt, 15 miles from home, and then proceeded in the dusk for one more mile.

The next day, April 1, with a strong following breeze and a sail to help us, we reached Hut Point after dark. We were both glad to be in and to get some sleep. By this time all hope of the return of the Southern Party had been given up. Cape Evans was separated from us by open water and it was then impossible to get help from that quarter while, for all we knew, Campbell and his party had still not been relieved and were somewhere on the coast. I regarded their relief at this time as being of prime importance. To effect this it was essential to get help from Cape Evans, as at Hut Point we had two sick men and two men who were capable of sledging at that time of the year. We watched the Sound anxiously for any chance of being able to get across the sea ice to Cape Evans. Almost every day it froze over in a thin sheet, only to be swept away by high winds. The temperatures recorded at this time of the year were 10° to 15° lower at Hut Point than they had been in the previous season.

On April 10 the two Bays, one between Glacier Tongue and the Hutton Cliffs on the peninsula and the other between the Glacier Tongue and Cape Evans, having frozen over, I decided to make along the peninsula with Keohane and Demetri, lower ourselves over the cliffs and make for Cape Evans. Leaving Cherry-Garrard necessarily at Hut Point to look after the dogs, we made our way along the peninsula and had only slight difficulty in lowering ourselves and the sledge over the cliffs with the Alpine rope. On this occasion our luck was most distinctly in. We had reached this place about 10 miles from Cape Evans at 2.30 in the afternoon; we then expected, owing to the bad surface of new sea ice, to have a pull lasting well on to 12 midnight, instead of which the ice had a firm and even surface and was devoid of any slush and ice-flowers such as are usual. We set sail before a strong falling breeze, and all sitting on the sledge had reached the Glacier Tongue in twenty minutes. We clambered over the Tongue, and our luck and the breeze still holding, we reached Cape Evans, completing the last seven miles all sitting on the sledge in an hour. There I called together all the members and explained the situation, telling them what had been done and what I then proposed to do, also asking them for their advice in this trying time. The opinion was almost unanimous that all that was possible had been already done. Owing to the lateness of the year and the likelihood of our being unable to make our way up the coast to Campbell one or two members suggested that another journey might be made to Corner Camp. Knowing the conditions which had lately prevailed on the Barrier, I took it upon myself to decide the uselessness of this.

April 11 and 12 were spent in preparing gear and securing provisions.

On April 13, about 10.30 in the morning, with Wright, Gran, Keohane, Williamson, and Demetri I started back to Hut Point. The surface of the sea ice had then completely changed and was covered with slush and ice-flowers; a trying blizzard started, and after a very hard pull we had to run for shelter to the Little Razorback Island. We camped there and had tea. Soon after, the blizzard abated somewhat and we got under way. We made very slow progress, and after a very hard day's pull could only reach the Glacier Tongue, seven miles from home. The next morning we awoke, made our way over the Tongue, and reaching the cliffs had some difficulty in getting up. The sledge was held at arm's length by four men while one clambered up and by the help of his knife eventually gained a sure footing and was able to help the others. Except for the steepness of the climb, the remainder of the journey to Hut Point was easy. There we found Cherry-Garrard greatly relieved at our return, as the ice had been blowing out of the Sound, but had luckily remained in in the two bays. We reached Hut Point on the 14th.

The 15th and 16th were occupied in drying gear and making up provisions for four weeks. I decided to take C. S. Wright, who was a skilled navigator, Petty Officer Williamson, and Keohane. The season was well advanced and a great part of the travelling and camping had to be done in the dusk.

On April 17 we started across the sea ice, and after 5 miles we reached some old sea ice which had probably been there for two years or more. We then proceeded over a very good surface through a cold day towards the pinnacled ice, and completed 13 miles for that day. The minimum for the night was minus 43°. We did not sleep very well and started breakfast at 7 a.m. in the dark. The temperature for the whole day was about minus 40°. We made good progress over this same old sea ice and luckily we were able to skirt the edge of the pinnacled ice. We camped finally about four miles from the Eskers on the western shore, four miles of new sea ice intervening between us and them. On this night there were five penguins on the old sea ice by our camp. This was disturbing, as it meant the near presence of open water. The minimum for the night was minus 45°. When the morning broke, we saw that a blizzard was impending and we knew it was a matter of speed if we were to cross the new sea ice in safety. Luckily the wind favoured us. We set sail and practically ran with the sledge for two miles before it. The wind then falling light our progress became very slow over a bad surface. To add to our anxiety we could see several Emperor penguins making towards the old sea ice and big leads opening and frost smoke rising from the breaking up of the new sea ice. Eventually we reached the Eskers in safety. We proceeded over a very bad surface from Butter Point for four miles and then, a strong blizzard setting in, we had to camp. This blizzard proved far from being a friend. With it the temperature rose to zero, and our clothing and our bags, which were already full of ice, became saturated, making us in a very uncomfortable state.

On the 20th in the morning, after 3 miles, we reached the depôt on the northern end of Butter Point. This depôt had been left there earlier in the season by the ship. We camped and had some tea. Having struck camp, while we were harnessing up Williamson exclaimed, 'Lord, look at that!' The sea ice at the foot of the Point was gradually breaking up and sailing out to sea. This meant that it was impossible for a party to travel up the coast to the relief of Campbell, and we necessarily had to turn back from this point. It also meant that it was impossible for Campbell and his party to make their way down the coast and that in all probability he and his party would have to winter at Evans Coves. The question of their travelling on such sea ice was infinitely more disturbing than the question of their wintering there.

As one instance of the loyal way in which I was supported during the whole of this season, I can quote the following: 'Wright, from the very first, had been entirely against this journey.

He had some knowledge of a previous sledge trip on the western coast. Not until after I had told him that we should have to turn back, did he tell me how thankful he was at the decision. He had come on this trip fully believing that there was every probability of the party being lost, but had never demurred and never offered a contrary opinion, and one cannot be thankful enough to such men.'

We depôted two weeks' provisions at Butter Point and started to make our way back to Hut Point, our only anxiety being lest the new sea ice had blown out in the blizzard which had delayed us at Butter Point. That night we camped near the northern end of the Eskers and awaited the morning with some anxiety. To our joy we found that the 4 miles of new sea ice was still in in part. Again with a favouring wind we set sail and ran before it for 2 miles. The wind again fell light, and to our consternation we saw the Emperor penguins walking solemnly toward the edge of the old sea ice, which probably meant that there was open water between us and it. But eventually we reached safety and camped for a meal, then in a bad light completed 6 more miles.

Next morning, the 22nd, a blizzard caused a late start. We made for the end of the pinnacled ice, hoping to find our ice still in. As we approached, dense volumes of frost smoke were seen arising from where it had been. This was serious, as it probably meant we should have to make our way through the pinnacled ice, an undertaking which meant several more days in the bad light and bad going. Luckily for the party, there was a narrow ledge or ice-foot projecting from the edge of the pinnacled ice. Alternately along this and along the edge of the pinnacled ice we made our way, stumbling and falling in the holes and capsizing the sledge. After 7 miles we made our way through, and although we could not then see our whereabouts, we knew the remainder of the journey would be pretty plain sailing.

On April 23 there was a blizzard in the morning, a very strong wind and low temperature. There were no land marks to steer by, and using the sastrugi for this purpose we only completed 3½ miles by 1 o'clock and then camped for a meal. Soon after, the weather cleared slightly and we started to make our way to Hut Point. We found that the sea ice had again gone out close to Hut Point, but by keeping well to the south and completing 15 miles, a very good march for the day, we arrived at Hut Point in the dark. I have never known a journey have such an effect upon a party in such a short time.

On the 23rd, the day we returned, we saw the sun for the last time until his return in August. The greater part of this journey was done in the dusk. Wright, owing to the low temperature, was unable to wear his glasses. The light being bad and he short-sighted, he marched under a very great disadvantage. I have spoken before of his loyalty and good-comradeship. Petty Officer Keohane behaved splendidly on the Barrier in the latter end of March and beginning of April and again on this journey. Williamson's conduct was also splendid in every way. The next few days we spent at Hut Point drying out our gear, which was badly iced, and getting some sleep, which we all needed. We began to realise that it was a question now of making the best of circumstances and waiting till the spring of the year before anything further could be done. At Hut Point Cherry-Garrard, Gran, and Demetri had remained, and their task of waiting had been by no means the easier one.

As winter drew on, we had now to return to the base. On April 28 Wright, Gran, and Keohane started to make their way back to Cape Evans over the sea ice. Soon after they had rounded the point it began to blow very stiffly and they ran for safety to the Glacier Tongue; they crossed very thin and bad sea ice, Wright having to go ahead at the full length of the Alpine rope. When they arrived eventually at Cape Evans it was dark and blowing a blizzard. They were lost on the Cape for some time, but eventually found the hut and were in safety.

On May 1 Cherry-Garrard, Demetri, Williamson, and I returned to Cape Evans with the two dog teams. There we started to settle in for the winter and gradually took up the winter routine.

Everything was well at the hut at Cape Evans and work, scientific and otherwise, had been proceeding as usual. We early realised that for the sake of everyone concerned the routine followed in the previous year must be continued in this as far as possible. It was a necessity for us to keep up our work and interests and exercise, so as to avoid slackness and depression and to keep fit and useful through the dark months. The North Bay had only frozen to within half a mile of the hut and had been continually freezing and blowing out.

The seven mules, which had been given by the Indian Government to Captain Scott to enable him to carry on further exploration in the second year, were in excellent condition. Lashly had received certain instructions from Captain Oates when Evans's party left them on the Plateau at 87° 37'. He had been in entire charge of the mules and continued so throughout the winter. Their condition throughout was splendid and spoke volumes for the care with which he looked after them. These mules were suggested to Captain Scott by Captain Oates, and they justified his hopes in every way. The mules had been exercised regularly whenever the weather permitted, and already the seven leaders had adopted their four-footed charges. The ship had also brought down fourteen new dogs. Three of these died soon after landing, and eventually only four of them proved to be of any use for sledging. A litter of pups had been added, but these died owing to their mother leaving them.

Debenham had been doing the meteorological work and Nelson, who was in charge, had carried out the magnetic observations. Crean was in charge of the sledges and sledging gear and Williamson had charge of the sewing-machine, with Keohane to help Crean and Williamson. We early appreciated the efforts of a really good cook in Mr Archer, who had been landed for this second year. Besides being a good cook he proved a good companion and was always lively and cheerful. Lieutenant Gran took charge of the stores and also of the four-hourly meteorological observations. He proved a most efficient stores officer and in his observations was continually trying to break previous records, which he was very often able to do in this exceptional season. Cherry-Garrard was again our editor for the *South Polar Times* and took over the care and preparation of all the ornithological and zoological specimens obtained. Hooper, the steward, took over the management of the acetylene plant, thereby relieving someone else of a very thankless task.

The mules were apportioned as follows:

To Nelson: Khan Sahib   To Gran: Lal Khan
To Crean: Rani   To Keohane: Begum
To Williamson: Gulab   To Hooper: Abdullah
To Archer: Pyaree

A regular night watch to take hourly observations of aurora, to look after the mules and to keep in the fires was also kept. Since our numbers were so much reduced the men were asked to take their nights, and to this they cheerfully agreed. We numbered altogether thirteen souls in the hut. Weekly lectures were arranged to be given by the various officers, and instead of confining these to merely scientific subjects, other items of interest were lectured upon.

On May 3rd to the 5th we had an exceptionally strong blizzard wind. In the evening the gusts recorded by the anemometer were between 70 and 88 miles an hour, a strength considerably over that of any previous observation. The ice was again blown from the North Bay. During the whole of the night the force of the gale increased, and toward morning it began to take off. When Gran checked the instrument at 8.30 a.m. it registered for 3 minutes the rate of 104 miles an hour, and by this time its force had abated considerably. It was exceedingly difficult at this time of the year to obtain any seals owing to the lack of ice in the South and North Bays.

Simpson had some hyacinth bulbs sent down to him, and under Hooper's care these, embedded in a basin full of white sawdust, burst into bloom and lasted for some considerable time.

It was strange at this time of the year to see the open water right up to the hut. The sky effects were beautiful towards the north at midday, and on a calm day their reflection from the open water was splendid.

Demetri and Keohane busied themselves in building a dog hospital. This was essential, as several of the dogs had not as yet recovered from their trip to the Barrier in March. It was large and comparatively warm and much appreciated by the invalids.

The exceptional weather with repeated blizzards of great force during the whole of May kept both man and beast very much confined to the hut. This one felt more than the previous year, as besides being confined to the hut, when it was possible to get exercise we could only do so for a short distance on the Cape, whereas in the previous year the sea ice had extended for some 30 miles to the north of us. There was now open water to the south,

Crean and Keohane had already started mending most of the sleeping-bags, which were in sad need of repair. Luckily the ship had left us with a good supply of reindeer skin and there was plenty to go round and fill up the bare patches in the sleeping-bags.

The mule gear which had been supplied by the Indian Government showed the very greatest forethought in every detail. There were only very slight alterations to be made, more especially in the texture of the gear. The mules had been supplied with a form of canvas snow-goggles, for the ponies in the previous year had suffered badly from snow blindness. These goggles saved the mules from this amount of discomfort when they were on the Barrier. We also realised that owing to their small hoofs they would probably have to use snow-shoes. These had been supplied, and on trying the mules with them most of the animals after a very short time took to them quite naturally.

Debenham had been given charge of all photographic gear; and was out continually taking photographs of general and scientific interest.

On May 10 Nelson lectured on the tides, the main interest of his contention being that with the greatest declination of the moon the movement of ice was more probable.

A never-failing source of amusement after dinner every night has been a form of bagatelle which is played on a mess table. The table was covered with a strip of green Willesden canvas stretched between two long boards which formed the cushions. Between these boards at the top of the table a bridge fits, having in it a number of holes. The object is to get the balls into these holes, the score being according to the number above the hole. A competition was arranged and the lowest scorer of the competition received the Jonah Medal. Having obtained this, he had to announce at luncheon each day 'Gentlemen, I am the Jonah.' This he continued to do until someone else had relieved him of the medal.

The ice in the North Bay now froze again to a thickness of 4 to 5 inches. Nelson started again to build his igloo on the ice in the South Bay to carry on his biological work. When he had pricked the ice the water came through and flowed over the floor of his igloo. The ice, being thin, was pressed down at the spot where the weight bore on it.

On May 13 we had a wonderful aurora display about 6 p.m. and this was believed to be the brightest that had been seen at Cape Evans. The greater part of the sky was covered, but the most vivid shafts ran north-east and south-west. Debenham tried with various exposures to photograph the phenomena, but unluckily failed to get any results. We started again our fish trap, which was let down by digging a hole through the ice; this was at first successful and we had a fair number of fish. The flesh of these fish was so sweet that they were, in the ordinary way, quite unpleasant eating. Archer, by soaking them first in vinegar and water, made them much more palatable. Keohane and Williamson, after a great deal of trouble, caught some of these same fish by hook and line.

On May 25 we had some slight excitement. Wright needed a lamp to heat his magnetic hut, and Nelson and he, while experimenting with one and increasing the pressure in the lamp to give a better flare, unluckily managed to burst it. Immediately the whole end of the table and part of the floor was a mass of flames. With blankets and a fire extinguisher these were soon put out and no harm done. Nelson, whose face was down by the lamp when the explosion occurred, had a very lucky escape. Our fish trap, which had been failing in the number of fish caught each day, was blown out to sea with the ice from the North Bay. This was a serious loss, but we managed with some wire, iron bars, and two hoops to make another but smaller one. About this time some of the geological specimens which had been brought back by the first and second return parties were handed over to Debenham. These had mainly been collected in the scattered moraine under the Cloudmaker. To his surprise and joy several fossils of plants and small marine animals were found in some of these.

One of the dogs, Vaida, who had been ill since his return, was allowed a certain amount of latitude; he frequently came into the hut and would take up his position there, appreciating the warmth and comfort and strenuously resisting ejection at any time. Altogether he regarded himself as having taken on the duty of a house dog.

On June 1, the ice appearing sound, Demetri and Hooper with a dog team went to Hut Point, doing the journey there and back in the same day. One of the dogs had been lost on our return to Cape Evans; but no trace of this animal was found on arriving there and he was never seen again.

The first week of June proved practically calm and we had our coldest temperatures of the winter.

However, as a little ice remained in the North Bay we were able to get more exercise for men and animals. From the 8th to the 13th we had a most exceptional blizzard, both for the warmth of temperature and the amount of drift. It was quite possible in this blizzard to move a few yards away from the hut and be lost for some considerable time. The ice again blew out and we had a wonderful show of phosphorescence in the sea. Once beneath the ice foot we saw a seal chasing a school of fish, the fish outlined with phosphorescence and the seal with a glowing snout and all his body bright, in hot pursuit.

In the previous season Wright had had great trouble in maintaining an even temperature for his pendulum observations. To overcome this a large hole was cut in the floor of the dark room and a kenyte boulder embedded in it, upon which the pendulum was set. With this arrangement he was able to take his observations more accurately and in greater comfort.

By this time the weather seemed to have broken and we had an almost continuous series of blizzards. Meanwhile we had noticed one peculiarity about the mules. The ponies in the previous year had refused to go out when there was any wind and drift blowing. The mules, on the other hand, objected strongly by kicking their stable and squealing if they were not taken out for exercise under these conditions.

On the 19th preparations were begun for our celebrations of Midwinter Day on June 22. Debenham was busy making the slides for a lantern lecture. Gran and Williamson were busy behind a blanket making a Christmas tree. This consisted of a central bamboo with lateral stems and the whole embedded in a pot of gravel. There was a present for everyone with an appropriate oration on its presentation. The whole was lighted with electric light, by arrangement with the physicist.

On June 22, Midwinter Day, Cherry-Garrard, our editor, presented us with another number of the *South Polar Times*, and the remainder of the afternoon was spent as a holiday in reading this, playing bagatelle, or making preparations for a happy evening. The whole hut was decorated with the Christmas tree, sledging flags, and some red bunting. A large white ensign was hung over all as a canopy. Nelson presented each member with a very pretty menu card. These were cut out of cardboard and painted to represent Adélie penguins.

The menu was:

Cape Evans
June 22nd, Midwinter's Day

Croûte Erebus   Amandes Sellés
Crême de Volaille Ferrar
Noisettes d'Agneau Darwinian
Centre Filet de Boeuf rôti
Asperges en Branches
Pommes de Terre Naturel
Poudin Noël   Pâté d'Eunice
Compôte de Fruits
Charlotte Russe glacée à la Beardmore
Buszard's Cake   Dessert

After dinner, when various healths had been drunk, Gran jumped out of the dark room dressed as a clown, with his face powdered and painted. His acting was splendid, with a joke for everybody and sometimes a piece of poetry which he declaimed to the men as they came forward to receive their presents. Gran made an excellent clown, and the whole entertainment went with a roar from beginning to end. Then Debenham put up his lantern and gave us a lot of pictures of all kinds: leaving Dunedin, in the pack, Cape Crozier, the Western Mountains, ponies, and many more. He had taken a lot of time and trouble over these slides and they were excellent and added to the enjoyment of everybody. The evening was closed by a sing-song. Each day now we knew meant one more towards the return of light and usefulness, and preparations were started for the future sledging season. After dinner I called together the members and told them what I proposed to do in the coming season, stating the reasons and asking for their criticism. Two alternatives lay before us. One was to go south and try to discover the fate of Captain Scott's party. I thought it most likely that they had been lost in a crevasse on the Beardmore Glacier. Whether their bodies could be found or not, it was highly desirable to go even as far as the Upper Glacier Depôt, nearly 600 miles from the base, in the hope of finding a note left in some depôt which could tell whether they had fulfilled their task or turned back before reaching the Pole. On general grounds it was of great importance not to leave the record of the Expedition incomplete, with one of its most striking chapters a blank. The other alternative was to go west and north to relieve Campbell and his party, always supposing they had survived the winter. If they had come through the winter, every day of advancing summer would improve their chances of living on in Terra Nova Bay. At the same time there was good prospect of their being ultimately relieved by the ship, if indeed she had not taken them off in the autumn. As for ourselves, it seemed most improbable that we could journey up the coast owing to the abnormal state of the ice. Instead of being frozen for the winter, the whole Sound to the north and west of Inaccessible Island was open water during July; the ice was driven out by the exceptionally strong and frequent winds, and there was little chance of a firm road forming for the spring. Under these conditions officers and men unanimously supported the decision to go south.

Nelson at the end of June had started some lectures upon heredity. These proved to be of great interest and led to several discussions amongst the men and officers. They were so popular that they had to be continued for three weeks. The weather in June as a whole was immeasurably worse than it had been in any previous season. Comparison of the records will show this in figures, both as regards wind and snow, though not in actual lowness of temperature. Our hut was becoming gradually snowed in. After these blizzards in the dark it was almost an impossibility to walk far in the camp because of the huge drifts. Pyaree started giving some trouble with her capped knee on her near fore-leg. This continued for some time and she was unable to get exercise and lost condition. The ice, which had been fairly permanent again, blew out in a large bight to the south of the Cape. In the afternoon now we occasionally saw some colour in the northern sky, a presage of the light that we were to have. One never appreciates fully the blessing of an amount of light until one has been through a good deal of darkness. This time also we started bagging off the rations for the future sledging season. Owing to the probable length of our search these were of considerable bulk.

On July the 16th we had probably the most beautiful day of the year. The whole northern sky was filled with opalescent clouds, and owing to some white ice instead of the black water in the North Bay, the increase of light seemed very appreciable. The mules were now exercised regularly on the ice in the South Bay, and by this means their leaders were able to take them over greater distances. Their condition began gradually to improve, and the way they had come through the winter so far reflected great credit on the care taken by Lashly.

On the 19th the plans for the Southern journey were laid before the other members. Debenham, who had been suffering from an old knee injury at football, and Archer were the two members who would have to remain by the hut.

It was a sad blow to both of them to realise their position, but they accepted it cheerfully. The plan was to provide enough provisions to enable two parties, each a unit of four, to ascend the Beardmore Glacier, and two dog teams with a unit of three men to return from some point not as yet settled. Of the men ascending the glacier, four were to remain at the Cloudmaker and collect geological specimens, photograph, and do survey work. They would then proceed to the foot of the glacier and continue doing this same work until the return of the others, for all this time they were needed as a support by the advance party. This advance party, the other unit of four, would ascend to the top of the glacier if it were necessary to go so far. On their return to the foot of the glacier both units would march home. At this time it was believed by most of us that an accident had occurred to the Southern Party, probably at the lower reaches of the Beardmore, in bad weather, and that sickness had nothing to do with the disaster.

As there was no food either for dogs, mules, or men in any of the depôts, the initial starting weights would have to be very large. To help as far as possible some small depôt journeys would be made in the spring. During the whole winter so far the cheerfulness of the party had been splendid under the most trying conditions, but there now seemed to be an added sprightliness with the return of light.

Nelson had been occupying his time by a very ingenious method of predicting occultations. He predicted altogether nearly fifty, but unfortunately was only able to get one or two observations. These observations were for obtaining the exact longitude. The whole Sound at this time to the north and west of Inaccessible Island was open water. We had two enormous drifts of nine to ten feet high leading from the door of the annexe down to the sea. The latter end of July the weather broke up entirely and we had a repetition of our usual blizzards for the season.

CHAPTER 4

In August, with the gradual return of light, we were able to get about more and consequently took more exercise. A small ski slope was made running down from the rear of the Hut and also a small jump was fixed by Gran. On fine days there was a continual stream of men labouring slowly up the slope and making their way down again with varying success. The sea ice conditions still continued bad and there was some doubt now as to whether we should be able to make our way over the sea ice to Hut Point.

On August 12 for the first time we saw the sun's rays on the summit of Erebus and the smoke rising from the crater was painted a beautiful pink. One of the difficulties that we had to encounter for the next sledging season was the lack of sledge-meters. We had only one left, but Lashly, our handy man, was trying his hand at the manufacture of another under the direction of Nelson. By means of a bicycle wheel and the front fork of a bicycle we got our lead and wheel, while the register was made from the meter attached to the dynamo. This looked exceedingly promising, and after it had been used over short distances gave very good results eventually. On the Barrier it proved of assistance up to One Ton Depôt and then had to be abandoned.

The new sledges, called Finnesskis, were the cause of much discussion. Six had been ordered from Hagen of Christiania, and these arrived with tapered runners, the breadth of the runner in front being 4 inches, diminishing to 2½ on the after part of the sledge. We tried these sledges with the old 12-foot, man-hauling over various surfaces and with equal loads. In every case the new sledges ran more easily, but it was impossible to judge if there was sufficient bearing surface for them with heavy loads on the soft Barrier surface. They eventually proved to be of the greatest service, and animals or men could move loads on these sledges which it was impossible for them to move with the ordinary 12-foot and broad runner. The idea of the sledge was that the broad front portion should run over and smooth and prepare the track for the after tapered portion.

There was very little alteration needed in any of the other gear. Each individual had his personal likes and dislikes and adapted his gear accordingly. In the rations there was only a very slight alteration, our old summit ration being adhered to with the addition of extra sugar, a stick of chocolate, and one onion per man per day.

On August 22 we celebrated the return of the sun with a special dinner, and ended up proceedings with a sing-song. It was not until the 23rd, however, that the sun was seen, and then only by Nelson, who saw its upper rim from the top of the ramp. Almost every day now we saw the earth shadows cast by Erebus and Mount Discovery. These looked like dark cones of shadow running across the sky from east to west.

During these bad conditions of ice in the winter we necessarily had to be careful of the dogs. Some of these were confirmed hunters, and it was through the ice going out during a blizzard that we lost the best leader that we had. Noogis was a dog who had been Demetri's leader on the southern journey in the early part of the year; he had never lost heart on that journey and had been a great factor in cheering the other dogs and getting them along as well as they did. In the earlier part of the year he had once before been taken out to sea by the ice blowing away, but on that occasion he made his way back by the ice-foot around the Barne Glacier. On this occasion he was blown out during the blizzard and we never saw him again.

Our feeding during this winter, with the idea of preventing scurvy, had a very welcome addition in the shape of fresh vegetables. These consisted of potatoes and onions which had been brought down by the ship. As the party was so reduced in numbers, this store lasted practically throughout the winter and proved very acceptable. In September we also had another addition in the shape of the Emperor penguins; they came up on the ice in the South Bay in very large numbers, and nearly every day for some time we were able to secure fresh food. The flesh of the Emperor penguin is better and much less unpalatable than seal; it was appreciated by the men where seal would only have been eaten as a preventive measure.

The number of dogs who were fit for work on the Barrier made exactly two teams. This left at the hut seven dogs who could work but were unable to stand the trials of a long journey. Debenham started to exercise these dogs for geological purposes around the hut. Small as the team was, it made up in obstinacy and trouble for its size.

The chief trouble was getting away from the Cape down a pretty steep ice-foot, and the old leader, Stareek, generally refusing to do his duty when he was within reach of the hut, their direction at first was uncertain.

On September 3, Wright, Debenham, Cherry-Garrard, and I made a small trip over the Barne Glacier to Cape Royds, Shackleton's winter quarters. Our main object was to secure a few luxuries and to leave some spirit and apparatus there for work to be done amongst the penguins in the summer. We found on arriving that the bays and the whole of the Sound as far as we could see were practically free from ice.

On September 5, during a stiff blow, our chimney caught fire. The chimney consisted of an upright piece which went through the hut about the middle. A galley and a stove were at either end of the hut; from each of these a funnel ran and connected with the central upright piece. The fire started at first in the centre and gradually spread down towards the galley or cooking range. We got the flames under control by covering the chimney on the outside with large slabs of snow, the inside of the hut meanwhile being full of smoke and smuts. After some trouble the funnel was disjointed, taken out and swept through.

During the worst time the funnel for nearly half its length was red-hot and glowing, and the heat inside the hut was very uncomfortable.

On the 6th, with the idea of giving the members exercise, Nelson, Gran, Crean, and Archer started for Cape Royds over the Barne Glacier. Gran made a complete list of all the stores at Shackleton's quarters and the party returned on the following day.

The exercise of the mules was now carried on over a longer period, sledges were made up and they were harnessed in and drew their loads on alternate days. The only mule that gave us any serious trouble was Gulab; but Williamson throughout was most tactful and painstaking with this mule, who proved eventually to be the best beast that we had. Pyaree's capped knee started now to give us a great deal of anxiety, and up to the last week in October before she started we thought that she would be unable to go. As it was, she went on to the Barrier with a stiff foreleg, but she worked splendidly as the strain wore off and proved to be the second best mule of the lot.

Owing to the uncertain condition of the ice it was essential to remove as many stores as possible to Hut Point. On September 18 to 22, a party went there with dog teams, taking down a load of stores and with the idea of putting the hut in order. The hut had nearly been buried by the inclement season, but after a great deal of digging had been done it was made more habitable. The hut at Cape Evans had been very much snowed up by this bad season and our roof in one part began to sag from the weight of snow upon it. This was continually removed and as continually was replaced by the next blizzard. During the remainder of this month several trips were made by the dog teams to Hut Point, taking down stores. The ponies also were given extra food so as to get them in better condition for their trip on the Barrier.

It was proposed after the previous year to make their allowance 11 lbs. per mule per day, a ration consisting of oil cake and oats in the proportion of two of oil cake to one of oats.

On September 26 we had a partial eclipse of the moon which we saw very clearly. The maximum shadow fell just before midnight, and we thought we should be unable to see it, for the moon rose behind clouds to the north of Erebus, but it cleared in time and Nelson was able to get his telescope fixed up. Our winter now was practically ended. With the return of light the health and cheerfulness of the party, which had been excellent throughout, improved still more, and we knew now that only a month intervened before we should be away on the Barrier. Scientific work had been carried on throughout the winter, although in certain branches this had been necessarily prohibited by the absence of sea ice.

On October 12 Debenham, Demetri, Cherry-Garrard, and I went down to Hut Point, and on October 14 took the two dog teams out to lay a depôt 12 miles south of Corner Camp. This consisted mainly of pony and dog food and was essential in order to relieve the ponies over the first four days of the journey, on which they would have to encounter heavy surfaces. On the return, as one of the dog teams was crossing a large crevasse, four of the dogs broke through the crust and the sledge was practically anchored by their weight. With the help of the other dogs these were gradually hauled out, popping out of the holes like corks from a bottle. As the sledge and team were on the crevasse at the same time it was fairly anxious work. The dogs bolted and a driving-stick was left by the edge of the crevasse. This was a good but unintentional mark by which to avoid it in future. The depôt was called Demetri Depôt in honour of the Russian dog-boy.

On October 19 four of the mules came down from Cape Evans to Hut Point, bringing loads; they did the journey splendidly and gave great promise of their future usefulness. Debenham meanwhile had been making a geological survey of the peninsula and Cherry-Garrard had been helping him.

On October 25 Cherry-Garrard and Demetri with two dog teams went out to Corner Camp, taking with them a further supply of dog biscuits and fodder. This was the last journey before we started south on October 29.

On October 29 the mules all came down with their leaders to Hut Point and everything was ready for a start on the journey south. It was decided to march at night as we had done in the previous season, so that the mules would be moving during this cold time and camp during the warm portion of the day.

At 7.30. p.m. on October 30 the seven mules and eight men making up the Pony Party started south. C. S. Wright was in command, as he was a skilled navigator. The mules and their leaders were as follows:

E. W. Nelson, leading Khan Sahib; T. Gran, leading Lai Khan; W. Lashly, leading Pyaree; T. Crean, leading Rani; T. Williamson, leading Gulab; P. Keohane, leading Begum; F. J. Hooper, leading Abdullah.

Wright was in command and went ahead, setting the course and standing by to give any help he could. The mules' weights up to Corner Camp would not exceed 500 lbs. This was because of the deep and bad surface usually occurring over this area. The tents were under Wright and Nelson. It was proposed to march twelve geographical miles every night, but, as their progress was uncertain, the question of this distance was left entirely to Wright's judgment.

Pyaree started lame, but within a few days had lost any slight trouble which she had. Gulab had proved that he would chafe easily with the breast harness, and in his case a collar was taken as well. Their first day they did twelve miles, camping about six miles to the S.E. of Safety Camp. Where the sea ice joined the Barrier there was a wide tide-crack, and Khan Sahib unluckily fell partially into this; he was a very quiet animal, and with the aid of an Alpine rope and hauling on his fore-legs they got him up and over on to the surface.

The next day they made good another twelve miles over a slightly worse surface, camping within six miles of Corner Camp.

Owing to the dogs' experience in the earlier part of the year, we realised that this area was more crevassed than it had been previously. I had left it to Wright's judgment as to whether the leaders of the mules were to be linked up by the Alpine rope in going over these last six miles. He thought it fit to do this and they proceeded in that order. The surface they encountered was exceedingly deep and heavy, and only two of the mules struck crevasses and these, luckily, without any mishap. The mules were so tired when they had finished the six miles to Corner Camp that Wright decided to remain there for half a day.

On November 1 the two dog-teams, with Cherry-Garrard, Demetri, and myself, started to follow the mules. The dogs' loads, which had been made out to allow about 75 lbs. per dog, proved to be heavy from the start; the progress was exceedingly slow and we completed fifteen miles for the first day. The next day, again over a very bad surface, we completed another fifteen miles and reached Corner Camp. There we had a very reassuring note from Wright. He said that the mules were going well together and, instead of having to be split up into fast and slow mules, they broke camp and pitched camp, with one exception, all together, for Khan Sahib, Nelson's mule, was peculiarly slow, and in the temperature we were encountering on the march Nelson found it of the greatest difficulty to keep himself at all warm. This mule would usually lose three-fourths of a mile on the others while they were completing two miles. Nelson invented a method of walking two steps forward and lumping one back, in order to keep his circulation up to the mark.

They proceeded, building cairns of snow at intervals of from two to four miles in order that we might follow their tracks.

I saw from the way that the dogs were going that we should have great difficulty, with their present weights, in catching the mules before they reached One Ton Depôt. On Wright's satisfactory report I decided to entrust everything to the mules and to use the dogs as a means of lightening their heavy loads. The mules' weights had increased from Corner Camp up to nearly 700 lbs. per mule. This was far in excess of any weights hauled by the ponies in the previous season, and here we saw the advantage of having tapered runners to our sledges. The beasts, with comparative ease, were able to move these heavy loads on the sledges, where they would have been unable to do so with the broad runners of the previous 12-foot sledge.

Wright proceeded the next day to Demetri Depôt, twelve miles south from Corner Camp. The mules here took on their full loads and proceeded south before we could get up to them. Here the remainder of the surplus weights of the dogs was left.

Kasoi, one of the dogs, had refused for that day to work; no amount of beating would induce him to do so. We therefore took him off the trace and tied him with the harness to the rear of the sledge. Demetri's team, who were following, realised that something was wrong with this dog: they pulled their very hardest with the idea of getting up to him and finishing him. Kasoi realised what this meant, and it decided him in favour of work as nothing else could have done. He resumed his pulling, and never slackened his trace afterwards.

On the night of the 4th and the morning of the 5th of November we had got on to a very good surface; we started early and light, in order to reach the mules before they had started, and this we eventually did after we had made our twelve miles. In view of their condition and the tired dogs I decided to give animals and men a day's rest at this place. The weather, which had been windy and drifting up to now, had begun to clear and would give the animals some chance of drying off, as well as having a good night's rest.

Gulab, Williamson's mule, had been badly chafed by the breast harness on his shoulder. Williamson had changed him to his collar and almost immediately after the first day of this he chafed again. Throughout the whole of his journey Williamson took the very greatest care of his animal and invented various new and clever designs for taking the weight of his draught off his chafed shoulder. Eventually Gulab's tail was brought as an aid to this. By means of a back strap connecting his collar and his tail most of the drag was taken off his shoulder and, under these conditions, the chafe began to heal.

About this time, as the lights were very strong, the mules began to show signs of snow-blindness. It was then that their snow-goggles were tried for the first time. We found that they were of the greatest use and generally stayed on while the mules were on their lines; they were of the greatest comfort to the animals.

The mules would not eat their ration of oil cake and oats at all. They showed a liking for everything except their ration. They would eat man or dog biscuits, tea-leaves and tobacco, ash and various portions of garments, with the greatest of relish, but they needed the utmost care and coaxing to be induced to touch their ration at all. They were picketed by their fore-legs, as the ponies had been in the previous year, and they showed the greatest ingenuity in getting themselves free and strolling about the camp, testing various articles of the store goods.

The same routine was kept by this party. The morning march was seven miles in length; they then camped and had tea, which lasted for about one hour and a half. When camp was struck, they marched on for five miles more, completing the twelve geographical miles for the day. Their speed on march was favourable compared with that of the ponies of the previous year. Our surfaces were so hard and good that the mules did not with their small hooves sink appreciably into the snow.

The dogs' weights here having been much reduced, they were able to relieve the mules to a large extent. The routine of the march was now changed: from one to two hours after the mules had started, the dogs followed them. The change in the dogs and in their rate of progress was now wonderful: when they had something to follow, and especially when the mules came into view, they proceeded during the whole of the day at a full gallop.

Abdullah, Hooper's mule, had constituted himself leader throughout, and continued so until his return from the Barrier towards the end of November. This was a difficult feat, as the first mule has always the added hardship of having to break the track.

The surface was extremely good, hard, and almost marbled, and the sledges followed the animals easily.

Each night, on camping, a wall was built for the mules, consisting of large slabs of hard snow dug in the Barrier; they were a considerable amount of trouble, but afforded shelter to the beasts from the wind and drift. The mules had so eaten their covers that it required much ingenuity to make these useful for protecting the beasts.

The day's rest had done everyone good, and on a glorious day we proceeded and soon finished the twelve miles for the day.

On the night of the 6th and 7th we started at 10.30, and, on a slightly worse surface, did seven miles up to lunch. All along this way we had been building cairns of snow at intervals of from two to four miles apart. The day, which was cloudy, cleared towards morning, and was much colder. During this time we were marching in temperature which ranged from minus 20° to the lowest of minus 29°. In the daytime, when the sun had reached its full height, the temperature would rise almost to zero.

On the night of the 7th and morning of the 8th of November we made the old Bluff Depôt in 79° South and re-built it, placing a new flag of black bunting on the pole. Here we left two boxes of dog biscuit for the dogs returning on their journey back from the south. The surface again continued good, and never in any previous experience had it been so hard and good as far south as this.

On the night of the 8th and 9th we continued over this same good surface, before a slight north-easterly wind and a cold day. The dogs had now again begun to fail. They seemed to lack enthusiasm and spirit; I believe that in their case they had had too much work upon the Barrier and were spiritless and easily depressed by the lack of anything to see. In the previous year we had had certain 'cuts' of land for the Bluff Depôt and Corner Camp. It was quite easy to see from these that both camps had changed their positions owing to the gradual movement of the Barrier, year by year. Approximately, and judging very roughly, the movement in either case had been about half a mile for the year.

On the night of the 9th and 10th we came again to a curious phenomenon of the Barrier surface. As the mules proceeded ahead of us loud crackling roars could be heard from time to time. These were caused by a subsidence of the surface over a large area, as an animal or man trod upon it. The depth of the subsidence was only a fraction of an inch, but the resulting report was exceedingly loud and startling, if unexpected. The mules soon settled down to the roars and became accustomed to them, but it was always a source of great interest to the dogs. As soon as one of these subsidences with its roar came to them they started off at full gallop, expecting at any moment some animal to appear. They had been accustomed in Siberia to dig out animals lying up snowed in. These subsidences were a great help and kept the dogs interested, and they ran very well.

On the night of the 10th and morning of the 11th we made One Ton Depôt, coming up five and three-quarters miles to it. I decided to give men and animals a half-day's rest here. It was a beautiful sunny and bright day but with some wind. Here we found the stores which had been left by Demetri and Cherry-Garrard. One of the tins of paraffin on top of the cairns had leaked and spoilt some of the stores placed at the foot of the camp. There was no hole of any kind in this tin.

Our progress up to this point had been made in a day and a half less time than it had taken us on the previous year, and that was with the mules drawing full loads for the whole of the time. There was no doubt that our surface had been infinitely better than in the previous season. Everything was favourable and the health of men and animals was splendid.

On the night of the 11th and morning of the 12th, after we had marched eleven miles due south of One Ton, we found the tent. It was an object partially snowed up and looking like a cairn. Before it were the ski sticks and in front of them a bamboo which probably was the mast of the sledge. The tent was practically on the line of cairns which we had built in the previous season. It was within a quarter of a mile of the remains of the cairn, which showed as a small hummock beneath the snow.

Inside the tent were the bodies of Captain Scott, Doctor Wilson, and Lieutenant Bowers. They had pitched their tent well, and it had withstood all the blizzards of an exceptionally hard winter. Each man of the Expedition recognised the bodies. From Captain Scott's diary I found his reasons for this disaster. When the men had been assembled I read to them these reasons, the place of death of Petty Officer Evans, and the story of Captain Oates's heroic end.

We recovered all their gear and dug out the sledge with their belongings on it. Amongst these were 35 lbs. of very important geological specimens which had been collected on the moraines of the Beardmore Glacier; at Doctor Wilson's request they had stuck to these up to the very end, even when disaster stared them in the face and they knew that the specimens were so much weight added to what they had to pull.

When everything had been gathered up, we covered them with the outer tent and read the Burial Service. From this time until well into the next day we started to build a mighty cairn above them. This cairn was finished the next morning, and upon it a rough cross was placed, made from the greater portion of two skis, and on either side were up-ended two sledges, and they were fixed firmly in the snow, to be an added mark. Between the eastern sledge and the cairn a bamboo was placed, containing a metal cylinder, and in this the following record was left:

'November 12, 1912, lat. 79 degrees, 50 mins. South. This cross and cairn are erected over the bodies of Captain Scott, C.V.O., R.N., Doctor E. A. Wilson, M.B., B.C., Cantab., and Lieutenant H. R. Bowers, Royal Indian Marine – a slight token to perpetuate their successful and gallant attempt to reach the Pole. This they did on January 17, 1912, after the Norwegian Expedition had already done so. Inclement weather with lack of fuel was the cause of their death. Also to commemorate their two gallant comrades, Captain L. E. G. Oates of the Inniskilling Dragoons, who walked to his death in a blizzard to save his comrades about eighteen miles south of this position; also of Seaman Edgar Evans, who died at the foot of the Beardmore Glacier. "The Lord gave and the Lord taketh away; blessed be the name of the Lord."'

This was signed by all the members of the party. I decided then to march twenty miles south with the whole of the Expedition and try to find the body of Captain Oates.

For half that day we proceeded south, as far as possible along the line of the previous season's march. On one of the old pony walls, which was simply marked by a ridge of the surface of the snow, we found Oates's sleeping-bag, which they had brought along with them after he had left.

The next day we proceeded thirteen more miles south, hoping and searching to find his body. When we arrived at the place where he had left them, we saw that there was no chance of doing so. The kindly snow had covered his body, giving him a fitting burial. Here, again, as near to the site of the death as we could judge, we built another cairn to his memory, and placed thereon a small cross and the following record: 'Hereabouts died a very gallant gentleman, Captain L. E. G. Oates of the Inniskilling Dragoons. In March 1912, returning from the Pole, he walked willingly to his death in a blizzard, to try and save his comrades, beset by hardships. This note is left by the Relief Expedition of 1912.'

It was signed by Cherry and myself.

From here I decided to turn back and to take, as far as possible, all the stores to Hut Point. I then thought that by any means that lay within our power we should try to reach Lieutenant Campbell and his party. As the sea ice would in all likelihood be impossible, we should probably have to take the route along the plateau, ascending the first Ferrar Glacier and making our way along the plateau as far as we were able.

On the second day we came again to the resting-place of the three and bade them there a final farewell. There alone in their greatness they will lie without change or bodily decay, with the most fitting tomb in the world above them.

Our journey back was uneventful. Two of the mules had to be killed because of their condition and to give food to the dogs. Five returned from the Barrier, and for the remainder of their days had as good a time as we could give them.

On the morning of November 25 two dog teams, with Cherry-Garrard, Demetri, and myself, having pushed ahead of the mules, reached Hut Point. Cherry went into the hut and returned with a letter and his face transformed. I think we had then the best news that any men could wish for many, many a long weary day. Campbell and his party, having all survived the winter, had made their way down, arriving at Hut Point on November 6.

We proceeded in all haste to Cape Evans, there to have the goodly sight of their rounding countenances. They had filled out wonderfully on the good and unusual food, and each and every-one was now heavier than he had ever been in his life. It was a sad home-coming for them after their hard time.

I can only here say that I can never be sufficiently grateful to all the members of the Expedition who were with me during this bad season, for their entire loyalty and good-fellowship; never one moment's trouble and always cheerful and willing.

THE ASCENT OF EREBUS, DECEMBER 1912

by Raymond Priestley

A party of six left Cape Evans on December 2, 1912, with the main object of surveying the old crater, and if time permitted making an ascent to the rim of the present active crater. It was originally intended that in the final climb Professor David's route should be followed, but our researches in the old crater led to the adoption of quite a different way, and one where a sledge could be pulled to a height of considerably over 9500 feet, at least 3000 feet higher than the Shackleton Expedition party were able to reach before being obliged to abandon theirs.

We left our Cape Royds camp (1000 feet above sea level) on December 4. It was not an ideal day for starting, and for the first 2000 feet of the ascent we groped from nunatak to nunatak through a thick cloud, and Debenham was unable to commence his plane table survey.

We lunched above this cloud belt, and although it swelled slowly upwards we were, with the exception of a very few minutes in the early afternoon, able to keep ahead of it until we camped beneath a prominent cone about 4,000 feet above sea level, which is well seen on the sky line from Cape Evans, and which would therefore be an important point of Debenham's survey, linking the portion of Erebus visible from Cape Evans and Cape Royds with the country beyond the shoulder, which was the last ridge visible from winter quarters.

As we were caught by the fog in the act of camping and the landmarks below had been blotted out all the afternoon by the belt of cloud, we were obliged to wait here until the weather cleared and we could fix the cone, and so persistent was the bad weather that it was not until 10 a.m. of the 7th that we struck Reflection Camp, as we had named it, and were able to proceed.

Our first objective, the Northern Nunatak, or Demetri's Peak as we afterwards named it, was within easy reach by lunch time, so I decided to camp at a large nunatak about a mile and a half from the peak and take a rope party to examine it. So far all the rocks we had passed had been the typical kenyte so familiar to us at Cape Royds, but we found ourselves now camped on basalt, an allied but distinct rock which was not seen by the Professor's party, who had kept close in to the main crater and had not attempted any side issues such as our present divergence. After lunch I took Gran, Abbott, and Dickason, leaving Debenham with Hooper to help him to continue his survey, and made straight for the peak, which we reached without crossing any bad country, though crevasses were numerous above our route.

We climbed the small triangular hill from bottom to top, making its height 300 feet, and from the top we obtained a good view and a photograph of the old crater and of a strongly seracced glacier which loomed up as a bad obstacle in our examination of the district.

The peak proved more interesting geologically than was expected, and we took back a good crop of specimens and photographs.

From here our route to the old crater itself proved steady, steep (for sledges), and uninteresting, and we camped on the gravel of a small nunatak on the lower side of the crater glacier at 5 p.m. on the 8th (8000 feet).

From this point Debenham was able to initiate the survey of the crater, and the next day all six of us carried one tent and equipment for three men a mile or two up the side of the glacier and established a camp in a gully nearly 9000 feet above sea level. After making this camp I took a rope party of four across and collected from the lower fang of the crater, while Debenham took Abbott and continued his plane table survey. What I saw from the crater side of the glacier decided me to make the final climb from a point about half a mile beyond the Gully Camp, and so I sent Gran with two of the men back for a supply of food from a depôt we had laid three or four miles back and almost on the Professor's route.

After lunch I returned with the other two, and we struck the single tent at our lower crater camp, collected all spare gear and depôted it and the extra food, and on the return of the other three we pulled the sledge with its skeleton equipment as far as the Gully Camp, where we spent the night.

On the morning of the 10th we again pulled out, and by 11.30 a.m. we were camped in the position from which I had decided to make the final ascent. After discussion with Debenham, I selected Gran, Abbott, and Hooper to accompany me to the top, leaving Debenham, who had slight mountain sickness, to continue his survey, and Dickason, who was feeling the height more than the other two men, to help him.

From here we were taking a single camping equipment – tent and poles, bags, inside cooker, primus, oil, and four days' provisions on full ration, and after this had been apportioned each man was permitted to take a reasonable amount of personal gear. All hands dragged the packs on the sledge some distance up the first snow slope, but the gradient soon became so steep that we were obliged to anchor the sledge with ice axes and assume our packs, while Debenham and Dickason tobogganed back to camp on the sledge.

By climbing about a hundred feet at a time and taking long spells we were able to make steady if slow progress up the rock ridges, which were here nearly continuous as far as the rim of the second crater. The only difficult bits to negotiate were when we were obliged to cross the snow-slopes from ridge to ridge, and these were only dangerous because, owing to scarcity of ice axes, the four of us were able to have but three between us, and I was never sure where the fourth man would fetch up if he slipped. This necessitated step cutting and slowed us up considerably, and it was not until three hours and a half after we had left the sledge that we reached the rim and saw the second crater stretching out in front of us.

Our first care was to select a good site for our camp, and after that was pitched to cook our evening meal and turn in. The clouds prevented our getting a view of the active crater and no photographs were possible. The only effect the height had on us as yet was to cause sleeplessness and a slight shortness of breath, but we were already beginning to experience some discomfort from the low temperatures, and the whole time we remained at or above this elevation the mercury remained obstinately below −10° F., and at one time registered −30° F.

The 11th saw us still shrouded in cloud and, except for a short walk in the immediate neighbourhood of the camp, we got nothing done; but Gran woke me at 1 o'clock in the morning of the 12th, to find the weather so magnificent that I roused all hands at once and we got breakfast, deciding to take time by the forelock and not risk a change of weather.

The only drawback to the morning was a low temperature, $-15°$ F. to $-18°$ F., and a cold southerly wind which gave us a good deal of trouble, as the high altitude very much decreased our chances of resisting frostbite. From the scenic point of view the volcano could not have been better, for it was very active, and the steam cloud was being carried steadily northward by the breeze. As we approached the active crater we secured photograph after photograph, and I also took several looking back at our camp and the old crater in the background, and at Mount Terror and Mount Bird. A good description of these two upper craters has already been given by Professor David, and repetition would be unnecessary and useless. The principal impression they have left on our minds is that of absolute bareness and desolation.

As our altitude increased we were more and more troubled with shortness of breath and fatigue, and were obliged to rest every hundred yards or so; but we reached the summit of the active cone within two or three hoars of leaving the camp, and while Gran made a cairn for the record I had prepared, I endeavoured with the help of Abbott and Hooper to light the hypsometer; but the breeze was too stiff and enfiladed the crater rim so that no adequate shelter could be obtained, and after wasting half a box of matches and getting several frostbitten fingers we were obliged to desist. Gran and I then took a series of photographs on the rim of the crater, but we were unable to see more than a few feet down because of the steam and sulphur vapour, which caused us considerable inconvenience even during the short time we spent on the rim, for every slight variation of direction of the wind resulted in our complete envelopment by the vapour, which was not too good to breathe in.

After a short while on top Hooper reported that his feet were frostbitten, and I at once ordered him back to camp, telling off Abbott to accompany him and to collect a rucksack full of pumice on his way down.

Gran and I continued slowly down the cone, collecting felspars as we went, and I had descended about 500 feet when I discovered to my annoyance that instead of the record we had left a tin of exposed films at the summit. Gran immediately volunteered to fetch this and place the real record, and as I wished to collect thoroughly I continued slowly on my way down. I had reached the second group of fumaroles and was beginning to photograph them by the time he should have reached the top, when there was a loud explosion, and amongst the smoke I could see large blocks of pumice hurled aloft. This eruption made me extremely anxious for Gran's fate, especially as he did not appear on the farther side of the smoke cloud as soon as he was due, so in spite of breathing trouble I made good speed up the hill, and had reached within fifty feet of the top in record time, and without a halt, when he strolled out of the steam cloud all serene and looking none the worse for his adventure. He had had a unique opportunity of observing an eruption of Erebus, and that the opportunity was not wasted can be seen from his description, which is as follows.

'Whilst making some notes of the things I had seen, I heard a gurgling sound come from the crater, and before I had realised what was happening I was enveloped in a choking vapour. The steam cloud had evidently been much increased by the eruption, and in it I could see blocks of pumiceous lava, in shape like the halves of volcanic bombs and with bunches of long drawn-out hair-like shreds of glass in their interior. The snow around me was covered with rock dust and the smoke was yellow with sulphur and disagreeable in the extreme.'

Gran was fortunate in not experiencing any worse effect of the eruption than a slight sickness during the next few days, which we both attributed to the sulphur vapour. I think of the two of us my own experience was the worse for, as he says later in his diary, 'It is no joke taking a mountain by storm, especially with the barometer standing at eleven inches.'

The hair-like lava I had already noticed on the slopes of the crater, and it is doubtless of the type known as Pele's hair.

Gran made his escape from the steam cloud on the western side of the mountain, and so was able to get a good view of the Western Mountains, and believed he could see a range stretching back and cutting across the plateau at about the latitude of Granite Harbour.

We then returned slowly to camp, collecting as we went, and arrived in about 9.30 a.m., to find that Hooper's feet had recovered and that Abbott had collected a fine lot of specimens.

After our return to camp we rested in our bags for a few hours, and then struck camp and glissaded down the 2000 feet till we rejoined Debenham and Dickason, covering in a few minutes a distance that had taken us three or four hours on our upward way. During our absence the latter had made good use of their time, finishing the survey of the old crater and collecting from moraines left by an ancestor of the crater glacier.

We spent the night camped here, and the next morning proceeded on our way down the mountain, using ice axes in rope grummets at the after end of the sledge as brakes and making such good way that the same day we picked up all our depôts, and camped within striking distance of Hooper's Shoulder, as we afterwards named the Southern Nunatak, in time for a late lunch.

In the afternoon Debenham, Abbott, and Hooper and I walked over to the shoulder, photographed it and collected from it, and by 6 p.m. we were back in camp.

The final descent was delayed until the 16th by bad weather, but on that date we pulled as near Cape Royds as we could take the sledges, and from there packed our own bags and such equipment as we required to Shackleton's Hut, where I reported to Lieutenant Campbell and gave him an outline of the trip.

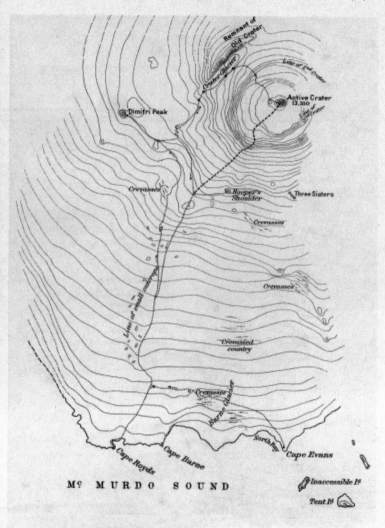

Remnant of Old Crater

Line of 2nd Crater

Crater Glacier

Active Crater 13,350

Dimitri Peak

Crevasses

Hooper's Shoulder

Three Sisters

Crevasses

Line of small moraine

Crevasses

Crevassed country

Crevasses

Barne Glacier

North Bay

Cape Evans

Cape Royds

Cape Barne

Inaccessible I^d

Tent I^d

M^c MURDO SOUND

SKETCH MAP OF
MOUNT EREBUS
showing routes of ascent,
from plane table map by
F. DEBENHAM.

NORTH (TRUE)

Route 1912.
Approx. route Prof. David, 1908.
Contour lines 250 ft very approximate.
Scale 2·7 miles to the inch (about)

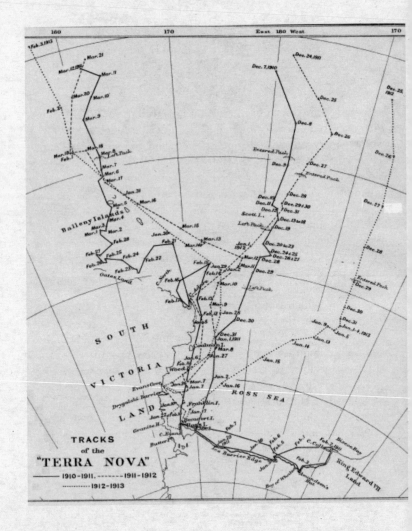

TRACKS
of the
"TERRA NOVA"
——— 1910-1911. ------- 1911-1912
·········· 1912-1913

VOYAGES OF THE *TERRA NOVA*

by Commanders E. R. G. R. Evans and H. L. L. Pennell

FIRST VOYAGE

To connect the thread of the story it is as well to run briefly over what occurred before Campbell landed at Cape Adare.

On January 28, 1911, Captain Scott and the southern depôt laying party having left, the ship proceeded for King Edward's Land with Lieutenant Campbell and his party on board. Ice preventing her from getting beyond Cape Colbeck, Campbell ran into the Bay of Whales, intending to land there; but finding Captain Amundsen had selected this site and built his hut here, he proceeded to the opposite extreme of Ross Sea to try and land on the north coast of South Victoria Land as far to the west as the ship could get. No landing place, however, could be found on this coast at all except at Cape Adare, Robertson Bay, where there is a moraine on which Borchgrevink wintered in 1898. There being no alternative he decided to build his hut here.

Feb. 18 *and* 19, 1911. *Cape Adare.* – During the 18th and 19th the work of landing the stores for Campbell's party was carried out as rapidly as possible, a dead flat calm lasting the whole time. Heavy pack ice, setting round the ship, prevented all communication with the shore between 1 and 2 p.m. on the 18th; and at 4 p.m. on the 19th the ship was again being pressed by the ice, only more heavily than on the previous day, so that it was necessary for her to steam to her anchor.

At 8 p.m. the order was given to weigh and stand off, and the night was spent by the ship in doing magnetic work, as fortunately the middle of Robertson Bay was clear of ice.

Feb. 20, 1911. – At 3.30 a.m. the moraine was again approached, and the watch that had been landed to work on shore were re-embarked. An adieu to Campbell's little party was hooted on the syren and the *Terra Nova* steamed to the N.N.W., in a calm, but with a rapidly falling barometer, to try and get round the pack that always extends north of North Cape.

Her orders were to explore to the west of North Cape as far as the coal supply allowed.

Six a.m. found her clear of the pack off the entrance to the bay. All hands set to to clear up the decks, batten down and prepare for bad weather, and it was well on in the forenoon before they were able to get any rest. By noon a strong wind was blowing from E.S.E. and freshening, and the sea was beginning to get up, so fires were banked and she was snugged down to lower topsails.

Blink appearing on the port hand, course was altered to north to keep away from it, when snow obscured everything.

Feb. 21, 1911, 68° 41' S., 168° 29' E. – At noon on the 21st course was altered to W., and shortly after the ship ran very close to an iceberg, which showed us that the range of vision, estimated at half a mile for ice, was considerably less than had been thought. During the afternoon she crossed Ross's track, the most westerly track in this sea up to date. At midnight steam was again put on the engines, the wind and sea having died rapidly and the weather cleared. A sounding was taken in 1435 fathoms and course altered to the S.W. to close S. Victoria Land again.

Feb. 22, 1911, 69° 10' S., 164° 30' E. – Bruce in the afternoon watch picked up some snow-capped mountains, and after this more peaks and lower land were quickly raised above the horizon, and a large number of icebergs appeared ahead. The ship was brought up by pack at 9 p.m. which stretched between her and the shore and parallel to the coast, as far as could be seen.

Though several attempts had been made, no ship previously had had the good fortune to get in sight of the coast on this longitude, so the luck of the *Terra Nova* was in this season.

This new coast-line discovered by Lieutenant Pennell has been christened Oates Land, after Captain L. E. G. Oates of the Inniskilling Dragoons.

The land was tantalisingly covered in cloud. Nothing could be done till the morning, and so the night was spent trawling and swinging for variation. A sounding gave 178 fathoms. The trawl was particularly interesting and made ample amends for the delay. As soon as it was light enough to see, we tried to close the land as the pack did not look especially heavy. Clouds still hid all except the lower land.

Feb. 23, 1911, 69° 29' S., 162° 49' E. – An hour and a half showed the futility of attempting to get through, and at 5 a.m. the attempt was given up, the ship being then 8000 yards from the end of a glacier tongue and in 134 fathoms of water. This tongue appeared to run down from snow-covered rounded hills, while behind it a rugged range of hills ran down to a point apparently forming the eastern point of a large bay, as away to the west could be seen high cliffs with outcroppings of rock, but everything in that direction was much obscured by mist or haze. The ship's position, fixed by sun and moon, was 69 43' S., 163 17' E.

Forty-seven icebergs could be counted from this spot, all being in the pack and probably mostly aground. This trend of the land to the northward would well account for the hang of the pack and icebergs north of North Cape.

At 8 a.m. the ship started to skirt the pack to the westward, noting what details could be made out of the coast, which were not many. The routine now was for Rennick to sound every forenoon and middle watch, and if in comparatively shallow water, as often as time could be spared. The sounding-machine was worked by hand, and on many nights was a cold and patience-trying job.

Feb. 24, 1911, 69° 4' S., 161° 19' E. – As she worked westward the pack pressed the ship out from the land, and in the afternoon a light fog and snow came down again. In the middle watch it blew a strong wind from the S.E., with thick snow, and she was hove to.

Feb. 25, 1911, 68° 50' S., 159° 11' E. – The snow stopped about 8 a.m., but the day was dull and one could not see far. Course was shaped S.S.W. and Feb. 25, by 2 the *Terra Nova* was stopped by pack with what appeared to be a miniature archipelago close to the southward. These turned out to be icebergs, probably aground, and some of large size, but when this was discovered the weather brightened and a cliffy coast-line was seen to the S.W. Following the pack along towards the land, it was soon seen that there was clear water inside the pack. This water extended, apparently, up to the land, and at one place the line of pack was not more than a mile broad. After sounding in 154 fathoms the ship was worked into the pack with high hopes of finding another place like Robertson Bay, which is often clear of pack, though the entrance is usually more or less guarded by it.

At 5 p.m., after an hour's struggle, the attempt was seen to be hopeless, the ship was only a third way through, and the pack grew heavier as she advanced. A light wind had sprung up and this had closed the pack, so that the ship was caught and unable to move at all. This was very disappointing and the position was not free from anxiety as, undoubtedly, there is a fair tidal stream in these waters, and grounded icebergs do not make pleasant neighbours in such circumstances.

As the sun got low the day improved, the clouds broke, and in the sunshine we had a good view of the land, though the upper parts of it were always shrouded in cloud. The ship appeared to be off a point (or angle) in the coast, apparently forming the western end of a large bay to the east of us. The coast was steep and rugged, half-bare rocky points separated by glaciers being the chief features. The hills behind did not appear to be very high, but this is only guess-work, as the higher land was obscured in clouds all the time and only occasionally a glimpse could be got when the clouds partially lifted in one spot or another. There was no movement in the ice in respect to the ship till 5 a.m., when Cheetham reported a general easing up, and shortly after the ship was able to turn and work out to the northward without unusual difficulty.

Feb. 26, 1911, 68° 57' S., 158° 53' E. – After taking bearings and making sketches from the edge of the pack we ran to the northward and north-westward, with pack on the port hand and the coast beyond the pack till 2 p.m., when the coast made a sharp bend to the westward, though the edge of the pack still continued to trend to the northward. While one of the soundings was being taken on this day a rorqual fouled the sounding wire in a most extraordinary manner, and for a short time there was quite an exciting and very novel sport of playing whale, which naturally ended by the wire parting.

This was the last we saw of the land, the pack not being finally cleared till in Lat. 64° 23' S. Many times false hopes were raised by the ship running into clear water and being able to turn west and even south of west towards where C. Hudson is marked on the charts, but invariably it was only a few hours before she would be turned and, as a general rule, each noon position was east of the previous one. On the whole, after leaving the coast, the floes were of a less formidable character than those found off the north shore of Victoria Land, but the interspaces were filled with slush or else frozen over with new ice. This made pack that earlier in the season would have been easily negotiable now absolutely impassable. The nights also were drawing out, and after dark the first appearance of pack had to be the signal to heave to till daylight, which often meant till 6 a.m., as the morning twilight was found very bad for picking a way through the pack.

The sea was now frozen over in the sort of large lakes or pools of still, open water that were found in this sea, and though this ice was never more than a few inches thick, it made a considerable difference to our speed.

March 2, 1911, 67° 35' S., 160° 16' E. – On March 2, while working through fairly loose pack, the wind that had been light westerly turned to E.N.E., with the immediate effect of closing the floes in, and the ship was completely held up. During that night the wind shifted again to the southward and so topsails and foresail were set. It was merely waste of coal to try and steam through this ice, but the steady pressure of the ship under sail let her gradually, though very slowly, work through; often held up by a floe for an hour or more, in the end she would manage to turn it and run ahead half a ship's length or so. This meant that in her wake was generally to be found a small pool of water clear of ice.

A number of whales (lesser rorquals) were in this pack, and they soon discovered this clear water and took advantage of it to come and blow; as there was not room for them to come up in the ordinary way, they had to thrust their heads up vertically and blow in a sort of standing-on-their-tails position. Several times one rested its head on a floe, not twenty feet from the ship, with its nostrils just on the water-line; raising itself a few inches, it would blow and then subside again for a few minutes to its original position, with its snout resting on the floe. The men amused themselves by pelting it with little bits of coal and other missiles, of which it appeared to be entirely unconscious. The grooves on their throats were plainly seen, quite clearly enough to count accurately; and sometimes even their moustaches could be distinctly made out, as also the white band on the flipper.

March 4, 1911, 67° 11' S., 160° 47' E. – Fortunately (or unfortunately) the whale gun was out of action, and so there was no necessity to try and procure a specimen for biological purposes. Whales kept close to the ship till noon on the 4th, when, the pack having eased up, steam was again put on the engines and she was able to make appreciable way.

March 5, 1911, 66° 37' S., 161° 42' E. – The ship passed only some ten miles west of Young Island (one of the Balleny Group), but although it was a sunny day all the Balleny Islands were covered in clouds, and no useful bearings could be taken.

At last, on March 8, when in 64° 23' S., 161° 39' E., she cleared the last of the pack, and in half an hour sooty albatross were round the ship, a sure sign that no pack was north of her.

The next fortnight was a struggle for the ship to keep to windward, the wind obstinately holding to the north side of west and generally blowing hard. Although so light, she was much stiffer than expected.

To the seaman of the present day used to iron ships it is a never-failing source of surprise and delight to see a wooden ship in a heavy sea. How nicely she rides the waves, like a living being, instead of behaving like a half-submerged rock.

The albatross and other deep-sea birds were a great pleasure; while south of Lat. 60° the pretty Hour-glass dolphin (first noticed by Dr Wilson in the *Discovery*) was often round the ship.

March 22, 1911, 56° 9' S., 159° 15' E. – On the 22nd, when ninety miles south of the Macquarie Islands, the long-hoped-for fair wind came at last and held till we made Stewart Island. On the 23rd steam was again raised.

The pumps had been a nuisance throughout, and during a gale on the 24th the trouble came to a head: the ship was heeling between 40 and 45 degrees and jumping about considerably, and only a little water could be got through the engine-room pumps. The hand pump had been kept going all night, but during the morning also choked, and as soon as there was a little water in the well, it lifted a plate in the engine-room during one of the ship's bad heels and let all the ashes and coal down into the well. Both bunker doors had to be shut and could not be opened with safety; engines were stopped and steam kept for the bilge pump, whose suction was with great difficulty kept partially free by Mr Williams. He kept a perforated enamel jug on the end of the suction, and stopping the pump every two or three minutes as the suction choked, removed and cleared the jug, replaced it and then restarted the pump; this process having to be kept up the whole time the hand pumps were being seen to. To accomplish his object Williams had to lie flat on the boiler-room plates, and when the ship listed to starboard, stretch right down with his head below the plates and clear as much coal away from round the suction as possible. This often meant that the water surged back before he could get his head out, and there can be few nastier liquids to be ducked in than that very dirty bilge-water.

Meanwhile for the hand pumps Davies had to take off the bottom lengths of the suction pipes, lift them, and clear them from below. To do this the flange rivets had to be bored out, and it took eight hours' incessant work to finish the job.

During the re-fitting at Lyttelton pumps and everything connected with them were thoroughly overhauled in all respects and never gave serious trouble again.

Paterson Inlet was made on March 28 and Lyttelton on April 1.

Throughout all her cruise the scientific side of the ship's work was undertaken as follows: Lillie had all the biological work and Rennick was solely in charge of the soundings, and it can be safely said that neither of them missed a single opportunity that offered.

Meteorological Log: Drake;

Zoological Log: Bruce;

Magnetic Log and Current Log: Pennell;

while the officer of the watch, at the time, kept a general lookout for anything of interest that might occur.

Lyttelton, April 1 *to July* 10 – The ship lay at Lyttelton for three months, undergoing a general and thorough refit. Rennick was employed the whole time in plotting as much of the surveying work carried out in the south as could be done in the time, and in preparing the charts for the forthcoming winter's cruise; while Bruce looked after the refit.

Here we should like to take the opportunity of thanking Mr J. J. Kinsey for the great trouble he always took to help the Expedition in every way that lay in his power.

July 10 to Oct. 10, 1911, Winter Cruise – The ship again left Lyttelton on July 10 for a three months' cruise, to carry out surveying work round the Three Kings' Islands and between this group and the extreme north of New Zealand.

Hereabouts rather troubled waters prevail, as the swell from the Tasman Sea to the west meeting that from the Pacific to the east often causes a confused swell even in calm weather. The routine was to sound all day and have Lillie's plankton nets over all night, while opportunities for trawling were always taken as they occurred, Lillie being ready any hour of the day or night. On the whole a very good biological collection was obtained.

Occasionally a visit was paid to Mangonui on the east coast to take in fresh provisions, but, as a rule, the ship was hove-to for the night.

Lillie gave a series of popular lectures on evolution, which aroused the greatest interest fore and aft and did a great deal to break the monotony of the time.

Rennick and Mr Williams very ingeniously adapted a motor (most generously lent by Mr Kinsey from a motorboat) to work the Lucas sounding machine, which quite trebled the ship's sounding efficiency.

Sounding work does not, as a rule, provide exciting incidents, the day when it is undertaken coming under one of two headings – suitable for work or unsuitable. On unsuitable days, if the wind was easterly, nothing could be done except to heave to and drift; if westerly, there was good anchorage inside North Cape (the extreme north-east point of New Zealand), and the whole company were on these occasions very thankful for the quiet days in the ship, in comparison with the tossing about experienced in easterly gales. Mr Williams was also able to take advantage of these days to clean boiler tubes.

Bay of Islands, Sept. 24–28, 1911 – The time away was strictly limited to the period covered by the insurance of the ship, and so, on September 22, she had to leave for Lyttelton. On the way down she called in at Russell, Bay of Islands, to take in fresh provisions and pick up her mail. Three days were spent here waiting for the mail and were much appreciated by everyone, as it is an exceedingly pretty and, historically, very interesting spot. Rennick without delay set about cleaning and painting the ship so that she might be presentable for Lyttelton, though frequent showers of rain did not help him.

Lillie and a companion walked over the peninsula to the tiny little Bay of Wangamumu, where there is a small whaling station belonging to Messrs Jaggers and Cook. After a delightful walk through the bush, which took some seven or eight hours instead of three or four as expected, they were lucky enough to find Mr Cook there himself, for he had arrived from the Southern Ocean only a few hours previously, and was preparing to commence whaling round this station.

Lillie was able to make arrangements to stay with them for a month.

On Thursday, the 28th, the *Terra Nova* weighed and proceeded south, calling at Wangamumu on the way, where Lillie was landed with all his paraphernalia for collecting and preserving specimens.

Kaikoura, Oct. 8, 1911 – The ship arrived off Kaikoura at daybreak on the 8th and, being now close to home and with three days' grace, was able to put in two days' sounding on the hundred-fathom line and so to fill up a rather serious blank on the charts. The coast scenery here, on a fine day, is magnificent, as the seaward Kaikoura mountains run close to the coast and there are very many striking snow-capped peaks in the range.

On October 10 the *Terra Nova* was once more berthed alongside the wharf at Lyttelton. It is only fitting here to acknowledge the real hospitality shown the Expedition by New Zealand. From the Prime Minister downwards all were anxious to help, and the extent of this help received both from individuals and Government departments can only be fully realised by the ship's party, who found all difficulties smoothed away for them as soon as they arose. Dr John Guthrie, M.D., of Lyttelton, took on the duty of honorary doctor, and Mr P. Strain, of Christchurch, volunteered as honorary dentist. The services of both gentlemen were frequently and gratefully invoked.

Lyttelton, Oct. 10 *to Dec.* 15, 1911 – The ship was rather over two months at Lyttelton, and the time was just sufficient. Rennick was able to finish the chart of the Three Kings and the ship's soundings by working hard at it, although the time was veryshort for such work.

The mules, given by the Indian Government, had arrived some weeks before the return of the ship and were enjoying themselves in the fields on Quail Island, while the fourteen Siberian dogs from Vladivostok arrived during October. Everything that care and foresight could do for the mules had been done before they left India, and the Expedition owes a deep debt of gratitude to Lieutenant George Pulleyn of the Indian army, in whose care they were, for the trouble taken over them. For some time before leaving India they had been exercised in rocking-boxes to develop the muscles especially brought into use by the motion of a ship; and their equipment, which was sent with them, had been thought out with the greatest care. As we had only seven mules, the stables were built over the fore-hatch on the foremost side of the ice-house, so that they all were in the open air.

The dogs travelled unattended from Japan, and the officers of the different ships in which the mules and the dogs travelled took every possible pains to keep them in good health, with the most happy results in both cases.

Mr James Dennistoun joined the Expedition here to take charge of the mules on the way south.

Lillie had a very fairly successful month at Wangamumu, as a good many whales were caught, all however of one species – the Humpback. On his return from there he went off to Mount Potts in the South Island, collecting fossil plants, being fortunate in obtaining some specimens of the early Mesozoic flora.

The programme for the cruise as far as could be foreseen and according to the outline given in Captain Scott's sailing orders to the ship was:

1. Pick up Campbell and party about January 1 at Cape Adare.
2. Re-land them in the vicinity of Wood Bay.
3. Relieve the geological party about January 15 at Granite Harbour.
4. Land mules, dogs, stores, &c., at Cape Evans.

5. Lay out various depôts according to the orders to be received at the Hut, in readiness for the next season's work.

6. Consistently with carrying out the above, to make biological collections, sound, and carry out other scientific work to as large an extent as possible.

Dec. 15, 1911. *Leaving Lyttelton.* – At daybreak on December 15 the ship slipped and proceeded with mules, dogs, and all relief stores on board. This year was the year of transport workers' strikes at home, and it was only the extreme energy and determination of our manager, Mr Wyatt, and the great consideration shown by the shipping companies, that enabled the stores to be shipped out in time. Until Christmas Day we had a high barometer and fine weather, with fairly light but continuous southerly winds. This made our progress slow, but the fine weather more than compensated for that.

Rennick sounded twice a day while on the New Zealand continental shelf and once a day afterwards, except for two and a half days round about Christmas, when the weather prevented this work being done.

The motor now worked without a hitch; without it the necessity of crossing the Southern Sea quickly, so as to save the animals, would have allowed very few soundings to be taken. The smooth sea also allowed the mules to be moved in their stalls, so that the stables could be properly cleaned out and thoroughly disinfected.

Dec. 24, 1911, 60° 39' S., 178° 39' E. – The Sunday before Christmas, just as we were going to lunch, Nigger, the cat, fell overboard. He had been baiting the dogs on the poop, got uncomfortably close to one and, jumping to avoid the dog, went overboard. Fortunately it was an exceptionally calm day; the sea boat was lowered, and Nigger, who swam pluckily, was picked up and the ship on her course again twelve minutes after the accident. He was quite benumbed with the cold, but was taken down to the engine-room and well dried, given a little brandy to drink, and by the evening was all right again.

Dec. 26, 1911, 63° 31' S., 173° 23' E. – The first berg was passed on Christmas Day in 61° 31' S., and the first belt of pack on the 26th in 63° 59' S. It was not, however, till the following evening that the real pack was met, and in the dog watches of the 28th it began to get heavy, eventually holding the ship up at 1 a.m. that night.

Dec. 29 and 30, 1911, 66° 46' S., 177° 48' E. – After once getting in the pack until they were landed, the mules were exercised at least twice, generally three times, a week. They were walked round and round the main hatch and nearly all of them used to take the opportunity to roll, which they greatly appreciated. With the numerous ring bolts, combing of the main hatch, and other obstructions, there was a certain amount of risk; fortunately there was no accident and the benefit they derived from being moved about justified the risk being taken.

The deck was always well covered with ashes, which were kept for the purpose instead of being thrown overboard when sent up from the boiler-room. Two or three of the mules were inclined to jump about a bit; Lal Khan, in particular, enjoying his outings a little too much, but Bruce always took charge of him and managed to keep him well under control.

Every day after leaving New Zealand the dogs were given a run round the upper deck, and whenever the ship was stopped in the ice they were exercised on a floe, which afforded plenty of excitement to the men as well as to the dogs.

Being held up in the pack always gives a good opportunity for work of different sorts to be done. Lillie has his plankton nets over, trying different depths; Rennick always sounds; and, if the sun comes out, observations for variation are taken with the landing compass on a floe outside the range of disturbance of the ship's iron; and, if a floe with ice that has not been splashed with salt water is near enough, the ship is watered, as there is no knowing when the next opportunity may occur to obtain fresh water.

During the 30th the floes were visibly breaking up, and in the morning watch of the 31st steam was again put on the engines and the ship able to make slow but steady progress.

Jan. 1, 1912, 68° 44' S., 178° 55' E. – In the early hours of the New Year the pack was left, and no more pack was met till the ship got to within five or six miles of Cape Adare at 9 a.m. on the 3rd.

Jan. 3 *and* 4, 1912. *Off Robertson Bay.* – Here very heavy pack was found and Robertson Bay was full of it, but by waiting for the chance she managed to get within a mile of the moraine on which the hut is built by 11.30; all inside this was heavy pack swiftly moving with the tidal stream. Nothing could be done, and with the satisfaction of seeing people moving about near the hut, we had to haul off to the centre of the entrance, where there was now a space of clear water. While waiting, Lillie got a satisfactory trawl in fifty fathoms – the first of the season.

At 4 p.m. the water on the north side of the moraine cleared sufficiently to allow of an attempt at landing, and after an hour's pushing through the pack she anchored close in, in seven fathoms.

Rennick and Bruce immediately went on shore with the cutter and whaler, and in spite of a nasty swell which was breaking on the beach were able to embark some of the stores.

In an hour and a half, however, the boats had to return, as the pack was setting towards the ship, and she had to weigh at once; it was not till 1 p.m. the next day that the pack gave signs of easing up again, and the ship took till 4.30 to work her way through and anchor again in the same position. The swell had now died down, and in two and a half hours Campbell and all his party, their collections, and all necessary stores were on board; just in time, for the pack was again setting on the ship.

Robertson Bay is not a nice place from the seaman's point of view. The tidal streams are strong, the pack ice heavy, there are very many grounded bergs about, and gales are frequent and fierce, while the uneven bottom suggests the likelihood of unknown pinnacled rocks. It was with great satisfaction, there-fore, that we left the bay with Campbell's party on board in excellent health and spirits.

Jan. 7, 1912, 75° 15' S., 168° 37' E. – More pack was found lying off the coast of South Victoria Land and kept the ship well off shore till about forty-five miles E.S.E. of the extremity of the Drygalski Barrier, when it became sufficiently loose to let her turn in towards the Drygalski and work through it. With hopes alternately raised and lowered as the pack eased up or became heavier, the ship at last got on the north side of the Barrier and into clear water; and during the first watch of the 8th was secured alongside the sea ice at the entrance to what is now called Arrival Bay, about six miles north of Evans's Coves.

The gear and a month's depôt for Campbell's party were immediately disembarked, and with hands from the ship to haul a depôt sledge, he was left on a moraine about one and a quarter miles from the ship.

Jan. 10, 1912, 76° 3' S., 165° 55' E. – The ship slipped immediately her party returned, and meeting a good deal of fog and snow had some difficulty in working through the pack on the way out, being eventually held up during the forenoon of the 10th and kept there for thirty-six hours; but in the end she arrived off Beaufort Island during the afternoon of the 12th.

Jan. 12, 1912, 76° 42' S., 167° 12' E. – The prospect was not encouraging, as there was nothing but heavy pack in the direction of Granite Harbour and across the whole entrance to McMurdo Sound. It was, however, a glorious day, and the opportunity was taken to swing ship for magnetic constants, take observations for variation on the ice, sound, and try to collect plankton. In the Antarctic seas the water is often so full of diatoms that the fine meshes of the plankton nets choke as soon as they are put over. This, by stopping the passage of water through the net, prevents it catching anything and so renders useless many opportunities for collecting that would otherwise be favourable.

Jan. 13 to *Feb.* 4, 1912. *In or near McMurdo Sound.* – Till February 4 nothing could be done. On January 13 fast ice was found to extend as far north as the southern end of Bird Peninsula; and, when it was possible to work through the pack towards Granite Harbour, fast ice was found on the 23rd to extend thirty miles from the head of this inlet.

These three weeks were one long succession of being caught in the pack and struggling to get out again. Whenever there appeared to be any change, the ship would steam over towards Granite Harbour or Cape Evans to look; for often it appeared as if the ice in the strait was really breaking up, but every time in reality it was found that only comparatively little had gone out.

The time, however, was not wasted: whenever in a workable depth, with steam up, Lillie had his trawl out and so got six or seven trawls. Rennick got a number of soundings, though of necessity not in any particular line, and there were several opportunities for swinging ship and observing variation on fast ice, while an interesting series of Giant Petrels was obtained, ranging from white to the comparatively dark varieties.

Mather, who had taken great trouble in New Zealand to perfect his taxidermy, skinned all the ship's specimens.

At last, on February 4, the ship was secured alongside fast ice off Cape Barne. Atkinson came off with a dog team and reported all well, and was shortly followed by Meares and Simpson. They informed us that the ice was bad between the ship and shore, and consequently did not stay long, but took the mails with them when they left.

Feb. 6–14, 1912. Off Cape Evans. – During the next two days two miles of ice went out in a gale, and in the first watch of the 6th the ship was at last secured alongside fast ice, with safe ice between her and Cape Evans.

The dogs went ashore at once, the mules were hoisted out early the next morning and soon were safely ashore, after being on board fifty-four days. It says much for Dennistoun's care of them that they landed in such good condition.

Sledging the stores on shore was commenced at once; but it was two and three-quarter miles to Cape Evans (i.e. five and a half miles on the round trip), so that the work was necessarily slow.

The unloading continued steadily till the 14th, with a break in the middle when a gale took another mile of ice out and so made work much quicker; but on the 14th the ice started breaking up and yet did not go out; nothing could be done, and as after a day no change took place the ship crossed over the Sound to Butter Point to see conditions in that direction. There were still nineteen tons of stores, including some coal, to be landed, but all the essentials were ashore.

Feb. 15, 1912. McMurdo Sound. – At Butter Point a note from Taylor (in charge of the geological party) was found, saying that his party had camped there and gone on the previous day. Following the coast south, this party was observed on the Blue Glacier, and they were soon on board, all well. It was fortunate that Taylor had realised early the impossibility of the ship reaching Granite Harbour and so had beaten a retreat south over the piedmont. His specimens he had been compelled to leave in a depôt at Granite Harbour.

Feb. 19, 1912, 75° 27' S., 166° 49' E. – Shortly after they were picked up it came on to snow and blow. Owing to the weather it was impossible to land this party at Cape Evans, so the ship turned north to pick up Campbell's team. Course was shaped direct for the extreme of the Drygalski Barrier, and the ship ran, with considerable pack to the east of her and loose pack in shore, until heavy ice ahead forced her to turn back on her course some twelve miles and then work through the eastern belt of pack.

The following extract is from the ship's journal.

'Following the edge of the pack north, it was seen to be very heavy and the blink gave no sign of open water inside it until the ship was east by north thirty-five miles from the end of the Drygalski, when there was a belt of pack some two miles broad and clear water inside, at any rate for some distance: this belt was entered at 2.30 p.m., and it shows the heaviness of the ice that she was not clear till past 9 o'clock (a speed of a third of a knot), although it was comparatively loose-looking pack.

'The wind was rising as she worked through this strip of pack, and soon after it came on to snow heavily. Nothing could be done but to remain under easy steam, to avoid the floes, if possible, and look out for bergs. Before midnight it was blowing storm force and objects were visible at only a few hundred yards.'

The storm continued for two days, the latter half without snow, when Mount Melbourne showed up in great beauty.

The open water the ship was in was about six miles broad, and though across the pack another lead (or possibly open water) could be seen, five miles or so distant, yet it was absolutely out of her reach.

The wind was steady in direction from the south-west, and the whole pack and ship drifted slowly but surely north until it became imperative to regain the open sea to avoid being caught in the *cul-de-sac* of Lady Newnes Bay.

Feb. 21, 1912, 75° 0' S., 169° 10' E. – Fortunately the retreat was open and the wind fair for taking it, and so on the 21st the ship had regained her freedom of action, but was no nearer to relieving Campbell. That evening the storm eased down and course was again shaped for the Drygalski Barrier, with the hope that the ice which had previously barred her way might have drifted past the end of the Barrier. The pack (now on the starboard hand) was followed south as closely as possible, though snow often shut in everything to a ship's length and compelled her to stop till it was clear enough again to see where she was going. Gradually she was able to alter more to the west and north of west, until in the middle watch (23rd) she had rounded the southern end of the pack, some 20 miles south of the Drygalski Barrier, and was steering north through light pancake ice with, of course, the heavy pack again to the eastward of her. The pancake ice gradually became heavier, but she was able to make two or three knots at sixty revolutions.

Feb. 23, 1912, 75° 43' S., 164° 20' E. – Tempted on by what appeared to be water sky ahead, she rather unexpectedly came to a dead stop about 4 a.m. and could not even go astern in her wake, as the pack east of her was pressing in towards the coast and so consolidating the pancake ice she was in. At the same time the weather cleared and showed the extremity of the Drygalski Barrier to be fifteen miles due north. The water sky proved to be a myth.

After six hours the pressure eased and the *Terra Nova* was able to turn, taking, however, four hours' struggle to do so, and it took another twenty-six hours to escape from the ice which, on the day before, she had taken three hours to pass through. The alternative of leaving the ship in the ice and letting her drift with it past the Barrier was too dangerous to be more than thought of and cast aside, owing to the probable severe pressure that would be encountered while passing the Barrier itself.

The ship immediately proceeded to Cape Evans in order to report and to embark those going home, as it was probable that she would have to spend the remainder of her time trying to relieve Campbell.

As far as Cape Bird the ship passed through sea covered with pancake ice, and Ponting was able to get some very interesting photos of it in different stages of growth. Fortunately this ice only reduced her speed by about two knots.

Feb. 25, 1912. *Cape Evans.* – After passing Cape Bird a strong southerly wind sprang up, so that great difficulty was experienced in making Cape Evans; but finally she anchored close in at 2 p.m. on the 25th, all the fast ice having gone out since she was last here. At 11 p.m. the gale lulled for a few minutes and a boat was sent ashore. Simpson at once came off with the news that Lieutenant

Evans was at Hut Point and seriously ill, and should be taken off as soon as possible.

Feb. 28, 1912. *Off Castle Rock.* – The gale came on again at once, and it was not till the first watch on the 28th that the ship could secure alongside the fast ice about ¼ mile north of Hut Point and Atkinson and his party were able to bring Evans on board. The opportunity was taken to land two sledge loads of stores that would be useful at *Discovery* hut.

The ship at once proceeded to Cape Evans, and by everyone on shore and aboard lending a willing hand the remainder of the stores (about nineteen tons) was landed in the boats between 2 a.m. and 7.30 a.m., in a perfect calm and beautiful weather.

Feb. 29, 1912, 77° 7' S., 166° 25' E. – As soon as the last boat came off, the ship left for Terra Nova Bay again. It was essential that Lieutenant Evans should have a doctor with him for a few days more and so Atkinson had to go in her, though it was quite likely that she might not be able to re-enter the Sound.

March 1 *and* 2, 1912. *Off Terra Nova Bay.* – Conditions off Terra Nova Bay had not improved, and the ship ran up and down outside the heavier pack trying it in places wherever a sign of weakness showed; but with always the same result, that after entering two or three miles through pack which gradually grew heavier she would be brought up. Once, indeed, she managed to work through to a position north-east seven miles from the end of the Drygalski Barrier, but even here she was 35 miles from her destination, and this was the last flicker of reasonable hope.

The following extract is from the ship's log.

'All day on outskirts of ice filling Terra Nova Bay and extending fifteen to twenty miles eastward from the extremity of the Drygalski Barrier. On the outskirts thin pancake and small, but very heavy, bay ice floes; the heavy floes becoming more numerous and the new ice heavier the farther the pack is entered, till heavy pack with interspaces all filled with snow slush forms an impenetrable barrier; in places this year's pancake, consolidated and up to one foot thick, in thick slush, forms equally impenetrable barrier owing to its viscous nature.'

March 3, 1912, 76° 2' S., 167° 26' E. – In the forenoon of the 3rd the ship was again headed for Cape Evans. From several miles north of Beaufort Island to nearly Cape Royds the ship was passing through pancake ice, refrozen into large solid sheets of very varying heaviness but often sufficient to reduce her speed fifty per cent. The wait at Cape Evans was very short; she was only delayed an hour embarking those members going home who had not been able to get on board before, together with Keohane, and then proceeded to Hut Point, where the ice had now broken away to within a quarter of a mile of the hut.

March 4, 1912. Off Hut Point. – Atkinson and Keohane were landed and a few stores taken to the hut. The ship then ran for the Glacier Tongue to complete with water, and shortly after 10 p.m. (the 4th) proceeded again for Terra Nova Bay.

Although only twenty hours had elapsed between the time she passed Cape Royds going south, and repassed it going north, the ice had materially thickened, and between Cape Bird and Beaufort Island she forced through with considerable difficulty. The condition off Terra Nova Bay had, if anything, grown worse, and this time the ship was held up when 20 miles E.N.E. of the Barrier.

March 7, 1912, 75° 5' S., 168° 43' E. – Finally, on March 7, taking into consideration the nature and extent of the pack and the time of the year, the conclusion was reluctantly come to that the ship could not reach Arrival Bay that season, and so she turned north.

March 8, 1912, 73° 32' S., 174° 12' E. – The next day a sooty albatross was around the ship – a most welcome sight, proving the absence of pack to north of her; and from now on large numbers of deep sea birds were always round the ship.

Mar ch16, 1912, 66° 44' S., 164° 48' E. – On the 15th and 16th the *Terra Nova* passed up the north-east side of the Balleny Islands, closer than any other ship had been able to get, except Balleny himself; but either it was foggy or else it snowed so persistently, that nothing was seen of them except on the 16th, when the fog suddenly rolled away for two hours and, through a rift in the clouds, a glimpse of Buckle Island was obtained – part of the side of a snow-capped mountain with the sun on it, a rarely beautiful sight, appearing to be quite detached from anything to do with the earth herself. Before this one of the beautiful little snowy petrels had appeared, telling of ice in the vicinity, so the course was altered more to the northward and, when the fog lifted, icebergs and smaller bits of ice were seen on the port hand. It is seldom these little birds are found away from the close vicinity of ice.

Fires were put out on the 18th, a good offing having been made, the position being 64° S., 160° 12' E.

March 24, 1912, 55° 51' S., 165° 49' E. – Between the 21st and the 25th it blew hard, the climax being reached on Sunday night (the 24th), when a severe storm was raging, the most severe encountered by the ship during her whole commission. It is a wonderful sight to see a comparatively small ship in a storm, particularly at night; the marvellous way she rides over waves that look as if they must break on board, together with the dense darkness in the heavy squalls, relieved only by the white crests of the waves as they break, is a sight that makes up for a considerable amount of discomfort.

March 26 *and* 27, 1912, 52° 20' S., 167° 33' E. – The gale was followed by two days' calm, when Ponting was able to cinematograph the birds feeding close under the ship's stern.

When off the coast of New Zealand a school of sperm whales was seen and followed for some time with the hopes of getting a photograph. The animals, however, were too shy for the ship to approach within reasonable photographic range.

April 1. *Akaroa.* – At daybreak on April 1 the ship entered Akaroa harbour to despatch the telegrams with the season's news. Here we learned of Amundsen's success in his undertaking.

On the 3rd she was berthed alongside the wharf in Lyttelton again, and, needless to say, received with true New Zealand hospitality.

The season had in many ways been a hard one for the engine-room department, but they never failed the ship in any of the difficulties in which she found herself, and, although conditions were often disheartening, the hands kept as willing and cheerful as if everything was going well.

Lieutenant Evans and Drake went home on Expedition business, the members of the shore party who had returned dispersed to their respective duties in civil life, and the men who had joined in New Zealand signed off temporarily for the winter.

Refitting and laying up the ship was hurried on as rapidly as possible and, by the help of the New Zealand Government, arrangements were made for the ship's party to survey Admiralty Bay in the Sounds.

The party were boarded at an accommodation house near French Pass and worked from motor launches, these latter being fitted with the ship's Lucas sounding machines.

The party consisted of thirteen, including officers, and three hands remained in the ship at Lyttelton as ship-keepers.

This work lasted from June 10 to October 15, when it was necessary to return to Lyttelton to prepare for the coming relief voyage.

On the whole for that part of New Zealand the weather this winter was unfavourable, but, in spite of this, a satisfactory amount of work was carried out.

On August 17 we had the great misfortune to lose Brissenden by drowning. He was buried on the hillside overlooking the bay, and a marble cross erected to his memory. Robert Brissenden was a first-class man, careful and reliable, besides being a very good messmate, and his loss was very much felt by all.

Dec. 14, 1912. *Lyttelton.* – The ship left Lyttelton at 5 a.m. on December 14, 1012. A crowd of friends had collected to bid us farewell and send last messages to our companions in Victoria Land.

At 7 p.m. that evening we discovered a wretched man stowed away in the lifeboat. On being questioned the stowaway said he was a rabbiter and anxious to make a voyage in the *Terra Nova*: he appeared to be about thirty-five years of age and not very intelligent. As there was no object in taking this man south we shaped course for the nearest port, Akaroa, in order to land him. Fortunately, the Norwegian barque *Triton* was sighted at midnight, and her courteous captain relieved us of our stowaway, promising to land him in Dunedin.

The programme for the third southward voyage included the running of a line of soundings from Banks Peninsula to a point in Lat. 60° S., Long. 170° W. Thence the ship was to proceed due south until the pack was reached, sounding twice daily. After entering the pack she was to continue to force her way southward, keeping approximately on the meridian of 165° W., to sound over the less known portions of the Ross Sea, and to determine the nature and extent of the pack ice in this unexplored region.

The earlier southern voyages had mostly been made in more westerly longitudes.

In conjunction with the ambitious deep-sea-sounding programme Lillie was to make a number of quantitative plankton stations, and obtain trawls whenever the occasion was suitable. We also hoped to add materially to our magnetic observations for Variation, Dip, and Total Force.

The programme was fairly well adhered to, and thanks to Rennick's expert handling of the Lucas machine we obtained several soundings of about 3000 fathoms, when less ardent hydrographers would have surrendered to the bad weather.

Dec. 17, 1912, 49° 12' S., 178° 14' E. – On December 17 the Antipodes Islands were passed, the ship labouring in the heavy sea and occasionally rolling her bulwarks under; it was not considered advisable to attempt a landing. These islands are visited twice a year by a Government steamer, and have been examined pretty thoroughly, although rather sketchily surveyed.

On this voyage the ship was infested with rats, but Cheetham, our boatswain, who has crossed the Antarctic Circle fourteen times, showed himself an adept at rat-catching and soon freed the ship from the pest. He used to throw the rats over the side, and the albatrosses and mollymawks would swoop down and devour the vermin in an incredibly short time. We had all kinds of rat-traps in use, and even used mouse-traps to catch the young.

Dec. 26, 1912, 63° 43' S., 166° 36' E. – On December 26, in Lat. 63° S., we passed the first iceberg of the voyage, an old disrupted berg, and as we advanced southward all kinds of icebergs were to be seen. The ice-log shows a greater number and variety of bergs on this than on the two preceding voyages.

Dec. 29, 1912, 69° 28' S., 166° 15' E. – The great belt of Antarctic pack ice was not reached until December 29, when we had attained the 69th parallel.

On comparison with the records of earlier voyages it will be seen that the northern limit of the pack this year lay two degrees farther south than found on voyages made in more western longitudes.

The only other Expedition that has explored this part of the Ross Sea was that under Sir James Ross, who found a line of compact hummocky ice in the same position in 1842; this confirmation throws some light on the trend of the pack in this quadrant.

We had expected to meet with pack ice on crossing the Antarctic Circle, and our expectations not being realised, the ship's company looked forward to an almost ice-free voyage to the Ross Sea.

Our hopes were frustrated. The day after entering the pack we encountered heavy bay ice, which retarded us to such an extent that we could scarcely make more than one mile an hour on our course. We had a tremendous struggle this season to get into the Ross Sea at all, and not until we had fought our way for over 400 miles did we really get through the pack.

The weather conditions this season were all that we could wish for, and we had plenty of time at our disposal to carry out our scientific programme. When our way was barred by temporary congestion of the pack Pennell, Rennick, and Lillie would all get ahead with magnetic, deep-sea sounding, and biological work, mostly under favourable conditions.

Occasionally the sea was so discoloured by diatoms that we might have been steaming in the Thames estuary, and then again the discoloured area would be succeeded by belts of beautiful blue water wherein one could see crab-eater seals diving under the ship.

Quite the most fascinating sight in the pack ice was the exhibition of swimming by two crab-eaters in the open water leads on New Year's Day. They followed the ship and disported themselves like dolphins; when we were forced to stop owing to the closeness of the pack the two seals rubbed themselves along the side of the ship.

We were disappointed at seeing no Ross seals this year, for we have secured no specimens of this animal at all.

Jan. 5, 1913, 71° 48' S., 166° 48' E. – By January 5 we had worked through 68 miles of pack, averaging only 24 miles a day, and burning over seven tons of coal for each daily run.

Now we were confronted by small belts of ice composed of floes 15 to 20 feet thick and 100 feet in diameter. This ice was so hard that the ship could not break it. Whenever we collided with a floe the *Terra Nova* shook fore and aft, the officer in the crow's nest experiencing the most violent concussions.

On this day a penguin chased us for over an hour, crying out ludicrously whenever one of us imitated its call. The little creature became quite exhausted, as we were steaming through lighter ice at the time and it had to swim steadily after us. The poor bird was unable to reach the ship, as the 'kick' of the propeller swirled it away whenever it caught us up. As often as this happened the penguin would struggle on to a floe and reel about like a drunken man, until finally it lay still, thoroughly defeated.

Jan. 6 *and* 7, 1913, 71° 48' S., 166° 48' E. – We were completely beset with ice on January 6 and 7, and the officers spent their time working for Lillie, obtaining plankton and water-bottle samples at many different depths.

Lillie put out his twenty-four mesh net at 1000 metres, and obtained a lot of specimens, including a fine jelly-fish.

Jan. 8, 1913, 71° 41' S., 167° 4' E. – On January 8, the ice opening up, we proceeded slowly on our way. We passed close alongside a low hummocky iceberg which had three Emperor penguins on it. They must have been there some weeks, as the surface of the berg was much soiled and the snow trodden about over a great area. The iceberg was too high for the birds to have regained had they once left it. Two of the Emperors were very thin; the third, an enormous bird, was moulting and one could not make out what sort of condition he was in.

Until January 14 progress was painfully slow, but on this day the ship worked through into looser ice. The pack was eventually cleared on January 16 in Lat. 74° 50' S., Long. 177° 15' E.

The night of January 17–18 was very still and a belt of stratus cloud settled down, forming a thick fog; the ship nevertheless was worked through small ice belts and she rounded Cape Bird on the morning of the 18th. About breakfast time the sun dispersed the mist and shone brightly. The now familiar features of McMurdo Strait were clearly outlined to the southward, and our stout little ship steamed at full speed past Cape Royds towards our winter quarters.

We had spent the last twenty-four hours in 'squaring up' and preparing our comfortable, if somewhat limited, accommodation for the reception of our comrades at Cape Evans. The mails were all sorted and each member's letters done up in pillow-slips with his name boldly printed thereon. We had only one piece of bad news, the death of poor Brissenden, for all the wives and relations were well, and eagerly looking forward to the return of the Expedition. Every telescope and binocular in the ship was levelled on the hut as Cape Evans opened out from behind the Cape Barne Glacier. The bay was free of ice and one or two figures were discernible outside the hut.

The ship rapidly closed the beach, and by the sudden lively movements of those ashore we knew that the *Terra Nova* had been perceived.

As we stopped engines a crowd collected before the hut and we could count nineteen men – it was an exciting moment.

The shore party gave three hearty cheers, to which the ship's company replied. The Commanding Officer, espying Campbell, shouted through a megaphone, 'Are you all well, Campbell?' At this our friends on shore became speechless, and after a very marked hush, which quite damped our spirits, Campbell replied: 'The Southern Party reached the Pole on January 18 last year, but were all lost on the return journey – we have their records.'

The anchor was dropped; Campbell and Atkinson immediately came off and told us in detail how misfortune after misfortune had befallen our gallant leader and his four brave comrades. We listened sadly to the story, and our feelings were too deep to be described. We had actually prepared the cabins for the reception of our lost companions, and it was with infinite sadness that the beds were unmade, the flags hauled down from our mastheads, and those undelivered letters sealed up for return to the wives and mothers who had given up so much in order that their men might achieve.

But however great our sorrow we had the consolation of pride in the magnificent spirit shown by the Polar Party. The manner in which these men died is in itself an eloquent description of their characters as we knew them. The absolute generosity of Captain Scott himself runs through his dying appeal to the nation and those letters of his with no word of blame or reflection on others for the disaster, though he could not know that scurvy had smitten the last supporting party, and that those who would have come were fettered by illness and the weather conditions that finally arrested the advance of the dog teams.

It was characteristic also that he did not forget the future of his Expedition, but left instructions and letters to the end that the scientific results should be fitly published.

The two devoted men who died side by side with Captain Scott were fine British types. Wilson was a wonderful fellow, whose magnificent judgment helped us all to smooth over the little troubles which were bound to arise from time to time, and who (it has been said before and let it be said again) by his own example and the influence of his personality was mainly responsible for the fact that there never was a quarrel or an angry word in the Expedition.

Bowers possessed an individuality that attracted his companions enormously. He was, besides being a very quick, clever worker, a humorist of the most pleasing type. He bore hardship splendidly and stood the cold probably better than anyone in the Expedition.

The conspicuous bravery of Oates was typical of the man. 'The Soldier' was really loved by the men. He had a dry wit that always left him uppermost in those exciting arguments that did so much to cheer us during the winter season. Patrick Keohane, a splendid Irish seaman, remarked to us as the details of the story were unfolded: 'Captain Oates did just what we all expected of him, sir; he was a fine man that, sir; not much talk about him, but chock full of grit.'

The fifth man of the Southern Party was a British bluejacket of the finest type, who had made himself invaluable. Edgar Evans was the sledge-master, and to him we owed the splendid fitting of our travelling equipment. He left a fine record of service, and his example will do a great deal for the younger seamen of the Royal Navy.

The *Terra Nova* remained at anchor off Cape Evans for thirty hours, and those on board did their best to help the Cape Evans party to settle down for the homeward voyage.

We heard that the shore party had that day (Jan. 18) commenced the work of preparation for a third winter; they were delighted to see us. A typical extract from the diary of a member may be quoted:

'*Jan.* 18.

> *Terra Nova* in sight
> Hurrah! Hurrah!
> Great Joy –
> Hurrah!

We are relieved, and God be thanked for that – Teddy* is on board the *Terra Nova*. Everything all right there.'

Immediately greetings had been exchanged and the situation thoroughly grasped, all hands packed and transported the specimens, collections, and equipment to the ship. We worked all night, and in twenty-four hours had removed our effects to the *Terra Nova*, and closed the hut after clearing it up and making a list of provisions and equipment.

* 'Teddy' refers to Lieut. Evans, who was not expected to live after his bad attack of scurvy.

We have left at Cape Evans an outfit and stores that would see a dozen resourceful men through one summer and winter at least.

On Sunday, January 19, at 5.20 p.m., the Expedition finally left Cape Evans and proceeded in the *Terra Nova* to Cape Royds, where a depôt of specimens left by Priestley's party on the Erebus journey was embarked.

We then steamed up the Sound towards Hut Point until brought up by the fast ice which still stretched out for nearly ten miles from the southern shores of McMurdo Sound.

Early on January 20 Atkinson set out with a party of seven to erect a cross in memory of our lost companions. It had been constructed by Davies of jarrah, an Australian wood.

This cross, 9 feet in height, now stands on the summit of Observation Hill, overlooking the Great Ice Barrier and in full view of the *Discovery* winter quarters.

IN

MEMORIAM

CAPT. R.F. SCOTT, R.N.

DR E.A.WILSON CAPT. L.E.G.OATES, INS.DRGS. LT. H.R.BOWERS, R.I.M.

PETTY OFFICER E. EVANS, R.N.

WHO DIED ON THEIR

RETURN FROM THE

POLE. MARCH

1912

TO STRIVE, TO SEEK,

TO FIND,

AND NOT TO

YIELD

The line chosen from Tennyson's 'Ulysses' was suggested by Cherry-Garrard. Atkinson's sledge team consisted of those who had taken part in the search for Captain Scott.

They took two days to convey the heavy wooden cross to the top of Observation Hill and erect it. It was well secured, and will remain in position for an indefinite time, as there is no dampness likely to cause rot in this high latitude.

During Atkinson's absence the ship's officers were employed surveying and carrying out magnetic work; the engineers took this opportunity of letting fires out and cleaning the boiler. Atkinson returned on the night of January 21, having put Hut Point in order and closed the old *Discovery* hut, which, like our own winter quarters, we have left well stocked with provisions and what equipment we could spare.

During the night of the 19th a large iceberg swept into McMurdo Sound and was carried by the current directly for us. Having no steam we had to set sail and stand away to the northward from the sea ice to which we were made fast. We had some excitement, as the wind was very light; the sails were just full enough to give us steerage way, and the great tabular iceberg drifted close across our stern.

The ship now proceeded towards Granite Harbour. Steam was ready by 5 a.m. on the morning of the 22nd, and encountering detached belts of ice we furled sail and worked close to the coast of Victoria Land.

At 2 p.m. the *Terra Nova* rounded Cape Roberts and secured to the fast ice off Granite Harbour.

Gran in charge of a party of six men went in to bring off a geological depôt left by Taylor and Debenham. It was a hard journey, 17 miles there and back. A big open lead had to be crossed *en route*, and Gran's men negotiated this by converting their sledge into a 'kayak', using a canvas cover which made quite a good boat out of the sledge. On their way home to the ship they had the fortune to get on to a loose ice floe with their two sledges. Ferrying in this fashion much time was saved, and the party returned hungry and tired but successful at 3 a.m. on January 23.

During the absence of this party some surveying work was accomplished, and the astronomical observations taken by the navigating officers in conjunction linked on the work of Griffith Taylor and Debenham to the main survey. Off shore soundings were obtained by Rennick with a view to throwing light on the neighbouring glacier movements. Pennell carried out magnetic observations, Lillie trawled with the Agassiz and obtained a fine haul, which included enormous sponges. In short, the usual bee-hive industry in the scientific work was maintained.

At 3.30 a.m. the sledge gear was brought on board by Gran's party; they had secured all Taylor's and Debenham's beautiful geological collections, consisting largely of fossils and coral. These specimens had been left here a whole year ago.

This accomplished, we hauled in our ice anchors and proceeded under steam as requisite for working through the pack which barred our way to the Drygalski Barrier.

At 11.30 a.m. the ice became so heavy that we were forced to turn round and return towards Granite Harbour.

All day we worked to clear out of the pack and made only fair progress, the floes being so big that our weight would not move them. The outlook was brighter at midnight, when we were doing 5 knots to the northeastward, the ice-fields being less compressed. The punching and butting through continued with varying success till 9 p.m. on January 24, when the Commander concluded that it was a waste of coal and unfair to the ship to proceed. We stopped, therefore, and banked fires.

After a delay of seven or eight hours Bruce reported the ice to be opening tremendously, and we accordingly proceeded on January 25, as soon as steam was ready. Very gradually the old ship worked towards Terra Nova Bay. Shortly after noon we won through into a very big open lead and could make five knots on our course. We stopped to sound at 8 a.m. and noon, the soundings showing 437, 625, and 515 fathoms. These soundings show a 'deep' which I believe Professor David rather suspected. They were really taken for his benefit.

By 3 a.m. on January 25 we had worked the ship through the ice near Campbell's winter quarters and secured to the sea ice which extended a quarter of a mile out from the piedmont. This was particularly solid and slippery, being quite free from snow. Although so close to the shore we found the depth 198 fathoms.

We sent a party away under Priestley to pick up the depôt of geological specimens; the remainder of the Expedition visited the igloo where Campbell and his party spent the previous winter.

The visit to the igloo revealed in itself a story of hardship that brought home to us what Campbell never would have told. There was only one place in this smoke-begrimed cavern where a short man could stand upright. In odd corners were discarded clothes saturated with blubber and absolutely black. The weight of these garments was extraordinary, and we experienced strange sensations as we examined the cheerless hole that had been the only home of six of our hardiest men. No cell prisoners ever lived through such discomfort. Most of the *Terra Nova*'s crew secured mementoes of their visit to this unparalleled habitation.

We left a depôt of provisions at the head of the Bay, its position being marked by a bamboo and flag. This depôt contains enough food stuffs to enable a party of five or six men to make their way to Butter Point, where another large depôt exists.

Very early on January 26 we left these inhospitable shores, and steaming E.N.E. to get clear of the ice belts which stream up the coast, we virtually gained the open Ross Sea by the evening, on the return voyage to New Zealand.

An attempt was made to close the Balleny Islands, which do not all appear to be correctly charted, but thick weather and adverse ice conditions prevented our accomplishing this.

The *Terra Nova* stood well to the westward, as shown in the accompanying track chart, until she was in a good position for making New Zealand.

It is interesting to note that in latitude 64° 15' S., longitude 159° 15' E. the *Terra Nova* passed close to an iceberg twenty-one geographical miles in length.

On February 2, in latitude 62° 10' S., longitude 158° 15' E., during thick weather, the ship was beset with icebergs and at slow speed steamed for six miles along the face of one huge berg. She was in a narrow channel out of which she could not work owing to the close grouping of detached icebergs which lay on the other hand.

This last season the ice conditions appeared to be the worst on record as far as the exterior ice was concerned, but close to Victoria Land we were never seriously hampered.

The biological, magnetic, and hydrographical work was continued on our homeward voyage, and on February 10, at 3 a.m., the ship reached Oamaru, a small port on the east coast of South Island, New Zealand. Here Lieutenant Pennell and Dr Atkinson were landed with the Commander's despatch, which was sent to the Central News for simultaneous distribution throughout the world.

The *Terra Nova* remained at sea until Wednesday, February 12, when she returned to Lyttelton.

Her entry into the harbour was very different from the happy return we had so looked forward to.

With flags at half-mast we steamed into the port and were berthed alongside the Harbour Board shed by Captain Thorpe, the harbour-master. Thousands came to meet us and quietly notified their sympathy, and for many days afterwards we received messages of condolence from all parts of the world.

The ship sailed from Lyttelton on her homeward voyage on March 13, 1913, under the command of Lieutenant Pennell. In the ward room, besides the Captain, were Rennick, Nelson, Lillie, Levick, Anderson, Mr Williams, and Mr Cheetham. When Bruce went home by mail steamer with Lady Scott, Nelson volunteered for the position of second mate, and proved himself a most efficient officer. Mr Gibson Anderson of Christchurch volunteered for the voyage, and was taken on for coal trimming.

The ship had thirteen dogs on board, going home as pets of various members. Davies built platforms for the dogs; these stood about ten inches off the deck and had a ledge three or four inches high, so that in wet weather the animals would be off the decks and in hot weather have air circulating under them, while, when the ship was rolling, they had the ledges to support themselves against. These platforms were a great comfort to them.

March 23, 1913, 56° 2' S., 156° 25' W. – It was intended to run down the Great Circle track to 56° South and then east along that parallel. The ship made a good run down to 56° South, but then met easterly winds, fortunately, however, being able to pass about fifteen miles north of where the Nimrod group is charted (from information we received nearly a hundred years ago), and got two soundings, both over 2000 fathoms. Captain Davis in the *Nimrod* on her way home in 1909 passed right over the charted position, but weather prevented them sounding. Either this group is charted a great deal out of position, or, what is more likely, does not exist at all.

North-east winds continuing, the ship was driven a good deal farther south than was intended and met with a considerable amount of fog and thick weather.

March 27, 1913, 58° 51' S., 142° 29' W. – On the 27th she passed three bergs, and another one on the 29th, but the weather all these days was so thick that ice could only be seen at a very short distance.

March 29, 1913, 58° 39' S., 134° 54' W. – On the 29th, however, she was able to alter to the north-east and soon to leave these rather uncomfortable latitudes.

There was a marked dearth of birds all across the Southern Ocean, great grey shearwaters and the little black-bellied petrels being the most common, while the mollymawks and sooty alba-tross were only occasional visitors.

Cape Horn was passed on April 11, in a strong gale; but as the ship entered the Straits Le Maire at daybreak the next morning the wind dropped and the sun rose over Staten Island, ushering in a beautiful day; and from here, with very little exception, fine weather was experienced all the way to England.

While crossing the shelf on which the Falkland Islands stand, Lillie was able to trawl, and once again after leaving Rio de Janeiro, for the last time on the commission, the catch in this case being almost entirely composed of swimming crabs.

Trawling probably caused more excitement and interest in the ship than anything else she did, and the instant a catch came in-board Lillie was surrounded by an interested group of men, very anxious to see if any startling novelty had at last been dragged up from the bottom.

Across the Atlantic the plankton nets were put over, when possible, for half an hour every night, and a good series of catches was made; the middle watch was chosen, as experience had shown the practical impossibility of entirely preventing garbage, ashes, &c., from being thrown overboard during the day, and the nets faithfully collected everything that went over. At night, however, after washing down the shoots and the ship's side where ashes had been thrown over, the haul was made and the net brought in absolutely clean.

Rio was reached on April 28, and the ship stopped here four days, coaling, taking in fresh provisions, and giving leave.

While crossing the Tropics the dog watches were taken in the stoke-hold by the after-guard. This gave each fireman a sixteen hours' spell free of watch two days out of every three: a great boon when the conditions are trying, as they undoubtedly are, in the engine-room and stokehold in the Tropics.

The ship called at Fayal in the Azores, in order to cable home, and anchored off Horta on June 2, She was placed in quarantine, much to our chagrin, though facilities were allowed for sending cables and getting provisions.

At last, on June 11, the ship dropped anchor in Crow Sound, Scilly Islands, where two days were spent painting and cleaning up, and on June 14 she arrived at Cardiff, exactly three years after leaving.

Here it only remains to acknowledge the exemplary conduct of the ship's company, fore and aft. Every member worked to help the Expedition forward loyally and cheerfully, accepting each position as it came, all hands doing their best to help matters forward and to see the humorous side of everything.

UNIVERSITAS ANTARCTICA!

Lecture on the Ross Ice Barrier by Captain Scott
June 7, 1911, 8 p.m. [from notes by Griffith Taylor]

1. *Flotation.* – Let us first of all consider the question of the flotation of the Barrier. There can be, I think, no doubt that it is afloat. On pages 417–420 in the *Narrative of the Discovery* will be found an account of the Ross Barrier, in which we read that its face is 360 miles long, and that the sea exceeds 1800 feet in depth along the greater part of this distance.

The ice wall is 150 feet high here in places, and we must allow for a much greater depth which is submerged below the level of the sea.

The ratio of submerged to visible ice appears to vary, and should be investigated on bergs in our vicinity. Even if it is 7 to 1, then the Barrier is afloat at its edge, and the same is of course the case if the ratio be taken as 4 to I. Professor David quotes an example of 1 to 1, but that is certainly exceptional.

It seems certain that there is a layer of water under the great Ice Barrier, which has five times the extent of the North Sea.

2. *Limits.* – We have several observations of the ice front, notably Ross in 1840, and the *Discovery* in 1902. The latter showed a recession in general of from 15 to 20 miles, with a maximum of

45 miles. In 1911, however, Pennell reported that the conditions appeared to have changed little during the last ten years.

This means that 45 miles at any rate must have been afloat. The Ross Sea does not get shallower so far as we know.

We must remember that the wall near Balloon Bight varies greatly in height. If the ratio of the edge of the Barrier above and below water line be taken as 1 to 4, then the ice sheet seems to vary in thickness from 70 to 700 feet, with an average of about 400 feet.

But it is quite conceivable that this sheet is extremely thin in places.

3. *Crevasses.* – These natural breaks in the continuity of the ice have been studied in some detail. We observe that they are radial near the Bluff and White Island. They have parallel sides, both in plan and section. No crevasses seem to occur more than 15 miles from the land. Curiously enough, none of these seem to have any great depth, for I saw platforms about 50 feet down, and rarely got a lead down beyond 8 fathoms (50 feet).

Let us compare an ice sheet over land with a similar sheet extending over water. In the first type one could not expect uncrevassed areas of any size if the ice were *moving* over the land (though we must remember that the *stationary* ice over the Plateau is not crevassed).

Again, over a sea surface the crevasses would only extend for a limited distance, in fact to sea-level, where they would freeze over. This may account for the limited depth observed.

Near the Barne and Shackleton Inlets the great lateral trench was filled with pools due to thaw waters, and this was 100 feet deep. If the sheet were 1000 feet thick, one would expect this 'rupture crack' to be much deeper.

4. *Temperature and pressure.* – The temperature in the crevasses seemed fairly constant near the land, but when farther away it seemed to rise with depth. This looks like the result of a sub-glacial sea.

The atmospheric pressures as taken on the journey to 82° S. varied very little from those at Hut Point:

At 79°, +0.045" difference At 81°, +0.06" difference
At 80°, +0.04" difference At 82°, −0.03" difference

The barometric gradient probably rises as one goes south, so that one cannot use the barometer to obtain accurate levels.

One could get equal (and useless) readings all the way if the change in *levels* corresponded to the change in barometric gradient.

In working up the meteorology notes, barometer figures based on Royds's journey – who went nearly parallel to the Barrier edge – were unfortunately used to obtain results for the Southern journey.

Finally, we may conclude that the tendency of all the facts is to support the 'Floating Barrier' theory.

5. *Movement of the Barrier.* – There is certainly not enough inclination in the Barrier ice sheet to account for its motion. The Bay of Whales (or Balloon Bight) has not moved much, and this may be taken as the eastern limit of the moving sheet. We don't of course know the extent of the ice sheet to the south-east.

Depôt A moved 608 yards in thirteen and a half months, which agrees closely with the 500 of movement observed by the *Nimrod*.

We must take note of the direction of movement observed, for this may not represent the total movement. It may give the minimum, and this result is very startling in view of the sluggish *land* glaciers.

Simpson suggests that the deposition of snow on the Barrier leads to an expansion due to the increase of weight. If it is 350 miles long and 400 feet thick, then the ratio of thickness to length is 1 to 5250. This can be adequately compared to a sheet of cardboard ⅛ inch thick and the length of this hut (50 feet).

The ice sheet can only move to the north. If we assume it moves 1000 yards, and that 175 square miles is the amount moved north, then the mass to be added to keep the breaking front about the same position is 11.7 cubic miles.

Let us consider the snow deposition. It is stated that about 4 inches of compressed snow falls per year. The blizzards evidently build up shallow flat hummocks here and there, and may cover the whole surface at the fourth effort.

The old *Discovery* Depôt was covered in 13 inches of old snow or 9 inches of ice.

If we assume the Barrier area is 350 x 350 miles, then we get a mass of 16.5 cubic miles.

The difference in these two interesting figures – 16.5 cubic miles and 11.7 cubic miles – may be due to an ablation of the under surface of the sheet by warm water. However, we may assume that there is sufficient snowfall on the Barrier to account for the movement, which is a fact of the first importance.

At the edge of the Barrier there is a curved ascent, and 'doming' is common in bergs. May not this curving be a result of the outward expansion?

The movement of the northern glaciers seems to be much greater than that of the Beardmore and southern glaciers. Perhaps it is six times as great. But the slow movement in the south may still be sufficient to account for the ice sheet's advance.

The fact that the great lateral trench keeps open looks as if rival motions were at work.

As far as 170° W., Campbell says that the 1911 survey showed the western edge of the Barrier face to be stable, and with no change like that since Ross's time. Of course there may be cata-strophic years. We know that icebergs are very plentiful in some years in the Southern Ocean. This last summer our Glacier Tongue broke away after remaining for many years.

6. [*Method of growth*]

7. *Mainland glaciers*. – There is very little evidence of large motion. David says the Nansen Glacier presses out the sea ice; but quite probably it is the other way, and due to the sea ice pressing against the Glacier Tongue. The movement of the glaciers is a measure of the pressure behind; they are, however, so cold in these regions that their movement is sluggish compared with those in temperate climes.

I do not think there is anything like 13 inches annual snowfall on the Ice Plateau. If there is recession along the coast, the same must obtain on the great Ice Plateau. The high level moraines decrease in height above the present surface of the ice, the débris being 2000 feet up near the coast and only 200 feet above near the plateau. However, the Beardmore from its great crevasses seems to show extra movement.

8. *The inland ice sheet.* – All our data are hypothetical – we are erecting an edifice of theoretical bricks! We may give it the area of two-thirds of the circle drawn with a radius of 1200 miles.

There seems to be a descent from 9000 feet at the Pole to 2000 near the edge, and then a rapid fall at the sea line.

We may surmise 50 to 100 yards movement per annum across the edge of the Plateau, with a thickness of 700 or 800 feet; but all this is merely a fine effort of the imagination!

The ice cliffs all round the continent seem much the same. The depths over the shelf at the edge seem of about the same order also.

We must remember that the new set of facts of the Great Plateau bounded by the new range of mountains was never thought of before 1903, and is not fully digested yet.

I believe that the snowfall increases towards the fringe of the plateau sheet.

These facts suffice to account for the outflow of Antarctic bergs. In latitudes 66° S. and 73° S. we find the same thickness of the ice cliffs. It must, however, be admitted that much of this theorising is very weak.

Finally, with regard to the question of the high continental Plateau and the land under the ice sheet I will ask the Physiographer to descant.

Discussion

As usual, Captain Scott called on the members in the order in which they sat at the table.

Oates commented on the difficulty of detecting differences in the Barrier level. He often saw herds of cattle on the ice surface which turned out to be débris of previous camps.

Wilson said that if the outward movement was due to a flattening of the Barrier mass, then he would expect the great Shackleton Inlet trench to fill up.

Wright suggested that it was aground before the great lateral trench was reached.

Taylor drew attention to the great amount of surface-sculpturing due, not to pressure, but to thaw waters and direct sun-melting. Some of the shallow crevasses might be due to this and not to movement or pressure – as on Butter Point.

If the Ferrar Tongue had grown since Captain Scott's visit, then these Antarctic glaciers were by no means sluggish. Might not the slope apparent at the edge of the Barrier be due to the greater weathering at the edge, due to the presence of warm waters and stronger winds? He suggested that the word 'glacierised' should be used for lands covered by glaciers instead of 'glaciated', which might be kept for land forms exposed on recession.

He discussed the probable structure of the continent, with 'block' coast near Ross Island and an 'Andean' Range near America. The level surface of the Plateau was largely due to the preservative action of the ice cap. But it would also seem to exhibit 'senile' features, due to a previous cycle of normal erosion.

Probably Antarctica was a primeval solid block of the earth's crust of the type known as a 'Shield'.

Nelson thought the increase in snow above would certainly be balanced by the solution below. He thought the face of the Barrier would be curved to the north, unless something were affecting it besides purely mechanical agents.

Simpson said that simply lowering thermometers into the crevasses was useless. They should be buried in ice in the crevasse sides.

Debenham said that the Admiralty Range was certainly not of a true Pacific type.

The meeting adjourned about 10 p.m., but a select group of debaters carried on the arguments until 12.15 a.m.

by *Griffith Taylor, B.Sc., B.E., B.A., F.G.S.*
(*Senior Geologist to the Expedition*)

It is always a wise principle in research to proceed from the known
to the unknown. So little has been written on the subject in
question that we should have almost a blank sheet were it not for
the geologists of Shackleton's Expedition, whose detailed work
is not yet published. Let us glance at a map of the South Polar
regions, however, and see if we can deduce any useful principles
from neighbouring lands.

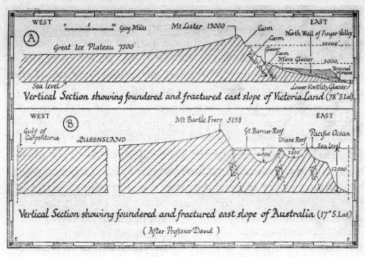

The physiography of the eastern coast of Australia has been
subjected to a somewhat detailed investigation during the last ten
years, with the result that it is found to exhibit splendid examples
of subsidence, trough faulting, and rivers 'drowned' by the sea.
Great slices of the coast have sunk below the waves fairly lately in

geological times, so that many of the great rivers of Eastern Australia now rise on the present coast (the old divide) and flow inland to the central lowlands. The features characteristic of this portion of the crust are therefore an elevated coastal region sloping gradually to the west and sharply truncated by 'faults' on the east.

Let us now journey southward to Antarctica and take a birdseye view of the coast of the Ross Sea and of the great mountain range which leads from the Ross Sea and McMurdo Sound almost to the Pole. We notice at once that this range extends almost due north and south, as was the case in Australia, that it practically constitutes the shore line, that it has a steep eastern slope – often dropping ten thousand feet in a few miles – and that it descends gradually on the west to a uniform land mass of a plateau type.

It seems evident that these points of resemblance are not accidental. The great earth movements which affected Australia in middle and late Tertiary times also affected Antarctica. A readjustment of equilibrium raised the west and depressed the east in both continents. The central portion of Australia, consisting of ancient rocks which have been planed down to a uniform level by the normal agents of erosion – by rivers, wind, &c. – is an example of a *peneplain*. It was formed in middle Tertiary times, and bears all the evidence of 'old age' in a land surface. As we have seen, it has been elevated and now the rivers are cutting it down again, forming canyons all round its coastal edges, and the 'cycle of erosion' has commenced anew. In Antarctica the land below the central ice plateau would appear to be a similar peneplain. The comparatively slight depth of the *outlet* glaciers seems to indicate that the ice cap is not very thick, probably one or two thousand feet only. The peneplain is, however, elevated to eight thousand feet instead of one to three thousand as in Australia.

It is, however, with the margin of the ice cap that these few pages are concerned. Just as in Australia beautiful canyons and falls have resulted from the attack of the weather on the margins of the plateau, so in Antarctica the ice rivers and agents of frost erosion have carved out their own characteristic topography.

We know from the fossils that warmer conditions existed in Mesozoic times in Antarctica, probably in early Tertiary times. Moreover, the elevation of the land so many thousand feet has undoubtedly given rise to a permanent refrigerating system of winds which has made Antarctic coasts much more inclement than they would have been with a less elevated interior.

There is practically no trace of *pre-glacial* topography such as might be shown by a moulding of the inland ice cap. We may picture the rock surface like that of upland Norway, as a gently rolling plateau. As the ice mantle covered Antarctica, occupying the more pronounced swellings first, and then spreading in lobes of ice down the broad depressions, we may imagine that a very little difference in the contour might determine the position of the great outlet glaciers where the ice cap drained away to the sea. In other words, the glacier valleys do not appear to owe much to pre-glacial topography.

Let us now survey the marginal mountain range and the ice plateau more closely. The plateau seems to rise to 11,000 feet near the South geographic Pole, and decreases gradually to the north, being about 7000 feet at the South magnetic Pole. The mountain ranges have peaks, such as Markham and Lister, rising to 15,000 and 13,000 feet respectively, but the average height is perhaps about 9000 or 10,000 feet, while for considerable stretches near Granite Harbour they are only 6000 or 8000 feet high. Every 20 or 30 miles this fairly continuous range is broken by a huge 'outlet' glacier. Many of these are now well known, such as the Beardmore, which is over 100 miles long and 30 miles wide, the Ferrar, Mackay, David, &c. They form the only routes from the coast to the interior, and were it not for the *ice falls* where the glacier covers some irregularity in its rock floor, or the more dangerous *crevassed areas*, where it sweeps round a corner, or receives the thrust of a large tributary, they would not be difficult to traverse with sledges. The grade is not very steep, and they are to some extent sheltered from the blizzard drift which is the great obstacle to Barrier and plateau journeys. Their detailed topography is, however, very different from that of an area subjected to 'normal' erosion.

The regions more especially investigated in the two sledge journeys of the Western Geological Parties in 1911 and 1912 were the following:

(a) The Ferrar and Taylor outlet glaciers (77° 40').

(b) The Koettlitz ice delta and its hinterland (78° 20').

(c) Granite Harbour and the Mackay outlet glacier (77°)

(d) The Great Piedmont Glacier between Granite Harbour and New Harbour (77° 20').

Each of these regions presented its own peculiar topography, and the four were diverse enough to embody almost the whole cycle of glacial erosion within their domain.

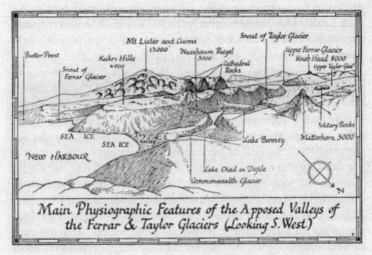

Main Physiographic Features of the Apposed Valleys of the Ferrar & Taylor Glaciers (Looking S. West)

(a) *The Ferrar and Taylor 'outlet' glaciers and the Dry Valley.* – These two glaciers are now connected by an ice col near Knob Head Mountain, but were originally distinct parallel glaciers draining the ice plateau. As one marches up the Ferrar Glacier and notes its crevasses and ice falls, one wonders what the rock floor is really like – under the ice river. Just 5 miles to the north is another glacier which furnishes the answer to this question, for the Taylor Glacier now stops short 25 miles from the sea, and in Dry Valley we see how all the other valleys will appear when the ice age shall pass away from Antarctica.

Starting from New Harbour at the mouth of Dry Valley, the latter presents a typical catenary cross-section. A splendid pair of walls with the characteristic slope of 33° defines the glacier trough. There is no large terminal moraine near the sea, which seems to denote a fairly uniform and perhaps rapid retrocession of the glacier. About 6 miles from the coast a narrow defile appears on the north side, but the rounded valley floor rises gradually to 2000 feet over the greater part of the trough. West of this point there is a sudden drop from the Nussbaum 'Bar' (or Riegel) into the next 'bowl' of the valley. This is filled with moraine material to the depth of several hundred feet, for the drainage of the 'bowl' is *away* from the sea to the salty waters of Lake Bonney. The defile previously mentioned is about 1500 feet deep, and would seem to be a water-cut gorge denoting an inter-glacial period.

Lake Bonney is about 3 miles long and is separated into two portions by a granite bar 500 feet high. This also is traversed by a narrow gorge on the northern side of the trough and is a smaller edition of the Nussbaum 'Bar' or Riegel. Then about ½ mile farther west we reach the snout of the Taylor Glacier, which appears to be overriding moraine material at its extremity. The surface of the latter rises 600 feet in a very short distance, and is carved into alcoves and gullies by the sun – all of these erosion features presenting a steep face to the north and a gently sloping one to the south. The thaw streams on the glacier and in the moraine-filled Dry Valley all flow to the N.E.

Visitors to Switzerland will recognise how closely this altern-ation of 'gorge', 'riegel', and 'bowl' recalls the classic glacial valley south of the Saint Gothard Tunnel. Moreover, Lake Lucerne owes its cross-like plan to the action of two parallel glaciers – one of which overflowed (near the Rigi) into the adjoining valley. The same process is being carried on today where the 'apposed' glaciers of the Ferrar and Taylor valleys are joined in Siamese-twin fashion south-east of Knob Head.

(b) The *Koettlitz Glacier* cascades over ice falls near Heald Island and reaches sea level while still 20 miles from its snout. This 20 miles of low-level glacier is extremely interesting, for it would appear to be a stagnant area whose chief characteristics are due to the action of thaw waters on an old glacier surface. The pinnacles, bastions, and bergs have been described in the preceding narra-tive. Here again the drainage is directed diagonally across the glacier to the north-east. Some movement has taken place, for the edge of uniform glacier sheet on the south is fringed by great bergs which are differently oriented, though all sealed in the extremely ancient water-cut labyrinth of ice which constitutes the north-west portion of the delta.

Below the scarp of the Royal Society Range is a hinterland of parallel valleys. These are about 10 or 12 miles long, and are in many cases occupied by small glaciers in the western half of the

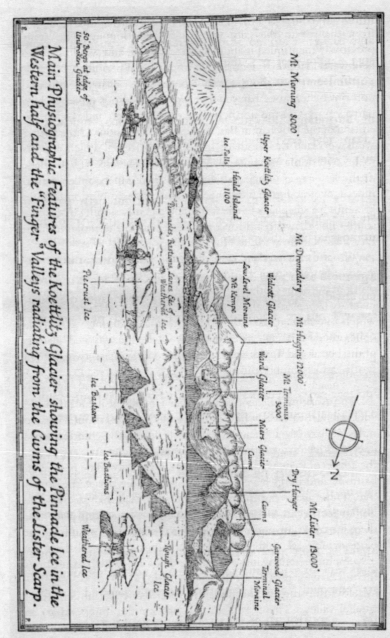

Mt Morning 8000'

Upper Koettlitz Glacier

Ice Falls

Heald Island 1100

Mt Dromedary

Walcot Glacier

Lowlevel Moraine

Mt Kempe

Mt Huggins 12000'

Ward Glacier

Mt Terminus 3000'

Miers Glacier

Cwms

Dry Hanger

Cwms

Mt Lister 13000'

Garwood Glacier

Terminal Moraine

Pinnacles, Bastions, Lanes Etc of Weathered Ice

Piecrust Ice

Ice Bastions

Ice Bastions

Weathered Ice

Rough Glacier Ice

50' Bergs at edge of Unbroken Glacier

N

Main Physiographic Features of the Koettlitz Glacier showing the Pinnacle Ice in the Western half and the "Finger" Valleys radiating from the Cwms of the Lister Scarp.

Koettlitz Glacier: physiographic features

valley. They are identical with the 'finger' valleys described in the reports on the glacial geology of the Rocky Mountains, U.S.A. Narrow ridges about 3000 feet high separate them. Some 'hang' a thousand feet above the Koettlitz. Characteristic hills, triangular in plan, occur where these valleys join, and all of them 'head' in beautiful cwms. Above these, cwms, and more cwms, fret the scarp of Mt Lister over the whole extent of its 10,000 feet face. There is little doubt that we have here an example of the way the glacial cycle commences its operations, for this is a fault scarp of comparatively recent date.

(c) *Granite Harbour*, like New Harbour, is probably a relic of the period of glacial maximum when the ice flood exerted tremendous erosive power on its bed, and was able to erode far below sea level. We shall, however, never be able to witness these maximum forces in operation. Because a dwindling river has little effect on the topography it would be foolish to deny the action of a great river in flood; just as our observations in the Antarctic on a nearly stagnant or receding glaciation are not to be taken as descriptive of the most active periods in glacial history.

The first feature that strikes the geologist is that as one proceeds north there is less and less land exposed below the snow and ice mantle. This implies, I think, that the precipitation in the south-west corner of McMurdo Sound is extremely little, and increases both northward and southward. The most striking feature in the harbour – the Ice Tongue – has been described in the narrative. The Mackay Glacier moves 3 feet a day, as already recorded. Mention must be made of the ridge separating the new glacier from the Devil's Punch Bowl. This has certainly been covered quite lately by the new glacier. The harder dykes are striated, but the ridge is for the most part covered with granite débris. There is practically no englacial rock débris in the glacier, so that one is led to the important conclusion that the floor of the new glacier is covered with rock débris and that no erosion is taking place under this fairly large glacier. What was the floor of the Mackay Glacier at its period of greater area is exposed in many places 1000 feet above the sea ice in the form of rock-strewn plateaux.

One of the most interesting features is the evolution of the cwm which is indicated on all sides in the steep faceted slopes. On

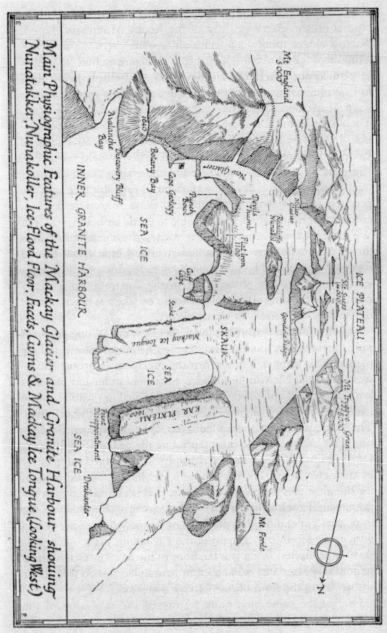

Main Physiographic Features of the Mackay Glacier and Granite Harbour showing Nunatakker, Nunakoller, Ice-Flood Floor, Facets, Cwms & Mackay Ice Tongue (Looking West)

Mackay Glacier and Granite Harbour: physiographic features

Discovery Bluff are the couloirs or chimneys; on Mt England these become somewhat funnel-shaped; on the face of the Kar Plateau they deepen to a definite if shallow bowl. They obviously only originate on steep slopes where the icy covering is shallow. Avalanche Bay and the Devil's Punch Bowl are respectively filled and empty cwms, both at sea level. Along the southern crest of the valley are giant cwms each with its own glacier. Here the Miller Glacier has cut through the divide and links the Mackay presumably to the upper Debenham Glacier. The walls are faceted, but not much faceting is visible – for the Mackay would seem to be filling its bed to a greater extent than the Ferrar or Taylor glaciers. Traces of a high level plateau at 3000 feet are evident all around Mt Tryggve Gran, and the ice sheet drains thence into large tributary glaciers such as the Cleveland.

The upland topography is of three types. There are mountains, such as Tryggve Gran, whose shape is due to their stratigraphy. This peak is flat-topped owing to the presence of a dolerite capping. Others exhibit the typical cusps of the Matterhorn type, due to cwms encroaching on three sides. Others again, such as Mt Forde, the Whale Back and Whitefinger, are now like giant *nunakoller*,* for the cusps have yielded to the smoothing action of frost erosion.

Scattered over the glacier are the *nunatakker** (such as Mount Suess) and *nunakoller** (Gondola Ridge and Redcliffs) which have been described in the narrative.

(d) Space does not permit of any adequate account of the *Great Piedmont Glacier*. It has a seaward edge some 200 feet thick over the land, and for a considerable portion its front would appear to be floating, for here the edge is but 30 feet above the sea ice (and presumably 200 feet below water level). It rises to some 2000 feet above the sea about 3 or 4 miles from the coast, and is beautifully moulded over hidden *nunakoller*. One or two of these project above the ice about a thousand feet, and the mountains behind exhibit beautifully the relation of lower glaciated slopes to cuspate peaks. The plane separating these topographic types is here about

* The two types of islands projecting through the ice sheet need to be distinguished. *Nuna-tak* is 'lonely *peak*', and I suggest *nuna-kol* (*fide* Gran) for the *rounded* ridges which have been covered by the ice-flood.

3000 feet high. Behind many of the rocky capes the piedmont appears to be nearly stagnant, or receding slowly, for the ice either begins to thicken very gradually or is greatly sun-weathered. In no case is there any evidence of pressure or 'overhang' on the capes, though the crevasses opposite the valley glaciers show some movement, no doubt due to the pressure of the latter.

In conclusion it will be of interest to trace the features accompanying the growth of an ice age as exhibited in Victoria Land. Near Cape Evans the change of a snow drift into a *glacieret*, and of the latter into a glacier, can be studied in many places. The later stages depend greatly on the topography. If the land is flat – i.e. part of an old peneplain – the ice sheet merely spreads out in great lobes, of which examples occur near the Solitary Rocks on the flattened slopes north of the Taylor Glacier. This grows larger and spreads out laterally, and, to my mind, plays a protective part, as in the Great Piedmont.

If, however, we are dealing with steep contours, the incipient glaciation – accompanied by water at this stage – cuts out couloirs and shallow cwms. The next stage is probably that represented by the scarp of Lister. Ultimately some cwms encroach on others and dominating 'finger valleys' are initiated. These ultimately become 'outlet' glaciers.

The 'outlet' glaciers rise to a maximum, overriding the slopes and carving out what later appear as shoulders or benches. At this period there is true glacial erosion. The *riegel* are overridden and planed down, the fiords are cut out, the lakes are deepened. Later the snowfall diminishes and the erosive power decreases, and the glaciers dwindle through all the stages recorded by Hobbs. The Beardmore Glacier with its tributaries largely entering at grade, the Mackay with a few 'hanging' glaciers, the Ferrar with a preponderating number of tributaries hanging on the slopes of the main trough, are examples of the earlier stages in this decline. The Koettlitz with its tributaries 5 miles back from the main glacier and the Taylor Glacier with its extraordinary ice-free outlet trough 25 miles long are later stages in the retrocession of the ice mantle.

THE GEOLOGICAL HISTORY OF SOUTH VICTORIA LAND

by F. Debenham, B.A., B.Sc.
(Assistant Geologist to the Expedition)

It is now nearly fifteen years since the first landing was made on the mainland of South Victoria Land, since which time four scientific expeditions have visited it and returned with geological information. This has been, or is being, published in the form of reports of a more or less technical character. Therefore it seems advisable that an attempt should be made to condense this information into a popular narrative of what actual changes that area has undergone in past time, so far as they are known.

The tale must necessarily be incomplete, for the difficulties confronting geological investigation in those regions are naturally considerable, but enough has been done to warrant a preliminary interpretation of the known facts.

South Victoria Land at the present day is marked on the map as a strip of coast running in a southerly direction from Cape Adare (Lat. 71°) and merging into King Edward VII Plateau in the region of the Beardmore Glacier (Lat. 83°–85°). As appears in the physiographic account, it consists for the most part of a high level plateau terminated along the coast by steep escarpments, more or less indented by the action of huge overflow glaciers. It includes several groups of volcanic islands, the chief of which is the Ross Archipelago (Lat. 77°–79°). But in this narrative we shall include the Ross Sea and the Great Ice Barrier in the region, as inseparably bound up with Victoria Land in its history.

The oldest rocks met with in South Victoria Land, forming its foundation, or 'shield', consist of gneisses, schists, quartzites, and crystalline limestones, much altered and folded by later earth-movements. On account of this alteration, much of their story is hidden from us, but we may compare them in age with the rocks of Western Australia or Eastern Canada – that is, they are of pre-Cambrian age. They were laid down for the most part by the agency of water, the schists and limestones being clays and chalks when they were formed. The sea-bottom on which these deposits collected was subject to continual up-and-down movements, changing the character of the deposit, for we find in rapid succession and in thin layers schists which were fine muds, next to quartzites which were sandbeds, and marbles which were either deep-water chalk deposits or shallow clear-water coral reefs.

On account of the complex folding of these beds, as well as the difficulty of obtaining a measurable section, we are unable to make any definite statement as to their thickness, but they cannot have been less than 15,000 to 20,000 feet. But figures are of little value, since there is no method of ascertaining what thickness of strata has since been denuded from the surface. The folding and heating of the rocks has since quite destroyed all evidence of the animal or vegetable life of that time, though numbers of small graphite particles, found in the crystalline limestones, may be the remnants of carbonaceous growth in the ancient coral reef.

Our earliest view, therefore, of the region is that of a sea bordered by land long since used up in forming these deposits of mud, sand, and limestone. The gneisses were in some cases huge intrusions of granite connected with the up-and-down movements referred to, and in other cases conglomerates, formed close to the coastline by waves or rivers. It is probable that there was life of the lower forms in these seas, their skeletons being now altered beyond all recognition.

Between the deposition of the crystalline schists and the next succeeding strata there is a vast gap, yet the mere existence of a gap in the geological record means something, and we may interpret it as marking a period of uplift in that area, so that it was dry land, and instead of receiving further deposits, became the source of deposits laid down in neighbouring seas. In the vast period of time that this gap represents, most of the alteration and folding of these rocks took place, for the later strata are comparatively undisturbed. The mechanics of these huge earth-movements are hidden from us, but they partook of the character of a shrinkage, and the strata were folded and plicated into only a fraction of their former horizontal extent. Further, the present directions of these folds tell us that the pressure came in a direction parallel to the Equator, the axes of the folds being nearly on a north and south line. However, with the opening of Cambrian times – a well-marked period in the earth's later history – the southern portion of our area was again below the sea, for in the Beardmore region we find beds of black limestone containing fossils of corals and of a primitive sponge-coral called Archaeocyathus. The northern portion of Victoria Land was still probably dry land. The limestone is of unknown thickness, but its character tells us something. From its purity we can argue a clear though comparatively shallow sea, while from a number of limestone breccias found, we know that after consolidation it was broken up in places by earth movements, or even volcanic eruptions, and afterwards re-cemented again. But after this period of deposition the land again emerged from the sea, and no legible record is found until much later. A record of a somewhat illegible kind exists in a comprehensive series of granites which occur in profusion along the whole of the present coastline. These are of infinite variety, and probably belong to many ages, but the majority seem to have been intruded after the Cambrian limestone and before the next succeeding strata. They were doubtless connected with the uplift of the whole region. In their intrusion through the pre-Cambrian schists they tore away and even assimilated huge blocks of schist and gneiss, which exist today as enclosures in the granite.

At the end of Palaeozoic, or beginning of Mesozoic times – that is, somewhat later than when the great coal measures of England were being formed – the whole of the Victoria Land region became an area of deposition of a very interesting kind. For belonging to this period we find a very well marked series of rocks, named by Mr Ferrar of the *Discovery* Expedition the Beacon Sandstone.

In the district visited by him, the Royal Society Range, the series is composed mainly of a dense sandstone with thin beds of shale, and is at least 2000 feet thick. Farther to the north the series is represented by a similar sandstone, but associated with beds of coral, shale, and limestone. In the Beardmore district it appears as limestone, calcareous sandstone, beds of coal, and shale. There can be little doubt that these all represent deposits of approximately the same period under slightly varying conditions.

In the Royal Society Range (Lat. 78°–79°) the sandstone itself tells us a good deal. The grains of sand are very well rounded, as though wind-worn, there is much false bedding, the shale bands are thin, and there are remains of fresh-water plants in these bands. From those facts we can postulate a low-lying area with sand dunes or desert sand in the neighbourhood, which was collected and redeposited, probably by water. A semi-arid climate prevented any great amount of animal or vegetable life, for there are no fossils in the sandstone. There are, however, worm markings, ripple marks, and the casts of sun cracks, all of which mean conditions such as now obtain in parts of the Gobi Desert. As far as is known, sea water had no part in this great series of deposits. Yet the climate varied according to both place and time, for in the Beardmore district there are many coal beds and thick shale deposits, marking probably a humid climate and a marshy topography. These conditions were repeated in a smaller degree in the Granite Harbour district and to the north. Throughout the whole area there must have been rapid, if not large, rivers, for the sandstone in places contains small pockets and bands of coarse conglomerate – a sign either of coastal sea action or of rapid rivers.

For this period, therefore, we may not be far wrong if we imagine a land somewhat approaching in conditions the Southern Sahara or the outskirts of the Gobi Desert. Too much emphasis must not be laid upon its desert character, however, for our only evidence for that is the wind-blown appearance of the sandgrains, and the absence of fossils in the sandstone itself. The same conditions probably held over what is now the Ross Sea and the Great Ice Barrier, these being formed at a much later period. The Beacon Sandstone series is the most important yet found in that quadrant of the Antarctic, for it is not only the latest sedimentary deposit of any magnitude, but it undoubtedly has locked up in it great stores of fossil evidence which have as yet hardly been touched by geologists.

In the absence of later sedimentary deposits, the more recent history of Victoria Land is somewhat hypothetical, but one very definite period stands out, marked by a geological phenomenon for which there are few analogies to be found in the world. Perhaps the most characteristic feature of the whole of Victoria Land is the existence in practically all parts yet visited of a line of dark level-bedded rock, which stands out on cliff faces, produces pinnacled mountains, and generally dominates the topography.

This is caused by intrusions of dolerite in the form of a sill, which from the district of its first description may be called the McMurdo Sill. From Lat. 71° down to Lat. 85°, and probably beyond, this dolerite is found, varying only slightly in character, and precisely similar in mode of occurrence. In places it occurs as one thick sill, nearly always columnar in form, up to 1500 feet in thickness; in others it splits into two or more sills of smaller size. In general it has intercalated itself between the strata of the Beacon Sandstone, but in some cases it has formed a sill through granite. In one particular district, that of the Ferrar Glacier, it forms a sill of 300 feet almost level bedded, dividing two very different types of granite. Its intrusion was for the most part quiet, and has left little effect, beyond a baking of the strata in its immediate vicinity. In places, however, it was evidently more violent, for huge blocks of granite or Beacon Sandstone are found in it, torn from their parent masses. The intrusion of these sills of molten rock probably raised the whole area to some extent, and prevented any further deposits. The true boundaries of the area intruded by the McMurdo Sill have not yet been located, but it can hardly be less than the size of the British Isles, and is probably much greater.

There is one more marked period in the history of South Victoria Land. Probably about the middle of Tertiary times that part of the crust was subjected to further shrinkage stress of an even kind, which ultimately resulted in a series of great breaks or faults along the present coast-line. On the upthrow side of the fault the land was slowly raised into the present plateau, while on the downthrow side the land was depressed below sea level, and now forms the Ross Sea and the sea bottom below the Great Ice Barrier. Simultaneously with, and probably as an effect of this faulting, there occurred a great outburst of volcanic energy along the line of break. At many points volcanoes were formed, the chief centres being the Ross Archipelago, the Cape Adare Peninsula, and the Balleny Islands. This outburst is now just dying out, only two volcanoes being still active – Mt Erebus on Ross Island, and Sturge Island in the Balleny Group. No recent deposits having been found, the later pages of the history of this area must come from its physiography, and cannot be treated of here.

For the work upon which this history is founded our thanks are due to the geologists of the various Antarctic Expeditions, chiefly Mr H. T. Ferrar, of the National Antarctic Expedition, and Professor T. W. Edgeworth David and Mr R. E. Priestley, of the British Antarctic Expedition, 1907–9. The 35 lbs. of specimens brought back by the Polar Party from Mt Buckley contain impressions of fossil plants of late Palaeozoic age, some of which a cursory inspection identifies as occurring in other parts of the world. When fully examined, they will assuredly prove to be of the highest geological importance.

SUMMARY OF GEOLOGICAL JOURNEYS

by F. Debenham, B.A., B.Sc.
(Assistant Geologist to the Expedition)

Owing to the early publication of this book before any of the material brought back has been examined, it is difficult to state the exact nature or importance of the geological results of the Expedition.

A summary of the work done will perhaps to some extent indicate its scope.

Of the three geologists accompanying the Expedition two were with the main party on Ross Island, Mr T. Griffith Taylor and Mr Frank Debenham. A third, Mr Raymond E. Priestley, was with the Northern Party, stationed the first year at Cape Adare, the second in the Mt Nansen region.

It had been among Captain Scott's original plans to maintain a geological party in the field during each sledging season, and this was carried out until the third season, when the Search Party took all available men.

The special geological journeys from the main base at Cape Evans were as follows.

In the autumn of 1911 a party of four, under Mr Taylor, spent six weeks in the foothills of the Royal Society Range, examining and surveying about eighty miles of coast line, including Dry Valley and the Ferrar and Koettlitz Glaciers. Mr C. S. Wright accompanied this party and studied ice phenomena under the most typical conditions.

The next summer another geological party under Mr Taylor spent three months on the coast to the north of McMurdo Sound, making their base at Granite Harbour. During this, probably the most comprehensive geological journey yet made in the South, a complete detailed survey of the coast and the hinterland was made both by theodolite and plane table.

The Mackay Glacier was ascended almost to its outfall from the plateau, and fossils associated with coal beds were found. A complete physiographic study of the region was made by Mr Taylor and some important measurements of glacier movement taken.

At the same time geological collections were being made on the Beardmore Glacier by various parties. The notes made by Dr Wilson and the specimens collected by him and by Lieutenant Bowers are perhaps the most important of all the geological results.

The plant fossils collected by this party are the best preserved of any yet found in this quadrant of the Antarctic and are of the character best suited to settle a long-standing controversy between geologists as to the nature of the former union between Antarctica and Australasia.

In December of 1912 a party of six under Mr Priestley ascended Mt Erebus by a new route and spent a fortnight on the upper slopes collecting and surveying. The positions of the former craters or calderas and of the fumerole areas were carefully mapped and much of the former history of the volcano ascertained.

In the Northern Party, stationed at Cape Adare for the first season, a journey chiefly geographical and geological was made along the coastline to the west. Owing to unfavourable ice-conditions the party was not able to go very far, but Mr Priestley was able to make a comprehensive collection of the slates and schists of the region, supplemented in the summer by the recent lavas of Cape Adare itself.

In the succeeding year, being landed by the ship at Evans Coves, the same party made a journey into entirely new country in the neighbourhood of Mt Melbourne and obtained further fossil evidence from the Great Beacon Sandstone Series.

Throughout his journeys Mr Priestley made a special study of local ice conditions which together with Mr Wright's work with the main party will furnish a very complete report on ice phenomena in the Antarctic.

From this summary it will be seen that the geological work of the Expedition was particularly comprehensive and was one of the chief items in the scientific syllabus of the Expedition. The mass of material brought back will be worked up and published in a special Geological Report.

NOTES ON ICE PHYSICS

by Charles S. Wright, B.A.

These notes deal with a very few only of the subdivisions falling under the heading 'Ice Physics', and are intended merely to give a popular survey of this interesting and by no means unimportant branch of scientific work.

As a practically new field of research, in the nature of things the work was largely observational in character, and until all the data are fully worked out all conclusions must be considered provisional and incomplete.

A consideration of the important place in the scheme of things occupied by the molecule known as H_2O would certainly lead one to give it the nickname of 'the mighty molecule'.

The climates of the earth are almost entirely controlled by water in one of its three forms. In the Northern Hemisphere we have long realised the effect of the Gulf Stream on our own lands; what then is the effect on the Southern Hemisphere of a stream of huge icebergs ever breaking off from the Antarctic continent and drifting northwards into low latitudes? Be it remembered that an iceberg at melting point is several times as efficient a reservoir of cold as an equal volume of water at the same temperature.

Consider only the simple case of an ocean current washing a natural ice barrier stretched across a strait and gradually eating its way through. How far-reaching will be the effect when the barrier is down! The whole history of the world might easily be changed by some such simple catastrophe.

Sea ice

Possibly foremost among the different forms of ice to be studied was that of sea ice – being fast ice* formed in autumn on the surface of the sea by the action of the cold air above it. The process

* Ice not in movement.

of freezing is a very interesting one to watch in cold, calm weather. As the temperature falls the sea becomes covered with small scale-like plate crystals up to one inch across of a delicate fern-like structure. They generally float flat upon the surface, but many are imprisoned in an approximately vertical position. After the surface becomes covered, the ice then grows in the ordinary way by accretion from below. In the initial stages, when the ice is only an inch in thickness, the felt-like mass on the surface has little rigidity, and even up to 3 inches thick moves freely up and down under the influence of a swell without losing its coherence in any way.

Sea ice is quite different in its properties from the ice formed on a pond or lake of fresh water, owing to the fact that some of the salt in solution in sea water is always imprisoned between the individual crystals in the sea ice. This imprisoned salt between the crystals does not freeze in contact with ice till a fairly low temperature is reached, and consequently sea ice when new and thin is never hard and rigid like fresh water ice. As a result ice even four or more inches thick is for sledging by no means safe, whereas the same thickness of fresh ice would be sufficient to support a regiment of soldiers.

In cold clear weather about thirty-six hours is required to form ice of this thickness, which is then of a dark slaty colour, but somewhat mottled owing to differences in transparency of the differently oriented crystals.

If the temperature of the air is below zero Fahrenheit, as the ice forms and while it is still only a couple of inches thick, the extruded salt on the surface commences to gather moisture from the air and grows upwards in beautifully shaped crystals, forming rosettes in almost infinite variety of structure, depending chiefly upon the conditions of temperature and humidity in the air above.

These 'ice flowers' have but a fleeting existence, however, for should the air temperature rise much above the temperature at which they were formed they melt again and collapse. Since the cryohydric temperature of common salt and water is zero Fahrenheit, it follows at once that no ice flowers can live above zero temperature (0° F.).

In the early part of the winter all additions to the thickness of the sea ice are due to conduction by the cold air above, but there is every reason to believe that later in the winter the sea ice grows to its great thickness of 8 and 9 feet largely by the deposition of frazil crystals from below.

There is very little growth from above due to deposition of snow.

After the first winter, when the Sound was completely frozen over, the ice was seen on the return of the sun to be buckled in the form of low waves two or three inches high and about 150 feet apart from crest to crest. This phenomenon was due evidently to the dilatation of the ice on rising temperatures and was remarkable by reason that in each hollow a tiny crack was visible and remained open until the disappearance of the ice – Nature's provision for helping the break-up of the sea ice after a severe winter. In mild winters when the outer Sound is kept free of ice no such cracks or waves appear.

Ice foot

During the autumn, while the sea is as yet open and the temperature low, the whole shore line becomes covered with a coating of frozen spray, which on account of its saline constituents remains wet and sticky at even comparatively low temperatures, and provides pendent masses in an infinite variety of form, from a very stubby icicle to the so-called foot-stalactites, due to constant accretion of snow drifting from one direction only. About the same time there is growing on all shallow shores a low platform a few feet above the surface of mean sea level. This growth is due partly to drifted snow consolidated by spray, partly to tidal action, and partly to growth direct from the waves and sea.

This ice foot later on becomes frozen clear to the bottom on shallow shores and remains fixed to the land during the winter, being separated by the working tide crack from the fast sea ice beyond.

Pack ice

Pack ice, in distinction to fast ice, is not bound to the shore, but moves under the influence of local currents and wind. In the Antarctic, pack ice is evidently seldom formed at sea and largely consists of fast ice which has been broken away and carried off to sea by blizzards or some such transporting agent. The pack extends in normal years in December from about 66° to 71° S. Lat., a distance of 300 miles from north to south, and at times evidently fills the whole width of the Ross Sea.

Pack may be heavy or light, closed or open – the latter conditions being entirely dependent on local winds and currents. Thus heavy pack if open may offer no insuperable bar to navigation, whereas in closed pack, whether heavy or light, little progress can be made by ships. Heavy pack is usually associated with hummocks or pressure ridges rising to a height of four or five feet above the general level of the floe. These hummocks and pressure ridges are called upon to furnish ice for cooking and other purposes in the pack, being comparatively free from salt, owing, as mentioned previously, to the fact that the salt in the ice goes into solution and drains away, whenever the temperature rises above zero.

Towards the end of February the Ross Sea becomes comparatively free of pack and offers no bar to navigation.

Snow

Precipitation from the atmosphere occurred always in the form of snow in these regions bordering on the continent; sometimes, when the temperature was high, in the form of delicate six-rayed stars, or at lower temperatures in the form of hexagonal plates, little granular balls, or at still lower temperatures fine needle-shaped forms.

Not long, however, do they keep this form after falling. Immediately 'the mighty molecule' starts its work, some crystals grow at the expense of others, the whole grows more compact, becomes hard, and while still containing much air is white and called névé. Later it completes its change by expelling the air and becomes the well-known blue ice.

During the summer one can see the whole transformation taking place before one's eyes in the course of a few days.

Crystal forms

Not only in the form of snow, however, do these crystal forms occur. In crevasses, on the roof of the stables, on windows, and so on, countless varied forms are to be seen, each single form corresponding to a particular temperature, humidity, change of temperature, and change of humidity. Every slight lowering of temperature deposits its appropriate form and quantity of ice crystals on every object exposed to these conditions.

Thus on ice ponds or other masses of ice, at times the crystals are so deposited as to outline the form of the massive crystals in the ice – at times so as to show the orientation of the crystals on the surface.

Probably the most beautiful form of crystal, and certainly the most distinctive one, was to be found in huge masses in all crevasses. Single crystals measured up to 2 inches across, and were built in the form of hollow pyramids.

Glaciers

It is, however, when in the form of glaciers that one appreciates to the full the power of 'the mighty molecule': huge valleys, 5, 10, 20, 30, even 50 miles wide, filled with moving ice, cut by this ice from the solid rock to a depth of thousands of feet – huge streams of ice moving by virtue of their own enormous weight at a rate of 30 feet a year even in the most dormant glaciers.

Hundreds of glaciers representing every type are to be found along the stretch of shore from Cape Adare to the Beardmore Glacier; some, like the Ferrar and Beardmore Glaciers, accommodating the outflow from the great ice plateau 9000 to 11,000 feet high, others flowing from local névé fields, and others little more than consolidated snow-drifts.

Owing to the fact that the 'snow-line' is at sea level, a very large proportion of the glaciers terminate in the sea and discharge bergs from their seaward faces as do many Greenland glaciers. More than this, however, the Antarctic glaciers, instead of coming to an end where they rest on the sea bottom, often preserve their entities as glaciers or streams of ice while projecting many miles into the open sea. Examples of this type are furnished by 'Glacier Tongue' between winter quarters and Hut Point, and by the Nordenskiold and Drygalski ice tongues farther north. This latter pushes its way into the sea a distance of about thirty miles and has a volume, on a rough calculation, of fifty thousand million cubic yards.

Probably the most interesting of the data collected on glaciers were connected with their interior structure, the size of the individual crystals, the amount of the imprisoned air in the form of air bubbles, the occurrence of silt bands and of bands of clear blue ice in horizontal layers, and the occurrence and distribution of crevasses and of pressure ridges in the glacier. This field, however, is much too large to enter upon in this place.

The Barrier

By far the most unique feature of the Antarctic is the occurrence of huge masses of floating ice, such as the Great Ross Barrier, which fills up the whole of the narrow end of the Ross Sea. This great sheet of floating ice has an average depth of probably 600 feet and presents an unbroken front to the sea 400 geographical miles in length with a depth from back to front of over 300 miles. The surface of the Barrier is comparatively level, and offers little obstruction to sledging. The yearly snowfall from observations by Captain Scott in the *Discovery* Expedition and from Sir Ernest Shackleton's work amounts to about eighteen inches of consolidated snow of density about $\frac{1}{2}$. From the same authorities we know that the yearly motion is in an east–north-easterly direction (close to Minna Bluff) at the rate of about 500 yards a year.

We have, moreover, data to show that no great change in the position of the seaward edge of the Barrier has taken place since the *Discovery* Expedition in 1901–04. Thus the Barrier may be considered for purposes of calculation as remaining *in statu quo* by virtue of the discharge of icebergs from its seaward face.

If this is so, we see that the volume of ice due to deposition,

$$18\tfrac{1}{2} \times \tfrac{1}{12} \times \tfrac{1}{3} \times 400 \times 2000 \times 300 \times 2000 = 12 \times 10^{10} \text{ cubic yards}$$

(taking width as 400 miles, and length 300), should be converted into a strip of ice on the seaward side 400 miles long, 500 yards wide, and 600 feet deep $= 8 \times 10^{10}$ cubic yards.

This agreement of observation is a remarkably close one and proves that our fundamental statement is very close to the truth.

It should here be pointed out that in the above calculation no allowance has been made for the effect of glaciers pushing the Barrier before them and so adding to the apparent motion. That is, it is assumed the Barrier moves under its own weight alone. Luckily the Barrier may be subjected to further calculation, being in the happy position of a mass of ice resting on a frictionless plane at freezing point. Thus with certain assumptions regarding the rather uncertain coefficient of viscosity of ice and a slight excursion into integral calculus, we can arrive at the conclusion that the Barrier under its own weight would each year push out a distance of from 100 to 500 yards – a distance at least of the same order of magnitude as that found by observation.

From this we see we are probably justified in neglecting the volume of ice added to the Barrier and carried down by glaciers from the plateau, and may treat the Barrier as an entity by itself.

Consider now the effect of such a Barrier in equilibrium, enclosed on three sides and exposed to a continuous snowfall. Without any further mathematics it is at once clear that the velocity of motion at the seaward edge must be very many times faster than the velocity at the shore farthest from the sea. The tendency of a continuous snowfall would be therefore to accumulate a much greater thickness of Barrier on the side farthest from the sea. That this is not so is shown by the barometric observations of the sledging parties, which furnish convincing proof that the Barrier is still afloat quite close to the landward end, and further that a very good current circulation obtains under this part, since the single circumstance capable of preventing an accumulation of snow is a corresponding melting action, which again can only be due to water underneath the Barrier.

Icebergs

It has been noted that the Barrier and also land glaciers may discharge ice into the sea in the form of bergs. Since no bergs were ever seen in McMurdo Sound except in the late summer months, it may almost be taken that the prime cause of the calving of bergs from the parent glacier is due to the melting action of the warm sea water.

Bergs met with in the Antarctic can best be roughly divided into barrier or tabular bergs and glacier bergs. The tabular berg is recognised by its flat tabular form, whereas the glacier berg seldom has such a regular profile and often is formed of deep blue ice in contradistinction to the dazzling whiteness of the barrier berg. The tabular berg has a height up to 200 feet above sea and at times reaches the enormous length of 21 miles – truly a floating island. After partial melting it usually becomes slightly tilted to one side, or develops enormous caverns due to the action of the waves. In the final stages it may overturn or even disintegrate and after prolonged exposure to the elements is hardly distinguishable from the glacier berg.

The general tendency of the currents in the Ross Sea is to carry these bergs northwards into the warmer water, so that in late summer the greatest accumulation of bergs occurs at a fairly low latitude. As a result also of their great heat capacity they are not associated at this time of the year with pack ice as they are in the early summer.

That the number and distribution of these enormous reservoirs of cold has a real effect upon the climate of Australasia can hardly be doubted, and it is therefore evident that a close study and analysis of the data on this subject may well give results of the very greatest value.

GENERAL PHYSICS

[*Simpson and Wright*]

by Charles S. Wright, B.A.

The field covered in pure Physics by the Expedition was by no means a small one. It may conveniently be divided as follows.

(a) *Magnetic observations*

These consisted in continuous photographic records by Eschen-hagen magnetographs of the elements N.S. (astronomical) force, E.W. force, and vertical force. These instruments were placed in a cave dug into an ice-drift a couple of hundred feet to the south-west of the hut at Cape Evans. This furnished the highly desirable advantage of a constant temperature condition, important in that the sensitiveness of the instruments is dependent upon temper-ature. The light in the cave was furnished by a small electric lamp run from accumulators in the hut. Time signals were recorded on the trace every two minutes by means of a clock fitted with electric contacts, kept also in the hut and compared daily with the standard chronometer.

The programme of magnetic work included 'quick runs' on international term days. 'Quick runs' are obtained when one moves the photographic paper at a much greater speed than usual, so as to have a more open time-scale. These were carried out at the same times by all magnetic observatories, in the hope that the com-parison of traces would give definite information regarding the origin of magnetic storms.

Magnetic storms, though frequent, are not of hourly occurrence, and it is a matter for congratulation that one of our largest storms (also recorded by Webb's instruments with Mawson) occurs during the course of a quick run.

In addition to almost complete traces furnished by the magneto-graphs, absolute observations were undertaken once a week for standardisation of the traces, while observations for sensitiveness of the magnetographs were carried out once a month.

Observations of stars or sun, for time signals and for rating of chronometers, were made on an average once every fortnight. During the whole of the second year the rate of the standard chronometer varied only from 0.17 second losing to 0.25 second gaining, a very fine performance considering the adverse conditions it had to contend against.

The complete hourly records of auroras, which have been shown to be connected with sun-spot phenomena and with magnetic storms, should when worked out give data of considerable value, especially when compared with the data collected by Priestley on the Northern Party.

(b) *Atmospheric electricity*
  b (1) Potential gradient
During the whole of the first year and part of the second (until the almost continuous blizzards made observations useless) records of the potential gradient of the atmosphere were made in the usual way by use of the self-recording Benndorff electrometers. Owing to the mechanical difficulties of such work in cold regions, recourse was had to the lately discovered element ionium as a collector of the air potential, this substance being furnished by the great kindness of Prof. Giesel.

An interesting effect, noticed almost immediately on setting up the apparatus, was that in high winds, even when there was only the slightest amount of very low drift, the collector became charged to such an extent that sparks ½ inch long were continuously emitted by the charged system.

In order to obtain an estimate of the mean absolute value of the earth's electrostatic field in the Antarctic, comparison eye observations were undertaken over the level surface of the sea ice, similar to those undertaken at Melbourne for determination of the absolute value of the potential gradient over the sea.* These observations gave for the Antarctic a mean value of the same order as those obtained in other latitudes and over the sea.

---

* 'Atmospheric Electricity over the Ocean', G, C, Simpson and C. S. Wright, *Proceedings of the Royal Society*, A., vol. 85, 1911.

b(2) Radioactivity of the air

Numerous observations on the radium content of the Antarctic air were made during the first year, using the same apparatus as was used for observations on sea air during the voyage of the *Terra Nova*. As might be expected (dry frozen surfaces can hardly disengage any great quantity of radium emanation), the variations in radium content were not large, but of the same order of magnitude as observed over the sea.

b(3) Natural ionisation in closed vessels

The paper before mentioned contains the results obtained on the voyage of the *Terra Nova* from England to New Zealand, of which the section on natural ionisation may be summarised as follows:

(i) Variations in natural ionisation are due primarily to varying amounts of radioactive products in the air (disengaged, chiefly at least, from land surfaces).

(ii) These radioactive products are too diffusely distributed in the atmosphere to have any direct effect on the natural ionisation, and only become operative when deposited in the neighbourhood of the experimental station by precipitation, or by the earth's electric field (potential gradient).

(iii) There exists a minimum value to this natural ionisation (about 4 ions per cc. per sec.) which has not by any method been reduced in value. This minimum would seem to be independent of the size or material of retaining vessel, and may therefore be best ascribed to a spontaneous breakdown of the enclosed gas, very similar to the spontaneous breakdown of radioactive substances.

From the above one can see that in places where the radium content of the air is very small (as over the sea), the variations in natural ionisation will also be small. Further work on the minimum value in the Antarctic (carried on in an ice cave at constant temperature) gave a value very slightly lower than that found over the sea, and showed, with a self-recording instrument, no variations greater than the probable errors of observation.

For further details of the above, and in respect to measurements of the ionisation of the air, the reader is referred to the paper before mentioned.

Samples of sea water were also collected from various depths for radium analysis, and will be worked out by Professor Joly, but the results are not yet available.

(c) *Pendulum observations*

It will be known to the general reader that the weight of any substance as measured by the pull of the earth upon it is not an invariable constant. Thus a piece of lead or other substance weighed at sea level on a spring balance would be heavier at the Pole than at the Equator by about 5 parts in 1000. This difference may be considered as partly due to the weakening, as one goes towards the Pole, of the centrifugal force of the earth's rotation, and partly due to the increased force of attraction by virtue of the flattening of the earth at the poles, and consequent shorter distance from the centre of attraction.

Dealing with such small differences in value of the gravity constant 'g', it becomes essential, if any theories are to be tested, that observations should be carried out with the most extreme accuracy.

The universal method of measuring 'g' is by noting the time of swing of a pendulum, and as absolute measurements are of the utmost refinement and delicacy, comparative measurements are nearly always undertaken, and referred to similar observations at the standard station in Potsdam.

The pendulums used were of Col. von Sterneck's pattern and are gilt, three in number, swinging from agate planes in two directions at right angles to one another. The pendulums are swung at atmospheric temperature and pressure, and corrections are applied to reduce to normal.

The time of swing is measured by the method of coincidences, with reference to a special clock making an electric contact each second. This clock is used as the standard and rated (if possible) to $\frac{1}{10}$ second in the day, by observation of stars at meridian transit.

With care the value of 'g' should be accurate, after all corrections are applied, to one part in a million, but under the particularly unfavourable conditions in the Antarctic it is doubtful if a much higher accuracy than 1 in 250,000 is obtainable.

The difficulties experienced with the instrument in the Antarctic, though apparently trifling at this distance, were very real at the time. For instance, observation on stars for clock rate was usually complicated by a temperature of −40° with a slight wind, quite sufficient to keep one nursing his nose, and to be very careful not to put one's eye to the telescope lest it freeze and remain there. Other little troubles, such as the stopping of the clock by a bodily shift of the wall of the hut upon which it was hung, also tended to reduce the accuracy of the observations.

During the first winter the pendulum observations were made in a small cave dug into an ice drift, but did not prove at all satisfactory, partly owing to the frost-fogging of the lenses and mirrors during the course of the observations and partly owing to the intense cold. There being more space in the hut during the second winter, a second series of observations was undertaken inside, a huge kenyte boulder being imported to serve as a solid base for the instrument. By cutting a hole through the floor of the hut and freezing the boulder to the frozen ground underneath, a very solid and rigid stand was formed. This second series was carried out in the dark room (by courtesy of Debenham), and the coincidences observed by telescope through a small window in the wall in order to reduce the temperature variation of the pendulums. The observations, though not equal to those obtainable in a fixed observatory, are quite concordant and should give sufficient data to substantiate definitely the theoretical formula at present in general use.

METEOROLOGICAL REPORT

by G. C. Simpson, D. Sc.

Captain Scott's great desire was that good scientific work should be done on the Expedition. He therefore did everything in his power to help those to whom he entrusted the work by giving them all possible facilities and large financial aid, and he allowed me to use all the money subscribed in my native town and country for the scientific work under my charge. In consequence no Expedition has gone out so well equipped with stores and instruments for physical investigation. The following short statement of work done at Cape Evans will give some idea of the completeness of the outfit.

(a) An almost unbroken record by self-registering instruments of: temperature (two instruments), barometric pressure, wind force (two instruments), wind direction, sunshine, electrical state of the atmosphere, and the three elements of terrestrial magnetism.

(b) Regular observations of the usual meteorological instruments.

(c) An investigation of the upper air by means of balloons both with and without instruments, by which knowledge has been gained of the temperature and air currents up to a height of over five miles.

(d) Weekly absolute determinations of the magnetic elements.

(e) Hourly observations of the aurora during the whole period when it was dark enough to observe.

(f) A close study of the optics of the atmosphere.

(g) Accurate determination of the value of gravity by means of pendulums.

(h) A very thorough study of ice, as it occurs both in the air and on the ground.

In addition to the above a valuable set of meteorological observations was made at Cape Adare.

It is impossible to discuss here, even briefly, the results obtained, but it is quite clear that many of them are new and unexpected.

Enough data have been collected to require many years for their adequate discussion by specialists. A few numerical results obtained during the first year are given in the table at the end of this article.

Throughout this book there have been constant references to temperature and wind – two meteorological factors which have been of vital importance to the members of the Expedition. It appears therefore that it would not be out of place to examine here these two factors from the scientific point of view to see what justification there was for the verdict passed on them from purely physiological experiences.

Temperature

The mean temperature at Cape Evans during the first year of our stay was −0.4° F., which compares with −1.3° F. found for the two years that the *Discovery* was in the same region. The corresponding temperature for a place in the same latitude in the Arctic is 2.5° F., thus the difference is not very great. The lowest temperature recorded at Cape Evans was −50° F., which is not particularly low, for many well inhabited towns in Alaska and Siberia experience lower temperatures every winter. The real severity of the Antarctic climate is not shown in its low minimum temperatures, but in its low maximum temperatures. The July temperature at the North Pole has been calculated to be 30° F., the mean temperature at Cape Evans during December 1911 and January 1912 was 21° F. Thus the summer temperature at our base station over 900 miles from the South Pole was 9° F. below the summer temperature at the North Pole itself. It is interesting to compare the mean temperature throughout the months of the year at Cape Evans with that of a station in the corresponding latitude in the northern hemisphere. The comparison is made in Table 1 on the next page.

Thus during the three summer months our temperature was more than 15° F. below what would have been experienced at a similar latitude in the Arctic. The low temperature during the summer in the Antarctic is one of the outstanding features of its climate and has not yet received a really satisfactory explanation.

As stated above, the lowest temperature experienced at Cape Evans was −50° F., but that was by no means the lowest met with by members of the Expedition. In July 1911 Wilson, Bowers, and Cherry-Garrard made a sledge journey on to the Barrier, and they experienced temperatures many degrees below those recorded at the same time at Cape Evans. The lowest temperature they encountered was −77° F., which is the record low temperature for the Antarctic and has only been surpassed in the Arctic at Werchojansk in Siberia − the coldest spot on the earth. That the Barrier is much colder than McMurdo Sound was made clear during the *Discovery* Expedition, but the temperature observations made by the Norwegian Expedition at Framheim have shown how great the difference really is. Framheim was only sixty miles nearer the Pole than Cape Evans, yet the mean temperature measured there was −13.4° F., that is 13° F. lower than the temperature experienced simultaneously at Cape Evans. The cause of the great difference of temperatures between the Barrier and McMurdo Sound is at present unknown, but it is hoped that the correct solution will be found when all the data have been discussed.

Table 1

Cape Evans 77° 35' S.		Northern stations 77° 30' N.		Difference
February	18.6	August	34.2	−15.6
March	6.2	September	21.4	−15.2
April	−1.4	October	2.1	−3.5
May	−11.0	November	−8.3	−2.7
June	−11.8	December	−16.6	4.8
July	−19.6	January	−23.1	3.5
August	−20.0	February	−23.3	3.3
September	−15.4	March	−19.5	4.1
October	−4.0	April	−5.4	−1.4
November	12.4	May	15.4	−3.0
December	21.5	June	33.1	−11.6
January	20.6	July	36.9	−16.2

Blizzards

It is a matter of experience, even in England, that great cold without wind is much easier to bear than a much higher temperature with wind. One does not wrap oneself in furs when going for a motor ride because of the cold, but because of the wind. It is the same in Polar exploration; the wind is the chief enemy, not the cold.

Those who, previous to reading this book, have read Amundsen's *South Pole* cannot but have been struck by the fact that while this book is full of descriptions and references to blizzards the word hardly appears in the other. It is very natural to ask the reason for this strange difference. The reason is an important one, and if it had been known previously the history of the conquest of the South Pole would have been very different. *One can now say definitely that the blizzards which have been so fateful to British Antarctic exploration are local winds confined to the western half of the Ross Barrier.* The meteorological observations made simultaneously at Framheim, Cape Evans, and Cape Adare have thrown a flood of light on to the nature of these winds, and although at the time of writing the observations have not been sufficiently discussed to give us a complete solution of all the problems connected with their origin, many points of general interest have appeared, and an attempt will be made to summarise them here.

The velocity of the wind can be recorded automatically without much difficulty, and this has been done at many observatories, so that we know the chief characteristics of the wind in most countries. In the Antarctic a continuous automatic record of the wind was obtained at Cape Evans; while at Cape Adare and Framheim frequent eye observations were made; we have therefore the data for an interesting comparison.

The character of the wind in the British Isles is found to be very similar at different stations. Calms are very seldom recorded, and at the other end of the scale winds of a greater velocity than 50 miles an hour are rare. There must therefore be some intermediate velocity which occurs most frequently. The records of three years have been taken for Yarmouth on the Norfolk coast, and the number of times winds of different velocities occurred counted.

The result of the count is shown in the second column of Table 2, from which it will be seen that at Yarmouth winds having a velocity of 4 miles an hour or less only occur on the average during 5.2 hours out of a hundred. The wind blows between 5 and 9 miles per hour for 23 hours out of the hundred, and velocities between 10 and 14 miles in the hour are met with during 28.4 per cent, of the time. Higher velocities than these occur less frequently, and during every hundred hours the wind blows at a greater velocity than 45 miles only during three-quarters of an hour.

Table 2
Frequency of winds

Wind velocity miles per hour	Yarmouth per cent.	Framheim per cent.	Cape Evans per cent.
0 to 4	5.2	42.2	29.8
5 to 9	23.0	25.9	16.0
10 to 14	28.4	16.1	8.1
15 to 19	19.0	8.0	7.7
20 to 24	11.5	3.6	7.5
25 to 29	5.7	1.9	7.8
30 to 34	3.0	1.4	7.4
35 to 39	2.1	0.6	5.9
40 to 44	1.5	0.3	4.7
45 to 49	0.7		2.9
50 to 54	0.0		1.5
55 to 59	0.0		0.7
> 60	0.0		0.2

The figures in the above table are plotted in Fig. 1, in which the thin line curve represents the data for Yarmouth. The curve shows clearly how the wind at Yarmouth blows most frequently with a velocity of about 10 miles an hour and that the frequency of higher and lower velocities falls off very rapidly on either side of the maximum. This curve is typical of all stations in the British Isles. In every case investigated, calms are of infrequent occurrence, while there is some velocity which occurs most frequently. The velocity which most frequently occurs varies from station to station, being least (about 5 miles an hour) at inland stations and greatest (about 10 to 15 miles an hour) at coast stations.

A similar analysis has been made of the winds at Framheim, the winter quarters of Captain Amundsen's Expedition. The results are shown in the third column of Table 1, and are plotted by a broken curve in Fig. 1. It will at once be seen that the result is entirely different from that obtained for Yarmouth. At Framheim calms were of frequent occurrence and the wind blew at 4 miles an hour or less during 42 per cent, of the total time. From this high percentage of calms winds of higher velocity fell off rapidly and regularly. It is important to notice that the shape of the curve for Framheim is similar to that of the curve for Yarmouth from

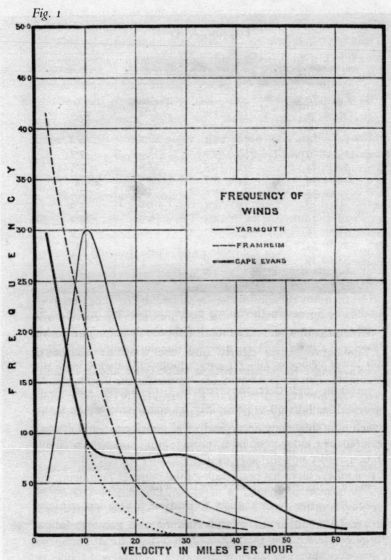

Fig. 1

FREQUENCY OF
WINDS

——— YARMOUTH

——— FRAMHEIM

——— CAPE EVANS

VELOCITY IN MILES PER HOUR

its highest point to its end. This shape is frequently met with in scientific work, and indicates that the change from maximum to minimum is regular without any outside factor influencing the natural change from stage to stage. It is the shape of the 'probability curve', that is, the curve which indicates the probability that anything will occur when it departs from a most probable value. The wind conditions shown in the Framheim curve are the ideal ones for Polar work, for the most probable wind is a calm, and the frequency with which higher velocities occur decreases rapidly and regularly as the velocities increase.

We will now turn to the results of a similar analysis for the winds recorded at Cape Evans. Column 4 of Table 1 contains the data, and they are plotted on the thick curve of Fig. 1. Here we have a curve which commences in a manner similar to that of Framheim: the most frequent winds are those with a velocity of less than 4 miles an hour, and higher winds are less frequently met with. In fact if one had the whole of the Framheim curve and only the first part of that for Cape Evans – as far as winds of 14 miles an hour – one would say they were similar and would complete the Cape Evans curve along the thin dotted line indicated in the figure, making it run parallel with the other two curves.

But that would be assuming that there was nothing abnormal in the region in which Cape Evans was situated, and that the winds were governed by the same laws as at Framheim. The real curve does not follow this ideal curve, but takes an entirely different shape. The frequency of winds greater than 15 miles an hour does not decrease with the velocity, for all winds with velocities between 15 miles an hour and 34 miles an hour occur with practically the same frequency. It is not until we reach higher velocities than 35 miles an hour that a decrease in frequency accompanies an increase in velocity. This shape of the curve indicates that there is some factor affecting the winds at Cape Evans which is not present at a normal station.

This factor is the blizzard. Superimposed upon the normal winds are the blizzard winds having velocities varying from 10 miles an hour up to over 60, in consequence of which high winds occur with a frequency out of all proportion to what would have occurred if there had been no blizzards.

Thus the shape of the wind curve for Cape Evans shows clearly that the blizzard is an abnormal phenomenon superposed upon the ordinary meteorological conditions, and the curve for Framheim that it does not occur there.

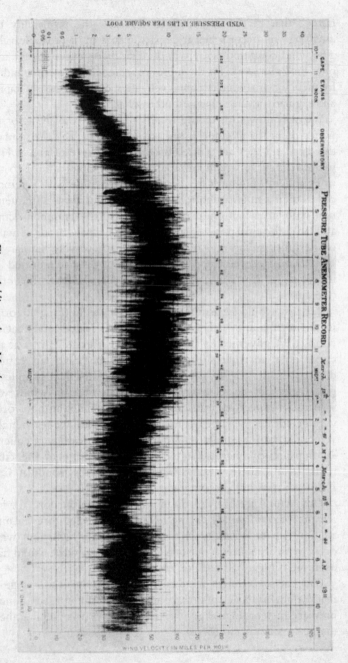

Fig. 2 A blizzard   March 12, 1911

The cause of the blizzards, their frequency, and the extent of country affected by them will be fully discussed in the scientific reports of the Expedition; here one is only interested in them in so far as they affected the fortunes of the members of the Expedition. The following table gives the number of hours blizzard winds were recorded at Cape Evans, and the mean temperature recorded while the winds were blowing.

Table 3
Number of blizzards recorded at Cape Evans
[a blizzard is taken as a southerly wind of 25 miles an hour or over]

	No. of hours with record	No. of hours of blizzard	Max. temp. during blizzards
February 1911	612	233	+16.4
March	744	404	+5.7
April	720	170	−1.7
May	744	72	−8.1
June	720	163	−0.9
July	744	258	−9.8
August	726	213	−6.3
September	720	198	−4.6
October	744	223	−1.4
November	720	215	+9.7
December	720	159	+22.6
January 1912	744	89	+23.8
February			
March			

It is only necessary to study this table for a few minutes to realise the conditions which had to be faced, and it explains why the fortunes of the sledging parties were affected so largely by the weather.

With regard to the extent of the country subjected to blizzards we cannot of course be very precise. Judging from Captain Amundsen's report they did not occur at Framheim, nor on the route he took to the Pole. Very high winds were occasionally experienced at Cape Adare, but they were in no way connected with our blizzards; as a rule when a blizzard was blowing at Cape Evans there was only a light southerly wind at Cape Adare. We know that typical blizzards were encountered at all points of Captain

Scott's route as far as the Beardmore Glacier. Whether the winds met with on the Plateau were connected with blizzards on the Barrier cannot be decided until a more thorough study has been made of the meteorological records kept by the different sledging parties. From the data at present available there appears no doubt that blizzards were confined almost entirely to the western half of the Ross Barrier.

The cause of the blizzards, and why they occur only over the western half of the Barrier, are questions which cannot at present be answered with any certainty. It appears, however, that the chief factors are the following: the air over the Barrier cools down much more than the air over the Ross Sea, and in consequence there is a region of relatively low pressure over the sea. Into this region the air from the Barrier tends to move, but owing to the large deflecting force of the earth's rotation so near to the Pole, the air cannot move from south to north but is driven towards the west.

The western boundary of the Barrier, however, is a range of lofty mountains which stop the westerly motion entirely. In consequence the pressure distribution becomes unstable and the tension is removed by a rush of air along the Western Mountains, through McMurdo Sound out into the Ross Sea. The evidence on which this explanation is based will be given in the scientific report.

In order to give some idea of the intensity of the blizzards a few records of one of the self-registering anemometers are reproduced. These records were taken by an instrument at the hut, and as the hut had been built in the most sheltered place available the records do not give the full force of the wind. The direction of the wind has been entered on the records, and in the line below the direction the time has been shown, as the time printed on the charts was not correct.

The record for March 12, 1911, is typical of the blizzards during the first months after our arrival, when the depôts were being laid and the first ponies were lost (Fig. 2).

The record for July 23, 1911, is interesting as this was the blizzard which nearly proved fatal to Wilson's party at Cape Crozier. The important thing to notice in this record is the extreme gustiness of the wind: in the hour between 7 p.m. and 8 p.m. the wind varied in velocity between 24 and 84 miles an hour (Fig. 3).

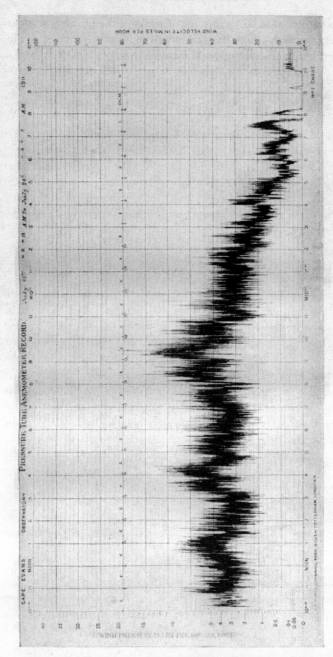

Fig. 3 A blizzard with gusts   July 23, 1911

One of the most dangerous peculiarities of the blizzards was the suddenness with which they commenced. Three examples of the sudden setting in of blizzards are shown in Fig. 4.

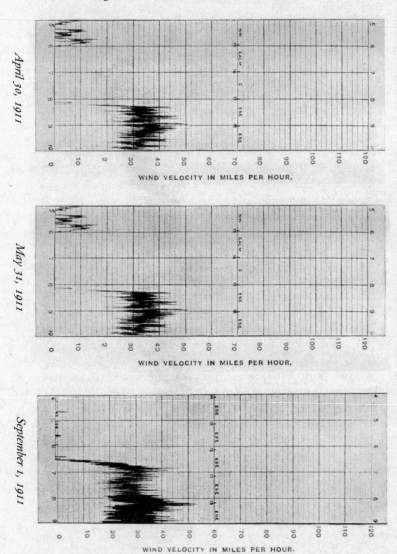

Fig. 4 Sudden commencements of blizzards

The following tables contain the chief meteorological results as far as they were worked out at the time of writing. The Framheim results, taken from Amundsen's *The South Pole*, have been included for ready reference.

Barometer

The barometer observations have been reduced to sea-level and normal temperature and gravity, except in the case of Framheim, which needs approximately .03 inch adding to reduce to sea-level (see Amundsen's *The South Pole*).

Wind

The Cape Evans wind amounts are from a continuous record by a self-recording Robinson anemometer.

The Framheim wind amounts are from observations made with a portable anemometer for a few minutes three times a day.

The Cape Adare wind was estimated on the Beaufort Scale and reduced to miles per hour by the equivalents used in the London Meteorological Office.

Maximum wind

The maximum wind is obtained as follows:

(a) Cape Evans. The highest amount of wind recorded in a complete hour; higher winds were always recorded in gusts.

(b) Framheim. The highest recorded reading of the hand anemometer.

(c) Cape Adare. The highest Beaufort number reduced to miles per hour.

Potential gradient

The values are the mean of those obtained during fine weather reduced to volts per metre over a level surface.

Cape Evans

	Barometer, inches			Temperature, °F			Wind, m.p.h.		Potential gradient
	Mean	Max.	Min.	Mean	Max.	Min.	Mean Vel.	Max. Vel.	
Feb.'11	29.31	29.64	28.96	18.7	33	0	23.6	61	
March	29.21	29.51	28.85	7.2	23	−7	25.7	57	75
April	29.32	29.80	28.82	−1.1	13	−18	15.9	55	73
May	29.23	29.84	28.26	−10.8	14	−29	12.0	54	62
June	29.11	29.82	28.65	−13.5	17	−37	13.2	56	72
July	29.08	29.55	28.52	−21.1	8	−50	18.5	66	84
Aug.	29.19	29.62	28.64	−20.8	15	−42	16.7	66	78
Sept.	29.16	29.85	28.29	−15.8	11	−37	14.5	57	105
Oct.	28.82	29.66	28.20	−3.5	8	−20	17.9	59	91
Nov.	29.63	30.15	28.98	+12.4	26	−2	16.1	43	89
Dec.	29.65	30.04	29.08	+22.0	32	+8	14.6	48	107
Jan.'12	29.43	29.64	29.05	+21.4	39	+10	10.9	54	98

Framheim

	Barometer, inches			Temperature, °F			Wind, m.p.h.		Potential gradient
	Mean	Max.	Min.	Mean	Max.	Min.	Mean Vel.	Max. Vel.	
April '11	29.80	29.80	28.69	−17.1	+12.2	−54.4	7.5	35.5	
May	29.02	29.66	28.02	−32.0	−4.0	−59.1	4.1	22.5	
June	28.88	29.54	28.50	−29.5	+12.9	−68.8	4.1	30.7	
July	28.86	29.51	28.24	−33.0	+10.4	−65.2	8.2	33.4	
Aug.	28.94	29.46	28.51	−48.1	−11.2	−73.3	6.8	34.1	
Sept.	28.90	29.46	28.04	−34.5	+15.8	−63.4	7.5	42.3	
Oct.	28.61	29.66	28.10	−10.6	+15.8	−40.3	12.3	36.8	
Nov.	29.49	30.01	29.08	−5.6	+22.7	−18.4	8.9	40.9	
Dec.	29.66	30.14	29.20	−20.9	+31.7	+1.8	8.2	40.9	
Jan.'12	29.36	29.62	29.01	−16.1	+27.5	+1.4	5.5	14.3	

Cape Adare

	Barometer, inches			Temperature, °F			Wind, m.p.h.		Potential gradient
	Mean	Max.	Min.	Mean	Max.	Min.	Mean Vel.	Max. Vel.	
March '11	29.12	29.42	28.75	20.6	28	10	10.0	63	
April	29.25	29.79	28.61	9.0	22	−8	8.4	74	
May	29.06	29.66	28.28	−0.3	24	−28	13.7	74	
June	29.11	29.70	28.63	−16.1	10	−35	5.7	63	
July	29.01	29.68	28.50	−14.9	9	−34	5.2	63	
Aug.	29.06	29.72	28.15	−13.4	12	−34	8.1	74	
Sept.	28.99	29.94	28.24	+0.2	20	−25	11.6	74	
Oct.	28.73	29.19	28.38	+6.2	26	−11	6.3	44	
Nov.	29.56	30.07	29.01	+19.9	31	+5	6.2	36	
Dec.	29.72	30.07	29.14	+28.3	39	+16	7.7	36	

SUMMARY OF BIOLOGICAL WORK CARRIED OUT ON BOARD THE *TERRA NOVA*, 1910–1913

by D. G. Lillie

Captain Scott, with his characteristic thoroughness, made it possible for scientific work to be carried out by the ship's party not only on their three summer visits to the Antarctic, but also during the two winters spent in New Zealand and on the outward and homeward voyages. As the early publication of this book makes it impossible to give any adequate account of the various biological results which may have been achieved, it is proposed to give here a brief summary of the collections brought home, together with a few notes concerning them, in order to help the general reader to form some idea of what he will find in the Biological Reports of this Expedition when they appear.

The outward and homeward voyages

Whenever opportunities occurred on the outward and homeward voyages between England and New Zealand, tow-nets of fine mesh and of various sizes were put overboard to catch the small animals and plants which drift about in the sea and form the staple food of the whalebone whales and of many birds and fishes.

These floating organisms, which include representatives of all the larger divisions of the animal kingdom, are spoken of collectively as the plankton. On some occasions the net was towed behind the ship for about half an hour to catch the floating population of the surface waters. Sometimes the ship was kept stationary and the net sent down by a sinker to 500 fathoms or less and hauled up again; by this means samples of those forms which live below the surface were obtained.

About 70 samples of the plankton were collected. They vary greatly in size; one catch hardly covers the bottom of a half-pound honey jar, while another requires two seven-pound fruit jars to contain it.

The size of a catch of course depends upon various factors, such as the size of the net, the time it was fishing, or the amount of water passing through it, and the quantity of plankton in the sea at the place where the haul was obtained.

A small number of sea-water samples were collected from various depths by means of the Nansen-Pettersson water-bottle. These were generally taken from the areas in which plankton samples were obtained. The object of these water samples is to ascertain the salinity of the sea at different points and at different depths.

Any change in the salinity means a marked change in the character of the plankton.

The plankton catches, when sorted, will doubtless be found to contain many new genera and species to add to the list of the known forms of living things. The vertical hauls, which were generally made for quantitative purposes, will help to increase our knowledge of the relative abundance of the plankton over the oceans of the world and at different seasons of the year. Isolated observations such as these may be of small value in themselves, but every expedition which collects such data thereby adds its quota to the gradually accumulating mass of evidence and brings the time for generalisation nearer to hand. A knowledge of the relative abundance of the food supply of the ocean is not only of scientific interest but of commercial importance.

On the homeward voyage two satisfactory hauls with the trawl were obtained, one off the Falkland Islands in a depth of 125 fathoms, and the other off Rio de Janeiro in 40 fathoms. The trawl scrapes the bottom of the sea, and brings up a fair sample of whatever animals and plants it can entrap or uproot.

So little scientific trawling has been done in the Southern Hemisphere that almost every haul has a chance of containing some creature hitherto unknown from the area in which the catch was obtained.

Animals which live at the bottom of the sea are known to zoologists as the benthos.

During the outward voyage a day was spent on the island of South Trinidad by several members of the Expedition, and collections of land plants, land spiders, insects, and marine coastal animals were obtained.

The collection of plants has been examined by Dr O. Stapf of Kew Herbarium, and found to contain some thirteen species which have not hitherto been recorded from the island. South Trinidad is a small volcanic island lying about 500 miles from the coast of Brazil, whence it has derived its scanty fauna and flora by means of such agents as winds, ocean currents, and birds. On the voyage home we actually saw one of these agencies at work. When the ship was rather more than a hundred miles from the Brazilian coast, to the southward of Trinidad, a large number of moths, belonging to about four species, were blown on board by a S.W. wind.

An up-to-date account of the fauna and flora of this island will be included in the Reports.

New Zealand

When the *Terra Nova* was engaged upon her three months' surveying in the neighbourhood of the Three Kings Islands, off the extreme north of New Zealand, some 80 samples of plankton and 32 samples of sea-water were obtained.

Seven successful trawls in depths varying from 15 to 300 fathoms yielded a good collection of benthos from this area.

During the first winter the ship's biologist spent five weeks at Mr Cook's whaling station near the Bay of Islands in the north of New Zealand; and in the second winter, through the kindness of Mr L. S. Hasle, four months were spent on two Norwegian floating factories which were exploiting the same waters. Three species of whalebone whales were examined and found to be identical with the three northern species – *Balaenoptera Sibbaldi*, the Blue Whale; *B. borealis*, Rudolphi's Rorqual; and *Megaptera longimana*, the Humpback Whale. About 30 specimens of the last species were examined. An embryo 2½ inches in length was obtained from a female humpback whale weighing about 60 tons.

While at the Bay of Islands an opportunity was taken of examining the inheritance of the pigment in several families of Maori-European half-castes. Sufficient data were collected to show that the phenomenon of Mendelian segregation evidently takes place.

Collections of fossil plants were made from several localities in the South Island of New Zealand, with a view to settling the geological age of the so-called 'glossopteris beds' of Mt Potts. From this material Dr E. A. Newell Arber* has been able to show that the oldest known plant-bearing beds in New Zealand are of Rhaeto-Jurassic age.

One volume of the Reports will be devoted to a description of these fossil flora, together with the fossil plants found by the Polar Party and others in the Antarctic.

An account of some undescribed collections of New Zealand Tertiary and Mesozoic marine invertebrates is to be included in the Expedition Reports.

The Antarctic

During the three summer voyages to the Antarctic a series of qualitative and quantitative plankton samples were taken between New Zealand and McMurdo Sound, and also in different parts of the quadrant visited by the ship.

The number of plankton samples obtained was 135. These comprise 27 collected during the first year, 48 the second year, and 60 the third year.

Also 96 samples of sea-water were obtained.

The increase in the relative size of the plankton catches as we left the warm seas around New Zealand and entered the cold waters of the far south was very marked. This increase was especially noticeable in the case of the diatoms. These minute plants became so numerous as to choke the meshes of the net after it had been fishing only five minutes. In the middle of pack ice the diatoms were much less numerous. This may have been due to the ice floes shutting out the sunlight or to an alteration in the salinity of the sea caused by the melting of the ice.

Some fifty samples of the muds and oozes from the bottom of the sea between New Zealand and the Antarctic were collected. A rough examination of some of these showed them to consist of the skeletons of diatoms and other inhabitants of the surface waters which had fallen to the bottom. These samples were obtained by letting down a weighted tube on the end of the

---

* Arber, *Proceedings of the Royal Society*, B. vol. 86, 1913; *Proceedings of the Cambridge Philological Society*, vol. xvii. part i. 1913.

sounding wire. The tube would sink vertically into the mud and bring up several inches of the deposit. Thus, if there were six inches of mud in the tube a sample taken from the bottom of the tube would come from about six inches below the surface of the sea floor.

In the Ross Sea it was found that many of the diatoms in a sample of mud taken from four inches below the surface of the deposit still contained their protoplasm and chlorophyll bodies. In other words, they were undecomposed.

When trawling in McMurdo Sound it was a common occurrence to find that nearly half the catch consisted of dead animals.

From an examination of the summer temperatures at various depths in several parts of the Ross Sea it was found that a temperature of +1° Centigrade was hardly ever reached. The usual temperature was slightly below 0° Centigrade.

At these low temperatures bacterial decomposition is at a minimum, and the food supply of the ocean remains in cold storage. However, a small amount of decomposition must take place to allow of the production of nitrates for the plants.

The abundance of plankton in Antarctic waters is shown by a brownish discolouration of the sea produced by the diatoms.

Another indication is given by large numbers of whalebone whales, which feed upon the plankton.

It is true that only about three species of whalebone whales were recognised south of the pack, but the number of individuals seen daily around the ship was very great. The two commonest species seen were *Balaenoptera Sibbaldi*, the Blue Whale, and *Balaenoptera rostrata*, the Pike Whale.

The large schools of killer whales, *Orca gladiator*, are an indirect indication of a plenteous food supply, because they feed upon seals and penguins, which in their turn live upon the plankton.

If it was fully realised by whalers that there is a natural reason for the abundance of whales in the cold waters of the Polar regions, they would not exploit warm seas such as that off the north of New Zealand with a 'trying out' plant suitable for South Georgia or the South Shetlands and so lose large sums of money.

Fifteen rich hauls with trawl and dredge in depths varying from 40 to 300 fathoms enabled a large collection of the benthos to be made. A striking feature of the marine fauna of the Antarctic is the extraordinary wealth of individuals, while the variety of forms does not appear to be very great. Also the large size to which some species attain as compared with their relatives in warmer seas is very marked.

This is, however, not the case with animals which require carbonate of lime, for the secretion of limy skeletons by members of the benthos seems to be at a minimum in the cold Antarctic waters. The shells of molluscs are small and fragile. Some sea-snails have no lime in their shells at all.

It requires the warm tropical seas for animals with calcareous skeletons to reach their vigorous growth.

Many of the bottom animals crawl over the sea floor and pass the nutritious mud through their digestive organs after the manner of earth worms; others take up a stationary vertical position, and by means of tentacles waft the falling diatoms into their mouths before they have time to reach the bottom.

Almost every trawl brought up quantities of large siliceous sponges covered with glassy spicules.

Good collections of sea-anemones, worms, urchins, starfishes, crustacea, sea-spiders, molluscs, and fishes were obtained. The collection of fishes has already been found to contain some new genera and several new species. There can be no doubt that many new forms will be found among the other groups.

Considerable quantities of three species of *Cephalodiscus* were obtained. These animals are of interest because they show signs of a distant relationship to the vertebrates, though their mode of life is very dissimilar. The minute individuals live together in colonies, and build up a gelatinous tree-like house.

The young forms of *Cephalodiscus* are very imperfectly known, and it is hoped that larval stages may be found among the material brought home, so that further light may be thrown upon the development of these curious animals.

In the last volume of the Biological Reports it is proposed to review the known marine benthos of the continental shelves of the globe in regard to its distribution in time and space. One of the objects of this inquiry will be to ascertain, as far as our present knowledge will permit, if there has been any tendency on the part of the benthos to originate in the Northern Hemisphere and migrate southward.

The work of Wallace on the distribution of land animals has shown that there appears to have been a tendency throughout the history of the earth for the land animals to originate in the Northern Hemisphere and gradually find their way south. The great belt of land which through long ages has almost encircled the northern half of the world seems to have been Nature's workshop for the evolution of types. These new forms spreading out from their points of origin had to find their way southward along the attenuated land areas of South America, Africa, and Australasia. Thus on account of their relative isolation these three southern continents became characterised by peculiar and in some cases comparatively primitive assemblages of animals. They became, as it were, behind the fashion. For instance, Australia today still has its marsupial population of kangaroos and such-like animals. In Europe marsupial types are only found as fossils, showing that they lived here millions of years ago in the Mesozoic ages of the earth's history, but have long since been exterminated and supplanted by newer types.

On account of the inadequate nature of the fauna of large parts of the Southern Hemisphere, man has had to stock these lands with northern animals.

Very few cases are known where land animals of a southern origin have advanced northwards. Whether this generalisation applies in the case of the marine benthos of the continental shelves presents an interesting field of inquiry. The collections brought home in recent years by the various Antarctic and other expeditions which have trawled in the Southern Hemisphere will, perhaps, make it possible to give some sort of answer to this question.

MARINE BIOLOGY — WINTER QUARTERS, 1911–1913

by E. W. Nelson

Before the collections have been examined it is difficult to say much about scientific results. The following is a very brief account of the biological work undertaken from the Cape Evans shore station during the two years the Expedition wintered there.

In the late summer of 1911 a trip was made across the Barne Glacier to Cape Royds.

The lakes in the vicinity of Sir Ernest Shackleton's winter quarters were covered with only a very few inches of ice, showing that, with the exception of Blue Lake, they had thawed out that summer. Clear Lake was tow-netted by cutting a long slit in the ice and dragging the tow-net backwards and forwards. Small catches were obtained containing chiefly unicellular algae and protozoa. A few rotifers were caught, but no specimens of the blood-red species *Philodina gregoria*, found in such quantity by Mr Murray, could be discovered. The masses of filamentous algae described by him are a constant feature of any lake frozen or thawed. Contrary to our expectation none of the larger lakes thawed out again during our stay.

On the return to Cape Evans an attempt was made to carry out a suggestion made by Mr E. T. Browne. The sea was not yet frozen over, and the idea was to drop a tow-net from a kite flown out over the sea and then pull the net in to shore. A kite was made and the net dropped about 250 yards out, but unfortunately small floating ice crystals choked the net and completely spoilt the catches.

After the sea had frozen over the general winter work was commenced. A hole was cut through the ice and a wall of ice blocks built round to afford some shelter from the wind. This hole had to be cut every day, freezing during the night to as much as two feet thick.

In the spring of 1911 (September) the sea ice at this point was 8 feet 3 inches thick.

The labour entailed in keeping the holes open was considerable, and the time taken in this work very appreciably curtailed the time available for making collections.

The position chosen was about three-quarters of a mile distant from the hut in the strait between Cape Evans and Inaccessible Island, the depth at this point being 100 fathoms.

Tow-nets of various sized mesh were set at varying depths, the current under the ice being sufficiently strong to allow them to fish satisfactorily as a stationary net. Very good catches were obtained, which were brought back to the hut in Thermos flasks. These flasks proved quite invaluable, since catches could be kept in perfect condition in the lowest temperatures which otherwise would have been ruined by crystals of ice forming and spoiling all the more delicate specimens.

The physical conditions under which these drifting or plankton organisms exist is of great importance, and observations were regularly taken with this end in view.

The Expedition was fortunate in possessing some very fine reversing thermometers made by Richter of Berlin, and these were used to determine the temperature of the sea. During the winter a reversing water-bottle was used to obtain samples of sea water for analysis, but with what success cannot be ascertained until the analyses have been carried out.

During the winter only one sample could be taken each day, as the instrument had to be taken back to the hut, thawed out, and thoroughly dried.

Soundings were also taken through cracks and seals' blow-holes, and these will be plotted on the charts.

During the first year a complete record was obtained with an automatic tide-gauge constructed and looked after by Mr Day. It might be mentioned here that the McMurdo Sound tides present some unusual features. Spring tides and neap tides are quite masked by the diurnal inequality of heights, depending on the declination of the moon. For example, with high declinations N. or S. the greatest rise and fall takes place, and there is only one high water and one low water in the twenty-four hours. But with the moon on the equinoctial there is much less rise and fall, and two high waters and two low waters are experienced.

Without entering upon any complex theory this phenomenon can be explained by the fact that with a high southerly declination the tide that would be normally caused by the inferior wave is so small as to be inappreciable to ordinary observation. With the moon at maximum northerly declination it would, of course, be the superior wave that would not appear. With the moon on the equator diurnal inequality disappears, and the two tides are experienced.

During the short summer before the work was interrupted by sledging and before the sea ice had broken up, the air temperature was warm enough to permit observations on the currents being taken with an Ekmann current meter. Series of measurements were obtained with this instrument which should prove of great interest.

Exceptionally severe weather characterised the second winter, and the fact that the sea ice was being constantly blown out made marine work impossible for extended periods.

Since a very complete tide record had been obtained during the first year, it was decided to convert the instrument used for this purpose, of which only one was available, into a seiche meter. One record was obtained and then the instrument was lost, owing to sea ice, which past experience had led us to believe was safe, blowing out and carrying the apparatus to sea. Otherwise the programme was similar to the previous year.

OUTFIT AND PREPARATION
by Commander E. R. G. R. Evans, C.B., R.N.

On September 13, 1909, Captain Scott published his plans for the British Antarctic Expedition of 1910, which he proposed to organise, equip, and lead.

His appeal to the nation, in fact to the Empire, for funds was heartily endorsed by the Press, and the first £10,000 was forthcoming by the spring of 1910. This amount was collected by Captain Scott and his *confrères* and was mainly subscribed by private individuals. The sums given varied from £1000 to 6*d.*, coming from people in all stations of life.

This nucleus fund was obtained only after the most strenuous efforts on the part of Captain Scott, but after the first £10,000 had been raised the Government grant of £20,000 followed, and the programme of the Expedition became more and more ambitious.

Government grants were subsequently made by the Australian Commonwealth, the Dominion of New Zealand, and South Africa, and Mr Samuel Hordern of Sydney contributed £2500 to swell the Australian contribution.

An office was taken and furnished at 36 Victoria Street, S.W., and here the preliminary organisation of the Expedition was carried out by Captain Scott, his second-in-command, and Dr Wilson, the Chief of the Scientific Staff.

The services of Mr F. R. H. Drake, R.N., a Paymaster in the Royal Navy, were obtained as Secretary to the Expedition, and this capable and energetic officer made himself so invaluable that he was eventually asked to take part in the Expedition itself.* Captain Scott was determined that this Expedition should be run on business lines; Sir Edgar Speyer kindly consented to act as Honorary Treasurer, and thanks to his sound advice the finance of the Expedition was used to the best advantage.

* During Mr Drake's absence on the Expedition Mr E. G. H. Evans became (honorary) acting secretary.

Messrs. James Fraser & Sons acted throughout as Honorary Auditors.

Mr George F. Wyatt was appointed business manager, and to him the Expedition owes a debt of gratitude for his expert selection of firms to supply provisions and equipment. Mr Wyatt was a perfect encyclopaedia in the matter of stores, and Captain Scott was delighted when he temporarily gave up his business in order that his whole time might be spent in assisting the Expedition.

Perhaps it would not be out of place to mention here some of the great firms who were selected to supply us with provisions.

Messrs J. S. Fry & Sons supplied our cocoa, sledging and fancy chocolate – delicious comforts, excellently packed and always in good condition.

Messrs Huntley & Palmer: ship's biscuit, fancy biscuit and cakes, and all the sledging biscuit which stood us so well and was so conveniently packed for travelling.

Messrs Colman of Norwich: flour and mustard, as in the *Discovery* Expedition.

Messrs Henry Tate & Sons: sugar, which was in perfect condition even after three years.

Messrs Peter Dawson, Ltd.: whisky.

Messrs Cooper, Cooper & Co.: 'The South Pole Tea', which, like the cocoa, helped us to accomplish our best marches.

Messrs Griffiths, Macalister & Co. of Liverpool supplied our tinned meats and general groceries.

Messrs Price's Patent Candle Co., Ltd.: candles, which were purposely made edible, though never eaten.

Messrs John Burgess & Son, Ltd.: pickles and condiments.

Messrs Abram Lyle & Sons, Ltd.: golden syrup.

Messrs Beach & Sons, Evesham: assorted jams.

Messrs Frank Cooper, Oxford: marmalade and preserved fruits.

Messrs Gillard & Co. Ltd.: pickles, sauces, and curried meats in tins.

The very good pemmican we used came entirely from J. D. Beauvais of Copenhagen, while Mr Maltwood of the Liebig Co. supplied Oxo and Lemco.

Messrs Shippams, Ltd., of Chichester supplied small potted meats and table luxuries for the outward voyage and for the base, and also delightful Christmas puddings.

Messrs Heinz & Co.: baked beans, tomato soups, and many relishes.

Messrs. Reckitt of Hull: starches and cleaning materials.

Messrs Gonzalez Byass & Co.: port and sherry, champagne (Heidsieck).

Messrs Simon Bros, of Northumberland Avenue: champagne (Moët & Chandon), Courvoisier cognac, and all liqueurs. The brandy was particularly well put up in suitable bottles for sledging.

Messrs Burroughs & Wellcome: the entire medical outfit and photographic chemicals.

The Wolsey Underwear Co. made all the underclothing, which could not be excelled.

Messrs Mandleberg of Manchester were responsible for our windproof clothing, which was in continuous use down South, and most satisfactory; also the tent material.

The Jaeger Co.: boots and blankets, and all our mattresses.

Messrs Benjamin Edgington, Ltd.: all the tents, over which they took an immense amount of trouble. The tents were made of Mandleberg material, which could not be beaten for lightness, strength, and efficiency.

In addition to the foregoing we were supplied with a range-finder by Messrs Barr & Stroud, standard compass and sounding machine by Messrs. Kelvin and James White, a fine player piano by the Broadwood Co., and two gramophones by the Gramophone Co., which brought a touch of home into the winter quarters of both parties, and often cheered both forecastle and wardroom of the *Terra Nova*.

Captain Scott, Lieut. Evans, and Mr Wyatt prepared separate provision lists and then met in committee to decide finally on the quantities and qualities of foodstuffs to be taken.

It was decided to add considerably to the kinds of stores taken on previous Expeditions, all believing in variety at the base stations. Thus, for example, we had three hundredweight of fancy chocolates for the shore parties, crystallised fruits, sweets, ginger, &c. Thanks to the magnificent generosity of the firms mentioned we practically obtained our provisions for nothing, and the packing of the stores was beyond all praise. So great was the interest taken by the employees of the provision firms that during the whole period of the Expedition we constantly came across little notes from the packers wishing us every success, &c. In two of Fry's cases were letters addressed to Captain Scott and the Second in Command, with new two-shilling pieces, to be returned if we thought fit to the packer in question, to hand down to his children, and so forth.

We were brought into close touch with the firms by visiting their works and actually seeing the goods packed in the 'Venesta' cases, which were, if possible, of no greater gross weight than 60 lbs., to facilitate handling.

Our tobacco was presented to the Expedition by the Imperial Tobacco Company, who also gave cigars and cigarettes. They took the greatest care to preserve this very important part of our stores, and the tobacco supply was undoubtedly the best and most generous that any Expedition has had.

The above-mentioned articles form only a part of the items of equipment necessary to a Polar Expedition with such an ambitious programme, and all this was arranged before we had collected our money or purchased a ship.

We had to obtain by purchase or otherwise ice-saws, anchors, picks and shovels, hides for soles of boots, &c., instruments of all descriptions for the various scientific purposes, lamps and lighting gear, books and mathematical tables, a library, oils and mineral grease, a colossal photographic outfit, stationery in gargantuan quantities, an efficient sledging outfit, harness and leather goods from John Leckie & Co. for our ponies and dogs, motor accessories for that part of our transport, &c., &c.

Our telescopes were presented by Lieut.-Col. J. W. Gifford of Oaklands Chard. He gave us a 3¼" equatorial telescope for which he calculated the lenses, and also a light 1¾" glass for the Southern Journey. Binoculars were provided by the staff.

Besides this we had great quantities of fishing gear, needles and scissors, knives, &c., from Milward's firm, and sewing machines from Singer's.

The Welsh Tin Plate and Metal Stamping Co. provided the majority of our cutlery, cooking apparatus, and mess traps free.

And then, lest anything should be forgotten, the Army and Navy catalogue was searched from cover to cover by the office staff for anything that might have been forgotten. Captain Scott *once* complained that we had forgotten to bring an article South – it was shaving soap; but it was produced forthwith from the 'annexe', as we called the store outside the big hut at Cape Evans.

Captain Scott, assisted by Lieutenant Campbell and Mr Gran, selected the sledging outfit, fur gloves, sleeping-bags, and finne-skoe, and Gran personally chose every pair of ski and inspected every sledge runner.

Mr Meares gave us some very sound advice on the preparation of the animals' harness and accoutrements, and the credit of this part of our equipment certainly belongs to him, while Captain Oates at his own cost provided the ponies' forage from New Zealand.

A more detailed description of the outfit will subsequently be published, but the nature of this narrative does not permit one to expand on the subject of fitting out.

The choice of a ship was made on September 22, 1909, and that day arrangements were made for the purchase of the steamship *Terra Nova*, the largest and strongest of the old Scottish whalers. Thanks to Messrs. C. T. Bowring & Co., we were able to secure the ship before we had raised a tenth of the necessary funds, and she was handed over to the Expedition on November 8, in the West India Docks. The *Terra Nova* was purchased for the Expedition by Messrs David Bruce & Sons for £12,500. This firm subsequently subscribed the amount of their commission on the transaction to the funds of the British Antarctic Expedition, and the owners (C. T. Bowring & Co.) subscribed £500 and greatly assisted Captain Scott to raise money in Liverpool for his enterprise.

The *Terra Nova* was handed over to the Second in Command to fit out while Captain Scott busied himself more with the scientific programme and the financial side of the Expedition. She was docked by the Glengall Ironworks Co., who altered her according to the specification which had been prepared to meet the requirements of the Expedition.

We had her rigged as a barque (her original rig), and on her upper deck a large well-insulated ice-house was erected. This was to hold 150 carcases of frozen mutton, and owing to its position, free from the vicinity of iron and with a good all-round view; the top of the ice-house was selected for mounting the standard compass and the Lloyd Creak pedestal for magnetic observations. We also mounted our range-finder here.

The galley was almost rebuilt and a new stove put in.

The forecastle was comfortably fitted up with mess-tables and lockers. A lamp-room was built, with paraffin tanks to hold 200 gallons for lighting purposes, and store-rooms, instrument room, and chronometer room were added.

The greatest alteration was made in the saloon, which was enlarged to accommodate twenty-four officers. This was scarcely luxurious accommodation, but it was always kept clean and the ventilation was good. Then a nice little mess was built for the warrant officers, of whom there were to be six.

Two large magazines and a clothing store were constructed in the between decks; these particular spaces were zinc lined to prevent damp creeping in.

It was found necessary to put a new mizzenmast into the ship, but on the whole she required alteration rather than repair.

All the blubber tanks were withdrawn and the hold spaces thoroughly cleaned and whitewashed.

A good chart-house was built above the wardroom and a large covered chart-table fitted up on the bridge.

The Glengall Co. were most anxious to meet us in everything and to push the alterations forward, and their work was efficient and not expensive.

Our original date of sailing was fixed for August 1, but by the united efforts of all concerned with the fitting out and stowing of the ship we halved the time apportioned for preparing the vessel, and the *Terra Nova* sailed on June 1.

The ship herself had to be provisioned and stored for her long voyage, and here again lists had to be prepared to meet every contingency. There were boatswain's stores, wire hawsers, canvas for sailmaking, carpenter's stores, cabin and domestic gear to be provided. The engineers had to purchase their stores together with a blacksmith's outfit. There were fireworks for signalling, whale boats and whaling gear, flags, logs, paint and tar, and a multitude of necessities to be thought of, selected, and not paid for if we could help it.

An invaluable collection of Polar literature, alike Antarctic and Arctic, was made for the Expedition by Admirals Sir Lewis Beaumont, G.C.B.; and Sir Albert Markham, K.C.B., and a beautiful library in miniature was presented to us by Mr Reginald Smith.

When we left London at 5 p.m. on June 1 probably the most strenuous part of the Expedition was over. This may sound strange, but the fitting out was carried on under such extraordinary conditions that we never knew whether the most trivial alteration could be permitted owing to the state of our finances.

During the year of preparation the *personnel* was chosen. We had something like eight thousand volunteers to select from, and, as one of the leading daily papers* stated, 'All sorts and conditions of men seem to have been imbued with a desire to earn Polar glory.' One man wrote that although he was a foreigner he was quite willing to become a British subject if Captain Scott would find him a berth. Of the fortunate men who were finally selected one may read elsewhere in this book, but there were naturally very many crowded out who were fit persons to have accompanied the Expedition.

One of these was Captain Ninnis, an enthusiast who would have been selected had not Captain L. E. G. Oates already been chosen. It will be remembered that he lost his life in the Mawson Expedition after proving himself to be eminently suitable for Polar work.

But even the eight thousand volunteers were disposed of eventually and the appointments made. The final selection was a happy one, and a vast amount of trouble was taken over this important matter.

The outward voyage of the *Terra Nova* hardened the men and taught them a good deal. Lifelong friendships were commenced, and the ship routine gave great opportunities for learning the characters and abilities of the members and for appreciating talents peculiar to various individuals. The different parties were selected from observation made on the long outward voyage.

It only remains to acknowledge the unbounded hospitality of the Cardiff citizens, with Mr Dan Radcliffe at their head, who docked and coaled the ship for us, gave freely in money and kind, and made their generosity so felt that Captain Scott promised that Cardiff should be the home port of the *Terra Nova*.

---

* *The Standard*, Sept. 17, 1909.

The closing words of this book must be a heartfelt acknowledgment from all concerned with Scott's Last Expedition, to the Antarctic Committee which has laboured so long and so disinterestedly to further the interests of the Expedition, of those who took part in it, and of those who were left desolate by its supreme achievement. That acknowledgment is most gratefully tendered to Sir Archibald Geikie, President of the Royal Society; to Lord Strathcona, Lord Howard de Walden, Lord Goschen, Sir George Taubman Goldie, Major Leonard Darwin, and Mr D. Radcliffe, who was invited to join at Commander Evans's request; above all, to Sir Edgar Speyer, who so ably and generously undertook the heavy duties of Hon. Treasurer; to Admiral Sir Lewis Beaumont, who gave unsparingly of his time and invaluable help; to Sir Clements Markham, the Father of Polar exploration, from whom Captain Scott assuredly drew much of his inspiration and encouragement; and to that close friend of Captain Scott, Mr Reginald Smith, K.C. In New Zealand the interests of the Expedition were admirably represented by Mr J. J. Kinsey, who became not merely its official representative but the trusted friend so warmly mentioned by Captain Scott and Dr Wilson. All the original members consented to join the Committee at Captain Scott's personal request, and their names were associated with his in the collection of funds for the equipment of the Expedition. Captain Scott himself undertook all the liabilities involved; he did not ask the Committee to share in these, albeit the Treasurer, with his characteristic generosity, gave him to understand that he would do much to see the venture through. Captain Scott, however, left a letter with Sir Lewis Beaumont giving him full authority to assume control of affairs should the ship be lost and a Relief Expedition become necessary. After Captain Scott's death the Committee translated into action Captain Scott's last appeal to the nation; the funds they raised were

united with the Lord Mayor's Fund, with the further aid of the
Lord Mayor, Lord Curzon of Kedleston, President of the Royal
Geographical Society, the Hon. Harry Lawson, and Alderman
and Sheriff Cooper; while Sir William Soulsby, Secretary to the
Lord Mayor, was indefatigable over the heavy business in connection with the national fund. These funds were supplemented
by a Treasury grant for the dependants of those who had lost their
lives in the service of the country. Such was the response of
the country and the Government to the appeal, that Captain
Scott's dying wish has been amply fulfilled. The Expedition has
discharged its liabilities; the dependants of the dead are well
provided for; the scientific results are to be fully worked out and
published under the auspices of the British Museum. His Majesty
the King received at Buckingham Palace all the members of the
Expedition who were in the country, and conferred upon all the
Antarctic medal, while officers and men of the Royal Navy have
had special promotion; and the Second in Command, Commander Evans, has been given the honour of C.B. The record is
one of public munificence and personal friendship which, could
they but have known it, would have greatly lessened the last cares
of the Southern Party as they awaited their lonely end.

APPENDIX: METEOROLOGICAL LOG

kept by Lieutenant Bowers on the Winter Journey
[reproduced from Mr Cherry-Garrard's diary]

The symbols used have the following meanings.

WIND:

Beaufort number	Description of wind	Velocity, m.p.h.
0	calm	0
1 2 3	light breeze	2 5 10
4 5	moderate breeze	15 21
6 7	strong wind	27 35
8 9	gale forces	42 50
10 11	storm forces	59 68
12	hurricane	75

WEATHER:

b. blue sky   f. fog   m. mist   s. snow
c. detached clouds   g. gloomy   o. overcast

	Time	Temperature	Wind	Weather
27 *June*	1.15 p.m.	−14.5 (off Glacier Tongue)	Breeze (E.) 3–4	
	6.00 p.m.		5	
	9.30 p.m.	−15	5	
28 *June*	7.45 a.m.	−24.5	1	b. c.
	1.30 p.m.	−26.5 (Hut Point)	1	b. c.
	8.00 p.m.	−44.5 (Barrier)		
		At Barrier edge a cold easterly air was flowing from surface on to sea ice.		
	9.10 p.m.	−47	0	b.
	minimum	−56.5		
29 *June*	9.00 a.m.	−49	1	b. c.
	1.00 p.m.	−50	1–2	b.
	7.30 p.m.	−50.2	1	b.
	minimum	−66		

	Time	Temperature	Wind	Weather
30 June	10.0 a.m.	−55	0	b.
	noon	Enough daylight for relaying sledges. Footmarks visible in soft surface for two hours.		
	2.00 p.m.	−61.6	1−2	b. c.
	9.00 p.m.	−66	0	b.
	minimum	−69		
1 July	10.00 a.m.	−66.6	1	b.
	3.00 p.m.		1	b.
	10.0 p.m.	−60.5	1	b.
	minimum	−65.2		
		Breeze during night, with slight drift.		
2 July	10.30 a.m.	−60.1	0	b. c.
	4.00 p.m.	−60.5	1	b. c.
		Light airs lasting until 4 p.m., when bank of fog formed over neck of peninsular. Later this dispersed to W.		
	9.15 p.m.	−65	0	b. c. m.
	minimum	−65		
3 July	11.00 a.m.	−52	0	b. c.
		Barrier surface featureless without sastrugi, as heavy as sand.		
	5.30 p.m.	−57.2	0	b. c.
	10.00 p.m.	−58.2	0	b. c.
	7.30 p.m.	Remarkably brilliant auroral display.		
	minimum	−65.4		
4 July	9.30 a.m.	−27.5	4	o. s.
		Weather very thick. No march. Overcast all day, with steadily falling snow. Wind 3−4, with occasional gusts from E.N.E. to S.E.		
	minimum	9.30 a.m. to 9.30 p.m., −44.5		
		9.30 p.m. to 9.00 a.m., −54.6		
	9.30 p.m.	−30	3	o. s.
5 July	9.00 a.m.	−55	2	c. b.
		Sky clearing; haze over W. slopes of Erebus.		
	2.00 p.m.	−56.5	1	c. b. f.
	9.00 p.m.	−60.1 (cloudy)	0	b. f.
	minimum	−75.3		
		At 6 p.m. a fog bank worked over the lower slopes of Erebus.		
6 July	9.30 a.m.	−70.2	0	b.
	9.00 a.m.	Clear weather, with patches of white haze.		
	noon	−76.8 (cloud 2)	0	b. m.
	4.00 p.m.	Fog lying over Barrier to E. all day. Ross Island clear. A bank of low stratus visible behind peaks of Terror and Terra Nova nearly all day, apparently almost stationary.		
	5.15 p.m.	−77 (carefully checked by Wilson)		
		−77.5 (other thermometer) (cloud 3) 0		b. m.
	minimum	−75.8		
7 July	midnight	−69	0	b. m.
		Low-lying mist (white) to N. and N.N.W.		
	2.00 p.m.	−68.3	0	b. m.
	7.30 p.m.	−55.4	1	f.

	Time	Temperature	Wind	Weather
7 *July*		At 2 p.m. slight haze. At 4 p.m. fog obscured Ross Island, working over lower slopes of Terror from E. At 10 p.m. halo round moon.		
	minimum	−59.8		
8 *July*	1.15 a.m.	−57.2	1	b. m. f.
		At 6.30 a.m. fog all over.		
	10.30 p.m.	−52.3	1	b. f. c.
	7.15 p.m.	−47	0	f. m. b.
		At 7 p.m. land obscured by thick fog; from 1 a.m. slight snow fell. Thick foggy weather.		
	minimum	−36.5		
9 *July*	11.00 a.m.	−36.7	2	o. f.
	1.30 p.m.	−29.2	0	o. f.
		At 1.30 p.m. the moon was invisible, and all objects were obscured by thick fog. During afternoon march noticed slight difference in character of the surface, the snow having been acted on by wind more than hitherto. Surface harder, with occasional small sastrugi.		
	7.00 p.m.	−29.5	1	o. f. s.
		Thick foggy weather, with snowy mist. Occasional light puffs of breeze from S.W.		
	midnight	−27	0	o. s. f.
		Camped on finding ourselves on or about pressure ridges. Snow falling. Nothing visible. Some hours after midnight commenced to blow strong from S. or S.W. Noise of ice pressure in vicinity of beneath camp.		
	minimum	−24		
10 *July*	noon	−24	6 to 8	o. s.
	11.00 p.m.		5 to 6	c. f. s.
11 *July*	10.00 a.m.	+7.8	5 to 9	o. s.
	noon		5 to 7	o. s.
	8.00 p.m.	+6.8	3 to 5	o. c.
12 *July*	6.00 a.m.		10	o. g. s.
	10.00 a.m.	+2.9	3 to 5	c. s.
	12.30 p.m.		2 to 4	c.
	7.30 p.m.	−2.8	4 to 8	c. b. s.
	10.00 p.m.		4 to 6	c. b. g. s.
13 *July*	4.00 a.m.	−12.2	2	b. c.
	6.00 a.m.	−18	1	b. c.
	9.10 a.m.	−22.3	1	b. c.
	3.00 p.m.		3	b. c.
	10.00 p.m.	−28.6	0	b. c.
	minimum	−35		
		When crossing top ridges of Terror it was found that a light breeze coming down the mountain side struck along the top of the ridge, and flowing each way caused a N.E. breeze on one side and a S.W. breeze on the other.		
14 *July*	2.00 a.m.		3	o. c.
	8.00 a.m.	−17.4	1	o. c. s.
	3.20 p.m.	−24.6	0–1	c. f.

	Time	Temperature	Wind	Weather
14 *July*	10.30 p.m.	−24.5	3	o. f. s.
		Weather thick and threatening.		
	minimum	−34.5		
15 *July*		During night fog and snow obscured everything.		
	10.30 a.m.	−19.2	3	c. f. s.
		Weather foggy, but clear sky overhead.		
	4.15 p.m.	−13	4	c. f.
	8.15 p.m.	−14.5	1	b. c.
		(800 feet high)		
	midnight	−19.2	0	b.
	minimum	−28.5		
16 *July*	8.45 a.m.	−24.8	0	b.
	5.40 p.m.	−25	3–5	c. f. b.
	midnight	−20.8	1	b. c.
17 *July*	3.00 a.m.	−23.3	0	o.
	noon	−19.5	3	c. m.
	6.30 p.m.	−22.1	3	b. c.
18 *July*		(unable to continue igloo)		
	6.00 a.m.	−27.3	4–5	b. c.
	9.00 a.m.	−26.5	5	b. c.
	4.00 p.m.		4–5	b. c.
	minimum	−37		
19 *July*	3.10 a.m.	−31.5	0	b. c.
	9.30 a.m.	−33.2	0	b.
	4.30 p.m.	−30	2	b. c.
		(among pressure ridges)		
20 *July*	3.00 a.m.	−28.3	2	b. c.
		(completed igloo)		
	9.00 a.m.	−27	3	b. c.
	5.30 p.m.	−23.3	4	b. c.
	8.00 p.m.	−24	6	b. c.
		(in pressure ridges)		
		During night wind increased to 8, falling towards 6 a.m. to 5.		
21 *July*	8.00 a.m.	20.4	3	o. c.
	noon		2	o. m.
	7.30 p.m.	23.7	1	c. b.
		Unsettled weather: pitched tent to leeward of hut.		
22 July (*Sat.*)		*Start of blizzard*: Friday afternoon.		
		Loss of tent early morning Saturday.		
	3.00 a.m.	Commenced blowing heavily from S., with little drift.		
	6.30 a.m.	−26.5	9–10	o.
		Heavy drift and wind in strong gusts; tent blown away.		
	a.m.	Collapse of blubber stove.		
23 *July*	9.00 a.m.	(all day wind blowing with almost continuous storm force – very slight lulls, followed rapidly by squalls of great violence. About noon roof carried away; storm continued with unabated fury all day – not much drift.		
	11 p.m.	Knoll visible; *loss of igloo roof*.		
24 *July*		Finding the tent.		
	6.30 a.m.		2	c. b.

	Time	Temperature	Wind	Weather
24 *July*	10.00 a.m.		3	c. b.
		From midnight squalls interspersed by short lulls to 9.		
	noon	Dull, cloudy, and unsettled appearance to S. Slight to gentle breeze all day.		
	6.00.p.m.	−12	4	c. b.
25 *July*		Start to return to C. Evans.		
	noon	−15.3 (breeze freshening)	4	o. b.
	2.00 p.m.	Breeze freshened to fresh gale; later to 9, and continued this for about ten hours, easing up towards morning.		
	3.00.p.m.	−17 (?)	8	o. c.
26 *July*	11.00 a.m.	−21.5	2–4	b. c.
		Wind fell light. Sky cleared. Among pressure ridges.		
	9.00 p.m.	−45	0	b.
27 *July*	9.00 a.m.	−46.3	0–1	b.
	5.00.p.m.	−46	0	b.
	9.00.p.m.	−47	0	b.
		At 9 a.m. clouds moving slowly over slopes of Terror from N.		
	minimum	−49.3		
28 *July*	8.30 a.m.	−47.2	0	b.
	3.00 p.m.	−40.3	0	b. c.
	8.00 p.m.	−38	3	b. c.
	minimum	−46.1		
29 *July*	5.30 a.m.	−42	0	b.
	2.30 p.m.	−43.8	2	b. c.
	9.00 p.m.	−45.3	1	b. c.
	minimum	−66.5		
30 *July*	9.00 a.m.	−65.3	0	b. c.
	3.00 p.m.	−63.2	0	b. c.
	8.30 p.m.	−61.8	1	b.
	minimum	−62.9		
31 *July*	9.00 a.m.	−57	0	b. c.
	3.00 p.m.	−43	1	b. c.
		Light airs off edge of Barrier as before. On approaching Gap considerable rise of temperature.		
	10.30 p.m.	−27	0	b. c.
		(Hut Point)		
	minimum	−27.8		
1 *Aug.*	3.30 a.m.	−27.3	6–7	b. c.
	8.00 a.m.	−28	0	b. c.
		During hours of daylight remarkable iridescent clouds to N. general colours opal.		
	5.30 p.m.	−31	1	b.
		(Glacier Tongue)		
		Off Inaccessible Island, northerly breeze 3, till arrived at Cape Evans.		

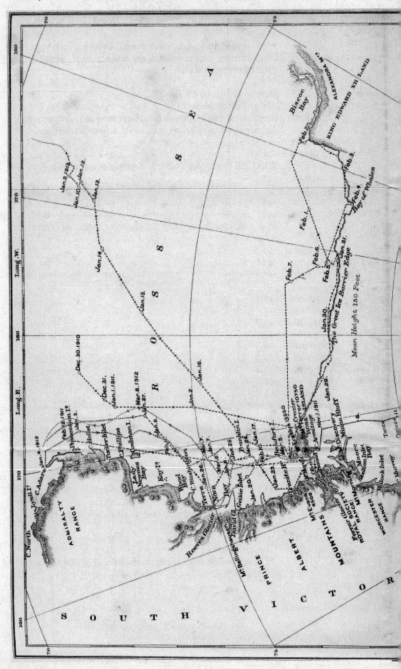

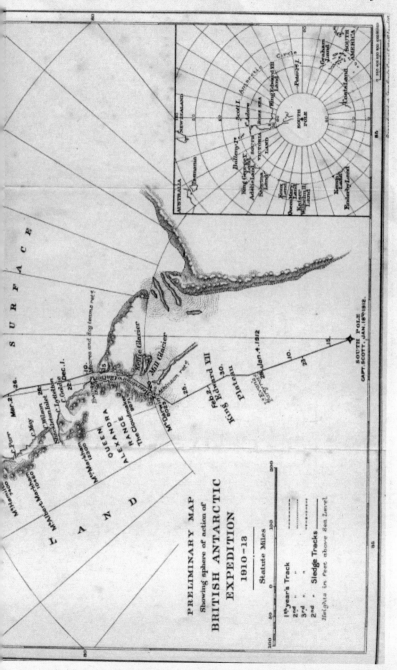